Explorations and Entanglements

Studies in German History

Published in association with the German Historical Institute, Washington, DC

General Editor:
Simone Lässig, Director of the German Historical Institute, Washington, DC, with the assistance of **Patricia Sutcliffe**, Editor, German Historical Institute

For a full volume listing, please see back matter

Explorations and Entanglements

Germans in Pacific Worlds from the Early Modern Period to World War I

Edited by

Hartmut Berghoff
Frank Biess
and
Ulrike Strasser

First published in 2019 by
Berghahn Books
www.berghahnbooks.com

© 2019, 2024 by Hartmut Berghoff, Frank Biess, and Ulrike Strasser
First paperback edition published 2024

All rights reserved. Except for the quotation of short passages
for the purposes of criticism and review, no part of this book
may be reproduced in any form or by any means, electronic or
mechanical, including photocopying, recording, or any information
storage and retrieval system now known or to be invented,
without written permission of the publisher.

Library of Congress Cataloging-in-Publication Data

Names: Berghoff, Hartmut, editor. | Biess, Frank, 1966- editor. | Strasser, Ulrike, 1964- editor. | German Historical Institute (Washington, D.C.)
Title: Explorations and entanglements : Germans in Pacific Worlds from the early modern period to World War I / edited by Hartmut Berghoff, Frank Biess, and Ulrike Strasser.
Description: New York : Berghahn Books, 2019. | Series: Studies in German history ; volume 22 | "Published in association with the German Historical Institute, Washington, D.C." | Includes bibliographical references and index.
Identifiers: LCCN 2018026353 (print) | LCCN 2018047226 (ebook) | ISBN 9781789200294 (ebook) | ISBN 9781789200287 | (hardback :¬alk. paper)
Subjects: LCSH: Germans--Pacific Area--History. | Pacific Area--Relations--Germany. | Germany--Relations--Pacific Area.
Classification: LCC DU28.1.G3 (ebook) | LCC DU28.1.G3 E97 2019 (print) | DDC 995/.00431--dc23
LC record available at https://lccn.loc.gov/2018026353

British Library Cataloguing in Publication Data
A catalogue record for this book is available from the British Library

ISBN 978-1-78920-028-7 hardback
ISBN 978-1-80539-327-6 paperback
ISBN 978-1-80539-438-9 epub
ISBN 978-1-78920-029-4 web pdf

https://doi.org/10.3167/9781789200287

Contents

List of Figures and Tables — vii
Acknowledgments — viii

Introduction: German Histories and Pacific Histories — 1
Ulrike Strasser, Frank Biess, and Hartmut Berghoff

Part I. Missionaries, Explorers, and Knowledge Transfer

1. German Apothecaries and Botanists in Early Modern Indonesia, the Philippines, and Japan — 35
   Raquel A. G. Reyes

2. A Bohemian Mapmaker in Manila: Travels, Transfers, and Traces between the Pacific Ocean and Germans Lands — 55
   Ulrike Strasser

3. German Naturalists in the Pacific around 1800: Entanglement, Autonomy, and a Transnational Culture of Expertise — 79
   Andreas W. Daum

4. Georg Wilhelm Steller and Carl Heinrich Merck: German Scientists in Russian Service as Explorers in the North Pacific in the Eighteenth Century — 103
   Kristina Küntzel-Witt

5. Johann Reinhold Forster and the Ship *Resolution* as a Space of Knowledge Production — 127
   Anne Mariss

6. Engineering Empire: German Influence on Chinese Industrialization, 1880–1925 — 153
   Shellen Wu

Part II. Expansion, Entanglements, and Colonialism in the Long Nineteenth Century

7. Expanding the Frontier(s): The Spreckels Family and the German-American Penetration of the Pacific, 1870–1920   171
   Uwe Spiekermann

8. Work and Non-work in the "Paradise of the South Sea": Samoa, ca. 1890–1914   195
   Jürgen Schmidt

9. German Women in the South Sea Colonies, 1884–1919   213
   Livia Rigotti

10. Sacrifice, Heroism, Professionalization, and Empowerment: Colonial New Guinea in the Lives of German Religious Women, 1899–1919   237
    Katharina Stornig

11. Rape, Indenture, and the Colonial Courts in German New Guinea   255
    Emma Thomas

12. The Trans-Pacific "Ghadar" Movement: The Role of the Pacific in the Indo-German Plot to Overthrow the British Empire during World War I   277
    Douglas T. McGetchin

13. The Vava'u Germans: History and Identity Construction of a Transcultural Community with Tongan and Pomeranian Roots   292
    Reinhard Wendt

    Epilogue
    German Histories and Pacific Histories: New Directions   309
    Matt Matsuda

Index   313

Figures and Tables

Figures

2.1	Klein's map as presented by Andres Serrano (1706), Gobierno de España.	61
2.2	Insulae Laos seu novae Philippinae, in: Stöcklein, Allerhand so lehr- als geist-reiche Brief, Bd. 1, Teil 6, f. 32.	68
5.1	Frontispiece of Francis Bacon, *Novum organum scientiarum* (1645).	132
7.1	Spreckelsville Mill: Maui's Economic Center—and headquarter of the Hawaiian Commercial and Sugar Company, 1890.	174
7.2	Fears of Inundation: Hawaii as the model for a Chinese invasion of the United States. Cartoon, 1883.	176
7.3	Covering the Pacific Ocean: Advertisement of the Oceanic Steamship Company, 1889.	180
7.4	Advertising the lovely Pacific, 1901.	181
7.5	Ho Yow (center right) and George T. Hawley (right behind him), representatives of the Chinese-American Commercial Company, at the St. Louis World's Fair, 1902, together with Congressman Richard Bartholdt (center left).	183
7.6	Claus Spreckels (left) as an independent player among nations-states. Cartoon, 1881.	185
10.1	"Sr. Valeria Dietzen in the coffin, 1917, PNG."	238
10.2	"On the stretcher of the missionary nun" (*An der Bahre der Missionsschwester*).	239

Tables

3.1	European Voyages into the Pacific.	92
3.2	Dramatis Personae.	94
9.1	Number of Germans over the age of fifteen in the South Sea colonies and in South West Africa, as at 1 January 1913.	214
9.2	White inhabitants over the age of fifteen in German South West Africa and German South Sea Colonies, as at 1 January 1913.	220

Acknowledgments

During the long period of its gestation, this volume has incurred many debts. We especially would like to thank the Thyssen-Foundation and the German Historical Institute (GHI), and we would like to acknowledge the support of the Department of History, the Division of Arts and Humanities, and the School of Global Policy and Strategy at UC-San Diego. Megan Murphy and—before it was abolished by the university—the Institute for International, Comparative and Area Studies (IICAS) at UCSD also provided essential support. Student assistants Sky Johnston and Teresa Walch, helped out with a range of important tasks. Susanne Fabricius of the GHI provided essential administrative support.

Chris Chappell and Marion Berghahn from Berghahn Books continued to believe in the project and displayed extraordinary patience. During the production process the manuscript was taken care of with great competence and enthusiasm by Soyolmaa Lkhagvadorj and Caroline Kuhtz from Berghahn Books. We also thank two anonymous readers for their comments, which led to a much-improved introduction. Finally, we are grateful to Sky and Virginia Johnston for their hard work in preparing the manuscript for submission.

Introduction
German Histories and Pacific Histories

Ulrike Strasser, Frank Biess, and Hartmut Berghoff

A volume exploring points of contact between Germans and Pacific worlds across the span of several centuries owes much to global history's ascent in the historical profession in the late twentieth century and early twenty-first century. As global historians have routinely breached conventional boundaries, they have inspired historians in other fields to also interrogate seemingly self-evident units of historical analysis and to consider connections between parts of the world that had long been treated in isolation within national historiographical traditions or area studies scholarship. Arguably, one of the most generative effects of global history in the profession at large is this greater freedom to reframe what constitutes meaningful frameworks for historical inquiry, so that we can pose previously unasked questions about dynamic interactions that have, over time, been taking place across unusual geographical clusters in distant parts of the world.[1]

This volume explores connections between spaces in and around the Pacific and Germans who traveled, explored, and settled in the Pacific, and thus, by implication, also the relationship between Pacific lifeworlds and the German lands from which these migrants journeyed to the Pacific. Looking across the span of the centuries from the early modern period to the eve of World War I, the varied contributions call attention to the long and deep history of German engagement and entanglement in this part of the world. In line with the more recent history on Germany's role in the world, the volume argues that the German presence in the Pacific was not limited to the relatively brief colonial period, and seeks to open up new perspectives on the German–Pacific dynamic.

If we assume for the moment the vantage point of colonial history, it would appear that Germans came late to a Pacific theater where other European players had been protagonists for centuries, forcing them to carve out a space amidst already

---

Notes from this chapter begin on page 26.

existing imperial structures. This volume, although it includes some contributions to the literature on German colonialism, on the whole takes a different approach. It highlights that Germans were not so much late to the European Pacific theater, but were already there, yet differently so. In the early modern period, Germans came alongside other Europeans, but they hailed from a decentralized empire and worked as non-imperial actors in the interstices of early modern European colonial powers. Accordingly, they brought with them a different European frame of reference and, in the Pacific, relied upon and developed more informal mechanisms of influence. The distinct nature of their engagement raises the question—albeit one whose answer far exceeds the scope of this or any single collection on the subject—whether the earlier articulations of informal German influence became the basis for later articulations of German colonial governance.

It is no easy task to open up new paths for researching and narrating the German–Pacific dynamic in the *longue durée*. The German lands and the Pacific Ocean basin are very different geographical spaces, and rather different chronologies have become attached to them in their respective historiographies. These chronologies have developed along two distinct arcs, which we will outline below, eluding attempts to subsume them under some kind of overarching narrative at this stage of research. Yet, as this volume highlights, the very divergences between Pacific histories and German histories, and the tensions inherent in exploring linkages between the two spaces, can render altogether new perspectives on both of them.

To begin with the German side of the story, this tale unfolds against the backdrop of a geographical area that was limited in size but shifted considerably over time, and against the backdrop of a historiography that oriented itself along the political evolution of this area. The German travelers, missionaries, entrepreneurs, and colonizers, whose footsteps and activities we trace here, hailed from a largely landlocked and highly fragmented center of Europe, one of the smallest continents. The German lands constituted a space whose borders did not fall along geographical features like rivers or mountains, but rather cut across distinct topographical zones, from river basins in the south to wooded highlands in the middle section and to the plains in the north ending at the Baltic Sea.[2] Moreover, one cannot locate "Germany" in any meaningful way without reference to the evolution of an overarching governmental structure that posited and solidified this geographical space as a political and cultural unity in the first place. Thus, to define the space of the German lands first of all means to take stock of the religious and political negotiations that forged, and at times fractured, their unity. Differently put, "Germany" as a political entity played out in a relatively small landlocked space and through intense negotiations among multiple institutional actors that led to distinct versions of empire and nation-state.

Not surprisingly then, these negotiations have provided a central plotline for German historiography. Historians have traced the medieval formation of the polycentric Holy Roman Empire of the German Nation in the force field of emperor, electors, and pope. They have recounted the empire's fluctuating fortunes during the tumultuous times of the Reformation period and ravages of the Thirty Years War, and the post-1648 shift in political balance as Calvinist Prussia rose to prominence and rivaled the Catholic imperial Austria-based Habsburg, first culturally and politically, and then also on the battlefield.[3] Likewise, historians have analyzed in detail the forces behind the empire's dissolution, and how in 1871, out of the conglomerate of nineteenth-century German polities, the Prussia-based German Empire emerged. That territorial unit too always constituted more than a German "nation-state." It became, from the 1880s onward, not only the basis for acquiring an overseas empire in Africa and in the Pacific but also for forming a continental "empire" of sorts, on the basis of the inclusion of non-German ethnic groups – Poles, Danes, and Alsatians – as well as through extending the territorial rule of a Prussian-based nation-state over areas with distinct and persistent regional identities, such as the South German states.[4] But while the boundaries of the "German lands" waxed and waned throughout these centuries, all along their size remained miniscule when paired with the Pacific Ocean world. At the height of the Holy Roman Empire's territorial extension, the German lands still barely exceeded the size of New Guinea, the largest island in the Pacific. Under Bismarck's German Empire, the area of Germany had shrunk to about two-thirds of this island alone.

If a landlocked territory of limited size circumscribed German society and culture, and political processes gave meaning to "Germany," water and vastness define the Pacific, leaving their mark on the cultures and societies emerging from and overlapping within it. Space and culture paired differently in this part of the world. The globe's largest body of water, the Pacific, fills one-third of the earth's surface; it is capacious enough to encompass the size of all continents combined. Together with the Asian and American landmasses that border the Pacific's blue expanse and the innumerable islands scattered across its waters, this ocean constitutes a force field in which societies and cultures evolved across time, their histories intersecting in shifting patterns and at varying points of density in response to both internal dynamics and external incursions. The much-touted Pacific Century of our present time is only the latest phase in an ancient process of dynamic interactions, dialogue, and conflict occurring across and beyond the Pacific Ocean basin.[5]

Any effort to pinpoint the chronological benchmarks of the complex histories unfolding in and around the world's largest ocean demands first of all that we make an important conceptual distinction between two different definitions of "the Pacific" that have organized knowledge and narratives about the topic. On the one hand, there is the Pacific as a "European invention," as Oskar Spate put it some ago.[6] The history of this Pacific begins with Magellan's inaugural act of naming it the "peaceful sea" in 1521, and proceeds in successive waves of mercantile and colonial intrusions that crested in nineteenth-century imperialism. To narrate this history inevitably implies rehearsing the histories of European empires in this part of the world. On the other hand, there is the Pacific that Matt Matsuda more recently has characterized in juxtaposition with the Pacific in Spate's sense or the Pacific as "a European project." Simultaneously drawing on and exploding the Braudellian ocean paradigm, Matsuda defines this Pacific as "multiple seas, cultures, and peoples, and especially the overlapping transits between them."[7] The histories of this Pacific are made up of the overlapping and intertwining of particular stories of the multiplicity of peoples traversing the big ocean, inhabiting littoral zones, islands, and waters, and being drawn together in shifting patterns through forms of cultural and economic exchange and contest. These histories precede the history of the European Pacific by many centuries and can be traced back to the ancient Polynesian voyagers whose far-flung journeys and settlements cast the first wide net of human communities across the blue expanse of the ocean.[8]

While we are mindful of the broader matrix of Pacific seas and societies and the newer literatures that have explored it, the focus of our volume rests elsewhere. It concerns itself primarily with revisiting the first approach, the history of the Pacific as a European imperial project, though the contributions also seek to engage, whenever possible, the second version and analyze the interaction of Pacific Islanders with the European presence. The respective areas of specialization and linguistic skills of our contributors pointed to this emphasis on the Pacific as a "European project" as the most sensible and credible choice for our undertaking. Yet we hope that the volume also opens up a dialogue with scholarship about the Pacific that is more fully grounded, including linguistically, in the lifeworlds of Pacific societies and cultures past and present. In this spirit, we invited Matt Matsuda to contribute an epilogue—for which we are immensely grateful—in which he offers an evocative reading of the volume's essays that gestures towards these possible connections.[9]

While the volume thus places the emphasis on the Pacific as a European project, it does so from a distinct vantage point that has been underdeveloped in the existing literature and that we believe aligns, from within European history, in fruitful ways with the focus within Pacific Studies on questions of contingency in colonial and imperial exchanges. Our volume focuses on the "German element" in the long history of European–Pacific encounters and entanglements, and it looks at Germans in the Pacific through the prism of transnational or global rather than imperial history. This focus on the Pacific as a European project from the perspective of Germans has its own intellectual rationale, which grows out of global history rather than imperial history. As global history encompasses the study of multiple forms of connections between different parts of the globe; it asks us to step outside the colonial and imperial frameworks that have organized knowledge about so many parts of the world, including but of course not limited to the Pacific Ocean basin. Global history furthermore has asserted the relevance of *all* parts of the world, and this assertion at once disavows Europe's singularity and demands its reinvigorated study from new vantage points. Global history, to be sure, has primarily concerned itself with decentering Europe and pushing back against Eurocentric biases in the record by expanding historical inquiry and its linguistic and professional bases into neglected areas of research. Yet, on the flipside, rewriting and refurbishing histories of Europe has also become crucial in seeking to tell the story of the globe anew and in a more balanced way.

This book offers a fresh look at the story of the "European Pacific" by turning the spotlight on a group of Europeans that did not formally join the imperial project until the late nineteenth century, when the German Empire acquired its first formal colonies. Nonetheless, since the early modern period, Germans operated in and around the Great Ocean within the interstices of other empires and the indigenous cultures of the Pacific. What role did Germans play in exploiting and exploring the Pacific? When and where did they bolster or mimic, when and where undercut or thwart the efforts of other Europeans? Is there such a thing as colonialism without colonies? How did Germans contribute to generating knowledge about the Pacific that blended local and European traditions and fed them into transnational networks of knowledge and power, including those in the German-speaking territories of Europe? And what do these activities in the Pacific tell us in turn about the global dimensions of German history? These are the types of questions this volume pursues to further qualify the "European" in understanding the Pacific as a "European project," as well as in "European Colonialism" and "European Imperialism."

The Pacific as a "European Project": Imperial Histories

To further elaborate our approach, we first need to turn to the existing historical literature on the Pacific as a European project. Generally speaking, since chronologies of empires have shaped this historiography, Europeans associated with those empires have received disproportionate attention. The German presence in the literature is confined to the late nineteenth century or the period of colonialism. A vibrant scholarship does of course exist on German colonialism, some of which we discuss below. For the earlier centuries, however, the storyline of the European Pacific has centered on the colonial and imperial undertakings of Europeans other than Germans. Although a full rehearsal of this story about the European expansion into the Pacific and integration of various subzones by far exceeds the scope of this introduction, it is possible to name the protagonists and sketch out at least five distinct stages of the plot. We will not attempt to insert Germans in these larger plotlines at this point or intimate how they might fit. Such a simple add-on would do little to shift the larger optics, as is the long-term goal, from a default focus on national narratives of European imperial expansion in the Pacific to more complex global and transnational narratives that trace how both imperial and non-imperial European actors became entangled in the complex histories unfolding in Pacific worlds.

The first act of the Pacific as a "European project" unfolded in the sixteenth century, as both Portugal and Spain, via different routes, pressed into the Pacific basin in search of spices, metals, and other riches. Their voyages took place at the very moment when indigenous transoceanic voyages had ebbed and the basin's inhabitants had turned their attention to local consolidations of power.[10] The Europeans came into a complex universe of already established trade networks and systems of political influence and tribute, one seafaring people among many. They were the most recent and hence least experienced arrivals, but they harbored grand ambitions. Nonetheless, it would take until the 1900s for Europeans to integrate and dominate more than limited subzones of the Pacific basin.[11]

Portugal's approach came via the Indian Ocean on the heels of Vasco de Gama's eastward voyages, illustrating the early interconnectedness of the worlds of the Indian and Pacific oceans. At the approximate boundary between these worlds sat the city of Malacca, in present-day Malaysia, which the Portuguese conquered in 1511 and used as a springboard into the Pacific. By 1521, they had gained a foothold in the Moluccas, the much-coveted Spice Islands, and from 1535 to 1575, when they were ousted from their base there, the Portuguese were effectively the hegemonic power in the spice trade, suppressing the authority of competing sultans and creating tighter links between Southeast Asian, Chinese, and western Pacific markets.[12]

Portugal's other main artery of influence ran through Macao, from where Portuguese traders were allowed to operate by Ming officials, who in turn could satisfy Chinese desires for spices and sandalwood while making a profit from the sale of silk and porcelain to the Europeans. Because China had also cut off direct trade with Japan, the Portuguese further became key intermediaries between the two countries. They delivered silver and copper from Japan to China, and they supplied Japan with Chinese porcelain, cloth, and iron, along with Europeans weapons and Jesuit missionaries, and Christianity soon took hold in Japan.[13]

In response to Portugal's successful forays, Spain dispatched Ferdinand Magellan on a quest for a westerly route to the riches of the East. Following the passage of the treacherous South American straits that now bear his name, Magellan's fleet progressed in the waters of a new ocean whose seemingly placid surface led the navigator to give it the often misleadingly tranquil name of "the Pacific." Magellan reached what is now Guam in 1521, before moving on to what became the Philippines, where he was killed in an armed conflict with locals.[14]

Spain's expansion into the Pacific made little progress thereafter until 1565, when Miguel Lopez de Legazpi began building alliances with local forces and recruiting indigenous soldiers, eventually conquering Luzon and founding Manila. Meanwhile, his pilot Andres de Urdanata fortuitously discovered a return route to the Americas, inaugurating the galleon ship trade that fused the eastern and western hemispheres into a global economic circuit linking the economies of Asia, the Americas, and Europe, and turning a subzone of the Pacific into "The Spanish Lake."[15] Silk, porcelain, ivory, spices, migrant laborers, and slaves traveled via Manila to Acapulco. Silver and people from the Americas flowed in the other direction, and a mere thirty years after the first galleon completed its journey across the Pacific, more silver left Acapulco than was traded across the entire Atlantic. In the wake of the many galleons plying the Pacific, cultures and societies in and around the Pacific basin underwent profound change. The Ladrones, at first a mere stopover on the route, were occupied by Spanish forces in 1668 and renamed the Marianas by Jesuit missionaries. After a series of brutal military conflicts, the island population was "reduced" on Guam, leading to the near-extinction of the indigenous Chamorros, the first Pacific Island population to fall victim to European colonization. The Manila galleons ran for two and a half centuries until 1815, and Spain held on to Manila and the Marianas until 1898.[16]

Act two of the early modern European commercial exploitation and colonization in the Pacific saw the rise of a different European protagonist. In the seventeenth century, Portugal and Spain found themselves surpassed by a rapidly expanding Dutch mercantile empire, led by the Dutch East India Company or VOC, an economic and military power unto itself. Like the Spanish in Manila, the Dutch encouraged the immigration of Chinese merchants and middlemen to their port city of Batavia (present-day Jakarta). Also like the Spanish, they took harsh action against islanders, decimating the population of the Banda island group in the heart of the Moluccas. Not all such deaths were by these direct actions; many indigenous people died of starvation when the Dutch replaced staple food sources with lucrative, highly controlled spice plantations, and restricted the production of certain spices to particular islands. The Dutch also pushed out the English when they took over the British station on Ran Island. They were able to dislodge their competitors by way of a consequential, long-distance land swap, trading Ran for Manhattan Island in the Atlantic. The Dutch monopoly on the Pacific spice trade would last until the nineteenth century.[17]

The second major venue of Dutch influence in and around the Pacific was Japan. Here, the Protestant, commercially focused Dutch took advantage of anti-Catholic sentiment and increased government centralization to help the Shogun remove Portuguese-sponsored missionaries and their converts. Between 1633 and 1639, Japan issued a series of edicts that amounted to a form of self-enclosure: no native-born Japanese were allowed to leave Japan, nor any foreigners to enter. Nagasaki, formerly a Jesuit stronghold, was the one port that remained accessible to both the Chinese and the Dutch. Being the only Europeans with permission to reside on nearby Deshima Island, the Dutch were able to access Japanese goods and culture and circulate them globally. They enjoyed this role as Japan's gateway to the larger world until the mid-nineteenth century.[18]

Exploratory voyages to farther regions of the Pacific Ocean form an important subplot of this larger story of Iberian and Dutch dominance. What drove these explorations was the quest for the rumored Great Southern Continent, where a plenitude of material riches and pagan souls allegedly awaited intrepid travelers. In the second half of the sixteenth century, Spanish navigators set out from the Americas and chanced upon—to use the European nomenclature—the Solomon Islands, the Marquesas, and islands belonging to the New Hebrides (now Vanuatu), making contact with peoples of Polynesia and Melanesia. In the early seventeenth century, Dutch rivals of the VOC braved the waters around South America to carve out a path to the riches of the Indies that lay beyond the VOC's monopoly. They sailed into the waters of the Tongan maritime empire, interacting with various island peoples along the way, eventually passing the northern coast of New Guinea. Some decades later, the Dutch explorer Abel Janszoon Tasman reached the island today known as Tasmania, off Australia's southern coast, and had an encounter with the Maori peoples of New Zealand. These journeys amounted to extraordinary feats of long-distance voyaging. Yet none of them resulted in commercial links or settlements, nor did they lead to sustained exploratory travel. The complex island worlds of Oceania remained beyond European reach, at least for the time being.[19]

Sustained exploration of the unknown came in the eighteenth century, and marks act three of the Pacific as a European project. The age of the Enlightenment brought large-scale, government-sponsored expeditions to the Pacific, blending newer scientific interests with the more long-standing commercial motivations that had first driven Europeans into Pacific waters. Europe saw the rise of scientific academies and the attendant proliferation of journals that delivered scientific information and travel reports to a growing number of readers. As print literature became a consumer product across Europe, it fueled the demand for novel discoveries, and turned the Pacific, the least explored region from a European point of view, into the "[e]ighteenth century's 'New World.'"[20] An increasingly systematic colonial science emerged, harnessing scientific inquiry to imperial projects, and pulling the Pacific and its peoples into its expanding circuit of knowledge production and imperial ambitions.[21]

Spain was an active participant, sponsoring large-scale scientific expeditions of naturalists and artists that resulted in, among other things, an enormous visual archive of the flora of the Philippines.[22] However, France and its English rivals clearly dominated this phase of state-sponsored Pacific exploration, embodied by such figures as Louis Antoine de Bougainville and James Cook; the latter was killed in Tahiti after exploratory journeys to map, among other things, the east coast of Australia and Hawaii. Russia was the third driving force behind the large-scale expeditions of the eighteenth century, with explorers like Vitus Bering expanding European knowledge of the Pacific exponentially, and reaching entirely new regions of what is today the US Pacific Northwest.[23] On the heels of these eighteenth-century expeditions, Europeans established an extensive zone of exchange among Asian, Oceanic, and American societies and their own back home. This would position them well for the nineteenth-century phase of Pacific–European relations, when the balance of power shifted in favor of the Europeans and propelled them into an even firmer position of hegemony.

In act four of the creation of the Pacific as a European project, the widely circulating reports of European voyages brought increasing global attention to the Pacific as a potential site of commercial expansion and geopolitical advantage. In the aftermath of the Napoleonic Wars (1799–1815), Pacific exploration and commercial activity increased as European powers searched for economic and strategic gains over their rivals.[24] New actors also appeared on the scene, with North American merchants particularly active.[25] American ships represented almost half of all merchant ships entering Californian waters during the first half of the nineteenth century, followed by British, Spanish, Mexican, and Russian vessels. Altogether, ships from more than twenty polities appeared off the California coast in the decades before the Gold Rush, reflecting broad international awareness of the Pacific's commercial opportunities.[26] Meanwhile, expanding trade connected the coastal regions of California and South America with Hawaii, which became increasingly important as a commercial traffic hub.

Sea otter fur and whale oil were among the commodities most desired by European and American consumers, leading to the near extinction of the Pacific sea otter population. Whaling along the Eastern Pacific coast, likewise, saw its heyday between the 1830s and 1850s and coincided with increased demand for whale oil due to the industrializing United States and Great Britain. Here too, American commercial interests abounded and accounted for seven hundred ships or three-fourths of the global whaling fleet.[27] The hunt for these natural resources, however, was not a purely Western enterprise but centrally depended on the skills of indigenous people, such as Aleut hunters in the sea otter trade and indigenous harpooners in whaling, as immortalized in the figure of Queequeq in Melville's *Moby Dick*.[28]

Chinese trade with the West remained highly supervised until the forceful "opening" of China for Western trade during the Opium Wars (1839–42, 1856–60), in which the British made use of their superior gunboats to overcome Qing prohibitions on the sale of opium. In the 1842 Treaty of Nanking, China was forced to cede Hong Kong to Britain, which also gained "most favored nation" trading status. Soon after, the United States and France followed this imperialist model and secured concessions on similar terms elsewhere in China. The "treaty port" became a widespread model that allowed foreigners to operate solely under the jurisdiction of their own consuls, living in separate, Europeanized sections of the port town that minimized encounters with indigenous people.[29] As treaty ports proliferated, they came to represent a new form of European power and dominance that remade the Pacific as a European project.[30]

The California Gold Rush in 1848 and the rapid incorporation of California into the United States in 1850 further accelerated the region's commercial integration. People from across the Pacific were able to arrive on the scene earlier than Americans from the East Coast,[31] a situation that only changed with the completion of the transcontinental railway in 1869. Improved communications and logistics, especially the spread of the steamship and railways and the widespread adoption of the telegraph, shrank time and distance in an unprecedented way and were key factors in the expansion of trade along the Pacific Rim and across the ocean.[32] "By 1850," writes David Igler, "the ocean's people, markets, and natural resources were thoroughly intertwined with the surrounding world."[33]

The commercial integration of the Pacific both preceded and enabled European powers' increasing formal imperial domination of the area, which marks the fifth and final act in the creation of the Pacific as a "European project." Great Britain, France, and, eventually, the United States had now replaced Spain, Portugal, and the Netherlands as dominant imperial powers, though the Dutch did expand and solidify their control over the Dutch East Indies—present-day Indonesia—following the bloody and protracted Aceh War (1873–1903).[34] To be sure, there was not one model for imposing Western imperial dominance on Pacific territories, just as Asian responses to Western intrusion varied widely depending on local circumstances. British control over Malay, for example, followed the explorations of adventurer James Brooke, and was only gradually formalized between 1874 and 1885,[35] while in New Zealand, the British exploited local division by signing the 1840 Treaty of Waitangi with indigenous Maori chiefs.[36] The French Empire in the Pacific emerged partly in response to British expansion. French domination over Tahiti was established in the French–Tahitian Wars (1843–46), while the nation's presence in the Indian Ocean also provided a base for further expansion into the Pacific. French colonial dominance in parts of Southeast Asia derived from a French missionary presence and Napoleon III's promise to protect the interests of French Catholics; by 1887, the territories that today encompass Vietnam, Laos, and Cambodia were combined in the "Union of Indochina."[37] As in other parts of the world, violence remained a persistent and integral feature of the European colonization of the Pacific. The demand of European settlers for land and grazing rights ultimately led to conflicts with local populations, such as the French faced with the Kanaks in the penal colony of New Caledonia.[38]

In the conventional imperial narrative of the Pacific as a European project, it is at this point that Germany and Germans join the action. Compared to other Western powers, German imperialism arrived late on the scene in the Pacific, as it did in Africa. As with other imperial players, German domination followed a previously established commercial presence—though compared to cases such as the Dutch, that presence was relatively recent. In Samoa, the foundation of German imperialism was the commercial expansion of the Hamburg trading firm J. C. Goddefroy and Son, which had established itself in 1857 and eventually controlled the Western Pacific copra trade.[39] With Bismarck's turn to colonialism in 1884/85, Germany acquired parts of northern New Guinea and the Bismarck Archipelago in 1885 as overseas territories. After the defeat of the Spanish in the Spanish–American War of 1898, the Northern Marianas, the Caroline Islands, Palau and the Marshall Islands also became German colonies. That same year, Germany secured a sphere of influence in the Shandong province in China.[40]

The second half of the nineteenth century also saw the United States solidify its status as an imperial power in the Pacific. With the arrival of Commodore Perry in Edo Bay in 1853, the United States forced Japan to end its 220-year-long seclusion. Initially motivated by the desire to protect shipwrecked soldiers and expand the commercial whaling industry into Japanese waters, the US eventually forced a series of treaties in 1854 and 1858 that granted concessions of extraterritoriality and favorable trading status, similar to those extracted by other Western powers from China. These provisions would eventually be extended to other European powers as well. Further US expansion in the Pacific centered on the Hawaiian Islands, which they eventually annexed in 1898. Hawaii became a US territory in 1900 and a state in 1950, with Pearl Harbor as the central base of the US Navy in the Pacific. The desire to have a permanent military and commercial presence in the Pacific underscored the increased importance of the region for US foreign and trade policy. The Spanish–American War of 1898 also saw the final replacement of Spanish rule by American rule in the region. Afterward, the US established colonial control over the Philippines during an increasingly brutal war in which an estimated two hundred thousand civilians perished, largely due to famine and disease.[41]

Finally, the creation of the Pacific as a European project also entailed the adoption of European form of control by one Asian power: Japan. In response to the threat posed by Western imperialism, the Meiji restoration in Japan pursued a "rich nation, strong military" approach. The expansion of the military sector as well as strategic investments in infrastructure and education led to state-led economic growth that eventually enabled Japan to become an imperial power itself. By both utilizing and challenging Western models, Japan developed what was in effect an imperialist anti-imperialism. It imposed an unequal treaty on Korea in 1876 and, following military victories in the Sino-Japanese (1894/95) and Russian–Japanese (1905) wars, annexed Korea as a colony in 1910. The Japanese military and government remained divided between rival models of imperial expansion: cooperation with Western powers on one hand, and challenging Western domination of the Pacific on the other.[42]

The Pacific as a "European" project did not thus lead to the domination of one single power over this vast space.[43] Instead, multiple empires competed for control over these territories and entered into a series of diverse arrangements with indigenous populations. Local responses to colonial intrusion varied widely, and yielded a wide variety of arrangements located on a spectrum between formal independence with a commercial presence (China, Thailand) and formal colonialism. The intensified colonial and commercial penetration also enhanced the exchange of people and products, ideas and knowledge. A more tightly integrated transoceanic labor market also emerged over the course of the nineteenth century. It built on earlier migratory patterns, yet it entailed more extensive labor migration across and within the Pacific. The establishment of large sugar plantations on Hawaii, and other cash crops such as copra on Samoa, demanded the steady supply of workers for a large labor force. Following the example of slavery in the cotton economy of the US South, various forms of unfree labor—from indentured servitude to blatant kidnapping and enslavement of Pacific Islanders (the infamous "blackbirding")—became widespread, occasionally with the collaboration of local chiefs. The British "Pacific Islander Protection Act" of 1872 sought to contain these practices, yet it remained weakly enforced. The British imported Indian laborers into Fiji to work on sugar plantations. Chinese and Japanese laborers, together with "blackbirded" Pacific Islanders, excavated guano along the costs of Peru and Chile, and on Hawaiian sugar plantations.[44] Chinese "coolie" workers built many American railways while Japanese laborers worked the fields of California. Labor migration thus constituted an increasingly common theme across the Pacific. "Remembering of laboring in foreign lands," as Matt Matsuda writes, "haunted almost all Pacific societies in the second half of the nineteenth century."[45]

World War I marked a caesura in the history of the Pacific as a European project. The global order was soon to be rearranged as the war helped to consolidate and accelerate anticolonial movements that called into question the entire European imperial project. (Germany's presence as a formal colonial power in the Pacific also ended with its defeat in World War I;[46] this moment accordingly marks a logical endpoint for this volume.) The mobilization of colonial soldiers in separate units such as the "Australian Brigade" and the "Defense of India Force" accelerated popular demands for greater autonomy or even independence. What the British proconsul Sir Harry Johnston stated in a presentation to the African Society in March 1919 applied to the Pacific as well: the war had brought a "revolt against white supremacy."[47] In part, this revolt resulted from the experience of the war as a truly global event. Thanks to the global networks of information through telegraphs and professional news agencies such as Reuters and the Associated Press, it was possible to follow the war virtually everywhere without much delay.[48] This global network of information was one reason for the heightened expectations that people in India, China, and Korea associated with the war and its outcome. US President Wilson's slogan of "self-determination" resonated broadly among colonized societies and sparked renewed demands for an end to Western imperialism. The disappointment of these hopes and the Western powers' reassertion of imperial control in the aftermath of the Paris Peace conference in 1919 profoundly discredited liberal political models. As a result, anti-colonial nationalists, such as the Vietnamese leader Ho-Chi Minh, turned to communism as an alternative.[49]

Germans in the Pacific: Earlier Entanglements, Formal Colonialism, and the *Longue Durée*

The imperial perspective outlined above has often driven scholarship on the European presence in the Pacific. As we have seen, Germans only tend to appear very late in this storyline, during the fifth stage with the formal acquisition of colonies in the late nineteenth century. This German colonial presence in the Pacific has become the subject of a quite extensive historical literature that has appeared steadily since the 1970s.[50] In recent times, Hermann Josef Hiery has synthesized some of this work into a handbook on the "German South Sea."[51] His and other recent scholarship do reflect a remarkable surge of interest in the history of German colonialism, which has begun to correct the hitherto predominant focus on German imperialism in Africa.[52]

Still, the predominant imperial framework has had unfortunate effects on scholarship on Germans in the Pacific. First, it is most densely concentrated on the period of formal colonialism and not systematically connected to research that has sought to highlight the German element in the European exploration and penetration of Pacific worlds for the precolonial period.[53] Moreover, within this dominant imperial framework, the German presence necessarily appears as late, short-lived, and relatively marginal. Measured against the British or French imperial presence, Germany's inevitably falls short.

By adopting a global perspective, this volume seeks to move away from the normative power of the imperial framework. Rather than focusing on German colonialism as late and short-lived, it seeks to bring into view the German presence in the Pacific as early and long—as different, as opposed to deficient. Our contributors connect this longer and distinct history to broader trends in global and transnational history as well as in German history to push toward a more nuanced assessment of Pacific–European encounters. To that end, the chapters assembled here move away from a purely state- or empire-centered approach to an actor-centered approach that brings into relief the variegated forms of German engagement with Pacific worlds since the sixteenth century. These engagements were not always precisely driven by a singular imperial interest, but more often unfolded in the interstices of empires in the plural or, in the case of German missionaries, paid heed to the dictates of another empire altogether: the empire of God.[54]

Adding previously neglected German actors and voices to the mix, our volume highlights that notions of a nationally cohesive Pacific such as "The Spanish Lake" prove to be fictions of a later age, both because they deny historical agency to myriads of indigenous actors and also because they gloss over the multiplicity of European actors involved in reshaping Pacific societies and cultures. A rather sizable contingent of Germans served under the Dutch VOC in Southeast Asia.[55] Raquel Reyes's contribution to this volume sheds light on the far-ranging networks of some of these men and their central role in forging connections between the Pacific and Europe. As part of the multinational Society of Jesus, many Germans served in Portuguese Asia and the Spanish Empire in the Pacific. Ulrike Strasser's chapter uses an exemplary case to highlight the intersecting migratory and information networks, imperial as well as religious, in which these Germans participated, crisscrossing seascapes and continents, and not confined to latter-day national boundaries.

What set Germans in the Pacific apart from other Europeans had a lot to do with the complex history of their homeland. These Pacific travelers not only shared a language, but a familiarity with specific institutional frameworks, cultural points of reference, and historical memories that distinguished them from other European actors. One need not resort to an essentialized, reified understanding of what it meant to be German, from the post-Westphalian early modern era to the high imperial period of the nineteenth and early twentieth centuries, to find meaningful threads of connection between the actors discussed and the specific historical situation of the German lands.

Let us name a few of the threads spun by our contributors. A recurring theme is the way in which Germans' more distant relationship to other imperial projects and Germany's status as a "latecomer" to nationhood and colonialism served as an advantage. It created the possibility for Germans to align themselves with whatever enterprises in the Pacific were best suited to help them achieve their own aims, whether that be saving souls, making scientific discoveries, building wealth, or fostering cultural ties. The contributions by Andreas Daum and Kristina Küntzel-Witt, for example, call attention to the notable degree of independence in thought and action that characterized German naturalists working in the Pacific in the employ of other empires.

This relative distance to European imperial projects also led at times to a critical attitude toward the more violent aspects of European intrusion as well as close relationship with the indigenous. Perhaps the best-known example is the German writer Adalbert Chamisso, who, on his voyages to the Pacific between 1815 and 1818, developed a "sense of alarm and compassion for all native communities around the Pacific," which was also illustrated in his famous friendship with the Hawaiian native Kadu.[56] In this volume, Anne Mariss sheds light on the importance of Polynesian informants to Johann Reinhold Foster's scientific exploits. Although Germans were also willing participants in the "othering" and exploitation of Pacific Islanders, their position in the Pacific differed in important and tangible ways from that of other Europeans who were tied earlier and more firmly to specific imperials projects.

Another thread of connection between German experiences back home and German experiences in the Pacific appears in the need to navigate decentralized and overlapping fields of political authority. Germans came from a tradition of comparatively more heterogeneous and decentralized polities with a tradition of religious (Christian) pluralism: the Holy Roman Empire before 1806, and the loose confederation of German states thereafter, arguably prepared Germans well for moving skillfully in a region of the world that also lacked a unifying central authority, had competing cultural and political constituencies, and traditions of negotiating difference among them. Germans were used to and skilled in communicating and interacting with a variety of authorities and to moving in different regional and national cultures, and were therefore better equipped to pursue their interest in the Pacific than other Europeans from more centralized overseas empires.

Related to this point, several chapters, such as the ones by Daum, Küntzel-Witt, and Mariss, show that Germans possessed qualities that made them desirable partners and collaborators for other Europeans. They were often graduates of an academic system that had, by the nineteenth century, become widely recognized as the most distinguished in the world. They possessed linguistic, communicative, and especially academic abilities that proved important soft skills for wielding power, and were indispensable for other European nations that otherwise had the longer experience in the hard business of colonialism and empire. In other words, German engagement with the European Pacific project was not so much deficient, with more successful imperial powers setting the implicit norm for success, but it was a different type of engagement. It was forged in a less monolithic polity, yet unified by structures of communication and education, asking us to nuance our view of the "European" presence in the Pacific by considering the complexities of imperial as well as non-imperial interactions between Europeans and Pacific societies and cultures.

This distinction between non-imperial and imperial forms of influence, although we have introduced it here to highlight the long yet distinct presence of German actors in the Pacific, also dovetails with the more recent literature on German colonialism. This recent scholarship has deliberately uncoupled the notion of colonialism from formal colonial power holding, and stressed the significance of more informal mechanisms of influence and control.[57] Once we expand the history of colonialism beyond territorial control and incorporate various means of wielding informal influence, both the early modern origins of German colonialism and its afterlife begin to look different. It allows for a greater sensitivity for a wide variety of connections and exchanges between Germans and the Pacific world, and between Germans and other imperial powers.

It further throws into relief forms of European influence in Pacific worlds that preceded German colonialism and, importantly, also extended beyond its formal end in 1918. As such, the deterritorialized German presence in the Pacific might actually have represented a more modern and innovative form of informal imperialism. The role of Germans in the Pacific can thus serve as a model and a historical precursor for very modern, and often very unequal, forms of transnational relations between the West and the global South that endure to this day.

By placing "Germans" and "Germany" into one analytical framework with the "Pacific" we hope to open up new lines of inquiry on both spaces. Beyond the distinct chronologies that have become attached to the histories of Germany and the Pacific, it is also possible to locate parallels and interconnections between these two vastly different spaces. During the early modern period, Jesuit missionaries, for example, conceived of saving souls in the Pacific as part of a broader evangelization effort that was essentially global in nature. From the order's point of view, the Holy Roman Empire, with its Protestant apostates and superstitious rural populations, was merely "another India." The Peace of Westphalia freed up growing numbers of German Jesuits to travel "the Indies" proper, including Pacific regions, and they began shaping the views of Germans back home about faraway places through letters and print media.[58] Over time Protestant missionaries, too, followed suit. The year 1648 therefore emerges as an important milestone not only of domestic reordering, but also of German engagement with the world beyond Europe. Newer scholarship on the internal history of the Holy Roman Empire, which has pushed against the tenacious notion of the empire as an unwieldy, inefficient, and failing political system that delayed Germany's entrance into modern nationhood, has offered a positive re-evaluation of 1648. Long portrayed as the death knell for the vitality of the Reformation period, and the moment when the Holy Roman Empire fell into moribund stagnation, the Peace of Westphalia in this perspective appears as a take-off for effective institutional rebuilding and much-needed reform, which laid the foundation for further political evolution and renewed sociocultural dynamism.[59] These internal innovations, on the one hand, and the intensified engagement with the non-European world, one the other, would appear to be two sides of the same coin of post-1648 renewal and dynamism.

Moving into the ensuing century, the commercial integration of the Pacific that David Igler discusses for the period from the mid-eighteenth to the mid-nineteenth century roughly coincided with the onset of the first phase of industrialization and commercial expansion in the German lands. To put it more provocatively, it might be possible to argue that Germans developed imperial ambitions and activities before or while becoming a nation-state. Uwe Spiekermann's chapter on the commercial expansion of the German-American

Spreckels family on the American West Coast and in the Pacific exemplifies such activities by non-state actors. Along similar lines, Reinhard Wendt's contribution shows how Pacific islands became the destination for the migration of ethnic Germans during the same period. The German model of imperial expansion differed from the British and French model in that the "trans" and the "national" appeared simultaneously rather than sequentially.[60] In this sense, it was perhaps more similar to the imperial expansion of, say, the Dutch in the eighteenth century, where the formation of the nation-state occurred simultaneously with imperial expansions.

One of the most innovative aspects of the transnational turn in historiography surely consists in the ways in which familiar narratives and chronologies begin to look different when essentially national (and often teleological) frameworks are dissolved. Thus the contributions in this volume also document how an idea of Germanness takes shape and is enacted in confrontation and cooperation with other European empires in the Pacific as well as with indigenous "others." Conversely, the considerable participation of Germans in transnational networks shows that competing visions of what it meant to be German were already being discussed in reference to the larger world—and to the Pacific more specifically. The volume provides further evidence of Sebastian Conrad's central insight, namely how "globalization" and the formation of the modern nation-state went hand in hand and mutually informed each other.[61] Or, as Geoff Eley put it more recently, "by thinking transnationally in advance of the national state's creation, we can observe the 'boundaries of German-ness' already being fashioned into place."[62]

This is also a central reason for why this volume crosses the conventional divide between the early modern and the modern periods. The early transnational or global ties and protonationalist conversations that our contributors uncover invite us to rethink the rise of nationalism in the nineteenth century as part of a longer and more complex history of German engagement with the extra-European world. They further contribute to a revised understanding of the origins of German colonialism, one that reaches back many centuries before the onset of formal colonialism in the late nineteenth century, and it points forward to non-state-driven forms of imperial presence in the postcolonial period. The volume thus also raises the question of whether the different German involvements in the early modern period helped usher in a different imperial presence in the nineteenth century. One cannot flatten the complexity of the precolonial period into a simplistic teleological prehistory of the colonial period; it followed its own historical logic, and included paths not taken. But it is notable that later German colonists, like the early modern missionaries and naturalists who preceded them, developed a wide variety of relationships that depended as much on local circumstances as on German interests and on relationships with other imperial powers. A long tradition of adjusting to local contexts and engaging with multiple authorities perhaps engendered a more flexible approach to colonial penetration and rule. Shellen Wu's contribution, for example, is suggestive in that it demonstrates how German engineers in China deliberately sought to develop more cooperative forms of imperialism in order to distinguish themselves from British and French competitors. Doug McGetchin, in turn, shows how German policy aligned with Indian anticolonialism in an effort to weaken the British Empire during World War I.

This is neither to downplay the well-known coercive dimension of German colonialism in the Pacific (or elsewhere) nor to overlook the active participation of early modern German Jesuit missionaries in the "othering" and oppressing island populations in the Spanish-controlled Pacific. Various contributors to the volume call attention to German colonial violence and dominance. They do so by focusing on mechanisms that simultaneously lay beyond and underpinned political rule and economic exploitation. Thus, the chapters by Katharina Stornig, Livia Maria Rigotti, and Emma Thomas locate struggles over religion, gender, and sexuality at the heart of the German colonial enterprise, while Jürgen Schmidt points to the ideological importance of a German "work ethic" to colonial governance. They also gesture toward what Geoff Eley called the "colonial effect"—that is, the myriad ways in which the colonial experience informed and shaped German society and culture at home.[63] Yet the colonial effect was not just a modern phenomenon, but, as this volume demonstrates, it was operative already in the early modern period, albeit in a more mediated way. German botanists, missionaries, and naturalists may have participated in the colonial adventures of others. Still, their reports from afar also fed into evolving conceptions of colonialism and Germanness back home.

By arranging contributions across the span of centuries of German presence in the Pacific, the volume finally invites reflection on the early modern and colonial roots of modern scientific exploration. German explorers of the eighteenth and nineteenth centuries at times self-consciously followed the paths of early modern missionaries, yet failed to acknowledge or even outright disavow their religious sources. The emergence of modern science and academic disciplines in Europe owed much to the earlier ethnographic, geographical, and botanical work of missionaries in the Pacific and to the indigenous informants whose local expertise was indispensable for missionaries and naturalists alike, even though neither group gave much credit to these indigenous knowledge brokers. In fact, "German science" about the Pacific, to put it bluntly, owed much to religion and indigenous peoples. These are only some of the connections and themes that can result from a more dynamic understanding of encounters and entanglements between Europeans and Pacific peoples, neither subsumed under the dictates of empire nor defined by clearly delineated geographical or chronological boundaries, but rather emerging and reverberating across multiple cultural domains both in the Pacific itself and back in Europe.

Contributions

Our contributors flesh out these larger themes from a variety of vantage points in richly textured case studies. Raquel Reyes opens the first section with an exploration of the motivations, activities, and networks of German apothecaries and botanists in early modern Indonesia, the Philippines, and Japan. She highlights how already in the early modern period commercially minded and scientifically inclined German naturalists contributed to the production of medical and scientific knowledge that became so important to the botanical prospecting of empires and global trade. Most of her subjects were active under the aegis of the VOC: Andreas Cleyer (1634–98), gentleman-soldier turned director of the Dutch medical shop in Batavia; Georg Everard Rumpf (1627–1702), gentleman-soldier turned naturalist of Ambon and the Spice Islands; and finally, Engelbert Kaempfer (1651–1716), a physician in VOC employed in Japan and Indonesia, and an avid student of medical practices. But there was also Georg Josef Camel, a Jesuit missionary-pharmacist in Manila, who devoted much time to gathering specimens and documenting plant life in the Philippines. What distinguished these Germans, according to Reyes, was the blend of entrepreneurial spirit with scholarly disposition. They maintained close ties to the European scholarly community while, at the same time, forging relationships with and relying on local informants who were knowledgeable in indigenous herbal medicines, such as native healers and Chinese herbalists. Men on the margins of empires, they made central contributions to emerging new European sciences.

The next chapter, by Ulrike Strasser, dovetails with several of the themes introduced by Reyes, such as the importance of learned Germans as knowledge brokers between indigenous life worlds and European empires. Strasser examines the history of the first European map of the Caroline Islands of Oceania, which was printed in multiple European countries and associated with a German Jesuit named Paul Klein (1652–1717). Originally from Bohemia, the highly educated Klein spent most of his life in Manila where he reached high offices and engaged in various intellectual pursuits, including botanical work in tandem with Georg Josef Camel as discussed by Reyes. The intersecting networks of the Spanish colonial empire, the far-flung transnational Society of Jesus, and the European Republic of Letters made it possible for German Jesuits like Klein to travel to the Pacific and for their materials to circulate back to Europe. Yet while the first European map of the Caroline Islands has been attributed to Klein, this version was actually a copy of a copy, with the original sketch provided by a group of Carolinian castaways using pebbles in the sand to communicate with the Europeans. Strasser highlights the cross-cultural exchange at the heart of this mapmaking enterprise, and the indispensable role of indigenous informants in the making of "European" knowledge. Highlighting the many hands involved in the making of this map and how various contributors were made invisible over time, Strasser points to some of the challenges of isolating a "German" contribution to early modern knowledge production in and about the Pacific, and calls attention to the transformation of knowledge during its journey from the Pacific to Europe.

Andreas Daum analyzes the German contribution to what he calls a "transnational culture of expertise" among explorers of the Pacific around 1800. Prussia, as the largest German state at that time, was not a maritime power, and German explorers therefore participated in the voyages of other European imperial powers, mainly Britain, France, and Russia. They include Johann Reinhold and Georg Foster, who sailed on James Cook's second voyage (1772–75) and whose publications inspired the journeys of the most famous of all German explorers, Alexander Humboldt, from 1799 to 1804. Yet Daum also identifies up to thirty less-well-known German naturalists who traveled on these voyages and made important and lasting scientific contributions to the study of the human and natural environment of the Pacific. Their apparent disadvantages of not being directly tied to European projects of imperial explorations eventually turned out to be fortuitous. German naturalists' academic training provided them with an expertise that was in high demand; their communicative and linguistic skills enabled them to convey their discoveries to a larger educated public. Finally, the Germans' pragmatic rather than ideological perspective entailed an "intellectual openness" and "relative autonomy" that allowed them to move beyond a merely imperial optic in their encounters with Pacific habitats. This stance the German scientists seem to have shared with German missionaries like Klein.

Following Andreas Daum's suggestion to "study individually" the "complex ways in which German travelers perceived and analyzed the natural habitats they observed in the Pacific," Kristina Küntzel-Witt examines closely the lives and contributions of two German explorers, Georg Wilhelm Streller and Carl Heinrich Merck. Like some of the explorers discussed by Daum, Streller and Merck sailed under a foreign flag, this time in the service of Russian explorations of the North Pacific. Having studied medicine and natural science at the University of Heller, Steller eventually moved to St. Petersburg and then participated in Vitus Bering's second Kamchatka expedition from 1773 to 1783. Based on Streller's diary, Küntzel-Witt reconstructs Streller's explorations of the natural fauna, his discovery of a now extinct sea cow named after him, as well as his encounter with indigenous people. Küntzel-Witt also examines Streller's conflicts with seamen on the ship who questioned his medical authority. A few years later, the German botanist and physician Carl H. Merck participated in the Billing-Sarychev expedition of the North Pacific from 1785 to 1794. Merck's collection of plants, herbs, and artifacts was eventually handed over to the Russian Academy of Science, though his diaries were not published and did not become widely known until the twentieth century. Küntzel-Witt's chapter thus rescues from near historical oblivion the contributions of two German scientists to the exploration of the North Pacific, while confirming Daum's thesis that these German explorers defined their "Germanness" mainly with respect to their academic training and superior level of *Bildung*. Their specific Germanness, to put it in stark terms, lay precisely in identifying themselves in the "universal" terms of scientific training and expertise. These were also precisely the qualifications that made them desirable participants in the imperial voyages of other European powers.

Anne Mariss's essay also offers a close-up look at German knowledge production by considering the ship as an incubator of knowledge. Like Daum and Küntzel-Witt, Mariss stresses the important role of Germans not just in the reception but also the production of knowledge about Pacific worlds. Like Reyes and Strasser, she emphasizes the role of the indigenous in the development of European epistemic concepts. Taking Johann Reinhold Foster's participation in the second Cook voyage (1772–75) as an example of a "microhistory of the global," Mariss examines the "social and material conditions of the processes of knowledge production in voyages of exploration." While Foster incorporated his discoveries in the field of the then dominant Linnean conceptual framework, the interests of the ship's commanding officers often limited the available time for the complete collection of specimens. Moreover, Foster's research was often influenced by, and depended on, the empirical observations of seamen on the ship, who were able to draw on past experiences. Seamen not only coined botanical and zoological terms still in use today but often also competed with naturalists in collecting specimens. Mariss's chapter thus points at conflicts between naturalists and seamen in the process of knowledge production, which is alluded to in Küntzel-Witt's chapter as well. Finally, Mariss's chapter highlights the role of indigenous people as important cultural intermediaries. Polynesians often served as crucial local informants for European naturalists like Foster, but occasionally they consciously withheld information and knowledge against what constituted European "bioprospecting" or "biopiracy" of the natural environment of the Pacific.

Knowledge transfers, which had been a major element in the premodern interaction between Germany and the Pacific worlds, continued well into the nineteenth and twentieth centuries, although new actors emerged alongside the missionaries, travelers, explorers, and scientists who made up the earlier European presence in the Pacific. Informal patterns of influence from preimperial days persisted and even expanded in the period of formal empire. Shellen Wu's chapter shows that engineers became important brokers of cultural and technological transfers and informal agents of empire in the modern period, when German universities not only trained those venturing outward, but hosted foreigners, initiating a two-way traffic between countries. Specifically, Wu examines the role of German engineers in building a formal and informal empire in China from 1880 to 1914. Chinese students attended German technological colleges and universities, while German engineers and scientists took up key positions in China's nascent industry and technological colleges. Although originally sent on a clandestine mission without *Reichstag* approval, German engineers crucially contributed to Germany's imperial presence in China by building infrastructure, mines, and factories. These engineers received an extremely attractive compensation and the full support of the German embassy. Since they made decisions about which machinery the Chinese purchased, these Germans were seen as important promoters of German products and crucial nodes of future business networks. As such, German engineers played an important role in the competition with other nations, notably the British, Belgians, Russians, and Americans, over access to the vast Chinese market.

Already in the early modern period, the economic integration of the Pacific constituted a central element of European expansion into the Pacific. In the modern period, German-American entrepreneurs were directly and significantly involved in this project. In exploring the economic ventures of the Spreckels family, Uwe Spiekermann analyzes a fascinating example of German-American business activity in the Pacific between 1870 and 1920. The Spreckels developed the Hawaiian sugar industry and created several shipping lines connecting, among others, San Francisco and Hawaii, and Australia and Samoa. Their wealth enabled them to play an important role in developing the infrastructure of West Coast cities such as San Francisco and San Diego. The example of the Spreckels reveals the German-American presence in the interstices of the expanding US empire in the Pacific: they were instrumental in advancing US interests in Hawaii, and their ships were deployed in US imperialist ventures in the Pacific. Spiekermann makes clear that their German descent significantly contributed to their business successes: they continued to rely on their contacts in and with Germany by recruiting German-trained engineers and thus made use of their technological expertise. Sometimes they even traveled back to Germany to learn about the latest cultivation methods and about new agricultural machinery. Technology transfer relied on personal networks and travel of individuals. Their belief in white supremacy led them to attempt to recruit—unsuccessfully—German and Scandinavian workers, but they ultimately relied on Chinese labor. In the end, their business success resulted from a genuinely transnational confluence of interconnected factors such as German technology, American capital, and Asian labor. This is a prime example of how private commercial actors of German descent were centrally involved in the gradual expansion of informal US imperialism in the Pacific.

By the late nineteenth century, Germans were not only involved in the imperial enterprises of other nations, they also appeared in the Pacific as colonizers in their own right. Focusing on Germans in Samoa, Jürgen Schmidt analyzes conflicting notions of work ethic. He reveals how German self-perceptions and perceptions of the colonized islanders shaped attitudes toward work on Samoa.

As the island was conceived as an abundant paradise of the South Sea, Germans more or less accepted what they perceived to be different attitudes toward work. Samoans refused to conform to European work schedules and were in a strong position to defend their autonomy because Germans—in the absence of soldiers and policemen—needed their voluntary cooperation. As a result, Germans colonizers engaged in the widely used practice of importing contract workers ("coolies") from China and Melanesia who had to work under harsh conditions and often did not renew their contracts after the initial three-year term. While German settlers often perceived Samoans as lazy, notwithstanding a high level of productivity on the island, they often overlooked similar attitudes among Germans. The climate and the autonomy of the remote colony precluded the retention of German patterns of work among colonial administrators and merchants. In a way, Samoans and Germans moved toward a cultural symbiosis at the expense of Chinese and Melanesian coolies.

Livia Maria Rigotti's chapter also looks at the interaction of Germans and indigenous people during the colonial period at the end of the nineteenth and the beginning of the twentieth centuries. She also calls attention to German women travelers to the Pacific, and together with the two following chapters by Stornig and Thomas opens up the exploration of gender dynamics in the German–Pacific encounter. Rigotti's chapter highlights the marked differences between African and South Sea colonies. Due to the remoteness of the South Sea and the small numbers of German settlers, racial divisions were not as rigid as in Africa. Indeed, interracial marriages and informal relationships of German men and indigenous women were quite common. These couples and their offspring were by and large socially accepted—or at least tolerated. Relationships of German women and indigenous men, however, remained rare and strictly taboo. The large surplus of men in the German colonial communities made it easier for German women to find a suitable co-ethnic as a partner. Social dividing lines lost much of the rigor they bore in Germany. Thus, marriages across social demarcations were common. The number of German women migrating to the South Sea remained small. Unless they were married to German colonists, most of the German women in the South Sea worked as nurses, but some were nuns, helpers of missions, educators, or cooks. Colonial or women's associations in Germany and religious missions supported these journeys because they considered the lack of women in the colonies as a major problem. The main rationale for the settling of women in the South Sea was the founding of German families and the prevention of "mixed marriages." Given the relative numbers of the sexes, this aim failed in many cases, and a culture of relative tolerance and even mutual integration developed—an untypical outcome for German colonies.

Katharina Stornig focuses on German missionary women in the Pacific, whose outlook in some respects resembled that of early modern German Jesuit missionaries. When Catholic nuns from Germany arrived in New Guinea in the late nineteenth century they needed to cooperate closely with indigenous women, especially in their work as educators and care givers. According to Stornig, their relationship was characterized by mutual assistance and by bitter conflicts. The latter revolved around questions of morality. Nuns perceived New Guinea as a highly sexualized space that posed multiple threats to Christian propriety. The nuns saw themselves as selfless sufferers and courageous evangelizers, often leading ascetic and highly disciplined lives. Their model of femininity collided with indigenous lifestyles. One field in which conflicts came to the boil was the corporal punishment of pupils, which the nuns perceived as "loving care." The nuns, like the Jesuits before them, also mediated European perceptions of New Guinea as they established a sphere of communication through letters and journal articles, which were printed in the Catholic press in Germany.

Emma Thomas looks at a very different group of women in German New Guinea, further complicating the gendered dynamics at play. Her essay focuses on female Pacific Islanders and other Asians who worked as indentured laborers for the Germans and thus represented one facet of widely practiced unfree labor in the colonies. Indentured labor was a key feature of colonial exploitation. Until 1914, about 85,000 New Guineans had been indentured to work on plantations for the colonial government or the missions. Most of them were men, which put the female laborers into a particularly vulnerable position. Recruitment was often involuntary, and there was a premium paid for single women as the massive surplus of men among the colonists and the indigenous workforce created a huge demand for women, both as domestic laborers and objects of sexual exploitation. Indeed, white colonists, as Thomas shows, believed themselves to have unrestricted access to the labor and the bodies of these women. The women were often the victims of gendered violence, including sexual assault and rape by both German colonists and male New Guinean laborers. When these cases were brought to the attention of the authorities and even became objects of court procedures, the male line of defense was to equate indentured women with prostitutes. Colonial courts sometimes convicted indigenous men but regularly acquitted Germans. White fantasies of the islanders' sexual permissiveness and promiscuity also added to this discourse, which legitimized gendered and racialized forms of violence.

A very different entanglement of Germans in trans-Pacific networks is the subject of Douglas T. McGetchin's chapter on the Ghadar movement that agitated on behalf of Indian independence in the United States and across the Pacific rim before and during World War I. McGetchin shows how a broad anti-British impetus led German diplomats as well as private citizens to lend material and logistic support to Indian nationalists in their struggles against British imperialism. Most of these plots eventually failed or needed to operate on increasingly hostile territory after the US entry into World War I in April 1917. Yet these activities nevertheless forged ties between German officials and Indian anti-imperialism that persisted into the post–World War I era when Weimar Berlin became an important hub for Indian nationalists. McGetchin thus succeeds in revealing a small if important German contribution to Indian nationalism that took shape across Pacific worlds.

A similarly small yet revealing form of the German presence in the Pacific is the subject of Reinhard Wendt's contribution. He traces the history of a transcultural diaspora of a group of ethnic Germans who migrated from Pyritz, Pomerania to Vava'u, a group of tropical islands in Tonga, in the second half of the nineteenth century, as well as the persistent cultural memory of this migration into the twentieth century. In a chain migration from the German lands, several community members followed a successful pioneer, established thriving businesses, forged economic contacts with surrounding territories, and gradually developed a hybrid Tongan–German identity, largely through intermarriage. As Wendt shows, this was a migration driven not by the push of a desperate situation at home but rather by the pull of a quite realistic appraisal by community members of the prospects for a better life in the South Pacific. It also preceded the formal establishment of Western colonialism in the South Pacific, with Tonga eventually becoming a British colony. World War I ended the "golden age" of a German transcultural diaspora in the South Pacific, but even after Vava'u Germans were dispersed throughout the Pacific, they managed to cultivate and preserve a cultural memory of Germanness throughout the remainder of the twentieth century. They thus provide another fitting example for the *longue durée* of a German presence in the Pacific worlds between Sydney and San Francisco, Auckland and Anchorage, that this volume as a whole seeks to bring into focus.

Ulrike Strasser is professor of history at the University of California, San Diego. She specializes in early modern Central Europe, religious history, gender history, and global history. Her publications include the award-winning monograph, *State of Virginity: Gender, Politics, and Religion in a Catholic State* (Michigan Publishing, 2004; paperback 2007).

Frank Biess is professor of history at the University of California, San Diego. He is the author of *Homecomings: Returning POWs and the Legacies of Defeat in Postwar Germany* (Princeton, NJ, 2006). He is currently completing a history of fear and anxiety in postwar West Germany.

Hartmut Berghoff is the director of the Institute of Economic and Social History at the University of Göttingen in Germany. He was the director of the German Historical Institute in Washington, DC from 2008 to 2015. He held various visiting positions at the Center of Advanced Study in Berlin, at Harvard Business School, Maison des sciences de l'homme in Paris, and at Henley Business School in the UK.

Notes

Many thanks go to Charles Parker, Jeremy Prestholdt, and Heidi Tinsman for their critical reading of an earlier draft and helpful suggestions for improvement. We further thank the two anonymous reviewers for pushing our thinking on some key issues.

1. For an overview of the field of global history and its effects on the discipline, see Douglas Taylor Northrop, *A Companion to World History*, Wiley-Blackwell Companions to World History (Chichester, UK: Wiley-Blackwell, 2012) and Patrick Manning, *Navigating World History: Historians Create a Global Past*, 1st ed. (New York: Palgrave Macmillan, 2003). For the early modern period, see Charles H. Parker, *Global Interactions in the Early Modern Age, 1400–1800*, Cambridge Essential Histories (Cambridge: Cambridge University Press, 2010).
2. See Thomas A. Brady, *German Histories in the Age of Reformations, 1400–1650* (Cambridge: Cambridge University Press, 2009), 12–14.
3. For the early modern period, see Brady, *German Histories*, and the magisterial two-volume account by Joachim Whaley. Joachim Whaley, *Germany and the Holy Roman Empire, Volume 1: Maximilian I to the Peace of Westphalia 1493–1648 & Volume II: Peace of Westphalia to the Dissolution of the Reich* (Oxford: Oxford University Press, 2012).
4. See also Edward R. Dickinson, "The German Empire: An Empire?" *History Workshop Journal* 66 (2008): 129–62.
5. The discovery of the Pacific as a space teeming with histories is inseparable from the larger trend of ocean history; see for example: Jerry H. Bentley, Renate Bridenthal, and Kären Wigen, *Seascapes: Maritime Histories, Littoral Cultures, and Transoceanic Exchanges*, Perspectives on the Global Past (Honolulu: University of Hawaii Press, 2007). Also, "AHR Forum: Oceans of History," *American Historical Review* 111, no. 3 (2006).
6. O. H. K. Spate, *Monopolists and Freebooters, The Pacific since Magellan*, Vol. 2 (Minneapolis: University of Minnesota Press, 1983); Spate, *The Spanish Lake, The Pacific since Magellan*, Vol. 1 (Minneapolis: University of Minnesota Press, 1979). Arif Dirlik speaks of a "EuroAmerica invention" in his critical engagement with the construction of this region, which extends into the twenty-first century. Arif Dirlik, *What Is in a Rim?: Critical Perspectives on the Pacific Region Idea*, 2nd ed. (Lanham, MD: Rowman & Littlefield, 1998), 4ff.
7. Matt K. Matsuda, *Pacific Worlds: A History of Seas, Peoples, and Cultures* (Cambridge: Cambridge University Press, 2012), quotation on 2; Matsuda, "AHR Forum: The Pacific", *American Historical Review* 111, no. 3 (2006): 758–80. See also Karen Wigen and Jessica Harland-Jacobs, eds., Special Issue: Oceans Connect, *Geographical Review* 89, no. 2 (1999); Nicholas Thomas, *Islanders: The Pacific in the Age of Empire* (New Haven, CT: Yale University Press, 2012); David Armitage and Alison Bashford, eds., *Pacific Histories: Ocean, Land, People* (Basingstoke, UK: Palgrave Macmillan, 2014).
8. For example: Ben R. Finney, *Voyage of Rediscovery: A Cultural Odyssey through Polynesia* (Berkeley: University of California Press, 1994); Patrick V. Kirch, *On the Roads of the Winds: An Archeological History of the Pacific Islands before European Contact* (Los Angeles: University of California Press, 2000).
9. Points-of-entry into the vast Pacific-based literature and its issues include: Malama Meleisea, "Pacific Historiography: An Indigenous View," *Journal of Pacific Studies* 4 (1978): 5–43; David Routledge, "Pacific History as Seen from the Pacific Islands," *Pacific Studies* 8, no. 2 (1985): 81–99; Doug Munro, "Who 'Owns' Pacific History? Reflections on the Insider/Outsider Dichotomy," *Journal of Pacific History* 28, no. 2 (1994): 232–37; Doug Munro and Brij V. Lal, *Texts and Contexts: Reflections in Pacific Islands Historiography* (Honolulu: University of Hawaii

Press, 2006); Paul D'Arcy, *The People of the Sea: Environment, Identity and History in Oceania* (Honolulu: University of Hawaii Press, 2006).
10. Matsuda, *Pacific Worlds*, 50ff.
11. Rainer F. Buschmann, *Oceans in World History*, 1st ed. (New York: McGraw-Hill, 2007). Buschmann sets 1850 as the tipping point for European dominance (see p. 97).
12. Ibid., 49–55, 81–83. For a comprehensive account of the Portuguese Empire in Asia, see Sanjay Subrahmanyam, *The Portuguese Empire in Asia, 1500–1700: A Political and Economic History*, 2nd ed. (Chichester, UK: Wiley-Blackwell, 2012).
13. Buschmann, *Oceans in World History*, 84–85.
14. Matsuda, *Pacific Worlds*, 57–58. Buschmann, *Oceans in World History*, 76–79. On the Marianas, see Robert F. Rogers, *Destiny's Landfall: A History of Guam*, Rev. ed. (Honolulu: University of Hawaii Press, 2011).
15. Thus the title of volume 1 of Oskar Spate's trilogy, which remains a key point of reference: Spate, *The Spanish Lake*.
16. Matsuda, *Pacific Worlds*, 114–26. Dennis Owen Flynn, Arturo Giráldez, and James Sobredo, *European Entry into the Pacific: Spain and the Acapulco-Manila Galleons*, The Pacific World (Aldershot, UK: Ashgate, 2001). On the Marianas, see Alexandre Coello de la Rosa, *Jesuits at the Margins: Missions and Missionaries in the Marianas (1668–1769)*, 1st ed., Routledge Studies in Cultural History (New York: Routledge, Taylor & Francis Group, 2016).
17. Matsuda, *Pacific Worlds*, 74–82; Parker, *Global Interactions*, 23–26. Spate, *Monopolists and Freebooters*.
18. Matsuda, *Pacific Worlds*, 88–102.
19. Matsuda, *Pacific Worlds*, 64–73, 83–87. There is of course a literature on each of these encounters, including paradigmatic studies such as: Greg Dening, *Islands and Beaches: Discourse on a Silent Land: Marquesas, 1774–1880* (Honolulu: University of Hawaii Press, 1980); Anne Salmond, *Two Worlds: First Meetings between Maori and Europeans, 1642–1772* (Honolulu: University of Hawaii Press, 1991).
20. Alan Frost, "The Pacific Ocean: The Eighteenth Century's New World," *Studies on Voltaire and the Eighteenth Century* 152 (1976): 779–822.
21. Tony Ballantyne, *Science, Empire, and the European Exploration of the Pacific* (Burlington, VT: Ashgate, 2004).
22. Daniela Bleichmar, *Visible Empire: Botanical Expeditions and Visual Culture in the Hispanic Enlightenment* (Chicago, IL: The University of Chicago Press, 2012).
23. O. H. K. Spate, *Paradise Found and Lost*, The Pacific since Magellan, Vol. 3 (Minneapolis: University of Minnesota Press, 1988). Matsuda, *Pacific Worlds*, 127–43. Buschmann, *Oceans in World History*, 86–93. Jane Samson, *British Imperial Strategies in the Pacific, 1750–1900*, The Pacific World (Aldershot, UK: Ashgate, 2003). Annick Foucrier, *The French and the Pacific World, 17th–19th Centuries: Explorations, Migrations, and Cultural Exchanges*, Pacific World (Aldershot, UK: Ashgate, 2005). Dorinda Outram, *Panorama of the Enlightenment* (Los Angeles: J. Paul Getty Museum, 2006).
24. David Igler, *Great Ocean: Pacific Worlds from Captain Cook to the Gold Rush* (New York: Oxford University Press, 2013), 139.
25. Lionel Frost, "The Economic History of the Pacific," in *The Cambridge World History: Volume 7, Part 1, Production, Destruction and Connection, 1750–Present*, ed. John McNeill and Kenneth Pomeranz (Cambridge: Cambridge University Press, 2015), 616.
26. Igler, *Great Ocean*, 25–26, 37.
27. Ibid., 118.
28. Ibid., 107; Matsuda, *Pacific Worlds*, 185–86.
29. Frost, "Economic History of the Pacific," 613, 20. In greater detail, James Hoare, *Japan's Treaty Ports and Foreign Settlements: The Uninvited Guests, 1858–1899* (Folkestone, UK: Japan Library, 1994).

30. Kenneth Pomeranz and Steven Topik, *The World That Trade Created: Society, Culture, and the World Economy, 1400 to the Present*, 2nd ed. (Armonk, NY: M.E. Sharpe, 2006), 6–8.
31. Frost, "Economic History of the Pacific," 615.
32. Ibid., 618.
33. Igler, *Great Ocean*.
34. Frost, "Economic History of the Pacific," 619–20. Elsbeth Locher-Scholten, "Imperialism after the Great Wave: The Dutch Case in the Netherlands East Indies, 1860–1914," in *Liberal Imperialism in Europe*, ed. Matthew Fitzpatrick (New York: Palgrave, 2012). Matsuda, *Pacific Worlds*, 197–98.
35. Matsuda, *Pacific Worlds*, 200–2. Frost, "Economic History of the Pacific," 620.
36. Matsuda, *Pacific Worlds*, 202–5.
37. Ibid., 210–11.
38. Ibid., 214.
39. Ibid., 228–29.
40. Horst Gründer, "Die Voraussetzungen des deutschen Kolonialismus," in *Die Deutsche Südsee, 1884-1914. Ein Handbuch*, ed. Herrman Joseph Hiery (Paderborn: Ferdinand Schöningh, 2001), 27–58. See also more comprehensively in Horst Gründer, *Geschichte der deutschen Kolonien* (Paderborn: Schöningh, 1985).
41. Matsuda, *Pacific Worlds*, 254; Paul A. Kramer, *The Blood of Government: Race, Empire, the United States & the Philippines* (Chapel Hill: University of North Carolina Press, 2006).
42. Matsuda, *Pacific Worlds*, 238–41.
43. Jürgen Osterhammel, *Die Verwandlung der Welt. Eine Geschichte des 19. Jahrhunderts* (Munich: C.H. Beck, 2009), 169.
44. Matsuda, *Pacific Worlds*, 220–27.
45. Ibid., 226.
46. Hermann Hiery, *The Neglected War: The German South Pacific and the Influence of World War I* (Honolulu: University of Hawaii Press, 1995).
47. Cited in Jörn Leonhard, *Die Büchse der Pandora: Geschichte des Ersten Weltkrieges* (Munich: C.H. Beck, 2014), 711.
48. Ibid., 707–8.
49. Erez Manela, *The Wilsonian Moment: Self-Determination and the International Origins of Anticolonial Nationalism* (New York: Oxford University Press, 2007).
50. See Hermann Hiery and John Mackenzie, eds., *European Impact and Pacific Influence: British and Gerrman Colonial Policy in the Pacific Islands and the Indigenous Response* (London: I.B. Tauris, 1997); Herrman Joseph Hiery and Hans Martin-Hinz, eds., *Deutsche und Chinesen in Tsingtau, 1897–1914* (Berlin: Deutsches Historisches Museum, 1999); Horst Hübner, *Kolonialverwaltung, Überseehandel Und Wissenschaftliche Forschung: Das Beispiel Der Ehemaligen Deutschen Schutzgebiete Im Stillen Ozean* (Bergisch Gladbach: 1-2-buch, 2008); John A. Moses and Paul Kennedy, *Germany in the Pacific and Far East, 1870–1914* (St. Lucia: University of Queensland Press, 1977); Herrman Joseph Hiery, *Das Deutsche Reich in Der Südsee (1900–1921): Eine Annäherung an Die Erfahrung Verschiedener Kulturen* (Göttingen: Vandehoeck & Ruprecht, 1995); Stewart Firth, *New Guinea under the Germans* (Melbourne University Press: Carlton Vic, 1982); Peter J. Hempenstall, *Pacific Islanders under German Rule: A Study of the Meaning of Colonial Resistance* (Canberra: Australian National University Press, 1978); John E. Schrecker, *Imperialism and Chinese Nationalism: Germany in Shantung* (Cambridge, MA: Harvard University Press, 1971).
51. Hermann Hiery, ed., *Die Deutsche Südsee 1884–1914. Ein Handbuch* (Paderborn: Ferdiand Schönigh, 2001).
52. See, for example, recent edited collections that do not include contributions on the Pacific, or treat the subject only very marginally: Volker Langbehn and Mohammad Salama, eds., *German*

Colonialism: Race, the Holocaust, and Postwar Germany (New York: Columbia University Press, 2011); Bradley Naranch and Geoff Eley, eds., *German Colonialism in a Global Age* (Durham, NC: Duke University Press, 2014). On this tendency in the historiography, see Hiery, *Das Deutsche Reich in Der Südsee*, 13. For an exception, especially regarding China, see Nina Berman, Klaus Mühlhahn and Patrick Nganang, eds., *German Colonialism Revisited: African, Asian, and Oceanic Experiences* (Ann Arbor: University of Michigan Press, 2014).
53. See Hanno Beck, *Germania in Pacifico: Der deutsche Anteil an der Erschließung des Pazifischen Beckens* (Wiesbaden: Steiner, 1970). More recently, see Hilary Howes, *The Race Question in Oceania: A.B. Meyer and Otto Firsch between Metropolitan Theory and Field Experiences, 1865–1914*. Frankfurt a.M.: Peter Lang, 2013; Elena Govor, *Twelve Days at Nuku Hiva: Russian Encounters and Mutiny in the South Pacific*. Honolulu: University of Hawaii Press, 2010.
54. Peter Reill, Comment for Session on "Germans in the Pacific, 1650 to 1850", German Studies Association Conference, San Diego, October 2016.
55. C. R. Boxer, *The Dutch Seaborne Empire, 1600–1800*, 1st American ed., The History of Human Society (New York: Knopf, 1965), 89–93.
56 56. Igler, *Great Ocean*, 129–130, 139–142.
57. As one paradigmatic example, see Sebastian Conrad, *German Colonialism: A Short History* (New York: Cambridge University Press, 2012). See also Nina Berman, *German Colonialism Revisited*.
58. Ulrike Strasser, "A Case of Empire Envy? German Jesuits and an Asia-born Saint from Colonial America," *Journal of Global History* (2007): 26–27.
59. Whaley, *Germany and the Holy Roman Empire*, 588–644.
60. Ibid., 30. Dickinson, "The German Empire: An Empire?"
61. Sebastian Conrad, *Globalization and the Nation in Imperial Germany* (New York: Cambridge University Press, 2006); David Armitage, *The Ideological Origins of the British Empire* (Cambridge: Cambridge University Press, 2000); Strasser, "Case of Empire Envy?"; Galaxis Borja and Ulrike Strasser, "The German Circumnavigation of the World: Missionary Writing and Colonial Identity Formation in Joseph Stöcklein's Neuer WeltBott," in *Reporting Christian Missions*, ed. Markus Friedrich and Alex Schunka (Wiesbaden: Harrassowitz, 2017), 73–92.
62. Geoff Eley, "Empire by Land or Sea: Germany's Imperial Imaginary, 1840–1945" in *German Colonialism in a Global Age*, ed. Geoff Eley and Bradley Naranch (Durham, NC: Duke University Press, 2014), 31.
63. Ibid., 37.

Bibliography

"AHR Forum: Oceans of History." *American Historical Review* 111, no. 3 (2006).
Armitage, David. *The Ideological Origins of the British Empire*. Cambridge: Cambridge University Press, 2000.
Armitage, David, and Alison Bashford, eds. *Pacific Histories: Ocean, Land, People*. Basingstoke, UK: Palgrave Macmillan, 2014.
Ballantyne, Tony. *Science, Empire, and the European Exploration of the Pacific*. Burlington, VT: Ashgate, 2004.
Beck, Hanno. *Germania in Pacifico: Der deutsche Anteil an der Erschließung des Pazifischen Beckens*. Wiesbaden: Steiner, 1970.
Bentley, Jerry H., Renate Bridenthal, and Kären Wigen, eds. *Seascapes: Maritime Histories, Littoral Cultures, and Transoceanic Exchanges*. Honolulu: University of Hawaii Press, 2007.

Berman, Nina, Klaus Mühlhahn, and Patrice Nganang, eds. *German Colonialism Revisited: African, Asian, and Oceanic Experiences*. Ann Arbor: University of Michigan Press, 2014.
Bleichmar, Daniela. *Visible Empire: Botanical Expeditions and Visual Culture in the Hispanic Enlightenment*. Chicago, IL: The University of Chicago Press, 2012.
Borja, Galaxis, and Ulrike Strasser. "The German Circumnavigation of the World: Missionary Writing and Colonial Identity Formation in Joseph Stöcklein's Neuer WeltBott." In *Reporting Christian Missions*, edited by M. Friedrich and Alex Schunka, 73–92. Wiesbaden: Harrassowitz, 2017.
Boxer, C. R. *The Dutch Seaborne Empire, 1600–1800*, 1st American ed., The History of Human Society, 89–93. New York: Knopf, 1965.
Brady, Thomas A. *German Histories in the Age of Reformations, 1400–1650*. Cambridge: Cambridge University Press, 2009.
Buschmann, Rainer F. *Oceans in World History*, 1st ed. New York: McGraw-Hill, 2007.
Coello de la Rosa, Alexandre. *Jesuits at the Margins: Missions and Missionaries in the Marianas (1668–1769)*, 1st ed., Routledge Studies in Cultural History. New York: Routledge, Taylor & Francis Group, 2016.
Conrad, Sebastian. *Globalization and the Nation in Imperial Germany*. New York: Cambridge University Press, 2006.
———. *German Colonialism: A Short History*. New York: Cambridge University Press, 2012.
D'Arcy, Paul. *The People of the Sea: Environment, Identity, and History in Oceania*. Honolulu: University of Hawaii Press, 2006.
Dening, Greg. *Islands and Beaches: Discourse on a Silent Land: Marquesas, 1774–1880*. Honolulu: University of Hawaii Press, 1980.
Dickinson, Edward R. "The German Empire: An Empire?" *History Workshop Journal* 66 (2008): 129–62.
Dirlik, Arif. *What Is in a Rim? Critical Perspectives on the Pacific Region Idea*, 2nd ed. Lanham, MD: Rowman & Littlefield, 1998.
Eley, Geoff. "Empire by Land or Sea: Germany's Imperial Imaginary, 1840-1945." In *German Colonialism in a Global Age*, edited by Geoff Eley and Bradley Naranch, 19–45. Durham, NC: Duke University Press, 2014.
Finney, Ben R. *Voyage of Rediscovery: A Cultural Odyssey through Polynesia*. Berkeley: University of California Press, 1994.
Firth, Stewart. *New Guinea under the Germans*. Carlton, Vic: Melbourne University Press, 1982.
Flynn, Dennis Owen, Arturo Giráldez, and James Sobredo. *European Entry into the Pacific: Spain and the Acapulco-Manila Galleons*, The Pacific World. Aldershot, UK: Ashgate, 2001.
Foucrier, Annick. *The French and the Pacific World, 17th–19th Centuries: Explorations, Migrations, and Cultural Exchanges*, The Pacific World. Aldershot, UK: Ashgate, 2005.
Frost, Alan. "The Pacific Ocean: The Eighteenth Century's New World." *Studies on Voltaire and the Eighteenth Century* 152 (1976): 779–822.
Frost, Lionel. "The Economic History of the Pacific." In *The Cambridge World History. Volume 7, Part 1, Production, Destruction and Connection, 1750–Present*, edited by John McNeill and Kenneth Pomeranz, 611–631. Cambridge: Cambridge University Press, 2015.
Govor, Elena. *Twelve Days at Nuku Hiva: Russian Encounters and Mutiny in the South Pacific*. Honolulu: University of Hawaii Press, 2010.
Gründer, Horst. "Die Voraussetzungen des deutschen Kolonialismus." In *Die Deutsche Südsee, 1884–1914. Ein Handbuch*, edited by Herrman Joseph Hiery, 27–58. Paderborn: Ferdinand Schöningh, 2001.

———. *Geschichte der deutschen Kolonien*. Paderborn: Ferdinand Schöningh, 1985.
Hempenstall, Peter J. *Pacific Islanders under German Rule: A Study of the Meaning of Colonial Resistance*. Canberra: Australian National University Press, 1978.
Hiery, Hermann. *Das Deutsche Reich in der Südsee (1900–1921): Eine Annäherung an die Erfahrung verschiedener Kulturen*. Göttingen: Vandehoeck & Ruprecht, 1995.
———. *The Neglected War: The German South Pacific and the Influence of World War I*. Honolulu: University of Hawaii Press, 1995.
———, ed. *Die Deutsche Südsee 1884–1914. Ein Handbuch*. Paderborn: Ferdinand Schönigh, 2001.
Hiery, Hermann, and Hans-Martin Hinz, eds. *Deutsche und Chinesen in Tsingtau, 1897–1914*. Berlin: Deutsches Historisches Museum, 1999.
Hiery, Hermann, and John Mackenzie, eds. *European Impact and Pacific Influence: British and German Colonial Policy in the Pacific Islands and the Indigenous Response*. London: I.B. Tauris, 1997.
Hoare, James. *Japan's Treaty Ports and Foreign Settlements: The Uninvited Guests, 1858–1899*. Folkestone, UK: Japan Library, 1994.
Howes, Hilary. *The Race Question in Oceania: A.B. Meyer and Otto Finsch between Metropolitan Theory and Field Experiences, 1865–1914*. Frankfurt a.M.: Peter Lang, 2013.
Hübner, Horst. *Kolonialverwaltung, Überseehandel und wissenschaftliche Forschung: Das Beispiel der ehemaligen deutschen Schutzgebiete im Stillen Ozean*. Bergisch Gladbach: 1-2-buch, 2008.
Igler, David. *Great Ocean: Pacific Worlds from Captain Cook to the Gold Rush*. New York: Oxford University Press, 2013.
Kirch, Patrick V. *On the Roads of the Winds: An Archeological History of the Pacific Islands before European Contact*. Los Angeles: University of California Press, 2000.
Kramer, Paul A. *The Blood of Government: Race, Empire, the United States & the Philippines*. Chapel Hill: University of North Carolina Press, 2006.
Langbehn, Volker, and Mohammad Salama, eds. *German Colonialism: Race, the Holocaust, and Postwar Germany*. New York: Columbia University Press, 2011.
Leonhard, Jörn. *Die Büchse der Pandora: Geschichte des Ersten Weltkrieges*. Munich: C.H. Beck, 2014.
Locher-Scholten, Elsbeth. "Imperialism after the Great Wave: The Dutch Case in the Netherlands East Indies, 1860–1914." In *Liberal Imperialism in Europe*, edited by Matthew Fitzpatrick, 25–46. New York: Palgrave, 2012.
Manela, Erez. *The Wilsonian Moment: Self-Determination and the International Origins of Anticolonial Nationalism*. New York: Oxford University Press, 2007.
Manning, Patrick. *Navigating World History: Historians Create a Global Past*, 1st ed. New York: Palgrave Macmillan, 2003.
Matsuda, Matt K. *Pacific Worlds: A History of Seas, Peoples, and Cultures*. Cambridge: Cambridge University Press, 2012.
———. "The Pacific." *American Historical Review* 111, no. 3 (2006): 758–80.
Meleisea, Malama. "Pacific Historiography: An Indigenous View." *Journal of Pacific Studies* 4 (1978): 5–43.
Moses, John A., and Paul Kennedy. *Germany in the Pacific and Far East, 1870–1914*. St. Lucia: University of Queensland Press, 1977.
Munro, Doug. "Who 'Owns' Pacific History? Reflections on the Insider/Outsider Dichotomy." *Journal of Pacific History* 28, no. 2 (1994): 232–37.

Munro, Doug, and Brij V. Lal. *Texts and Contexts: Reflections in Pacific Islands Historiography.* Honolulu: University of Hawaii Press, 2006.

Naranch, Bradley, and Geoff Eley, eds. *German Colonialism in a Global Age.* Durham, NC: Duke University Press, 2014.

Northrop, Douglas Taylor. *A Companion to World History,* Wiley-Blackwell Companions to World History. Chichester, UK: Wiley-Blackwell, 2012.

Osterhammel, Jürgen. *Die Verwandlung der Welt. Eine Geschichte des 19. Jahrhunderts.* Munich: C.H. Beck, 2009.

Outram, Dorinda. *Panorama of the Enlightenment.* Los Angeles: J. Paul Getty Museum, 2006.

Parker, Charles H., *Global Interactions in the Early Modern Age, 1400–1800,* Cambridge Essential Histories. Cambridge: Cambridge University Press, 2010.

Pomeranz, Kenneth, and Steven Topik. *The World That Trade Created: Society, Culture, and the World Economy, 1400 to the Present,* 2nd ed. Armonk, NY: M.E. Sharpe, 2006.

Rogers, Robert F. *Destiny's Landfall: A History of Guam,* Rev. ed. Honolulu: University of Hawaii Press, 2011.

Routledge, David. "Pacific History as Seen from the Pacific Islands." *Pacific Studies* 8, no. 2 (1985): 81–99.

Salmond, Anne. *Two Worlds: First Meetings between Maori and Europeans, 1642–1772.* Honolulu: University of Hawaii Press, 1991.

Samson, Jane. *British Imperial Strategies in the Pacific, 1750–1900,* The Pacific World. Aldershot, UK: Ashgate, 2003.

Schrecker, John. E. *Imperialism and Chinese Nationalism: Germany in Shantung.* Cambridge, MA: Harvard University Press, 1971.

Spate, O. H. K. *The Spanish Lake, The Pacific since Magellan.* Vol. 1. Minneapolis: University of Minnesota Press, 1979.

———. *Monopolists and Freebooters, The Pacific since Magellan.* Vol. 2. Minneapolis: University of Minnesota Press, 1983.

———. *Paradise Found and Lost, The Pacific since Magellan.* Vol. 3. Minneapolis: University of Minnesota Press, 1988.

Strasser, Ulrike. "A Case of Empire Envy? German Jesuits and an Asia-born Saint from Colonial America." *Journal of Global History* (2007): 23–40.

Subrahmanyam, Sanjay. *The Portuguese Empire in Asia, 1500–1700: A Political and Economic History,* 2nd ed. Chichester, UK: Wiley-Blackwell, 2012.

Thomas, Nicholas. *Islanders: The Pacific in the Age of Empire.* (New Haven, CT: Yale University Press, 2012.

Whaley, Joachim. *Germany and the Holy Roman Empire, Volume 1: Maximilian I to the Peace of Westphalia 1493–1648 & Volume II: Peace of Westphalia to the Dissolution of the Reich.* Oxford: Oxford University Press, 2012.

Wigen, Karen, and Jessica Harland-Jacobs, eds. *Geographical Review* 89, no. 2 (1999). Special Issue: Oceans Connect.

Part I

MISSIONARIES, EXPLORERS, AND KNOWLEDGE TRANSFER

Chapter 1

GERMAN APOTHECARIES AND BOTANISTS IN EARLY MODERN INDONESIA, THE PHILIPPINES, AND JAPAN

Raquel A. G. Reyes

Introduction

In the Spanish and Dutch colonies in the Pacific of the early modern period, Germans were among the many foreigners who served as missioner priests, soldiers, and sailors employed by the Catholic religious orders, the Spanish Crown, and the Dutch East Indies Company, the *Vereenigde Oost-indische Compagnie*, better known as the VOC. Foreign recruits generally had a lamentable reputation, and men from Germany and Scandinavia were particularly numerous. VOC company officials often complained that they were being sent debauched men who collectively constituted a base and dissolute rabble. Four German naturalists and apothecaries, however, broke this sorry mold and stood above the uncouth hordes: Georg Everard Rumpf (1627–1702), better known by his Latinized name Rumphius, whose prodigious work in the Spice Islands, Ambon and the Moluccas earned him the epithet "Pliny of the Indies"; Andries Cleyer (1634–98), the ambitious and opportunistic director of the *medicinale winkel*, or medical shop in Batavia, the capital of the Dutch East Indies; Engelbert Kaempfer (1651–1716), the physician, scholar-adventurer who voyaged to the Indies, Siam and Japan; and lastly, the Jesuit brother Georg Josef Camel (1661–1706), a skillful herbalist based at Spanish Manila, after whom the camellia flower (*thea japonica*) is named. Through their efforts, a phenomenal amount of biota was collected and described; plants traveled in and around Asia, from and to Europe; and for the first time, information on the natural history, medical practices, and even social customs and cultural myths of the Philippines, Indonesia, Japan, and adjacent areas came to be known. What were the contexts, motivations and

---

Notes from this chapter begin on page 48.

processes involved in amassing all this scientific knowledge? This chapter focuses on the "German connection" in early modern natural history, and tracks the entwined interests of empires, global commercial enterprises, the transmission of local knowledge, and individual entrepreneurial spirit. The developments in botany and natural history discussed here exemplify the spirit of the Scientific Revolution, and are not seen as precursors of the later German Enlightenment or the emergence of the disciplines of ethnography and ethnology.[1]

Empire, Commerce, and Global Botanizing

In the early modern period, every major European power nursed a grandiose but simple ambition: to secure all-important sea routes to the spices, silks, and other riches of the East. Ownership of the Moluccas, better known as the Spice Islands, and control of the trade in cinnamon, cloves, nutmeg, and pepper—that is, the spice trade, then the most lucrative trade in the world—figured centrally in dreams of an empire in the Pacific and motivated extraordinary voyages, from Christopher Columbus (1451–1506) to Vasco da Gama (1469–1524). Arguably, the Dutch came closest to realizing this dream. Soon after their arrival in the Indonesian archipelago around 1600, they wrested control of the Moluccas from the Portuguese. A couple of years later they created the formidable VOC, turned the port city of Jayakerta, on western Java, into the capital city of Batavia and the main Asian headquarters of the VOC, established trading arrangements with the Japanese on the artificial island of Deshima in the port of Nagasaki in Japan, and, through ruthless "total war" campaigns, enforced a trade monopoly on nutmeg, cloves, and mace on the Spice Islands, in addition to securing much of the trade in pepper and cinnamon. At their zenith, VOC territories and trading posts stretched between the Cape of Good Hope and Japan, and six million pounds of black pepper were being imported to the Netherlands annually.[2]

As the Dutch ascended, Spain, in comparison, suffered her share of setbacks: she had lost her crucial claim to the Moluccas and the spice trade to Portugal in 1529. But she was far from being outdone. Spain had gained a foothold in the Pacific by colonizing the Philippine archipelago and, thanks to the ingenuity of the circumnavigator and Augustinian friar Andrés de Urdaneta (1498–1568), had discovered a fast and efficient return route across the Pacific to Mexico, a factor critical to the commercial success of the Spanish colonial enterprise in the Pacific. Urdaneta had sailed from the Visayan island of Cebu in central Philippines and, climbing between thirty-seven and thirty-nine degrees, his ship caught the prevailing westerlies across the Pacific, skirted the California coast, and reached Acapulco in Mexico with a total journey time of four months. With this route secured, Spain established the mighty Trans-Pacific galleon trade with the first of the 'Manila galleons' sailing for Acapulco in 1572, and the last in

1815.³ Departing from the Spanish colonial capital city of Manila, on the island of Luzon in the Philippine archipelago, galleon ships annually set forth eastwards to Acapulco, bringing Chinese silks, spices, porcelain, and other treasures, to return loaded with silver from Spanish America. The galleons were the richest ships in the world and, through the Trans-Pacific trade, Spain came to dominate commerce with America and Europe in both silk and spices. Luxuries and precious merchandise from the East, demanded by New Spain and Europe, were traded in New Spain in exchange for American silver desired by China. Neither demand outweighed the other. The significance of this demand and supply commerce, and the route taken to facilitate it, was far reaching. Not only did two world regions come into contact with one another for the first time through the direct exchange of goods, but this Trans-Pacific trade influenced the histories of four continents—Europe, the Americas, Asia, and Africa.⁴ Moreover, the Manila–Acapulco voyages facilitated important botanical exchanges. Coconuts from the Philippines taken aboard Manila galleons were responsible for the introduction and spread of modern coconut populations in Mexico and southwards to Peru.⁵ The return voyages introduced many New World plants to Southeast Asia: cereals and beans, maize, sweet potato, fruiting trees, peppers, peanuts and pineapple, medicinals, ornamentals, textile plants,⁶ and even vanilla, which reached the Philippines from possibly Guatemala or El Salvador.⁷

Botanical prospecting, or the quest for plants, went hand in hand with voyaging, conquest, trade, and scientific exploration. Recent scholarship has established that the development of botany, including the processes involved in finding, procuring, and accumulating detailed information about valuable foreign plants, was an intimate bedfellow of European colonialism, territorial expansion, and long distance trade.⁸ Cinchona, for example, obtained from the Peruvian bark trees *Cinchona officinalis*, yielded the precious anti-malarial quinine, which determined the success or failure of European colonizing in tropical areas. In the mid-eighteenth century, France sought to undercut the Spanish monopoly on cinchona by stealing seedlings from Spanish territories.⁹

Historians have, of late, given much attention to the connective tissues that bind science, commerce, and state politics.¹⁰ In the mid-eighteenth century, Spain sought to inventorize resources and produce highly detailed information on her overseas possessions. Major, scientific, circum-global expeditions were launched in which plant collecting played an integral role. Five of the fifty-six expeditions organized by the Spanish Crown from 1750 to 1800 were solely focused on plant collecting.¹¹ Spanish scientific exploration excelled most notably in the field of botany. Naturalist-botanists who sailed on the expeditions sponsored by the Crown sent thousands upon thousands of floral and faunal specimens to Spain, completed equal numbers of folio botanical illustrations, and wrote detailed descriptions of new specimens, valuable woods, precious resins and gums, medicinals, curiosities, fish, and other marine life. One of the most ambitious and scientifically important expeditions to be organized by the Spanish Crown was by the brilliant 34-year-old Italian-born naval officer Alejandro Malaspina in 1789.[12]

Botanizing, *herborizando*, fulfilled several objectives: it responded to the overarching ambitions of a surveillance state, indeed it helped visualize Spain's sprawling empire; it repudiated accusations of scientific and intellectual backwardness leveled at her by other Europeans; and it enabled the exploitation of commercially profitable plants and the discovery of new plants for medicine and scientific purposes.[13]

This work did not just fall on state-sponsored expeditions and the scholarly teams of naturalist-botanists and artists who enlisted. Although they worked independently, receiving no funding from the state for botanical research, members of religious orders were key actors. Catholic missionaries who were dispersed throughout the Spanish empire, and clerics who lived amongst local communities and were dedicated to humanitarian service and charged with ministering to the sick, compiled herbals and wrote huge sprawling works known as *historía* and *relación* that included long, detailed sections on plants and animals.[14]

Yet, this vast accumulation of knowledge was kept secret, largely due to an enduring "bureaucratic culture of secrecy," *arcane imperii*, long upheld by the Spanish monarchy. Knowledge, it was thought, could only be circulated in manuscript form amongst the trusted, a strategy that would effectively obstruct the ambitions of imperial rivals—or so it was reasoned.[15]

The Dutch, at least in terms of official VOC company policy, did not share the Spanish state's appetite for global botanizing and inventorizing in quite the same way. By the mid-seventeenth century, the Dutch had secured their reputation as pioneers in many areas of science, medicine, and natural history, and had less to prove in terms of scientific endeavor and intellectual prowess. Governors of the VOC in the Dutch Republic, the Gentlemen Seventeen, as well as high government officials in Batavia, the Council of the Indies, appreciated scientific curiosity. VOC employees interested in natural history were encouraged to undertake botanical exploration and to publish their research on natural history and medicine. This resulted in many landmark works on the flora and fauna of the New World, Africa, and Asia, by luminaries that included: Hendrik Adriaan van Reede tot Drakenstein (1636–91), appointed the commissioner general in Ceylon, Malabar, Surat, Coromandel, and Bengal; Jacobus Bontius (1591–1631), physician, apothecary, and medical inspector of VOC territories (both of the above published under the aegis of the VOC); and the German-born naturalist, painter, and illustrator, Maria Sybilla Merian (1647–1717), who, working independently, published *Metamorphosis insectorum Surinamensium ofte verandering der surinaamsche insecten* in 1705.[16]

Back in Europe, the acquisitive desire for things from distant places held Europeans in thrall. European audiences were delighted and intrigued by and materially profited from botanicals, things from nature (*naturalia*), curiosities and rarities—the marvelous (*mirabilia*), those that originated from strange places (*exotica*), and human-made artifacts (*artificialia*). Treated as wondrous, their ownership and display in European museums and private curiosity cabinets symbolized the power, wealth, and cosmopolitan tastes of their owners, and made clear the global reach of rulers and their empires.[17]

Botanical prospecting, or the quest for plants, was of interest to sovereigns, governments, and a wide spectrum of people—medical practitioners of all kinds, apothecaries who sought out information as well as specimens for the manufacture, sale, and use of medicines, gardening enthusiasts and horticulturalists, wealthy collectors, and intellectuals who harbored a professional or even an amateur curiosity toward exotic botany, natural history, and collecting. Not even Europe's colder climes posed an impediment to the cultivation of tropical botanicals. In Groningen, one of the most northerly provinces of the Netherlands, a professor of botany had managed to raise bananas in a purpose-built hothouse and was cultivating cinnamon and nutmeg trees, or so the Royal Society in London was informed in 1682. In 1687, at Leonen aan de Vecht in the province of Utrecht, the affluent owner of a spectacular estate garden had succeeded in growing the first ever pineapple fruit in Europe.[18] In Paris, at the Jardin du Roi, established in 1635, displays of rare and exotic plants celebrated French overseas possessions and the superiority of French thinking, particularly with regard to the accumulation of new pharmacopeia and medical knowledge.[19] By the late eighteenth century, approximately sixteen hundred botanical gardens were being cultivated in Europe, and were requiring replenishment and the constant acquisition of accurate information.

Plant collecting also gave rise to a gamut of practices and technologies—identification and naming (taxonomy), classification, mapping floral habitats, drawing and descriptive writing, transportation, transplanting, and acclimatization. Adding to these methods, the German physician Daniel Gottlieb Messerschmidt (1684–1735), in the employ of Peter the Great, devised double-entry bookkeeping, as an astonishingly accurate way of recording the natural things he found on his seven-year expedition to Siberia.[20]

While these developments unfolded in Europe, there was, however, a more immediate need for botanical prospecting in colonial outposts in Asia. In the Dutch and Spanish entrepôts of Batavia and Manila, Europeans arrived debilitated from the long sea voyage between Europe and Asia, afflicted with a host of illnesses from scurvy and typhus to malnutrition. Further, the tropical climate, various expeditions and military sieges, and new diseases such as malaria and beriberi, all took a terrible toll upon sailors, soldiers, and government officials. Moreover, Manila was an unsanitary and crowded city with an acute shortage of fresh water, especially among the poor. Epidemics struck the city with alarming frequency: smallpox swept through the population in 1656 and 1705; and in

1668 an unnamed epidemic was reportedly widespread and resulted in a high number of deaths.[21] In Batavia, Bontius himself survived dysentery and beri-beri when the city was under siege in 1628 and 1629. His second wife and eldest son were not so lucky—she died from cholera in 1630 and he in 1631, from *kinderpoxkens*, which may have been measles.[22] By the late seventeenth century, VOC trade with Asia was reportedly costing about seven thousand European lives per year.[23] Provisioning their overseas establishments with medicines imported from Amsterdam was not only proving costly, but they often arrived in a deteriorated state. Finding alternatives from locally sourced pharmacopeia to treat the sick offered the cheapest solution by far. This presented a unique opportunity for enterprising Germans with an interest in botany and natural history.

Cleyer and Batavia's *medicinale winkel*

Andries Cleyer is known for a pioneering work on Chinese pulse doctrine entitled *Specimen Medicinae Sinicae*. Published in 1682, the book carries translations of Chinese medical thinking, methods of pulse taking for diagnosis and prognosis, and an annotated list of Chinese medicinals. Cleyer is credited as the sole editor—but the work, it transpired, was not his own. It was born from the efforts of two Jesuit missionaries in China: Michal Boym (1612–59), a Polish linguist and botanist, and author of several works on Chinese medicine, flora, and fauna; and Philippe Couplet (1623–93). The latter had undertaken extensive research on Chinese philosophy, science, and medicine, and had regularly corresponded with Cleyer. Moreover, in preparing the work for publication, Cleyer received substantial assistance from the erudite Dutch physician and botanist Willem Ten Rhijne (1647–1700), an authority on Japanese moxibustion and with whom he had collaborated since the 1670s. Ten Rhijne was also unacknowledged in the *Specimen Medicinae*, and the two eventually had an acrimonious falling out, with Ten Rhijne accusing Cleyer of slander.[24]

Cleyer was smart. He possessed an astute understanding of the fertile context in which plant collecting took place, and how it stimulated groundbreaking botanical research. He knew that the expert reputation of apothecaries largely depended on their knowledge of exotic drugs and substances in which they dealt. He knew that finding substitutions for imported medicine required not only a search for plants, but also the compilation of a great deal of botanical information. Cleyer was no botanist and he had a poor command of Latin, but he was well placed to spur on the hunt for specimens.

In the handful of years between enlisting with the VOC in 1661 as a gentleman soldier and arriving in Batavia in 1664 as a medical practitioner, Cleyer had financially and socially enriched himself. He started modestly—while head of the Batavian Latin school he made easy money distilling chemical medicines for the medical shop—but by the early 1680s he occupied all the important medical positions in Batavia. He also made several trips as a merchant to Deshima, where he engaged in commercial skullduggery and amassed a fortune. When the Japanese authorities discovered what he was up to, he was expelled from Japan and his cohorts were punished by crucifixion. He otherwise escaped unpunished and, with his wealth, built himself one of the grandest houses in Batavia. He established a garden tended by fifty slaves and brought over a German gardener named Georg Meister who worked for him for almost a decade. Cleyer's botanical notes and drawings on Japanese flora, which were later published in Germany under his name, seem to have come from the hand of his gardener.[25]

Cleyer's career took off in 1667 when he was appointed the new director of the VOC medical shop in Batavia. The city was at the heart of the action—here ships departed for and returned from Europe, India, and the Far East. Information about Asia and decisions about trade and personnel all coursed through Batavia. The shop itself supplied all the medical chests to VOC ships and trading posts in the East. Cleyer's appointment enabled him to control all medical activities in Batavia and to exert influence practically everywhere the VOC operated.

As chief *apotheker*, Cleyer requested VOC stations at the Cape, Ceylon, and Coromandel to send medicinal plants and preparations of them. They duly complied, and both the shop and VOC medical chests were supplied with many exotic botanicals originating from their vast Asian networks, many of which were herbs and drugs known in Ayurvedic and other traditional medicines—sarsaparilla, bitter colocynth apples, *nux vomica* (from which strychnine was later derived), and the plum-like myrobalans fruit. Learned personnel, notably fellow Germans, were also brought over from Europe—Paulus Hermann (1645–95), who had qualified in medicine from Padua, arrived in Ceylon in 1672 where he undertook botanical research. Hendrik (or Heinrich) Claudius (about 1655–97), a talented chemist born in Breslau, was personally funded by Cleyer to go to the Cape in 1682 to start a herbarium, collect *naturalia*, and paint local flora.

Finally, Cleyer's networks served him well, and facilitated the flow of knowledge between Asia and Europe. His correspondence with Christian Mentzel, court physician to Friedrich Wilhelm, elector of Brandenburg, for instance, gained him membership to the Academia Naturae Curiosorum (later known as the Leopoldina), the academic society for naturalists and physicians in German-speaking areas. This was possibly to reward Cleyer for sending Mentzel herbs with which to treat Wilhelm's gout. Through Mentzel, Cleyer sent a wealth of information to Europe, from an illustrated treatise on leprosy to drawings and observations on Japanese plants, which saw print in the Academia's journals. Of course, Kaempfer and Rumphius were also acquaintances of Cleyer. On Cleyer's recommendation, Rumphius was made a member of the Academia in 1680 and, through the society's journal, published a selection of his articles, *observationes*, over a period of fifteen years.

If personal gain may be seen to have mixed rather too freely with scientific curiosity in Cleyer, there can be no doubt that he and his position in Batavia's medical shop gave impetus to the movement of plants, people, and information. Cleyer prompted all sorts of activities: the involvement of men of industry and learning; expanded lines of inquiry and channels through which information flowed; and gardens and herbariums doubling up as research centers. All of this resulted in a dynamic accumulation of detailed and accurate information that benefited science and commerce.

Camel, Kaempfer, and Rumphius Find Things Out

In 1688, Cleyer's German gardener, Georg Meister, returned to the Netherlands, taking with him quantities of plants from the Batavian garden, including a camphor tree from Japan. At the same time, Georg Josef Camel was journeying to Manila; Engelbert Kaempfer had just joined the VOC as a ship's physician and was leaving Persia for southern India, a voyage that would eventually take him to Southeast Asia and Japan; and Rumphius was recovering from a terrible fire that had destroyed his home in Ambon, together with partial copies of his manuscript *Herbarium Amboinense*. Camel, Kaempfer, and Rumphius, like Cleyer, seized whatever opportunities came their way, and each showed considerable entrepreneurial spirit and an indomitable will. But these three ranged far wider and deeper in their scientific enquiries than Cleyer. How did they find things out?

Born in the Moravian city of Brno, Camel joined the Society of Jesus in 1682 and was in his late twenties when he, along with other Moravian and Bohemian missionaries, reached Manila. Trained in pharmacy, he was assigned to the Jesuit college where he worked hard as the college *infirmarian*, caring for his sick colleagues and preparing remedies. He established a garden where he planted rare and medicinal herbs, and a pharmacy that became renowned as much for the variety of remedies it supplied as for Camel's skill as an apothecary and his solicitous ministrations to the impoverished sick. The Jesuit Pedro Murillo Velarde (1696–1753), professor of theology, canon law and an accomplished mapmaker, praised Camel's service in glowing terms:

> The doors of the pharmacy were always wide open to the poor, toward whom the brother always exercised the most generous charity. He not only gave them various medicines but administered these medicines himself and cured their ills and ailments … Nor did he limit his charity to those nearby in Manila or its environs. He sent … drugs even to the natives and poor people of the Visayan islands, for whom he always had a special affection.[26]

In 1695 Camel was appointed apothecary, and four years later, in recognition of his botanical expertise, was accorded the title *botanicus*. Camel kept up a lively correspondence with botanists in Asia and England. Willem Ten Rhijne was a cordial contact in Batavia who introduced him to Cleyer and Hermann in Ceylon. The manuscript volume entitled "Icones fruticum et arborum Luzonis" describing low-growing plants, vines, shrubs, and trees appears to be a product of collaboration between Camel and Ten Rhijne.[27] Camel's communications with Samuel Browne, an English surgeon in Madras, brought him to the attention of John Ray and James Petiver, prominent members of the Royal Society in London who received Camel's work with much enthusiasm and interest. Camel sent Ray and Petiver quantities of specimens of flora and fauna collected from all over the Philippine archipelago, as well as thousands of notes and drawings, only portions of which appeared in the Society's *Philosophical Transactions*. Descriptions of plants, insects, minerals, shells, and corals, a body of work titled "Historia stirpium insula Luzonis et reliquarum Philippinarum," also appeared as an appendix in Ray's *Historia Plantarum* (1704). Pablo Clain (or Paulus Klein, 1652–1717), another German Jesuit who had arrived in Manila ten years before Camel, noticed the latter's assiduous letter writing to European savants and his diligence in sending them his observations and collections. Clain shared Camel's interest in ethnobotany, indigenous medicines, and medical practices, and went on to publish an acclaimed work on common illnesses and their local remedies in 1712.[28]

Manila at the time was a medical marketplace.[29] Most religious orders had their own priories where the sick could receive treatment; a royal hospital staffed by a physician, an apothecary and surgeons, and equipped with sick wards treated Spaniards; the Misericordia extended their medical aid to slaves and accommodated destitute women; the barefooted Franciscans working as "physicians, surgeons, and apothecaries … carry[ing] out marvelous cures in medicine and surgery," administered a hospital called Santa Ana for natives "suffering from all kinds of ailments";[30] and at Balete, the Hospital de San Lázaro served leprosy sufferers.[31] In addition there were a variety of indigenous healers, Chinese doctors and apothecaries. Referring to the Chinese quarter of the city, Bishop Salazar observed how "in this Parian we find doctors and druggists with advertisements written out in their own tongue in their shops which tell the public what they sell."[32] Elaborating further on the extent of Chinese medical knowledge, the Minnanese(Hokkien)-speaking Dominican missioner priest Father Juan Cobo (1546–92) noted: "They [the Chinese] know about the heartbeat and they heal with herbs, many of which are known in Castile. They do not bleed the patient but burn him in certain members with the use of certain herbs," a procedure that was perhaps moxibustion.[33]

Camel mingled freely with Manila's various types of medical practitioners and seems to have been knowledgeable about local pharmacopeia used both by indigenous and emigrant Chinese. He is known to have sent Chinese herbs to London that had been introduced into the Philippines.[34] He corrected remedies that had been prepared by local healers, as Murillo Velarde remarked: "It happened occasionally that … the *curanderos* [native shamans]—of whom there are plenty here without science or art—prescribed a bigger dose than the case required. At such times the brother would alter the prescription, reducing it to the proper dosage, with very good results."[35]

It is not known whether Camel mastered any Philippine languages, but his evident familiarity with local languages seems to be the key to the way in which he acquired knowledge. Camel's incorporation of local names of Philippine plants as conveyed to him by local informants, most likely by indigenous healers, often provides the best route toward identification. The recorded local names that appear in Camel's descriptions are largely in Tagalog, although in many instances Camel indicates the names by provinces, and frequently includes local names common to the Visayas. Camel was the first to have described and named "*Strychnos Ignatii* Berg." (St. Ignatius' bean), a seed from a vine from which the crystalline, alkaloid poison strychnine is derived, and to bring the plant to the attention of European pharmacology. He called the bean "Igasud seu Igasur," following the name by which it was known by the local inhabitants of Catbalogan, Samar, in the Philippines where it grew in profusion. The seeds were valued locally for their active tonic properties and thought to act as an aphrodisiac.[36] Camel had dispatched drawings and observations of this important plant, and his writings were translated into Italian and German. Camel's dried specimen was the first appearance in Europe of this Philippine source of strychnine. Sold in Europe at fabulous prices, a few of the seeds may have found their way to the grand ducal *spezieria* or pharmacy of Princess Anna Maria Luisa de Medici (1667–1743). She was the only daughter of Cosimo III de Medici, the Grand Duke of Tuscany, and had returned to her native Florence after her husband's death in Germany. The princess had collected over two hundred 'recipes' constituting culinary recipes, medicinal remedies and therapeutics, based on ingredients available at the court pharmacy. Notably, Camel's St. Ignatius' bean is recommended to "lower the monster of women" by inserting the beans into the vagina.[37]

Camel had an ear for the sound of the vernacular tongue. His inclusion of foreign specimens, notably plants originating from the Americas that had been early introductions into the archipelago, provide good examples of the ways in which the original Aztec name underwent modification or corruption. There are numerous examples of plants of American origin known by a local variant of their Aztec name, such as "*cacaloxochitl mexicanoru*". A flower commonly planted in and around cemeteries all over Southeast Asia, and introduced into the colony by the Spaniards in the sixteenth century, *calachuchi cacaloxochitl* (*Plumeria rubra*, frangipani), now bears the indigenized name "*calachuchi*" in the Philippines, which is manifestly derived from the Aztec one.[38]

Camel's travels seem to have been restricted to within the Philippines where he lived for almost two decades, remaining there until his death at the age of 45, caused, according to Murillo Velarde, by diarrhea. Kaempfer, by contrast, was exceedingly well traveled. Appointed secretary to the Swedish legation, he journeyed through the Russian and Persian courts, and after four years took the decision to travel on to the Far East, gambling that he would have better prospects with the VOC. He arrived in Batavia in 1689 and, after a short, professionally precarious period, accepted the position of physician at Deshima. He arrived there, after a brief sojourn in Siam, in 1690, just shy of his fortieth birthday.

Kaempfer's reputation was established by a work he published in 1712 entitled *Amoenitatum Exoticarum* (Exotic medical pleasantries). The book contained many insightful observations of Persia and Japan in the periods he lived there, namely from 1683 to 1687 and from autumn 1690 to autumn 1692. Upon returning to Europe, he became a personal physician to the Count of Lippe, whom he served for twenty-four years. After Kaempfer's death, Hans Sloane of the Royal Society bought all of Kaempfer's drawings and manuscripts, and in 1727 published his account of Japanese life, customs, history, and politics in English translation under the title *History of Japan*, which was an instant bestseller.[39]

The *Amoenitatum* gave many insights on the Japanese tea ceremonies and the medical practices of moxibustion and acupuncture, defined by Kaempfer as Japanese cures for colic. Most notably, one section was devoted to Japanese flora. Four hundred and twenty plants were described, many of them new discoveries. He is famously known to have produced the first botanical description of the gingko biloba tree and to establish its characteristic name. He describes the strength and texture of the gingko's wood, its seasonal changes, and compares it to a walnut tree, and its fruit to large pistachios. Remarks on the culinary uses of the nuts suggests this information came from local informants: "Eaten after a meal, the kernels promote digestion … therefore they are never missing in the dessert of a sumptuous meal. They also serve as an ingredient in several dishes after one took away their bitter taste by cooking or roasting."[40] Kaempfer sent the first gingko seeds to Europe; they were planted in the university gardens in Utrecht, where it continues to flourish today.

From the mid-seventeenth century until the nineteenth century, the VOC factory in Deshima was the only entry point for Europeans into Japan. Once a year the Dutch were obliged to travel to Edo (Tokyo) to present gifts to the ruling shogun who would decide the conditions of trade and set prices. The two-month mission presented the only opportunity for Europeans to see the country. Kaempfer undertook the journey twice, enabling him to describe what he saw and gather as much information as he could. He smuggled out town plans and maps;[41] botany, cartography, descriptions of the land and its inhabitants, and aspects of medicine which all received his close attention. Kaempfer's descriptions were respected for their authenticity, and his works stood as a contribution to the exchange of medical knowledge and its dissemination between Japanese and Europeans.⁴² The vivid details he includes suggest he had been privy to a deeper knowledge of the country than would ordinarily be expected. How was this possible? Flattery and generous servings of European liqueurs seem to have helped; also, his readiness to satisfy Japanese curiosity by answering questions on all manner of subjects from European medicine to astronomy and mathematics. Kaempfer admits: "No one refused to give me information to the best of his knowledge, even concerning the most forbidden matters, provided I was alone with him."⁴³ Most important of all, however, was his entire dependence on Japanese informants, for Kaempfer did not speak a word of Japanese. His acquaintance with a young man, an 'educated youth' who acted not only as his interpreter but also aided him in gathering material, was particularly significant.⁴⁴ The man's name was Imamura Gen'emon Eisei (1671–1736), acknowledged by Dutch merchants as "the hub around which everything turns."⁴⁵

Unlike Kaempfer, Rumphius was no transient and had no need of an interpreter. He came to love Ambon and the Moluccas. He immersed himself in the islands' communities, learned their languages and lived a long and productive life with them for almost fifty years (1654–1702). Throughout his writings, Rumphius refers to the opinions of Chinese, Malay, Javanese, Ternatan, and Balinese informants. In this way it is easy to understand how Rumphius found things out.

Rumphius traveled to the Netherlands from Germany in 1645. As Cleyer had done, he began his career by enlisting with the VOC as a gentleman soldier. He arrived in Ambon, in the Moluccas, by way of the Cape in 1654. He was twenty-seven years old and had been hired to supervise the construction of fortifications. After five years, during which time he learnt Portuguese and Malay, he changed tack. He transferred to the civil branch of the VOC and became a merchant, an *onderkoopman*, securing a lucrative posting on Hila.⁴⁶

By the early 1660s, Rumphius had begun to work seriously on a complete natural history of Ambon and, before the decade was out, he had dedicated himself to research. His VOC superiors recognized the importance of his undertaking and gave him their support: books and scientific instruments were shipped to him on VOC vessels, paid clerks and draughtsmen assisted him, and he was given an appointment that amounted to a generous sinecure. Moreover, from around 1677 to 1682, he was paid handsomely to collect curiosities for Cosimo III de Medici.

Rumphius enjoyed fame and esteem from his peers during his lifetime. He was elected to the prestigious German scientific society the Academia Naturae Curiosorum in 1681, and he produced two of the most brilliant works on natural history to have appeared in the early eighteenth century, both published posthumously—*D'Amboinsche Rariteitkamer* (The Ambonese Curiosity Cabinet, 1705), and the six-volume *Het Amboinsche kruid-boek* or *Herbarium Amboinense* (Ambonese Herbal, 1741–50). Yet he endured personal disasters and setbacks.

He became blind around 1670; the original manuscript of his Herbal was lost in a shipwreck; and his partner, a local woman known only as Susanna, by whom he had two children, a son and a daughter, was tragically killed in an earthquake together with their daughter in 1674. Susanna assisted him in his botanical research and he named a rare orchid the "Susanna Flower" in her honor.

Rumphius enjoyed an astonishing level of intimacy with his local informants. With their help he made many discoveries, from them he was able to ascertain a range of differing opinions and make comparative judgments, and due to them he learnt about aspects of everyday life that were highly personal in nature. Ambonese women, for instance, taught him recipes which utilized the soccum capas tree (perhaps *Mangifera foetida* Lour.), which helped post-partum women;[47] he learnt how an infusion of *moernagels* or cloves when given to young brides aided in closing "up their nature, which will make them more pleasing to their men";[48] and the *Flos Coeruleus*, or blue clitoris flower, had some culinary use. Rumphius was gripped. Dwelling at length on the delicate blue flower, the naturalist writes that the natives cook and eat the flowers with coconut milk, resulting in a weak, mildly sweet porridge. More commonly, the flowers were used to color cooked rice blue "because the Indians consider it elegant to serve cooked rice in three or four colors." That said, Rumphius was fascinated by the flower's nomenclature. These names, he notes, were rather immodest: in Malay it was called *Bonga Calente* or *kelentit*, which means "clitoris" though it could also refer to the female genitals. In Ternatan, the flower was known as *Saja Cotele* or *Bokyma Cotele*, which, as Rumphius explained, pertained to the Flos Clitoridis or Clitoris Principissae, or "that part of the female conch, which the Muslims circumcise in Women, to wit both the Lips." Here, he used the Latin "*nymphaea*" and may have had the vulva's labia minora in mind; he also referred to the clitoris with the Dutch word *kittelaar*, meaning "to tickle" or more literally "the tickler." And, in a bid to further clarify, he added: "the folds that are displayed in the opened conch, and which resemble this flower more."[49]

Conclusion

The quest for plants prompted all sorts of activities: the involvement of men of industry and learning; the expansion of lines of inquiry and channels through which information flowed; and the establishment of gardens and herbariums doubling up as research centers. All of this resulted in a dynamic accumulation of detailed and accurate information that benefited science, commerce, and imperial goals.

What are the common threads that draw Cleyer, Camel, Kaempfer, and Rumphius together? First, each man may be said to have possessed an entrepreneurial spirit—in the sense that they immersed themselves fully in the context of their own particular circumstances, exploiting opportunities and taking initiatives. Second, we should think of these men as knowledge producers. The knowledge that was conveyed about plants and the natural world of the Philippine and Indonesian archipelagoes and Japan was a product of a multitude of interlinked factors—of travel (people, texts, and objects); of networks and connections between like-minded people and between friends; and most crucially, of dependence on local informants. Third, and most profoundly, the common methods each man employed in their researches—gathering and collecting, drawing, the exchange of information through letter writing, the willingness to send specimens—were the practices, strategies, and conventions integral to the commerce in global scientific knowledge that distinguished the period that has come to be known as the "scientific revolution."

Raquel A. G. Reyes is an associate research fellow in the Department of History, School of Oriental and African Studies, University of London. She works on the history of science and medicine, history of gender and sexuality, and trade and cultural innovation in early modern Southeast Asia, with particular reference to the Philippines. She is the author of *Love, Passion and Patriotism: Sexuality and the Philippine Propaganda Movement* and *Sexual Diversity in Asia c.600–1950* (co-editor). She is also a columnist for the *Manila Times*.

Notes

1. See, for instance, John H. Zammito, *Kant, Herder, and the Birth of Anthropology* (Chicago, IL: University of Chicago Press, 2002); Hans F. Vermeulen, *Early History of Ethnography and Ethnology in the German Enlightenment: Anthropological Discourse in Europe and Asia, 1710–1808* (Leiden: Ridderkerk, 2008).
2. The scholarship on the Dutch trading empire is vast. Recent works include Jan J. B. Kuipers, *De VOC: een multinational onder zeil, 1602–1799* (Zutphen: Walburg Pers, 2014); Lodewijk Wagenaar, *Aan de Overkant: ontmoetingen in dienst van de VOC en WIC 1600–1800* (Leiden: Sidestone Press, 2015); Robert Parthesius, *Dutch Ships in Tropical Waters: The Development of the Dutch East India Company (VOC) Shipping Network in Asia 1595–1660* (Amsterdam: Amsterdam University Press, 2007); Femme S. Gaastra, *The Dutch East India Company: Expansion and Decline* (Zutphen: Walburg Pers, 2003); and Kees Zandvliet, *The Dutch Encounter with Asia 1600–1950* (Zwolle: Rijksmuseum Amsterdam and Waanders Publishers, 2002).
3. Benito J. Legarda, Jr., *After the Galleons: Foreign Trade, Economic Change and Entrepreneurship in the Nineteenth-Century Philippines* (Quezon City: Ateneo de Manila University Press, 1999).
4. Dennis O. Flynn, Arturo Giráldez, and James Sobredo, eds., *European Entry into the Pacific: Spain and the Acapulco–Manila Galleons* (The Pacific World: Lands, Peoples and History of the Pacific, 1500–1900, Vol. 4 (Aldershot: Ashgate Variorum, 2001), xvii; O. H. K. Spate, *The Spanish Lake* (London: Croom Helm, 1979); Dennis O. Flynn, Lionel Frost and A. J. H. Latham, eds., *Pacific Centuries: Pacific and Pacific Rim History since the Sixteenth Century*

(London: Routledge, 1999); Birgit Tremml-Werner, *Spain, China and Japan in Manila, 1571–1644: Local Comparisons, Global Connections* (Amsterdam University Press, 2015); Arturo Giraldez, *The Age of Trade: The Manila Galleons and the Dawn of the Global Economy* (London: Rowman & Littlefield, 2015). See also selected essays in *Revista de Cultura*, International Edition 17, January 2006 (Instituto Cultural de Macao). On slavery and the trans-Pacific trade, see Tatiana Seijas, *Asian Slaves in Colonial Mexico: From Chinos to Indians* (New York: Cambridge University Press, 2014).

5. Hugh Harris, "Key to Coconut Cultivation on the American Pacific Coast: The Manila–Acapulco Galleon Route (1565–1815)," *Palms* 56, no. 2 (2012): 72–77.
6. Corazon S. Alvina and Domingo A. Madulid, *Flora Filipina: From Acapulco to Manila* (Manila: Art Post Asia, National Museum of the Philippines, 2009), 11.
7. Pesach Lubinsky, et al., "Neotropical Roots of a Polynesian Spice: The Hybrid Origin of Tahitian Vanilla, *Vanilla Tahitensis* (ORCHIDACEAE)," *American Journal of Botany* 95, no. 8 (2008): 1040–47.
8. Londa Schiebinger and Claudia Swan, eds., *Colonial Botany: Science, Commerce, and Politics in the Early Modern World* (Philadelphia: University of Pennsylvania Press 2005), 3.
9. Ibid., 1.
10. David Arnold, *Science, Technology and Medicine in Colonial India* (Cambridge: Cambridge University Press, 2000); several art historical studies on the Mughal empire, for instance Som Prakash Verma, *Flora and Fauna in Mughal Art* (Bombay: Marg Publications, 1999); Harold J. Cook, *Matters of Exchange: Commerce, Medicine, and Science in the Dutch Golden Age* (New Haven, CT: Yale University Press, 2007); Londa Schiebinger, *Plants and Empire: Colonial Bioprospecting in the Atlantic World* (Cambridge, MA: Harvard University Press, 2004); Schiebinger and Swan, *Colonial Botany*; Londa Schiebinger, "Forum Introduction: The European Colonial Science Complex," *Colonial Science* Special Issue, *Isis* 96 (2005): 52–55; Jorge Cañizares-Esguerra, *Nature, Empire and Nation: Explorations of the History of Science in the Iberian World* (Stanford, CA: Stanford University Press, 2006); Roy MacLeod, ed., *Nature and Empire: Science and the Colonial Enterprise*, Special Issue, *Osiris* 15 (2000). See also selected essays in the Variorum volumes: Ursula Lamb, ed., *The Globe Encircled and the World Revealed*, Vol. 3 (Aldershot: Ashgate Variorum, 1995); Felipe Fernández-Armesto, ed., *The Global Opportunity* (An Expanding World: The European Impact on World History 1450–1800), Vol. 1 (Aldershot: Ashgate Variorum, 1995); and Sanjay Subrahmanyam, ed., *Merchant Networks in the Early Modern World, 1450–1800*, Vol. 8 (Aldershot: Ashgate Variorum, 1996).
11. Chiyo Ishikawa, ed., *Spain in the Age of Exploration 1492–1819* (Seattle, WA: Seattle Art Museum, University of Nebraska Press, 2004), 171–72.
12. On the Malaspina Expedition in the Philippines, see Raquel A. G. Reyes, "Collecting and the Pursuit of Scientific Accuracy: The Malaspina Expedition in the Philippines, 1792," in *Science and Empire: Dutch Science around 1800 in Comparative Perspective*, ed. Peter Boomgaard, (New York: Palgrave Macmillan, 2013), 63–88.
13. Daniela Bleichmar, *Visible Empire: Botanical Expeditions and Visual Culture in the Hispanic Enlightenment* (Chicago, IL: University of Chicago Press, 2012); Daniela Bleichmar et al., eds., *Science in the Spanish and Portuguese Empires 1500–1800* (Stanford, CA: Stanford University Press, 2009).
14. Notable examples are: Juan de Plasencia, *Relacíon de las Costumbres los Tagalos* (1589); Francisco Colin, *Labor Evangelíca* (1604); Pedro Chirino, *Relacíon de las Islas Filipinas* (1663); and Francisco Combes, *Historia de las Islas de Mindanao, Jolo y sus adjacentes* (1667). See Ignacio Francisco Alcina, *History of the Bisayan People in the Philippine Islands* [1668], edited by Cantius J. Kobak and Lucio Gutierrez (Manila: University of Santo Tomas Publishing House, 2005).
15. Jorge Cañizares-Esguerra, "Introduction", in Bleichmar et al., *Science in the Spanish and Portuguese Empires*, 1.

16. See Johannes Heniger, *Hendrik Adriaan van Rheed tot Drakenstein (1636–1691) and Hortus Malabaricus: A Contribution to the History of Dutch Colonial Botany* (Rotterdam: Balkema, 1986); Ella Reitsma, *Maria Sybilla Merian and Daughters: Women of Art and Science* (Amsterdam: Rembrandt House Museum, 2009); and Harold J. Cook, "Global Economies and Local Knowledge in the East Indies: Jacobus Bontius Learns the Facts of Nature," in Schiebinger and Swan, *Colonial Botany*, 100; Christina Skott, "Linnaeus and the Troglodyte: Early European Encounters with the Malay World and the Natural History of Man," *Indonesia and the Malay World* 42 (2014): 141–69.
17. Work on European collecting and collecting practices is vast. Some prominent examples are: Thomas DaCosta Kaufmann, *The Mastery of Nature: Aspects of Art, Science, and Humanism in the Renaissance* (Princeton NJ: Princeton University Press, 1993); John Elsner and Roger Cardinal, eds., *The Cultures of Collecting* (Cambridge, MA: Harvard University Press, 1994); Lorraine Daston and Katherine Park, *Wonders and the Order of Nature 1150–1750* (New York: Zone Books, 1998); Paula Findlen, *Possessing Nature: Museums, Collecting, and Scientific Culture in Early Modern Italy* (Berkeley: University of California Press, 1994); Nicholas Jardine, Emma Spary, and J. A. Secord, eds., *Cultures of Natural History* (Cambridge: Cambridge University Press, 1996); Anthony Grafton and Nancy Siraisi, *Natural Particulars: Nature and the Disciplines in Europe* (Cambridge, MA: MIT Press, 1999); Pamela H. Smith and Paula Findlen, eds., *Merchants and Marvels: Commerce, Science and Art in Early Modern Europe* (London: Routledge, 2002). Eddy Stols, Werner Thomas, and Johan Verberckmoes, eds., *Naturalia, Mirabilia e Monstrosa en los Imperios Ibéricos* (Leuven: Leuven University Press, 2007); also Part 3, chapters 9, 10 and 11 in Claire Farago, ed., *Reframing the Renaissance: Visual Culture in Europe and Latin America, 1450–1650* (New Haven, CT: Yale University Press, 1995). I thank Thomas DaCosta Kaufmann for bringing this book to my attention.
18. Cook, *Matters of Exchange*, 327.
19. Chandra Mukerji, "Dominion, Demonstration, and Domination: Religious Doctrine, Territorial Politics, and French Plant Collection," in Schiebinger and Swan, *Colonial Botany*, 20–33.
20. Anke te Heesen, "Accounting for the Natural World: Double-Entry Bookkeeping in the Field," in Schiebinger and Swan, *Colonial Botany*, 238–51.
21. Linda Newson, *Conquest and Pestilence in the Early Spanish Philippines* (Honolulu: University of Hawaii Press, 2009), 127.
22. Cook, "Global Economies," 102.
23. Cook, *Matters of Exchange*, 178.
24. Ibid.
25. Ibid., 321.
26. Quote from Pedro Murillo Velarde, *Historia de la Provincia de Philipinas de la Compañía de Jesús* (Manila: Imprenta Compañía de Jesús, 1749), 892–93, in Horatio de la Costa, S.J., *The Jesuits in the Philippines 1581–1768* (Cambridge, MA: Harvard University Press, 1961), 557.
27. Raquel A. G. Reyes, "Botany and Zoology in the Late Seventeenth-Century Philippines: The Work of Georg Josef Camel, SJ, 1661–1706," *Archives of Natural History* 36(2) (2009): 262–76.
28. Pablo Clain, *Remedios Fáciles Para Diferentes Enfermedades* (Manila: Imprenta del Colegio de PP. Domenicos de Santo Tomás, 1712).
29. This phrase, which refers to the interaction of medical pluralism and commerce, is owed to Harold J. Cook who pioneered its use as a tool of historical investigation.
30. Antonio de Morga, *Sucesos de las Islas Filipinas* [1604], trans. by J. S. Cummins (Cambridge: Cambridge University Press for the Hakluyt Society, 1971), 284–85.
31. Newson, *Conquest and Pestilence*, 127.
32. Bishop Salazar quoted in Alfonso Felix, Jr., *The Chinese in the Philippines 1570–1770*, Vol. 1 (Manila: Solidaridad Publishing House, 1966), 125.

33. Ibid., 138. On Father Juan Cobo, see also Eugenio Menegon, *Ancestors, Virgins and Friars: Christianity as a Local Religion in Late Imperial China* (Cambridge, MA: Harvard University Asia Center for the Harvard Yenching Institute, 2009), 54.
34. Reyes, "Botany and Zoology," 266; Leo A. Cullum, "Georg Josef Kamel," *Philippine Studies* 4 (1956): 319–39.
35. Quote from Pedro Murillo Velarde, *Historia*, in de la Costa, *The Jesuits in the Philippines*, 557.
36. *S.Ignatii* is highly toxic and is known to contain 2.5% to 3% of total alkaloids of which two-thirds is strychnine. Strychnine is so deadly that half a grain has proved fatal to man. I. H. Burkhill, *A Dictionary of the Economic Products of the Malay Peninsula*, Vol. II (London: Crown Agents for the Colonies, 1935), 2091–95.
37. Ashley Buchanan, "The Recipe Collection of the Last Medici Princess," 29 January 2013. Retrieved September 2015 from http://recipes.hypotheses.org/788.
38. Reyes, "Botany and Zoology," 269.
39. Engelbert Kaempfer, *Kaempfer's Japan: Tokugawa Culture Observed*, trans. by Beatrice M. Bodart-Bailey (Honolulu: University of Hawaii Press, 1999).
40. Engelbert Kaempfer, *Ameonitatum exoticarum politico-physico-medicarum fasciculi V*, 811.
41. Detlef Haberland, *Engelbert Kaempfer 1651–1716: A Biography* (London: The British Library, 1996), 81.
42. Cook, *Matters of Exchange*, 374.
43. Haberland, *Engelbert Kaempfer*, 67.
44. Ibid.
45. Ibid.
46. H. C. D. de Wit, "Georgius Everhardus Rumphius," in *Rumphius Memorial Volume*, ed. H. C. D. de Wit (Baarn: Uitgeverij en Drukkerij Hollandia, 1959).
47. Rumphius, *Ambonese Herbal*, trans. by E. M. Beekman, Vol. 1, (New Haven, CT: Yale University Press, 1992), 353.
48. Rumphius, *Ambonese Herbal*, Vol. 2, p. 11.
49. Rumphius, *Ambonese Herbal*, Vol. 3, p. 563.

Bibliography

Alcina, Ignacio. *History of the Bisayan People in the Philippine Islands* [1668]. Edited by Cantius J. Kobak and Lucio Gutierrez. Manila: University of Santo Tomas Publishing House, 2005.

Alvina, Corazon S., and Domingo A. Madulid. *Flora Filipina: From Acapulco to Manila*. Manila: Art Post Asia; National Museum of the Philippines, 2009.

Arnold, David. *Science, Technology and Medicine in Colonial India*. Cambridge: Cambridge University Press, 2000.

Bleichmar, Daniela. *Visible Empire: Botanical Expeditions and Visual Culture in the Hispanic Enlightenment*. Chicago, IL: University of Chicago Press, 2012.

Bleichmar, Daniela, et al., eds. *Science in the Spanish and Portuguese Empires 1500–1800*. Stanford, CA: Stanford University Press, 2009.

Buchanan, Ashley. "The Recipe Collection of the Last Medici Princess," 29 January 2013. Retrieved September 2015 from http://recipes.hypotheses.org/788.

Burkhill, I. H. *A Dictionary of the Economic Products of the Malay Peninsula*. Vol. II. London: Crown Agents for the Colonies, 1935.

Cañizares-Esguerra, Jorge. *Nature, Empire and Nation: Explorations of the History of Science in the Iberian World*. Stanford, CA: Stanford University Press, 2006.

Carneiro de Sousa, Ivo. "A Primera Viagem Histórica da Globalização: 'Peregrinatio', Pecado, Sexualidade e Mentalidade Mercantil: discutindo o libro de Antonio Pigafetta sobre a grande viagem de Fernão de Magalhães," *Revista de Cultura* (International Edition) 17 (January 2006): 54–66.

Clain, Pablo. *Remedios Fáciles Para Diferentes Enfermedades*. Manila: Imprenta del Colegio de PP. Dominicos de Santo Tomás, 1712.

Cook, Harold J. *Matters of Exchange: Commerce, Medicine, and Science in the Dutch Golden Age*. New Haven, CT: Yale University Press, 2007.

———. "Global Economies and Local Knowledge in the East Indies: Jacobus Bontius Learns the Facts of Nature." In *Colonial Botany: Science, Commerce, and Politics in Early Modern World*, edited by Londa Schiebinger and Claudia Swan, 100–119. Philadelphia: University of Pennsylvania Press, 2005.

Cullum, Leo A. "Georg Josef Kamel," *Philippine Studies* 4 (1956): 319–39.

Daston, Lorraine, and Katherine Park. *Wonders and the Order of Nature 1150–1750*. New York: Zone Books, 1998.

de la Costa, Horatio, S.J. *The Jesuits in the Philippines, 1581–1768*. Cambridge, MA: Harvard University Press, 1961.

de Morga, Antonio. *Sucesos de las Islas Filipinas* [1604]. Trans. by J. S. Cummins. Cambridge: Cambridge University Press for the Hakluyt Society, 1971.

de Wit, H. C. D. "Georgius Everhardus Rumphius." In *Rumphius Memorial Volume*, edited by H. C. D. de Wit, 1–26. Baarn: Uitgeverij en Drukkerij Hollandia, 1959.

Elsner, John, and Roger Cardinal, eds. *The Cultures of Collecting*. Cambridge, MA: Harvard University Press, 1994.

Farago, Claire, ed. *Reframing the Renaissance: Visual Culture in Europe and Latin America 1450–1650*. New Haven, CT: Yale University Press, 1995.

Felix, Alfonso, Jr. *The Chinese in the Philippines 1570–1770*. Vol. 1. Manila: Solidaridad Publishing House, 1966.

Fernández-Armesto, Felipe, ed. *The Global Opportunity* (An Expanding World: The European Impact on World History 1450–1800) Vol. 1. Aldershot: Ashgate Variorum, 1995.

Findlen, Paula. *Possessing Nature: Museums, Collecting, and Scientific Culture in Early Modern Italy*. Berkeley: University of California Press, 1994.

Flynn, Dennis O., Lionel Frost and A. J. H. Latham, eds. *Pacific Centuries: Pacific and Pacific Rim History since the Sixteenth Century*. London: Routledge, 1999.

Flynn, Dennis O., Arturo Giráldez and James Sobredo, eds. *European Entry into the Pacific: Spain and the Acapulco–Manila Galleons*. The Pacific World: Lands, Peoples and History of the Pacific, 1500–1900, Vol. 4. Aldershot: Ashgate Variorum, 2001.

Gaastra, Femme S. *The Dutch East India Company: Expansion and Decline*. Zutphen: Walburg Pers, 2003.

Giraldez, Arturo. *The Age of Trade: The Manila Galleons and the Dawn of the Global Economy*. London: Rowman & Littlefield, 2015.

Grafton, Anthony, and Nancy Siraisi. *Natural Particulars: Nature and the Disciplines in Europe*. Cambridge, MA: MIT Press, 1999.

Haberland, Detlef. *Engelbert Kaempfer 1651–1716: A Biography*. London: The British Library, 1996.

Harris, Hugh. "Key to Coconut Cultivation on the American Pacific Coast: The Manila–Acapulco Galleon Route 1565–1815." *Palms* 56, no. 2 (2012): 72–77.

Heniger, Johannes. *Hendrik Adriaan van Rheed tot Drakenstein 1636–1691 and Hortus Malabaricus: A Contribution to the History of Dutch Colonial Botany*. Rotterdam: Balkema, 1986.

Heesen, Anke te, "Accounting for the Natural World: Double-entry Bookkeeping in the Field." In *Colonial Botany: Science, Commerce, and Politics in Early Modern World*, edited by Londa Schiebinger and Claudia Swan, 237–252. Philadelphia: University of Pennsylvania Press, 2005.

Ishikawa, Chiyo, ed. *Spain in the Age of Exploration 1492–1819*. Seattle, WA: Seattle Art Museum and University of Nebraska Press, 2004.

Jardine, Nicholas, Emma Spary, and J. A. Secord, eds. *Cultures of Natural History*. Cambridge: Cambridge University Press, 1996.

Kaempfer, Engelbert. *Ameonitatum exoticarum politico-physico-medicarum fasciculi V*. (Limgoviae [Lemgo]: Typis & Impensis Henrici Wilhelmi Meyeri, Aulae Lippiacae Typographi 1712)

———. *Kaempfer's Japan: Tokugawa Culture Observed*. Translated by Beatrice M. Bodart-Bailey. Honolulu: University of Hawaii Press, 1999.

Kaufmann, Thomas DaCosta. *The Mastery of Nature: Aspects of Art, Science, and Humanism in the Renaissance*. Princeton, NJ: Princeton University Press, 1993.

Kuipers, Jan J. B. *De VOC: Een multinational onder zeil, 1602–1799*. Zutphen: Walburg Pers, 2014.

Lamb, Ursula, ed. *The Globe Encircled and the World Revealed*. Vol. 3. Aldershot: Ashgate Variorum, 1995.

Legarda, Benito J., Jr. *After the Galleons: Foreign Trade, Economic Change and Entrepreneurship in the Nineteenth-Century Philippines*. Quezon City: Ateneo de Manila University Press, 1999.

Lubinsky, Pesach, Kenneth M. Cameron, María Carmen Molina, Maurice Wong, Sandra Lepers-Andrzejewski, Arturo Gómez-Pompa, and Seung-Chul Kim. "Neotropical Roots of a Polynesian Spice: The Hybrid Origin of Tahitian Vanilla, *Vanilla Tahitensis* ORCHIDACEAE." *American Journal of Botany* 95, no. 8 (2008): 1040–47.

MacLeod, Roy, ed. *Nature and Empire: Science and the Colonial Enterprise*. Special Issue, *Osiris* 15 (2000).

Menegon, Eugenio. *Ancestors, Virgins and Friars: Christianity as a Local Religion in Late Imperial China*. Cambridge, MA: Harvard University Asia Center for the Harvard Yenching Institute, 2009

Mukerji, Chandra, "Dominion, Demonstration, and Domination: Religious Doctrine, Territorial Politics, and French Plant Collection." In *Colonial Botany: Science, Commerce, and Politics in Early Modern World*, edited by Londa Schiebinger and Claudia Swan, 19–34. Philadelphia: University of Pennsylvania Press, 2005.

Newson, Linda. *Conquest and Pestilence in the Early Spanish Philippines*. Honolulu: University of Hawaii Press, 2009.

Parthesius, Robert. *Dutch Ships in Tropical Waters: The Development of the Dutch East India Company VOC Shipping Network in Asia, 1595–1660*. Amsterdam: Amsterdam University Press, 2007.

Reitsma, Ella. *Maria Sybilla Merian and Daughters: Women of Art and Science*. Amsterdam: Rembrandt House Museum, 2009.

Reyes, Raquel A. G. "Botany and Zoology in the Late Seventeenth-Century Philippines: The Work of Georg Josef Camel, SJ, 1661–1706." *Archives of Natural History* 36, no. 2 (2009): 262–76.

———. "Collecting and the Pursuit of Scientific Accuracy: The Malaspina Expedition in the Philippines, 1792." In *Science and Empire: Dutch Science around 1800 in Comparative Perspective*, edited by Peter Boomgaard, 63–89. New York: Palgrave Macmillan, 2013.

Rumphius. *Ambonese Herbal* [1741]. Translated by E. M. Beekman, 3 vols. New Haven, CT: Yale University Press, 1992.

Schiebinger, Londa. "Forum Introduction: The European Colonial Science Complex." *Colonial Science*, Special Issue, *Isis* 96 (2005): 52–55.

———. *Plants and Empire: Colonial Bioprospecting in the Atlantic World*. Cambridge, MA: Harvard University Press, 2004.

Schiebinger, Londa, and Claudia Swan, eds. *Colonial Botany: Science, Commerce, and Politics in the Early Modern World*. Philadelphia: University of Pennsylvania Press, 2005.

Seijas, Tatiana. *Asian Slaves in Colonial Mexico: From Chinos to Indians*. New York: Cambridge University Press, 2014.

Skott, Christina. "Linnaeus and the Troglodyte: Early European Encounters with the Malay World and the Natural History of Man." *Indonesia and the Malay World* 42 (2014): 141–69.

Smith, Pamela H., and Paula Findlen, eds. *Merchants and Marvels: Commerce, Science and Art in Early Modern Europe*. London: Routledge, 2002.

Spate, O. H. K. *The Spanish Lake*. London: Croom Helm, 1979.

Stols, Eddy, Werner Thomas, and Johan Verberckmoes, eds. *Naturalia, Mirabilia e Monstrosa en los Imperios Ibéricos*. Leuven: Leuven University Press, 2007.

Subrahmanyam, Sanjay, ed. *Merchant Networks in the Early Modern World, 1450–1800*. Vol. 8. Aldershot: Ashgate Variorum, 1996.

Tremml-Werner, Birgit. *Spain, China and Japan in Manila, 1571–1644: Local Comparisons, Global Connections*. Amsterdam: Amsterdam University Press, 2015.

Verma, Som Prakash. *Flora and Fauna in Mughal Art*. Bombay: Marg Publications, 1999.

Vermeulen, Hans F. *Early History of Ethnography and Ethnology in the German Enlightenment: Anthropological Discourse in Europe and Asia, 1710–1808*. Leiden: Ridderkerk, 2008.

Wagenaar, Lodewijk. *Aan de Overkant: ontmoetingen in dienst van de VOC en WIC 1600–1800*. Leiden: Sidestone Press, 2015.

Zammito, John H. *Kant, Herder, and the Birth of Anthropology*. Chicago, IL: University of Chicago Press, 2002.

Zandvliet, Kees. *The Dutch Encounter with Asia 1600–1950*. Zwolle: Rijksmuseum Amsterdam and Waanders Publishers, 2002.

Chapter 2

A Bohemian Mapmaker in Manila

Travels, Transfers, and Traces between the Pacific Ocean and German Lands

Ulrike Strasser

Mapping the world's largest ocean and the islands peppering its blue vastness was a Herculean task for the many Europeans who followed in Magellan's footsteps to explore the waters he had first christened "the Pacific." From the sixteenth century onward, a steady trickle of knowledge flowed from Pacific regions back to Europe in the form of reports, specimens, and maps. It grew into a stream of information over the centuries, leading up to the famous Cook–Forster voyages. Alan Frost aptly termed the Pacific "the eighteenth century's New World" to capture its lure for Europeans.[1]

The Caroline Islands were among the many places that called to Europeans in the eighteenth century. They first appear on a European map in print in Madrid in 1706. Andres Serrano, a Spanish Jesuit, published the map as part of a report he had authored on the discovery and planned evangelization of the islands. He credited a German Jesuit named Paul Klein with having created it.[2] Originally from Bohemia, Klein was stationed in Manila, and his map had traveled from there to find its way into print in Spain, France, England, and Germany, and possibly elsewhere. As it happened, though, Klein had never visited the islands in question. He placed them based on information he had learned from a group of Carolinian castaways—Klein referred to them as Palaos—who were shipwrecked in the Philippines in 1696. The prevailing currents and winds had caused such unintended landings by Palaos islanders on Philippine shores before, but Klein's 1696 encounter with these particular castaways stood out for the information and publicity it generated.[3] The castaways laid out pebbles in the sand to provide a sketch of their island world, offering key data for the 1706 map that appeared in Klein's name.

This chapter takes the case of the Klein map, its origins in the Pacific, and its reception and redactions in Europe to illuminate several broader themes of

---

Notes from this chapter begin on page 71.

relevance to this volume. To begin with, this story sheds light on the multiple networks—religious, political, communicative—that brought a Jesuit like Klein from Bohemia to the Pacific, and his map back to Europe. It illustrates that the Holy Roman Empire of the German nation, in spite of its lack of colonies, was plugged into transnational circuits of information and the flow of people moving through the Spanish Empire to its Pacific frontier. The history of the making and fortune of Klein's map further turns the spotlight on the wide range of people, including indigenous informants, who produced geographic information about the Pacific in their respective local contexts, and often collaboratively. It highlights how difficult, albeit not altogether impossible, it is to isolate "German" influences from those of other ethnic groups, European and indigenous, when studying Pacific cross-cultural exchanges in the early modern period.

These arguments will be fleshed out in three sections: the first will introduce Paul Klein in the context of Jesuit cartographic endeavors and of a notable increase in the number of Germans in the order's Spanish overseas missions; the second will focus on the key role of Palaos islanders in the making of Klein's map, probing this European map for traces of indigenous spatial perspectives; and the third will trace the fortunes of Klein's map in different European countries, including the German lands from which he first ventured in the Pacific.

Missionary Mapmaking: Paul Klein's *Carta* of the Palaos

The Jesuits controlled one of the largest transnational information and communication networks in the early modern world and counted first-rate cartographers among their ranks.[4] Thus it makes sense that a Jesuit from Bohemia became associated with creating the first European map of the Caroline Islands. Europeans indeed owed the cartographic conquest of vast areas of the "New World" to missionaries in the Society of Jesus. In the seventeenth century, an increasing number of Jesuits venturing abroad hailed from German-speaking lands; many of them were chosen precisely for the superb mathematical and geographical skills that had been learned in their home colleges.[5] Klein's activities in the Philippines took place against the backdrop of these larger phenomena.

Jesuit geographical knowledge was second to none at the time. Prior to the establishment of state-run academies in Europe in the eighteenth century, Jesuit colleges were key training centers for cartography. The Jesuit curriculum *ratio studiorum* entailed instruction in surveying techniques and mapmaking, together with teaching geography.[6] Geography dealt with places and peoples, fusing modes of inquiry and knowledge classification that evolved into the separate disciplines of cartography and ethnography in modern times.[7]

Since the fifteenth century, and in particular since the appearance of Ptolemy's *Geographica* in Western Europe, a new notion of the earth as a sphere wrapped in a web of latitudinal and longitudinal lines had begun to upend Jerusalem's former pride of place as the geometrical center. A view of the world as a unified space began to take hold instead. The European voyages of discovery and exploration served to fill in the precise contours of this newly imaged world, filling in blank spaces with precise detail.[8]

Although Jesuit missionaries shared these scientific interests and participated in the mapping of the earth, it is important to note that their ultimate motivation differed from those of other explorers. Theirs was a quest for salvation, of self and other,[9] and this overarching intention influenced why and how they mapped space. There was the practical necessity of surveying a terrain before the evangelization of its inhabitants. There was also, on a deeper level, a sense of co-shaping the course of salvation history by helping expand Christianity around the globe. Already the medieval Church understood itself as universal, yet its universalism lacked the geographic specificity that came to characterize the Jesuits' sense of being called to global evangelization.[10] Apocalyptic readings of time infused this new globalism. The accelerated speed of discoveries supposedly signaled the imminent end of time. Once Christianity came to envelope the entire world, the eschatological clock would grind to a halt. Jesuits thus busily named, mapped, and classified the lands they encountered, reading each geographical environment for signs that pointed to its place in salvation history, and marking the progress of that history.[11]

Taken together, this truly global sense of mission and the exceptional educational possibilities of the Society meant that the Jesuits soon achieved the status of star cartographers among the religious orders. In Spanish America, Jesuits who, often alone, ventured beyond the fortified colonial towns to carry the gospel into the countryside also carried out the most extensive mapping of these remote areas, whose labor was not surpassed until the large-scale national mapping projects at the turn of the twentieth century.[12]

In the seventeenth century, more and more Jesuits from the German lands of Central Europe journeyed to the Spanish overseas empire. Although the Spanish Crown limited the numbers of non-Iberians admitted to the colonial territories, at times prohibiting foreign participation altogether, the urgent need for personnel repeatedly led to a loosening of restrictions.[13] In addition, the Crown held missionaries from dynastic allies, such as the Austrian Habsburg, in relatively high regard: they classified such missionaries as "reliable" rather than "suspicious" foreigners. Thus about one thousand Jesuits, or 26 percent of all Jesuits in the seventeenth-century Spanish overseas empire, came from German lands; and between 5 and 10 percent of them ended up working in the empire's Pacific parts.[14] As non-Iberians, they were routinely assigned to areas far beyond the colonial urban centers the Spaniards preferred. In rural areas, the Germans could apply the excellent mapping skills they had acquired at the order's Central European colleges.[15]

Paul Klein's travels to the Pacific coincided with the greater influx of Germans into the Spanish Empire. He was born in Eger in Bohemia in 1652,[16] only two years before the Spanish Crown apportioned one-fourth of available missionary appointments to non-Spaniards as a way of redressing the chronic shortage of missionaries in its colonial territories. In 1667, Klein began his novitiate at the age of seventeen in Brno. University studies in Prague followed, and in 1675 he dispatched a first letter from there to Rome petitioning to be sent to the Indies.[17] The same year brought another change in admission policies as Maria Anna of Austria, widow of Philip IV and regent of the Spanish Empire, spurred on by her Austrian Jesuit confessor, further eased the conditions of missionary participation for non-Spaniards. She set the quota at one-third, and waived the year-long residency requirement in the province of Toledo in favor of a flexible regulation that made it possible for foreigners to board the first available ship for the long overseas passage.[18]

Nonetheless, it took Klein years to reach the Philippines from Prague. Three years after his first letter he succeeded in his application, having stressed the completion of his theological studies and his readiness for the mission in a letter of January 1678.[19] Six months later, Klein was at sea, transiting across the Mediterranean from Genoa to Spain and then from Cadiz across the Atlantic to Vera Cruz. Next, he proceeded on the back of a mule across the Mexican highlands to the Jesuit residence San Borgia, near Mexico City, and then to Acapulco to await the annual departure of the Manila galleon.[20] Another hundred days of open ocean, this time the Pacific, and Klein landed in Manila. Three lengthy sea journeys later, and it was the middle of 1682.

Klein spent the next thirty-five years until his death in Manila in 1717 living and working in the island world of the Philippines.[21] From 1687 to 1696 and 1716 to 1717 he served as professor of moral theology at the main college in Manila. He also served as prefect of studies at the residential college of Jan Jose in Manila from 1690 to 1701, when he became its vice-rector. After a stint as rector of the college in Cavite, Klein reached the peak of his career in 1708, when he became provincial for the entire Philippine province, encompassing the Philippines proper, the missions on the Marianas, and the evangelization of the Palaos Islands, the archipelago he had first mapped around the turn of the century.[22]

Linguistic and cultural boundary crossings characterized Klein's missionary life from start to finish. As a subject of the Austrian Habsburgs, the Bohemian Jesuit occupied a position on the colonial grid that differed from the position of his Spaniard confreres: he negotiated a doubly unfamiliar world, the world of indigenous culture and of Spanish political rule.[23] Colonial officials and Spanish Jesuits were not without prejudices toward non-Spaniards, although, as Klein's own career trajectory documents, those views did not necessarily get in the way of holding high offices. Klein eventually published in Spanish under the hispanized name of "Pablo Clain." He chose this name at a time when Germans no longer needed to alter their names to ease passage into Spanish colonial society,[24] suggesting a high degree of acculturation later in life.

Some indigenous people also distinguished between Central European Jesuits and Spanish Jesuits. They believed the Spanish fathers to be more closely allied with the colonial state and hence preferred dealing with non-Spaniards. Perhaps this was a factor in why, in 1684 in Manila, a spiritually ambitious mestiza chose Klein as her spiritual director. Under his guidance, Ignacia del Espiritu Santo, as this daughter of a Filipina and Chinese came to call herself, established the Philippine's first female congregation for mestizas and Filipinas in a house neighboring Klein's college.[25]

Klein's high level of education facilitated his engagement with the diverse populations of the Philippines. Regulations for the province stipulated that its missionaries had to acquire at least one indigenous language to the satisfaction of their superior.[26] Klein exceeded this expectation. His first work in Spanish (already a foreign language for him), a medical and pharmaceutical handbook of three hundred pages, was published in Manila on rice paper in 1713. Aimed at aiding other missionaries who worked in the far-flung island world, the manual presented a comprehensive overview of regional diseases and instructions for preparing medicines. Klein explained in a preface that he added an "index of remedies with explanations and instructions for applying them because he [Klein] often used the vernacular tongue of the Philippine people which one may not understand."[27] In addition to Spanish and Latin, the index listed relevant terminology in Tagalog, Visayan, and Pampanga. A year later, the Bohemian wrote and published an explication of Christian doctrine in Tagalog. Translations from Latin, French, and Spanish into Tagalog followed in subsequent years and, over time, Klein developed an entire *vocabulario tagala*, which was published posthumously and remains a linguistic benchmark to this day.[28]

Klein's talents as a cross-cultural translator certainly also justified his assignment early in 1697 to travel to Samar in the Visayan part of the Philippines and meet the stranded Palaos Islanders who would help him place their life world on a map. Jesuit Provincial Antonio Tuccio ordered Klein to interview the castaways and explore the possibility of "introducing the light of the Holy Gospel" to the unknown archipelago.[29] In this instance even the polyglot Klein required assistance. He did not speak the Palaos language and came to rely on two women, earlier Palaos castaways who had been on Samar for many years, who translated the new arrivals' conversation into Visayan for him. The lengthy letter Klein dispatched on 10 June 1697 to the order's general in Rome to present his findings and request support for evangelizing the islands reveals this. The two female translators remain nameless, as do all the indigenous informants whom Klein referenced in his account.[30]

The women were not the only mediators of the castaways' geographical information. After the initial gathering of information, Klein returned to Manila in

1697. Meanwhile, Francesco Pradella, another Jesuit and resident of Samar, was ordered to question the castaways again about the exact number and location of islands. This time, the Palaos used pebbles on the beach as a visual aid for depicting all the islands of their archipelago that they knew from firsthand experience. Pradella copied the outline of the pebbles spread out on the sandy beach onto paper and sent it to Klein in Manila.[31]

Multiple moments of translation and transfer thus marked the final cartographic product. The first European map of the Palaos archipelago, although credited to Klein and indeed brought into circulation by him, was a copy of a copy, since Klein had worked off another Jesuit's sketch of the Palaos's pebble arrangement. The original stemmed from the islanders themselves; they alone knew the represented space from experience. Their unique perspective left traces on the European cartographic record, to which we now turn.

Navigating Island Worlds: European and Indigenous Imaginings of Oceanic Spaces

A scant and lopsided historical record seriously complicates attempts to reconstruct the Palaos past. There are very few sources to begin with, and existing materials stem from the quills of Europeans like Klein, who inevitably offer outsider perspectives.[32] This makes it very challenging to avoid replicating the colonial trope of the ahistoricity of non-Western people and render indigenous people as individual historical actors rather than members of a timeless "island culture."[33]

There are ways of at least mitigating, even if not fully overcoming, such methodological difficulties. It is possible to read the European sources against the grain, and draw on recent postcolonial and anthropological literature to reconstruct possible islander perspectives. Brownen Douglas's reflections on Pacific source materials are particularly instructive in this respect. Arguing that the European representations were shaped not only by European points of view but by the "dialectic of discourse and experience" that haunts all cross-cultural encounters, Douglas urges scholars to comb the European record for "countersigns" that encapsulate the indigenous participation and agency in those encounters, and decode them for their underlying meaning.[34]

Clearly the cross-cultural encounter that made Klein's map possible had shaped it, and it bears the direct imprint of Palaos perspectives. The very existence of the map, however, adds another interesting twist to this source. While Palaos navigators knew perfectly well their way around a far-flung archipelago of some 1,500 miles,[35] their knowledge system consisted entirely of highly complex mental maps, which they passed down orally from generation to generation. When Klein made the first European map of the region by relying on indigenous data instead of firsthand knowledge, he thus also created the first lasting material

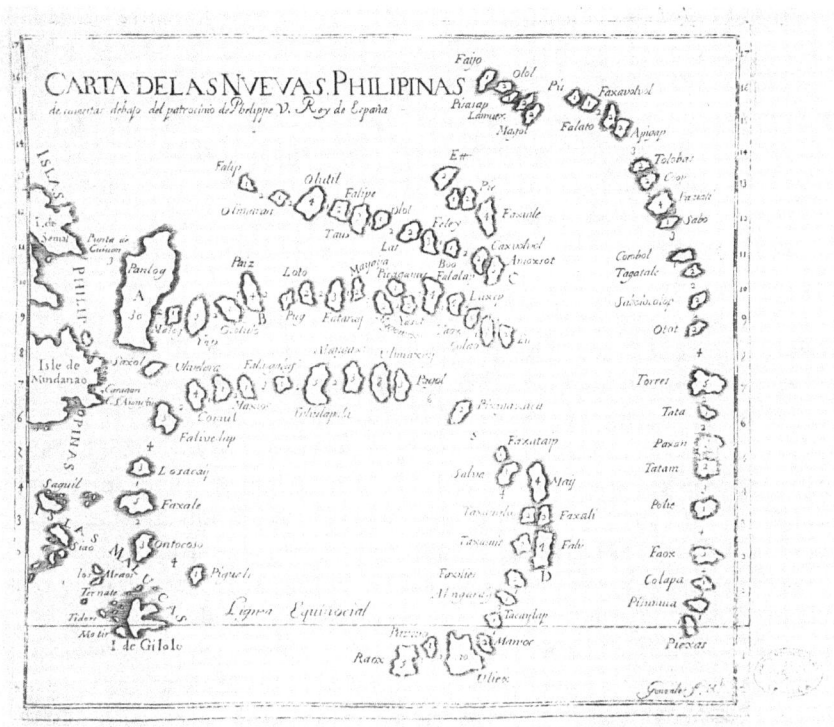

Figure 2.1: Klein's map as presented by Andres Serrano (1706), Gobierno de España. Ministerio de Cultura, Archivo General de Indias, AGI, MP-Filipinas 15- Carta de las Nuevas Filipinas: Islas Palaos. Published with permission.

representation of the islanders' mental maps. In this instance—distortions in Klein's translation of the islanders' information notwithstanding—the Jesuit left a historical record where otherwise none would have existed.[36]

Like a time capsule, Klein's map contains two competing visions of oceanic space that we can roughly characterize as "European" and "islander." This is not to suggest that the heterogeneous perception of the many individuals that compose each one of these broad groups can be flattened into a single, collectively held worldview. With respect to this cartographic artifact, however, we can identify two distinct spatial perspectives that can be said to be more broadly characteristic of European explorers and missionaries on the one hand, and of Palaos navigators on the other.

Islander navigators, in essence, imagined their surrounding from the perspective of a seafarer in a canoe who charted his course with his eyes low on the horizon. The navigator watched for the rising and falling of certain stars and constellations that could guide him or her toward the island of destination. This navigational system pivoted upon sure knowledge of the relevant constellations for each island—what is known as a "star compass." In addition to these celestial reference points, navigators picked islands that lay to one side of the course or the other as reference points, and tracked their successive passage, triangulating between the stars, the reference islands, and the island of destination.[37]

By contrast, European navigators charted their course with instruments and sea charts, and they did so in reference to fixed star positions that allowed them to determine their own location at a particular moment in time. Progress was measured by imagining oneself from an aerial point of view, or God's eye, moving across a grid of longitude and latitude that enveloped the world. To create a European cartographic representation based on the islanders' cognitive maps, then, meant translating a practice-oriented horizontal view into a vertical perspective derived from Euclidian geometry.

Klein's visual depiction of the archipelago still bore the residues of the islanders' spatial experiences. Jesuit mapmakers in the Spanish Indies often baptized places with Christian names, but each of the eighty-seven individual islands on this map bear Palaos names. The indigenous toponymy marks the de facto limits of European access to, never mind control over, the depicted space. More centrally still, the size of the islands and the distances between them do not adhere to the rules of European geometry. Both are expressed numerically. This numbering system derived directly from the Palaos experience of the island space. Their navigators measured distances in sailing days rather than in sea miles.[38] The numbers on the islands recorded the time it took for circumnavigation; the numbers noted between islands indicated the time required for transit from one island to the next. For example, thirty days to travel around Panlog or two days to journey to the neighboring island of Malog.

The islanders "how long" instead of the European "how far" emphasized the accessibility of islands and the connectedness of the archipelago. In precolonial days, inter-island voyages were frequent, and islanders experienced the biggest ocean on the planet not as a divide or an obstacle to connection but as a relay and medium for exchanges, a vision the Tongan scholar and writer Epeli Hau'ofa tried to recapture programmatically in his 1994 essay "Our Sea of Islands."[39] Historical research has evidence of strong inter-island relations, notably in the Western Carolines where an elaborate regional system of tribute was in place. This Carolinian exchange system initially extended to the Marianas as well. The connection was severed once the Carolinians learned of the Spanish conquest of the Marianas and the brutal treatment of the local Chamorro population. This severing of ties was only a first instance of the profound boundary drawings that accompanied the establishment of a European colonial presence in the region. It eventually culminated in outright prohibitions of inter-island canoe travel.[40]

The days had yet to come when Europeans put an ideological finish on this geopolitical reconfiguration and attached the geographic label of smallness

("Micronesia") to the world of separate islands that they had created in the first place. But already in Klein's time, and his writing, one sees a kernel of the perception of the ocean as an isolating force that undergirded these later developments. For Central Europeans who had developed their sense of environment in a place where the land dwarfed the water, the Pacific must have appeared a monstrous disruption of natural territorial connections. Even to European men from a seaborn empire like Spain, the Pacific presented itself as a formidable barrier, not a connector, between far-flung destinations. When the Spanish captain reached a group of Carolinian islands in 1721, he christened them "Garbanzo islands"—a metaphor that evokes chickpea-size land fragments floating on a soup of open sea. Spaniards also began referring to the Carolinian archipelago as *islas encantadas* (mystery islands) in a phrase reflective of the islands' lure as well as their status as virtually unattainable objects.[41]

In other words, the connecting lanes and orientation points that islanders perceived in the open sea remained obscure to the European eye. It is thus not surprising that Klein depicted parts of their archipelago as more divided than they actually were, and divided islets linked within atolls into separate entities.[42] It is arguably much more interesting that the Jesuit retained any traces of the islanders' spatial vision at all by including their numbering system instead of completely transforming their temporal experience of crossing a connected sea into a geometric representation of separate bodies of land. The particular bend of some islands' arcs in Klein's map may even reflect the islanders' horizontal perspective in setting a course.[43]

At any rate, Klein's map reveals itself as a hybrid system of signs. It complies only partially with the growing demand for accuracy and semiotic homogeneity that one finds in Europe at the time, including instead traces of the islanders' geographical gaze. The map was obviously the result of a cross-cultural conversation about a space that only one of the conversation participants knew experientially. That Klein engaged in this conversation was directly linked to his view of the theological significance of this oceanic space. In his letter to the Jesuit general, he interpreted the Palaos shipwreck as a sign that "God arranged and ordered the discovery and ... conversion of these peoples in this time."[44]

As Jesuits knew all too well, though, God's intentions were one thing, the order's capabilities another. After Klein's fact-finding mission, the Philippine Jesuits tried to launch the evangelization of the Palaos but soon discovered that they lacked enough money and suitable high seas vessels. These were typical start-up difficulties for which the Jesuits sought a typical solution: they dispatched an emissary to Europe to round up the requisite funds and logistical support. The man for this mission was Andres Serrano, the Spanish Jesuit who first introduced Klein's map to Europe's courts and print culture.

Klein's Map Goes to Europe: Court Audiences and Print Publications

The arrival of Klein's map in Europe coincided with two larger trends that helped pave the way for its reception: first, in the realm of politics, cartography's emergence as a technology of rule at European courts; and, second, in the realm of print, the proliferation of missionary periodicals that garnered a broad, educated readership beyond their immediate denominational circles.

Andres Serrano's three major European destinations were the Roman curia, the Bourbon courts of Louis XIV in Paris, and those of his grandson Philip V in Madrid. He successfully obtained the fiat of Pope Clement XI as well as securing the financial and political support of the two kings for the archipelago's evangelization. Serrano subsequently published the above-mentioned treatise *Breve Noticia del Nuevo Descubrimiento de las Islas Pais o Palaos* in Madrid, which included copies of the papal letters and royal decrees issued in support of the mission, Klein's map, and a version of his report.

Serrano's assemblage of materials in the *Breve Noticia* reveals that he made a set of telling redactions to Klein's materials. These changes served to persuade European monarchs to invest resources in the exploration and subjugation of distant Pacific islands. While the German's account had referenced the poverty of the Palaos, Serrano promised the exact opposite: a rich bounty of spices and metals. The Spaniard deduced the availability of these riches from the islands' geographic location, specifically their proximity to islands already under European influence: "We believe that said islands do not lack various riches, like gold, silver, pearls, metal, and aromatic spices, for they are located virtually on the same latitude with the Moluccas, Borneo, Mindanao, New Guinea, Papua, and other islands which have an abundance of such riches."[45] This presentation played right into the abiding desire of the Spanish Crown to find the famed golden temples of Solomon, and it sparked hope that the newly discovered archipelago would be identical to the legendary island paradise of Rica de Ora and Rica de Plata, imagined to be somewhere near Japan.[46]

In a related move, Serrano gave Klein's cartographic creation its title: *Map of the New Philippines Discovered under the Patronage of Philip V*, a characterization that was both flattering and exhortative given the de facto limits of European control in the region. Klein's map already included a section of the Philippines, which the title cast as the old Philippines, suggesting a natural progression of the empire's claims eastward. The map further included parts of the Moluccas, the much-coveted spice islands under the control of the Dutch—a visual reminder of the colonial competition, and evocative of Serrano's promise of comparable riches on the neighboring "New Philippines." Serrano's title, we might say, functioned as a paratext that pushed a particular reading of Klein's map as a call to colonial action.

This was a timely message to European monarchs. In the sixteenth and seventeenth centuries, rulers across Eurasia discovered the usefulness of cartography to governance.[47] In Europe, a medieval notion of rule based on control over people gave way to an early modern view of rule as grounded in a place or territorial sovereignty.[48] It led to the creation of new offices and institutions that wielded cartography as a technology of rule.[49] In Spain in 1571, the Crown appointed a special chief cosmographer, Juan Lopez de Velasco, to its Council of the Indies, and charged him with the task of mapping the entire overseas territories. He developed a questionnaire that local officials in all parts of the Spanish Indies had to answer. Their answers arrived in Spain in the form of both a report (*relacion*) and a drawing (*pintura*), whereupon the chief cosmographer tried to streamline the information into a single cartographic work of entirely unprecedented scope. This project epitomizes the broader "colonization of space" that Walter Mignolo has traced for the Spanish Empire—that is to say, the introduction of European territorial and spatial modalities (Christian place names, Euclidian geometry) that accompanied and legitimated the political conquest of space and the erasure of indigenous worlds.[50]

Klein's materials and Serrano's presentation fit right into this established tradition of Spanish colonial mapmaking. Klein had gathered the data in conversation with indigenous people in the Spanish Indies and produced both a written report and a visual depiction. Serrano brought the materials to Europe and, tweaking some of the contents, offered the monarchy a way to fill in a blank spot on the colonial master map.

Cartography was also in vogue at the French court. Since the relocation of star astronomer Giovanni Cassini from Italy to France in 1668, the country had established itself as Europe's center of surveying and mapmaking techniques. Domestically, Louis XIV had launched a first comprehensive national survey, resulting in a detailed *Carte de France*. Gazing toward the wider world, he asked his royal academy with its cutting-edge astronomical observatory to map the entire globe and situate every known place on a cartographic grid.[51] As members of the largest transnational institutional network of the time, Jesuits were often the only Europeans who could provide information from faraway lands to the royal academy's resident geographers, who rarely even left Paris. Add to this that rare maps were prized objects among courtly collectors, and it makes sense that Louis XIV, as the sources tell us, gazed at the map of the New Philippines delivered by Serrano "with enormous pleasure," and questioned Serrano about the islands for several hours.[52]

Whatever Klein thought of Serrano's editorial work, the Bohemian must have been pleased with the effect of the Palaos map on the Bourbon kings. Upon his election as provincial of the Philippine province, Klein himself was able to hand the royal decrees ordering the exploration of the archipelago over to the colonial authorities in Manila. Between 1708 and 1712, colonial officials and Jesuits in the Pacific made at least nine attempts to land on the Palaos islands. Not a single one succeeded. The one that came closest was the 1710 expedition by the Spanish captain-general Francisco Padilla. He was able to land near the island now known as Sonsorol, and dispatch a boat, with two Jesuits aboard, to its shore. Yet strong currents and winds soon drove Padilla's fleet far to the north, forcing him to leave the priests behind without any provisions. Several ill-fated rescue missions followed. Andres Serrano joined one such rescue team, only to drown in a shipwreck off the very islands he had popularized in Europe. Islanders killed the two stranded priests.[53] The spectacular failure of these Pacific missions highlights the distinction, common to colonial maps, between the symbolic appropriation of a space and its actual physical control.[54]

Meanwhile, back in Europe, Klein's map was making additional appearances in print. Scientific journals and missionary periodicals were taking off during the early Enlightenment, and Klein's materials surfaced in both types of publication, a reflection of the overlap between these two publishing markets in terms of content and authorship. In 1708, Klein's map thus appeared in the Philosophical Transactions of the Royal Society with a preface by French Jesuit Charles Le Gobien, editor of the famous missionary journal *Lettres Edifiantes et Curieuses*, which had featured Klein's materials the previous year.[55]

The London-based scientific journal regularly featured articles by geographers and mapmakers, yet it usually prized maps first and foremost for accuracy grounded on firsthand observation. In this case, however, it emphasized the unorthodox genesis of the map and the lack of scientific accuracy. Le Gobien's preface advertised the ethnographic rather than the scientific dimension of the map to its readership. It related the story of how the Palaos had communicated by laying out pebbles on the beach, and added the following punch line: "and this is the map, thus traced out by the Indians, that is here ingraved [sic]."[56] Although it was of course not "the" map that the Palaos had traced, but rather Klein's cartographic translation in its highly mediated print version that appeared in *Philosophical Transactions*, Le Gobien claimed authorship for the Palaos. Authorship, however, was not to be mistaken for accuracy according to European standards: "Not that I can warrant for the exactness of [the map]," Le Gobien continued; "When our missionaries shall have travelled to these Islands ... there will be found a great many things in it that will need correction."[57]

One such correction to the Palaos map was made in German lands. It was featured prominently in the premier Catholic missionary periodical *Der Neue Welt-Bott*, the first serialized publication of German Jesuit reports from all over the world. Between 1726 and 1763, forty installments of *Welt-Bott* appeared, amounting to over 4,500 folio pages packed with print and some visual materials.[58] The publication was first launched in Augsburg, the nodal point in Germany's national and international trade network, center of its publishing industry, and gateway for information arriving from the Spanish Americas.[59]

Like the *Lettres Edifiantes* and the contemporary Protestant *Halle'sche Berichte*, the *Neue Welt-Bott* pursued a dual aim of combining the edifying with the educational to appeal to a confessional audience as well as a broader interested public. Joseph Stöcklein, the founding editor, pitched the journal in a prologue to the general reader as a form of travel writing, praising the genre's particular value to Germans:

> [E]verything that comes from foreign lands to Germany (*Teutschland*) tickles our appetite for knowledge more than do all domestic rarities, ... in this respect accounts of the world and of travels no doubt deserve pride of place; after all, a curious reader, without taking a step, can sit at home and wander the entire world merely by reading these kinds of writings, whereby he can acquire an almost complete knowledge of the entire globe with no danger, costs, or effort.[60]

This was a text for German armchair travelers and resident scholars, published in the vernacular to broaden its appeal. *Teutsch* is in fact a key term in this journal, functioning as a marker of a shared identity based on culture and language, not a fixed location or origin, thus uniting missionaries abroad and readers at home, and creating an imaginary global community of Germans. The journal's selections and editorial comments suggested that this German cultural conquest of the world was a natural consequence of the superiority of Germans vis-à-vis various others, including other European powers.[61]

Joseph Stöcklein apparently judged that German readers would have a strong interest in the Pacific. The *Welt-Bott*'s first issue opened with materials about Pacific regions, setting a pattern for subsequent issues. Stöcklein's thematic focus provides one reason for the inclusion of the Klein materials in his journal. The *Welt-Bott*'s editor furthermore professed a particular interest in delivering cutting-edge geographical information to his readers. In the above-cited preface, he compared the accounts printed in his journals with the maps of the Ancients, with their "invented places and names." The *Welt-Bott*, by contrast, presented factual reports about "[t]he discovery of previously either unknown or largely unknown places through which our missionaries personally travelled, yes, through personal observation measured, described, and recorded on land-charts."[62]

Paul Klein's Palaos map was included in installment six of the *Welt-Bott*.[63] Stöcklein had a simple remedy for the fact that Klein had never been to the archipelago: like a true resident geographer of his time, he assessed the available evidence, including information compiled during Padilla's 1710 expedition, and redacted Klein's map so that it that no longer suffered from "the mistakes of the poor barbarians," meaning Klein's Palaos informants.[64] Stöcklein recalculated the longitudinal and latitudinal coordinates and adjusted the East–West range of the map. He moreover converted all distances into German sea miles and removed the numbering system from the map, instead expressing all distances geometrically by increasing the size of islands with larger numbers and

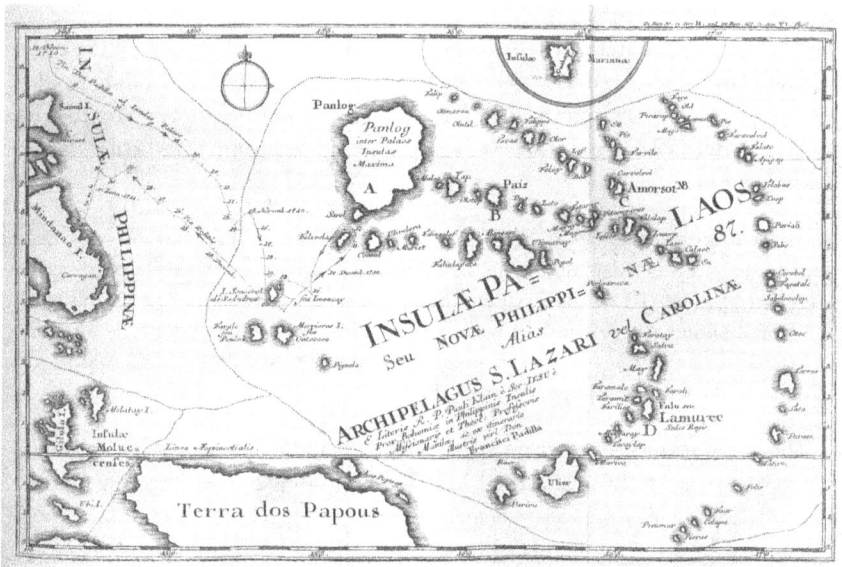

Figure 2.2: Insulae Laos seu novae Philippinae, in: Stöcklein, Allerhand so lehr- als geist-reiche Brief, Bd. 1, Teil 6, f. 32. Niedersächsische Staats- und Universitätsbibliothek Göttingen. Published with permission.

decreasing the size of islands with smaller numbers. The islanders' "how long" thus disappeared as the European's "how far" took over in the visual representation. Stöcklein also recorded Padilla's itinerary—the most successful European foray in the region—in his redacted map, projecting the intended expansion of European influence onto his cartographic representation.[65]

If cultural translation entails, as Peter Burke claims, "a double process of decontextualization and recontextualization, first a reaching out to appropriate something alien and then domesticating it,"[66] Stöcklein in Germany completed the process of domesticating the indigenous spatial conceptions that Klein had only begun in the Pacific. But it would be a mistake to assume that work on the colonial periphery made a missionary cartographer inevitably more susceptible to indigenous perspectives than an armchair geographer in Germany. A brief look at the map that came to replace Klein's makes this plain.

In 1720, Antonio Cantova, an Italian Jesuit, had the fortune of encountering another group of Palaos castaways on the Mariana Islands. He stayed for eight months and acquired the language skills to obtain, without translators or other go-betweens, a fuller picture of the Palaos and their world. The result was an ethnography that far exceeded Klein's in detail, and a new map that superseded Klein's to become the benchmark for future European mapmaking endeavors in the region. When Charles de Brosses synthesized the existing European information about the Pacific and its island world in his *Histoire de Navigation aux Terre Australes* in 1736, he printed Cantova's map, not Klein's, although he featured a version of the Bohemian's account of the Samar castaways.[67] Thereafter, Klein's written geographical record appeared periodically, but once again uncoupled from the visual record and sometimes even without proper attribution. Notably, it appeared in Volume 10 of Matthias Christian Sprengel and Johann Reinhold Forster's *Neue Beiträge zur Völker- und Länderkunde*, with Cantova mistakenly listed as the author.[68]

The history behind Cantova's map is in itself complex and deserves a detailed treatment. Suffice it to say here that his representation was closer to the cartographic sensibilities of someone like Stöcklein, who never left Europe. Indigenous spatial conceptions found no place in Cantova's map. It was an entirely geometrical representation of the island space on a longitudinal and latitudinal grid. In addition, Cantova grouped the islands into geographical units—or five provinces, as he called them. The map included a wind rose as was customary on portolan charts, and marked suitable locations for dropping anchor offshore to further aid European navigators. This kind of detail helps explain why the Cantova map served as the geographical point of reference for the expedition of Henry Wilson in the late eighteenth century, as well as those of Otto von Kotzebue and Adalbert von Chamisso in the early nineteenth century.[69] It also led the mapmaker himself to the Palaos, and made him, in 1731, the first European missionary to found a mission station on the islands. This proved to be an abortive enterprise. Islanders hostile to his conversion efforts killed him after a few months, repositioning the Palaos Islands as a space beyond European reach until the British reached the archipelago half a century later, thus ending all efforts of evangelization until the twentieth century.[70]

Conclusion

The story of the first map of the Caroline Islands and its German maker highlights three intersecting networks that tied early modern Germany into the Pacific world: the transnational Society of Jesus with its global aspirations and far-flung mission stations; European colonial structures of military power, finance, and transportation, enabling the flow of people and information between Europe and other parts of the world; and finally, closer to home, Germany's network of editors, publishers, printers, readers, and participants in the European Republic of Letters. The combined effects of these networks brought a Bohemian to Manila, and his map back to Madrid, Rome, Paris, London, and his native Germany, where it produced a view of an ocean space that the vast majority of his contemporaries never visited, but it now became part of their geographical and political horizon.

The story of Klein's map further shows that geographic knowledge production by missionaries, including those from German lands, played into European colonial expansion. Jesuits contributed to the "colonization of space" in Mignolo's sense when they offered their cartographic services to colonial authorities or brought a new map of Pacific islands to Europe's kings with a request to lay claim to the lands. It seems no coincidence, however, that the Iberian Andres Serrano delivered the map of the German Jesuit to the court in Madrid. Germans like Klein did not have their own political presence in the Pacific, making it inevitable that their contributions to the colonial knowledge economy would be mediated and filtered through by others. On the flipside, the more tenuous position of Germans like Klein meant that they always remained representative of different constituencies rather than of Spanish colonial society. This positionality, combined with their generally high level of education, may have made German Jesuits especially suitable brokers of cross-cultural exchange.

The case of Klein's map finally suggests that geographic knowledge about the Pacific was produced by a wide range of people mainly in local context, and often collaboratively. The story of German geographic knowledge production about the Pacific begins long before the all-male naturalist explorers of the eighteenth century; it begins among the peoples of the Pacific themselves. Local knowledge—both knowledge articulated in a particular place and about a particular place—could find its way into the emerging European knowledge systems. In Klein's map, we see a blending of European and Palaos spatial perspectives, a record of alternate and competing conceptions of oceanic space in the early modern world. Over time, however, only some of these knowledge makers received authorial credit, whereas the role of others was disavowed. The female translators who facilitated Klein's first interview with the Palaos remain nameless in his account. Stöcklein, the editor of *Welt-Bott*, happily printed Klein's map but dismissed "the ignorant barbarians" who knew the geographic location from experience. Johann Reinhold Forster later used Klein's ethnography in his scientific publication together with Cantova's map, but credited only the Italian and not the German Jesuit. Progressive erasures and disavowals have thus haunted the very process of knowledge production about the Pacific and continue to do so to this day, demanding that we take an attitude that is both skeptical and humble in seeking to highlight "German" contributions to the making and understanding of Pacific worlds.

Ulrike Strasser is professor of history at the University of California, San Diego. She specializes in early modern Central Europe, religious history, gender history, and global history. Her publications include the award-winning monograph, *State of Virginity: Gender, Politics, and Religion in a Catholic State* (Michigan Publishing, 2004; paperback 2007).

Notes

An earlier version of my research on Klein's map appeared in German. See Ulrike Strasser, "Die Kartierung der Palaosinseln: Geographische Imagination und Wissenstransfer zwischen europäischen Jesuiten und mikronesischen Insulanern um 1700," *Geschichte und Gesellschaft* 36 (2010): 197–230.

1. Alan Frost, "The Pacific Ocean: The Eighteenth Century's New World," *Studies on Voltaire and the Eighteenth Century* 152 (1976): 779–822.
2. Andres Serrano, *Breve Noticia del Nuevo Descubrimiento de las Islas Pais o Palaos ...*, Madrid, 1706. An excerpt of Serranos's account was printed separately: Andres Serrano, *Noticia de las Islas Palaos, Impresa en Madrid (?) [sic!]*, in 1705. Ahora nuevamenta reimpresa. Ano de 1895, in *Archivo del Bibliofilo Filipino por W. E. Retana. Tomo Segundo*, Madrid 1896, 161–73. A version may have appeared in 1705 as well. See Robert Streit and Johannes Dindinger, *Missionsliteratur von Australien und Ozeanien, 1525–1950* (Bibliotheca Missionum, Vol. 21, Freiburg, 1955), 65–66.
3. Francis X. Hezel, "Early European Contact with the Western Carolines, 1525–1750," *Journal of Pacific History* 7 (1972): 26–44. See also: idem, *The First Taint of Civilization: A History of the Caroline and Marshall Islands in Pre-Colonial Days, 1521–1885* (Honolulu: University of Hawaii Press, 1983); idem, *Foreign Ships in Micronesia: A Compendium of Ship Contacts with the Caroline and Marshall Islands 1521–1885* (Saipan: published in cooperation with the Trust Territory Historic Preservation Office and the US Heritage Conservation and Recrecation Service, 1979); and Alexandre Coello de la Rosa, *Jesuits at the Margins: Missions and Missionaries in the Marianas, 1668–1769* (New York: Routledge, 2016), 177–221.
4. Steven J. Harris, "Mapping Jesuit Science: The Role of Travel in the Geography of Knowledge," in *The Jesuits: Cultures, Sciences, and the Arts, 1540–1773*, ed. John W. O'Malley et al. (Toronto: University of Toronto Press, 1999), 212–40; idem, "Jesuit Scientific Activity in the Overseas Missions, 1540–1773," *Isis* 96, no. 1 (March 2005): 71–79.
5. Luke Clossey, *Salvation and Globalization in the Early Jesuit Missions* (Cambridge: Cambridge University Press, 2008), especially 142, 153, 138, and 208–9.
6. Mary Sponberg Pedley, *The Commerce of Cartography: Making and Marketing Maps in Eighteenth-Century France and England* (Chicago, IL: University of Chicago Press, 2005) 26–29; Lesley B. Cormack, "Maps as Educational Tools in the Renaissance," in *The History of Cartography. Volume 3: Cartography in the Renaissance, Part 1*, ed. David Woodward (Chicago, IL: University of Chicago Press, 2007), 630.
7. Laura Hostetler, *Qing Colonial Enterprise: Ethnography and Cartography in Early Modern China* (Chicago, IL: University of Chicago Press, 2005), 23. On the development of the science of geography in a modern geopolitical context, see Jürgen Osterhammel, *Die Verwandlung der Welt: Eine Geschichte des 19. Jahrhunderts* (Munich: C.H. Beck, 2009), 131–43.
8. Norman J. W. Thrower, *Maps & Civilization: Cartography in Culture and Society* (Chicago, IL: University of Chicago Press, 1996), 39–90; Evelyn Edson, *Mapping Time and Space: How Medieval Mapmakers Viewed Their World* (London: British Library Board, 1999).
9. Clossey, *Salvation and Globalization*, especially 120–23.
10. Ibid., 8.
11. Ibid., 91–102.
12. David Buisseret, "Spanish Colonial Cartography, 1450–1700," in *The History of Cartography*, Volume 3: Cartography in the Renaissance, Part I, ed. David Woodward (Chicago, IL: University of Chicago Press, 2007), 1148.
13. Bernd Hausberger, *Jesuiten aus Mitteleuropa im kolonialen Mexiko: Eine Bio-Bibliographie* (Vienna: Oldenbourg, 1995), 34–37.

14. Clossey, *Salvation and Globalization*, 149 and 153 (for numbers, calculations are mine).
15. Buisseret, "Spanish Colonial Cartography," 1148.
16. For a short biography, see Hausberger, *Jesuiten aus Mitteleuropa*, 220–21.
17. Letter from 9 September 1678, Archivum Romanum Societatis Jesu (ARSI), F.G., 756 Bohemia, f. 119. On letters of application from German Jesuit provinces, see Christoph Nebgen, *Missionsberufungen nach Übersee in drei deutschen Provinzen im 17. und 18. Jahrhundert* (Regensburg: Schnell & Steiner, 2007).
18. Horacio de la Costa, *The Jesuits in the Philippines, 1581–1768* (Cambridge, MA: Harvard University Press, 1961), 439.
19. Letter from 1 December 1678, ARSI, F.G., 756 Bohemia, f. 125.
20. Hausberger, *Jesuiten in Mitteleuropa*, 47–50. Clossey, *Salvation and Globalization*, 147–49.
21. De la Costa, *The Jesuits in the Philippines*, 62.
22. Ibid., 507–8.
23. J. Michelle Molina and Ulrike Strasser, "Missionary Men and the Global Currency of Female Sanctity," in *Women, Religion and Transatlantic World*, ed. Danna Kostroum and Lisa Vollendorf (Toronto: University of Toronto Press, 2009), 158–79. Hausberger, *Jesuiten aus Mitteleuropa*, 87–92.
24. On the earlier practice of involuntary name changes, see Clossey, *Salvation and Globalization*, 34.
25. De la Costa, *Jesuits in the Philippines*, 508.
26. Ibid., 262.
27. On this manual, see Renée Gicklhorn, *Missionsapotheker: Deutsche Pharmazeuten im Lateinamerika des 17. und 18. Jahrhunderts* (Stuttgart: Wissenschaftliche Verlagsgesellschaft, 1973), 65–70. See also Raquel Reyes's contribution in this volume.
28. A list of Klein's writings is included in "J. S. Arcilla" in *Diccionario histórico de la Compañía de Jesús: Biográfico-temático, 4 Vols.*, ed. Charles E. O'Neill and Joaquín María Domínguez (Rome, 2001), Vol. 3, 2201–2. On the "politics of translation" in imperial contexts and "translation as a passage to conversion," see Vincent L. Rafael, *Contracting Colonialism: Translation and Christian Conversion in Tagalog Society under Early Spanish Rule* (Durham, NC: Duke University Press, 2001). An edition of Klein's linguistic manual can be found in the Fondo Filipinas des Arxiu Històric de la Companyia de Jesus Catalunya in Barcelona: VOCABULARIO DE LA LENGUA TAGALA COMPUESTO POR LOS PADRES PABLO CLAIN, FRANCISCO IANSENS Y IOSEPH HERNANDEZ, LOS TRES DE LA COMPAÑÍA DE IESUS. Imprimió por primera vez en Manila, año 1754.
29. Serrano, *Noticia de las Islas Palaos*, 166–67.
30. A first printed version appeared in French in Charles Le Gobien, Histoire Des Isles Marianes, Nouvellement converties à la Religion Chrestienne; & de la mort glorieuse des premiers Missionnaires qui y ont prêché la Foy Paris, 1700, Appendix, 395–410.
31. Archivo General de Indias, Filipinas, Legajo 251, Testimonio Nr. 5, bes. f. 19r–21v. Parts are reprinted in German and Spanish in Augustin Krämer, *Ergebnisse der Südsee-Expedition 1908–1910: II. Ethnographie: B. Mikronesien, Band 3: Palau*, ed. Georg Thilenius; Augustin Krämer, Palau, 1. Teilband (Hamburg, 1917).
32. For a survey of available sources, see Francis X. Hezel, "Catholic Missions in the Caroline and Marshall Islands: A Survey of Historical Materials," *Journal of Pacific History* 5 (1970): 213–27.
33. For critical perspectives on the historical record and its uses, see the works by Greg Dening, especially *Islands and Beaches: Discourse on a Silent Land, Marquesas, 1774–1880* (Honolulu: University of Hawaii Press, 1980); Nicholas Thomas, "Partial Texts: Representation, Colonials and Agency in Pacific History," *The Journal of Pacific History* 25, no. 2 (1990): 139–58; Doug Munro and Brij V. Lal, eds., *Texts and Contexts: Reflections in Pacific Island Historiography*

(Honolulu: University of Hawaii Press, 2006); Anne Salmond, *Two Worlds: First Meetings between Maori and Europeans, 1642–1772* (Honolulu: University of Hawaii Press, 1991).
34. Brownen Douglas, "In the Event: Indigenous Countersigns and the Ethnohistory of Voyaging," in *Oceanic Encounters*, ed. Margaret Jolly, Serge Tcherkezoff, and Darrell Tryon (Canberra: The Australian National University Press, 2009), 175–98.
35. This is large even by the standards of seafarers. See Hezel, *First Taint of Civilization*, 51.
36. Thomas Suárez also points this out: Suárez, *Early Mapping of the Pacific: The Epic Story of Seafarers, Adventurers, and Cartographers who Mapped the Earth's Greatest Ocean* (Singapore: Periplus Editions, 2004), 182.
37. For a detailed discussion of this highly complex system presented here in simplified terms, see Ben Finney, "Nautical Cartography and Traditional Navigation," in *The History of Cartography. Vol. 2, Book 3: Cartography in the Traditional African, American, Arctic, Australian, and Pacific Societies*, ed. David Woodward and John B. Harley (Chicago, IL: University of Chicago Press, 1998), 443–92. Also, Paul Hambruch, *Die Schiffahrt auf den Karolinen- und Marshallinseln* (Berlin: Ernst Siegfried Mittler und Sohn, 1912), 1–40.
38. Suárez, *Early Mapping of the Pacific*, 184–85.
39. Epeli Hau'ofa, "Our Sea of Islands," *The Contemporary Pacific* 6, no. 1 (1994): 148–61.
40. Paul D'Arcy, "Connected by the Sea: Towards a Regional History of the Western Caroline Islands," *The Journal of Pacific History* 36, no. 2 (2001): 163–82. Compare also, D'Arcy, *The People of the Sea: Environment, Identity and History in Oceania* (Honolulu: University of Hawaii Press, 2006).
41. Hezel, *First Taint of Civilization*, 45.
42. Suárez, *Early Mapping of the Pacific*, 184.
43. Finney, *Nautical Cartography*, 452.
44. Quoted from the German version that appeared in Joseph Stöcklein, *Allerhand so lehr- als geistreiche Brief, Schrifften und Reis-beschreibungen, welchen von denen Missionariis der Gesellschaft Jesu aus beyden Indien, und andern über Meer gelegenen Ländern seit An. 1642 biss auf das Jahr 1726 in Europa angelangt seynd*. Erster Bund oder die 8. Erste Teil, Augsburg und Grätz: Verlag Philip, Martins und Joh. Veith seel. Erben, 1726, Letter Nr. 37, folios 5–8; quote from folio 6.
45. Serrano, *Noticia de las Islas Palaos*, 167 (translation mine).
46. Coelle, *Jesuits at the Margins*, 180.
47. Hostetler, *Qing Colonial Enterprise*, 4 and 74.
48. On the nexus between territoriality and maps, see Jörg Dünne, "Die Karte als Operations- und Imaginationsmatrix: Zur Geschichte eines Raummediums," in *Spatial Turn: Das Raumparadigma in den Kultur- und Sozialwissenschaften*, ed. Jörg Dünne and Tristan Thielmann (Bielefeld: Transcript, 2008), 1–69.
49. Richard L. Kagan and Benjamin Schmidt, "Maps and the Early Modern State: Official Cartography," in *The History of Cartography. Volume 3: Cartography in the Renaissance, Part 1*, ed. David Woodward and John B. Harley (Chicago, IL: University of Chicago Press, 2007), 661–80.
50. Walter Mignolo, *The Darker Side of the Renaissance: Literacy, Territoriality, and Colonization* (Ann Arbor: University of Michigan Press, 1995), especially 243–86. Mignolo, "The Movable Center: Geographical Discourses and Territoriality during the Expansion of the Spanish Empire", in *Coded Encounters: Writing, Gender and Ethnicity in Colonial Latin America*, ed. Francisco Xavier Cevallos-Candau (Amherst: University of Massachusetts Press, 1994), 15–45.
51. Pedley, *Commerce of Cartography*, especially 26. Also Florence Hsia, "Jesuits, Jupiter's Satellites, and the Academie Royale des Sciences," in *The Jesuits: Cultures, Sciences, and the Arts, 1540–1773*, ed. John W. O'Malley et al. (Toronto: University of Toronto Press, 1999), 241–57.
52. The experience of "pleasure" at the sight of maps is a topos in the literature, speaking to the quasi-magical aura surrounding the first cartographic representations of an area and turning them

into coveted objects for court collectors. Kagan and Schmidt, "Maps and the Early Modern State", especially 661 and 679.
53. For a brief summary of events, see Hezel, "Catholic Missions," especially 216–17.
54. Jess Edwards, "Wie liest man eine frühneuzeitliche Karte?" in *Text – Bild – Karte: Kartographien der Vormoderne*, ed. Jürg Glauser et al. (Freiburg: Rombach, 2007), 102.
55. Charles Le Gobien, ed., *Lettres Edifiantes et Curieuses Ecrites des Missions Etrangeres par quelques Missionnaires de la Compagnie de Jesus* (Paris: N. Leclerc, 1707).
56. Charles Le Gobien, "An Extract of Two Letters from the Missionary Jesuits, concerning the Discovery of the New Philippines-Islands, with a Map of the Same," in *Philosophical Transactions XXVI* (London, 1708), 197.
57. Ibid.
58. Galaxis Borja and Ulrike Strasser, "The German Circumnavigation of the World: Missionary Writing and Colonial Identity Formation in Joseph Stöcklein's *Neuer Welt-Bott*," in *Reporting Christian Missions*, ed. Markus Friedrich and Alex Schunka (Wiesbaden: Harrassowitz Verlag, 2017), 73–92. Renate Dürr, "Der '*Neue Welt-Bott*' als Markt der Informationen? Wissenstransfer als Moment jesuitischer Identitätsbildung," *Zeitschrift für historische Forschung* 34, no. 3 (2007): 441–66. Bernd Hausberger, "El padre Joseph Stöcklein o el arte de inscribir el mundo a la fe," in *Desde los confines de los imperios ibéricos*, ed. Karl Kohut, Torales Pacheco, and María Cristina (Mexico: DF, 2007), 631–62.
59. Galaxis Borja, *Jesuitische Berichterstattung über die Neue Welt: Zur Veröffentlichungs-, Verbreitungs- und Rezeptionsgeschichte jesuitischer Americana auf dem deutschen Buchmarkt* (Göttingen: Vandenhoeck & Ruprecht, 2011).
60. Stöcklein, Allerhand so lehr- als geistreiche Brief, Bd. 1, Allgemeine Vorrede zum gesamten Werk, unpaginated.
61. Borja and Strasser, "German Circumnavigation"; Also Ulrike Strasser, "A Case of Empire Envy? German Jesuits Meet an Asian Mystic in Spanish America," *Journal of Global History* 2 (2007): 32–40.
62. Stöcklein, Allerhand so lehr- als geistreiche Brief, Bd. 1.
63. Ibid., Teil 6.
64. Ibid., Brief des Verfassers, Nr. 127, Folio 1–6, quote Folio 2.
65. See also Suárez who compares the Le Gobien version of the map that was published in the Philosophical Transaction to Stöcklein's redacted version. Suárez, *Early Mapping of the Pacific*, 185.
66. Peter Burke, "Cultures of Translation in Early Modern Europe," in *Cultural Translation in Early Modern Europe*, ed. Peter Burke and Ronnie Po-chia (Cambridge: Cambridge University Press, 2007), 10.
67. Charles de Brosses, *Vollständige Geschichte der Schiffahrten nach den grösstentheils unbekannten Südländern. Mit Karten. Aus dem Französischen des Herrn Praesidenten de Brossess übersetzt. Mit Anmerkungen begleitet und mit verschiedenen Zusätzen versehen von Johann Christoph Adelung* (Halle, 1767). Tom Ryan, "'Le Président des Terres Australes': Charles de Brosses and the French Enlightenment Beginnings of Oceanic Anthropology," in *Science, Empire and the European Exploration of the Pacific*, ed. Tony Ballantyne (Aldershot, UK: Ashgate, 2004), 247–77. For context on this publication, see also Christiane Küchler Williams, *Erotische Paradiese: Zur europäischen Südseerezeption im 18. Jahrhundert* (Göttingen: Wallstein Verlag, 2004).
68. Matthias Christian Sprengel and Georg Forster, eds., *Neue Beiträge zur Völker- und Länderkunde, 10. Teil* (Leipzig 1792).
69. Suárez, *Early Mapping of the Pacific*, 186–91.
70. Hezel, *First Taint of Civilization*, 57–59. Krämer, *Palau*, Erster Teilband, 106.

Bibliography

Borja, Galaxis. *Jesuitische Berichterstattung über die Neue Welt: Zur Veröffentlichungs-, Verbreitungs- und Rezeptionsgeschichte jesuitischer Americana auf dem deutschen Buchmarkt.* Göttingen: Vandenhoeck & Ruprecht, 2011.

Borja, Galaxis, and Ulrike Strasser. "The German Circumnavigation of the World: Missionary Writing and Colonial Identity Formation in Joseph Stöcklein's *Neuer Welt-Bott.*" In *Reporting Christian Missions*, edited by Markus Friedrich and Alex Schunka, 73–92. Wiesbaden: Harrassowitz Verlag, 2017.

Buisseret, David. "Spanish Colonial Cartography, 1450–1700." In *The History of Cartography, Volume 3: Cartography in the Renaissance*, edited by David Woodward, 1143–71. Chicago, IL: University of Chicago Press, 2007.

Burke, Peter. "Cultures of Translation in Early Modern Europe." In *Cultural Translation in Early Modern Europe*, edited by Peter Burke and Ronnie Po-chia, 7–38. Cambridge: Cambridge University Press, 2007.

Clossey, Luke. *Salvation and Globalization in the Early Jesuit Missions.* Cambridge: Cambridge University Press, 2008.

Coello de la Rosa, Alexandre. *Jesuits at the Margins: Missions and Missionaries in the Marianas, 1668–1769.* New York: Routledge, 2016.

Cormack, Lesley B. "Maps as Educational Tools in the Renaissance." In *The History of Cartography, Volume 3: Cartography in the Renaissance*, edited by David Woodward, 622–36. Chicago, IL: University of Chicago Press, 2007.

D'Arcy, Paul. "Connected by the Sea: Towards a Regional History of the Western Caroline Islands." *The Journal of Pacific History* 36, no. 2 (2001): 163–82.

———. *The People of the Sea: Environment, Identity and History in Oceania.* Honolulu: University of Hawaii Press, 2006.

de Brosses, Charles. *Vollständige Geschichte der Schiffahrten nach den grösstentheils unbekannten Südländern. Mit Karten. Aus dem Französischen des Herrn Praesidenten de Brosses übersetzt. Mit Anmerkungen begleitet und mit verschiedenen Zusätzen versehen von Johann Christoph Adelung.* Halle, 1767.

de la Costa, Horatio, S.J. *The Jesuits in the Philippines 1581–1768.* Cambridge, MA: Harvard University Press, 1961.

Dening, Greg. *Islands and Beaches: Discourse on a Silent Land, Marquesas, 1774–1880.* Honolulu: University of Hawaii Press, 1980.

Douglas, Brownen. "In the Event: Indigenous Countersigns and the Ethnohistory of Voyaging." In *Oceanic Encounters*, edited by Margaret Jolly, Serge Tcherkezoff, and Darrell Tryon, 175–98. Canberra: The Australian National University Press, 2009.

Dünne, Jörg. "Die Karte als Operations- und Imaginationsmatrix: Zur Geschichte eines Raummediums." In *Spatial Turn: Das Raumparadigma in den Kultur- und Sozialwissenschaften*, edited by Jörg Dünne and Tristan Thielmann, 1–69. Bielefeld: Transcript, 2008.

Dürr, Renate. "Der '*Neue Welt-Bott*' als Markt der Informationen? Wissenstransfer als Moment jesuitischer Identitätsbildung." *Zeitschrift für historische Forschung* 34, no. 3 (2007): 441–66.

Edson, Evelyn. *Mapping Time and Space: How Medieval Mapmakers Viewed Their World.* London: British Library Board, 1999.

Edwards, Jess. "Wie liest man eine frühneuzeitliche Karte?" In *Text – Bild – Karte: Kartographien der Vormoderne*, edited by Jürg Glauser and Christian Kiening, 95–130. Freiburg: Rombach, 2007.

Finney, Ben. "Nautical Cartography and Traditional Navigation." In *The History of Cartography. Vol. 2, Book 3: Cartography in the Traditional African, American, Arctic, Australian, and Pacific Societies*, edited by David Woodward and John B. Harley, 443–92. Chicago, IL: University of Chicago Press, 1998.

Frost, Alan. "The Pacific Ocean: The Eighteenth Century's New World." *Studies on Voltaire and the Eighteenth Century* 152 (1976): 779–822.

Gicklhorn, Renée. *Missionsapotheker: Deutsche Pharmazeuten im Lateinamerika des 17. und 18. Jahrhunderts*. Stuttgart: Wissenschaftliche Verlagsgesellschaft, 1973.

Hambruch, Paul. *Die Schiffahrt auf den Karolinen- und Marshallinseln*. Berlin: Ernst Siegfried Mittler und Sohn, 1912.

Harris, Steven J. "Jesuit Scientific Activity in the Overseas Missions, 1540–1773." *Isis* 96 no. 1 (March 2005): 71–79.

———. "Mapping Jesuit Science: The Role of Travel in the Geography of Knowledge." In *The Jesuits: Cultures, Sciences, and the Arts, 1540–1773*, edited by John W. O'Malley et al., 212–40. Toronto: University of Toronto Press, 1999.

Hau'ofa, Epeli. "Our Sea of Islands." *The Contemporary Pacific* 6, no. 1 (1994): 148–61.

Hausberger, Bernd. *Jesuiten aus Mitteleuropa im kolonialen Mexiko: Eine Bio-Bibliographie*. Vienna: Oldenbourg, 1995.

———. "El padre Joseph Stöcklein o el arte de inscribir el mundo a la fe." In *Desde los confines de los imperios ibéricos*, edited by Karl Kohut, Torales Pacheco, and María Cristina, 631–62. Mexico: DF, 2007.

Hezel, Francis X. "Catholic Missions in the Caroline and Marshall Islands: A Survey of Historical Materials." *Journal of Pacific History* 5 (1970): 213–27.

———. "Early European Contact with the Western Carolines, 1525–1750." *Journal of Pacific History* 7 (1972): 26–44.

———. *The First Taint of Civilization: A History of the Caroline and Marshall Islands in Pre-Colonial Days, 1521–1885*. Honolulu: University of Hawaii Press, 1983.

———. *Foreign Ships in Micronesia: A Compendium of Ship Contacts with the Caroline and Marshall Islands, 1521–1885*. Saipan: published in cooperation with the Trust Territory Historic Preservation Office and the US Heritage Conservation and Recreation Service, 1979.

Hostetler, Laura. *Qing Colonial Enterprise: Ethnography and Cartography in Early Modern China*. Chicago, IL: University of Chicago Press, 2005.

Hsia, Florence. "Jesuits, Jupiter's Satellites, and the Academie Royale des Sciences." In *The Jesuits: Cultures, Sciences, and the Arts, 1540–1773*, edited by John W. O'Malley et al. 241–57. Toronto: University of Toronto Press, 1999.

Kagan, Richard L., and Benjamin Schmidt. "Maps and the Early Modern State: Official Cartography." In *The History of Cartography, Volume 3: Cartography in the Renaissance*, edited by David Woodward, 661–80. Chicago, IL: University of Chicago Press, 2007.

Krämer, Augustin. *Ergebnisse der Südsee-Expedition 1908–1910: II. Ethnographie: B. Mikronesien, Band 3: Palau*, edited by Georg Thilenius. Hamburg: 1917.

Le Gobien, Charles. "An Extract of Two Letters from the Missionary Jesuits, Concerning the Discovery of the New Philippines-Islands, with a Map of the Same." *Philosophical Transactions XXVI*, 189–99. London, 1708.

―――. *Histoire Des Isles Marianes, Nouvellement converties à la Religion Chrestienne; & de la mort glorieuse des premiers Missionnaires qui y ont prêché la Foy.* Paris: Ne Pepie, 1700.

―――, ed. *Lettres Edifiantes et Curieuses Ecrites des Missions Etrangeres par quelques Missionnaires de la Compagnie de Jesus.* Paris: N. Leclerc, 1707.

Mignolo, Walter. *The Darker Side of the Renaissance: Literacy, Territoriality, and Colonization.* Ann Arbor: University of Michigan Press, 1995.

―――. "The Movable Center: Geographical Discourses and Territoriality during the Expansion of the Spanish Empire." In *Coded Encounters: Writing, Gender and Ethnicity in Colonial Latin America*, edited by Francisco Xavier Cevallos-Candau, 15–45. Amherst: University of Massachusetts Press, 1994.

Molina, Michelle J., and Ulrike Strasser. "Missionary Men and the Global Currency of Female Sanctity." In *Women, Religion and Transatlantic World*, edited by Danna Kostroum and Lisa Vollendorf, 158–79. Toronto: University of Toronto Press, 2009.

Munro, Doug, and Brij V. Lal, eds. *Texts and Contexts: Reflections in Pacific Island Historiography.* Honolulu: University of Hawaii Press, 2006.

Nebgen, Christopher. *Missionarsberufungen nach Übersee in drei deutschen Provinzen im 17. und 18. Jahrhundert.* Regensburg: Schnell & Steiner, 2007.

Osterhammel, Jürgen. *Die Verwandlung der Welt: Eine Geschichte des 19. Jahrhunderts* Munich: C.H. Beck, 2009.

Pedley, Mary Sponberg. *The Commerce of Cartography: Making and Marketing Maps in Eighteenth-Century France and England.* Chicago, IL: University of Chicago Press, 2005.

Rafael, Vincente L. *Contracting Colonialism: Translation and Christian Conversion in Tagalog Society under Early Spanish Rule.* Durham, NC: Duke University Press, 2001.

Ryan, Tom. "'Le Président des Terres Australes': Charles de Brosses and the French Enlightenment Beginnings of Oceanic Anthropology." In *Science, Empire and the European Exploration of the Pacific*, edited by Tony Ballantyne, 247–77. Aldershot, UK: Ashgate, 2004.

Salmond, Anne. *Two Worlds: First Meetings between Maori and Europeans, 1642–1772.* Honolulu: University of Hawaii Press, 1991.

Serrano, Andres. *Breve Noticia del Nuevo Descubrimiento de las Islas Pais o Palaos* …. Madrid, 1706.

―――. *Noticia de las Islas Palaos, Impresa en Madrid (?) [sic!]*, in 1705. Ahora nuevamenta reimpresa. Ano de 1895, in *Archivo del Bibliofilo Filipino por W. E. Retana. Tomo Segundo,* 161–73. Madrid, 1896.

Sprengel, Matthias Christian, and Georg Forster, eds. *Neue Beiträge zur Völker- und Länderkunde, 10. Teil.* Leipzig, 1792.

Stöcklein, Joseph. *Allerhand so lehr- als geistreiche Brief, Schrifften und Reis-beschreibungen, welchen von denen Missionariis der Gesellschaft Jesu aus beyden Indien, und andern über Meer gelegenen Ländern seit An. 1642 biss auf das Jahr 1726 in Europa angelangt seynd.* Erster Bund oder die 8. Erste Teil, Augsburg und Grätz: Verlag Philip, Martins und Joh. Veith seel. Erben, 1726.

Strasser, Ulrike. "A Case of Empire Envy? German Jesuits Meet an Asian Mystic in Spanish America." *Journal of Global History* 2 (2007): 23–40.

Streit, Robert, and Johannes Dindinger. *Missionsliteratur von Australien und Ozeanien, 1525–1950.* Bibliotheca Missionum, Vol. 21. Freiburg: Herder, 1955.

Suárez, Thomas. *Early Mapping of the Pacific: The Epic Story of Seafarers, Adventurers, and Cartographers who Mapped the Earth's Greatest Ocean.* Singapore: Periplus Editions, 2004.

Thomas, Nicholas. "Partial Texts: Representation, Colonials and Agency in Pacific History." *The Journal of Pacific History* 25, no. 2 (1990): 139–58.
Thrower, Norman J. W. *Maps & Civilization: Cartography in Culture and Society*. Chicago, IL: University of Chicago Press, 1996.
Williams, Christiane Küchler. *Erotische Paradiese: Zur europäischen Südseerezeption im 18. Jahrhundert*. Göttingen: Wallstein Verlag, 2004.

Chapter 3

GERMAN NATURALISTS IN THE PACIFIC AROUND 1800
Entanglement, Autonomy, and a Transnational Culture of Expertise

Andreas W. Daum

Introduction

In the decades around 1800, naturalists from the German-speaking territories of Europe were present in various areas of the vast oceanic space we commonly reduce to a single word: the Pacific. They all traveled under the flags of other countries and had hardly any nominal authority. Yet these men (no women yet) from Rostock and Zurich, Westphalia and Danzig, made a difference, and their disadvantages turned out to be strengths.[1] The German naturalists contributed in significant ways to understanding Pacific spaces and habitats. They did so with an intellect and a mindset that allowed them to balance, on the one hand, their relative autonomy in pursuing scientific research and, on the other, their entanglement with the interests of the imperial powers that sponsored them. As a result, these men became important interlocutors in the increasingly global traffic of knowledge and of objects collected along their routes. The German naturalists helped to create epistemic networks and a transnational culture of expertise, both of which bridged political divides in Europe. They also mobilized public interest in the Pacific among a variety of German-speaking audiences.

The dual question of whether these men may, indeed, be called "Germans" and whether there was something distinct about them as Germans is more difficult to answer. To arrive at a tentative answer, I will first take a bird's-eye view of the role that experts of natural history played in the Pacific around 1800, and highlight the underlying context of rivalries between Europe's imperial powers. The second part of this chapter focuses on the German speakers among the colorful cohorts of Pacific naturalists. Finally, a comparative perspective allows us

---

Notes from this chapter begin on page 96.

to qualify more precisely what being German meant in the exploration of the Pacific.

Pacific Explorations and the Transnational Networks of Naturalists

Setting aside short-distance voyages and trips that explored only the coastlines of the Americas and Asia, large-scale Pacific journeys around 1800 were mostly part of circumnavigations of the globe. Only the great powers of the Eurasian continent—Great Britain, France, Spain, and Russia—were able to finance and sustain such endeavors, which always stretched over several years.[2] Imperial rivalries dominated the Second Age of Discovery, as Western interpreters have dubbed the decades between about 1760 and 1840. There was no Germany that could have participated in them. Prussia was still a regional power confined to Central Europe; German (and Prussian) naval power and oceanic projects emerged only after 1871.[3]

From the 1730s on, Europe's maritime powers began to scramble for territorial possessions, geostrategic advantages, and economic profits in the Pacific. Their competition revolved around acquiring and exploiting raw materials, goods, and food: wood and fur from the Northern Pacific rim; spices, tea, and coffee from India and East Asia; pork and fruit from Tahiti; and many more. At stake, too, were profits to be gained from trading in other commodities such as textiles produced in Europe. The governments and trade companies behind this drive aimed to connect existing hubs of commerce as well as to open new markets in Asia, the Americas, and later Oceania. Along North America's Pacific coast, the Russian emissaries clashed with their Spanish counterparts, who, in turn, competed with British and French claims. The global British–French conflict was only temporarily contained by the Treaty of Paris in 1763, following the Seven Years' War. In turn, this agreement drove the Spanish Empire to secure its interests along the Pacific rim.

The stage was thus set to turn Pacific spaces, often thousands of miles apart from each other, into venues for international conflict. Yet, most of the expeditions to these multiple Pacific worlds[4] were not devoted to a singular cause but pursued a variety of goals. The study of the natural habitats along the way was an integral part of such "mixed use" voyages and never separated from the political or economic profit that could be gained. Table 3.1 (at the end of the chapter) shows thirty voyages that fit this profile. Their sponsorship reflects the dominance of the British–French rivalry, encapsulated by the two outstanding navigators of the era, James Cook (1728–79) and Louis-Antoine Bougainville (1729–1811). Ten out of these thirty voyages sailed under British command, nine under a French flag, Spain backed two voyages,[5] and eight served Imperial Russia. The United States only began large-scale maritime explorations in 1838.

These voyages needed naturalists, to use the contemporary umbrella term for individuals who were qualified to study a broad spectrum of natural phenomena. They were experts in branches of so-called natural history—areas that later became the subject of distinct scholarly disciplines such as botany, geology, zoology, and hydrology. The national governments and naval authorities carefully selected the naturalists they sent overseas and provided them with a broad charge. It included the assignment to draw maps and mark areas of natural resources, measure climate and water conditions, collect and dissect specimens, evaluate the profitability of cultivating certain plants, and document the customs of the people they encountered on islands or along coastlines. However, in most of the cases the multitalented men shouldering these tasks could not even determine the destination of the dried plants and other objects they brought home, nor publish a travelogue without the consent of the governments that had sent them to the Pacific.

These naturalists were crammed together with seamen, missionaries, commercial traders, and medical doctors on ships that set out to the western and southwestern areas of the Pacific and to Australia. They reached islands in the central and southern Pacific, explored the northern Pacific along the Russian coast, the Bering Strait, and Alaska, and studied the Pacific rim from Alaska to Mexico and South America. All these areas became "contact zones" for encounters between Europeans and non-Europeans,[6] as much as a turf for clashes and communication among the European travelers themselves. This overlap between different kinds of asymmetrical encounters had a particular impact on the traveling naturalists. They were committed to remaining loyal to their commander, and many of them shared the political ambitions of the nation supporting them. But they, and especially the Germans among them, were not simply accomplices of colonial endeavors.[7]

For certain, British and French expeditions relied on the vast expertise accessible in their home countries. Joseph Banks, the English naturalist and long-time president of London's Royal Society, the Scottish botanist Robert Brown, and Charles Darwin are examples of young researchers who earned their stripes on oceanic expeditions launched by Great Britain. Their French counterparts included the botanical expert Philibert Commerçon, who accompanied Louis de Bougainville on France's first circumnavigation of the world in 1766–69; his assistant Jeanne Baret, for a long time the only woman on such a voyage (she initially disguised herself as a man);[8] and the marine hydrologist Louis Duperrey, who served on Louis de Freycinet's voyage in the years 1817–20.

Still, scholarly competence mattered at least as much as political allegiance when hiring a naturalist. This need for expertise explains why British, Russian, and Spanish expeditions into the Pacific also drew on naturalists from other

European regions. The Swedish botanist Daniel Solander, who worked for the British Museum in London, and his Finnish colleague Herman Spöring joined Joseph Banks on James Cook's first world voyage of 1768–71.[9] Anders Sparrman, another botanist from Sweden, collaborated with Johann and Georg Forster on James Cook's second voyage in 1772–75. There was the Austrian Ferdinand Bauer, who specialized in botanical drawings and accompanied Matthew Flinders in 1801–3 on the first circumnavigation of Australia.[10] The Dane Morten Wormskjold participated in the Russian *Rurik* expedition of 1815–18. He explored the fauna of Greenland and Kamchatka, the large Russian peninsula in the northwest Pacific.

Furthermore, the expert status of these naturalists both allowed and required from them to stay intellectually and socially connected among each other, which contributed to the transnational character of their network. The measurements they took, the analysis of specimens they collected, their assessment of the correctness of previous astronomical observations—in short, the practices that occupied much of their everyday life—all relied on epistemological conventions set by Europeans. They included the Linnean, binary nomenclature used for classifying plants, the standards of measurement generated by instruments that were traded among the participating countries, and an anatomical language suited to describe and compare animal species, their features, and variations.

These methodological conventions were based on what may be called a "Western" epistemology. As critics have rightly pointed out, the Europeans did not map a terra incognita. Often enough, they encountered existing layers of indigenous, colonial, and "creole" knowledge.[11] Moreover, the actual objects of study, especially botanical specimens, migrated with their investigators and were replanted and recategorized elsewhere, only to be redistributed again, traveling around the globe in the form of new specimens, drawings, printed descriptions, or other, newly acquired epistemic status.

All these practices and migrations unfolded in a continuous process of rereading scholarly literature that circulated across political borders, though with a clear preference for knowledge generated by European savants. A small part of this knowledge could be stored onboard in the form of books and manuscripts, which, too, traveled the Pacific. The much larger part, however, had to be memorized and communicated—often with intervals of many months, if not years—through correspondences that were maintained with colleagues across Europe, the Americas, and Asia.

The naturalists' knowledge thus drew as much on the places they traveled to as on virtual spaces such as publications, diaries, lectures given and heard, and especially on growing webs of correspondence.[12] All these factors generated a translocal and interpersonal network that began to connect Hawaii and Berlin, the Easter Islands and London, the Bering Strait and St. Petersburg. It was a web of contacts and transfers, of written and spoken knowledge as well as objects, that began to draw on globally dispersed locations. This network defies any retrospective separation between "central" versus "peripheral" spaces.[13]

German Explorers in the Pacific

In what ways did the German-speaking naturalists figure in this network and in the exploration of the Pacific around 1800? Who were they, and what kind of Germans are we dealing with?

As mentioned already, the German-speaking naturalists all sailed under the flag of other European countries. This basic fact might partially explain why the German speakers have lived a shadow existence in the accounts of Pacific exploration, setting aside Georg Forster and Alexander von Humboldt, who have assumed an almost iconic status in the narratives of world traveling. Yet, the cohort of German-speaking naturalists had a surprising presence in the Pacific, both in terms of numbers (in relation to the overall number of expeditions) and of contributions to Pacific research.[14] I have arrived at a sample of about thirty individuals, though it is impossible to provide exact figures. Table 3.2 (at the end of the chapter) lists them and their major travelogues individually.

The first Germans exploring the Pacific might have been among the crews that accompanied the Portuguese Ferdinand Magellan and the Spaniard García de Loaysa on their journeys in the years 1519–26. A century later, Adolph Decker from Strasbourg authored the first German-language report on a Pacific journey. In the seventeenth century, Japan attracted the most interest among Germans. Engelbert Kaempfer, born in Westphalia, stood out among them. Based on firsthand observations, Kaempfer compiled a comprehensive historical geography of Japan.[15] Although published initially in English, French, and Dutch, his survey of the history and nature of Japan had a profound influence on subsequent research in Germany, which culminated in the work of Philipp Franz von Siebold. When Christian Wilhelm von Dohm published in 1777 a German version of Kaempfer's seminal studies, Carl Friedrich Behrens had already alerted the German public to the South Pacific Easter Islands, which he had visited—supposedly as the first European—while traveling on a Dutch ship in 1722.

During the period of systematic Pacific exploration, the naturalists from German-speaking territories, as from other countries, were hired as reporters on duty. As so often, Alexander von Humboldt was an exception. He traveled for his own sake, financed largely by his family fortune, albeit under the protection of the Spanish Empire. For the others, Great Britain and Imperial Russia offered the best opportunities to reach the Pacific. Both countries launched circumnavigations of the world and were more open than France to the idea of bringing along qualified naturalists with different national backgrounds.

Carl Friedrich Behrens, Johan Georg Gmelin from Tübingen, and the Franconian Georg Wilhelm Steller served as naturalists on the Russian Great Northern Expedition which took off in 1733 under the command of the Danish-born Vitus Bering. While Behrens and Gmelin focused on the geography of Siberia, Steller explored the northern Pacific rim. Forty years later, the Pomeranian Johann Reinhold Forster and his son Georg crossed the Pacific when they circumnavigated the globe on Cook's second voyage in 1772–75. Their journey marked a new beginning in the history of Germans in the Pacific.

The Forsters integrated knowledge and practices of natural history emerging from the German-speaking territories of Europe into the growing transnational network of Pacific experts. Johann Reinhold's plan to publish his account of the voyage failed due to conflicts with the British sponsors. Yet the voluminous travelogue authored by his son became a stunning success. *Travel Around the World*, published in English in 1777 and translated into German by 1780, introduced the German public to the South Pacific (at that time called *Südsee*, southern sea) and brought the search for the land surrounding the South Pole into the limelight.

Georg Forster's narrative impressed children and teenagers, among them the young Humboldt, as well as adult readers and many scholars. The literary quality of this page-turner is stunning, as was Forster's ability to merge observations on the ocean's natural features with ethnological and sociological portraits of the island inhabitants. The sympathetic description of Tahiti, which seemed to stand in clear contrast to more critical remarks on other Polynesian societies, struck a special chord with readers, and resonated well into the twentieth century. Many readers took Forster's depiction as the image of a counterworld with a "natural" and free life. Yet, the popularization of this German *Südsee Enthusiasmus* (enthusiasm for the South Pacific) largely ignored Forster's fine-grained observations.[16] In fact, *Reise um die Welt*, as the German title ran, offered an abundance of sophisticated materials about the Pacific's natural history. It invited subsequent travelers to pursue Pacific studies in a continuous comparison with other habitats around the world.[17] Ultimately, the various trajectories that characterized the broad reception of Forster's account all nourished the growing interest in the Pacific in the German-speaking culture of Europe.

Georg Forster's literary success as a Pacific traveler has overshadowed the role that other German naturalists played in the Pacific. Forster himself used the observations made by two German seamen who sailed with James Cook on his third voyage to the Pacific in 1776–80.[18] Much more important was Thaddäus Haenke. He is largely forgotten today due to the paucity of his writings, the lack of archival evidence, and the repercussions of nineteenth-century, Prussian-dominated *kleindeutsch* thinking. Haenke was born in 1761 in northern Bohemia, then part of the Habsburg Empire. He stood in age between Georg Forster and Humboldt. Haenke's tireless activities as a naturalist in South

America were surpassed only by Humboldt's, and Haenke made it far deeper into the Pacific. In 1790 Haenke did a stint on the voyage of the Italian Alessandro Malaspina, whom the Spanish Crown had charged with a scholarly expedition around the world.[19] His and the Forsters' zigzagging between, on the one hand, studies of oceanic organisms, maritime climate, and water currents, and, on the other, coastal excursions and inland explorations, generated a template that all subsequent Pacific naturalists followed.

Alexander von Humboldt placed the systematic, empirically founded study of the interrelationship between all natural phenomena and human societies in the center of his research agenda, which he fleshed out on his American journey in the years 1799–1804. Historians of science have summarized his approach in the term "Humboldtian Science."[20] Humboldt had initially planned to cross the Pacific from the Americas to the Philippines, and to return to Europe from there via the Persian Gulf. He conversed with Louis-Antoine der Bougainville, the aging commander of the first French circumnavigation of the world, and almost joined the Pacific journey of Nicolas Baudin, France's foremost global navigator, which Baudin finally embarked on in 1800.[21] Ultimately, Humboldt and his companion Aimé Bonpland traveled on their own. They spent only forty-seven days, out of five years, in Pacific waters while traveling from Peru to Mexico in 1802–3, a record that hardly seems to qualify them as Pacific explorers.

Although Humboldt never found the time to fully interpret or publicize his oceanic studies, they deserve attention. Humboldt made important observations on the existence of a mid-Pacific oceanic current, distinguished from its mid-Atlantic counterparts by colder temperatures. He himself did not use term "Humboldt Current," and the latter remained disputed among scholars. Instead, Humboldt spoke of the Peruvian current, which he compared to the Gulf current.[22] He also suggested creating a link between the Pacific and the waters of the Mexican Gulf (i.e., ultimately the Atlantic Ocean), and investigated plankton organisms, oceanic fish, and seabirds. Humboldt blended these and other data, concerning everything from sea climate to nautical astronomy, into his attempt to draft a "physics of the earth."[23] He astutely grasped the need to establish a network of simultaneous, comparative oceanic measurements conducted by ships equipped with the latest technology.

A few months after Humboldt landed on the Pacific coast of Mexico in August 1803, another big player appeared on the scene: from the Baltic port of Kronstadt, Russia launched her first sea voyage around the world under Captain Adam von Krusenstern. Already Tsar Catherine II (r. 1762–96) had gone beyond the exploration of the northern Pacific authorized in earlier decades. Her successors now made Russia reach out massively toward the Pacific.[24] In 1803, Krusenstern followed the example of French and British voyages and steered the *Nadeshda* via the Atlantic and Cape Horn to the Pacific.[25] A look at his voyage adds important angles to the narrative of German-speaking naturalists in the Pacific. Once again, the primacy of expertise led a government to tap into the transnational networks that oceanic naturalists had established by 1800. Krusenstern set an example by hiring a whole team of highly qualified naturalists. Russia cherished, in particular, expertise provided by the German-speaking elite in the Baltic provinces. More than rival governments, the Tsarist rulers offered German-speaking naturalists opportunities for participation in oceanic journeys.

Six out of the seven major expeditions into the Pacific launched by Russia in the first three decades of the nineteenth century sailed under the command of Baltic Germans (see Table 3.1). Otto von Kotzebue, who had served as one of the *Nadeshda*'s naturalists and was related to Krusenstern's family (and, yes, son of August von Kotzebue who was assassinated in 1819), commanded the *Rurik* expedition of 1815–18. A decade later, he steered another Russian ship around the world. In between, Fabian Gottlieb von Bellinghausen, who had also accompanied Krusenstern in 1803, led the *Vostok* into the South Polar region and provided evidence for the existence of the Antarctic continent.[26] Ferdinand von Wrangel added a world voyage in 1825–27 to the already impressive Russian record. All four naval commanders came from German-speaking families in or close to Estonia. Russia's last great Pacific explorer, Fyodor Litke, also had a German background. Throughout his life he spoke German better than Russian.

Neither the prominence of the Baltic region as a turf for recruiting experts nor specifically the German influence was coincidental. For centuries this region had been a hub of multiethnic encounters, trade routes, and naval commerce. The port cities of Riga in Livonia and Reval in Estonia offered young men favorable conditions to acquire nautical skills. Reopened as a Russian imperial institution in 1802, the University of Dorpat, today's Tartu, was heavily influenced by the leading German university in Göttingen. It provided the chance to acquire knowledge about the world—and all courses were held in German.[27]

The German families in the Baltic regions, who often derived from the regional nobility, both profited from this education and fed into it.[28] This background and their multifaceted outlook on the world qualified them for the goals the Tsarist regime was pursuing in Asia and the Pacific. Krusenstern took over the directorship of the Russian naval school for aspiring officers in St. Petersburg prior to his world voyage, after he had already visited India and China. Only later did attempts to invent national traditions clearly categorize the Pacific expeditions of Krusenstern, Kotzebue, Bellinghausen, and Litke as solely "Russian."

The Russian-Baltic-German commanders themselves knew better. For their journeys, they preferred to recruit naturalists from German-speaking Europe. The Swiss-born astronomer Johann Kaspar Horner assisted Krusenstern on the *Nadeshda*, as did the naturalist and medical doctor Georg Heinrich von Langsdorff from Rhine-Hesse, who had attended school in the Alsace and spent some time in Portugal before setting out to the Pacific. They communicated in German among themselves and with their colleague Wilhelm Gottlieb Tilesius, born in Thuringia, who added his skills as a zoologist to Krusenstern's expedition, and provided drawings. The ability to draw quick sketches of nature and of the inhabitants of Pacific islands was among the most cherished talents on such journeys. For this purpose, Kotzebue's *Rurik* expedition hired the German-Russian Louis Choris.[29] Kotzebue made another fortuitous choice, which might appear more unusual in retrospect: he enlisted Adelbert von Chamisso as a botanist.

At that time Chamisso had already distinguished himself as a literary writer. The French-born author had just published *Peter Schlemihl*. In this brilliant, enigmatic story, the protagonist dares to bargain with the devil, sells his shadow, and—after a series of adventures—happens to acquire seven-league boots. With their help he storms around the world and follows the routes of some of the most famous sea voyages of the time. Schlemihl is particularly fascinated by Southeast Asia, though he must succumb to the geographical realities of the South Pacific. Even the miraculous boots are insufficient to hop over the enormous distances separating South America, the polar region, the Polynesian islands, and Australia.[30] Aboard the *Rurik*, Chamisso did not make it to that part of the Pacific either. But he was compensated by a route that led him to Hawaii. Chamisso thus complemented his reputation as a literary writer with his newly gained status as a Pacific traveler, an expert on Hawaiian languages, a botanist, and the author of a seminal work on an invertebrate ocean animal, the *salpa tunicate*.[31]

On the *Rurik*, Chamisso found a congenial naturalist-companion in Johann Friedrich von Eschscholtz, a Baltic German and graduate of the university in Dorpat. Eschscholtz anticipated some of Darwin's studies of coral reefs and conducted important research on a family of beetles, the *elateridae*, and their larvae (wireworms), which he dissected in the Pacific. Some years later he was hired again by Kotzebue on his next Pacific journey.[32] This time he joined Emil Lenz, a Baltic-German expert in the study of magnetism, the mineralogist Ernst R. Hofmann, born in Dorpat, and the astronomer Ernst Wilhelm Preuss, born in the Lausitz and later director of an observatory near the Baltic cost. Comparable positions were occupied on Fyodor Litke's Pacific voyage in 1826–29 by the Baltic-German botanist Karl Heinrich Mertens, the mineralogist Alexander Postels from Dorpat, and the ornithologist Heinrich von Kittlitz, born in Breslau.

Competences and Expertise, Intercultural Dialogues and Ambiguities

Any in-depth narrative of the German-speaking naturalists in the Pacific would need to take into account the broad spectrum and multiethnic composition of this pool of dramatis personae. It would also need to investigate further the dynamics of their transnational networks, which profoundly influenced the resonance that their Pacific travelogues enjoyed on the growing market of public knowledge in the period around 1800.³³ Yet even an overview invites an attempt to demarcate the qualities of these naturalists in a comparative perspective.

Although their overall number appears modest in retrospect, the German-speaking naturalists were anything but a negligible factor in the Pacific at this time. Their history needs to be read against the long list of disadvantages that characterized, at first glance, German-speaking societies in their potential for Pacific explorations. In contrast to their counterparts in Britain, France, and Spain, the naturalists from Westphalia and Berlin did not represent a maritime nation. They were not part of an empire that could draw on long traditions of overseas travel, capitalize on vast nautical experience, or make use of an existing imperial network of colonial and trade outposts.

By the turn of the nineteenth century, the German-speaking Pacific naturalists were still lacking the state-sponsored infrastructure that fostered scholarship in global natural history in the centers of Europe's great powers.³⁴ Berlin and Göttingen had no botanical repositories that could come close to what Kew Gardens, near London, and the collections in Paris and Madrid were offering. It was no coincidence that Johann von Eschscholtz donated his extensive collection of Pacific species to the University of Dorpat. The Breslauer Heinrich von Kittlitz delivered hundreds of stuffed bird species to the Russian Academy of Science. Thousands of the plant species that Humboldt brought back from his American journey made it to Berlin, but the scientific analysis of this collection could never be completed there. Naturalists found more favorable conditions for research in Vienna, with natural history collections in nearby Schönbrunn.³⁵

Furthermore, the Germans had no navy and no institution like Britain's Royal Society that could connect the dots of scientific, economic, and political outreach, and collaborate closely with an imperial fleet. Only in the course of the nineteenth century did Germany generate a strong set of institutions—not only universities but also extra-university research centers—that managed to absorb, reinterpret, and publish the knowledge of natural scientists, and were soon admired for that capacity around the world.

And yet, in spite of such deficits and disadvantages, the traveling German-speaking naturalists were in demand. They were anything but provincials whom fortuitous circumstances allowed to set off to the Pacific. They offered key competences for Pacific research, and the results of their research mattered. Unlike scholars such as Johann Friedrich Wilhelm Otto and Heinrich Berghaus who studied the Pacific in the seclusion of their private libraries, the traveling naturalists exploited firsthand observations and generated novel insights into the natural history of the Pacific. They continuously refined their scholarly expertise on their journeys.

Georg Wilhelm Steller researched the indigenous languages of Kamchatka and investigated the organism of a colossal—and soon to be extinct—maritime mammal, named after him: "Steller's sea cow" (*Hydrodamalis gigas*.) Over time, such research has come to be appreciated for its contribution to the history of evolution. Humboldt was among the first to describe the meteorological anomalies in the Pacific coastal region, specifically the reoccurring increase in water and air temperature in the central-eastern part of the Pacific—what we call El Niño today. This is even more remarkable since Humboldt did not sail the Pacific coastline during an El Niño period.[36]

Wilhelm Gottfried Tilesius's studies on *Infusoria*, microscopic organisms he found in ocean water, were instrumental in establishing modern plankton research. Eschscholtz and Adelbert von Chamisso proved the existence of an alternation of generations (*Generationswechsel*) in organic nature through their investigations of *salpae*, invertebrate ocean organisms in the Pacific.[37] After returning from Kotzebue's *Rurik* expedition, Chamisso spent most of his life on botanical studies in Berlin. Alongside his research on electromagnetism, Emil Lenz provided the scholarly world with insights into the salt content of different oceanic areas; and Heinrich von Kittlitz added knowledge about rare and soon to be extinct bird species.

This list of scholarly achievements could easily be expanded. They were, as I want to suggest, grounded in exactly those conditions that only appear deficient at a superficial look. The German naturalists were well trained, and often self-taught, in the study of nature. They capitalized on their access to *Bildung*, education and self-training, and to knowledge about nature that was on an upswing in the German-speaking territories. Their expertise grew out of local centers of education and emerged from the training in applied knowledge and everyday practices of natural history cultivated under the umbrella of *Kameralwissenschaften* (Cameralism: the comprehensive study of the practical needs of states). This expertise was formed in academies devoted to trade issues, and mining colleges such as the one in Freiberg/Saxony, as much as in lectures in Göttingen or later Berlin. It also profited from travels throughout Europe, as in the case of Georg Forster and Alexander von Humboldt. All these factors provided the German naturalists with the sensory skills, technology, and analytical categories needed to explore the Pacific. This equipment supported their expert status. It fit a market demand that was needed in the Bering Strait, along the coasts of Australia, and in the Pacific waters near California and Peru.

In addition, the Germans in the Pacific could master those foreign languages that set the standard for scholarly discussions—Latin, French, and English—and they had command of a language that was on its way to becoming a new lingua franca of academic discourse and an entry billet to the emerging success model called research university.[38] This linguistic competence was not only relevant for scholarly discussions. It also nourished the communicative mobilization in the German-speaking territories of Europe from the late eighteenth century on. More and more institutions and media began to popularize geographical and scientific knowledge: reading societies and libraries, salons of the enlightened elite, a growing network of natural history associations, and an expanding print market for journals and books.³⁹ They began to spread the naturalists' expertise at home and, more broadly, in the transatlantic world. They coupled it with the enormous popularity of adventure stories along the lines of Daniel Defoe's *Robinson Crusoe*.

This new dynamic left its imprint on the transatlantic book market (see Table 3.2). By the early nineteenth century, readers who were confined to the German language could easily find translations of the major Pacific travelogues originally published by James Cook or Louis-Antoine Bougainville. Likewise, some of the German-speaking naturalists published their findings on oceanic voyages first in English, French, Latin, or Russian, only to witness German translations later; examples include Georg Forster's *Voyage Round the World* and Humboldt's *Relation historique du voyage aux régions équinoxiales du nouveau continent*. Krusenstern's account of his world voyage was published almost simultaneously in Russian and German. Karl Heinrich Mertens published some of his studies in St. Petersburg—and in the German language.

Finally, the German naturalists' lack of experience in imperial warfare, as opposed to some of the British and French naturalists, and their position as observers of, not participants in, the systems of colonial exploitation, were no disadvantage in pursuing their task. Instead, these deficits allowed them to maintain an intellectual openness and relative autonomy when they encountered the Pacific. Unlike what the focus on Georg Forster's much-described idealization of selected South Pacific societies suggests, to take only one example, his impressions of the sexual freedom practiced among the Tahitians were accompanied by his critique of other bodily practices in the Pacific, as well as the sexual violence practiced by seamen aboard his ship. Forster continually reflected on the injustice the Europeans had exported to the Pacific.⁴⁰ Humboldt was even more pointed in his critique of the colonial system he encountered in Spanish America. He explicitly questioned the terminology of racial, cultural, and gender differences that other European writers maintained at his time.⁴¹

The Pacific journeys, framed by the interests of the powers that sponsored them, turned the German naturalists to some extent into insiders of imperial endeavors. Yet, at the same time, they remained outsiders. This ambiguity deserves to be emphasized, too, in response to postcolonial studies in their emphasis on the discursive constructions of race, gender, and power that guided Europeans in their perceptions of the Pacific, and accounted for much of the Pacific's astounding presence as a trope in the minds of elites as well as broader social strata in Europe and North America. Still, the attention paid to the establishment of systems of control and power, following Michel Foucault, and the emphasis on the construction of stereotypes and "otherness," taking Edward Said's critique of "Orientalism" as a model, are hardly sufficient to explain the complex ways in which the German travelers perceived and analyzed the natural habitats they observed in the Pacific. The German naturalists did not simply have the myopic view of people who looked at the world with "imperial eyes" and catered to "colonial fantasies."⁴²

Many of them operated with finely calibrated lenses and promoted an intercultural dialogue—in variations and with contradictions and limits set by their commitment to European culture, all of which deserve to be studied individually.⁴³

Identity in a Shared Culture of Knowledge

Ultimately then, we are left with the question of what it meant to be German around 1800. In response, we may refer to the plurality of German-speaking territories in Europe and include our new appreciation of the flexibility of the Holy Roman Empire as a meaningful framework for generating German identities. However, the history of the German-speaking naturalists in the Pacific points toward a definition of Germanness that goes beyond criteria developed along the lines of territorial, ethnic, or political borders, or one that focuses on an individual's commitment to a nation.

At least for the men considered here, being a German naturalist primarily meant possessing a set of skills in the study of natural history, combined with broader communicative and scholarly competences. This generated an expertise that capitalized on the strengths of knowledge practices in the German-speaking countries. It was constituted by the global, transregional traffic of knowledge and natural history objects alike. This deterritorialized identity and the migratory mode of acquiring knowledge were the preconditions for studying the territories these naturalists were sent to. Only the trained gaze of observers who were able to balance distance from and familiarity with their subject matters could deliver the results that they were asked to provide.

The German naturalists' mode of studying nature was neither apolitical nor exempt from national interests or European prejudices. It was entangled with the political and commercial interests of the imperial powers, such as in identifying profitable ways of utilizing specific plants. This mode could be reconciled with new political alliances, as the activities of the naturalists and naval commanders from the German-speaking Baltic regions demonstrate. But scientific exploration had a logic of its own too, and was more than a "handmaiden" of empires.⁴⁴

The German-speaking botanists, geologists, zoologists, and artists in the Pacific might be best described as pragmatists rather than ideologues, and they were hired exactly for this reason. Forster, Humboldt, and Chamisso; Krusenstern, Kotzebue, and Bellinghausen; Steller, Horner, Lambsdorff, Eschscholtz, and Tilesius—all were interlocutors in a shared, transnational culture of expertise. They were wanderers between globally dispersed locations rather than emissaries of imperial governments alone, and Humboldt does not fit this template anyway. These men ultimately became intellectual migrants due to their travels, their communication with others across political divides, and thanks to the broad resonance of the resulting publications.

Table 3.1: European Voyages into the Pacific. This table concentrates on major European-sponsored voyages that included a scholarly component and, in most cases, were accompanied by naturalists charged with recording, measuring, and analyzing the Pacific's habitats. The table highlights the German-speaking naturalists, and includes a special case: Humboldt's Pacific voyage.

Years of Journey	Ship and Consort Ship	Sponsored by	Commanders (excluding consort ships) and Naturalists Aboard (in selection)
1733–43	*Saint Peter* and *Saint Paul*	Russia	"Great Northern Expedition" (Second Kamchatka Expedition) Vitus Bering accompanied by Georg Wilhelm Steller and, for inland research, by Carl Friedrich Behrens and Johann Georg Gmelin
1766–68	*Dolphin* and *Swallow*	Britain	Samuel Wallis
1766–69	*La Boudeuse* and *L'Étoile*	France	First French circumnavigation of the world Louis-Antoine Bougainville
1768–71	*Endeavour*	Britain	James Cook (first world voyage) accompanied by Joseph Banks, Charles Green, Daniel Solander, and Herman Spöring
1772–75	*Resolution* and *Adventure*	Britain	James Cook (second world voyage) accompanied by Johann Reinhold Forster, Georg Forster, and Anders Sparrman
1776–80	*Resolution* and *Discovery*	Britain	James Cook (third world voyage) accompanied by German shipmen Heinrich Zimmermann and Barthold Lohmann
1785–88	*La Boussole* and *L'Astrolabe*	France	Jean François (de Galaup) de La Pérouse
1789–94	*Descubierta* and *Atrevida*	Spain	Alessandro Malaspina accompanied in 1790–93 by Thaddäus Haenke
1791–93	*Providence* and *Assistant*	Britain	William Bligh
1791–94	*Recherche* and *Espérance*	France	Joseph Bruni d'Entrecasteaux accompanied by French naturalists
1791–95	*Discovery* and *Chatham*	Britain	George Vancouver
1800–4	*Le Géographe* and *Naturaliste*	France	Nicolas Baudin
1801–3	*Investigator*	Britain	First circumnavigation of Australia Matthew Flinders accompanied by Robert Brown and Ferdinand Bauer

1802–3	*La Castora* and *Atlante*	Spain	Part of the American journey by Alexander von Humboldt and Aimé Bonpland
1803–6	*Nadeshda* and *Neva*	Russia	First Russian circumnavigation of the world Adam von Krusenstern accompanied by F. G. von Bellinghausen, Johann Caspar Horner, Otto von Kotzebue, Georg Heinrich von Langsdorff, Hermann Ludwig von Löwenstern, and Wilhelm Gottlieb Tilesius
1815–18	*Rurik*	Russia	Second Russian circumnavigation of the world Otto von Kotzebue accompanied by Adelbert von Chamisso, Johann Friedrich von Eschscholtz, and Ludwig Choris
1817–19	*Kamchatka*	Russia	Vasily Golovnin accompanied by Ferdinand von Wrangel and Fyodor Litke
1817–20	*Uranie* and *La Physicienne*	France	Louis Claude de Freycinet
1819–21	*Vostok* and *Mirny*	Russia	F. G. von Bellinghausen
1822–25	*La Coquille*	France	Louis Isidore Duperrey
1823–26	*Predpriyatiye*	Russia	Otto von Kotzebue accompanied by Johann Friedrich von Eschscholtz, Ernst Hofmann, Heinrich von Kittlitz, H. F. Emil Lenz, and Ernst Wilhelm Preuss
1824–25	*Blonde*	Britain	George Anson Byron
1825–27	*Krotky*	Russia	Ferdinand von Wrangel
1825–28	*Blossom*	Britain	Frederick William Beechey
1826–29	*L'Astrolabe*	France	Jules Dumont d'Urville
1826–29	*Senyavin* and *Moller*	Russia	Fyodor Litke accompanied by Heinrich von Kittliz, Karl Heinrich Mertens, and Alexander Postels
1829–32	*La Favorite*	France	Cyrille Pierre Théodore Laplace
1831–36	*Beagle*	Britain	Robert FitzRoy accompanied by Charles Darwin
1836–37	*La Bonite*	France	Auguste-Nicolas Vaillant
1838–42	*Vincennes* and *Peacock*	United States	United States Exploring Expedition Charles Wilkes William Levereth Hudson (*Peacock*)

Table 3.2: **Dramatis Personae.** This table includes the German-speaking naturalists on the Pacific journeys as well as those German-Baltic commanders who headed Russian expeditions into the Pacific. The individuals are listed according to birth year. The second column highlights in an abbreviated form the first German-language publication of their major travelogues, which in several cases were preceded by a French- or English-language edition.

Engelbert Kaempfer (1651–1716)	*Engelbert Kämpfers Geschichte und Beschreibung von Japan,* ed. Christian Wilhelm Dohm, 1777
Carl Friedrich Behrens (1701–1747)	*Carl Friedrich Behrens Reise nach den unbekandten Süd-Ländern und rund um die Welt,* 1728 *Der wohlversuchte Süd-Länder, das ist: ausführliche Reise-Beschreibung um die Welt,* 1738
Georg Wilhelm Steller (1709–1746)	*Ausführliche Beschreibung von sonderbaren Meerthieren mit Erläuterungen,* 1753 *Beschreibung von dem Lande Kamtschatka,* 1774 *G. W. Steller's Reise von Kamtschatka nach Amerika,* 1793
Johann Georg Gmelin (1709–1755)	*Flora Sibirica sive Historia plantarum Sibiriae,* 1747–49 *Voyage en Sibérie,* 1767
Johann Reinhold Forster (1729–1798)	*Johann Reinhold Forster's und Georg Forster's Beschreibungen der Gattungen von Pflanzen, auf einer Reise nach den Inseln der Süd-See,* 1779
Johann Georg Forster (1754–1794)	Also see above under Johann Reinhold Forster *Johann Reinhold Forster's Reise um die Welt während den Jahren 1772 bis 1775,* 1778–80
Ferdinand Lukas Bauer (1760–1826)	Besides his drawings, Bauer's written contributions to the study of the Pacific were mainly published in English and Latin.
Thaddäus Haenke (1761–1816)	Haenke only authored a few, condensed articles.
Alexander von Humboldt (1769–1859)	Humboldt did not publish a separate account of the Pacific part of his American journey, but included references to the *Südsee* in several of his publications.
Wilhelm Gottlieb Tilesius von Tilenau (1769–1857)	A Russian-language edition was published in 1813: *Naturhistorische Früchte der ersten kaiserlich-russischen unter dem Kommando des Herrn von Krusenstern glücklich vollbrachten Erdumseeglung*
Adam Johann von Krusenstern (1770–1846)	*Reise um die Welt in den Jahren 1803, 1804, 1805 und 1806,* 1810–12
Johann Kaspar Horner (1774–1834)	Horner did not publish a major Pacific travelogue.
Georg Heinrich von Langsdorff (1774–1852)	*Bemerkungen auf einer Reise um die Welt in den Jahren 1803 bis 1807,* 1812
Hermann Ludwig von Löwenstern (1771–1836)	*Eine kommentierte Transkription der Tagebücher von Hermann Ludwig von Löwenstern (1777–1836),* trans. Joan Moessner, 2005

Fabian Gottlieb von Bellinghausen (1778–1852)	*Forschungsfahrten im südlichen Eismeer, 1819–1821*, 1902
Adelbert von Chamisso (1781–1838)	*Bemerkungen und Ansichten auf einer Entdeckungs-Reise unternommen in den Jahren 1815 – 1818*, 1821 *Reise um die Welt mit der Romanzoffischen Entdeckungs-Expedition in den Jahren 1815–18*, 1836
Otto von Kotzebue (1787–1846)	*Entdeckungs-Reise in die Süd-See und nach der Berings-Straße*, 1821 *Neue Reise um die Welt in den Jahren 1823, 24, 25 und 26*, 1830
Johann Friedrich von Eschscholtz (1793–1831)	*Zoologischer Atlas, enthaltend Abbildungen und Beschreibungen neuer Thierarten während des Flottcapitains von Kotzebue zweiter Reise um die Welt*, 1829-33
Louis Choris (1795–1828)	Choris provided illustrations for Kotzebue's and Chamisso's narratives of the *Rurik* voyage and authored two accounts in French that presented his artistic depictions with separate comments: *Voyage pittoresque autour du monde*, 1822 and *Vues et paysages des régions équinoxiales*, 1826.
Philipp Franz von Siebold (1796–1866)	Among Siebold's many studies on Japan, often published in Latin, is *De historia naturalis in Japonia statu*, 1826
Karl Heinrich Mertens (1796–1830)	*Untersuchungen über den inneren Bau verschiedener in der See lebender Planarien*, 1833 Mertens's observations were incorporated in Litke's travelogue.
Ferdinand von Wrangel (1796–1870)	*Physikalische Beobachtungen des Capitain–Lieutenant Baron von Wrangel während seiner Reisen auf dem Eismeere*, 1827 *Reise des K. R. Flotten-Lieutenants F. v. Wrangel längs der Nordküste von Sibirien und auf dem Eismeer*, 1839
Fyodor Petrowitsch (Friedrich Benjamin) Litke (Lütke) (1797–1882)	*Viermalige Reise durch das nördliche Eismeer auf der Brigg Nowaja*, 1835
Friedrich Wilhelm Heinrich von Kittlitz (1799–1874)	Among Kittlitz's many publications about his observations in the Pacific is *Denkwürdigkeiten einer Reise nach dem russischen Amerika, nach Mikronesien und durch Kamtschatka*, 1858
Ernst Reinhold Hofmann (1801–1871)	Hofmann did not provide a major travelogue.
Alexander Postels (1801–1871)	Postels' observations were incorporated in Litke's travelogue.
Heinrich Friedrich Emil Lenz (1804–1865)	Lenz did not provide a major travelogue.

Andreas W. Daum is professor of history at the State University of New York at Buffalo. He has published books on German and international history, including *Wissenschaftspopularisiernung im 19. Jahrhundert* [Popularizing science in the nineteenth century] (1998) and *Kennedy in Berlin* (2008). He is currently working on Alexander von Humboldt.

Notes

1. Apothecaries, missionaries, surgeons aboard ships, and representatives of trade companies are related groups of travelers; some of them undertook serious scholarly studies of the Pacific. Ida Pfeiffer, born in 1797 in Vienna, might have been the first German-speaking woman to travel the Pacific. She participated in two circumnavigations of the globe, in 1846–48 and 1851–55, and developed a keen interest in the natural history of the regions visited. Amalie Dietrich, born in 1821 in Saxony, who explored Australia, followed in this line of tradition.

    I wish to thank Peter Paret, Peter H. Reill, and Sherry Foehr for providing valuable feedback on earlier versions of this chapter.

2. Jacques Brosse, *Great Voyages of Discovery: Circumnavigators and Scientists, 1764–1843*, transl. Stanley Hochman (New York: Facts on File Publications, 1983); O. H. K. Spate, *Paradise Found and Lost* (Minneapolis: University of Minnesota Press, 1988); Roy MacLeod and Philip F. Rehbock, eds., *Nature in its Greatest Extent: Western Science in the Pacific* (Honolulu: University of Hawaii Press, 1988); MacLeod and Rehbock, eds., *Darwin's Laboratory: Evolutionary Theory and Natural History in the Pacific* (Honolulu: University of Hawaii Press, 1994); Margaret Lincoln, *Science and Exploration in the Pacific: Europe Voyages to the Southern Oceans in the Eighteenth Century* (Woodbridge: Boydell, 1998), though hardly mentioning the German naturalists; Keith R. Benson and Philip F. Rehbock, eds., *Oceanographic History: The Pacific and Beyond* (Seattle: University of Washington Press, 2002); Annick Foucrier, ed., *The French and the Pacific World, 17th–19th Centuries: Discoveries, Migrations and Cultural Exchanges* (Aldershot: Ashgate Varioum, 2003); David Igler, *The Great Ocean: Pacific Worlds from Captain Cook to the Gold Rush* (Oxford: Oxford University Press, 2013).

3. Hermann J. Hiery, *Das Deutsche Reich in der Südsee (1900–1921): Eine Annäherung an die Erfahrungen verschiedener Kulturen* (Göttingen: Vandenhoeck & Ruprecht, 1995); and Hiery, ed., *Die deutsche Südsee 1884–1914: Ein Handbuch* (Paderborn: Schöningh, 2001).

4. See Matt K. Matsuda, *Pacific Worlds: A History of Seas, Peoples, and Cultures* (Cambridge: Cambridge University Press, 2012); and David Armitage and Alison Bashford, eds., *Pacific Histories: Ocean, Land, People* (Basingstoke: Palgrave Macmillan, 2014).

5. This number alone is deceptive. Spurred by Cook's outreach into the Pacific, the Spanish Empire under Carlos III kept a close eye on America's Pacific coastline and undertook several other explorations along the Pacific rim; see Robin Inglis, "Successors and Rivals to Cook: The French and the Spaniards," in *Captain Cook: Explorations and Reassessments*, ed. Glyndwr Williams (Woodbridge: Boydell, 2004), 172–78.

6. This is the emphasis in Mary Louise Pratt, *Imperial Eyes: Travel Writing and Transculturation*, 2nd ed. (London: Routledge, 2008).

7. This observation needs to be separated from any valuation of their worldview as imbued (or not) with colonial or racist ideas, as emphasized by postcolonial studies. See, in addition to Pratt, Susanne Zantop, *Colonial Fantasies: Conquest, Family, and Nation in Precolonial Germany, 1770–1870* (Durham, NC: Duke University Press, 1997); Russell A. Berman, *Enlightenment*

or Empire: Colonial Discourse in German Culture* (Lincoln: University of Nebraska Press, 1998); Miriam Kahn and Sabine Wilke, "Narrating Colonial Encounters: Germany in the Pacific Islands," *Journal of Pacific History* 42, no. 3 (December 2007): 293–97; Sabine Wilke, "Performing Native Cultures in the 'South Sea': Mythical Images of Others in Early German Contact Narratives," *Pacific Coast Philology* 42, no. 2 (2007): 169–80.
8. Glynis Ridley, *The Discovery of Jeanne Baret: A Story of the High Seas, and the First Women to Circumnavigate the Globe* (New York: Crown Publisher, 2010).
9. Edward Duyker, *Nature's Argonaut: Daniel Solander, 1733–1782, Naturalist and Voyager with Cook and Banks* (Carlton South, Vic.: Miegunyah Press, 1998).
10. Marlene J. Norst, *Ferdinand Bauer: The Australian Natural History Drawings* (London: British Museum, 1989); Peter Watts, Jo Anne Pomfrett, and David Mabberley, *An Exquisite Eye: The Australian Flora & Fauna Drawings 1801–1820 of Ferdinand Bauer* (Glebe, NSW: Historic Houses Trust of New South Wales, 1997).
11. See Daniela Bleichmar, *Visible Empire: Botanical Expeditions and Visual Culture in the Hispanic Enlightenment* (Chicago, IL: The University of Chicago Press, 2012), 147–48; and with a fundamental critique of Western epistemology, Jorge Cañizares-Esguerra, *Nature, Empire, and Nation: Explorations of the History of Science in the Iberian World* (Stanford, CA: Stanford University Press, 2006).
12. See Regina Dauser et al., eds., *Wissen im Netz: Botanik und Pflanzentransfer in europäischen Korrespondenznetzen des 18. Jahrhunderts* (Berlin: Akademie Verlag, 2008).
13. A reassessment of this outdated dichotomy is offered by Daniela Bleichmar et al., eds., *Science in the Spanish and Portuguese Empires, 1500–1800* (Stanford, CA: Stanford University Press, 2009).
14. See Hanno Beck, *Germania in Pacifico: Der deutsche Anteil an der Erschließung des Pazifischen Beckens* (Mainz: Akademie der Wissenschaften und der Literatur, 1970); Gerhard Kortum, "Germania in Pacifico: Humboldt, Chamisso and Other Early German Contributions to Pacific Research, 1741–1876," in *Oceanographic History: The Pacific and Beyond*, ed. Keith R. Benson and Philip F. Rehbock (Seattle: University of Washington Press, 2002), 107–17; and Harry Liebersohn, *The Traveler's World: Europe to the Pacific* (Cambridge, MA: Harvard University Press, 2006).
15. Gerhard Bonn, *Engelbert Kaempfer (1651–1716): Der Reisende und sein Einfluss auf die europäische Bewusstseinsbildung über Asien* (Frankfurt a.M.: Lang, 2003).
16. See Hermann J. Hiery and John M. MacKenzie, eds., *European Impact and Pacific Influence: British and German Colonial Policy in the Pacific Islands and the Indigenous Response* (London: I.B. Tauris, 1997); and Gabriele Dürbeck, *Stereotype Paradiese: Ozeanismus in der deutschen Südseeliteratur 1815–1914* (Tübingen: Niemeyer, 2007).
17. Gerhard Steiner already articulated this caveat in his edition of Georg Forster, *Reise um die Welt* (Frankfurt a.M.: Insel, 1967, new edition 1983), 1029.
18. Beck, *Germania in Pacifico*, 41–42.
19. See Hans Schadewaldt, "Thaddaeus Haenke (1761–1817), österreichischer Arzt und Naturforscher, und seine Beobachtungen während der Weltreise Malaspinas in den Jahren 1789–1794 in Südamerika und im Pazifik," *Die medizinische Welt*, 11 April 1964: 883–93; and Alexander von Humboldt, *Amerikanische Reise*, 6th ed., ed. Hanno Beck (Wiesbaden: Edition Erdmann, 2009), 47–50, 258–61.
20. Susan Faye Cannon, *Science in Culture: The Early Victorian Period* (New York: Science History Publications, 1978), 73–110; Michael Dettelbach, "Humboldtian Science," in *Cultures of Natural History*, eds. N. Jardine, J. A. Secord, and E. C. Spary (Cambridge: Cambridge University Press, 1996), 287–304; Andreas W. Daum, "Alexander von Humboldt, die Natur als 'Kosmos' und die Suche nach Einheit: Zur Geschichte von Wissen und seiner Wirkung als Raumgeschichte," *Berichte zur Wissenschaftsgeschichte* 23 (2000): 243–68.

21. Alexander von Humboldt, *Reise in die Äquinoktial-Gegenden des Neuen Kontinents*, Vol. 1, ed. Ottmar Ette (Frankfurt a.M.: Insel, 1991), 16, 47–48.
22. Alexander von Humboldt, *Schriften zur physikalischen Geographie*, 2nd ed., ed. Hanno Beck, (Darmstadt: Wissenschaftliche Buchgesellschaft, 2008), 169–77, 206–11.
23. Kurt-Reinhard Biermann, "Alexander von Humboldt und das Projekt einer Verbindung zwischen Atlantik und Pazifik," in *Miscellanea Humboldtiana* (Berlin: Akademie Verlag, 1990), 69–72. In French Humboldt used the term "physique du monde," in German several variations: see the terms "Physik der Welt," "Theorie der Erde," "Physikalische Geographie," and "Physik der Erde" in Humboldt, *Reise in die Äquinoktial-Gegenden*, 12 and 15.
24. Erich Donnert, "Russische Entdeckungsreisen und Forschungsexpeditionen in den Stillen Ozean im 18. und beginnenden 19. Jahrhundert," in *Europa in der frühen Neuzeit: Festschrift für Günter Mühlpfordt*, Vol. 6, ed. Erich Donnert (Weimar: Böhlau, 2002), 837–67; Simon Werrett, "Russian Responses to the Voyages of Captain Cook," in *Captain Cook*, ed. Glyndwr Williams (Woodbridge: Boydell, 2004), 179–97.
25. A scholarly biography of Krusenstern, as of other German-Baltic navigators, is long overdue. Some orientation is offered by Ewert von Krusenstjern, *Weltumsegler und Wissenschaftler: Adam Johann von Krusenstern, 1770–1846. Ein Lebensbericht* (Gernsbach: C. Katz, 1991); Erwin Seppelt, *Adam Johann von Krusenstern: Ein Porträt* (Rostock: BS-Verlag, 2009).
26. Here, too, we only have sparse information; see Anto Juske, *Estonian-Born Admiral F. v. Bellingshausen, the Discoverer of Antarctica* (Tallinn: Infotrükk, 2003).
27. Peer Hempel, *Deutschsprachige Physiker im alten St. Petersburg: Georg Parrot, Emil Lenz und Moritz Jacobi im Kontext von Wissenschaft und Politik* (Munich: Oldenbourg, 1999), 72–79, 248–49; Erich Donnert, *Die Universität Dorpat-Jurev, 1802–1918: Ein Beitrag zur Geschichte des Hochschulwesens in den Ostseeprovinzen des Russischen Reiches* (Frankfurt a.M.: Böhlau, 2007), 120–60.
28. See Heide W. Whelan, *Adapting to Modernity: Family, Caste and Capitalism among the Baltic German Nobility* (Cologne: Böhlau, 1999).
29. Donnert, "Russische Entdeckungsreisen," 851–52; Niklaus R. Schweizer, ed., *Journal des Malers Ludwig York Choris* (Berlin: Lang, 1999). See also the profound work by Bleichmar, *Visible Empire*.
30. Adelbert von Chamisso, "Peter Schlemihls wundersame Geschichte," in Adelbert von Chamisso, *Sämtliche Werke in zwei Bänden*, Vol. I (Munich: Winkler, 1975), 13–67. See Matthias Glaubrecht, "Naturkunde mit den Augen des Dichters: Mit Siebenmeilenstiefeln zum Artkonzept bei Adelbert von Chamisso," in *Korrespondenzen und Transformationen: Neue Perspektiven auf Adelbert von Chamisso*, eds. Marie-Theres Federhofer and Jutta Weber (Göttingen: V&R Unipress, 2013), 51–76.
31. See Igler, *Great Ocean*, 129–43; and Matthias Glaubrecht and Wolfgang Dohle, "Discovering the Alternation of Generations in Salps (Tunicata, Thaliacea): Adelbert von Chamisso's Dissertation "De Salpa" 1819 – its Material, Origin and Reception in the Early Nineteenth Century," *Zoosystematics and Evolution* 88, no. 2 (2012): 317–63.
32. Tatiana Arkadevna Lukina, *Johann Friedrich Eschscholtz, 1793–1831*, trans. Wilma C. Follette (Mill Valley, CA: Follette, 2009).
33. Andreas W. Daum, "Varieties of Popular Science and the Transformations of Public Knowledge: Some Historical Reflections," *Isis* 100 (June 2009): 319–32.
34. See Richard Drayton, *Nature's Government: Science, Imperial Britain, and the "Improvement" of the World* (New Haven, CT: Yale University Press, 2000).
35. Hans Walter Lack, *Alexander von Humboldt and the Botanical Exploration of the Americas* (Munich: Prestel, 2009).
36. Kortum, "Germania in Pacifico," 109; Gerhard Kortum, "Humboldt und das Meer: Eine Ozeanographiegeschichtliche Bestandsaufnahme," *Northeastern Naturalist* 8, Special Issue 1 (2001): 91–108.

37. See endnote 31.
38. Andreas W. Daum, "Wissenschaft and Knowledge," in *Germany 1800–1870*, ed. Jonathan Sperber (Oxford: Oxford University Press, 2004), 137–61.
39. Thomas H. Broman, "The Habermasian Public Sphere and 'Science in the Enlightenment,'" *History of Science* 36 (1998): 123–49; Andreas W. Daum, *Wissenschaftspopularisierung im 19. Jahrhundert: Bürgerliche Kultur, naturwissenschaftliche Bildung und die deutsche Öffentlichkeit, 1848–1914*. 2nd ed. (Munich: Oldenbourg, 2002); Philippe Despoix and Justus Fetscher, eds., *Cross-Cultural Encounters and Constructions of Knowledge in the 18th and 19th Centuries: Non-European and European Travel of Exploration in Comparative Perspective* (Kassel: Kassel University Press, 2004).
40. Forster, *Reise um die Welt*, 206, 296, 302, 332–33, 411, 431, 442–43, 653, 673.
41. See Humboldt's remarks on the early stages of the American journey in Humboldt, *Reise in die Äquinoktial-Gegenden*, 260, 341, 378–79, 394, as well as his scathing critique of slavery in Alexander von Humboldt, *Political Essay on the Island of Cuba*, eds. Vera M. Kutzinski and Ottmar Ette (Chicago, IL: University of Chicago Press, 2011).
42. See the studies by Pratt and Zantop cited in endnotes 6 and 7.
43. The reports by German-speaking naturalists and captains on Russia's Asian expeditions offer an important, yet undervalued source; see Doris Posselt, ed., *Die große nordische Expedition von 1733 bis 1743: Aus Berichten der Forschungsreisenden Johann Georg Gmelin und Georg Wilhelm Steller* (Munich: C. H. Beck, 1990); Otto von Kotzebue, *Zu Eisbergen und Palmenständen: Mit der "Rurik" um die Welt 1815–1818* (Lenningen: Edition Erdmann, 2004); and Friedrich Litke, *Viermalige Reise durch das nördliche Eismeer: Auf der Brigg Nowaja Semlja in den Jahren 1821–1824*, ed. Claudia Weiss (Wiesbaden: Edition Erdmann, 2014).
44. Jorge Cañizares-Esguerra, "Introduction," in Bleichmar et al., *Science in the Spanish and Portuguese Empires*, 1.

Bibliography

Armitage, David, and Alison Bashford, eds. *Pacific Histories: Ocean, Land, People*. Basingstoke: Palgrave Macmillan, 2014.

Beck, Hanno. *Germania in Pacifico: Der deutsche Anteil an der Erschließung des Pazifischen Beckens*. Mainz: Akademie der Wissenschaften und der Literatur, 1970.

Benson, Keith R., and Philip F. Rehbock, eds. *Oceanographic History: The Pacific and Beyond*. Seattle: University of Washington Press, 2002.

Berman, Russell A. *Enlightenment or Empire: Colonial Discourse in German Culture*. Lincoln: University of Nebraska Press, 1998.

Biermann, Kurt-Reinhard. "Alexander von Humboldt und das Projekt einer Verbindung zwischen Atlantik und Pazifik." In *Miscellanea Humboldtiana*, 69–72. Berlin: Akademie Verlag, 1990.

Bleichmar, Daniela. *Visible Empire: Botanical Expeditions and Visual Culture in the Hispanic Enlightenment*. Chicago, IL: The University of Chicago Press, 2012.

Bleichmar, Daniela, et al., eds. *Science in the Spanish and Portuguese Empires, 1500–1800*. Stanford, CA: Stanford University Press, 2009.

Bonn, Gerhard. *Engelbert Kaempfer (1651–1716): Der Reisende und sein Einfluss auf die europäische Bewusstseinsbildung über Asien*. Frankfurt a.M.: Lang, 2003.

Broman, Thomas H. "The Habermasian Public Sphere and 'Science in the Enlightenment.'" *History of Science* 36 (1998): 123–49.

Brosse, Jacques. *Great Voyages of Discovery: Circumnavigators and Scientists, 1764–1843*. Translated by Stanley Hochman. New York: Facts on File Publications, 1983.
Cañizares-Esguerra, Jorge. *Nature, Empire, and Nation: Explorations of the History of Science in the Iberian World*. Stanford, CA: Stanford University Press, 2006.
Cannon, Susan Faye. *Science in Culture: The Early Victorian Period*. New York: Science History Publications, 1978.
Chamisso, Adelbert von. "Peter Schlemihls wundersame Geschichte." In *Sämtliche Werke in zwei Bänden*, Vol. 1, 13–67. Munich: Winkler, 1975.
Daum, Andreas W. "Alexander von Humboldt, die Natur als 'Kosmos' und die Suche nach Einheit: Zur Geschichte von Wissen und seiner Wirkung als Raumgeschichte." *Berichte zur Wissenschaftsgeschichte* 23 (2000): 243–68.
———. "Varieties of Popular Science and the Transformations of Public Knowledge: Some Historical Reflections." *Isis* 100 (2009): 319–32.
———. "Wissenschaft and Knowledge." In *Germany 1800–1870*, edited by Jonathan Sperber, 137–61. Oxford: Oxford University Press, 2004.
———. *Wissenschaftspopularisierung im 19. Jahrhundert: Bürgerliche Kultur, naturwissenschaftliche Bildung und die deutsche Öffentlichkeit, 1848–1914*. 2nd ed. Munich: Oldenbourg, 2002.
Dauser, Regina, Stefan Hächler, Michael Kempe, Franz Mauelshagen, and Martin Stuber, eds. *Wissen im Netz: Botanik und Pflanzentransfer in europäischen Korrespondenznetzen des 18. Jahrhunderts*. Berlin: Akademie Verlag, 2008.
Despoix, Philippe, and Justus Fetscher, eds. *Cross-Cultural Encounters and Constructions of Knowledge in the 18th and 19th Centuries: Non-European and European Travel of Exploration in Comparative Perspective*. Kassel: Kassel University Press, 2004.
Dettelbach, Michael. "Humboldtian Science." In *Cultures of Natural History*, edited by N. Jardine, J. A. Secord, and E. C. Spary, 287–304. Cambridge: Cambridge University Press, 1996.
Donnert, Erich. "Russische Entdeckungsreisen und Forschungsexpeditionen in den Stillen Ozean im 18. und beginnenden 19. Jahrhundert." In *Europa in der frühen Neuzeit: Festschrift für Günter Mühlpfordt*, Vol. 6, edited by Erich Donnert, 837–67. Weimar: Böhlau, 2002.
———. *Die Universität Dorpat-Jur̓ev, 1802–1918: Ein Beitrag zur Geschichte des Hochschulwesens in den Ostseeprovinzen des Russischen Reiches*. Frankfurt a.M.: Lang, 2007.
Drayton, Richard. *Nature's Government: Science, Imperial Britain, and the "Improvement" of the World*. New Haven, CT: Yale University Press, 2000.
Dürbeck, Gabriele. *Stereotype Paradiese: Ozeanismus in der deutschen Südseeliteratur 1815–1914*. Tübingen: Niemeyer, 2007.
Duyker, Edward. *Nature's Argonaut: Daniel Solander, 1733–1782, Naturalist and Voyager with Cook and Banks*. Carlton South, Vic.: Miegunyah Press, 1998.
Forster, Georg. *Reise um die Welt* [Travel Around the World, 1777]. Frankfurt a.M.: Insel, 1983.
Foucrier, Annick, ed. *The French and the Pacific World, 17th–19th Centuries: Discoveries, Migrations and Cultural Exchanges*. Aldershot: Ashgate Variorum, 2003.
Glaubrecht, Matthias. "Naturkunde mit den Augen des Dichters: Mit Siebenmeilenstiefeln zum Artkonzept bei Adelbert von Chamisso." In *Korrespondenzen und Transformationen: Neue Perspektiven auf Adelbert von Chamisso*, edited by Marie-Theres Federhofer and Jutta Weber, 51–76. Göttingen: V&R Unipress, 2013.

Glaubrecht, Matthias, and Wolfgang Dohle. "Discovering the Alternation of Generations in Salps (Tunicata, Thaliacea): Adelbert von Chamisso's Dissertation 'De Salpa' 1819 – its Material, Origin and Reception in the Early Nineteenth Century." *Zoosystematics and Evolution* 88, no. 2 (2012): 317–63.

Hempel, Peer. *Deutschsprachige Physiker im alten St. Petersburg: Georg Parrot, Emil Lenz und Moritz Jacobi im Kontext von Wissenschaft und Politik*. Munich: Oldenbourg, 1999.

Hiery, Hermann J. *Das Deutsche Reich in der Südsee (1900–1921): Eine Annäherung an die Erfahrungen verschiedener Kulturen*. Göttingen: Vandenhoeck & Ruprecht, 1995.

———, ed. *Die deutsche Südsee 1884–1914: Ein Handbuch*. Paderborn: Schöningh, 2001.

Hiery, Hermann J., and John M. MacKenzie, eds. *European Impact and Pacific Influence: British and German Colonial Policy in the Pacific Islands and the Indigenous Response*. London: I.B. Tauris, 1997.

Humboldt, Alexander von. *Amerikanische Reise*, 6th ed., edited by Hanno Beck. Wiesbaden: Edition Erdmann, 2009.

———. *Political Essay on the Island of Cuba*, edited by Vera M. Kutzinski and Ottmar Ette. Chicago, IL: University of Chicago Press, 2011.

———. *Reise in die Äquinoktial-Gegenden des Neuen Kontinents*, Vol. 1, edited by Ottmar Ette. Frankfurt a.M.: Insel, 1991.

———. *Schriften zur physikalischen Geographie*, 2nd ed., edited by Hanno Beck. Darmstadt: Wissenschaftliche Buchgesellschaft, 2008.

Igler, David. *The Great Ocean: Pacific Worlds from Captain Cook to the Gold Rush*. Oxford: Oxford University Press, 2013.

Inglis, Robin. "Successors and Rivals to Cook: The French and the Spaniards." In *Captain Cook: Explorations and Reassessments*, edited by Glyndwr Williams, 172–78. Woodbridge: Boydell, 2004.

Juske, Anto. *Estonian-Born Admiral F. v. Bellingshausen, the Discoverer of Antarctica*. Tallinn: Infotrükk, 2003.

Kahn, Miriam, and Sabine Wilke. "Narrating Colonial Encounters: Germany in the Pacific Islands." *Journal of Pacific History* 42, no. 3 (2007): 293–97.

Kortum, Gerhard. "Germania in Pacifico: Humboldt, Chamisso and Other Early German Contributions to Pacific Research, 1741–1876." In *Oceanographic History: The Pacific and Beyond*, edited by Keith R. Benson and Philip F. Rehbock, 107–17. Seattle: University of Washington Press, 2002.

———. "Humboldt und das Meer: Eine Ozeanographiegeschichtliche Bestandsaufnahme." *Northeastern Naturalist* 8, Special Issue 1 (2001): 91–108.

Kotzebue, Otto von. *Zu Eisbergen und Palmenstränden: Mit der "Rurik" um die Welt 1815–1818*. Lenningen: Edition Erdmann, 2004.

Krusenstjern, Ewert von. *Weltumsegler und Wissenschaftler: Adam Johann von Krusenstern, 1770–1846. Ein Lebensbericht*. Gernsbach: C. Katz, 1991.

Lack, Hans Walter. *Alexander von Humboldt and the Botanical Exploration of the Americas*. Munich: Prestel, 2009.

Liebersohn, Harry. *The Traveler's World: Europe to the Pacific*. Cambridge, MA, 2006.

Lincoln, Margaret. *Science and Exploration in the Pacific: Europe Voyages to the Southern Oceans in the Eighteenth Century*. Woodbridge: Boydell, 1998.

Litke, Friedrich. *Viermalige Reise durch das nördliche Eismeer: Auf der Brigg Nowaja Semlja in den Jahren 1821–1824*, edited by Claudia Weiss. Wiesbaden: Edition Erdmann, 2014.

Lukina, Tatiana Arkadevna. *Johann Friedrich Eschscholtz, 1793–1831*. Translated by Wilma C. Follette. Mill Valley, CA: Follette, 2009.
MacLeod, Roy, and Philip F. Rehbock, eds. *Darwin's Laboratory: Evolutionary Theory and Natural History in the Pacific*. Honolulu: University of Hawaii Press, 1994.
———. *Nature in its Greatest Extent: Western Science in the Pacific*. Honolulu: University of Hawaii Press, 1988.
Matsuda, Matt K. *Pacific Worlds: A History of Seas, Peoples, and Cultures*. Cambridge: Cambridge University Press, 2012.
Norst, Marlene J. *Ferdinand Bauer: The Australian Natural History Drawings*. London: British Museum, 1989.
Posselt, Doris, ed., *Die große nordische Expedition von 1733 bis 1743: Aus Berichten der Forschungsreisenden Johann Georg Gmelin und Georg Wilhelm Steller*. Munich: C. H. Beck, 1990.
Pratt, Mary Louise. *Imperial Eyes: Travel Writing and Transculturation*, 2nd ed. London: Routledge, 2008.
Ridley, Glynis. *The Discovery of Jeanne Baret: A Story of the High Seas, and the First Women to Circumnavigate the Globe*. New York: Crown Publisher, 2010.
Schadewaldt, Hans. "Thaddaeus Haenke (1761–1817), österreichischer Arzt und Naturforscher, und seine Beobachtungen während der Weltreise Malaspinas in den Jahren 1789–1794 in Südamerika und im Pazifik." *Die medizinische Welt* (11 April 1964): 883–93.
Schweizer, Niklaus R., ed. *Journal des Malers Ludwig York Choris*. Berlin: Lang, 1999.
Seppelt, Erwin. *Adam Johann von Krusenstern: Ein Porträt*. Rostock: BS-Verlag, 2009.
Spate, O. H. K. *Paradise Found and Lost*. Minneapolis: University of Minnesota Press, 1988.
Watts, Peter, Jo Anne Pomfrett, and David Mabberley. *An Exquisite Eye: The Australian Flora & Fauna Drawings 1801–1820 of Ferdinand Bauer*. Glebe, NSW: Historic Houses Trust of New South Wales, 1997.
Werrett, Simon. "Russian Responses to the Voyages of Captain Cook." In *Captain Cook*, edited by Glyndwr Williams, 179–97. Woodbridge: Boydell, 2004.
Whelan, Heide W. *Adapting to Modernity: Family, Caste and Capitalism among the Baltic German Nobility*. Cologne: Böhlau, 1999.
Wilke, Sabine. "Performing Native Cultures in the 'South Sea': Mythical Images of Others in Early German Contact Narratives." *Pacific Coast Philology* 42, no. 2 (2007): 169–80.
Zantop, Susanne. *Colonial Fantasies: Conquest, Family, and Nation in Precolonial Germany, 1770–1870*. Durham, NC: Duke University Press, 1997.

Chapter 4

GEORG WILHELM STELLER AND CARL HEINRICH MERCK
German Scientists in Russian Service as Explorers in the North Pacific in the Eighteenth Century

Kristina Küntzel-Witt

At the beginning of the eighteenth century, the North Pacific and the Arctic region had still not been explored at all. They were blanks on the European maps, and so cartographers and other scientists became increasingly interested in the region. It was even discussed if there might be a land connection from the Asian to the American continent.[1] At the same time, the always energetic tsar of Russia, Peter the Great (1672–1725), noticed that his government did not know much about Eastern Siberia, or its frontiers. Peter became acquainted with the discussion about the question of a land connection between Asia and America during his stay in Western Europe in 1716 when he met Gottfried Wilhelm Leibniz (1646–1716), who was one of the leading scientists of the "Enlightenment" in Germany.[2] Peter the Great was fascinated by Leibniz's ideas, and started to bring a new system of education and academic life to Russia.[3] Leibniz was deeply interested in this question of a land connection and discussed the problem with Peter. After this meeting and the encounter with the French geographer Guillaume Delisle [or de l'Isle] (1675–1726) in Paris in the same year, the tsar began to think about the usefulness of mapping Siberia and its coastline.[4]

After his return home, Peter sent at first the "geodesists" Ivan M. Evreinov and Fedor F. Luzhin to Kamchatka, where they were to map the peninsula and search for a passage through to the Pacific. Evreinov and Luzhin came back to St. Petersburg in 1722, their travel having been especially useful in respect to mapping the position of the Kurile Islands.[5]

After their return, the German scientist and doctor of medicine, Daniel Gottlieb Messerschmidt (1685–1735), was engaged by Peter the Great to explore Siberia and map it. Messerschmidt spent seven years in Siberia from 1720 to 1727. For some time, the Swedish officer and prisoner of war Johann Tabbert von

---

Notes from this chapter begin on page 118.

Strahlenberg (1676–1747), a German by origin, accompanied Messerschmidt. After his return to Stockholm, Strahlenberg published a famous book about Siberia, including a map that became very well known.[6] Messerschmidt was not so lucky. When he returned to St. Petersburg, Peter the Great was dead and the political climate had changed. He was pressed to give all his materials to the newly founded Academy of Science and could publish nothing by himself.[7]

Because of Peter the Great's policy of opening up Russia for foreigners and his ambitious project to establish an academic life in his empire, many German scientists came to the new capital St. Petersburg and started to work for the Academy of Science. The far-sighted tsar died suddenly in February 1725 before the academy was officially opened, but his successors, although never as ambitious as Peter, did not change the plans for this important scientific institution, which was in contact with other European academies in Paris and Berlin and with the British Royal Society. Russia was without a single university at this time. There were only some theological higher institutions, but no secularized institutions of higher education. Nonetheless, the history of the academy is a history of success in the eighteenth century, despite it being a politically unsteady time during which there was no educational system upon which the academy could be based and from which it could draw members. During the entire century, the academy depended on foreign scientists, and many of them were Germans by origin. This situation produced numerous conflicts, with the intense disputes between Gerhard Friedrich Mueller (1705–83) and the famous Russian universal scientist Mikhail V. Lomonosov (1711–65) over the origin of the Russian nation being the most striking example.[8]

On the other hand, it was the period before the emergence of nation-states, and the Germans often came from different regions with different sovereignties and, very often, also different beliefs. It is clearly not an easy task to define their "German" identity,[9] but at least the language and the cultural background were important for them. On the other hand, it should not be forgotten that they defined themselves primarily as "scientists."

Two German scientists of this period are the main focus of my research. Both were members of the Russian expeditions through the North Pacific during the eighteenth century, and the reception of their work is a very complex story that is worth being told because their reports are the first authentic descriptions of the North Pacific, the Aleutian Islands, and the Alaskan coast. They are also dramatic reports, but they were almost forgotten in Germany, especially Merck's travelogue.

Georg Wilhelm Steller (1709–46) and Carl Heinrich Merck (1761–99), both naturalists and doctors of medicine, explored the North Pacific in the eighteenth century while they were serving the Russian state. Georg Wilhelm Steller crossed the Pacific from Kamchatka to Kayak Island in 1741; and Carl Heinrich Merck explored the North Pacific and the Aleutian Islands in 1790 and 1791. It is time to bring them back into scientific discourse and restore their public remembrance—they were not forgotten because their work was not worth remembering, but because of their early deaths. As a result, their materials and works were not published during their lifetime, nor for a long time afterward. Recently the diaries of Merck[10] were published for the first time in German, as was a part of Steller's diary which had been lost for almost 250 years in the Archive of the Russian Academy of Science in St. Petersburg.[11] It is astonishing, but the reception of their works was even better in North America than in Germany.[12]

For instance, the only biography about Steller was published by the American biologist Leonhard Stejneger of the Smithsonian Institution in 1936 and not much discussed in Germany, perhaps because of the time it was published.[13] In recent decades we have not had an annotated scientific publication of Steller's report from his voyage with Bering in 1741 besides Orcutt Frost and Margritt Engel's in 1988, which followed the tradition of the publication of Bering's voyages by Frank A. Golder in 1922, a milestone in the documentation of the legendary expedition.[14] On the one hand, it is of course only natural that American and Alaskan scientists were more interested in the history of the first exploration of the North Pacific,[15] which is well illustrated by the impressive publication in three volumes of Basil Dmytryshyn, E. A. P. Crownhart-Vaughan, and Thomas Vaughan.[16] On the other hand, the relative disregard of Steller and especially Merck for such a long time in Germany deserves an explanation, as a biography of Merck is still lacking.

The Second Kamchatka Expedition, 1733–43

In the eighteenth century, the picture of Siberia and the North Pacific in Western Europe changed fundamentally, thanks to the large expeditions to Siberia and Alaska, the so-called First and Second Kamchatka Expeditions, from 1725 to 1729 and 1733 to 1743 respectively, under the leadership of the Danish captain-commander, Vitus Jonasson Bering (1681–1741).

The First Kamchatka Expedition started in 1725 shortly after the death of Peter the Great. The instructions had been made by Peter, but he died unexpectedly in February without regulating the reign after his death. Vitus Bering's charge was to search for a land connection between Asia and America and to map the coastline. Bering started to serve in the Russian Navy already during the Great Northern War against Sweden. Economic motivations also played a role in the expedition, but they were not directly expressed.[17] On this first expedition, the Russian captain Aleksei Chirikov (1703–48) accompanied Bering, as he would again on the second expedition. By land they reached the Sea of Ochotsk, crossed it by ship, and then sailed the coastline of Kamchatka to the north until they came very close to the American coast and near "Cap

Dezhnev," as it is called today. Because of a thick fog, however, they did not see the opposite coast and so thought that the whole expedition was unsuccessful. Bering returned to St. Petersburg and tried to persuade the government to send another expedition to the Pacific to explore a passage to America. In many respects it is quite astonishing that the new Russian empress Anna Ivanovna (1693–1740) continued this project and even broadened it, as Anna's reign is not famous for farsighted policy as much as heavy nepotism. She was accused of being under a German influence from her counsellor Biron (or Büren), a noble Baltic German, who gave the period the name "*bironovshchina*," which carried an unfriendly connotation.[18]

The Russian expeditions were not primarily focused on economic prospects, but were much more "imperial projects"—the country should be explored and mapped for its own sake, as large portions of Eastern Siberia were still a "terra incognita" for the government. The Second Kamchatka Expedition differed considerably from the first one, because the Academy of Science became involved in the project whereas the first expedition had mainly been a military project. In the end, nearly three thousand people were engaged and it lasted for almost ten years. It was the most expensive expedition of the Russian Empire in the eighteenth and nineteenth centuries.

On the second expedition, Bering and Chirikov were supposed to search again for a passage through the Pacific Ocean, but this time with a course set more to the south and not along the coastline to the north. Captain Martin Spanberg (or Spangberg) (1696–1761), a Dane, was to go even further south down the coastline to search for a passage to Japan. Several other groups of mariners were sent down the large Siberian rivers to go to the coast and map the coastline from the Pechora to Kamchatka, itself a very ambitious and dangerous project. All these different groups, which belonged to the Russian Navy, needed years to fulfill their tasks, and many members lost their lives when they encountered scurvy, as Bering and Chirikov did on their passage to America.[19]

A special academic group accompanied the whole expedition and explored Siberia. To this group belonged the German scientists Gerhard Friedrich Mueller, Johann Georg Gmelin (1709–55), Georg Wilhelm Steller (1709–46), and the French astronomer Louis Delisle de la Croyère.[20] Later they were joined by the historian Johann Eberhard Fischer (1697–1771).

Georg Wilhelm Steller and His Passage to Alaska

Steller is one of the main subjects here, because he was the first West European scientist to step onto Alaskan soil. Stejneger's biography gives a good impression of Steller's personality and his work, but it was never translated into German. There is only a short biographical sketch by Gmelin, which was published in

German shortly after Steller's death.[21] Steller died unexpectedly on his way back from Siberia to St. Petersburg in November 1746 and so could not publish any of his materials. Only a very few of his writings were published, which was soon after his death.[22]

Today, we know much more about him and his works because of the launch in the 1990s of a large edition of the materials from the Second Kamchatka Expedition organized by Wieland Hintzsche from the Franckeschen Stiftungen in Halle, Germany and the archive of the Academy of Science in St. Petersburg. On the anniversary of Steller's birth in 2009, for example, a part of his diary from his way back from Kamchatka to Tjumen' was published, having been lost for 250 years.[23] Also, in Halle the International Society of Georg Wilhelm Steller was founded.[24] Why is Halle so active in respect to Steller? Because Steller had studied in Halle and had contact there with the "Waisenhaus" of August Herrmann Francke, one of the leading figures of pietism in the early eighteenth century, before he left Germany to find a job as a scientist in Russia. Steller was born in Franken in Windsheim, but not much is known about his childhood or family, who were originally called Stöller. He started his studies early, at first with theology in Wittenberg and then in natural sciences and medicine in Halle. After completing a profound scientific education, he left Germany in 1734 to find an appointment in St. Petersburg. At first, he worked for Archbishop Theophan of St. Petersburg until the archbishop's death in September 1736. He was then engaged to join the Kamchatka Expedition to help or replace the other German naturalist Johann Georg Gmelin, who had fallen ill after being in Siberia for three years.[25] The other German scientists, Mueller and Gmelin, had left St. Petersburg in 1733, so they did not know Steller personally before he arrived in Siberia to meet them and get his instructions from his elder colleagues, who were already professors at the academy. Officially, Steller was then called an "Adjunct of the Academy."

The historian Gerhard Friedrich Mueller and the botanist and naturalist Johann Georg Gmelin were on their way through Siberia with a large entourage. They took with them their own library, a good supply of wine (especially from the Rhine), and their cooks and servants. Steller's arrangement stood in stark contrast to their way of traveling; Gmelin described it with the following words, after they met for the first time:

> He was not troubled about his clothing. As it is necessary in Siberia to carry along one's own housekeeping outfit, he had reduced it to the least possible compass. His drinking cup for beer was the same as his cup for mead and whiskey. Wine he dispensed with entirely. He had only one dish out of which he ate and in which was served all his food. For this he needed no chef. He cooked everything himself and that with so little circumstance that soup, vegetables and meat were put into the same pot and boiled together. Smoke and smell in the room in which he worked did not affect him. He used no wig and no powder; any kind of shoe or boot suited him.[26]

Gmelin's biographer Robert Gradmann characterized Steller with the words: "A foolhardy 'go-getter', impulsive and full of life, but also passionately in love with science; tough and indefatigable, unassuming as a child and frugal to a degree; blessed with an indestructible humour [that] nothing could overcome, and which rose more triumphantly the more hopeless and miserable the outward circumstances might appear."[27]

Orcutt Frost maintains that Steller in some way represented a "new type" of scientific explorer that afterwards became more popular. He writes, "In his self-sufficiency, his love of nature, his predilection for preaching, his reputation as a loner, his respect for aboriginal peoples, and his zest for science, he anticipates Henry David Thoreau and John Muir by more than a century."[28]

It is a pity, but we have no portrait of Steller and not many descriptions about his figure; only average height and brown hair are mentioned. Stejneger suggests that his appearance was less remarkable than his conduct, or his colleagues would have noted it. And although Gmelin and Mueller really embodied another type of scientist, who too worked hard and left an immense corpus of writings, they were quite impressed by the younger Steller. They wrote: "In the matter of his observations he was exceedingly exact and so indefatigable in all his undertakings that in this respect we need not have the slightest anxiety. It was no hardship for him to go hungry and thirsty a whole day if he was able to accomplish something advantageous to science."[29] Steller was hungry for success. He was very pleased that Mueller and Gmelin did not want to go to Kamchatka so that he himself could explore the peninsula undisturbed; he even sent the Russian student Krasheninnikov away, who had been there before him and later published a description of the peninsula.[30]

At Kamchatka, Vitus Bering offered that Steller participate in the expedition to America as a physician onboard the *St. Peter* and, of course Steller, agreed. The other ship, the *St. Paul*, crossed the Pacific under the command of Chirikov. On board was Louis Delisle de la Croyère (ca. 1687–1741), who died of scurvy shortly before he could return to Kamchatka. Louis was the brother of the famous Guillaume Delisle. Guillaume Delisle kept in contact with the Russian court after his encounter with Peter the Great and later sent his younger brother Joseph-Nicolas Delisle (1688–1768) as a leading astronomer and geographer to the Academy of Science in St. Petersburg. Delisle was accompanied by his other brother Louis.

Without question, Guillaume Delisle's influence on his younger brother Joseph-Nicolas Delisle was great. The latter drew a map of the North Pacific based on his famous brother's studies, and Bering and Chirikov took this map on the expedition that Louis Delisle de la Croyère accompanied as an astronomer. The map showed three large islands: "Jeso", "Compagnieland" (or Staten Island), and "da Gama-Land." Jeso later turned out to be the Japanese island of Hokkaido, and the other two islands did not exist at all.[31] Bering wanted to reach them and therefore chose a course to the south. Instead of 1,400 sea miles, the passage required 3,500 sea miles, resulting in much wasted time in search of imaginary islands.[32]

Bering and Chirikov discovered the islands of the Aleutians, but on different routes because they were separated after a heavy storm at the beginning of the voyage. Owing to incorrect navigation, the voyage to America lasted too long and the ships were hit hard by scurvy. Furthermore, they could not remain in America during the winter, because they did not have enough provisions with them as a result of the sinking of the ship with supplies in a storm crossing the Sea of Ochotsk.[33] Bering was therefore eager to return as fast as possible to Kamchatka when they reached the Kayak Island in July 1741.

Only because of the need for fresh water did Bering allow some members of his crew to leave the *St. Peter* in a small boat. Steller could only go with them after a dispute with the captain-commander, and said afterwards, "We have come only to take American water to Asia."[34] It is astonishing, especially in regard to Russian history, but the Russian mariners did not claim any territory for their state when they landed. The vast empire, always eager to enlarge itself, made this first expedition without raising a flag. Half a century later, the German scientist Peter Simon Pallas (1741–1811) wrote, "It is incomprehensible that there was no thought of real exploration [or] taking possession of the land discovered; one might almost conjecture that the general instructions issued must have been insufficient, or that in so distant parts all subordination and discipline had vanished."[35]

Thus, it appears that Bering had no detailed instructions about what he should do when he reached the American coast, and it is also apparent that the preparations were not sufficient. But Steller made the best of it. Although he was only allowed to leave the *St. Peter* for one day when they reached Kayak Island on the American coast on 20 July 1741, he not only used those few hours to gather a whole collection of plants and herbs, but also found a hearth and a place where provisions had been buried. From the contents he could derive something of the living conditions of the inhabitants. He found, for example, salmon in birch bark containers, yarn made of grass to make nets, bark fiber to serve as emergency food rations, arrows, and a drill, which led him to suggest that the people of Alaska and Kamchatka must be related.

A bird, which Steller recognized from the literature as an Eastern Blue Jay (*Cyanocitta cristata*), convinced him that they really had reached the American continent. Steller collected the results of his botanical research in a plant catalogue with 145 species: "Catalogus plantarum intra sex horas in parte Americae septemtrionalis…" His collected herbs actually saved his life on the way home by preventing scurvy; the sailors, however, would not accept herbal remedy and became ill.

Six weeks later, on the way back to Kamchatka, the *St. Peter* called at Nagai, one of the Shumagin Islands, in search of fresh water. There again Steller had only one day, 30 August 1741, to examine the island. Nagai Island looked like a treeless desert and Steller had a serious dispute with the mariners about the fresh water, because he thought the pond they chose to take the water from was too close to the shoreline and contained salty water. This turned out to be true and was another cause of later troubles for the *St. Peter*. When they visited the island, one of the mariners, Nikita Shumagin, died and another five men could not work at all. Sixteen others were already infected, and Bering himself could not leave his cabin anymore. Scurvy was onboard the ship and every day it became worse.[36] Later, the islands were named after Shumagin. Steller collected plants and herbs, and wanted to cure the scurvy with them, but the mariners did not follow his advice and so the epidemic went on. By the end of the journey the ship was almost inoperable because so many sailors were unable to work.[37]

On Bird Island in the outer Shumagins, Steller was able to go ashore again, along with Sven Waxell, Bering's first officer. This was the first time he had left the ship without a conflict.[38] Steller's relationship with the seamen was anything but easy.[39] They would not accept his advice and his knowledge when he wanted to treat them with his herbs. After Steller treated Bering, he got better for a short time and could leave his cabin, but this success had no consequences; how Steller had managed the scurvy epidemic was forgotten shortly afterwards.[40]

Steller's relationship with the Russian navigator Sofron Khitrov was especially bad. Steller blamed him for choosing the southerly course that had led them to the American coast too late.[41] With other officers too, such as the Swede Waxell, Steller had a lot of disputes. His journal is full of reproaches against them, which also reflects that Bering was too weak to manage these conflicts.[42]

Another day they met some Aleutians in a kayak, which Steller later described in great detail as being extremely light and seaworthy.[43] This encounter with the indigenous people was not without difficulties. They wanted the seamen to come with their boat to the beach, but it was considered to be too rocky and the Russian mariners feared that the boat would be destroyed. In the end they fired weapons into the air to get rid of the Aleutians and to free their Chukchen translator, whom the Aleutians had tried to take.[44]

After this short encounter with the indigenous population, Steller's report becomes more and more dramatic. Heavy storms and unfavorable winds made the journey quite difficult for the increasingly miserable crew; unable to climb up the masts, the vessel became almost impossible to sail. Waxell, the de facto commander because Bering was incapacitated, wrote in his report about his anxieties concerning passing the strait with only a few healthy sailors:[45]

> I could not move anymore on deck, without holding on somewhere. It was useless to set the sails, because in the end I would have had nobody to get them down. And it was late in the year, October and November, with heavy storms and long dark nights, not to mention the snow, hail, and rain. … The pair of men who could still move

were so weak that they could not work anymore. They pleaded that they should be dispensed from work, because they were without any strength. They wished for a fast death so they would not suffer anymore. They told me that they would prefer to die than to live so wretchedly. We had no fresh water, and were very miserable. Our ship was like a dead tree trunk, with nobody sailing it; so we drifted from one direction to another, depending on the waves and the wind.[46]

Like this they drifted on the ocean until 4 November, when they discovered land. They were unsure if it was Kamchatka.

In the end, later that month, the *St. Peter* was shipwrecked on Bering Island—at that time an unknown island off the coast from Kamchatka. They believed at first, however, that they had landed on the shore of Kamchatka. The condition of the crew had worsened, including Bering himself. The captain-commander died on 8 December on this island, which was later named after him, as was the strait they had crossed. What about Steller? He tried to save as many members of the crew as he could with his herbs and started to explore the unknown island. What made him famous afterwards is that he discovered a "sea cow" (*Hydrodamalis gigas*). Its meat became extremely valuable for the stranded group and helped them to survive. The sea cows would not survive for long after the encounter; Russian hunters, the so-called *promyshlenniki*, pursued them so excessively to get their meat that the cows were last seen in 1768. On Bering Island, Steller wrote a book "De bestiis marinis…". This was the only publication published shortly after his death, and it made him famous—at least in the eighteenth century.[47]

Bering Island could have easily been the grave of Steller too. Yet his colleagues' description of him as "indefatigable" proved to be right: after examining the island during the winter, Steller started to build a small boat from the wreck of the *St. Peter* in the spring, and finally in August he and the rest of the crew—forty-six of the original seventy-seven seamen—left the shabby island for Kamchatka. During their time on Bering Island, the relations between Steller and the sailors started to improve because they learned that he could really help them, and he even cured their scurvy with herbs he collected on the island.[48]

The survivors earned themselves a living by hunting sea otters, whose pelts were extremely valuable. Steller wrote that they hunted more than seven hundred sea otters and that their meat also helped them to survive.[49] The sailors earned quite a fortune when they returned to Kamchatka with the pelts, and soon afterwards Russian *promyshlenniki* followed their example and started to hunt the sea otters on Bering Island and later on the Aleutian Islands. Eventually this led to the extinction of the sea cows, because the hunters needed their meat.[50]

Steller did not then return directly to St. Petersburg, but stayed in Kamchatka for three years and collected huge amounts of plants and ethnographic materials. He died in 1746 in Tjumen' of a fever. His description of Kamchatka was published in German for the first time in 1774 by Johann Benedict Scherer, but was shortened and largely rewritten.[51] It was based on a manuscript that Steller had handed over to Johann Eberhard Fischer, who partook in the expedition because Mueller fell ill. Fischer still possessed the manuscript in 1769 and then Pallas made a copy from it as well as Scherer. Pallas published the manuscript from Steller's journey with Bering in 1793.[52] Frost holds the opinion that Pallas changed much of the original—he shortened all criticisms of the Russian regime, he "improved" the German of Steller, and he rearranged parts of the journal for a better understanding. So, it was changed decisively and does not show many of the sarcastic comments that were so typical of Steller.[53] A summary of Steller's journal was published in English by the British traveler, chaplain, and historian William Coxe at the end of the eighteenth century. Coxe became a close friend of Gerhard Friedrich Mueller when he was in Russia, and a good acquaintance of Pallas.[54]

After the return of the expedition, a hot debate started in Western Europe about its geographical results. The brother of Louis Delisle de la Croyère, Joseph-Nicolas Delisle, did not believe the discoveries of Bering and Chirikov, and after his return to Paris from St. Petersburg in 1747 he published a pamphlet contradicting the results of the Second Kamchatka Expedition, together with a map on which the three islands of Jeso, Compagnieland and da Gama Land were still drawn.[55] Joseph-Nicolas only received the materials from his brother, who was on the ship with Chirikov. Thus Delisle thought that Bering had been shipwrecked shortly after he lost Chirikov and not on his way back from America, and he even wrote that Bering never reached America.

The Russian government was not at all amused by this publication and asked Gerhard Friedrich Mueller to write an argumentation against Delisle. Mueller published it anonymously in 1753 in the "Nouvelle Bibliothèque Germanique" and called it "Lettre d'un Officier de la Marine Russienne à un Seigneur de la Cour concernant la Carte des nouvelles Découvertes au Nord de la Mer du Sud, & le Mémoire qui y sert d'explication publié par Mr. De l'Isle. A *Paris* en 1752. *Traduit de l'Original Russe.*"[56] It was later translated into English and German, and was disputed in the scientific world. Mueller corrected some of Delisle's mistakes, proving that Bering had reached Alaska and died on his return from this perilous journey.[57] For this correction, Mueller drew on Steller's journals and materials from his journey with Bering. Maybe because Mueller answered anonymously, the debate did not stop but, to the contrary, ran on for decades.[58]

Carl Heinrich Merck on the Billings–Sarychev Expedition in the North Pacific

In the years following the very expensive Second Kamchatka Expedition no similar project was organized, but the Russian *promyshlenniki* made several excursions to the Commander Islands, the Aleutians, and the Kurile Islands, always in search of valuable pelt—especially from the sea otter because in Siberia the hunting grounds were almost empty. These Russian adventurers needed to find new resources for hunting, and Steller and his companions showed them a dangerous but feasible way to make a fortune. This led to the extinction of the sea cow and a dangerous reduction of sea otters, polar foxes, and other animals in the North Pacific.[59]

In 1785 the Russian government started another attempt to explore the North Pacific under Catherine II (1729–96), who in many respects followed the example of Peter the Great in regard to imperial policy. Under Catherine the Great the Russian Empire conquered Ukraine, and with the foundation of Odessa had the port on the Black Sea that Peter I had always wanted. In Central Asia, Russia also grew, and it seems it was only a matter of time before Russia would pay the North Pacific more attention again. In reality, this policy was probably more a reaction to Spanish expeditions and James Cook's third circumnavigation of the globe from 1776 to 1780. Cook started to explore the North Pacific in order to examine the Russian geographical data from Bering's expedition, because he was also interested in the ongoing geographical discussion. The British admiralty was interested in the region after they heard of the Russian penetration of the Aleutians and the Spanish expeditions along the American coast to Vancouver Island in 1774 and 1775 (without landing). The Spanish expedition was in turn a reaction to the expansion of the Russian *promyshlenniki*.[60] This Russian approach further south was one of the main reasons why the Spanish Crown launched several attempts to explore the Pacific coast further north from southern California, which they had not attempted for centuries due to economic difficulties and ongoing conflicts with the Indians.[61]

That Cook died on this expedition in 1779 in Hawaii, murdered by the indigenous population, is well known. Less known is that he wanted to explore the North Pacific on this expedition with the goal of finding a passage to the Arctic Ocean. Cook's lieutenant Charles Clerke followed as commander, but he did not survive the attempt to pass through the Bering Strait into the Arctic Ocean. In the end, this part of the expedition ended unsuccessfully, but the coastline of Alaska was mapped.[62] A description of this legendary journey was published afterwards by the American sailor John Ledyard who tried later to cross Russia on foot and then cross the Pacific to reach America.[63] He was arrested in Irkutsk in 1788 and taken out of Russia on the order of Catherine II, who did not want a foreigner to get such intensive knowledge of Russia.[64]

The British naval officer Joseph Billings (1761–1806) partook in Cook's third circumnavigation of the globe. He was afterward engaged by Catherine the Great to lead the expedition of the Russian government to the North Pacific, together with the Russian marine officer Gavriil Andreevich Sarychev (1763–1831). Billings was already familiar with the Pacific Ocean thanks to his travels with Cook and Clerke.

Sarychev, although still young when the expedition started in 1785, also was an experienced sailor. He had been educated in the "Marinekorps" in Kronshtadt by St. Petersburg, and made his first voyage in 1778 from Kronshtadt to Reval (Tallinn) in Estonia, followed by many different expeditions into the Baltic Sea and the Mediterranean. Because of his special interest in hydrography he was chosen to be the second commander of the expedition.

The so-called Billings–Sarychev expedition can be characterized as a truly "imperial" project, and was obviously a reaction to Cook's exploration of the North Pacific and the above-mentioned Spanish expedition along the American coast. When the French expedition of Jean-François de Galaup de La Pérouse started in August 1785 in Brest, the preparations for the Billings-Sarychev expedition had already begun. It took La Pérouse almost two years to reach the North Pacific. In 1787 he mapped Sachalin, the Kurile Islands, Kamchatka, and Alaska, and made many explorations, but in 1788 his ships *Astrolabe* and *Boussole* sank near the Solomon Islands in the South Pacific.[65] His translator Jean Baptiste de Lesseps left the expedition at the end of September 1787 in Petropavlovsk, and returned through Russia to Paris, where he published a description of his travels with La Pérouse in 1790.[66]

In comparison with the era of the Second Kamchatka Expedition, the North Pacific was almost crowded with expeditions of the leading European empires, and the "run" to new territories seems to have extended to the North Pacific as circumnavigations became quite *en vogue*. After the turn of the century, several Russian circumnavigations started—no doubt inspired by Cook and his spectacular successes.

The German historian Martina Winkler recently published an interesting article in which she tries to prove that the Russian government understood the North Pacific at that time as their territory of influence, and that the Russian government was very interested in securing the North Pacific as their "dominion." In this view they were more interested in the American coastline than the continent, although there were economic reasons as well.[67] A serious economic factor was the advance of the Russian fur trade to Alaska. The Aleutian Islands were less and less profitable for the *promyshlenniki*, so they turned to Alaskan territories for hunting.[68]

The German physician and botanist Carl Heinrich Merck (1761–99) partook in Billings's expedition unexpectedly. Merck followed the tradition of his family and studied medicine from 1780 until 1784 in Gießen and Jena. The family business of Merck from Darmstadt is still one of the most important pharmaceutical firms in Germany. Carl Heinrich Merck finished his studies with a dissertation about the anatomy and physiology of the spleen. Then he left Germany for St. Petersburg because his uncle Johann Heinrich Merck (1741–91), a friend of Johann Wolfgang von Goethe and participant in the court in Hessen-Darmstadt, had intense contacts with the court in Russia where he spent some time in 1773.[69]

Carl Heinrich received an invitation from Catherine II to come to Russia and work there as a physician, and so the young Merck went to St. Petersburg in 1785. He left the Russian capital after some weeks for the Siberian city of Irkutsk near the Baikal Sea, where he was engaged as a physician.[70]

While he was working in a hospital in Irkutsk he was asked to join the expedition, after the intended participant, French colleague Eugène Melchior Louis Patrin, fell ill. Merck left Irkutsk after only one day of deliberation, and on 15 May 1786 followed Billings on the expedition to the Pacific. Like the scientists on the Second Kamchatka Expedition, he received a doubled salary of 1,600 roubles, a very good income at that time, and he was promised a lifelong pension as well as ennoblement—all in all, not at a bad employment for a young man.

His advisor in scientific matters became the aforementioned Peter Simon Pallas—another German physician, botanist, and naturalist from the Academy of Science in St. Petersburg. Pallas had served at the academy since 1767 and was well acquainted with Gerhard Friedrich Mueller and the results of the Second Kamchatka Expedition. He even published the previously mentioned edition of Steller's report, and hence was familiar with Eastern Siberia and the North Pacific.[71] He carried out several of his own expeditions through Siberia and the Central Asian steppe, and was a very well respected naturalist in Europe and a member of the Royal Society in London.[72]

After a month, Billings quite laconically informed Pallas, who had previously written his instructions for Patrin, that he had engaged Merck instead of the French scientist.[73] At first Billings gave Merck these old instructions for Patrin, but on 30 September 1786 Pallas wrote Merck his own instructions, full of advice on how to collect botanical, zoological, and ethnographical material, and with the order to write an extensive report of his travels.[74]

Carl Heinrich Merck needed to wait four years until, in 1790, he could leave the coast of Kamchatka on the *Slava Rossii* together with Billings and Sarychev, and cross the Pacific. Several difficulties had hindered an earlier departure. At first they attempted to go from the mouth of the Kolyma into the East Siberian Sea and from there made a passage through the Bering Strait to the Pacific Ocean. They searched for a shorter passage along the Siberian coast, but this ended shortly afterward at the cape Baranii Kamen as the ice was much too heavy to be navigable. Therefore, in autumn 1787, the expedition returned to Jakutsk; and with the sailors at the end of their physical strength, stayed there over winter.[75] During his time in Jakutsk and the following year in Ochotsk, Merck made a lot of observations and came into frequent contact with the Jakut indigenous population.[76]

During the year 1789, two ships were built in Ochotsk to cross the Sea of Ochotsk, virtually the same way that Bering, Chirikov, and Spanberg had chosen some fifty years earlier. Only one ship, the *Slava Rossii*, could leave Ochotsk, and after a survey of five Kurile Islands, the expedition reached Petropavlovsk on

Kamchatka and stayed there the next winter. Merck used the time for smaller expeditions to collect materials, and he made further observations such as those of the hot water springs on the peninsula. Finally, the real adventure started when they left Kamchatka in May 1790 on the *Slava Rossii* and sailed for five months along the Aleutians, the Shumagins, and the islands Kad'jak (Kodiak) and Kayak, to Alaska.[77]

Merck had much more time for his collections of plants, herbs, and indigenous artifacts than Steller, and sent them all to the Academy of Science in St. Petersburg. The following year, Sarychev made another trip to the Alaskan coast,[78] while Billings together with Merck traveled to the coast of the Chukchi Peninsula in the utmost northeastern region of Siberia, where Merck could make extremely interesting observations of the Chukchi, which had not yet been truly conquered by the Russians at that time.[79] His report about their time with the Chukchi is a unique and impressive source about the living conditions and the different ethnic population of the Chukotka peninsula.[80] In comparison to the Bering expeditions, the Billings–Sarychev expedition was much better prepared with provisions, and not nearly as dramatic as Steller's passage to America.

Merck returned to St. Petersburg in 1794, and married a Russian woman there. In 1797 he spent some time visiting his hometown of Darmstadt, but then returned to Russia in 1798. Merck died unexpectedly from a stroke in St. Petersburg in 1799. He was only thirty-eight years old, and nothing was published of his materials from the expedition.

The biggest portion of his collections and diaries were given to Pallas. Shortly before his death, Pallas returned to Berlin and took a lot of his materials to Germany. For a long time, Merck's diary disappeared, but it suddenly reappeared in an used book store in Leipzig where it was sold in 1936. How it found its way to Leipzig is unclear, but the Merck family finally bought it and the original is still in their archive in Darmstadt.

A few years later, the secretary of Billings, Martin Sauer, published a report of the expedition which was well known in the Western hemisphere, and Gavriil Sarychev's report became popular in the Russian Empire.[81] Maybe this is part of the reason why Merck's materials, albeit much more detailed, were not published. By the time Pallas got the materials he was no longer a young man and his health had suffered from his own long expeditions. Perhaps this is another reason why Merck's reports were not published by the academy.

In recent years, Dittmar Dahlmann and his younger colleagues from the University of Bonn, especially Diana Ordubadi, have edited Merck's travel reports and his descriptions of the Chukchi people in German. And so, after two hundred years, Merck and his rich manuscripts are coming back into our scientific memory in Germany.[82]

Conclusion

Georg Wilhelm Steller and Carl Heinrich Merck were two of the first men to cross the dangerous and rough North Pacific. Steller was with his companions on the first passage from Asia to America. Later Billings, Sarychev, and Merck mapped the whole region including all the different groups of islands. They were the first to explore the flora and fauna of this region, with its extreme living conditions and climate. Particularly Merck's achievements were almost depressingly undervalued at least in Germany, as one of the first explorers of the North Pacific. This is changing, but for more than two hundred years the history of the exploration of the North Pacific was written with no more than a mention of his name. Now we should add something, because Merck's published diaries contain many materials of particular interest for ethnologists, but also other specialists like biologists.[83]

His contemporaries often characterized Merck as a very modest man. In his diary personal commentaries are rare—in contrast to Steller's vivid language. Merck knew that his reports would be given to Pallas and the academy, but this was perhaps only one reason why his comments are so sparse. He was a different type of scientist than Steller—almost shy and very cautious with his comments on indigenous people and their habits. His personality is not so visible as Steller's in his diaries, whose reporting is so dramatic and full of conflicts and dangers. On the other hand, Merck's observations are very often without prejudices. In this respect he seems to strive for more "objectivity" in his works than was usual at this time. Being a different type of character, he also did not write about serious conflicts between him and Billings or the Russian sailors. This is a notable contrast to Steller's diary, but there are some similarities as well.

Both scientists were engaged by the Russian state when they were quite young and without a name in the scientific world, but they were very well educated with a rather broad field of interest, and their minds were open to all novelties on their way through Siberia and the Pacific. Did they define themselves as Germans? This is a difficult question. First and foremost, they defined themselves as scientists—this is quite obvious. Nevertheless, their German origin was important to them, as their mentalities were different than those of their Russian colleagues. The Russian seamen showed some distrust of Steller because he was not a sailor, and also because he was a foreigner. The question is, whether or not many of the conflicts developed because the Russian sailors were not as well educated as the Germans and therefore there was less in common between them. The language posed no hindrance since Steller and Merck were familiar with Russian. The really difficult question is whether the educational barrier, the different rank in society, or the different nationality was the most important reason for the distance between the German scientists and their Russian crews. In the end, they needed each other on their dangerous journeys, and all their achievements were possible only because they worked together.

Kristina Küntzel-Witt is a historian of Eastern Europe. She is in the process of completing her *Habilitation* at the University of Hamburg with a project about "Siberia and the Northeast Passage in West European Historiography in the Eighteenth Century." Her PhD dissertation focused on the development of the Russian city of Nizhnii Novgorod between 1890 and 1930. In 2008/9, she held a fellowship from the Max Weber Foundation of the German Historical Institutes, with research stays in London, Paris, and Moscow.

Notes

1. Paul Pulver, *Samuel Engel: Ein Berner Patrizier aus dem Zeitalter der Aufklärung 1702–1704* (Bern: Haupt 1937), 223–25; see also Kristina Küntzel-Witt, "Wie groß ist Sibirien? Die russischen Entdeckungen im Pazifik und die Kontroverse zwischen Joseph Nicholas Delisle, Samuel Engel und Gerhard Friedrich Müller im 18. Jahrhundert," in *Osteuropa kartiert – Mapping Eastern Europe*, ed. Jörn Happel and Christophe von Werdt (Berlin: Chronos 2010), 162.
2. Dittmar Dahlmann, *Sibirien: Vom 16. Jahrhundert bis zur Gegenwart* (Paderborn: Schöningh, 2009), 112.
3. For a short survey about enlightenment in Russia, compare: Michael Schippan, *Die Aufklärung in Russland im 18. Jahrhundert* (Wiesbaden: Harrasowitz, 2012); Gabriela Lehmann-Carli et al., "Einleitung: Aufklärungsrezeption und Bildungskonzepte in Rußland," in *Russische Aufklärungsrezeption im Kontext offizieller Bildungskonzepte (1700–1825)*, ed. Gabriela Lehmann-Carli et al. (Berlin: Spitz, 2001), IX–XXXVI; and the works of Larry Wolff, especially his monograph *Inventing Eastern Europe: The Map of Civilization on the Mind of the Enlightenment* (Stanford, CA: Stanford University Press 1995), and his article "The Global Perspective of Enlightened Travelers: Philosophic Geography from Siberia to the Pacific Ocean," *European Review of History / Revue Européenne d'histoire* 13 (2006): 437–53.
4. Guillaume Delisle was at this time famous for his maps of Northern America; see Lucie Lagarde, "Le Passage du Nord-Ouest et la Mer de l'Ouest dans la Cartographie française du 18e Siècle, Contribution à l'Etude de l'Ouevre des Delisle et Buache," *Imago Mundi* 41 (1989): 25. See also the monograph of Nelson-Martin Dawson, *L'Atelier Delisle. L'Amerique du Nord sur la table à dessin. Avec la collaboration de Charles Vincent* (Sillery, Quebec: Septentrion, 2000).
5. Dahlmann, *Sibirien*, 112.
6. Johann Tabbert von Strahlenberg, *Das nord- und östliche Teil von Europa und Asia, In so weit solches Das gantze Rußische Reich mit Siberien und der grossen Tatarey in sich begreiffet* (Stockholm 1730).
7. His diaries were published more than two hundred years later in the GDR in four volumes: Eduard Winter and Nikolai A. Figurovskij, eds. *D. G. Messerschmidt – Forschungsreise durch Sibirien 1720–1727* (Berlin: Aufbau, 1962–68).
8. The literature about this debate is almost endless; see for example: Peter Hoffmann, *Gerhard Friedrich Müller (1705–1783): Historiker, Geograph, Archivar im Dienste Russlands* (Frankfurt

a.M.: Peter Lang, 2005), 195–201; Joseph Lawrence Black, *G.F. Müller and the Imperial Russian Academy* (Kingston, ON: McGill-Queen's University Press 1986), 109–11.

9. Compare the brief remarks of Heinz Duchhardt in his foreword to *Russland, der Ferne Osten und die "Deutschen"*, ed. Heinz Duchhardt (Göttingen: Vandenhoeck & Ruprecht, 2009), 1–3. There are a lot of studies about Germans in Russian service beginning with the school of Eduard Winter in eastern Germany, but most of these works are very descriptive and do not ask or could not ask for a "German identity." For example, in St. Petersburg an edition of Germans in Russia exists under the title *Nemtsi v Rossii* by Galina Smagina, a project that started in the 1990s and still continues.

10. Carl Heinrich Merck, *Das sibirisch-amerikanische Tagebuch aus den Jahren 1788–1791*, ed. Dittmar Dahlmann et al. (Göttingen: Wallstein, 2009); Merck, *"Beschreibung der Tschucktschi, von ihren Gebräuchen und Lebensart," sowie weitere Berichte und Materialien*, ed. Dittmar Dahlmann, Diana Ordubadi, and Helena Pivovar (Göttingen: Wallstein, 2014).

11. *Georg Wilhelm Steller—Johann Eberhard Fischer: Reisetagebücher 1738 bis 1745*, ed. by Wieland Hintzsche in cooperation with Heike Heklau, (Halle: Franckesche Stiftungen, 2009). Wieland Hintzsche is preparing another part of Steller's journal for publication.

12. Carl Heinrich Merck, *Siberia and Northwestern America, 1788–1792: The Journal of Carl Heinrich Merck, Naturalist with the Russian Scientific Expedition Led by Captains Joseph Billings and Gavriil Sarychev, Translated by Fritz Jaensch* (Kingston, ON: Limestone Press, 1980).

13. Leonhard Stejneger, *Georg Wilhelm Steller: The Pioneer of Alaskan Natural History* (Cambridge, MA: Harvard University Press, 1936).

14. Orcutt W. Frost, ed., *Georg Wilhelm Steller: Journal of a Voyage with Bering 1741–1742* (Stanford, CA: Stanford University Press, 1988); Frank Alfred Golder, *Bering's Voyages: An Account of the Efforts of the Russians to Determine the Relation of Asia and America, in Two Volumes* (American Geographical Society, Research Series No. 1). Volume I: *The Log Books and Official Reports of the First and Second Expeditions 1725–1730 and 1733–1742* (New York: American Geographical Society, 1922); Volume II: *Steller's Journal of the Sea Voyage from Kamchatka to America and Return on the Second Expedition 1741–1742. Translated and in part annotated by Leonhard Stejneger* (New York: American Geographical Society, 1925). See, also, Golder's earlier publication: *Russian Expansion on the Pacific 1641–1850: An Account of the Earliest and Later Expeditions Made by the Russians along the Pacific Coast of Asia and North America; Including Some Related Expeditions to the Arctic Regions* (Cleveland, OH: Arthur H. Clark Co., 1914).

15. See also James R. Gibson, "Die Stellersche Seekuh und das russische Vordringen von Sibirien nach Amerika 1741–1768," in *Europa in der Frühen Neuzeit. Festschrift für Günter Mühlpfordt,6*, ed. Erich Donnert (Weimar: Böhlau, 2002), 963–78.

16. Basil Dmytryshyn, E. A. P. Crownhart-Vaughan, and Thomas Vaughan, *Russia's Conquest of Siberia 1558–1700*; *Russian Penetration of the North Pacific Ocean 1700–1797*; *The Russian American Colonies 1798–1867*. To Siberia and Russian America, North Pacific Studies series, vols. 9–11. (Portland, OR: Western imprints, 1985–89).

17. There was a hot debate between Raymond H. Fisher and his Russian colleague Boris P. Polevoj over the question of whether there were any economic reasons or not; see Raymond H. Fisher, *Bering's Voyages: Whither and Why?* (Seattle: University of Washington Press 1977); Boris P. Polevoi, "Glavnaja zadacha pervoi kamchatskoi ekspeditsii po zamyslu Petra I.," *Voprosy geografii Kamchatki* 2 (1964): 88. Carol Urness argued convincingly that mapping was the main goal of the expedition; see her chapter "The First Kamchatka Expedition in Focus," in *Under Vitus Bering's Command: New Perspectives on the Russian Kamchatka Expeditions*, ed. Peter Ulf Møller and Natasha Okhotina Lind (Aarhus, Denmark: Aarhus University Press, 2003), 17.

18. The era of the *bironovshchina* is quite well researched; one of the latest and best written studies is a biography by Igor V. Kurukin, *Biron* (Moscow: Moladaja Gvardia, 2006).

19. Dahlmann, *Sibirien*, 135.

20. Croyère just took the name of his mother to make a heritage from his grandfather, but he was a direct brother of Guillaume, even though the other name has led a lot of writers to think that he was just a half-brother; see Dawson, *Atelier Delisle*, 21.
21. Johann Georg Gmelin, *Leben Herrn Georg Wilhelm Stellers gewesenen Adjuncti der Kayserlichen Academie d Wissenschaften zu St. Petersburg* (Frankfurt a.M.: without publisher, 1748).
22. Georg Wilhelm Steller, *Georg Wilhelm Stellers ausführliche Beschreibung von sonderbaren Meerthieren, mit Erläuterungen und nöthigen Kupfern versehen* (Halle: Kümmel, 1753).
23. Hintzsche, *Georg Wilhelm Steller—Johann Eberhard Fischer: Reisetagebücher 1738 bis 1745*.
24. Founded by Wieland and Elisabeth Hintzsche, with annual meetings; see: www.steller-gesellschaft.de
25. Stejneger, *Georg Wilhelm Steller*, 86.
26. Ibid., 146–47.
27. Quoted after Stejneger, *Georg Wilhelm Steller*, 147.
28. Orcutt W. Frost, introduction to *Georg Wilhelm Steller: Journal of a Voyage with Bering 1741–1742* (Stanford, CA: Standford University Press, 1988), 18. The sexual side of Steller's personality describes Jörn Happel in his article "Unter Ungeziefer und 'Wilden': Sibirien-Reisende im 18. Jahrhundert," *Jahrbücher für Geschichte Osteuropas* 61 (2013): 11–12.
29. Quoted after Stejneger, *Georg Wilhelm Steller*, 148.
30. Stepan Krasheninnikov, *Opisanie zemli Kamčatki*. 2 toma (St. Peterburg: Akademia, 1755). A first translation into German was printed in 1766.
31. See Aleksandr I Andreev, *Trudy G.F. Millera o Sibir*, in *G.F. Miller Istorija Sibiri, t. 1, izd. Rossijskaja Akademija Nauk*, Moscow: Vostochnaja literatura (1937) 2005 (3rd ed.), 109; Leonid Breitfuss, "Early Maps of North-Eastern Asia and of the Lands around the North Pacific. Controversy between G.F. Mueller and N. Delisle," *Imago Mundi* 3 (1939): 92.
32. Breitfuss, "Early Maps," 92. Delisles' statements about the location of the three islands are published in a memorandum for Vitus Bering from 6 October 1732. See Wieland Hintzsche, ed., *Dokumente zur 2. Kamčatkaexpedition 1730–1733: Akademiegruppe* (Halle: Francke, 2004), 49.
33. Dittmar Dahlmann, "Einleitung," in *Johann Georg Gmelin: Expedition ins unbekannte Sibirien. Herausgegeben, eingeleitet und erläutert von Dittmar Dahlmann* (Sigmaringen: Thorbeke 1999), 51–55.
34. Frost and Engel, *Steller*, 64.
35. Frost and Engel, *Steller*, chapter 2, note 10, 192. "Es ist unbegreiflich, dass an keine ernstliche Untersuchung und Besitznehmung des entdeckten Landes hat gedacht werden wollen; und fast sollte man muthmassen daß die ertheilte allgemeine Instruction unzulänglich gewesen seyn müsse, oder daß in so entfernten Gegenden alle Subordination und Furcht verschwunden" (translation by Margritt Engel).
36. Frost, Introduction, 22.
37. Ibid.
38. Frost and Engel, *Steller*, 99.
39. Ibid., 57.
40. Frost, Introduction, 23.
41. Frost and Engel, *Steller*, 95.
42. Ibid., 50.
43. Ibid., 97.
44. Ibid., 101.
45. Sven Waxell, *Die Brücke nach Amerika. Abenteuerliche Entdeckungsfahrt des Vitus Bering 1733–1743. Reisebericht seines ersten Offiziers und Stellvertreters Sven Waxell ergänzt durch Beschreibungen des mitreisenden Naturforschers G.W. Steller*, ed. Anni Carlsson (Olten, Switzerland: Walter, 1968), 85.

46. Ibid., 85. "Ich selbst konnte mich an Deck kaum bewegen, ohne mich festzuhalten. Es war nutzlos, viele Segel aufzuziehen, denn im Notfall hätte ich niemanden gehabt, der die Segel eingeholt hätte. Dazu kam die späte Jahreszeit, Oktober und November, mit heftigen Stürmen und langen, dunklen Nächten, von Schnee, Hagel und Regen ganz zu schweigen. ... Die wenigen Leute, die sich noch auf den Beinen hielten, waren ganz entkräftet und daher nicht gewillt, zu arbeiten. Sie baten in der Regel, man möge sie mit der Arbeit verschonen, weil sie keine Kraft mehr hätten. Sie wünschten nur, durch einen raschen Tod erlöst zu werden. Sie sagten mir, sie wollten lieber sterben als auf diese elende Weise weiter vegetieren. Frisches Wasser fehlte uns auch, kurz, wir befanden uns im größten Elend. Unser Schiff schwamm wie ein Stück totes Holz, niemand lenkte es, wir trieben hierhin und dorthin, wie Wind und Wellen wollten" (translation by Küntzel-Witt).
47. Steller, *Georg Wilhelm Stellers ausführliche Beschreibung von sonderbaren Meerthieren*.
48. Frost and Engel, *Steller*, 148.
49. Ibid., 145.
50. Dahlmann, *Sibirien*, 101–4.
51. Georg Wilhelm Steller, *Georg Wilhelm Stellers gewesenen Adjuncto und Mitglied der Kayserl: Academie der Wissenschaften zu St. Petersburg Beschreibung von dem Lande Kamtschatka dessen Einwohnern, deren Sitten, Nahmen, Lebensart und verschiedenen Gewohnheiten herausgegeben von J.B.S. [Johann Benedikt Scherer] mit vielen Kupfer* (Frankfurt: Fleischer, 1774).
52. Georg Wilhelm Steller, "Reise von Kamtschatka nach Amerika mit dem Commandeur-Captain Bering hrsg. und bearbeitet von Peter Simon Pallas," *Neue nordische Beyträge zur physikalischen und geographischen Erd- und Völkerbeschreibung, Naturgeschichte und Ökonomie*: vols. 5, 6 (1793). See also the inspiring work of Ryan Tucker Jones, *Empire of Extinction: Russians and the North Pacific's Strange Beasts of the Sea, 1741–1867*. Oxford: Oxford University Press, 2014.
53. Frost, "Introduction," 29–32.
54. William Coxe, *Account of the Russian Discoveries between Asia and America: To Which Are Added the Conquest of Siberia and the History of the Transactions and Commerce between Russia and China* (London: Nichols, 1780).
55. Henry R. Wagner, *Cartography of the Northwest Coast of America to the Year 1800. Vol. 1* (Berkeley: University of California Press, 1937), 140–42, 159–61.
56. *Nouvelle Bibliothèque Germanique* 13(3) (1753): 46–87.
57. Breitfuss, "Early Maps," 93. Compare too: Peter Hoffmann, *Ostsibirien und Nordpazifik in der zweiten Hälfte des 18. Jahrhunderts: Die Diskussion um die Ausdehnung Asiens* (Frankfurt a.M.: Peter Lang, 2013), 97–102.
58. Küntzel-Witt, "Wie groß ist Sibirien," 166, 170, 171.
59. Dahlmann, *Sibirien*, 103.
60. Dittmar Dahlmann, Anna Friesen, and Diana Ordubadi, "Einleitung Carl Heinrich Merck und die Erforschung des nordöstlichen Sibiriens und des nordostpazifischen Raumes," in *Carl Heinrich Merck: Das sibirisch-amerikanische Tagebuch aus den Jahren 1788-1791*, ed. Dittmar Dahlmann, Anna Friesen, and Diana Ordubadi (Göttingen: Wallstein, 2009), 18–19.
61. Bernd Hausberger, "Das Eigenleben einer angeblichen Peripherie. Lateinamerika," in *Die Welt im 17. Jahrhundert*, ed. Bernd Hausberger (Vienna: Mandelbaum, 2008), 105.
62. Dahlmann, Friesen, and Ordubadi, "Einleitung Carl Heinrich Merck," 21.
63. John Ledyard, *Journal of Captain Cook's Last Voyage to the Pacific Ocean, and in Quest of a North-West Passage, between Asia & America. Performed in the Years 1776, 1777, 1778 and 1779* (Hartford, CT: Patten, 1783).
64. Dahlmann, Friesen, and Ordubadi, "Einleitung Carl Heinrich Merck," 21, note 36; compare: Stephen D. Watrous, ed., *John Ledyard's Journey through Russia and Siberia 1787–1788: The Journals and Selected Letters* (Madison: University of Wisconsin Press, 1966), 50.

65. Dittmar Dahlmann, Friesen, and Ordubadi, "Einleitung Carl Heinrich Merck," 25.
66. Jean Baptiste-Barthelemy de Lesseps, *Travels in Kamtschatka, during the Years 1787 and 1788. Translated from the French of M. De Lesseps, Consul of France, and Interpreter to the Count de la Perouse, Now Engaged in a Voyage Round the World, By Command of His Most Christian Majesty.* In two volumes. London, 1790. Reprint, New York: Arno 1970. See Dittmar Dahlmann, Friesen, and Ordubadi, "Einleitung Carl Heinrich Merck," 25, note 47.
67. Martina Winkler, "Another America: Russian Mental Discoveries of the Northwest Pacific Region in the Eighteenth and Early Nineteenth Centuries," *Journal of Global History* 7(1) (2012): 36–37.
68. For a history of Russian America, see: Ilya Vinkovetsky, *Russian America: An Overseas Colony of a Continental Empire, 1804–1867* (Oxford: Oxford University Press, 2011).
69. Dittmar Dahlmann, Friesen, and Ordubadi, "Einleitung Carl Heinrich Merck," 33.
70. Ibid., 31–33.
71. See James R. Masterson and Helen Brower, eds. *Bering's Successors 1745–1780: Contributions of Peter Simon Pallas to the History of Russian Exploration toward Alaska.* Seattle: University of Washington Press, 1948.
72. Folkwart Wendland, *Peter Simon Pallas (1741–1811): Materialien einer Biographie*, 2 vols. Berlin: de Gruyter, 1992.
73. Dahlmann, Friesen, and Ordubadi, "Einleitung Carl Heinrich Merck," 44.
74. Ibid., 47.
75. Ibid., 49.
76. Ibid., 54.
77. Ibid., 55. Meanwhile the dissertation of Diana Ordubadi about the expedition is published, see Diana Ordubadi, *Die Billings-Saryčev-Expedition 1785–1795: Eine Forschungsreise im Kontext der wissenschaftlichen Erschließung Sibiriens und des Fernen Ostens* (Göttingen: V&R unipress, 2016), especially 139–185 and her article "'Brennendes Eis, jeden Traum verscheuchende Stürme und merkwürdige Fremde…': Carl Heinrich Merck und sein Beitrag zur Erforschung des russischen Nordens im Rahmen der Billings-Saryčev-Expedition 1785–1795." In *Russland, der Ferne Osten und die "Deutschen"*, edited by Heinz Duchhardt. Göttingen: Vandenhoeck & Ruprecht, 2009: 79–96.
78. Gavriil A. Sarychev, *Account of a Voyage of Discovery to the North-East of Siberia, the Frozen Ocean and the North-East Sea* (Amsterdam: N. Israel, 1969). The first Russian edition was published in 1802, followed by a translation into German in 1806 and English in 1807.
79. Merck, *"Beschreibung der Tschucktschi."*
80. Merck collected, for example, huge wordlists of the different dialects of the indigenous population; ibid., 414–515.
81. Martin Sauer, *An Account of a Geographical and Astronomical Expedition to the Northern Parts of Russia: For Ascertaining the Degrees of Latitude and Longitude of the Mouth of the River Kovima, of the Whole Coast of the Tshutski, to East Cape... by Commodore Joseph Billings, in the Years 1785, etc. to 1794* (London: Cadell and Davies, 1802).
82. Merck's journal was published and translated in English in 1980 by Fritz Jaensch, *Carl Heinrich Merck, Siberia and Northwestern America.*
83 The same can be said about the first publication of Gerhard Friedrich Mueller's ethnological studies, which are published now for the first time by Wieland Hintzsche, ed., *Gerhard Friedrich Müller: Ethnographische Schriften I.* edited by Wieland Hintzsche and Aleksandr Christianovič Élert in cooperation with Heike Heklau. Halle: Franckesche Stiftungen, 2010. It was also published in Russian by Élert and Hintzsche in 2009.

Bibliography

Andreev, Aleksandr I. "Trudy G.F. Millera o Sibir." In *G.F. Miller Istorija Sibiri, t. 1, izd. Rossijskaja Akademija Nauk*, 66–149. Moscow: Vostochnaja Literatura, (1937) 2005.

Black, Joseph Lawrence. *G.F. Müller and the Imperial Russian Academy*. Kingston, ON: McGill-Queen's University Press, 1986.

Breitfuss, Leonid. "Early Maps of North-Eastern Asia and of the Lands around the North Pacific: Controversy between G.F. Mueller and N. Delisle." *Imago Mundi* 3 (1939): 87–99.

Coxe, William. *Account of the Russian Discoveries between Asia and America: To Which Are Added the Conquest of Siberia and the History of the Transactions and Commerce between Russia and China*. London: Nichols, 1780.

Dittmar Dahlmann, "Einleitung", in *Johann Georg Gmelin: Expedition ins unbekannte Sibirien. Herausgegeben, eingeleitet und erläutert von Dittmar Dahlmann*, 7–84. Sigmaringen: Thorbeke, 1999

———. *Sibirien: Vom 16. Jahrhundert bis zur Gegenwart*. Paderborn: Schöningh, 2009.

Dahlmann, Dittmar, ed. *Johann Georg Gmelin: Expedition ins unbekannte Sibirien. Herausgegeben, eingeleitet und erläutert von Dittmar Dahlmann*. Sigmaringen: Thorbeke, 1999.

Dahlmann, Dittmar, Anna Friesen, and Diana Ordubadi. "Einleitung Carl Heinrich Merck und die Erforschung des nordöstlichen Sibiriens und des nordostpazifischen Raumes." In *Carl Heinrich Merck: Das sibirisch-amerikanische Tagebuch aus den Jahren 1788–1791*, edited by Dittmar Dahlmann, Anna Friesen, and Diana Ordubadi, 7–86. Göttingen: Wallstein, 2009.

Dawson, Nelson-Martin. *L'Atelier Delisle. L'Amerique du Nord sur la table à dessin. Avec la collaboration de Charles Vincent*. Sillery, Quebec: Septentrion, 2000.

de Lesseps, Jean Baptiste-Barthelemy. *Travels in Kamtschatka, during the Years 1787 and 1788. Translated from the French of M. De Lesseps, Consul of France, and Interpreter to the Count de la Perouse, Now Engaged in a Voyage Round the World, By Command of His Most Christian Majesty*. In two volumes. London, 1790. Reprint, New York: Arno, 1970.

Dmytryshyn, Basil, E. A. P. Crownhart-Vaughan, and Thomas Vaughan, eds. *Russia's Conquest of Siberia 1558–1700; Russian Penetration of the North Pacific Ocean 1700–1797; The Russian American Colonies 1798–1867*. To Siberia and Russian America, North Pacific studies series, vols. 9–11. Portland, OR: Western imprints, 1985–89.

Duchhardt, Heinz. "Vorwort." In *Russland, der Ferne Osten und die "Deutschen."* Edited by Heinz Duchhardt, 1–3. Göttingen: Vandenhoeck & Ruprecht, 2009.

Fisher, Raymond H. *Bering's Voyages: Whither and Why?* Seattle: University of Washington Press, 1977.

Frost, Orcutt W. "Introduction." In *Georg Wilhelm Steller: Journal of a Voyage with Bering 1741–1742*, edited by Orcutt W. Frost, 3–33. Stanford, CA: Stanford University Press, 1988.

Gibson, James R. "Die Stellersche Seekuh und das russische Vordringen von Sibirien nach Amerika 1741–1768." In *Europa in der Frühen Neuzeit: Festschrift für Günter Mühlpfordt. Band 6, Mittel-, Nord-und Osteuropa*, edited by Erich Donnert, 963–78. Weimar: Böhlau, 2002.

Gmelin, Johann Georg. *Leben Herrn Georg Wilhelm Stellers gewesenen Adjuncti der Kayserlichen Academie d'Wissenschaften zu St. Petersburg*. Frankfurt a.M.: without publisher, 1748.

Golder, Frank Alfred. *Bering's Voyages: An Account of the Efforts of the Russians to Determine the Relation of Asia and America in Two Volumes.* New York: American Geographical Society, 1922, 1925.

———. *Russian Expansion on the Pacific 1641–1850: An Account of the Earliest and Later Expeditions Made by the Russians along the Pacific Coast of Asia and North America; Including Some Related Expeditions to the Arctic Regions.* Cleveland, OH: Arthur H. Clark Co., 1914.

Happel, Jörn. "Unter Ungeziefer und 'Wilden': Sibirien-Reisende im 18. Jahrhundert." *Jahrbücher für Geschichte Osteuropas* 61 (2013): 1–25.

Hausberger, Bernd. "Das Eigenleben einer angeblichen Peripherie. Lateinamerika," In *Die Welt im 17. Jahrhundert*, edited by Bernd Hausberger, 99–130. Vienna: Mandelbaum, 2008.

Hintzsche, Wieland, ed. *Dokumente zur 2. Kamčatkaexpedition: Akademiegruppe.* Quellen zur Geschichte Sibiriens und Alaskas aus russischen Archiven 4, 2. Halle: Franckesche Stiftungen, 2004.

———, ed. *Georg Wilhelm Steller—Johann Eberhard Fischer: Reisetagebücher 1738 bis 1745.* Quellen zur Geschichte Sibiriens und Alaskas aus russischen Archiven 7. Halle: Franckesche Stiftungen 2009.

———, ed. *Georg Wilhelm Steller—Stepan Krašeninnikov—Johann Eberhard Fischer: Reisetagebücher 1735 bis 1743.* Quellen zur Geschichte Sibiriens und Alaskas aus russischen Archiven 2. Halle: Franckesche Stiftungen 2000.

———, ed. *Gerhard Friedrich Müller: Ethnographische Schriften I*, edited by Wieland Hintzsche and Aleksandr Christianovič Èlert with cooperation from Heike Heklau. Quellen zur Geschichte Sibiriens und Alaskas aus russischen Archiven 8. Halle: Franckesche Stiftungen, 2010.

Hintzsche, Wieland, Thomas Nickol, and Ol'ga Novochatko, eds. *Georg Wilhelm Steller: Briefe und Dokumente 1739.* Quellen zur Geschichte Sibiriens und Alaskas aus russischen Archiven 3. Halle: Franckesche Stiftungen, 2001.

Hoffmann, Peter. *Gerhard Friedrich Müller (1705–1783): Historiker, Geograph, Archivar im Dienste Russlands.* Frankfurt a.M.: Peter Lang, 2005.

———. *Ostsibirien und Nordpazifik in der zweiten Hälfte des 18. Jahrhunderts: Die Diskussion um die Ausdehnung Asiens.* Frankfurt a.M.: Peter Lang, 2013.

Jones, Ryan Tucker: *Empire of Extinction: Russians and the North Pacific's Strange Beasts of the Sea, 1741–1867.* Oxford: Oxford University Press, 2014.

Krasheninnikov, Stepan. *Opisanie zemli Kamčatki.* 2 volumes. St. Peterburg: Akademia, 1755.

Küntzel-Witt, Kristina. "Wie groß ist Sibirien? Die russischen Entdeckungen im Pazifik und die Kontroverse zwischen Joseph Nicholas Delisle, Samuel Engel und Gerhard Friedrich Müller im 18. Jahrhundert," In *Osteuropa kartiert – Mapping Eastern Europe*, edited by Jörn Happel and Christophe von Werdt, 155–72. Berlin: Chronos, 2010.

Kurukin, Igor V. *Biron* (Zhizn' zamechatel'nich lyudei. Seriya Biografii No. 968). Moscow: Molodaja Gvardia, 2006.

Lagarde, Lucie. "Le Passage du Nord-Ouest et la Mer de l'Ouest dans la Cartographie française du 18e Siècle, Contribution à l'Etude de l'Ouevre des Delisle et Buache." *Imago Mundi* 41 (1989): 19–43.

Ledyard, John. *Journal of Captain Cook's Last Voyage to the Pacific Ocean, and in Quest of a North-West Passage, between Asia & America. Performed in the Years 1776, 1777, 1778 and 1779.* Hartford, CT: Patten, 1783.

Lehmann-Carli, Gabriela, Michael Schippan, Birgit Scholz, and Silke Brohm. "Einleitung: Aufklärungsrezeption und Bildungskonzepte in Rußland." In *Russische Aufklärungsrezeption im Kontext offizieller Bildungskonzepte (1700–1825)* (Aufklärung und Europa hrsg. v. Martin Fontius), IX–XXXVI. Berlin: Spitz, 2001.

Masterson, James R., and Helen Brower, eds. *Bering's Successors 1745–1780: Contributions of Peter Simon Pallas to the History of Russian Exploration toward Alaska*. Seattle: University of Washington Press, 1948.

Merck, Carl Heinrich. *"Beschreibung der Tschucktschi, von ihren Gebräuchen und Lebensart," sowie weitere Berichte und Materialien*, edited by Dittmar Dahlmann, Diana Ordubadi, and Helena Pivovar. Göttingen: Wallstein, 2014.

———. *Siberia and Northwestern America, 1788–1792: The Journal of Carl Heinrich Merck, Naturalist with the Russian Scientific Expedition Led by Captains Joseph Billings and Gavriil Sarychev*, Translated by Fritz Jaensch. Kingston, ON: Limestone Press, 1980.

———. *Das sibirisch-amerikanische Tagebuch aus den Jahren 1788–1791*, edited by Dittmar Dahlmann et al. Göttingen: Wallstein, 2009.

Mueller, Gerhard Friedrich. "Lettre d'un Officier de la Marine Russienne à un Seigneur de la Cour concernant la Carte des nouvelles Découvertes au Nord de la Mer du Sud, & le Mémoire qui y sert d'explication publié par Mr. De l'Isle. A *Paris* en 1752. Traduit de l'Original Russe." *Nouvelle Bibliothèque Germanique* 13(1) (1753): 46–87.

Ordubadi, Diana: "'Brennendes Eis, jeden Traum verscheuchende Stürme und merkwürdige Fremde…': Carl Heinrich Merck und sein Beitrag zur Erforschung des russischen Nordens im Rahmen der Billings-Saryčev-Expedition 1785-1795." In *Russland, der Ferne Osten und die "Deutschen"*, edited by Heinz Duchhardt, 79–96 Göttingen: Vandenhoeck & Ruprecht, 2009.

——— *Die Billings-Saryčev-Expedition 1785–1795: Eine Forschungsreise im Kontext der wissenschaftlichen Erschließung Sibiriens und des Fernen Ostens. Mit einer Übersichtskarte*. Kultur- und Sozialgeschichte Osteuropas/Cultural and Social History of Eastern Europe, edited by D. Dahlmann et al. 4. Göttingen: V&R unipress, 2016.

Polevoi, Boris P. "Glavnaja zadacha pervoi kamchatkoi ekspeditsii po zamyslu Petra I." *Voprosy geografii Kamchatki* 2 (1964): 88–94.

Pulver, Paul. *Samuel Engel: Ein Berner Patrizier aus dem Zeitalter der Aufklärung 1702–1704*. Bern: Haupt, 1937.

Sarychev, Gavriil A. *Account of a Voyage of Discovery to the North-East of Siberia, the Frozen Ocean and the North-East Sea*. Amsterdam: N. Israel, 1969.

Sauer, Martin. *An Account of a Geographical and Astronomical Expedition to the Northern Parts of Russia: For Ascertaining the Degrees of Latitude and Longitude of the Mouth of the River Kovima, of the Whole Coast of the Tshutski, to East Cape … by Commodore Joseph Billings, in the Years 1785, etc. to 1794*. London: Cadell and Davies, 1802.

Schippan, Michael. *Die Aufklärung in Russland im 18. Jahrhundert*. Wiesbaden: Harrasowitz, 2012.

Stejneger, Leonhard. *Georg Wilhelm Steller: The Pioneer of Alaskan Natural History*. Cambridge, MA: Harvard University Press, 1936.

Steller, Georg Wilhelm. *Georg Wilhelm Stellers ausführliche Beschreibung von sonderbaren Meerthieren, mit Erläuterungen und nöthigen Kupfern versehen*. Halle: Kümmel, 1753.

———. *Georg Wilhelm Stellers gewesenen Adjuncto und Mitglied der Kayserl: Academie der Wissenschaften zu St. Petersburg Beschreibung von dem Lande Kamtschatka dessen Einwohnern, deren Sitten, Nahmen, Lebensart und verschiedenen Gewohnheiten herausgegeben von J.B.S. [Johann Benedikt Scherer] mit vielen Kupfer*. Frankfurt: Fleischer, 1774.

———. *Journal of a Voyage with Bering 1741–1742*. Translated by Orcutt W. Frost and Margritt A. Engel. Stanford, CA: Stanford University Press, 1988.

———. "Reise von Kamtschatka nach Amerika mit dem Commandeur-Captain Bering hrsg. und bearbeitet von Peter Simon Pallas." In *Neue nordische Beyträge zur physikalischen und geographischen Erd- und Völkerbeschreibung, Naturgeschichte und Ökonomie*, vols. 5, 6. St. Petersburg, Leipzig: Logan 1793.

Urness, Carol. "The First Kamchatka Expedition in Focus." In *Under Vitus Bering's Command: New Perspectives on the Russian Kamchatka Expeditions*, edited by Peter Ulf Møller and Natasha Okhotina Lind, 17–33. Aarhus, Denmark: Aarhus University Press, 2003.

Vinkovetsky, Ilya. *Russian America: An Overseas Colony of a Continental Empire, 1804–1867*. Oxford: Oxford University Press, 2011.

von Strahlenberg, Johann Tabbert. *Das nord- und östliche Teil von Europa und Asia, In so weit solches Das gantze Rußische Reich mit Siberien und der grossen Tatarey in sich begreiffet, In einer Historisch=Geographischen Beschreibung der alten und neuern Zeiten, und vielen andern unbekannten Nachrichten vorgestellet*. Stockholm: Strahlenberg, 1730.

Wagner, Henry R. *Cartography of the Northwest Coast of America to the Year 1800. Vol. 1*. Berkeley: University of California Press, 1937.

Watrous, Stephen D., ed. *John Ledyard's Journey through Russia and Siberia 1787–1788: The Journals and Selected Letters*. Madison: University of Wisconsin Press, 1966.

Waxell, Sven. *Die Brücke nach Amerika. Abenteuerliche Entdeckungsfahrt des Vitus Bering 1733–1743. Reisebericht seines ersten Offiziers und Stellvertreters Sven Waxell ergänzt durch Beschreibungen des mitreisenden Naturforschers G. W. Steller*, edited by Anni Carlsson. Olten, Switzerland: Walter, 1968.

Wendland, Folkwart. *Peter Simon Pallas (1741–1811): Materialien einer Biographie*, 2 vols. Berlin: de Gruyter, 1992.

Winkler, Martina. "Another America: Russian Mental Discoveries of the Northwest Pacific Region in the Eighteenth and Early Nineteenth Centuries." *Journal of Global History* 7(1) (2012): 27–51.

Winter, Eduard, and Nikolai A. Figurovskij, eds. *D. G. Messerschmidt – Forschungsreise durch Sibirien 1720–1727*. Berlin: Aufbau, 1962–68.

Wolff, Larry. "The Global Perspective of Enlightened Travelers: Philosophic Geography from Siberia to the Pacific Ocean." *European Review of History / Revue Européenne d'histoire* 13 (2006): 437–54.

———. *Inventing Eastern Europe: The Map of Civilization on the Mind of the Enlightenment*. Stanford, CA: Stanford University Press, 1995.

Chapter 5

Johann Reinhold Forster and the Ship *Resolution* as a Space of Knowledge Production

Anne Mariss

Introduction

Johann Reinhold Forster (1729–98) is chiefly known for having served as official naturalist during the second expedition to the Pacific (1772–75) under the command of James Cook (1728–79). In fact, he was only engaged in this capacity following a conflict about the available space onboard Cook's vessel HMS *Resolution*. In May and June 1772, the events that finally led to Forster's engagement came thick and fast.[1] The wealthy nobleman Joseph Banks (1743–1820), the naturalist on the first voyage (1768–71), had been engaged for the second expedition as well, but due to the hardship experienced on his first circumnavigation he had demanded more comfortable quarters for himself and his entourage of assistants and servants. Banks wished to be quartered in the Great Cabin, which by right was the captain's, so an additional roundhouse had to be constructed on deck to accommodate Cook. These alterations made the vessel, a Whitby collier, top heavy and thus unseaworthy, and they had to be demolished. Beside himself with anger about this development, Banks protested to parliament and the king.[2] Unwilling to accept this affront by a civilian, Lord Sandwich, the First Lord of the Admiralty, used his good relations with the prime minister, Lord North, in order to find an adequate substitute for Banks. On 8 June 1772, in a letter to the prime minister, Sandwich recommended Forster as "one of the fittest persons in Europe for such an undertaking."[3]

This chapter is not so much concerned with the complex social hierarchies aboard Cook's vessels; rather, it presents an analysis of the ship as a space of knowledge, in which, however, social negotiation processes took place as well.

Notes from this chapter begin on page 145.

Being unable to discuss the complex shipboard hierarchy in more detail in the present context, I will limit myself to pointing out the great variety of nationalities and social ranks onboard Cook's ships. The presence of the naturalists contributed considerably to the conflicts on board *Resolution*; since they were civilians, the officers of the Royal Navy had no or only very limited jurisdiction over them. In the course of the second voyage, conflicts, sometimes of a fierce nature, between Forster and the ship's company were frequent.

In the context of a culturally oriented global history that is centered on actors, the ship lends itself as a focal point for combining the macro-historical perspective of the world and its oceans, and the micro-historical one of shipboard life and the isles and coasts where the ship was landing.[4] Taking a spatial view of the dynamics that ensued from the insoluble entanglement of land or island, sea and ship opens up new perspectives on the conditions, possibilities, and limitations of the production of knowledge in natural history on voyages around the world. Not only shipboard conditions, but also the movement of the ship itself through space, from island to island, shaped the knowledge generated during these voyages. The ship as a *space in motion* or *in transit* is always connected to the sea on which it sails and the various environments it touches, such as the icy Antarctic, the shallow waters of the littoral zone, and the islands and ports where it makes landfall. Ships were not, as the French sociologist and philosopher Bruno Latour would have it, mere "tracers," which charted the contours of all "discovered" land or means of transport. According to Latour, the ship as such is not important; it may very well sink, as long as the documents generated onboard survive and reach their destination.[5] Certainly, Latour is not entirely wrong in this. But what he does not take into account is that the production of knowledge is tied inseparably to the ship as a space of knowledge. The ship, through its spatial characteristics and its movement through space, structured the production of knowledge onboard. In addition, the social conditions onboard influenced the production of knowledge in the field of natural history. Michel Foucault interpreted the ship as a "placeless place" and as "the heterotopia par excellence,"[6] but other approaches have turned out to be more fertile, especially within transatlantic history. These conceptual approaches view the ship as social space and as a "living, micro-cultural, micro-political system in motion."[7] With this in mind, I view the ship as a mobile and permeable space of knowledge, in which knowledge in the shape of texts, images, and objects was stored, transported, and transferred, and which itself, through its spatial conditions, influenced the production of knowledge. On the one hand, this spatial perspective makes it possible to focus on the ship as social microcosm and "contact zone" (Pratt) for different actors and groups—the seamen, midshipmen, and officers; the civilian scientists; and the inhabitants of the different Pacific islands—and thus to analyze the social and cultural conditions of knowledge generated during sea voyages.[8] On the other hand, utilizing the ship as focal point allows for an analysis of the problematic side of knowledge-generating procedures on sea voyages, as well as the material conditions under which they took place.

On the basis of these thoughts, this chapter focuses on the social and material conditions of the processes of knowledge production on voyages of exploration. The European participants of Cook's voyages will be considered as well as the local actors. The cooperation between naturalists, seamen, and Polynesian actors was essential for ensuring that surveys of the discovered regions and their exotic flora and fauna were as complete as possible. At the same time, this need for cooperation was the source of innumerable conflicts, which had their origin in the social and cultural heterogeneity of the *Resolution*'s company as well as in their conflicting interests. The following questions are central: Which conditions on board the ship shaped the generation of knowledge about foreign peoples and natural environments? What did the everyday life of the naturalists onboard look like? And finally, which actors took part in the process of knowledge production? Answers to these questions can be found in Johann Reinhold Forster's *Resolution Journal*, which provides insights into everyday practices of knowledge onboard the vessel, and is therefore an indispensable source for the historiography of the enlightened culture of knowledge in a global context.

From Clergyman to Explorer: Johann Reinhold Forster as an Actor of Eighteenth-Century Natural History

Among his contemporaries, Johann Reinhold Forster had the reputation of being one of the most famous German polymaths and natural historians. He is known chiefly for taking part in Cook's second voyage which, like the first expedition, had the aim of searching for the mythical continent *terra australis incognita*, which geographers such as Alexander Dalrymple believed to be located in the Southern Hemisphere. James Cook's three voyages between 1768 and 1780 form a turning point in British as well as in global history, and have to be understood as an Enlightenment project under the standard of contemporary ideals of augmenting knowledge and striving for improvements in the context of civilization. However, Cook's voyages were not solely concerned with charting and exploring unknown parts of the world; they also marked the beginning of territorial appropriation by the British Crown in the Pacific. While Johann Reinhold Forster's engagement as official naturalist on Cook's second voyage was due to a conflict about the space onboard ship, it was anything but a coincidence. Forster senior had long striven to become one of the most respected naturalists of his time. For a long time, he was overshadowed—at least in German-language historiography—by his son Georg Forster (1754–94) and his *Voyage around the World* (*Reise um die Welt*), which was the literary account of Cook's second voyage. Forster's strong discord with Cook and the Royal Navy about the publication of the official account of the voyage also earned Forster senior the doubtful reputation of a "tactless Philosopher."[9]

Forster's socio-professional rise is nonetheless noteworthy. After studying theology in Halle, he had been appointed vicar of the parish of Hochzeit (Wislina) near Nassenhuben (Mokry Dwór). During his time there, he married and started a family; at the same time, he followed his strong interest in universal history and applied himself intently to the study of ancient Near Eastern languages, history, geography, and natural history. In the context of Catherine II's efforts of colonization, Forster was called to Russia in 1765 in order to inspect the newly founded settlements in the southeast of the huge empire, and to study the country's natural history. The Russian expedition, which at first had appeared so promising, turned out to be a financial disaster for Forster, since in his report to the authorities he criticized the poor living conditions of the German settlers. In the ensuing conflict with the local authorities, Forster departed without having received any pay, and emigrated to England, at first taking only his eldest son Georg. In England, he succeeded rather quickly in establishing himself as a scholar. He taught French, natural history, and mineralogy at the Dissenter's Academy in Warrington—his handwritten course catalogues, which date from this time, offer profound insight into the contemporary understanding of the study of nature as a useful science.[10] Forster made a name for himself especially with the translation of travelogues into English. His son Georg, who by now was fluent in the English language, was of invaluable assistance to him in this undertaking.[11] With these translations, Forster quite literally inscribed himself in the minds of the learned public of his day. After the naturalist Banks withdrew from the second voyage under Cook's command, the admiralty appointed the German scholar as official naturalist, as described above. It was only shortly before the anchor was weighed that Cook learned "that Mr John Reinhold Forster and his Son Mr George Forster were to imbark with me, gentlemen skill'd in Natural history and Botany but more especially the former, who from the first was desireous of going the Voyage and therefore no sooner heard that Mr Banks had given it up then he applied to go."[12]

After returning safe and sound from the exploration of the Pacific, a bright future seemed at first to await the two travelers, who were celebrated for their voyage with Cook. A future career in Forster's adopted homeland of England seemed to be in the offing, but this hope was destroyed in the course of the next few years. The fiasco surrounding the publication of the official account, the ensuing financial strains and the circumstance that Johann Reinhold Forster became a persona non grata with his patrons finally led to the family's return to Germany. In February 1779, Forster was appointed professor of natural history and mineralogy at his alma mater in Halle. As warden of the Botanical Gardens, he figured prominently in its rebuilding in the 1780s, as well as in the establishment of an academic natural history collection. His private collection of natural and artificial curiosities from the South Sea as well as his extensive library was a visitor attraction in Halle and served as a teaching collection for students. Forster died on 9 December 1798 in Halle. He had suspected that he did not have long to live; in fact, he had diagnosed himself—correctly—with arteriosclerosis half a year before his death. Forster is buried in the town cemetery in Halle.

Knowledge Production Onboard HMS *Resolution* in the Pacific

Early modern natural history and European expansion were inextricably entangled with each other. Thus, in his vision of a "Great Instauration" of the arts and sciences (*Instauratio magna*, 1605 and 1623) Francis Bacon explicitly referred to overcoming the geospatial borders of Europe and the exploration of the world. The expansion of natural history did not only take place on the level of geographical discoveries. While technical improvements in the telescope allowed scholars to cast a glance at the infinite universe, the microscope enabled naturalists to discover new, minuscule worlds. These media were crucial for the production and dissemination of empirical knowledge about nature since they transmitted observations from the field of natural history. Among the documents published were charts, drawings, sketches, and paintings, and especially the journals written during the voyages, which were published as travelogues, often richly illustrated, and made knowledge about foreign worlds accessible to an interested European public. Another mainstay of natural history "on the road," apart from the documentation of empirical observations, was the collection, preservation, and drawing of natural objects, since they functioned as carriers of knowledge about natural history. The collection of specimens, their taxidermic and visual preservation as well as the exchange of objects were an important catalyst of the globalization of knowledge in the eighteenth century.

Natural history, more than any other science in the eighteenth century, did not limit itself to learned literature, but was characterized by a wide spectrum of practices necessary to the worldwide documentation, description, and categorization of nature, and the mobilization of knowledge about it. A great number of people of diverse cultural and social origin, who were not naturalists in the narrow sense of the term, were involved in the often arduous acquisition of natural objects especially, but also in the drawing, conservation, and transport of them. Thus, practices of natural history on voyages around the world must be understood as a project to which many different actors contributed.[13] During Cook's first voyage, the naturalist Joseph Banks was already accompanied by an entourage of assistants, among them Daniel Solander, one of the so-called Linnaean Apostles, the painters Sidney Parkinson and Alexander Buchan, and Herman Spöring Jr., a Finnish student of Linnaeus. Banks was furthermore accompanied by four servants who helped him in the collection of natural objects. Johann

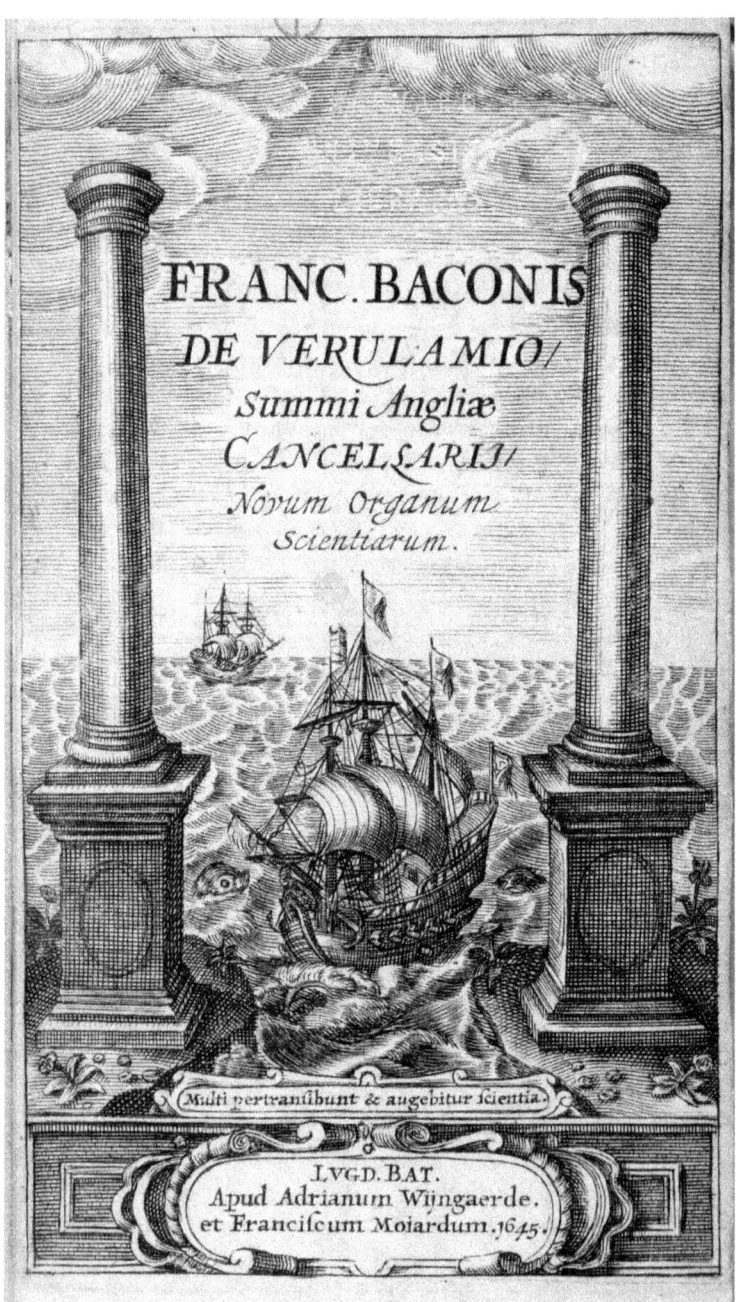

Figure 5.1: Frontispiece of Francis Bacon, *Novum organum scientiarum* (1645). Image source: Houghton Library, Harvard University, call number EC.B1328.620ib. Published with permission.

Reinhold Forster, on the second voyage, could not afford this luxury and only took his servant Ernst Scholient, who was educated in natural history and helped Forster in collecting natural objects. Georg Forster accompanied his father more or less gratis, "both as a Naturalist & a tolerable Draughtsman well qualified for to assist me."[14] Traveling scholars relied on their assistants, draftsmen, and servants, who were schooled in natural history, in order to be able to deal with the amount of collected material, and to be able to study it while still "on the road." The empirical analysis, then, did not take place only after the objects had been transferred to the "metropolis," but immediately onboard, making the ship a kind of floating natural history collection, in which collected objects were described, drawn, and preserved.

In addition to the natural history "team," the ship's company of the *Resolution* was involved in the process of empirical observation and the collection of knowledge. In contrast to the naturalists' assistants and the painters, the seamen working the vessels in the employ of early modern explorers have hardly been studied as involved in the production of knowledge in their own right.[15] A lack of sources (few handwritten documents by ratings have come down to posterity), is a primary reason for this lacuna.[16] Additionally, seamen's corpora of knowledge are not easy to reconstruct, since they consisted of knowledge seldom put into written form, but rather passed on orally or acquired through hands-on experience onboard. In the fields of cartography, marine zoology, and meteorology especially, the naturalists had to draw on the experiences of the professional seamen. The part played by the local actors whom the European travelers encountered on their voyages should likewise not be underestimated. For a long time, traditional history of science as well as older imperial history ignored the connection between the emergence of the new sciences and the European expansion, or assumed an "exportation" of European technologies and knowledge to the regions discovered by Europeans. More recently, however, the mutual entanglements of the different parts of the world in the process of knowledge production have been brought into focus. Central questions in this perspective are the connection between power and knowledge, methods of mobilizing knowledge, and the agency of local actors. The historiographical challenges of such a globally oriented history of knowledge lie in unlocking new corpora of sources and in reading against the grain the existing sources written by Europeans.[17]

The Naturalists' Work Onboard the Resolution

During the three years of Cook's second voyage between 1772 and 1775, the naturalists were chiefly occupied with the painstaking collection, documentation, preservation, and drawing of natural objects. Already during the stay at the Cape of Good Hope, where the *Resolution* and her consort *Adventure* took on stores before sailing through Antarctic waters, the Forsters undertook daily excursions during which they collected incredible amounts of thitherto unknown animals and plants. They quickly realized that their allocated task of compiling an, if possible, complete "catalogue of nature" was hardly manageable without further assistance. With Cook's permission, Forster engaged the Swedish naturalist and Linnaean apostle, Anders Sparrman (1748–1820), whom he paid out of his own pocket. The very limited time ashore (only 290 of 1,100 days in total) was used to collect material and make observations. As soon as the ship made landfall at an island, all three naturalists went ashore, either together or separately, in order to collect as many specimens as was humanly possible. Back onboard, Georg Forster was mainly engaged in drawing the material collected during these excursions, while Sparrman and Forster senior described and classified. A typical entry in Forster's *Resolution Journal* is, for instance: "I collected several plants, some of which were new ones. Next day my Son began to draw & Mr Sparman [sic] to describe the plants. … I collected several Shells & plants. In the morning I described the new Shag & a new Lark, & George drew the Shag & a new *Bat*, which we had got."[18] Johann Reinhold Forster viewed himself as warden and coordinator of this inventory of natural history—a time-consuming labor, which took place mainly after the excursions and onboard, where the instruments and books necessary for the description, drawing, and conservation were kept.[19]

The "hunt for plants" upon which the Forsters embarked with Sparrman was rooted firmly in the idea of a global inventory and categorization—if possible without gaps—of the plant and animal kingdoms. For several years now, the economic and political dimensions of procedures in the field of natural history have been studied intensely. Londa Schiebinger and Claudia Swan fittingly describe the multilateral relationship between botany, politics, and colonialism as the "Colonial Politics of Botany."[20] Historians agree that procedures of knowledge production in natural history were not some kind of precondition or pre-existing instrument for controlling nature and man in the service of the imperial state. Instead, natural history and imperialism are viewed as interlocking mechanisms that are part of the same complex historical process:

> Colonial botany—the study, naming, cultivation, and marketing of plants in colonial contexts—was born of and supported European voyages, conquests, global trade, and scientific exploration. The expanding science of plants depended on access to ever farther-flung regions of the globe; at the same time, colonial profits depended largely on natural historical exploration and the precise identification and effective cultivation of profitable plants.[21]

In a similar vein, Simon Schaffer in his afterword to *Visions of Empire* concludes: "Natural Histories provided accounts of economy and government which were widely deployed in political debate. Political management relied on the skills of naturalists and artists."[22]

Natural historians hoped to discover plants that promised to have economic and/or medical uses, and whose cultivation in Europe seemed possible. Thus, botany—and with it the entire Linnaean system—became a scholarly discipline of the highest political significance in almost all of Europe. Johann Reinhold Forster was an ardent admirer of the Swedish naturalist and his *Systema Naturæ*. Employing the Linnaean method of classification for their botanizing during Cook's second voyage, however, presented the naturalists with considerable problems. In order to adequately classify a plant, the flower as well as the male and female organs or the male and female plants as well as the correct number of stamina and pistils and their positions relative to each other were required. Finding the flowers of a plant with leaves and seeds was especially difficult because of the short duration of the stays on most islands, and posed a great challenge for the naturalists. In addition, the flowers of one and the same tree were subject to some variation; at times, the seeds, which would have enabled a complete classification, were lacking. Thus, although the naturalists did encounter an abundant vegetation in New Zealand in March 1773, the botanical "harvest" was still meagre, much to Forster's disappointment, because the unripe fruit and withered leaves meant he could not classify the unknown plants.[23]

Considerable difficulties in compiling a global inventory of nature arose from the conflicting interests of the naturalists and the commanding officers. Conflicts between them usually ensued if islands that promised rich findings in the field of natural history were passed by, or if the stay—in the opinion of the naturalists—was too short to collect a sufficient number of specimens. Longer sea passages without making landfall, too, were frustrating for the naturalists onboard. The depth and temperature of the water were measured frequently, but the study of the submarine fauna was nigh impossible—only by using nets and fishing rods could living specimens be brought onboard, and even this was frequently impracticable if the ship was moving at speed. The naturalists were often angry when the ship continued on its course with a complete disregard for important discoveries in the field of natural history. On 8 June 1774, the lieutenant of marines, John Edgcumbe, shot an unknown species of whale "but one did not wish to interrupt the speedy course of the ship although this would have provided a significant link to complete the chain that leads to knowledge of natural history,"[24] as Sparrman describes in his account.

The regular quarrels between the *Resolution*'s company and the naturalists, then, were classic conflicts of interest between two parties. While Cook's aim was to make exact charts of the discovered coastlines, agreeable to his orders from the admiralty, the naturalists longed to make every trip ashore in order to collect plants, hunt animals, and describe the landscape as well as its inhabitants. However, despite some frustrations, the time spent together onboard was frequently productive and filled with discussions between the seamen and the naturalists, as we will see next.

Seamen as Actors of Knowledge

During the voyage, the seamen, midshipmen, and officers not only fulfilled their roles as nautical professionals who navigated the ship, maintained it in good condition and organized the smooth running of everyday shipboard life; they also acted as interpreters, shared their linguistic and cultural knowledge with the naturalists, and were involved in the collection of plants and the hunt for animals. In the context of Johann Reinhold Forster's studies of the Polynesian languages, the knowledge of those seamen who had already been in the South Seas during Cook's first voyage was indispensable. When compiling his own vocabulary of the South Sea languages, Forster for instance drew on the vocabulary book kept by William Brougham Monkhouse, the ship's surgeon of the first expedition, who had died during the voyage in 1770, as well as on that of Midshipman Isaac Smith (1752–1831).[25] During the voyage, an important part as interpreter and intermediary fell to marine corporal Samuel Gibson: according to Forster, his command of the Polynesian languages was better than anyone's onboard.[26] Often, the naturalists' work was integrated into regular shipboard routine. Richard Pickersgill (1749–79), the *Resolution*'s first lieutenant, who was an excellent marksman, left the animals he shot to Forster, so that he could classify them. Frequently, however, the naturalists had to hurry in classifying and sketching the fish, birds, and mammals before they ended up in the cook's pot.

The entries in Forster's journal hint at the procedural character of the production of knowledge in the field of natural history onboard the *Resolution*, and show that knowledge about specific natural phenomena circulated among the seamen. Due to the considerable spatial mobility of seamen, the knowledge they acquired—either randomly or purposely—in one place traveled around the world with them. It is highly probable that there was a purposeful oral exchange of knowledge about certain natural phenomena and objects among the seamen to augment their own knowledge about the sea as the space in which they worked and lived, and to minimize risks and dangers caused by hostile environments. When part of the ship's company suffered fish poisoning in July 1774, for instance, Lieutenant Robert Cooper noted in his journal that he had observed a similar phenomenon on a voyage in the Caribbean, and remembered: "[A] similar accident happen'd when I was in the Pts Louisa at Tobago in the West Indies with Adml Tyrrell by eating the same kind of Fish … whereby many of the Officers & people were seized in like manner."[27]

The seamen were not only well traveled; they were also multiethnic or multicultural, which was another factor that contributed to the broad base of knowledge about different natural phenomena among them. Onboard Cook's vessels *Endeavour, Resolution, Adventure,* and *Discovery* was a heterogeneous mixture of nationalities; and during the voyage, too, seamen of different nationalities were frequently signed on, such as a seaman from Hanover, who appears in the ship's muster as John Hendrick.[28] During the first passage of the Antarctic sea in the winter of 1772/3, Forster and Cook profited from the presence of two seamen onboard the *Resolution* who had been in Arctic waters before. In their speculations concerning the origin and characteristics of the icebergs in the Antarctic sea, Cook and Forster drew on the knowledge of these men and compared it to their own.[29] Having spoken with the seamen, both Forster and Cook tried to develop their own theories about the icebergs. Forster adopted the expressions that the seamen had told him for the formations of ice, such as pack ice and tabular icebergs, and concluded: "From what I have seen, read, & heard, I find there are three different kinds of Ice."[30] Seeing—reading—hearing: this trinity was characteristic of the process of knowledge production onboard the *Resolution*. The naturalists compared their own experience with written information in the books and magazines that traveled with them in the ship's library, and then complemented this body of knowledge with the information they received from the seamen. Because the seamen were so well traveled, they could contribute observations from different parts of the world that lay at considerable distances from each other, and make comparisons.

That seamen took an active interest in phenomena observed on the world's oceans is evident not only in Forster's journal entries but also in many zoological and botanical terms still in use today: supplejack (*rhipogonum scandens*),[31] coalfish, leatherjacketfish and bottlenose dolphin are all terms created by seamen.[32] The naturalists did not always approve of these names that were coined by the seamen and often inspired by conspicuous external characteristics of the plants and animals they described.[33] Forster's *Resolution Journal* frequently mentions such names, some of which the naturalists adopted, while they corrected or outright rejected others. The most problematic factor, from the point of view of the naturalists, was the fact that the creation of names by the seamen was not based on any scientific system—or on any system at all, for that matter.

The process of knowledge production onboard the *Resolution* was characterized by an insoluble entanglement of learned "book knowledge," empirical observations, and the experiential knowledge of the seamen.[34] The naturalists did not reject the latter as a matter of course. On the contrary, especially in the eighteenth century, when the seas were for the most part still unknown, the naturalists depended on the zoological knowledge of the seamen. Aware of the gaps in their own knowledge, the naturalists respected the seamen as global agents of knowledge transfer, and realized that they needed the seamen as a source of knowledge in order to augment their own. However, the experiential knowledge of the seamen and that of the naturalists was only compatible to a certain degree. In the eyes of the naturalists, for knowledge to be reliable and thus "true," it had to be verifiable in situ with the assistance of empirical observation or the books held in the ship's library. Despite their cooperation onboard the ship, naturalists and seamen cannot be seen as a homogenous group in pursuit of the same interests. The collection of exotic curiosities and natural objects, in particular, was a repeated source of conflict, since it created a rivalry between them—but this topic exceeds the scope of this chapter.[35]

Intermediaries Onboard the Resolution

During his three voyages of exploration in the Pacific, Cook was sometimes accompanied by Polynesian travelers who, because they lived onboard for some time, were mentioned in some detail in the accounts of the voyages. Most notable among these were the Polynesian scholar and navigator Tupaia (ca. 1725–70); the Polynesian Mai (ca. 1753–79), who on the second voyage sailed to London with Captain Tobias Furneaux in the *Adventure*, and who received considerable publicity in Europe as the seeming incarnation of the "noble savage"; and Hititi (or Hitihiti or Ohedidee, also called Maheine), who traveled onboard the *Resolution* for a while. Although these three Polynesian travelers had fundamentally different biographies and went onboard the European ships with entirely different aims, all three of them operated as cultural brokers and intermediaries. They assisted the Europeans considerably in collecting knowledge and natural objects, were an invaluable help in navigation, and acted as translators and interpreters and thus as mediators of the foreign natural environment, language, and culture.[36] Like the Polynesian scholar and navigator Tupaia, Hititi was originally from the island of Raiatea and lived in exile in Tahiti, where he met the strangers from Europe.[37] Hititi was not as skilled a navigator as Tupaia, but he, too, was educated in the Polynesian techniques of navigation, and made a stick chart during Cook's second voyage.[38] His mnemonic chart hints at the self-understanding of the Polynesian travelers who accompanied Cook on his voyages. Seafarers and navigators were well-respected personages in Polynesian society. Probably, Hititi, too, wanted to boost his standing among Tahitians by going on a journey in the *Resolution*.[39] He did change his original travel plans and, in the end, remained in Raiatea, but during Cook's second voyage he acted as cultural mediator, interpreter, and informant in the field of natural history, similar to Tupaia. The Forsters profited from Hititi for nine months: he went onboard the *Resolution* in September 1773 and returned to Raiatea in June 1774. During this period, the Forsters drew, time and again, on his knowledge to find out the names of islands, animals, and plants. When Cook sailed for the Antarctic a second time, in the winter of 1773/4, to continue his search for the hypothetical *terra australis*, the Forsters used the endless hours onboard to ask him about the meaning of religious and cultural customs in Polynesian society, an undertaking that proved to be rather difficult due to communication problems.[40] Communication with local informants was a common feature of voyages of exploration and of knowledge production in intercultural contexts.[41] Forster also relied on local informants when compiling his above-mentioned vocabulary of the Polynesian languages, in addition to the written and oral testimonies of several seamen. In his *Observations*, Forster explicitly refers to the part the Polynesians travelers onboard played in his acquiring the language, without, however, mentioning any names.[42] Forster emphasizes most strongly Hititi's role as a mediator of knowledge in his Polynesian vocabulary: he was the most important source for systematizing Forster's ethnolinguistic observations.[43]

However, Forster's views of local informants was highly ambivalent. He accorded central significance to some of his informants in the context of knowledge production—if, in his opinion, they were of a certain social rank and standing, and thus educated people. He also admired the islanders for their keen senses as, in his eyes, they still lived in an uncorrupted state of nature. On 5 November 1773, Forster reported enthusiastically that during an outing near Ship Cove, a small bay in Queen Charlotte Sound (New Zealand), Hititi had shot a bird with a musket, a weapon he had never used before. According to Forster, it was altogether astonishing "how acute senses these Nations have: in *Otahaitee* the Natives often shewed me Ducks or Snipes or other birds, where none of us could distinguish any."[44]

With reference to the relationship between Banks, Tupaia, and Mai, Vanessa Smith has written about intercultural friendship in the context of encounter.[45] Something similar could be said about the relationship of the Forsters and Hititi. The term "friendship" is certainly fitting, if one remembers that this ideal was really a double-edged sword. Similar to the customs of the republic of letters, the "useful friendship" of intercultural context served to create equality among unequal people, and to promote intellectual and cultural exchange, while sociocultural boundaries were supposed to remain intact. The Forsters valued their friend Hititi as an informant and a partner in communication, while at the same time frequently adopting paternalist attitudes when describing his behavior as naive or uninformed in a childlike way. Several of the local informants were thus perceived as able to meet the European explorers on an eye to eye level and were treated with respect. They were admired for their uncorrupted senses, but the scope of their understanding of the world, in the Eurocentric conception of knowledge as championed by the Forsters, remained limited. The knowledge received from local informants was viewed mainly as a means to verify and legitimize the Europeans' own procedure of generating knowledge based on empirical observation during the voyage.

Bioprospecting in the Pacific

In addition to the better-known Polynesian travelers like Tupaia and Hititi, many other local actors of knowledge, whose names are unknown to history, supplied the European naturalists with valuable material and knowledge from the field of natural history during their crisscrossing of the Pacific. Often, this was material that would otherwise have remained unknown to the Europeans. Forster's *Resolution Journal* abounds with hints that the Polynesians shared their knowledge about flora and fauna, which had been collected over the course of centuries, with the naturalists. In Tahiti, in August 1773, the islanders brought the naturalists specimens of black nightshade (*Solanum nigrum*) and red flowering coral tree (*Erythrina*).[46] A few days later, the naturalists found a specimen of *Calophyllum inophyllum*, or Indian laurel, which was not in flower and was thus difficult to classify. The islanders informed the naturalists that the tree was called "Tamanoo" and had white, fragrant flowers; they also gave them a container of its seeds.[47] There are innumerable further examples of the interaction between the local informants and the keen naturalists; a list of these would fill many pages.

Cook's Pacific voyages are part of the global bioprospecting, which had its beginnings in the early modern era and entailed the appropriation of local knowledge and its classification after European parameters.[48] The term "bioprospecting," that is, the exploration and commercialization of biological resources, may be a modern coinage, but it adequately describes the exploitation of global biodiversity and local knowledge—a process that gained significant momentum in the eighteenth century.[49] The feminist science theoretician and environmental activist Vandana Shiva criticizes the inherent Eurocentrism of the term bioprospecting, because it suggests that value was added only through a European "discovery" of natural resources.[50] With this criticism in mind, it would also be possible to describe the naturalists of the eighteenth century as globally active "biopirates," because they, with a mandate from the state, searched for natural resources that they claimed for mercantilist, economic reasons, and appropriated without regard for intellectual property rights or territorial claims.

Forster's journal often gives the impression that the Polynesians were only too willing to assist him in the arduous task of compiling an inventory of nature, despite adverse conditions such as difficult terrain and tropical heat. Complacently, the German naturalist praised the hospitality of the Tahitians, who, according to him, welcomed the Europeans as friends, provided accommodation, gave them food, and carried them through the surf to the ship's boats, without ever demanding anything in return.[51] Forster's description of the Tahitians and their friendly or "servile" behavior to the Europeans points to several aspects of his experience of alterity and his perception of the foreign culture, which he tried to integrate into his worldview. In the course of the Enlightenment, the different peoples and cultures of the world were compared to a large human family. In the context of this integrative conceptualization it was possible to envision different "stages of development" and devise a socio-anthropological legitimation for them. According to this concept, the Europeans in the "Old World" had already reached a higher stage in this process and had at their command the knowledge and technologies necessary to make them an adult and rational member of this family, while the so-called "infantile" nations in the "New Worlds" in the East and West remained at a less progressed stage of development.

The idea of the perfectibility of man was an inherent feature of the enlightened understanding of mankind and is mirrored in Forster's reflections on the relations between Europeans and "primitive peoples." He did criticize the Europeans' exaggerated feeling of superiority, while at the same time defending the European claim for superiority on the basis of more advanced technological developments in the "Old World." Enlightened philanthropy and imperial bioprospecting thus stood in an ambivalent relationship. The knowledge of indigenous peoples was valued and utilized wherever possible to augment the European body of knowledge; simultaneously, indigenous knowledge was supposed to occupy a subordinate position to European knowledge because it was, as such, locally specific, and only achieved universality—and thus universal value—at the hands of the Europeans.

However, as Forster had to learn in a rather painful way during the voyage, not every person in the world was ready to share their knowledge or their resources with foreign arrivals. Indigenous informants who did not understand the Europeans or were reticent were often described as "wild," "uncivilized," or "underdeveloped." For the inhabitants of Tierra del Fuego, "the most wretched & dirty of all human beings,"[52] Forster felt nothing but contempt: despite repeated requests, they did not volunteer the names of certain things, which Forster flatly interpreted as stupidity. Quarrels, sometimes of a violent nature, occurred again and again during the voluntary or enforced cooperation between local informants and naturalists, as shown by the incident on the island of Tanna. The *Resolution* was at anchor off the island when the volcano Yasur erupted ash, slack, and stones. The naturalists were impatient to climb the mountain and observe the volcano's activities with the assistance of a thermometer and barometer, to study its flora and to make drawings. The inhabitants of the islands were suspicious of the strange activities of the naturalists, who dug holes at the foot of the volcano to take the temperature with their instruments. The Tannese asked the naturalists "not to stir much in the *Avernus*, for it could take fire."[53] Forster had originally planned to climb the volcano further, but realized "that the Natives had been artfull enough to bring us a great way from their habitations, where they dislike the Sight of Strangers."[54] The next day, Forster again wanted to climb the mountain, in order to get an overview of the island and the surrounding archipelago. As his party got under way, it was stopped by the Tannese who willingly showed them the way. However, according to Forster, who angrily noted the event in his *Resolution Journal*, the Europeans soon realized that they had been "misled," since the Tannese had shown them the wrong way—one that led them back to the ship.[55] The indigenous people tried with all their might to keep the Europeans from their settlements and their holy sites in the vicinity of the volcano, leading them past at a sufficient distance not to break the *tapu* of these places.

The *tapu* (in Hawaii: *kapu*) was a body of rules widespread in Polynesia which decreed certain places, things, creatures or people to be untouchable or sacred. Cook described the *tapu* during his third Pacific voyage (1776–80) as "Taboo." The Polynesian "food taboo," for instance, regulated that women and men as well as low-ranking and high-ranking social groups—according to their degree of "holiness" (or possibly power or *mana*)—were not to eat together; this is but one facet of this complex body of rules that the Europeans did not understand, or only very insufficiently. The behavior of the islanders, which Forster interpreted as a lack of comprehension, a misunderstanding or a cozenage, can be interpreted as an intentional withholding of information, with reference to the term "agnotology"[56] coined by Robert Proctor: "We need to think about the conscious, unconscious, and structural production of ignorance, its diverse causes and conformations, whether brought about by neglect, forgetfulness, myopia, extinction, secrecy, or suppression."[57] Ignorance, as well as knowledge and information, have to be seen as products of specific cultural practices which have to be put in their respective historical and sociocultural contexts. From this perspective, the intentional refusal to understand, the concealment, the lying, and the misleading can be interpreted as the expression of a specific agency with which the islanders protected and successfully asserted their interests against the Europeans. By purporting ignorance or a lack of linguistic comprehension, the islanders made use of the room for maneuver that offered itself in the situation of intercultural encounter: those versed in natural history consciously did not pass on information—or passed on incorrect information—about plants and animals to the Europeans; guides took detours during excursions, led the foreigners to different places, and controlled their movements through space. The islanders' scope of action widened further through the possibility of demanding material rewards in return for the knowledge they shared with the Europeans. Frequently, information was not shared readily, but actively bartered for objects. Local actors of knowledge did not at all conceive of themselves as mere sources of information, but expected material rewards for their hospitality and services. Culturally different notions of ownership and property carried particular potential for conflict. In return for their hospitality and the knowledge shared, the islanders appropriated the material possessions of the Europeans—the Europeans often demanded the return of "stolen" items, threatening violence or the taking of hostages.[58] It was very nearly impossible to draw a line between the mutual exchange of presents, which often preceded the establishment of contact, and the subsequent bartering trade, which according to European notions had to follow certain rules. The differences between presents, trade goods, and "freely available" natural resources were anything but clear.

Conclusion

For a long time, global or imperial history favored the sea powers of Spain, Portugal, the Netherlands, England, and France and their colonies as subjects of study. In contrast, the Holy Roman Empire and other "continental" powers without formal overseas territories appeared to have long remained untouched by the European expansion in the early modern era. The idea, however, that the Holy Roman Empire as a space of knowledge was mainly in a recipient capacity, and that the scholars there were content to only reflect on ideas and discourses of the New World, has to be revised.[59] Recent historiography has dedicated more and more attention to the circumstance that it was not only "colonial fantasies" and discourses about the other that were important to learned society in the empire but also more informal structures.[60] Knowledge about far-flung regions such as the Pacific was not mainly transmitted through official institutions, but rather or even chiefly through actors of knowledge and their transnational networks. Via these globally organized exchange networks, knowledge about foreign worlds such as the Pacific circulated, in the shape of letters, question catalogues, texts, images, and natural objects. Processes and developments of global history thus had a bearing on more than the colonial powers. Therefore, it is necessary to reimagine the Holy Roman Empire as part of a larger European process of entanglement and interconnection, and to place it in the context of global history. Such a history of polycentric relations can be conceived as a micro-history of the global, with the aim of viewing every subject of study, be it an actor, a village or a region, in the context of its respective relations to the rest of the world.[61]

Due to his part in Cook's second Pacific voyage as official naturalist, Johann Reinhold Forster was one of these German "global players" of the eighteenth century. Through the publication of Georg Forster's *Voyage* (1777), as well as Johann Reinhold Forster's own *Observations* (1778), ideas of the peoples living in the Pacific, their cultures, and the natural environment were disseminated in Europe, where they had lasting influence on European discourses of the self and the other. One instance of this is the Polynesian concept of the *tapu* (taboo), which, through Cook's voyages, was integrated into modern European culture; another is the purported promiscuity of the Polynesian women, which inspired nineteenth-century European notions of the South Seas as an erotic paradise, as painted in Gaugin's famous tableaux.

With regard to the role of Forster as one of the German naturalists who had traveled the world in the eighteenth century, his vast collection of natural specimens and artificial curiosities he made during the Pacific voyage is even more significant. Even if Forster did not have the expected success with his published travelogues, he took part in the dissemination and circulation of knowledge about the Pacific World through his vast collection. The exchange of natural objects and artificial curiosities within Forster's far-reaching network circulated knowledge in the German-speaking regions and beyond. Forster's material and textual resources thus contributed to the formation of knowledge about the Pacific natures and cultures within Europe.

The sources show Johann Reinhold Forster as a historical protagonist; however, he was not left to his own devices, but was—as the analysis of the ship as a space of knowledge production was able to show—to a considerable extent dependent on others, among them especially the seamen, the Polynesian intermediaries, and further islanders who often remained anonymous. The analysis of the ship as a space of knowledge showed that the generation of knowledge was only possible through the cooperation of innumerable actors. The *Resolution* as a historically specific space of knowledge brings into focus the contributions of the naturalists' assistants and servants, as well as those of the mariners, seamen, local actors, and intermediaries. This collaborative process of knowledge production onboard HMS *Resolution*, however, was characterized by imponderables and conflicts. Among these were the climatic conditions and the difficulties in obtaining the sought-after specimens. The conflicting interests of the naturalists, on the one hand, and the ship's company and the Royal Navy as the institution responsible for the expedition, on the other, meant that the compilation of an inventory of nature turned into an arduous undertaking. The knowledge that the seamen had acquired in their travels was a valuable resource for the naturalists, which they did not leave unused but compared it to their own bodies of knowledge. The cooperation between naturalists and local actors was as productive as it was conflictual. Intercultural encounters in specific spaces such as the ship make evident that global knowledge could only be produced with the assistance of indigenous actors, who helped in the collection of natural objects, supplied information about local terms for plants and animals, and their usage, and acted as interpreters and guides. At the same time, not all local informants cooperated willingly with the European travelers, but rather made use of their specific agency by consciously concealing their knowledge, not resolving misunderstandings, and misleading foreigners.

In sum, the example of Johann Reinhold Forster and the ship *Resolution* as a space of knowledge makes plain that it is possible to write a global history as a history of global entanglements between different parts of the world by looking at a specific actor in relation to the social environments and space(s) he traversed.

Anne Mariss has been a research assistant with the Department of Early Modern History at the University of Regensburg since October 2016. From 2013 to 2016, she held different positions as a research assistant at the University of Tuebingen. Previously she was a PhD candidate with the graduate school "Dynamics of Space and Gender" at the University of Kassel. Her PhD thesis has won a translation prize award, and will be published with Lexington Books in 2018.

Notes

This chapter is based on my German language dissertation *"A World of New Things": Praktiken der Naturgeschichte bei Johann Reinhold Forster* (Frankfurt a.M.: Campus 2015), which will be published in the series *Empires and Entanglements in the Early Modern World*, edited by Ulrike Strasser and Charles H. Parker with Lexington Books (Rowman & Littlefield) in 2018. My thanks go to Lena Moser (Tuebingen) for the translation of this text, and to the editors of this volume for their helpful comments.

1. Cf. Johann Reinhold Forster, *The Resolution Journal of Johann Reinhold Forster*, Vol. I, ed. Michael E. Hoare (London: Hakluyt Society, 1982), 123–27, for his own version of events.
2. Banks's long letter of 30 May 1772 to Lord Sandwich is illuminative in this context. In it, he explains his angry reaction to the admiralty's negative answer as necessary "to avoid the appearance of inconsistency, and to justify my conduct in the Eyes of the publick & your Lordship". Banks to Sandwich, London, 30 May 1772. Joseph Banks, *The Indian and Pacific Correspondence of Sir Joseph Banks, 1768–1820*, Vol. I, ed. Neil Chambers (London: Pickering and Chatto, 2008), 117.
3. Cited in Joseph Stuart Gordon, *Reinhold and Georg Forster in England, 1766–1780* (Durham, NC: PhD dissertation, Duke University 1975), 153.
4. See the introduction by Klein/Mackenthun, 'The Sea is History', in Bernhard Klein and Gesa Mackenthun, eds., *Sea Changes: Historicizing the Ocean* (New York: Routledge, 2004), 10.
5. Cf. Bruno Latour, "Die Logistik der Immutable mobiles," in *Mediengeographie. Theorie—Analyse—Diskussion* (*Medienumbrüche* 26), ed. Jörg Döring and Tristan Thielmann (Bielefeld: transcript, 2009), 117. For an English version see: Bruno Latour, "Visualisation and Cognition: Drawing Things Together," in *Knowledge and Society: Studies in the Sociology of Culture Past and Present* 6 (1986): 1–40.
6. Michel Foucault, "Of Other Spaces: Utopias and Heterotopias," in *Rethinking Architecture: A Reader in Cultural Theory*, ed. Neil Leach (New York: Routledge, 1997), 336.
7. Paul Gilroy, *The Black Atlantic: Modernity and Double Consciousness* (Cambridge, MA: Harvard University Press, 1995), 4. For a sociohistorical perspective on the "Red Atlantic", see Marcus Rediker, *Between the Devil and the Deep Blue Sea: Merchant Seamen, Pirates, and the Anglo-American Maritime World, 1700–1750* (Cambridge: Cambridge University Press, 1987).
8. Mary Louise Pratt defines *contact zones* as "social spaces where cultures meet, clash, and grapple with each other, often in contexts of highly asymmetrical relations of power, such as colonialism, slavery, or their aftermaths as they are lived out in many parts of the world today." Mary Louise Pratt, "Arts of the Contact Zone," *Profession* (1991): 33–40. For Pratt's concept of contact zones, see also her book *Imperial Eyes: Travel Writing and Transculturation* (London:Routledge, 1992), 6–7.
9. For the background of the quarrel, see Michael E. Hoare, *The Tactless Philosopher: Johann Reinhold Forster (1729–98)* (Melbourne: Hawthorn Press, 1976), 151–204.
10. Forster, *Lectures on Natural History*. SBB. Ms. germ. oct. 22a. See also Mariss, *"A World of New Things"*; as well as Michael Dettelbach, "'A Kind of Linnaean Being': Forster and Eighteenth-Century Natural History," in Johann Reinhold Forster, *Observations Made during a Voyage round the World*, ed. Nicholas Thomas et al. (Honolulu: University of Hawaii Press, 1996), lv–lxxiv.

11. As Ludwig Uhlig points out in his biography of Georg Forster, it was actually the son who was the author of these translations into English, while the father mainly analyzed the accounts in reference to natural history. Cf. Ludwig Uhlig, *Georg Forster: Lebensabenteuer eines gelehrten Weltbürgers (1754–1794)* (Göttingen: Vandenhoeck & Ruprecht, 2004), 36.
12. James Cook, *The Journals of Captain James Cook on his Voyages of Discovery*, Vol. I, ed. John C. Beaglehole (Cambridge: Hakluyt Society at the University Press, 1955), 8.
13. Cf. the programmatic article by Bettina Dietz, "Making Natural History: Doing the Enlightenment," *Central European History* 43 (2010): 25–46; as well as Londa Schiebinger, *Plants and Empire: Colonial Bioprospecting in the Atlantic World* (Cambridge, MA: Harvard University Press, 2004), 46–50, for a case study.
14. Forster, *Resolution Journal*, I, 123.
15. For more details on the connection between seafaring and maritime bodies of knowledge, see Margaret Deacon, *Scientists and the Sea, 1650–1900: A Study of Marine Science* (London: Academy Press, 1971); Daniel Finamore, ed., *Maritime History as World History* (Salem, MA: Peabody Essex Museum, 2004); Daniela Bleichmar, ed., *Science in the Spanish and Portuguese Empires, 1500–1800* (Palo Alto, CA: Stanford University Press, 2008); Maria Fusaro, ed., *Maritime History as Global History* (*Research in Maritime History* 43) (St. John's, Newfoundland: Internat. Maritime Economic History Assoc., 2010).
16. The reason for this was not that most seamen were illiterate, but that any documents written during the voyage where confiscated by admiralty order before the ship's return to port. Of Cook's three voyages, some accounts by seamen were published anonymously and have survived—for instance, those of James Magra (also called Matra) and John Marra, and the *Reise um die Welt* (Voyage around the world) of sailor Heinrich Zimmermann, who signed on for the third voyage.
17. Cf. Sujit Sivasundaram, "Sciences and the Global: On Methods, Questions, and Theory," *Isis* 101(1) (2010): 147–54.
18. Forster, *Resolution Journal*, II, 283. "Mr Sparman went ashore to collect plants for my George to draw them, & I brought a new creeping umbellated plant" (ibid., 287).
19. Cf. ibid., 286. Cf. also the entry of 28 June 1774: "Mr Sparman & my Son stood in the Afternoon on board, in order to draw, describe, & bring plants overside. I & a Sailor went ashore & collected plants & found a few new ones, which I delighted in" (ibid., III, 542).
20. Londa Schiebinger and Claudia Swan, eds., *Colonial Botany: Science, Commerce, and Politics in the Early Modern World* (Philadelphia, PA: University of Pennsylvania Press, 2005).
21. Ibid., 2.
22. Simon Schaffer, "Visions of Empire: Afterword," in *Visions of Empire: Voyages, Botany, and Representations of Nature*, ed. David P. Miller and Peter H. Reill (Cambridge: Cambridge University Press, 1996), 336.
23. Forster, *Resolution Journal*, II, 241.
24. Anders Sparrman, "Anders Sparrman's Journal: Sweden, South Africa, New Zealand, French Polynesia, Tonga, Fiji, Vanuatu, New Caledonia, Easter Islands, Marquesas Islands, Argentina," in *The Linnaeus Apostles: Global Science and Adventure*, Vol. 5, ed. Lars Hansen (London: IK Foundation, 2007), 406.
25. The manuscript with the title *Vocabularies of the Language spoken in the Isles of the South-Sea & of the various Dialects which have Affinity to it* (1774) is located in the manuscript department of the Staatsbibliothek Berlin under the shelf mark Ms or. oct. 62. It is partially reproduced in the essay of a librarian by the name of Moser, "Nachschrift von einer Handschrift J. R. Forster's in der Kön. öffentlichen Bibliothek zu Stuttgart," *Serapeum: Zeitschrift für Bibliothekswissenschaft, Handschriftenkunde und ältere Literatur* 3 (1840): 33–38. The manuscript obtained by Moser must be a copy of the original, as emerges from his analysis of the manuscript. On Forster's manuscript, see Karl H. Rensch, "Forster's Polynesian Linguistics," in Johann Reinhold Forster,

Observations Made during a Voyage round the World (Honolulu: University of Hawaii Press, 1996), 383–400; and for the collective task of understanding the Polynesian languages, see Anne Mariss, "Sprache und (Miss-)Verstehen: Formen kollektiver Wissensproduktion im Umfeld der zweiten Cook-Expedition (1772–75)," in *Georg Forster-Studien* 19 (2014), ed. Stefan Greif and Michael Ewert, 45–78.

26. Cf. Forster, *Resolution Journal*, II, 242.
27. Qtd. after Cook, *Journals*, II, 470.
28. Cf. Forster, *Resolution Journal*, IV, 732f. Cf. also Cook, *Journals*, II, 883.
29. Cf. Forster, *Resolution Journal*, II, 194f. Cook, too, noted down the information of his men. Cf. Cook, *Journals*, II, 63.
30. Forster, *Resolution Journal*, II, 199.
31. Cf. ibid., 277.
32. Cf. ibid., 295.
33. Cf. ibid., 270.
34. On the role of books, images, and texts for the production of knowledge during the voyage, see Anne Mariss, "A Library in the Field: The Use of Books aboard the Ship *Resolution* during Cook's Second Circumnavigation, 1772–1775," in *Understanding Field Science Institutions*, ed. Helena Ekerholm et al. (Sagamore Beach, MA: Science History Publications, 2018), 41–70.
35. Cf. Nicholas Thomas, "Licensed Curiosity: Cook's Pacific Voyages," in *The Cultures of Collecting*, ed. John Elsner and Roger Cardinal (London: Reaktion Books, 1994), 116–36; as well as Mariss, *"A World of New Things"*.
36. On this topic cf. e.g., Simon Schaffer, ed., *The Brokered World: Go-betweens and Global Intelligence, 1770–1820*, Uppsala Studies in History of Science 35 (Sagamore Beach, MA: Science History Publications, 2009); Sebastian Jobs and Gesa Mackenthun, eds., *Agents of Transculturation: Border-crossers, Mediators, Go-betweens*, Cultural Encounters and the Discourses of Scholarship 6 (Münster: Waxmann, 2013).
37. Concerning Tupaia, cf. Anne Salmond, *The Trial of the Cannibal Dog: Captain Cook in the South Seas* (London: Allen Lane, 2003); Glyn Williams, "Tupaia: Polynesian Warrior, Navigator, High Priest—and Artist," in *The Global Eighteenth Century*, ed. Felicity Nussbaum (Baltimore, MD: Johns Hopkins University Press, 2003), 38–51; Joan Druett, *Tupaia: Captain Cook's Polynesian Navigator* (Santa Barbara, CA: Praeger, 2011). For Hititi, see also Laure Marcellesi, "(Re-)Appropriating Trinkets: How to Civilize Polynesia with a Jack-in-the-Box," in *Eighteenth-Century Thing Theory in a Global Context: From Consumerism to Celebrity Culture*, ed. Ileana Popa Baird and Christina Ionescu (Farnham: Ashgate, 2014), 249–68.
38. Cf. Georg Forster, *Voyage round the World: In His Britannic Majesty's Sloop, Resolution, Commanded by Capt. James Cook, during the Years 1772, 3, 4, and 5* (London: White, 1777), Vol. I, 530.
39. Georg Forster reported in his *Voyage* that Hititi had collected a substantial number of curiosities "which he was well convinced would give him weight among his countrymen; and he had acquired such a variety of new ideas, and seen so many distant and unknown countries, that he was persuaded he would attract and demand their attention. The prospect of being courted by every body, and the idea of distinguishing himself by his intimacy with us, by his acquaintance with our manners, and above all, by making use of our fire arms for his diversion, gave him infinite pleasure." Ibid., II, 49.
40. Forster, *Resolution Journal*, III, 435.
41. For an approach located in the history of Christian mission, cf. Renate Dürr, "Early Modern Translation Theories as Mission Theories: A Case Study of José de Acosta 'De procuranda indorum salute' (1588)," in *Cultures of Communication: Theology of Media in Early Modern Europe and Beyond*, ed. Helmuth Puff, Ulrike Strasser, and Christopher Wild (Toronto: University of Toronto Press, 2017), 209–27.

42. Cf. J R. Forster, *Observations Made during a Voyage round the World*, ed. Nicholas Thomas et al. (Honolulu: University of Hawaii Press, 1996), 249.
43. J. R. Forster, *Vocabularies of the Language spoken in the Isles of the South-Sea & of the various Dialects which have Affinity to it; with some Observations for the better Understanding of them, collected by John Reinhold Forster F.R.S.* (1774), 3.
44. Forster, *Resolution Journal*, III, 419.
45. Cf. Vanessa Smith, "Banks, Tupaia, and Mai: Cross-cultural Exchanges and Friendship in the Pacific," *Parergon* 26, no. 2 (2009): 139–60; Smith, *Intimate Strangers: Friendship, Exchange and Pacific Encounters (Critical Perspectives on Empire)* (Cambridge: Cambridge University Press, 2010).
46. Cf. Forster, *Resolution Journal*, II, 326.
47. Cf. ibid., 333.
48. The term "bioprospecting" is derived from the term "prospection," commonly used in mining and the mineral oil industry, where it describes the search for and exploration of mineral resources.
49. Concerning this, cf. Schiebinger, *Plants and Empire*, esp. 73–100.
50. See Vandana Shiva, *Biopiracy: The Plunder of Nature and Knowledge* (Boston, MA: South End Press, 1997); as well Alfred W. Crosby, *The Columbian Exchange: Biological and Cultural Consequences of 1492* (Westport, CT: Greenwood, 1972) for a more markedly historical perspective; also Crosby, *Ecological Imperialism: The Biological Expansion of Europe, 900–1900.* (Cambridge: Cambridge University Press, 1986).
51. "It is amazing how willing they always were to carry us on their backs through the Surf into the boats, or across a river, though often they got no retribution for it. Nothing is here more common than hospitality" (Forster, *Resolution Journal*, III, 395).
52. "Their Language seemed to us very unintelligible; & though I pointed to many things, in order to get the Names of them, they seemed to be too stupid for the signs" (Forster, *Resolution Journal*, IV, 698).
53. Avernus is the name of a crater lake near Pozzuoli, but had been used since antiquity to describe places were pestilential fumes rise from the earth.
54. Ibid., IV, 600.
55. Forster, *Resolution Journal*, IV, 601.
56. Robert Proctor and Londa Schiebinger, eds., *Agnotology: The Making and Unmaking of Ignorance* (Stanford, CA: Stanford University Press, 2008). The term describes the cultural production of ignorance as well as its study. Agnotology was consciously conceptualized as a counterweight to epistemology, so as to be able to study the precondition for ignorance. "My hope for devising a new term was to suggest the opposite, namely, the historicity and artifactuality of non-knowing and the non-known – and the potential fruitfulness of studying such things" (ibid., 27).
57. Ibid., 3.
58. Nicholas Thomas, *Entangled Objects: Exchange, Material Culture, and Colonialism in the Pacific* (Cambridge, MA: Harvard University Press, 1991).
59. Susanne Zantop, *Colonial Fantasies: Conquest, Family, and Nation in Precolonial Germany, 1770–1870* (Durham, NC: Duke University Press, 1997); Hans-Jürgen Lüsebrink, "Von der Faszination zur Wissenssystematisierung: die koloniale Welt im Diskurs der Aufklärung," in *Das Europa der Aufklärung und die außereuropäische koloniale Welt*, ed. H.-J. Lüsebrink (Göttingen: Wallstein-Verlag, 2006), 9–18; Yomb May, "Imperiale Diskurse: Forschungsreisen des 18. Jahrhunderts als Antizipation des Kolonialismus," *KulturPoetik* 7, no. 2 (2007): 284–305; Anja Hall, *Paradies auf Erden? Mythenbildung als Form von Fremdwahrnehmung: der Südsee-Mythos in Schlüsselphasen der deutschen Literatur* (Würzburg: Königshausen & Neumann, 2008).
60. For a discussion of studies on this topic, cf. Dürr et al., "Forum: Globalizing Early Modern German History," *German History* 31 (2013): 366–82.

61. For a theoretical approach see Natalie Zemon Davis, "Decentering History: Local Stories and Cultural Crossings in a Global World," *History and Theory* 50, no. 2 (2011): 188–202; and Hans Medick, "Turning Global? Microhistory in Extension," *Historische Anthropologie* 24, no. 2 (2016): 241–52.

Bibliography

Anon. [James Magra or Matra]. *A Journal of a Voyage round the World in His Majesty's Ship Endeavour, in the Years 1768, 1769, 1770, and 1771; Undertaken in Pursuit of Natural Knowledge, at the Desire of the Royal Society*. London: T. Becket and P. A. de Hondt, 1771.

Anon. [John Marra]. *Journal of the Resolution's Voyage, in 1772, 1773, 1774 and 1775*. Dublin: Caleb Jenkin and John Beatty, 1776.

Banks, Joseph. *The Indian and Pacific Correspondence of Sir Joseph Banks, 1768–1820*, 4 vols., ed. Neil Chambers. London: Pickering and Chatto, 2008–11.

Bleichmar, Daniela, ed. *Science in the Spanish and Portuguese Empires, 1500–1800*. Stanford, CA: Stanford University Press, 2009.

Cook, James. *The Journals of Captain James Cook on his Voyages of Discovery*, 4 vols., ed. John C. Beaglehole. Cambridge: Hakluyt Society at the University Press, 1955–67.

Crosby, Alfred W. *The Columbian Exchange: Biological and Cultural Consequences of 1492*. Westport, CT: Greenwood, 1972.

———. *Ecological Imperialism: The Biological Expansion of Europe, 900–1900*. Cambridge: Cambridge University Press, 1986.

Davis, Natalie Zemon. "Decentering History: Local Stories and Cultural Crossings in a Global World." *History and Theory* 50, no. 2 (2011): 188–202.

Deacon, Margaret. *Scientists and the Sea, 1650–1900: A Study of Marine Science*. London: Academy Press, 1971.

Dettelbach, Michael. "'A Kind of Linnaean Being': Forster and Eighteenth-Century Natural History." In *Johann Reinhold Forster: Observations Made during a Voyage round the World*, ed. Nicholas Thomas et al., lv–lxxiv. Honolulu: University of Hawaii Press, 1996.

Dietz, Bettina. "Making Natural History: Doing the Enlightenment." *Central European History* 43 (2010): 25–46.

Druett, Joan. *Tupaia: Captain Cook's Polynesian Navigator*. Santa Barbara, CA: Praeger, 2011.

Dürr, Renate. "Early Modern Translation Theories as Mission Theories: A Case Study of José de Acosta 'De procuranda indorum salute' (1588)." In *Cultures of Communication: Theology of Media in Early Modern Europe and Beyond*, ed. Helmuth Puff, Ulrike Strasser, and Christopher Wild, 209–27. Toronto: University of Toronto Press, 2017.

——— (with Ronnie Hsia, Carina Johnson, Ulrike Strasser, and Merry Wiesner-Hanks). "Forum: Globalizing Early Modern German History." *German History* 31 (2013): 366–82.

Finamore, Daniel, ed. *Maritime History as World History*. Salem, MA: Peabody Essex Museum, 2004.

Forster, Georg. *Voyage round the World: In His Britannic Majesty's Sloop, Resolution, Commanded by Capt. James Cook, during the Years 1772, 3, 4, and 5*. London: White 1777.

Forster, Johann Reinhold. *Lectures on Natural History & especially on Mineralogy Part the 1st containing the Introductory Lectures & the Earths & Stones, with the Petrefactions or all the true Fossils, began to be read & composed 1767 & 1768*. Staatsbibliothek Berlin. Ms. germ. oct. 22a.

———. Ms or. oct. 62. *Vocabularies of the Language spoken in the Isles of the South-Sea & of the various Dialects which have Affinity to it; with some Observations for the better Understanding of them, collected by John Reinhold Forster F.R.S.* 1774.

———. *The Resolution Journal of Johann Reinhold Forster*, 4 vols., ed. Michael E. Hoare. London: Hakluyt Society, 1982.

———. *Observations Made during a Voyage round the World*, ed. Nicholas Thomas et al. Honolulu: University of Hawaii Press, 1996.

Foucault, Michel. "Of Other Spaces: Utopias and Heterotopias." In *Rethinking Architecture: A Reader in Cultural Theory*, ed. Neil Leach, 330–36. New York: Routledge, 1997.

Fusaro, Maria, ed. *Maritime History as Global History* (*Research in Maritime History* 43). St. John's, Newfoundland: Internat. Maritime Economic History Assoc., 2010.

Gilroy, Paul. *The Black Atlantic: Modernity and Double Consciousness*. Cambridge, MA: Harvard University Press, 1995.

Gordon, Joseph Stuart. *Reinhold and Georg Forster in England, 1766–1780*. Durham, NC: PhD dissertation, Duke University, 1975.

Hall, Anja. *Paradies auf Erden? Mythenbildung als Form von Fremdwahrnehmung; der Südsee-Mythos in Schlüsselphasen der deutschen Literatur*. Würzburg: Königshausen & Neumann, 2008.

Hoare, Michael E. *The Tactless Philosopher: Johann Reinhold Forster (1729–98)*. Melbourne: Hawthorn Press, 1976.

Jobs, Sebastian, and Gesa Mackenthun, eds. *Agents of Transculturation: Border-crossers, Mediators, Go-betweens* (Cultural Encounters and the Discourses of Scholarship 6). Münster: Waxmann, 2013.

Klein, Bernhard, and Gesa Mackenthun, eds. *Sea Changes: Historicizing the Ocean*. New York: Routledge, 2004.

Latour, Bruno. "Die Logistik der Immutable mobiles." In *Mediengeographie. Theorie—Analyse—Diskussion* (*Medienumbrüche* 26), ed. Jörg Döring and Tristan Thielmann, 111–44. Bielefeld: transcript, 2009.

———. "Visualisation and Cognition: Drawing Things Together." In *Knowledge and Society: Studies in the Sociology of Culture Past and Present* 6 (1986): 1–40.

Lüsebrink, Hans-Jürgen. "Von der Faszination zur Wissenssystematisierung: die koloniale Welt im Diskurs der Aufklärung." In *Das Europa der Aufklärung und die außereuropäische koloniale Welt*, ed. H.-J. Lüsebrink, 9–18. Göttingen: Wallstein-Verlag, 2006.

Marcellesi, Laure. "(Re-)Appropriating Trinkets: How to Civilize Polynesia with a Jack-in-the-Box." In *Eighteenth-Century Thing Theory in a Global Context: From Consumerism to Celebrity Culture*, ed. Ileana Popa Baird and Christina Ionescu, 249–68. Farnham: Ashgate, 2014.

Mariss, Anne. "A Library in the Field: The Use of Books aboard the Ship *Resolution* during Cook's Second Circumnavigation, 1772–1775." In *Understanding Field Science Institutions*, ed. Helena Ekerholm et al. Sagamore Beach, MA: Science History Publications, 2018.

———. *"A World of New Things": Praktiken der Naturgeschichte bei Johann Reinhold Forster*. Frankfurt a.M.: Campus, 2015.

———. "Sprache und(Miss-)Verstehen: Formen kollektiver Wissensproduktion im Umfeld der zweiten Cook-Expedition (1772–75)." In *Georg Forster-Studien* 19 (2014), ed. Stefan Greif and Michael Ewert, 45–78.

May, Yomb. "Imperiale Diskurse: Forschungsreisen des 18. Jahrhunderts als Antizipation des Kolonialismus." *KulturPoetik* 7, no. 2 (2007): 284–305.

Medick, Hans. "Turning Global? Microhistory in Extension." *Historische Anthropologie* 24, no. 2 (2016): 241–52.
Moser. "Nachschrift von einer Handschrift J. R. Forster's in der Kön. öffentlichen Bibliothek zu Stuttgart." *Serapeum: Zeitschrift für Bibliothekswissenschaft, Handschriftenkunde und ältere Literatur* 3 (1840): 33–38.
Newell, Jennifer. *Trading Nature: Tahitians, Europeans, and Ecological Exchange*. Honolulu: University of Hawaii Press, 2010.
Pratt, Mary Louise. "Arts of the Contact Zone." *Profession* (1991): 33–40.
———. *Imperial Eyes: Travel Writing and Transculturation*. London: Routledge, 1992.
Proctor, Robert, and Londa Schiebinger, eds. *Agnotology: The Making and Unmaking of Ignorance*. Stanford, CA: Stanford University Press, 2008.
Rediker, Marcus. *Between the Devil and the Deep Blue Sea: Merchant Seamen, Pirates, and the Anglo-American Maritime World, 1700–1750*. Cambridge: Cambridge University Press, 1987.
Rensch, Karl H. "Forster's Polynesian Linguistics." In Johann Reinhold Forster. *Observations Made during a Voyage round the World*, 383–400. Honolulu: University of Hawaii Press, 1996.
Salmond, Anne. *The Trial of the Cannibal Dog: Captain Cook in the South Seas*. London: Allen Lane, 2003.
Schaffer, Simon. "Visions of Empire: Afterword." In *Visions of Empire: Voyages, Botany, and Representations of Nature*, ed. David P. Miller and Peter H. Reill, 335–352. Cambridge: Cambridge University Press, 1996.
———, ed. *The Brokered World: Go-betweens and Global Intelligence, 1770–1820* (Uppsala Studies in History of Science 35). Sagamore Beach, MA: Science History Publications, 2009.
Schiebinger, Londa. *Plants and Empire: Colonial Bioprospecting in the Atlantic World*. Cambridge, MA: Harvard University Press, 2004.
Schiebinger, Londa, and Claudia Swan, eds. *Colonial Botany: Science, Commerce, and Politics in the Early Modern World*. Philadelphia, PA: University of Pennsylvania Press, 2005.
Shiva, Vandana. *Biopiracy: The Plunder of Nature and Knowledge*. Boston, MA: South End Press, 1997.
Sivasundaram, Sujit. "Sciences and the Global: On Methods, Questions, and Theory." *Isis* 101(1) (2010): 146–58.
Smith, Vanessa. "Banks, Tupaia, and Mai: Cross-cultural Exchanges and Friendship in the Pacific." *Parergon* 26, no. 2 (2009): 139–60.
———. *Intimate Strangers: Friendship, Exchange and Pacific Encounters* (*Critical Perspectives on Empire*). Cambridge: Cambridge University Press, 2010.
Sparrman, Anders. "Anders Sparrman's Journal: Sweden, South Africa, New Zealand, French Polynesia, Tonga, Fiji, Vanuatu, New Caledonia, Easter Islands, Marquesas Islands, Argentina." In *The Linnaeus Apostles: Global Science and Adventure*, Vol. 5, ed. Lars Hansen. London: IK Foundation, 2007.
Thomas, Nicholas. *Entangled Objects: Exchange, Material Culture, and Colonialism in the Pacific*. Cambridge, MA: Harvard University Press, 1991.
———. "Licensed Curiosity: Cook's Pacific Voyages." In *The Cultures of Collecting*, ed. John Elsner and Roger Cardinal, 116–36. London: Reaktion Books, 1994.
Uhlig, Ludwig. *Georg Forster: Lebensabenteuer eines gelehrten Weltbürgers (1754–1794)*. Göttingen: Vandenhoeck & Ruprecht, 2004.

Williams, Glyn. "Tupaia: Polynesian Warrior, Navigator, High Priest—and Artist." In *The Global Eighteenth Century*, ed. Felicity Nussbaum, 38–51. Baltimore, MD: Johns Hopkins University Press, 2003.

Zantop, Susanne. *Colonial Fantasies: Conquest, Family, and Nation in Precolonial Germany, 1770–1870*. Durham, NC: Duke University Press, 1997.

Zimmermann, Heinrich. *Heinrich Zimmermanns von Wißloch in der Pfalz, Reise um die Welt, mit Capitain Cook*. Mannheim: Schwan, 1781.

Chapter 6

ENGINEERING EMPIRE
German Influence on Chinese Industrialization, 1880–1925

Shellen Wu

The Age of Exploration initially brought Europeans to the Pacific as traders, adventurers, and missionaries. By the nineteenth century, in addition to trading companies, the British, French, and the Russian empires, and other European states, sponsored scientific expeditions with the dual missions of collecting scientific knowledge as well as increasing the scope of their imperial territories. European presence in the Pacific, and in East Asia in particular, followed larger historical developments, including the rise in importance of sea power and trade, the development of the nation-state, and, by the nineteenth century, the unleashing of the transformative processes of industrialization across the globe.

The considerable literature on imperialism and European colonies in the Pacific has focused attention disproportionately on the roles of science and religion in the European encounter with Asia, largely overlooking the contributions of an essential actor in the spread of industrialization around the world: the engineer. This chapter offers a partial corrective by examining the contributions of some of the earliest German engineers who worked in China in the late nineteenth and early twentieth centuries. The historian of science Margaret Jacob traced to the early modern period and the industrial revolution in eighteenth century Britain the rise of a new kind of professional, one imbued with a mechanical view of the world.[1] The engineers who emerged from this first wave of industrialization subsequently helped to spread their knowledge and skills across continental Europe and, along with the expansion of European empires, around the world.

The development of the engineering profession shows how specific historical trends fostered its growth and created a social niche for its members. As the German states recovered from Napoleonic occupation in the first half of the nineteenth century, they laid the foundations for industrialization in the

---

Notes from this chapter begin on page 166.

following decades. Friedrich Krupp opened the Krupp cast steelworks in 1811, although the business did not prosper until under the leadership of his son Alfred in the 1840s. The first German train lines were constructed in the 1830s, and August Borsig opened his locomotive factory in Berlin in 1837. Concurrently, in the decade between the mid-1820s and mid-1830s, nearly all the German states sponsored the founding of technical schools.[2] At the same time that educational reforms were transforming the universities into centers of advanced research and development, technical education received a boost. German educators saw the new modes of production as the only salvation to lift Germany from economic backwardness and overpopulation.[3] These technical schools created a steady supply of skilled workers for new industries in Germany and abroad. These efforts paved the way for rapid German industrialization in the second half of the nineteenth century, but also set the stage for the export of German expertise overseas, in particular to East Asian countries in search of their own economic miracles.

The Prussian state carefully cultivated the image of Germany as the leading producer of technical institutions and scientific and technological advances. From the late nineteenth century into the 1920s, the Prussian Ministry of Culture kept careful track of foreign students studying at technical schools in Germany as well as visitors to various institutions of higher learning.[4] In 1904, when the Qing official Duan Fang secured funding to send eighty Chinese students to study in Europe, the German Consulate in Nanjing immediately updated officials in the Foreign Ministry in Berlin as to any of these students who could potentially attend German institutions.[5] The records also reveal that in the years from 1908 to 1912, over thirty Chinese students studied in various Berlin and Hannover schools. Language issues proved difficult to overcome—although Chinese students enrolled in schools, none matriculated with degrees in that four-year period. Government and school officials at various institutions discussed making special testing arrangements for these foreign students, while others bemoaned the dilution of the worth of a German degree should foreign students be passed without undergoing the full rigor required at these prestigious institutions. Considerable handwringing and debate between officials and educators continued into the 1920s without leading to a satisfactory solution.[6]

For short-term visitors, on the other hand, German technical institutions became a mandatory stop on their tour of Europe. Japanese visitors, whether they were engineers or professors in institutions in Japan or for the South Manchurian Railroad on the Asian mainland, regularly wrote to the Foreign Ministry to request tours of laboratories and schools in Germany. At times the sterling reputation of German technical education worked against the instructors at these institutions. So many foreign visitors "dropped by" without appointment that it caused considerable grumbling among the teachers, who saw the steady stream of visitors as a source of disruption during instructional time.[7]

Such grumbling from instructors aside, it was clear that the German state encouraged and actively sought to foster Germany's reputation as the prime training ground for engineers. In East Asia, the Foreign Ministry not only cultivated this reputation but also went a step further. Starting in 1886 a series of secret memorandums circulated in Berlin between Reich Chancellor Otto von Bismarck's office and the Ministry of Public Works.[8] At the behest of the German ambassador to China, Max von Brandt (1835–1915),[9] Bismarck's office requested that the Ministry of Public Works provide a list of around twelve railway engineers to send to China and learn the language. Once in China, these engineers would be affiliated with the embassy and provide German economic interests with an added advantage against the rivalry of other states. As originally conceived, these engineers would "create an advantage for German industry by placing them in the first line of consideration for the building of railroads."[10] Since the Ministry of Public Works could only access those engineers already working in the state railroad bureaucracy, and who, moreover, were willing to leave their secure positions for an extended and possibly dangerous assignment on the other side of the world, the task proved difficult. The ministry eventually supplied four names, two high-ranked railway engineers, Scheidtweiler and Assman, and two lower-ranked employees, Küster and Löhr. The four men left for China in 1887 under the guise of translation interns for the embassy. The small and treacherous diplomatic community in Beijing at the time, according to Brandt, necessitated the subterfuge. The German plan called for the placement of engineers in Chinese industrial works, where they would be in direct competition with engineers from Britain, France, Belgium, and the United States.

In Asia, and China in particular, German efforts encountered the more firmly entrenched diplomatic and trade interests of the British and French empires. By the 1880s, the German Foreign Ministry had become increasingly concerned with the advancement of German interests. The longtime German ambassador to China, Max von Brandt, took a particularly aggressive stance regarding German industries in China, stating that he "takes the view that the work of diplomats nowadays in countries such as China is in the first line one of national economic [interest], that is, to forcefully demand the sales of the industrial products."[11] Given the possibility of opposition, the plan to send railway engineers to China remained a secret, not only to the other European powers in China, but also to the Reichstag. Funding for the program came out of the chancellor's discretionary funds, precluding the need for Reichstag approval. The engineers signed agreements for a minimum of five years of service in China, with a pay of 500 marks a month for the higher-ranked engineers, and 300 marks for the lower-ranked.[12]

This first small coterie of engineers arrived at an opportune time. From the Chinese vantage point, in the nearly five decades since the First Opium War (1839-1842), the debate over the role of Western knowledge had reached a critical point. By the 1860s, the devolution of power from the court to provincial leaders during the devastating Taiping Rebellion (1850–62) had allowed certain provincial leaders like Li Hongzhang and Zhang Zhidong to develop their alternate centers of powers, with extensive entourages of secretaries and consultants (*mufus*) now also containing Western advisors. These provincial leaders and their advocates at court recognized the importance of technical expertise to the success of their industrial projects. Foreign engineers helped to construct railroads and industries in China until a sufficient force of Chinese technicians had been developed.

When the Qing general and statesman Zuo Zongtang established the Fuzhou Shipyard and Naval Academy in 1866, the first such institution in China, he hired a team of French engineers under the direction of Prosper Giquel to oversee the technical aspects.[13] Similarly, in the 1870s at the Jiangnan Arsenal in Shanghai and Li Hongzhong's various industrial projects in Tianjin and northeast China, Qing officials relied on groups of foreign engineers.[14] So when Germany launched its bid to dominate the supply of foreign technical consultants in China in the 1880s, they were following behind the footsteps of the French and British. To catch up with the presence of other nationals in Chinese industries and arsenals, therefore, required a particularly aggressive push on the part of the German Foreign Ministry.

Starting in the 1870s, Li Hongzhang in the northeast and Zhang Zhidong in the treaty port city of Hankou began supporting large-scale industries, in recognition of Western technological superiority. Their efforts followed closely behind the establishment of coastal arsenals in Fuzhou and Shanghai in the late 1860s. The first modern Chinese industries developed under the auspices of "official supervision and merchant management," or the *guandu shangban* system. The system developed out of the government salt monopoly, and operated on the assumption that private enterprise best handled the logistics of commerce while government officials looked out for state and public interests. The fiscal weakness of the Qing central government and the devolution of power to provincial power centers, however, effectively placed control of these industries in the hands of a few reformers, with funding coming from provincial sources. Aside from funding issues, the structure at the top of the industries little affected the day-to-day running of the factories and mines. Instead, control rested in the hands of the technical staff, and until World War I it was almost entirely foreign.

Zhang Zhidong began planning a modern ironworks in the 1880s while serving as governor general of Guangdong, several decades after the first large-scale efforts to import Western science and technology had commenced along the coast. In a lengthy memorial from 1885 on the question of naval defenses, Zhang repeatedly invoked the need for both educational initiatives and the importation of technology. After discussing the manufacturing specifications of armament factories in England, Germany, and the United States, Zhang observed that, "the wealth and power of foreigners rely entirely upon their coal and iron. China's [deposits] of coal and iron far surpasses the rest of the world."[15] At this juncture, Zhang advocated the establishment of an official bureau (*kuangwu ju*) to handle mining affairs and the recruitment of merchants to develop coal and iron deposits.

In 1889, Zhang ordered machinery from England for a planned iron foundry. When he was appointed governor general of Hu-Guang, the machinery followed him northward to the river port city of Hankou on the Yangzi River. At the time, Zhang believed that both coal and iron resources would be readily available in Hubei.[16] In Hubei he selected a site across from his Yamen offices with a large river-front access and room for expansion, which formed the heart of what later became the Hanyeping Coal and Iron Company.[17] The company name combined the names of the three pillar industries under its auspices: Hanyang Iron Foundry, Daye Iron Mines, and Pingxiang Coalmines. In addition to the ironworks, Zhang built an arsenal, a cotton mill, and mines to supply fuel for the foundry. He also planned railway lines, launching an ambitious bid for modern industries in the Chinese interior.

In northeastern China during the same period, Li Hongzhang opened Kaiping Mines in 1877. The first railway in China was built in 1881 to facilitate the transport of coal from Kaiping, and stretched 10 km from Tangshan to Xugezhuang. The engineer in charge of that project, an Englishman named Kinder, eventually became head engineer of the China Railway Company. All of these projects required the purchase of everything from cement to heavy machinery, and even coal, before the building of infrastructure to link the major coal deposits in the interior of the country to the industries on the coast. To oversee these projects, Zhang and Li hired foreign experts.

The potential development of a China market drew the interest of steel and machinery producers across Europe and America. In the 1880s and 1890s, in particular, Germany looked for export markets for its burgeoning heavy industries. At this juncture, four railway engineers arrived in China in 1887/88.[18] Of the four men, the Prussian state building master (*Regierungsbaumeister*) Peter Scheidtweiler proved particularly adept at learning the Chinese language, in addition to already possessing good English skills. By the end of 1889, the German legation in Beijing, in cooperation with its consulate in Guangzhou, arranged for Scheidtweiler to travel to Shanghai to meet one of Zhang Zhidong's private secretaries.

As Brandt had hoped for, Zhang engaged Scheidtweiler's services for Tls. 200 per month, with an additional Tls. 100 during the months he had to travel for work. (At the contemporary exchange rates, Tls. 200 amounted to approximately 960 marks, Tls. 300 to 1,350 marks.) "Your duty," Max von Brandt informed Scheidtweiler in November 1889, "is to gain the trust of the [secretary] and through him, the Governor-general [Zhang Zhidong], and where possible to win influence, if not the placement of technical advisors, and seize for German industries the imminent building of railroads."[19] In addition to his Chinese pay, Scheidtweiler retained the 500 marks the German legation paid him as a "translator intern" and 20 marks per day when he traveled for work, as legislated by the Prussian legal code for civil employees of his rank. The Chinese pay was already high for a railway engineer. For the next six years while he served Zhang Zhidong and drew a second income from the German legation, Scheidtweiler did exceedingly well financially. In November 1890, Brandt observed with some acerbity that during the previous six months Scheidtweiler had earned at least 2,100 marks per month, thus drawing a higher pay than the chief engineer of the China Railway Company, the Englishman Mr. Kinder, and members of the diplomatic service, including himself.[20]

At the Hanyang iron foundry in Hankou, Scheidtweiler found himself in an international community of technical experts working for Zhang Zhidong, including Belgian, English, and fellow German nationals. The technical staff was largely isolated from the Chinese population. These men brought with them knowledge from their previous employment in their respective countries; the Englishmen who had worked at the Teesside Ironworks recommended the import of English machines, while the Germans argued for the superiority of German drills and locomotives. Despite the high pay, personnel turnover was extremely high, due in large part, according to Scheidtweiler, to most foreign employees' inability to communicate with Chinese officials and the unfamiliarity of the surroundings. In this regard, the "translators" trained by the German embassy staff immediately possessed an advantage. For a number of years, the Belgian workers were the chief competition for the Germans. Emile Braive, a Belgian national and self-titled "China Inspector General of Mines," had previously worked for the Belgian legation and secured large orders for the Belgian company Cockerill. To justify his double income, Scheidtweiler intrigued against the other foreign nationals and advocated the superiority of German industrial products.

Scheidtweiler soon earned Brandt's respect by both ingratiating himself to his Chinese superiors and directing large orders to German companies: 30,000 marks for German pumps, 160,000 marks for German coke ovens, and 40,000 marks for German dynamite added up to an impressive list. In the years 1890–91 alone, Scheidtweiler reported orders originating from Germany totaling 1.17 million marks, including 48,000 marks for cement, and 119,000 marks for locomotives and workshop tools.[21]

During the period of Scheidtweiler's tenure, rumors surfaced in the German community in Hankou that Scheidtweiler was ordering large amounts of unnecessary equipment for his own enrichment. Brandt, extremely pleased with Scheidtweiler's diligent advocacy of German industries, dismissed these rumors as idle gossip spread by trading firms, who were losing contracts and their cut of profits when Scheidtweiler directly contacted factories in Germany. Whether or not Scheidtweiler personally benefited from the extent of his orders, his successor Heinrich Hildebrand pointed out in his reports that upon inspection by a seasoned mining engineer, a number of expensive German machines had turned out to be superfluous.

German mines, like Chinese ones, on average encountered more faulting than British coalmines.[22] The more powerful (and expensive) German drills and pumps, for example, better suited the conditions at Hanyang. As a trained railway engineer, educated in the highly specialized German system, Scheidtweiler lacked any real expertise in mining. He was certainly not qualified to order mining equipment, even with the best of intentions. His exceptional track record of promoting German industries, however, ensured the success of the "translator intern" program.

In 1893, Scheidtweiler was joined at Hanyang by fellow German national Heinrich Hildebrand, who had headed to China with a second group of four engineers in the "translator intern" program.[23] Scheidtweiler returned to Germany in 1894 with high commendations from the German embassy in China and the Foreign Ministry, a promotion to railway construction and operations inspector (1891), a double pension for the period of his service in China, and a small fortune from his extra income. Peter Scheidtweiler's success story contrasted markedly with the misfortunes of the three colleagues who had accompanied him to China. The fate of this small sample of foreign technicians in China likely reflects trends in the broader foreign population in China, with disease and homesickness claiming most expatriates.

The other higher-ranked engineer, Assman, never learned sufficient Chinese, and lacking as well the English language skills necessary to work for the predominantly British merchant communities in Shanghai and Hong Kong, he failed to make any headway in employment in China. He made several trips to explore the possibilities of building a railway line in Manchuria, but, unlike Scheidtweiler, did not manage to win the patronage of any high-level Qing officials. Eventually in 1891 he requested release from his service in China to work for the Royal Railway Service of Siam, where, however, he soon died of malaria.[24] The lower-ranked technician Löhr worked under Scheidtweiler for a time at Hanyang before requesting to return to Germany due to bad health. Küster taught at the German-run railway school in Tianjin under the patronage of Li Hongzhang. Upon his return to Germany in 1895 he could only find work in the same rank as when he had left eight years previously. He sent the Foreign Ministry long reports with detailed charts projecting lost income because of his lack of promotion during his six and a half years in China, and decrying the injustice of his situation after sacrificing for his fatherland. Finally, the Railway Administration of Saarbrücken, where he had a new position, fired him for refusal to work.[25]

Early in 1894 Heinrich Hildebrand began working for Zhang Zhidong. The capital and political consensus needed for the long-planned railroads of China had yet to fully materialize and Hildebrand found most of Zhang's foreign employees scrounging for work. Hanyang Ironworks idled for the lack of coke. The globalization of industrialization created opportunities for those with technical skills. At the same time, the demand for coking coal had pushed the technology of mining forward by the need for deeper shafts and refining processes. Geological conditions determine whether surface or deep underground mining would be more suitable for particular coal seams, but in general in places with long histories of mining, surface deposits would be exhausted first. By the nineteenth century, large underground mines required sophisticated drainage and ventilation systems, wagons and tracks for conveying coal underground to the surface, and in the near vicinity of the pithead, coal washing equipment to remove surface dirt and impurities, and therefore also lower the cost of transportation.[26] Economic development, political boundaries, and nature combined to limit or encourage industrial development. The Ruhr valley, for example, had risen to prominence in the first half of the nineteenth century due to the fortuitous conjunction of easy river transport and wide availability of coking coal.[27]

Initially, mining engineers attempted to find ready sources of coal in Hanyang's immediate vicinity. The coalmines at Manganshan in Hubei, close to the Tayeh Iron Mines, however, failed to deliver usable coking coal and were eventually abandoned with heavy losses due to wasted machinery and time.[28] Chemical analysis of coal deposits in Hubei uniformly found high levels of sulfur. In order to keep the ovens at Hanyang working, large amounts of coke had to be imported from Kaiping or even more expensive foreign sources. Coal available for sale in Shanghai came from Taiwan, Japan, Australia, and England.

China possessed highly lucrative deposits of coal, and by the 1870s a large demand already existed in Asia. However, the successful exploitation of these natural resources required large investments of capital, not only in modern machinery at the mines but also in infrastructure, railroads, and docks to bring the product to the international market. To achieve coking coal with high carbon content and low levels of contaminants also required coal washing and refining processes. Certainly Li Hongzhang at Kaiping and Zhang Zhidong recognized the importance of coalmines as the fuel source for industry and railroads. The infrastructure and supply network, however, took time to develop—and enormous capital investments.

The search for coal became the top priority at Hanyeping in the early 1890s. In the same period, the devaluation of silver had nearly doubled the cost of British engineers, who were paid in pound sterling rather than the local currency. The lack of progress in the search for coal added to the incentive for Qing officials to replace them with cheaper and equally competent German mining engineers. Both Scheidtweiler and Hildebrand requested that the Foreign Ministry send out mining engineers from Germany to take charge of Hanyang. In February 1892, Scheidtweiler summarized the problem in his regular report to Brandt:

"Thus far, my experience in China indicates that in the near future the building of railroads in China will always be in connection with mining. For example, the Tianjin Railroad has to thank as its source Kaiping Mines, and the railroads on Taiwan have essentially as their purpose the transportation of coal to the coast."[29] With barely enough work for one higher-ranked railway engineer, Scheidtweiler decided to make a graceful exit and return home.

Within the foreign diplomatic circles, at least, Hildebrand's role as a German agent became an open secret. Nevertheless, he gained the trust of his Chinese superiors, and in May 1896 was named the technical leader of Zhang's planned Shanghai–Wusong–Nanjing railway. His influence brought into Chinese employment two other German engineers trained by the embassy and his brother Peter Hildebrand, also a Prussian railway engineer. Severe financial problems forced Zhang Zhidong to sell the Hanyang Ironworks and related mines. After stalled negotiations with, among others, the German company Krupp, and a French-Belgian consortium, the merchant official Sheng Xuanhuai became Hildebrand's new employer in 1896. Hildebrand remained confident that his leading position under Sheng could foster closer Sino-German ties.

Despite Hildebrand's enthusiasm, in November of 1896 the new German ambassador Baron Edmund von Heyking reported to Chancellor Schillingsfürst that their "outlook for participation in the building of trains in China is worse than it has ever been."[30] Chinese railways, with the lucrative prospect of large industrial orders and high-interest loans, had attracted enormous interest and pressure from the British, Russians, French, and Americans. At a private audience with Li Hongzhang, Heyking reported with pleasure the presence of a photograph in Li's private sitting room of Li's meeting with Bismarck. However, Li refused to make any concrete promises to the German ambassador. When the British won the financing contract for the Shanghai–Wusong–Nanjing railroad, Hildebrand and the German engineers he recruited immediately fell from favor.

Unbeknownst to the German engineers in China, naval and court circles in Berlin had already formulated plans for the seizure of a treaty port in China. The Sino-Japanese War exposed Chinese vulnerability in the northeast. In 1897, the murder of two German Catholic missionaries in Shandong province provided the necessary pretext for the German government to make territorial and other compensation demands. In December 1897, the Reichstag was informed that Jiaozhou's acquisition was a fait accompli. In the same month, the first Naval Bill was introduced to the parliament. By March 1898, the Reichstag would pass the bill and allot 400 million RM to the construction of an imperial navy. China became the new arena for the balance of power among European empires. From 1885 to 1898, German policy in East Asia had transitioned from indirect economic influence to full-blown imperialism. For engineers like the Hildebrand brothers, their experience under Qing employment made for an easy transition to the planned German railway lines in Shandong. Representing the Shandong

Railway Company, the subsequent years saw Heinrich Hildebrand as director of operations, responsible for negotiating the railway protocols with then governor of Shandong, Yuan Shikai.

Railway engineers like Scheidtweiler and Hildebrand at Hanyang gave way to mining engineers. In one example of how recruitment worked during this period, in November 1891 the Qing merchant official and Li Hongzhang's protégé, Sheng Xuanhuai, corresponded with the German consul in Zhifu, Dr. Lenz. Sheng requested the German consul's recommendation for a suitably qualified mining engineer for employment in a planned mining enterprise in Shandong province. Sheng requested that the engineer have the appropriate credentials and familiarity with coal and iron mining, capable of surveying and machine maintenance, and knowledgeable about the smelting process. For these and any further skills, the said engineer would be well compensated and given free accommodations, although Sheng could not guarantee a European-style house.

With alacrity Dr. Lenz forwarded Sheng's request to the German ambassador in Beijing, Max von Brandt, and to the Foreign Ministry in Berlin.[31] A German mining engineer placed in a position of leadership, even in a Chinese mine, would not only ensure a steady stream of confidential reports regarding progress at the mine, but might also steer future orders of heavy machinery, worth millions, to German firms, as the precedence of German agents at Hanyang had shown. This example shows one way in which Sheng Xuanhuai, Li Hongzhang, and Zhang Zhidong acquired technical experts from abroad. In cases of a specific need, they also contacted the Qing legation in Berlin to inquire about candidates for an open position. Once in Qing employment, German engineers sang the praises of German industry and encouraged the hiring of other Germans, in some instances personally wiring companies in Germany to send employees. At the height of German success in China, not only Hanyang but also industries established by Li Hongzhang fell under heavy German influence.

The German firm Krupp reaped handsome profits from supplying weapons to the Qing, in addition to military advisors and engineers. The railway engineer Küster, for example, worked under a representative from Krupp named Baur at the Tianjin Railway School. In addition to his duties at the Imperial Chinese Maritime Customs, the German-national Gustav Detring served as an unofficial advisor to Li Hongzhang. One reporter for the *Shanghai Mercury* complained in 1893 that "'Made in Germany' on every article is now the motto of the day in Tientsin, and unless things bear these magic words the Viceroy [Li Hongzhang] and Haikwan Taotai will have none of them."[32]

In the search for a viable coal source, the German Gustav Leinung became the longest-serving foreign engineer in Hanyeping Coal and Iron Companies. Leinung had started his employment as a superintendent of Tayeh Iron Mines in Hubei before joining another German mining engineer in the exploration of local mines at Pingxiang in 1896. The town lay on the border between Hubei and Jiangxi provinces, in close proximity to water transportation. Before branch lines connecting the mining area to main railway lines had been built, Pingxiang delivered approximately thirty thousand tons of coal per year by water. Locals had been mining coal in the region since the Tang dynasty (618–907), although before the arrival of Hanyang engineers, operations remained small scale, with shallow shafts and limited production.[33]

According to Leinung's estimates, Pingxiang was located in a basin about three miles wide with ten coal seams, five of them workable and with a total thickness of eight meters. "The quantity of coal contained in this range … is estimated to amount to over 500 million tons, sufficient to supply the mines with coal for more than two hundred years at a daily output of 8,000 tons. The coal, besides being a good steam and blacksmith coal, is specially a splendid coking coal, containing 20–30 percent bitumen, yielding a very firm coke."[34] A solution finally appeared for Hanyang's fuel shortage problem.

At the high point of his career, Leinung had a team of fifteen fellow German mining engineers under his control, as well as a mining academy. A reporter visiting the mines in 1905 described the valley as a German "colony" nestled improbably in the Chinese interior.[35] On the evening of his visit, the reporter witnessed a friendly game of bowling between two five-man teams of German staff members. Based on Leinung's extensive correspondence, including a long-standing friendship with Heinrich Cordes, a representative of the Deutsch Asiatische Bank in China, his sincerity in serving the Chinese could not be doubted. Having devoted nearly twenty years of his life to Pingxiang coalmines and played an essential role from its founding, Leinung strongly identified with its success. In 1907, during a financial crisis at the mines, he personally attempted to attract German funding for the ironworks.[36]

The collapse of the Qing dynasty in 1911 barely interrupted the rush to exploit mineral resources by both foreign and Chinese enterprises. The new Republican government initially attempted to establish the study of geological sciences along a German model. However, the precarious state of Chinese politics and finances after the fall of the Qing bode ill for new education ventures. In 1913, the Ministry of Agriculture and Commerce hired the German geologist and mining engineer Dr. Friedrich Solger to head a planned school of geology. Before traveling to China, Solger sought assurance of proper compensation from the German embassy, should things fall through with the Chinese government. His caution proved prescient. By the time Solger actually arrived in Beijing in November of that year, the money for the new geological school had fallen through, and the students who had passed an entrance exam were either sent home or transferred to Peking University. Solger, however, hardly sat idle for lack of work—he left immediately on expeditions to Shandong and Henan, specifically to Zhangde in Henan province, where the new president of the Republic, Yuan Shikai, showed an interest in expanding the existing mines into a large modern mining enterprise. While Solger occupied himself with expeditions, requests for his services poured in from both his Chinese employers and the German embassy. Throughout 1914, various consuls in the German Foreign Ministry requested Solger to conduct thorough studies of deposits, including the iron ore potential in Shanxi and Henan provinces.

By July 1914, not only the German embassy but also the Prussian Geological Institute in Berlin were showing interest in Solger's whereabouts. Earlier in the year, word had circulated in the diplomatic circles in Beijing of Chinese plans to conduct a geological survey of the entire empire. Von Maltzan, at the German embassy, wrote of the plans that

> Participation in such a comprehensive planned geological survey of the whole of China could be used by us in numerous ways. Through the survey, we would be in possession of valuable information about the mineral treasures of China earlier than everyone else; with this work we would receive leadership of the mining section of the Ministry of Agriculture and Commerce, and through that perhaps could even lead to future German participation in the opening up of mining in China.[37]

Both the Germans and the Chinese recognized the importance of this practical application of geology. As early as 1897, Gustav Detring, a German member of the Imperial Chinese Maritime Customs, had memorialized the throne advocating the establishment of a Chinese mining institute, and further requesting a concession for a syndicate of German manufacturers and capitalists to build railroads and open mines in China. In his memorial, Detring openly criticized Zhang Zhidong's ironworks, accusing the reformer of failing to calculate the costs of smelting iron at Hanyang.[38] Detring's memorial had no visible impact on the court, although a year later the Germans would acquire their concessions in Shandong by force.

Nor were the Germans alone in appreciating the stakes of the "Great Game." An editorial in the *Hongkong Telegraph* of 22 April 1898 decried that,

> It is a matter of the greatest import that Hong Kong secures a cheap coal supply … Hong Kong has hitherto subsisted on its shipping trade. There are many indications that its future growth and prosperity depend upon its adaptability to become a great industrial center. Our German neighbors of yesterday at Kiaochow [Jiaozhou] and our French neighbors of the week before in Tonkin, do not evidently believe in the inutility of getting mining rights in Shantung or Yunnan. Are we to be indifferent…?[39]

In this tense, competitive atmosphere, the news that the Chinese government had hired the Swedish geologist Dr. J. G. Andersson for the China Geological Survey (founded in 1913) brought consternation from Beijing to Berlin. Andersson had studied at the University of Uppsala, and had served as the director of the Swedish National Geological Survey before receiving the invitation to work in China. The head of the Prussian Geological Institute immediately wrote to Professor Andersson with congratulations, and requested a meeting should the honored colleague be passing through Berlin on his way to China (Andersson sent his heartfelt regrets). From the field, Solger wrote angry responses to inquiries from the German legation, stating that his contract stipulated that he be the only European hired by the Chinese ministry. By July, the legation had assured Berlin that Dr. Solger, and only Dr. Solger, was employed for the geological survey, while Dr. Andersson would only be a consultant and would have nothing to do with the survey.[40]

The correspondence between Berlin and a Dr. Kneiper in Qingdao returned to the subject of a proposed China Geological Institute, which would rely on German guidance and expertise. The Prussian Land Ministry went so far as to draw up a full draft of a constitution for a Chinese geological survey, detailing the need for a systematic survey of China and calling for twenty-five large maps on a 1:1,000,000 scale. While Solger involved himself with plans for a Richthofen Institute for German China Research, Dr. Behaghel and Mr. Korndörfer proposed plans for the "German Engineer Bureau of China."[41] As the *Kölnische Zeitung* pointed out in 1911, "it would be a great business mistake if we Germans do not try with all our might to plant our companies in China and insure our industries' participation in the opening up of China."[42] The gist of all these various efforts, alongside China's own efforts at legal reforms and the establishment of new institutions, underlines geology's central role in both modern state building and the "Great Race" for empire. And in this "Great Race" which played out across China, engineers were the protagonists.

In their work in East Asia, German engineers played essential roles in the globalization of industrialization. They worked in some of China's first industrial enterprises, establishing business ties and markets in Asia for German industrial machinery, which to this day enjoys a sterling reputation for quality and precision. What does it mean to be a German overseas? In the first modern industrial enterprises established in late nineteenth-century China, German engineers not only oversaw the purchase of industrial equipment and the running of mines and factories, but also actively promoted the superiority of the German technical education system and industries in the homeland. Brandt and other members of the German diplomatic corps in China worked closely with engineers, recognizing in their technical skills the entry into positions of authority within Chinese-owned industries. The promise of the vast China market beckoned. A small group of German engineers answered the call, and in turn helped to bring China into a global network of industrialized states.

Shellen Wu is associate professor of history at the University of Tennessee, Knoxville. Her first book, *Empires of Coal: Fueling China's Entry into the Modern*

World Order, 1860–1920, was published with Stanford University Press in 2015. She has published articles in *The American Historical Review*, *International History Review*, and other leading journals in history and Asian studies.

Notes

1. Margaret C. Jacob, *Scientific Culture and the Making of the Industrial West* (Oxford: Oxford University Press, 1997), 8.
2. Karl-Heinz Manegold, *Universität, Technische Hochschule und Industrie: Ein Beitrag Zur Emanzipation Der Technik Im 19. Jahrhundert Unter Besonderer Berücksichtigung Der Bestrebungen Felix Kleins*. Schriften Zur Wirtschaft- und Sozialgeschichte. Edited by Wolfram Fischer. Vol. 16 (Berlin: Duncker & Humblot, 1970), 43.
3. Ibid., 16.
4. GStA PK. I. HA Rep. 76, Sekt 1. Tit. XII Nr. 3 Bd. 1 and 2 and 3; 1874–1920s.
5. GStA PK. I. HA Rep. 76, Sekt 1. Tit. XII Nr. 3 Bd. 3.
6. GStA PK. I. HA Rep. 76 Va, Sekt 1. Tit. X Nr. 6.
7. GStA PK. I. HA Rep. 76, Sekt 1. Tit. XII Nr. 3 Bd. 3. Letter dated 31 October 1923.
8. These internal memorandums are recorded in BA R901 / 12932, "Die Entsendung deutscher Eisenbahntechniker nach China," Politisches Archiv d. Auswärt. Amts (Oct. 1886–Dec. 1887).
9. Brandt was part of the Prussian mission to East Asia in 1860, for which Richthofen served as part of the science team. A numbers of participants in the mission later served in high government posts and influenced the course of German involvement in China. Count Eulenburg, leader of the mission, later became minister of the interior. Even at this early date, Eulenburg broached the idea of a German leasehold in China, an idea Qing officials quickly dismissed. A number of other members of the mission eventually attained high positions within the navy, which directly contributed to the lingering interest in acquiring a naval port in China.
10. BA R901 / 12932 (Oct. 1886–Dec. 1887), 8.
11. Vera Schmidt, *Die Deutsche Eisenbahnpolitik in Shantung 1898–1914*. Veröffentlichungen Des Ostasien-Instituts der Ruhr-Universität Bochum (Wiesbaden: Otto Harrassowitz, 1976), 47.
12. BA R901 / 12932 (Oct. 1886–Dec. 1887), 55.
13. Although Rawlinson examines Chinese naval development in general, he focuses in particular on the French influence at the Fuzhou Shipyard. John L. Rawlinson, *China's Struggle for Naval Development, 1839–1895* (Cambridge, MA: Harvard University Press, 1967), 45.
14. For the operation of the Jiangnan Arsenal from the 1870s through the Sino-Japanese War, see Meng Yue, "Hybrid Science *versus* Modernity: The Practice of the Jiangnan Arsenal," *East Asian Science, Technology, and Medicine* 16 (1999): 13–52; also Benjamin Elman, "Naval Warfare and the Refraction of China's Self-Strengthening Reforms into Scientific and Technological Failure, 1865–1895," *Modern Asian Studies* 38, no. 2 (2004): 283–326.
15. Zhang Zhidong, *Zhang Wenxiang gong quan ji* 張文襄全集 [The complete works of Zhang Zhidong](Taipei: Wen hai chu ban she, 1963), *zou yi* (memorials), 11.16–24.
16. Ibid., *dian du* (telegrams), 12.39.
17. The founding and decline of Hanyeping Iron and Coal Works is well documented and studied as a case study of early Chinese industries. Albert Feuerwerker, *China's Early Industrialization: Sheng Hsuan-Huai (1844–1916) and Mandarin Enterprise* (Cambridge, MA: Harvard University Press, 1958); Albert Feuerwerker, *Studies in the Economic History of Late Imperial China*. Michigan Monographs in Chinese Studies (Ann Arbor: Center for Chinese Studies The University of Michigan, 1995); Jeff Hornibrook, "Local Elites and Mechanized Mining in

China: The Case of the Wen Lineage in Pingxiang County, Jiangxi," *Modern China* 27, no. 2 (April 2001).
18. BA R 901 / 12933.
19. BA R 901 / 12934, "Die Entsendung Deutscher Eisenbahntechniker Nach China," Politisches Archiv d. Auswärt. Amts (Jan. 1889–Jun. 1890).
20. Ibid. (Jun. 1890–Feb. 1891), 137.
21. BA R 901 / 12937, "Die Entsendung Deutscher Eisenbahntechniker Nach China," Auswärtiges Amt. Handelspol. Abt. (Oct. 1891–Apr. 1892), 83.
22. Faulting results in the fracturing of veins of mineral deposits and makes mining more difficult. A vein of coal, for example, might continue at a different depth.
23. BA R 901 / 12939 (Dec. 1892–May 1893).
24. BA R 901 / 12936 (1891–1892).
25. BA R 901 / 12943 (Sep. 1895–Apr. 1896), 42.
26. Warrington Smyth, *A Treatise on Coal and Coal Mining* (London: Virtue Brothers and Co., 1867).
27. Martin F. Parnell, *The German Tradition of Organized Capitalism: Self-Government in the Coal Industry* (Oxford: Clarendon Press, 1994), 12.
28. The search for coking coal not only drew the attention of Qing officials, but also proved of interest as an issue of practical geology in Europe. An update on the search for coal appeared in a mining journal published in Berlin: *Zeitschrift für praktische Geologie*, Vol. 7 (1899), 342–43.
29. BA R901 / 12938.
30. BA R 901 / 12945, 127.
31. BA R 9208 / 1265, 1–16.
32. BA R 9208 / 569, "Industrielle Unternehmungen, Syndikate," (Mar. 1888–Jan. 1899), 175.
33. *Hanyeping Gongsi Zhi* 汉冶萍公司志 [History of Hanyeping Company], ed. Hubei shen ye jing zhi bian hui wei yuan hui 湖北省冶金志编绘委员会 (Huazhong ligong daxue chuban she, 1989), 60–61.
34. BA R 9208 / 1289, "Bergwerks Konzession der Firma Carlowitz & Co.," Acta der Kaiserlich Deutschen Gesandtschaft für China (1 Jan. 1914–31 Mar. 1907), 76.
35. BA R 901 / 4998, Auswärtiges Amt. Abt. Handels u. Schiffs Asien (1903–12), 20.
36. BA R9208 / 1273, 220.
37. BA R 9208 / 1278, 68.
38. BA R 9208 / 1265, 152.
39. BA R 9208 / 1265, 210.
40. In Chinese accounts a different story emerges. Solger appeared to be an eccentric and isolated man during his time in China. Andersson's contributions to Chinese geology would prove far greater in the long run, particularly in the nascent field of paleontology.
41. BA R 9208 / 655 and BA R 9208 / 1277, 219.
42. BA R 9208 / 1276, 285.

Bibliography

Elman, Benjamin. "Naval Warfare and the Refraction of China's Self-Strengthening Reforms into Scientific and Technological Failure, 1865–1895." *Modern Asian Studies* 38, no. 2 (2003): 283–326.
Feuerwerker, Albert. *China's Early Industrialization: Sheng Hsuan-Huai (1844–1916) and Mandarin Enterprise*. Cambridge, MA: Harvard University Press, 1958.

———. *Studies in the Economic History of Late Imperial China*. Michigan Monographs in Chinese Studies. Ann Arbor: Center for Chinese Studies The University of Michigan, 1995.

Hornibrook, Jeff. "Local Elites and Mechanized Mining in China: The Case of the Wen Lineage in Pingxiang County, Jiangxi." *Modern China* 27, no. 2 (April 2001): 202–28.

Hubei shen ye jing zhi bian hui wei yuan, ed. *Hanyeping Gongsi Zhi*. Wuchang: Huazhong ligong daxue chubanshe, 1990.

Jacob, Margaret. *Scientific Culture and the Making of the Industrial West*. Oxford: Oxford University Press, 1997.

Manegold, Karl-Heinz. *Universität, Technische Hochschule Und Industrie: Ein Beitrag Zur Emanzipation Der Technik Im 19. Jahrhundert Unter Besonderer Berücksichtigung Der Bestrebungen Felix Kleins*. Schriften Zur Wirtschaft- Und Sozialgeschichte. Edited by Wolfram Fischer. Vol. 16. Berlin: Duncker & Humblot, 1970.

Meng, Yue. "Hybrid Science *Versus* Modernity: The Practice of the Jiangnan Arsenal." *East Asian Science, Technology and Medicine* 16 (1999): 13–52.

Parnell, Martin F. *The German Tradition of Organized Capitalism: Self-Government in the Coal Industry*. Oxford: Clarendon Press, 1994.

Rawlinson, John L. *China's Struggle for Naval Development 1839–1895*. Cambridge, MA: Harvard University Press, 1967.

Schmidt, Vera. *Die Deutsche Eisenbahnpolitik in Shantung 1898–1914*. Veröffentlichungen Des Ostasien-Instituts der Ruhr-Universität Bochum. Wiesbaden: Otto Harrassowitz, 1976.

Smyth, Warrington. *A Treatise on Coal and Coal Mining*. London: Virtue Brothers and Co., 1867.

Zhang, Zhidong. *Zhang Wenxiang Gong Quanji: [Zou Yi; Dian Zou]* Jindai Zhongguo Shiliao Congkan. Edited by Wang Shunan. 10 vols. Taipei: Wenhai chuban she, 1970.

Part II

EXPANSION, ENTANGLEMENTS, AND COLONIALISM IN THE LONG NINETEENTH CENTURY

Chapter 7

EXPANDING THE FRONTIER(S)
The Spreckels Family and the German-American Penetration of the Pacific, 1870–1920

Uwe Spiekermann

The "Germans" in the Pacific—this catchy title implies the existence of a clear-cut "German element" to be easily distinguished from other groups, nationalities, and ethnicities.[1] This chapter will present a more flexible perspective of "German" presence in the Pacific region—not only because there was no German citizenship before 1934,[2] but also because "Germans" in the Pacific could come from very different regions and backgrounds: Hanseatic merchants, travelers, and immigrants from quite different states were only some of the myriads of hybrid structures of "Germanness" and/or "German-Americans" in the Pacific world during the late nineteenth and early twentieth centuries.[3] In this chapter, I will focus on one of the most prominent German-American families on the west coast—the Spreckels. Their entrepreneurial spirit integrated large portions of the Pacific region into the global economy, and made this region attractive and even fashionable in the United States and in Germany. I will use the Spreckels family as an example for three main reasons: first, this will allow for discussions on the contributions of German-American immigrants to the economic and cultural penetration of the Pacific regions from the 1870s; second, it helps to analyze private initiative as a temporary substitute for state activity in the "Age of Empire"; and third, it enables looking to informal empires of business, and integrating the interaction between state representatives and business circles into our understanding of the changes in the Pacific, starting from the late nineteenth century.

Notes from this chapter begin on page 187.

Sugaring of Hawaii

The Spreckels family was already an economic power in California in the 1870s. Similar to several neighbors and relatives, Claus Spreckels (1828–1908) left his northern German home village of Lamstedt in 1846 to seek a better life in the United States.[4] He started working as a clerk and retailer in Charleston, South Carolina, and continued his career in the dry goods and alcohol trade, first in New York City and, from 1856, in San Francisco. Integrated into a family network of several brothers and many relatives, he invested his profits first in beer brewing and afterward in sugar refining. The Bay Sugar Refining Company, incorporated in 1864, and the 1867 California Sugar Refinery Company were starting points of an immensely profitable business career, which set Claus Spreckels in a dominant position in sugar production in the American West from the mid-1870s. In 1869, his taxable income was already $113,833 and in 1874 he was listed as one of San Francisco's millionaires.[5] Claus Spreckels, naturalized in 1855, was a leading representative of German-Americans in California. He spoke English, but with a heavy accent, was married to a German wife from his home region, sent several of his sons to Germany for education, and was an integral part of San Francisco's German-American community, where his brother Peter Spreckels (1839–1922) held leading positions.[6] At the same time, however, he crossed the borders of the ethnic niche community and was proud of being a Californian and an American. Spreckels had a dual identity, co-organizing both the Fourth of July parade and the republican torchlight procession on 4 September 1871, the anniversary of the Battle of Sedan.[7] This was not only an individual passion but was also functional for business, because he could act as an intermediary, linking German and American business interests.

This became important when the Reciprocity Treaty between the independent Kingdom of Hawaii and the United States opened up new horizons from 1876.[8] Having at first fought fiercely against this trade agreement, he sent his eldest son John D. Spreckels (1853–1926) to the Sandwich Islands to explore business prospects. Trained in chemistry and mechanical engineering at the Polytechnic School in Hanover, he had become superintendent of the California Sugar Refinery in 1873 and received additional business training during a brief apprenticeship at the Bremish trade house Hackfeld & Co. in Honolulu in 1876.[9] Based on his son's pilot surveys, Claus Spreckels went to Hawaii in 1876. The Reciprocity Treaty gave high incentives for investments into sugar cultivation, because every pound of sugar exported from the islands to the United States was subsidized with two cents by the American taxpayer. While the regular price of raw sugar was around eight cents per pound at that time, this was an attractive incentive for foreign investors. Spreckels bought several smaller sugar plantations on Oahu and the Big Island, purchased the vast majority of the Hawaiian crop, and established his San Francisco refinery as the center for converting Hawaiian raw sugar into white and brown sugar.[10]

Spreckels' main and most ambitious project, however, was the conversion of Maui, the second largest island of the kingdom, into a sugar island.[11] The Hawaiian Commercial Company, incorporated in 1878 and reincorporated in 1882 as the Hawaiian Commercial and Sugar Company, was to become the largest cane sugar plantation not just in the Pacific but worldwide.[12] This, indeed, was an immense endeavor; and Spreckels had to face severe skepticism and even laughter from the Californian business community. The main problem was to buy sufficient land to secure the water supply of the new plantation ground. Maui's climate and geological structure offered the best chances for a profitable agribusiness. Money, robust business methods, and his close relationship to King Kalakaua allowed Spreckels to secure the plain crownlands of the island; but these were arid regions, as sufficient water was only available in Maui's volcanic areas. Irrigation was necessary to start large-scale cane sugar cultivation; and Spreckels managed this based on general plans, developed by him, his son, and some American business partners.[13]

The later sugar king of Hawaii could obtain the German-American hydraulic engineer Hermann Schüssler (1842–1919) for this task. He was born in Rastede, near Oldenburg, where he attended the Prussian military academy from 1859 to 1862.[14] Afterward he studied civil engineering in Zurich and Karlsruhe, and emigrated to California in 1864. In the San Francisco bay area, he was engaged as a chief engineer for the Spring Valley Water Works, but was also doing contract work for the Virginia City and Gold Hill Water Company and the Sutro Tunnel Company. Based on these credentials, he arrived, together with Claus Spreckels and additional investors, in Honolulu in May 1878 and began his work in Maui in June 1878.[15] He organized a surveying party, "consisting of an assistant, eight natives, a Japanese cook and a mule driver."[16] Schüssler took two weeks to make a survey of the canal and ditch routes, including the pipes, their strength, and the water reservoirs. He suggested the construction of a narrow-gauge railroad through the plantation and with lateral branches. Afterward he went first to Pittsburgh and then to the San Francisco Risdom Iron Works to order the steel and the pipes for use in construction of the ditch. Together with additional material, they were shipped to Maui in December 1878. At that time, Schüssler was already directing a team of several managers and foremen, four hundred workers, one hundred head of oxen, and sixty mules.[17] In total, forty-five miles of canal and around twenty tunnels were built. Schüssler left the kingdom in early October 1879, and returned to California where he remained, although he was later consulted to construct water works for the city of Tokyo.[18]

The irrigation system was the cornerstone for the large-scale cane sugar cultivation by Spreckels' Hawaiian Commercial and Sugar Company, which used Maui's center for business purposes.[19] It was a milestone for Maui: "The dry

Figure 7.1: Spreckelsville Mill: Maui's Economic Center—and headquarter of the Hawaiian Commercial and Sugar Company, 1890. Library of Congress, Washington, DC. (http://www.loc.gov/pictures/item/hi0004.photos.058707p/) Library of Congress, Prints & Photographs Division, HABS, Reproduction number "HABS HI,5-SPRK,1–2." Published with permission.

valley of a few years ago has become a mine of wealth, a bonanza, pouring out its ceaseless flood of treasure."[20] The monoculture around the newly founded company town Spreckelsville triggered one-sided economic growth, which even today is shaping the island's landscape apart from beaches, resorts, and tourist destinations.[21] In parallel, the green central lands of Maui became an important element of the first vertically integrated sugar firm in the world, because Spreckels organized not only the production and manufacturing of cane sugar, but also the transport and finance. His western sugar empire was based on sound economic ground, and in the late 1880s the German-American sugar king[22] could even compete with the American Sugar Refining Company, the so-called Sugar Trust—at that time, the company with the second largest capitalization in the United States.

Multicultural Repopulation of the Hawaiian Kingdom

The sugaring of Maui, the Big Island, and Oahu was decisive for the population of the Pacific region with Europeans and the opening of the labor market to Chinese and Japanese contract workers.[23] The Spreckelsville Mill became the center of a network with several thousand contract plantation workers and approximately 200 to 300 white specialists.[24] Spreckels' early investments set an end to the traditional system of crown lands and community properties.[25] The cash nexus led to a rapid redistribution of land and water rights to foreign investors, although the legal changes had already been launched in the early 1850s.

Labor migration changed the ethnic structure of the Hawaiian kingdom fundamentally—a kingdom with only 80,578 inhabitants in 1884 and a shrinking indigene population.[26] Labor was scarce and Spreckels tried to attract "white" labor to work at his plantations, although this was more expensive; in 1879 he paid his 125 "white" employees $3–4 per day, while his 100 Chinese workers received only $10–12 per month.[27] But Spreckels realized that economic rationality had to be balanced with widespread prejudices against "yellow" immigrants both by indigene population and "white" immigrants.[28]

In 1881, Hackfeld & Co. organized a first transport of 127 Germans, most of them from Thuringia, followed by a second tranche of 180 a year later.[29] Additional ships were planned in 1883, according to an advertisement in the newspaper *Gothaer Tageblatt* trying to attract additional workers; but such contract work was harshly criticized by German newspapers, because they "actually degrade free-born Germans to the level of coolies and negroes, rendering them useless to the Fatherland they have left, turning them from men into merchandise and practically using them as human manure for the properties of the sugar planters."[30] Even the German parliament discussed the matter, and the lawmakers agreed that plantation work in Hawaii would degrade German labor and German laborers.[31] Spreckels hired some of the seven to eight hundred German immigrants who arrived in April 1883, although it is not clear how many. Most of them, however, were promoted to more responsible positions in the hierarchical world of Pacific plantations.

Together with his business partner William G. Irwin, Claus Spreckels also hired five hundred Norwegians in 1881, "but they were accustomed to northern climate only."[32] Most of them left the country after a short time. Portuguese immigrants from the volcanic islands of Madeira and then the Azores seemed to be a working alternative, although the passage cost the planter about $100 per person, while the contract workers had to agree to a three-year employment with a salary of about $1 per day.[33] This immigration was predominantly managed by the German-born merchant Abraham Hoffnung, who came to Hawaii via Canada, and eventually became a Hawaiian charge d'affaires and settled in

Figure 7.2: Fears of Inundation: Hawaii as the model for a Chinese invasion of the United States. Cartoon, 1883. *The Wasp* 10 (1883), 5 May, 16.

London.³⁴ The Spreckels used their own resources as well—for instance, when they chartered the steamer *City of Paris*, which brought 824 immigrants from Saint Michael to Honolulu in 1884.³⁵

These workers, indeed, could be accustomed to the hard work in the cane fields. Based predominantly on Spreckels experiences, the Hawaiian Planters' Labor and Supply Co. encouraged "the further immigration of Portuguese and Chinese."³⁶ When Portuguese immigration was interrupted in early 1882, Claus Spreckels thought of taking up to two thousand Japanese workers, and offered "to represent the Hawaiian Government in Japan in immigration questions."³⁷ This, however, was not accepted and the tide turned in favor of Chinese immigrants. From 1884, Spreckels used ships of his own line to import them to Hawaii.³⁸ Similar to other planters, he did not accept restrictions by the Hawaiian state, which tried to cap the transports to twenty persons per month.³⁹ In 1891, twelve hundred Chinese laborers were employed by the Hawaiian Commercial and Sugar Company, in addition to six hundred workmen of other nationalities. They were "imported from every part of the earth," among them Japanese, who arrived first in 1884.⁴⁰ In 1912, the Kilauea Plantation Company, owned by John D. Spreckels and his brother Adolph B. Spreckels (1857–1924), had a labor force of 385 Japanese, 97 Filipinos, 59 Portuguese, 41 Puerto Ricans, 29 Chinese, 18 Koreans, and 6 Hawaiians.⁴¹ Claus Spreckels was definitely not the first planter to import coolie workers—this was likely Hackfeld & Co., importing Chinese workers already in 1852.⁴² But he surely became the largest buyer of cheap labor;

and the sheer quantity fundamentally changed the ethnical composition of the islands.

The consequences of this multicultural repopulating of Hawaii were not limited to this small country in the Pacific. The nativist debate in the United States, resulting in several exclusion acts, starting in California, was shaped by the ethnic transitions in Hawaii, predominantly by the influx of Chinese laborers. In San Francisco, the German-American immigrant Claus Spreckels was denounced as a "Chinese lover" and "the biggest, dirtiest labor thief that ever cursed" California.[43] Denis Kearney, Irish immigrant and head of the nativist Workingmen's Party, threatened to kill him, was brought to court, charged to pay a fine of $1,000 and imprisoned for six months.[44]

Spreckels' success underlined ethnic and racist stereotypes. Coming to the islands and developing their economy within only a few years supported ideas of white supremacy. The South Sea was perceived as an underdeveloped region and a civilizing task for the emerging Western colonial nations. Claus Spreckels, who often compared the indigene Hawaiians with children, would have agreed to such widespread racism.[45] In this particular case, however, it was perhaps even more important that models of population and repopulation practiced in Hawaii were used in the Western states as well. Models and procedures, developed in the periphery, helped to change and reconfigure the centers—namely, when they were still frontier states like California.[46] Claus Spreckels used similar methods of labor recruitment in California's Salinas Valley when he started large-scale beet sugar production there in the late 1890s. For some decades the sugaring of central California had similar effects to the sugaring of Maui. As with his Watsonville beet sugar factory, founded in 1887, Claus Spreckels first tried to convince "white" farmers to grow beets and to guarantee a steady flow of raw material for his Watsonville beet sugar refinery.[47] This failed, however, and from the early 1890s more than two-thirds of the work was done by Chinese and Japanese contract workers.[48] In Salinas, Claus Spreckels bought huge areas of land for beet cultivation. Again, he tried to attract "white" labor first. In cooperation with Salvation Army commander Frederick Booth-Tucker, in 1897 he founded a settler community for 150 farmers of German origin at Fort Romie, near Soledad in Monterey County.[49] This was a successful experiment "in colonizing the poor of the great cities upon idle land."[50] But this was insufficient to fill the gaps for supplying by far the largest beet sugar factory in the United States. While the neighborhood of the factory, namely the company town Spreckels, was predominately "white," the farm work was overwhelmingly done by Japanese immigrants. California established a kind of "colonial economy."[51] Economic models, developed in the Pacific periphery, shaped California's transition to a multicultural and multiethnical state.

Such economic cooperation and exploitation was closely related to additional cultural transfers. The Pacific region was not only used, but it became fashionable as well. Especially in the 1910s, younger members of the Spreckels family were attracted by the exotic world of the South Sea and Japan. These trendsetters of the smart set promoted Pacific traditions, fashions, and lifestyles as an integral part of leisure-class pleasures. Good examples of this were Japanese gardens built at Coronado at the backside of John D. Spreckels' Glorietta Bay property, and at the Hillsborough mansion of Howard Spreckels.[52] For the younger Spreckels, who defined themselves as Californians and members of an international smart set, it became fashionable to use the exoticism of the Pacific. In 1916, John D. Spreckels Jr.'s second wife, Sidi Spreckels Wirt, posed in a kimono in the Japanese garden at Coronado and made sure that these images were spread widely in the press.[53] Meanwhile, his first wife, Edith Huntington Wakefield Spreckels, departed indefinitely to Tahiti, to enjoy the ease of the South Sea.[54] Later, such cultural exoticism was even used for commercial purposes—for instance, in an advertisement for Cream of the Wheat, where Gertrude Spreckels, the daughter of Howard Spreckels, was posing in the Hillsborough Japanese garden.[55]

An Industrious and a Beautiful Ocean: The Spreckels Shipping Lines

Such cultural adoptions were no coincidence but a result of earlier commercial penetration of the Pacific Ocean. The Spreckels family founded several sea transportation firms, connecting important destinations in the Pacific. Sugar was at the forefront. Having first chartered vessels by the holding firm of John D. Spreckels & Bros., founded in 1878 and incorporated in 1880, the Spreckels family incorporated the Oceanic Steamship Company in 1881, which started buying, constructing, and chartering nearly a dozen freight sailing ships.[56] Known as "the Spreckels line," it carried, on a regular basis, raw sugar from Hawaii to the San Francisco sugar refinery, and then merchandise back to the islands.

In 1882, however, the company expanded its Pacific business. A first large steamer was chartered, followed by two new steamers, built in Philadelphia. They were combined freight and passenger ships, carrying up to 2,300 tons and 104 passengers on every passage.[57] This allowed the expansion of the passage to Australia and New Zealand. When the American Pacific Steamship Company withdrew their vessels from this passage in 1885, the Spreckels purchased two additional steamers and established a regular service from San Francisco to the British colonies via Honolulu, first in cooperation with the Union Steamship Company of New Zealand, and then from 1901 in their own right.[58] In addition, they took over the mail service to Oceania, carrying post from London to Honolulu, Auckland, Sydney and some South Sea islands. Parallel, John D. Spreckels & Bros. established a freight charter line from San Francisco to

Newcastle, New South Wales. In 1889, they were the largest coal importer to the American West, importing 200,000 tons annually to California.[59]

Such trade gave important incentives for the development not only of San Francisco, but other Californian cities. San Diego is perhaps the most prominent example. In 1887, John D. Spreckels made his first visit to this town, at that time a community of forty thousand inhabitants suffering severely from recession and failed speculation. He explored the local port and negotiated about a regular steamship line from San Diego to the British colonies in Australia and New Zealand.[60] Although the latter failed, John D. Spreckels and his brother Adolph B. Spreckels incorporated the Spreckels Bros. Commercial Company in 1887, which became a symbol of their faith in the town's future.[61] A 15,000-ton coal wharf was constructed in 1888 and port facilities were improved.[62] Together with many other investments by the Spreckels family, best known of them perhaps the Hotel del Coronado,[63] this connected San Diego to the trade routes of the West—to California, Oregon, Canada, Australia, and New Zealand. Until the 1920s, Spreckels Bros. Commercial Company remained the largest regional supplier of coal, oil, cement, and fertilizers, all necessary for the development of San Diego and its vicinity.

More important for the development of the Pacific region, however, was the Spreckels line, the Oceanic Steamship Company. It became the leading American shipping company in the South Pacific trade and the only regular carrier between San Francisco and Hawaii, Australia, New Zealand, Samoa, and Tahiti. This was promoted not only by the Spreckels family, but also by the Hawaiian kingdom, the Australian and New Zealand colonies, and later on even by the United States, who all paid subsidies to the Spreckels line for carrying the British mails from London to the Pacific commonwealth. Although American by citizenship, private business served those willing to pay for these services. This was a difficult task in the late nineteenth century, when shipping lines became a matter of national prestige and imperial pride. The Spreckels line included American, Hawaiian, and British ships, although finally the US shipping acts led to Americanization and limited her ability to compete with British lines.

The commercial penetration of the Pacific region was not, however, only founded on freight business. On a long perspective, perhaps even more important was the active promotion of Hawaii and the South Sea as a tourist destination.[64] The steamships of the Spreckels line offered quite comfortable cabins for travelers—and their owners were proud of being able to compete with the standards defined on the transatlantic routes.[65] Oceanic Steamship advertisements presented what are today quite common ideas of a sunny South Sea and a relaxed way of living. The company propagated the easy world of "Aloha," promoted surfing and "luau," and made wedding tours to the Sandwich Islands fashionable. This started in the early 1880s, long before air travel and cheap fares made this region an affordable tourist destination, even for middle-class customers.

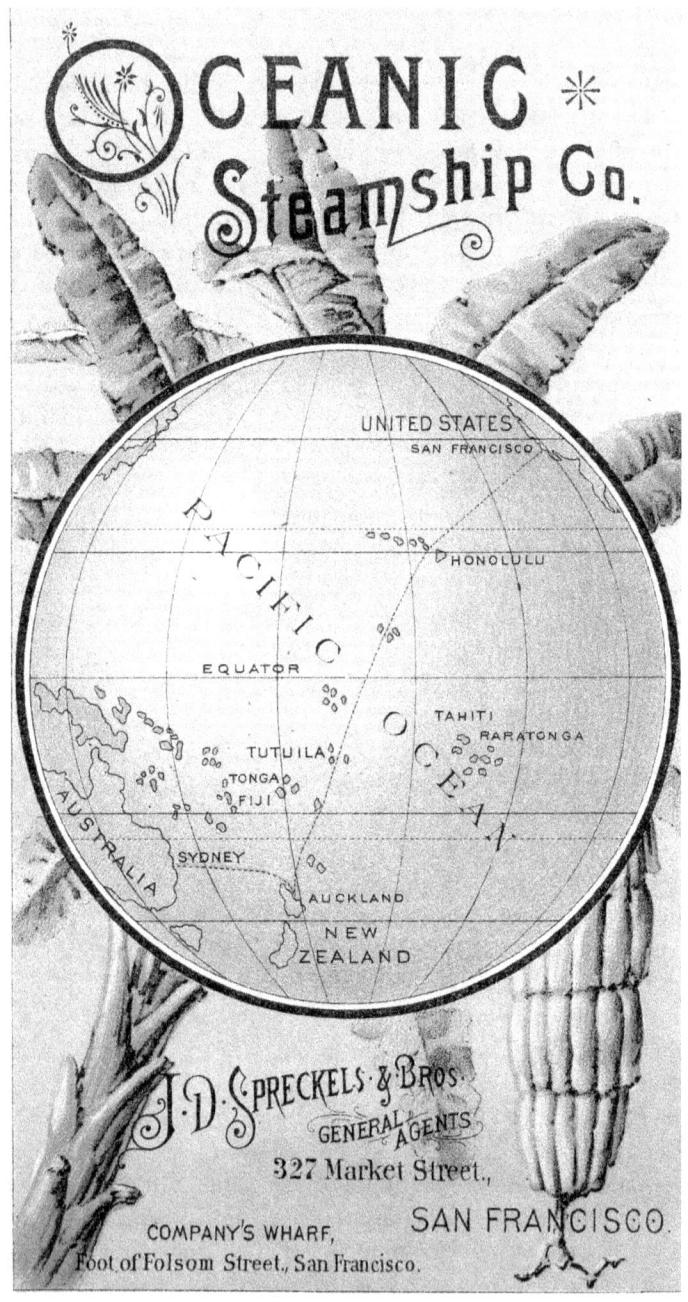

Figure 7.3: Covering the Pacific Ocean: Advertisement of the Oceanic Steamship Company, 1889. *Ports of San Diego, Portland, Puget Sound, Vancouver Island, Burrand Inlet, and Honolulu,* ed. J. D. Spreckels & Bros. (San Francisco: no publisher, 1889), 62.

Figure 7.4: Advertising the lovely Pacific, 1901. *The World's Work* 31, 1901/2, advertisement 56.

The Spreckels line was linked to early package deals, which offered passage, hotel, excursions, and entertainment for a flat rate.[66] In this period, the Spreckels family and their partner William G. Irwin established a notable local entertainment, the Honolulu Music Hall, which later becoming the Opera House.[67]

It is important to realize that not only explorers or travelers created standardized images of the Pacific region. Commercial firms, like the Spreckels line, established and used many of the images still in our minds today when we are envisaging this part of the world. The Spreckels family integrated not only Pacific cash crops and raw materials into a globalized economy but created new integrated and global networks for upper-class tourism, while at the same time offering Pacific dream worlds to the excluded rest.

Again, such models of touristic development of the periphery not only shaped the Pacific world but the countries of origin as well. In the Spreckels case, the Hotel del Coronado is perhaps the most prominent example of the interactions between peripheries and centers. Bought in 1889, the Spreckels established it as a leading resort for the smart set, offering hunting and fishing, golf and polo, beach life and an indoor swimming pool, all before the turn of the century.[68] In a parallel manner, in 1900 John D. Spreckels founded Coronado Tent City as a middle-class tourist destination, and advertised Coronado as a beautiful city, a place for rest and pleasure.[69]

Selling US Products in the Pacific: The Chinese-American Commercial Company

While the Spreckels line focused on the southern Pacific, other family members attempted to push the commercial frontiers even farther to the West, following the enunciation of an open-door policy in China in 1899. The million-dollar Chinese-American Commercial Company, financed by Claus's youngest son Rudolph Spreckels (1871–1958) and other San Francisco investors, is the most prominent example. Incorporated in August 1902, its purpose was to establish commercial museums in China and San Francisco, and to sell US and Chinese products in both countries.[70] For this endeavor, the company hired one of the most prominent Chinese diplomats, Consul General Ho You from San Francisco.[71] The 32-year-old son of a wealthy and prominent Guangzhou family had studied law at Cambridge and in Hong Kong, was a representative of Cantonese merchant interests, and a pronounced supporter of more intense trade relations with the United States: "The Government of China … is favorable to progress and is desirous of extending throughout the empire the light of Western knowledge and of adopting and applying to the industrial and strategic advantages of the country those marvelous benefits which Western thought has wrested from nature and brought under the control of man."[72] His task was twofold: first, he should pave the road to the Chinese market, dominated by local agents and traders; and second, his language skills and extensive business networks should provide US manufacturers with necessary market information.

Ho You had already supported the idea of a Pacific Commercial Museum in San Francisco in 1900, provided by the local chamber of commerce to develop the Pacific trade.[73] Collecting information and presenting American goods seemed to be a profitable way for American manufacturers to enjoy the benefits of European colonization without having to bear its financial or military costs. The initiative was part of more nuanced efforts to open up the Chinese market for "Western" technology and goods in a less aggressive way than that of the colonial powers, including Germany. Similar efforts of Japanese companies were successful.

The Philadelphia Commercial Museum served as an example for this endeavor.[74] But while this institution offered the broadest possible range of foreign goods, the Chinese-American Commercial Company added an idea practiced successfully by the Stuttgart *Exportmusterlager*: manufacturers should establish such institutions in foreign countries and negotiate directly with foreign clients.[75]

Together with general manager George T. Hawley, the Chinese representative of the Spreckels interests visited the St. Louis World's Fair to promote the Chinese-American Company and to attract American manufacturers. Further

Figure 7.5: Ho Yow (center right) and George T. Hawley (right behind him), representatives of the Chinese-American Commercial Company, at the St. Louis World's Fair, 1902, together with Congressman Richard Bartholdt (center left). "Mr. Ho Yow in St. Louis," *World Fair's Bulletin* 3 (1902), no. 12, 9.

trips through the East resulted in exclusive agencies for staple products like flour and lumber, and modern consumer goods, for instance canned food, beer, hardware, cotton fabrics, and electrical goods.[76] The company opened a commission house in Hong Kong in late 1902, "but from some untoward circumstances intervening it has been wound up and disposed of to local interests here."[77] Eventually, the company was a failure, mainly because the Russo–Japanese War hit trade interests significantly, among them special favors the firm was enjoying from several steamer lines.[78] Rudolph Spreckels' investment did not pay, but the Chinese-American Commercial Company demonstrated the interest of the Spreckels in foreign and complex Pacific markets with very different business cultures.

A functional equivalent for commercial museums were international and world fairs, which created dream worlds of innovation, progress, and modernity from the mid-nineteenth century.[79] Members of the Spreckels family were not only regular visitors of world fairs but their business interests in the United States and the Pacific region generated generous support of similar events in California. The 1915 San Francisco Panama–Pacific International Exposition, the official world fair, was supported by Adolph B. and Rudolph Spreckels with $25,000 each.[80] The unofficial world fair of that year, the 1915 San Diego Panama–California

Exposition, was promoted by a one-million-dollar company, headed by John D. Spreckels. When unrest in the board of directors led to a temporary suspension of this initiative in 1911, it was due to Ulysses S. Grant Jr.'s and John D. Spreckels' money and commitment, that the exposition finally took place in the newly constructed Balboa Park.[81] Both exhibitions, although affected by World War I, gave potential customers in the Pacific region and other places a good idea of California's economic performance.

Private Actors in the Age of Empire: The Naval Industrial-Military Complex in San Francisco and San Diego

Private entrepreneurs, like the Spreckels, had to continuously deal with the emerging modern state, or "Leviathan 2.0," as Harvard historian Charles Maier has coined this phenomenon from the 1870s.[82] Due to the penetration and colonization of the American continent, the United States was a belated imperialist nation in the Pacific.[83] However, after the annexation of Hawaii and the Philippines in 1898, the informal empire in the Caribbean and the establishment of Roosevelt's "White Fleet," the American state largely affected private enterprises.[84]

The Spreckels shipping interests cooperated with the US federal state from the early 1890s. Most of their steamers were on the US naval lists as auxiliary cruisers, and were built in accordance with requirements of US naval laws.[85] Some of the Spreckels tugboats, stationed in Honolulu and San Francisco, were equipped as potential torpedo and dispatch boats during the Spanish–American War in 1898.[86] Managed by the holding firm of J.D. Spreckels & Bros., these mid-sized boats, with a length of up to 150 feet and a 15 knots speed, were not only crucial for running the large ports but could also be used for coastal defense and catching merchant ships.[87] This seems to demonstrate a close and dependent relation to the US government.

This, however, is only half the story. The Spreckels interests were relevant and independent factors in the Pacific theater from the mid-1880s.[88] In 1885, for instance, British and Russian representatives tried to purchase some Spreckels steamers for use in the event of a war between these two powers.[89] In 1889, the conversion of the steamers into cruisers was discussed to fight German cruisers in Samoa.[90] In 1891, the US government tried to lease ships from the Spreckels line to intervene with them as troop carriers in the Chilean Civil War. In addition, the conversion of steamers to cruisers and the largest tugboat to a torpedo boat was discussed.[91] Finally, in 1892, Spreckels steamers were discussed to potentially ply against Britain in the event of a war over the Bering Sea dispute. San Francisco journals imaged a yacht fleet of San Francisco's Pacific Yacht Club put into commission, including the commodores John D. and Adolph B. Spreckels.[92]

Figure 7.6: Claus Spreckels (left) as an independent player among nations-states. Cartoon, 1881. *The Wasp* 7 (1881), 64.

Any war service of Spreckels ships could be avoided. But the interest of the great powers in the property of a private company demonstrates their role as a quite independent power, at a time when the US federal government was not willing to invest heavily in a Pacific navy. The latter was pushed by business interests all over the United States from the late 1880s. For instance, the Oceanic Steamship Company's steamers were discussed in relation to becoming part of a naval militia, a plan propagated by the Naval Reserve Committee of the New York Chamber of Commerce.[93] But a naval reserve was not established until 1915.

The decade of independent strategic relevance of the Spreckels shipping interests in the Pacific theater ended with the Spanish–American War in 1898. The US fleet was regularly supported by the Spreckels tugboats, and steamers were used for troop transports to the Philippines in 1898.[94] Such service was offered for only slightly reduced fees. Thereupon, the Hearst Press, competitor of John D. Spreckels' newspaper the *San Francisco Call*, questioned the loyalty of the German-American businessman.[95] The intensified engagement of the federal government in the Pacific theater, however, caused additional problems for private enterprise. While the Spreckels supported (but ultimately failed) plans for massive subsidies of American merchant ships in the West, they had to renegotiate their mail contracts with New Zealand and Australia in 1901 because the Oceanic Steamship Company's steamers had to be registered as US ships because foreign ships were excluded from shipping mail to the new US territory of Hawaii.[96] This significantly weakened its position in the competition for prolonging the Pacific mail service.[97]

There is insufficient space to delve deeper into the close but often informal cooperation of the Spreckels' interests in San Francisco and their steel and shipping interests on the American Pacific coast, demonstrated not only by the industrial cluster at San Francisco's Protero district. A very prominent example was again San Diego, where John D. Spreckels' enthusiasm for marine interests resulted in the sale of the bay's North Island to the US Navy in 1917, after he had built up and maintained the infrastructure for the navy's presence on his private grounds for two decades.[98] Today, this is the Pacific port for US aircraft carriers. John D. Spreckels, a stalwart Republican, was closely linked to the early military-industrial complex in Washington, DC and in California, and to all presidents, and secretaries of state and of war.[99] He stood at the beginning of the growing importance of military interests in San Diego and became one of the most active proponents of a strong US presence in the Pacific, to protect his interests in Hawaii and the Philippines. From 1923, he was vice president of the Pacific Foreign Trade Council,[100] and, until his death in 1926, John D. Spreckels was pushing such business interests.

Conclusion

The example of the Spreckels family proves the relevant role German-American immigrant entrepreneurs played in the economic transformation of the Pacific regions, its integration into global networks of trade and tourism, and the creation of widely circulated images of the South Sea. Although the leading representatives of the family were fully aware that they were perceived as actors of one of the imperial nations competing for influence in the Pacific regions, they demonstrated that private business remained an important and relatively independent factor during the "Age of Empire."[101] As German-Americans, however, the Spreckels family were important intermediaries, who gave German companies and investors additional business opportunities. World War I, however, brought an end to this hybrid structure, not only because it set an end to the German colonial experience in the Pacific, but also because the networks between Germans and German-American actors were weakened and often cut off. This private business perspective has to be added to common narratives on the end of German colonial rule in the Pacific.

Uwe Spiekermann teaches history at the University of Göttingen, Germany. His research interests include consumption, retailing, nutrition, and knowledge. Among his eleven books are *Künstliche Kost: Deutsche Ernährung von 1840 bis heute*; *Immigrant Entrepreneurship: The German-American Experience since 1700* (coeditor). He is currently writing a history of the German-American Spreckels family.

Notes

1. For a long while such essentialism was undisputed in "academic" literature on Germans in Hawaii, f.i. Nikolaus Rudolf Schweizer, "Hawaii und die Deutschen," in *Die Deutsche Südsee 1884–1914*, ed. Hermann Joseph Hiery (Paderborn: Schöningh, 2000), 725–36.
2. In Germany the states remained sovereign with their individual nationality laws until the 1934 law on the recompilation of the empire (*Gesetz über den Neuaufbau des Reichs*) constituted a mandatory German citizenship. The 1913 Nationality Law of the German Empire and States had already established a German citizenship, but this was mostly derived from the citizenship of one of the German states, not acquired through the German federal government. Cf. Dieter Gosewinkel, *Einbürgern und Ausschließen: Die Nationalisierung der Staatsangehörigkeit vom Deutschen Bund bis zur Bundesrepublik Deutschland* (Göttingen: Vandenhoeck & Ruprecht, 2001); Eli Nathans, *The Politics of Citizenship in Germany: Ethnicity, Utility and Nationalism* (Oxford: Berg, 2004).
3. Cf. Krista O'Donnell, Renate Bridenthal, and Nancy Reagin, eds., *The Heimat Abroad: The Boundaries of Germanness* (Ann Arbor: University of Michigan Press, 2005).

4. Uwe Spiekermann, "Claus Spreckels: A Biographical Case Study of Nineteenth-Century American Immigrant Entrepreneurship," *Business and Economic History Online* (2010).
5. *San Francisco Chronicle*, 26 June 1869, 4; "San Francisco Millionaires," *London-American Register*, 31 October 1874, 6.
6. On Peter Spreckels, a banker, investor, and millionaire in his own right, see Uwe Spiekermann, "An Ordinary Man among Titans: The Life of Walter P. Spreckels," in *Immigrant Entrepreneurship: The German-American Experience since 1700*, ed. Hartmut Berghoff and Uwe Spiekermann (Washington, DC: GHI, 2016), 264–66.
7. "The Glorious Fourth," *San Francisco Chronicle*, 20 June 1871, 2; *San Francisco Abend Post*, 30 August 1871, 2.
8. Cf. David M. Pletcher, *The Diplomacy of Involvement: American Economic Expansion across the Pacific, 1784–1900* (Columbia: University of Missouri Press, 2001), 46–66.
9. *San Francisco Directory* (San Francisco: Henry G. Langley, 1874), 620; "Claus Spreckels, the Sugar King, is Dead," *Hawaiian Gazette*, 29 December 1908, 3. Paradoxically, nothing can be found on this firm or many other German-owned businesses in Hawaii in Stewart G. Firth, "German Firms in the Pacific Islands, 1857–1914," in *Germany in the Pacific and Far East, 1870–1914*, ed. John A. Moses and Paul M. Kennedy (St. Lucia: University of Queensland Press, 1977), 3–25; for additional information, see Stefan Manz, "America in Global Context: German Entrepreneurs around the World," in *Immigrant Entrepreneurship: German-American Business Biographies, 1720 to the Present*, Vol. 3, ed. Giles R. Hoyt and the German Historical Institute.
10. *San Francisco News Letter* 29 (1878/79), 27 July, 20; *Pacific Commercial Advertiser*, 29 April 1879, 2; *Pacific Commercial Advertiser*, 6 September 1879, 3; *The Planters' Monthly* 1 (1882), 134; Charles R. Buckland, "Report of the Agent of the Boston Exhibition," *Pacific Commercial Advertiser*, 7 July 1883, 3.
11. Uwe Spiekermann, "Das gekaufte Königreich: Claus Spreckels, die Hawaiian Commercial Company und die Grenzen wirtschaftlicher Einflussnahme im Königtum Hawaii, 1875–1898," in *Tatort Unternehmen: Zur Geschichte der Wirtschaftskriminalität im 20. und 21. Jahrhundert*, ed. Hartmut Berghoff, Cornelia Rauh, and Thomas Welskopp (Berlin: De Gruyter Oldenbourg, 2016), 49–53; Carol A. MacLennan, *Sovereign Sugar: Industry and Environment in Hawai'i* (Honolulu: University of Hawaii Press, 2015); C. Allan Jones and Robert V. Osgood, *From King Cane to the Last Sugar Mill: Agricultural Technology and the Making of Hawai'i's Premier Crop* (Honolulu: University of Hawaii Press, 2015).
12. "Incorporations," *Sacramento Daily Union*, 3 October 1878, 3; "A Serious Mistake," *San Francisco Chronicle*, 16 November 1883, 3.
13. Cf., although with some mistakes, Jessica B. Teisch, *Engineering Nature: Water, Development, and the Global Spread of American Environmental Expertise* (Chapel Hill: University of North Carolina Press, 2011), 137–41.
14. Cf. Warren D. Hanson, *San Francisco Water and Power: A History of the Municipal Water Department & Hetch Hetchy System*, rev. ed. (San Francisco: SF Public Utilities Commission, 2005), 8; Gray Brechin, *Imperial San Francisco: Urban Power, Earthly Ruin* (Berkeley: University of California Press, 2006), 79–80, although Schüssler is presented here as a "Swiss" citizen; "A Water-Systems Engineer and Architect of Dams," *The Daily Journal*, 8 June 2009.
15. *Pacific Commercial Advertiser*, 25 May 1878, 2; *Pacific Commercial Advertiser*, 1 June 1878, 2.
16. "Mr. Spreckles [sic] Projected Enterprise on Maui," *Pacific Commercial Advertiser*, 12 October 1878, 3.
17. John S. Hittell, *The Commerce and Industries of the Pacific Coast* (San Francisco: A.L. Bancroft, 1883), 548.
18. *Pacific Commercial Advertiser*, 4 October 1879, 2; *Sacramento Daily Record-Union*, 10 May 1880, 2.

19. "The Hawaiian Commercial and Sugar Company's Estate at Spreckelsville, Maui, H.I.," *The Planters' Monthly* 8 (1889): 68–75.
20. *Pacific Commercial Advertiser*, 31 January 1880, 2.
21. On the latter, see Mansel B. Blackford, *Fragile Paradise: The Impact of Tourism on Maui, 1959–2000* (Lawrence: University Press of Kansas, 2000). In 2016, however, sugar plantation was phased out by Alexander & Baldwin, successor of the Spreckels family.
22. German-Americans often perceived Claus Spreckels as a pioneer of Germans in Hawaii: "Deutsche in Hawaii," *Scranton Wochenblatt*, 4 December 1902, 6.
23. Edward Bechert, *Working in Hawaii: A Labor History* (Honolulu: University of Hawaii Press, 1985); Ronald Takaki, *Pau Hana: Plantation Life and Labor in Hawaii, 1835–1920* (Honolulu: University of Hawaii Press, 1983).
24. "Spreckelsville Plantation, Hawaiian Islands," *Northern Star*, 26 July 1882, 2; Jacob Adler, *Claus Spreckels: The Sugar King in Hawaii* (Honolulu: Mutual Publishing, 1966), 69–79.
25. John M. Van Dyke, *Who Owns the Crown Lands of Hawai'i?* (Honolulu: University of Hawaii Press, 2008).
26. Helen Jennings, ed., *Chronology and Documentary Handbook of the State of Hawaii* (Dobbs Ferry, NY: Oceana, 1978), 9; Dirk Hoerder, *Cultures in Contact: World Migrations in the Second Millennium* (Durham, NC: Duke University Press, 2002), 394.
27. "What Claus Spreckels Says," *Pacific Commercial Advertiser*, 6 December 1879, suppl., 5 (Hawaiian Commercial Company only).
28. "The Danger of Unrestricted Chinese Immigration," *Pacific Commercial Advertiser*, 30 August 1879, 3.
29. *Honolulu Advertiser*, 17 October 1882, 2.
30. "The Slave Traffic," *San Francisco Chronicle*, 3 June 1883, 8; based on a *Welt Post* (Leipzig) article.
31. *Stenographische Berichte über die Verhandlungen des Reichstages*, Leg. V, Sess. II 1882/83, vol. 2 (Berlin: Pindter, 1883), 1496–98 (Kapp).
32. "Hawaiian Sugar," *Chicago Daily Tribune*, 13 November 1882, 8.
33. For a more general perspective see A[uguste] Marques, "Portuguese Immigration to Hawaiian Islands," in *Hawaiian Almanac and Annual for 1887*, ed. Tho[ma]s F. Thrum (Honolulu: Press Publishing, 1886), 74–78; John Henry Felix and Peter F. Senecal, *The Portuguese in Hawaii* (Honolulu: no publisher, 1978). Until 1887, nearly 11,000 Portuguese immigrants, mostly families, went to Hawaii.
34. W[illiam] D[e Witt] Alexander, *Kalakaua's Reign: A Sketch of Hawaiian History* (Honolulu: Hawaiian Gazette, 1894), 28; Gerald Tulchinsky, *Taking Root: The Origins of the Canadian Jewish Community* (Hanover: Brandeis University Press, 1993), 64–65.
35. *Der Deutsche Correspondent*, 3 June 1884, 3.
36. "Report of the Secretary of the Planters' Labor and Supply Company," *The Planters' Monthly* 2 (1883), 185–94, here 192.
37. *The Planters' Monthly* 1 (1882), 141–42, here 141; "Report of the Secretary of the Planter's Labor and Supply Company," *The Planters' Monthly* 1 (1882), 176–88, here 184.
38. *Daily Alta California*, 6 January 1884, 7.
39. "The Sandwich Islands," *Argus*, 19 February 1884, 10.
40. "Chinese Emigration to Hawaii," *North China Herald*, 31 July 1891, 9.
41. Carol MacLennan, "Kilauea Sugar Plantation in 1912: A Snapshot," *Hawaiian Journal of History* 41 (2007): 19.
42. Richard Hawkins, "Hackfeld, Heinrich," in *Immigrant Entrepreneurship: German-American Business Biographies, 1720 to the Present*, vol. 2, edited by William J. Hausman and the German Historical Institute. Last modified 13 February 2017. http://www.immigrantentrepreneurship.org/entry.php?rec=285.

43. "The Sand-Lot Party's Spokesman," *Daily Alta California*, 11 March 1880, 1.
44. "Kearney in Court," *Daily Alta California*, 13 May 1880, 1.
45. "The Kanakas are simply children. There is a gap between them and the whites which cannot be bridged" ("Spreckels Arrives, But Undecided," *Chicago Daily Tribune*, 4 May 1893, 4).
46. Cf. Richard A. Walker, *The Conquest of Bread: 150 Years of Agribusiness in California* (New York: New Press, 2004).
47. "A Beet-Sugar Refinery to be Built at Watsonville," *Daily Alta California*, 6 November 1887, 5. During the first season, Spreckels made contracts with 163 farmers ("Fighting a Trust," *Daily Alta California*, 3 September 1888, 1). Many of them, however, complained about the heavy manual labor and the continuous need to deal with the hoe. Those who remained in business, hired farmworkers. At the same time, Claus Spreckels tried to make contracts with larger ranches, depending on contract workers. A detailed analysis of the early beet sugar industry in California was given by Richard Steven Street, *Beasts in the Field: A Narrative History of California Farmworkers, 1769–1913* (Stanford, CA: Stanford University Press, 2004), 307–33, while he has discussed the Watsonville case only briefly (ibid., 361–62).
48. Adolph B. Spreckels stated "that 95 per cent of the labor of beet raising at Watsonville is done by American laborers" ("Japan Moderates its Demands," *Chicago Daily Tribune*, 10 June 1897, 3). An examination by the labor commissioner, however, came to the result that two-thirds of the cultivation work was done by approximately one thousand Chinese and Japanese ("In Beet Fields," *Pacific Commercial Advertiser*, 31 July 1897, 2).
49. "Rural Homestead Plan," *New York Times*, 21 May 1897; "To Colonize the West," *Ogden Standard Examiner*, 28 August 1897, 1.
50. "Abolish the Poor," *Chicago Daily Tribune*, 12 December 1897, 35.
51. Carey McWilliams, *Factories in the Field: The Story of Migratory Farm Labor in California* (Berkeley: University of California Press, 1999), 88.
52. A Japanese tea garden was already an attraction at the 1894 Midwinter Exposition in San Francisco's Golden Gate Park. Richard W. Amero, *Balboa Park and the 1915 Exposition* (Charleston, SC: History Press, 2013), 149.
53. *Washington Post*, 16 April 1916, RP2.
54. "Mrs. Wakefield's Newest Fad," *The Wasp* 72 (1916), 4 March, 8; "The Wakefields Depart," *The Wasp* 72 (1916), 15 April, 7. Although Mrs. Wakefield returned to San Francisco after some months, she continued sojourning in Tahiti: "The Marriage of Mrs. Lily Holbrook," *The Wasp* 100 (1920), 24 January, 9.
55. *The Parents' Magazine* 6 (1931), 29.
56. Jacob Adler, "The Oceanic Steamship Company: A Link in Claus Spreckels' Hawaiian Sugar Empire," *Pacific Historical Review* 29 (1960): 257–69.
57. "The New Steamship Line," *Pacific Commercial Advertiser*, 22 April 1882, 4; "Two New Steamships," *San Francisco News Letter* 33 (1882/83), 15 July, 1.
58. *Coshocton Age*, 25 July 1885, 2.
59. "John D. Spreckels & Bros.," *Daily Alta California*, 7 July 1889, 12. The Spreckels also imported coal from Japan, but the volume remained relatively low (*Daily Alta California*, 18 June 1888, 2). Other bulk freight was lumber and cement. Coal was also imported by chartered ships from Liverpool.
60. "The San Diego Terminus," *San Francisco Merchant* 18 (1887), 24 June, 72.
61. "San Diego to be the Headquarter," *Los Angeles Herald*, 5 August 1887, 1; "Articles of Incorporation of the Spreckels Brothers Commercial Company," *Yuma Daily Sun*, 12 October 1949, 5.
62. *The Great Southwest* 1 (1889), no. 3, 8; ibid., no. 6, 9.
63. *Hotel Del Coronado History* (Coronado, CA: Hotel Del Coronado Heritage Department, 2013).

64. An overview is offered in Bryan Farrell, *Hawaii: The Legend that Sells* (Honolulu: University of Hawaii Press, 1982).
65. "The O.S.S. Co's Steamer 'Mariposa,'" *San Francisco Merchant* 10 (1883), 27 July, 320; *San Francisco News Letter* 34 (1883/84), 5 January, 3.
66. "Amusements," *Los Angeles Herald*, 9 December 1891, 4.
67. "The Music Hall," *Pacific Commercial Advertiser*, 18 August 1883, 2; "The Honolulu Theatre," *San Francisco Merchant* 10 (1883), 14 September, 480. After it was destroyed by fire in 1895, the Spreckels and Irwin built a new opera house: see "Review of Operations for 1896," *Pacific Commercial Adviser*, 2 January 1897, 1. The Spreckels also financed the Hilo Hotel in 1903 to develop Big Island for tourism; this was a failure, however, and had to close in 1904 ("Hilo Hotel," *Hilo Tribune*, 15 May 1903, 4; "The Hotel Proposition," *Hilo Tribune*, 15 July 1904, 2).
68. C.B. Goodell, "Musings at San Diego Bay," *Ogden Standard Examiner*, 4 April 1891, 4.
69. Richard V. Dodge, *Rails of the Silver Gate: The Spreckels San Diego Empire* (San Marino, CA: Golden West, 1960), 31. Cf. William H. *Wilson, The City Beautiful Movement (Baltimore, MD: Johns Hopkins University Press, 1989)*.
70. "Trade with China," *Los Angeles Times*, 14 August 1902, 3; "Will Invade the Orient," *San Francisco Chronicle*, 14 August 1902, 3. In contrast to his father, who regularly cooperated with German-Americans, the new company was an endeavor of established Yankee bankers and some representatives of the consumer good export industries.
71. Guenter B. Risse, *Plague, Fear, and Politics in San Francisco's Chinatown* (Baltimore, MD: Johns Hopkins University Press, 2012), 52–53.
72. "Chinese Consul General Would Increase Trade," *San Francisco Call*, 14 July 1900, 2. The *Call* was owned by John D. Spreckels.
73. "Will Help the Pacific Museum," *San Francisco Chronicle*, 31 March 1900, 14.
74. Richard Waterman, "The Movement for Museum Extension," *Chicago Daily Tribune*, 14 July 1901, 13.
75. Details on both institutions can be found in Séverine Antigone Marin, "Introducing Small Firms to International Markets: The Debates over the Commercial Museums in France and Germany, 1880–1910," in *The Rise of Marketing and Market Research*, ed. Hartmut Berghoff, Philip Scranton, and Uwe Spiekermann (Houndmills, UK: Palgrave Macmillan, 2012), 128–51.
76. "George M. Hawley has Sold Out," *San Diego Union*, 3 November 1902, 5. The Union Steamship Company was also owned by John D. Spreckels.
77. *Commercial Relations of the United States with Foreign Countries during the Year 1903*, vol. 2 (Washington: Government Printing Office, 1904), 416.
78. "Trade Dull in Far East," *Salt Lake Telegram*, 22 January 1904, 7; "Company Quits Business," *Oregonian*, 23 January 1904, 14.
79. Alexander C. T. Geppert, *Fleeting Cities: Imperial Expositions in Fin-de-Siècle Europe* (Houndmills, UK: Palgrave Macmillan, 2013). John D. Spreckels' *San Francisco Call* had already tried to promote a San Francisco exposition in 1900 ("Worth of all Support," *Oakland Tribune*, 22 February 1898, 4).
80. "The Old San Francisco Spirit Still Lives," *The Wasp* 63 (1910), 7 May, 13; *San Francisco Call*, 29 April 1910, 1.
81. "The Money and the World's Fair," *Oakland Tribune*, 27 February 1910, 17; "Panama Fair Heads Quit," *Ogdensburg Journal*, 20 June 1911, 4.
82. Charles S. Maier, *Leviathan 2.0: Inventing Modern Statehood* (Cambridge, MA: Belknap, 2012).
83. Arthur Power Dudden, ed., *American Empire in the Pacific: From Trade to Strategic Balance, 1700–1992* (Aldershot, UK: Ashgate, 2004).

84. Hawaii became a US territory on 30 April 1900, but sovereignty had already been transferred on 12 April 1898. American dominance surely started earlier, with the acquisition of the Pearl Harbor naval base in 1887 as an important milestone.
85. "Prospective Ships," *Los Angeles Herald*, 5 June 1890, 1; "On the Naval List," *San Francisco Morning Call*, 26 January 1892, 2. The United States also supported the transition from coal to oil burning briefly after the turn of the century ("Alameda to Use Oil," *Hilo Tribune*, 9 May 1902, 8; *Chicago Daily Tribune*, 5 October 1902, 42).
86. "Tug Boats in Uncle Sam's Service," *Oakland Tribune*, 14 April 1898, 8.
87. "The Epidemic Still Rages," *Ogden Standard Examiner*, 24 December 1895, 1.
88. At that time the United States had already started the rebuilding of their navy, but it remained far behind the leading European powers, at least until the Spanish–American War of 1898. Cf. Paul H. Silverstone, *The New Navy, 1883–1922* (New York: Routledge, 2006).
89. "The English War Preparation," *Manchester Evening News*, 21 April 1885, 4; "'Alameda' and 'Mariposa,'" *Daily Alta California*, 23 April 1885, 1. For a short while, John D. Spreckels expected that the vessels would be purchased by the British on his terms (*Sacramento Daily Union*, 24 April 1885, 2), but eventually the two powers found a diplomatic compromise.
90. "Spreckels' War Ships," *Daily Alta California*, 2 February 1889, 2.
91. "Tracy Seeking Ships," *Chicago Daily Tribune*, 24 December 1891, 1; "Chilean Brutality," *Los Angeles Herald*, 22 December 1891, 1.
92. *San Francisco News Letter* 43 (1891), 3 October, 24; *The Argonaut* 30 (1892), 4 April, 2–3, here 3.
93. "Naval Militia," *Los Angeles Herald*, 5 December 1888, 6; "Vorschlag zur Gründung einer Marine-Miliz," *Der Deutsche Correspondent*, 6 December 1888, 1.
94. "Merritt is Leader," *Chicago Daily Tribune*, 5 June 1898, 3; "U.S. Dispatch Boat," *Hawaiian Gazette*, 14 October 1898, 6; "Shipping Reports," *Sydney Morning Herald*, 21 February 1899, 8.
95. "Two Kinds of Men," *Salt Lake Herald*, 23 June 1898, 4.
96. "The Oceanic Steamship Company," *Sydney Morning Herald*, 11 March 1901, 5; "The San Francisco Mail Service," *Sydney Morning Herald*, 13 March 1901, 8. John D. Spreckels went to Sydney to discuss this problem with officials.
97. "Carriage of Mails," *Examiner*, 21 July 1904, 4.
98. *Los Angeles Herald*, 6 October 1901, 10; "U.S. Gets Spreckels' Island at $6,098,333," *Oakland Tribune*, 31 December 1921, 8.
99. "Visits San Diego Forts," *Nevada State Journal*, 29 July 1913, 3.
100. "Delegation Secures Foreign Trade Convention," *San Francisco Business* 7 (1923), November 23, 23; "Pacific Foreign Trade Council to Meet Here in March," *San Francisco Business* 12 (1926), January 13, 15.
101. Eric Hobsbawm, *The Age of Empire 1875–1914* (New York: Vintage Books, 1989).

Bibliography

Adler, Jacob. *Claus Spreckels: The Sugar King in Hawaii*. Honolulu: Mutual Publishing, 1966.
———. "The Oceanic Steamship Company: A Link in Claus Spreckels' Hawaiian Sugar Empire." *Pacific Historical Review* 29 (1960): 257–69.
Alexander, William De Witt. *Kalakaua's Reign: A Sketch of Hawaiian History*. Honolulu: Hawaiian Gazette, 1894.
Amero, Richard W. *Balboa Park and the 1915 Exposition*. Charleston, SC: History Press, 2013.

Bechert, Edward. *Working in Hawaii: A Labor History*. Honolulu: University of Hawaii Press, 1985.
Blackford, Mansel B. *Fragile Paradise: The Impact of Tourism on Maui, 1959–2000*. Lawrence: University Press of Kansas, 2000.
Brechin, Gray. *Imperial San Francisco: Urban Power, Earthly Ruin*. Berkeley: University of California Press, 2006.
Dodge, Richard V. *Rails of the Silver Gate: The Spreckels San Diego Empire*. San Marino, CA: Golden West, 1960.
Dudden, Arthur Power, ed. *American Empire in the Pacific: From Trade to Strategic Balance, 1700–1992*. Aldershot, UK: Ashgate, 2004.
Farrell, Bryan. *Hawaii: The Legend that Sells*. Honolulu: University of Hawaii Press, 1982.
Felix, John Henry, and Peter F. Senecal. *The Portuguese in Hawaii*. Honolulu: no publisher, 1978.
Firth, Stewart G. "German Firms in the Pacific Islands, 1857–1914." In *Germany in the Pacific and Far East, 1870–1914*, ed. John A. Moses and Paul M. Kennedy, 3–25. St. Lucia: University of Queensland Press, 1977.
Geppert, Alexander C. T. *Fleeting Cities: Imperial Expositions in Fin-de-Siècle Europe*. Houndmills, UK: Palgrave Macmillan, 2013.
Gosewinkel, Dieter. *Einbürgern und Ausschließen: Die Nationalisierung der Staatsangehörigkeit vom Deutschen Bund bis zur Bundesrepublik Deutschland*. Göttingen: Vandenhoeck & Ruprecht, 2001.
Hanson, Warren D. *San Francisco Water and Power: A History of the Municipal Water Department & Hetch Hetchy System*, rev. ed. San Francisco: SF Public Utilities Commission, 2005.
Hawkins, Richard. "Hackfeld, Heinrich." In *Immigrant Entrepreneurship: German-American Business Biographies, 1720 to the Present*, Vol. 2, edited by William J. Hausman and the German Historical Institute. Last modified 13 February 2017. http://www.immigrantentrepreneurship.org/entry.php?rec=285.
Hittell, John S. *The Commerce and Industries of the Pacific Coast*. San Francisco, CA: A.L. Bancroft, 1883.
Hobsbawm, Eric. *The Age of Empire 1875–1914*. New York: Vintage Books, 1989.
Hoerder, Dirk. *Cultures in Contact: World Migrations in the Second Millennium*. Durham, NC: Duke University Press, 2002.
Hotel del Coronado History. Coronado, CA: Hotel Del Coronado Heritage Department, 2013.
Jennings, Helen, ed. *Chronology and Documentary Handbook of the State of Hawaii*. Dobbs Ferry, NY: Oceana, 1978.
Jones, C. Allan, and Robert V. Osgood. *From King Cane to the Last Sugar Mill: Agricultural Technology and the Making of Hawaii's Premier Crop*. Honolulu: University of Hawaii Press, 2015.
MacLennan, Carol. "Kilauea Sugar Plantation in 1912: A Snapshot." *Hawaiian Journal of History* 41 (2007): 1–34.
———. *Sovereign Sugar: Industry and Environment in Hawai'i*. Honolulu: University of Hawaii Press, 2015.
Maier, Charles S. *Leviathan 2.0: Inventing Modern Statehood*. Cambridge, MA: Belknap, 2012.
Manz, Stefan. "America in Global Context: German Entrepreneurs around the World." In *Immigrant Entrepreneurship: German-American Business Biographies, 1720 to the Present*. Vol. 3, edited by Giles R. Hoyt and the German Historical Institute. Last modified 25 September 2014. http://www.immigrantentrepreneurship.org/entry.php?rec=187.

Marin, Séverine Antigone. "Introducing Small Firms to International Markets: The Debates over the Commercial Museums in France and Germany, 1880–1910." In *The Rise of Marketing and Market Research*, edited by Hartmut Berghoff, Philip Scranton, and Uwe Spiekermann, 128–51. Houndmills, UK: Palgrave Macmillan, 2012.

McWilliams, Carey. *Factories in the Field: The Story of Migratory Farm Labor in California*. Berkeley: University of California Press, 1999.

Nathans, Eli. *The Politics of Citizenship in Germany: Ethnicity, Utility and Nationalism*. Oxford: Berg, 2004.

O'Donnell, Krista, Renate Bridenthal, and Nancy Reagin, eds. *The Heimat Abroad: The Boundaries of Germanness*. Ann Arbor: University of Michigan Press, 2005.

Pletcher, David M. *The Diplomacy of Involvement: American Economic Expansion across the Pacific, 1784–1900*. Columbia: University of Missouri Press, 2001.

Risse, Guenter B. *Plague, Fear, and Politics in San Francisco's Chinatown*. Baltimore, MD: Johns Hopkins University Press, 2012.

Schweizer, Nikolaus Rudolf. "Hawaii und die Deutschen." In *Die Deutsche Südsee 1884–1914*, edited by Hermann Joseph Hiery, 725–36. Paderborn: Schöningh, 2000.

Silverstone, Paul H. *The New Navy, 1883–1922*. New York: Routledge, 2006.

Spiekermann, Uwe. "Claus Spreckels: A Biographical Case Study of Nineteenth-Century American Immigrant Entrepreneurship." *Business and Economic History Online* (2010). Retrieved 15 July 2018 from http://www.thebhc.org/sites/default/files/spiekermann.pdf.

———. "Das gekaufte Königreich: Claus Spreckels, die Hawaiian Commercial Company und die Grenzen wirtschaftlicher Einflussnahme im Königtum Hawaii, 1875–1898." In *Tatort Unternehmen: Zur Geschichte der Wirtschaftskriminalität im 20. und 21. Jahrhundert*, edited by Hartmut Berghoff, Cornelia Rauh, and Thomas Welskopp, 47–66. Berlin: De Gruyter Oldenbourg, 2016.

———. "An Ordinary Man among Titans: The Life of Walter P. Spreckels." In *Immigrant Entrepreneurship: The German-American Experience since 1700*, edited by Hartmut Berghoff and Uwe Spiekermann, 263–84. Washington, DC: GHI, 2016.

Street, Richard Steven. *Beasts in the Field: A Narrative History of California Farmworkers, 1769–1913*. Stanford, CA: Stanford University Press, 2004.

Takaki, Ronald. *Pau Hana: Plantation Life and Labor in Hawaii, 1835–1920*. Honolulu: University of Hawaii Press, 1983.

Teisch, Jessica B. *Engineering Nature: Water, Development, and the Global Spread of American Environmental Expertise*. Chapel Hill: University of North Carolina Press, 2011.

Tulchinsky, Gerald. *Taking Root: The Origins of the Canadian Jewish Community*. Hanover: Brandeis University Press, 1993.

Van Dyke, John M. *Who Owns the Crown Lands of Hawai'i?* Honolulu: University of Hawaii Press, 2008.

Walker, Richard A. *The Conquest of Bread: 150 Years of Agribusiness in California*. New York: New Press, 2004.

Wilson, William H. *The City Beautiful Movement*. Baltimore, MD: Johns Hopkins University Press, 1989.

Chapter 8

WORK AND NON-WORK IN THE "PARADISE OF THE SOUTH SEA"

Samoa, ca. 1890–1914

Jürgen Schmidt

Introduction

Notions of work and labor have undergone radical transformation in recent years. Different processes and reasons for this development come into play. First of all, the European perspective on work, workers, and working classes was explicitly criticized for its exclusive emphasis on the male breadwinner and on wage labor. Other forms of work—in the household, unpaid work—remained largely marginalized.[1] Second, the strict borderline between work and non-work has become more and more blurred.[2] To take only one example from professions that have played a central role in Samoa's history from the eighteenth century onward: What work did European explorers of the Pacific perform? Was their traveling a form of work or—leaving bad traveling conditions aside—a kind of leisure, and an escape from the expected routines of everyday work? Third, work and labor—as seen from a European or Western perspective—was seriously challenged by colonial perspectives. How could working-class history be written on a global scale if research only focuses on the free wage laborer, meaning the development toward a market-based society and economy where a worker could negotiate his wage and workplace autonomously? This conception of labor entails its own difficulties (for example, how "free" was the free wage laborer on the labor market?) But it also leaves out all forms of unfree labor such as slavery and indentured servitude, which became important especially outside of Europe and in conjunction with the global spread of a market-based economy.[3]

These different strands inform this chapter about work and non-work in Samoa in the late nineteenth and early twentieth centuries. Samoa as a research field was

---

Notes from this chapter begin on page 207.

chosen because one can find different perspectives, perceptions, and practices of work in a nutshell. Accordingly, the chapter does not describe Samoa's history under German rule or give a complete history of different work practices in Samoa. Rather, it analyzes discourses and imaginations of work observed and performed on this Pacific island. How was work perceived and constructed in the special context of Samoa? What are the interrelations and connections between "German-specific" work ethics and practices in Samoa?

The chapter emphasizes the specificity of the island, which, like other Polynesian islands, was seen in Germany and Europe as a kind of paradise.[4] Alongside the colony of Togo in Africa, Samoa was the only German colony that was not dependent on subsidies from the German state in the last decade under colonial rule. In addition, the colonial system was characterized by a paternalism that tried to protect the Samoans from the "danger" of modernity and secure their traditional culture. But despite Samoa's exceptionalism within Germany's colonial system, one has to be careful not to portray the colonial situation in too harmonious a manner. Traditional leadership, for example, was transformed and recast to suit the needs of the colonizers. On the other hand, these fundamental structural changes pacified the formerly conflict-ridden Samoan society. On the one hand, Samoans experienced probably the most advanced self-administration in Germany's colonial empire. On the other hand, after a small group of Samoans wanted to reinstall previous forms of self-government, hierarchies, and administration in 1908/9, seventy of them were banished and sent to Saipan in the Mariana Islands—more than two thousand miles away. However, although this uprising was a clear conspiracy against the colonial state and system, no insurgents were sentenced to death.[5]

The first section of the chapter gives a short overview of Samoa's economic and social history in the nineteenth century. The following sections address the questions posed by describing five different types of work found in Samoa.

Historical, Economic, and Social Background of Samoa's Colonization

German economic activities on this Pacific island began in the late 1840s and became more stabilized by 1856 when the German trading company Godeffroy from Hamburg established a permanent branch office in Apia. This laid the foundation for a German community besides the already existing British and American communities. The Godeffroy Company was mainly focused on trading in its first years of existence on Samoa, but from 1864 onward became an important landowner and established plantations. The first attempts at integration into the global market were made with cotton because there was a cotton shortage during the American Civil War. In the cotton industry during this period, new producers like India, Egypt, and Brazil entered the market, and Samoa's cotton only remained relevant for a brief period. Against the global players, Samoan plantations had little chance of producing enough profitable cotton, although according to a British report, in 1878 German enterprises exported cotton worth 1 million Mark from Samoa and Tonga—40 percent of the overall export from both islands.[6]

The most important product from the 1870s onward was copra, the dried meat of the coconut used to extract coconut oil. The leading trading agents of the Godeffroy Company, August Unshelm and Theodor Weber, were experimenting with switching the transport from coconut oil to the dried meat, which would facilitate transportation and reduce costs. Under Theodor Weber, who was in charge of Godeffroy Company in Samoa from the year 1864, this change was successfully realized. Copra became the main export good from Samoa. Especially under the successor of the Godeffroy Company, the Deutsche Handels- und Plantagen-Gesellschaft (DHPG, German Trade and Plantation Society), copra dominated exports from Samoa. Between 1900 and 1906, between 95 and 99 percent of the value of the entire export goods from Samoa was from copra; in 1907 this fell below the 90 percent mark for the first time, and by 1913 it had fallen below 80 percent.

The decline of copra exports from Samoa corresponded with the growth of cacao, which grew from 0.4 percent in 1900 to 9.2 percent in 1908, reaching almost 20 percent by 1913.[7] This increase was facilitated by another social and economic development: the migration and settlement of small-scale plantation owners from the late 1890s onward. While the German Trade and Plantation Society and the colonial administration never favored a transformation of the Pacific islands into a German settler colony, the situation changed with the growing characterization of Samoa as a paradise island, and a place where one could easily make one's fortune. These new settlers mainly invested in cacao and rubber plantations.[8]

Although Samoa became more attractive as a residence, in total figures the German population on the island was never bigger than any small village in contemporary Germany. From 1902 to 1914 the number of Germans increased from 151 to 373. Europeans and Americans together totaled 600 in 1914; about 100 of them were female, but only 10 percent were of "marriageable age," as an official statistic noted in 1914. The 1914 statistics also classified 1,000 people as "half-castes"; but this only comprised those children who were officially acknowledged by their white fathers. In 1911, about 34,000 Samoans were living on the Samoan islands.[9]

Self- and External Perception of Work, Work Attitudes, and Working Conditions: Five Types of Work in Samoa

In the following section I will synthesize different forms of work according to self- and external perception of work, work attitudes, and real working conditions according to five types.

Samoans

Work among Samoans was adjusted to their needs and climatic conditions. Due to the climate, there existed only a limited possibility for food storage. On the other hand, the climate did not make it necessary to stock food. The rhythm of work was different from European forms of work. A German agronomist described that Samoans only needed to till the fields of yam and taro on Fridays, as they received other food as a gift from nature.[10] However, while this Samoan pattern and perception could be found in very different tropical regions, the view with regard to Samoa and its inhabitants was different than in other colonial contexts, even within the Pacific world. In Melanesia, for example, a very strict labor regime was installed, and inhabitants of German New Guinea were forced to work on plantations.[11]

One reason for this segregation between Melanesian and Samoan work attitudes lay in racism,[12] which also included the attempt to "whiten" the Samoan natives during the nineteenth century, as George Steinmetz has pointed out. While Samoans were described with color attributes like brown or bronze, Melanesians were seen as black and dark.[13] As a result, two different spaces were constructed: the dark and dangerous zone of New Guinea where headhunters lived and cannibalism occurred, and the bright and relatively peaceful place of Samoa. There enmities between different tribes could be observed, too, but they were interpreted in "modern" terms of struggles about political power and influence—and with the help of German regulation and intermediation these conflicts could be overcome. The Samoans were transformed into "noble savages."[14]

Such fundamentally different constructions of behavior and culture influenced the view on work. While the perception of Melanesian work fitted into the usual colonial stereotype of the lazy native, who had to be educated by forced regimented work, the attitude to Samoan work was more ambivalent. First of all, Samoan work was interpreted as part of the paradisiac natural state, somehow admired as an alternative to the predominant working conditions in the "civilized" colonial center. Franz Reinecke, botanist and anthropologist, even drew parallels between German students and Samoans by quoting a *Burschenschaft* song describing the idealistic students' carefree living, and whose "life-course is love, air and the tone of songs," which in Reinecke's eyes was a reality for Samoans.[15]

Therefore, such forms of work were accepted and regarded as a kind of "laissez faire" in a Garden of Eden: "All attempts to accustom the Samoans to regular work failed due to the natural idleness of these kind people," described travel novelist Otto Ehlers in 1895.[16] According to this conception, laziness among Samoans was a shortcoming, but one Germans had to forgive because the Samoans were such kind and pleasant people. It was the perspective of a good-tempered father who could only view his children with affection. A few years later, Richard Deeken agreed with Ehlers' perception of Samoan working attitudes: "The Samoans possess everything in opulence what they need to fulfill their needs. Hence, they feel no tendency for regular, constant work." Deeken, a former lieutenant, was one of the most influential promoters of Samoa as a new and huge space for German settlers, and he activated many of the stereotypes of Samoa as a paradise in the Pacific.[17] Because these "salvage colonists" refused force as a means to bring Samoans to work, a kind of obliging resignation was the predominant tone among these authors. A change in the working attitudes and work ethics of the Samoans would "primarily depend upon the Samoans themselves."[18]

Although the acceptance of Samoan working attitudes was an important discourse, one also has to point to the fact that this attitude was highly controversial and that more critical voices existed, too. The ambivalence with regard to the work of Samoans could be found even within one text of a single author. Ferdinand Wohltmann, professor of agronomy, who admitted in his book about his "Samoa exploration" that the "adjustment" and "upheaval" of the Samoans to modern production forms and modern culture was up to the Samoans, emphasized in the same text that Germany "hardly seized our colonies to allow the natives to live a free, comfortable life in a land of milk and honey." That Samoans, due to high leasing receipts for land, could live in a status of "well-off pensioner" was unacceptable for him and not compatible with the "interest to educate the natives." Frieda Zieschank, the spouse of a German settler, expressed the opinion that efforts should be taken to train and to educate the Samoans to work. Especially the small-scale German settlers arriving from the end of the nineteenth century needed a cheap labor force, and demanded steps toward a forced labor system.[19]

Yet, the opposite was the case. After West Samoa officially became a German colony in 1900, the German imperial governor of Samoa, Wilhelm Solf, protected Samoans from such demands. Samoan chiefs pointed out in a petition in 1903 to Governor Solf: "It is practice that nobody on these islands is doing menial work. … It is true that Samoans are very strong workers, but it is against our custom that a Samoan is doing slavery work."[20] However, Samoans were obliged to work in street and infrastructure building projects—and Samoans needed an income to pay the taxes which amounted to twelve Mark for the male head of a household and four Mark per year for unmarried male Samoans (which went up to eight in 1906).[21]

This brings us to some aspects of Samoan working situations and its varieties. First, Samoans adapted traditional work to new methods. The traveler and writer Otto Ehlers described in his 1895-published book that some fishermen were still standing up to their necks in the waters of the bays and throwing their nets, while others were going by boat further away from the coastline and using dynamite for fishing. This dangerous but effective form of fishing guaranteed a surplus beyond self-consumption, and opened the opportunity for Samoan fishermen to act as merchants on the market. In addition, Samoans adjusted to capitalist and colonial conditions by leasing land to settlers and the German administration.[22]

Second, that the accusation of laziness was nothing more than a prejudice becomes obvious with regard to concrete production figures. In 1912, of about 11,000 tons of copra only 3,300 were gathered and processed in the plantations of the German Trade and Plantation Society, while the rest came from Samoan plantations and was sold by the Samoans to the DHPG.[23]

Third, Samoans in general did not refuse to work for Europeans but they knew about their importance and value for the mostly German settlers and traders. They used their strong bargaining position to demand daily wages of up to four Mark (after about 1900) which corresponded to wages in Germany. Consciousness of their power, not subordinating under a contract, and only working on a daily basis with the autonomy to leave the workplace when they had earned enough, or thought that they could earn more at another workplace, created not only anger among German settlers, but reinforced their picture of lazy Samoans.[24]

Finally, Samoan chiefs and leaders who were responsible for the Samoan self-administration got paid for their political and administration activities and functions. These expenses were covered by the Samoan taxes, as was typical of indirect rule within German colonialism.[25]

Beachcombers

With Christian Kracht's novel *Imperium*, published in 2012, the social figure of the dropouts in the South Sea at the turn to the twentieth century became well known to a broader public.[26] The character of the dropout has accompanied Samoan history almost since the first permanent European settlement. In 1856 the commander of the America Pacific fleet reported that in Apia a "state of society" existed "that beggars all description; composed of a heterogeneous mass of the most immoral and dissolute foreigners that ever disgraced humanity; principally composed of Americans and Englishmen, several of whom had been Sidney [sic] convicts."[27] In German travel reports, the social figure of the "beachcomber" showed up again and again. Siegfried Genthe speaks in his travel report of "imbruted whites (*verwilderten Weißen*)", who in language, clothing and way of living "are more wogs (*Kanaken*) than Europeans" and live out their addiction to drunkenness, debauchery, and laziness.[28] Richard Deeken, who wanted to make Samoa a settler colony, was drawing the picture of those already existing small-scale settlers who only had one aim, to continue their life "in sweet idleness and celebrate cozy lovers' trysts (*Schäferstündchen feiern*) with beautiful Samoans or even more dangerous half-caste mermaids."[29] The fear of hybridity, a dimension that Thomas Schwarz emphasizes, is obvious in such paragraphs. But it is also the fear of a lazy society that loses its merits as a nation of work, effort, and success. Beachcombers were seen as an alarming and "dubious class" consisting mainly of adventurers and colonial dropouts of English, American, and Australian origin. The Germans wanted to distance themselves from them. However, since some of the new settlers did not have enough capital to start careers as plantation owners, a number of Germans also probably entered the beachcomber social group.

To cite in the context of beachcombers a more insightful and empathic voice, Ernst von Hesse-Wartegg described the life of the very few Europeans who lived more or less isolated on the southern beaches of Samoa, and were married to Samoan women: "The good McFarlan ... has in his loneliness learned to be happy in his own way. He became a Samoan."[30] These were the forgotten drop-outs who, as Franz Reinecke pointed out, became through the "mild climate and the natural innocence" of Samoa "harmless" people themselves if alcohol abuse did not revive their savagery again. On the other hand, there were some well-known dropouts, like August Engelhardt on the small island of Kabakon in the Bismarck Archipelago described by novelist Christian Kracht. With Engelhardt's writings and his alternative lifestyle, worshipping the sun and the coconut, he became popular in the media and found followers and admirers in Europe after 1900. A small community of members of the "Order of the Sun" even settled on Kabakon.[31]

German Employees and Officials in Public Service and Business

German employees and officials in public services and business were not used to working in a tropical climate. But it was not only the climate that shaped working conditions and habits in Samoa, which were so different to those that prevailed in Germany. The huge distance from the colonial homeland guaranteed a high degree of autonomy for the German administration and companies in Samoa. Samoa, for example, was not connected with the submarine telegraph cable before World War I. Telegrams to Samoa were sent to the nearest cable station in Honolulu or Auckland, and from there they were transported as normal letters to Samoa.[32]

Before he came to Samoa, the merchant August Unshelm worked for the Godeffroy Trading Company in Valparaiso, Chile. He stated in the 1850s: "We don't work here like oxen as in Germany, rather the working time is adjusted to the requirements." Usually the employees worked six to eight hours per day, and only in the week before a steamer was due to arrive with letters and orders did they have "to work like hell" (*höllisch viel zu thun*). There is no evidence as to whether Unshelm kept this working rhythm after arriving in Samoa. However, as he took greater responsibility for trade in Samoa, he applied German working attitudes to his employees. Unshelm described both a captain of a skiff and an employee who worked in a store in Apia as "slowcoach" (*Bummler*). Both were dismissed. In contrast to them, another employee was described as "energetic" and "active," and Unshelm hoped that he also would be "persistent."[33]

While values and attitudes of work from the German context were upheld in the colonial context, Samoan reality obviously changed working conditions. Perhaps the most revealing fact is that even under official colonial rule in Samoa no standard time existed. Every Saturday at noon a cannon shot was the only orientation. While time in Germany became the most important measurement to rate and pay work, time lost its work-shaping function in the colony. "The notion of 'hurry' gets totally lost here," noted Frieda Zieschank. And Siegfried Genthe realized, after his arrival in the capital Apia, that "[h]ere everything take time, twice or three times as long as at home, and it is not a little piece of work to walk along the main street" and have a small chat with all acquaintances.[34]

A report on the state of health of German police secretary Schaaffhausen indicated that he was suffering from his uncomfortable office, which was constantly sweltering. It said he could continue his work in Samoa without problems if, rather than permanent office work, he could fulfill his service as much as possible outdoors.[35] While at home the pride in German accuracy and the quality of work was praised and supercharged by national traditions,[36] in the Samoan colony the opposite practice of work challenged these notions of German "quality work."

German Settlers

A similar ambivalent development occurred with respect to the German small-scale settlers: great plans and visions to turn Samoa into a settler colony faced a sober reality. The attempt, as proposed by Richard Deeken and others, was grounded on a political strategy to give the Pacific colony more weight in Germany. This idea challenged the politics of the colonial administration on the island under German governor Wilhelm Solf and the economic monopoly of the German Trade and Plantation Society. Since only a limited part of the island, the so-called plantation district of Apia, could be sold or leased (and most parts were under control of the DHPG), the idea of a German settler colony was nothing more than a chimera. Even when in 1909 the ban to sell land to foreigners was relaxed, this did not change the general impression. In addition, Richard Deeken, as an important promoter of the settlement movement, underestimated the necessary initial investments, so that even those Germans who wanted to start as plantation owners could soon fall into financial crisis.[37] Indeed, besides the

German Trading and Plantation Society, "None of the New German planters or firms was financially successful." Even two bigger plantation societies, the "Deutsche Samoa-Gesellschaft" and the "Safata-Samoa-Gesellschaft," could never pay a dividend. In 1904, nearly three-quarters of all foreign plantation enterprises had less than 200 acres of land. Governor Solf complained about "inferior elements" who came to Samoa after the island became attractive in Germany.[38] "Inferior" was definitely not the social status of those who wanted to start a planter career: a lot of them came from the middle classes or had been military officers. They had neither experience in (tropical) agriculture nor were they educated in this subject. Images of a master, who was investing money and earned the profits while other people did the work, definitely played a role in the decision making of Germans to move to Samoa. Deeken and other authors suggested—at least implicitly—this colonial attitude that becoming a plantation owner was an easy way to make a living in the colony.

When a young, well-educated middle-class son wrote to the Colonial Department of the Foreign Office in Berlin that he wished to settle on Samoa, but due to a lack of connections asked the office for support, the civil servant in the *Reichskolonialamt* pulled no punches and wrote the remark: "It is not the Foreign Office's duty to act as a labor agency for clerks."[39] A kind of adventurousness, simplemindedness, and exoticism gave the impression of success without much work.

Coolies

Someone had to do the work—and these were migration contract workers, so-called "coolies."[40] As mentioned, a large-scale plantation system by the Godeffroy Company had been started in the 1860s. Samoans worked on a daily wage mainly in forest clearance, and from the late 1860s onward coolies from the Kingsmill (now Gilbert) Islands were brought to the plantations. Between 1867 and 1871, 353 workers were registered. In the 1870s, workforce migration increased dramatically. Between 1873 and 1880, 2,735 workers were recruited, and after 1879 they also came from the New Hebrides (Vanuatu) and the Solomon Islands. Between 1881 and 1885, 1,472 contract workers came, mainly from different Melanesian regions—most of them from New Britain in the Bismarck Archipelago. From 1888 onward, Germany and Great Britain granted exclusively to the DHPG the right to recruit contract workers for Samoa from the Bismarck Archipelago and the Solomon Islands. Melanesian coolies came on the basis of a three-year contract, and worked and lived in very bad conditions. The death rate was high; employers had the right of physical coercion and most of the coolies did not renew their contracts after three years.[41] Desertion in Samoa was high, hence in the 1890s at some plantations convict stations were established and a kind of labor camp was implemented (*Strafarbeiterabtheilung*).

Still, in 1912 the German Imperial District Officer reported from a recruitment expedition along the shore of "Südneupommern" (South New Britain) that the "relationship with the indigenous people" was "very annoying." In nearly every village the vessels called at, "the inhabitants flew in the bush and only with a great deal of effort we could bring some people to stop, mainly old men and former workers."[42] But the Melanesian coolies not only used the exit strategy to avoid contract labor. Those who signed a contract and came to Samoa also raised their voices. For example, the British consul of Samoa emphasized in a letter to his German colleague in 1895 that coolies stood under British protection and that a worker from the Gilbert Islands had complained about exceeded working hours, unhealthy nutrition, and "an overseer named Vesa whips them from on horseback."[43]

The situation of the Chinese coolies who, from 1903, came regularly to Samoa was both similar and different to the Melanesian ones. The main similarity was the form of a three-year contract the workers had to sign before they went to Samoa. It guaranteed a wage on a monthly basis, free lodging, nutrition, and transportation. Another similarity was that the Germans looked at both groups with equal disgust, mistrust, and racial arrogance. Frieda Zieschank noted in her diary, for example, that in contrast to Samoan workers one had to show the Melanesian and Chinese "in a blunt way who was the master" (*schroff den Herrn zeigen*).[44] The treatment of Chinese coolies who arrived with the first two coolie transports was especially harsh. Even the German governor, Solf, complained about "incorrectness" (*Ungehörigkeiten*), and expressed his impression that the settlers wanted to "economize this, what before they had reluctantly to give to the Samoan workers."[45] The attitude toward both coolie groups was typical for colonial economic systems. Only the exploitation of their work counted. When the first 298 coolies and "4 free artisans" arrived in May 1903 the *Samoanische Zeitung* described them as "apparently most excellent worker material."[46]

But there were also differences. First of all, the Chinese coolies were mainly employed in small groups at small-scale plantations of the new German settlers, who had been the main group to pressure the start of the Chinese coolie trade. Therefore the conditions of the coolies differed and were dependent upon the individual attitudes of the German settlers. In addition, the distribution of Chinese workers by lot in small groups to different settlers caused troubles, because those from the same home region or even relatives and friends were separated.[47]

But the decisive difference between the two coolie groups was that, from about 1905 on, the Chinese coolies found support from their nation-state and the Chinese public. The working and living conditions of contract workers in German Samoa was more and more criticized in the Chinese media and therefore the Chinese administration had to react. Chinese civil servants came to Samoa to inspect the conditions, and in 1909 a Chinese consulate was installed.

Intense German–Chinese diplomatic complications were one result of this shift in Chinese attention. The contracts the workers had to sign became more and more elaborate and contained new clauses that helped to improve the situation of the workers in Samoa. This struggle for improvement could also lead to cultural crossovers or entanglements, as can be seen in the fact that from 1911 on the Chinese could enforce that not only did contract workers not have to work on the few high Chinese holidays, but also on all German holidays, even the emperor's birthday.[48]

In addition, the legal status of the Chinese coolies was hotly disputed. The Chinese diplomats wanted Chinese people to be treated like Germans, and for this reason they denied the right to punish workers if they "walk in idleness."[49] When the Colonial Office argued in 1913 that according to the German "Servant's law" (*Gesindeordnung*) such punishment was legal, common, and usual, the Chinese could not resist and they gave the Germans a critical lesson in German history. The Chinese Embassy in Berlin told the Foreign Office on 4 July 1914 in a verbal note: "As much as is known here, the law was mainly passed so as to rule better the partly crude and uncivilized rural workers." In general, such a comparison was, according to the Chinese Embassy, totally misleading, because the *Gesindeordnung* was much milder compared to what the Chinese contract workers were having to suffer in Samoa.[50]

The working conditions of the Chinese coolies definitely improved after establishing regular inspection travels by Chinese officials and the implementation of a consulate. Nevertheless, a lot of misuse could still be found, and in the German discourse the settlers feared that step by step they would lose their ability to force coolies to work. On the other hand, settlers depended on the Chinese workforce, and they and the German governor in Apia knew that recruitment in China could only be successful if they accepted the improvements to the contracts and the conditions in a positive way. Nevertheless, the treatment of the Chinese and Melanesian coolies stood in harsh contrast to the attitudes and realities of work with regard to the Samoans.

Conclusion

By analyzing different perceptions of and attitudes toward work and working conditions, this chapter has demonstrated the puzzling coexistence of patterns of "work" and "non-work." Even basic distinctions from a Western concept of work became blurred when, for example, Ferdinand Wohltmann described the Samoan attitude to work in categories of play and fun.[51] As if Wohltmann wanted to illustrate that he was in no way affected by such work ethics, he ended his three-page itinerary of his South Sea travel with the following lines: "[June] 17th, midnight 12:10 return to Bonn (10 o'clock in the morning beginning of lecture)." The disciplined German work ethics prevailed over the alluring paradise working habits: Less than ten hours after his return from his world tour, Wohltmann stood in the auditorium and fulfilled his duties as professor. That other forms of interconnectedness of work and non-work were possible—which the German protagonists did not perceive at all—illustrates a scene described by travel novelist Otto Ehlers. Ehlers, who again and again pointed to the idleness and missing persistence of the Samoans, visited a plantation far away from the capital Apia by Samoan rowboat with representatives of the German Trade and Plantation Society. The owner of the plantation brought not only food and "good beverages" onboard, but also ice—"an outrageous luxury in Samoa." After lunch "a general sleepiness arises which does not infect our [four Samoan] oarsmen. They continue to work in the killer heat without taking a rest only for a minute; and the regularity of their movements puts us completely to sleep."[52]

The Samoan exceptionalism within the German colonial system had a lot to do with the exoticism the "paradise island" in the Pacific played in the view of the book authors and colonial administrators. But power-related and economic structures were also of importance. First of all, the indirect colonial rule in Samoa was stable, and after Samoa became a German colony the Samoans voluntarily handed over rifles and weapons to the German administration for a premium. However, neither German military nor police were stationed in Samoa, and German warships rarely came to the island. Therefore, German colonial authorities sought to avoid direct (or violent) confrontation, although after about 1900 the Samoan resistance movements against fundamental changes to the traditional societal and political structures of Samoa were weak and rare. If, however, the colonizers had applied pressure to try to change the work ethics of Samoans, it would have influenced "fa'a Samoa"—the Samoan way of life and traditions—to such a degree that resistance could have been expected. Therefore in view of the two main actors—the German Trading and Plantation Society and the colonial administration— it was best for economic reasons: to limit German migration to Samoa; to focus mainly on the trade between Samoans (who produced copra on their own collectively organized plantations) and the DHPG; to limit land sale and land lease to a minimum; and to let Samoans and Germans live in their own spheres. Melanesian and Chinese coolies had to pay the price for this "salvage colonialism" (George Steinmetz).

Jürgen Schmidt is working at the International Research Center "Work and Human Lifecycle in Global History" at Humboldt University Berlin, and at the Institute for the History and Future of Work in Berlin and at Lake Constance. Recently, he published *Brüder, Bürger und Genossen: Die deutsche Arbeiterbewegung zwischen Klassenkampf und Bürgergesellschaft 1830–1870* (J. H. W. Dietz, 2018) and the English translation of his biography of August Bebel (IB Tauris, 2018).

Notes

This is a slightly revised version of my article "Arbeit und Nicht-Arbeit im 'Paradies der Südsee': Samoa um 1890 bis 1914," *Arbeit – Bewegung – Geschichte. Zeitschrift für Historische Studien* 15 (2016), issue II/2016, pp. 7–25.

1. See especially Jürgen Schmidt, *Arbeiter in der Moderne: Arbeitsbedingungen Lebenswelten, Organisationen* (Frankfurt a.M.: Campus, 2015), esp. 69ff.; Andrea Komlosy, *Arbeit: Eine globalhistorische Perspektive. 13. bis 21. Jahrhundert* (Vienna: Promedia, 2014); Kathi Weeks, *The Problem With Work: Feminism, Marxism, Antiwork Politics, and Postwork Imaginaries* (Durham, NC: Duke University Press, 2011).
2. See in general: André Gorz, *Reclaiming Work: Beyond the Wage-Based Society* (London: Polity Press 1999), 86f.; Chris Rojek, *The Labour of Leisure: The Culture of Free Time* (London: SAGE, 2010). Critical with the idea of work as enjoyment in modern IT and media jobs is Svenja Flaßpöhler, *Wir Genussarbeiter: Über Freiheit und Zwang in der Leistungsgesellschaft* (Munich: Deutsche Verlags-Anstalt, 2011).
3. See Marcel van der Linden, *Workers of the World: Essays toward a Global Labor History* (Leiden: Brill, 2008).
4. Reinhard Wendt, "Die Südsee," in *Kein Platz an der Sonne: Erinnerungsorte der deutschen Kolonialgeschichte*, ed. Jürgen Zimmerer (Frankfurt a.M.: Campus 2013), 45ff.
5. Central for German colonialism in the Pacific are the works of Hermann Joseph Hiery: idem, *Das Deutsche Reich in der Südsee (1900–1921): Eine Annäherung an die Erfahrungen verschiedener Kulturen* (Göttingen: Vandenhoeck & Ruprecht, 1995); idem, ed., *Die deutsche Südsee 1884–1914: Ein Handbuch* (Paderborn: Schöningh, 2001); Peter Hempenstall, "Grundzüge der samoanischen Geschichte in der Zeit der deutschen Herrschaft", in *Die deutsche Südsee 1884–1914*, ed. Hermann Joseph Hiery (Paderborn: Schöningh, 2001), 702–4; Sebastian Conrad, *Deutsche Kolonialgeschichte* (Munich: Beck, 2012), 32f., 61; Winfried Speitkamp, *Deutsche Kolonialgeschichte* (Stuttgart: Reclam, 2014), 65f., 142f.
6. Malama Meleisea, *The Making of Modern Samoa: Traditional Authority and Colonial Administration in the Modern History of Western Samoa* (Suva, Fiji: Institute of Pacific Studies of the University of the South Pacific, 1987), 33, 35f.; Sven Beckert, *King Cotton: Eine Globalgeschichte des Kapitalismus* (Munich: Beck, 2013); Aleš Skrivan, "Das hamburgische Handelshaus Johann Cesar Godeffroy & Sohn und die Frage der deutschen Handelsinteressen in der Südsee", *Zeitschrift des Vereins für Hamburgische Geschichte* 81 (1995), 131; Hempenstall, "Grundzüge," 691. Cotton was first planted because it could be plowed soon after planting, while it took up to eight years before coconuts could be harvested; see Otto E. Ehlers, *Samoa, die Perle der Südsee, à jour gefaßt* (Berlin: Verlag von Hermann Paetel, 1895), 129.
7. Hiery, *Das Deutsche Reich*, 211.
8. Matthew P. Fitzpatrick, *Liberal Imperialism in Germany: Expansionism and Nationalism, 1848–1884* (Oxford: Berghahn Books, 2008), 84.
9. Hermann Joseph Hiery, "Die deutsche Verwaltung Samoas 1900–1914," in *Die deutsche Südsee 1884–1914*, 650, 656; Hiery, *Das Deutsche Reich*, 41; Thomas Schwarz, *Ozeanische Affekte: Die literarische Modellierung Samoas im kolonialen Diskurs* (Berlin: TEIA, 2013), 88f.; Livia Loosen, *Deutsche Frauen in den Südsee-Kolonien des Kaiserreichs: Alltag und Beziehungen zur indigenen Bevölkerung, 1884–1919* (Bielefeld: transcript, 2014). For the topic of "half-castes" see, with further literature, Roland Samulski, "Die Sünde im Auge des Betrachters—Rassenmischung und deutsche Rassenpolitik im Schutzgebiet Samoa 1900 bis 1914," in *Rassenmischehen—Mischlinge—Rassentrennung: Zur Politik der Rasse im deutschen Kolonialreich*, ed. Frank Becker

(Stuttgart: Franz Steiner Verlag, 2004), 329–56; Evelyn Wareham, *Race and Realpolitic: The Politics of Colonisation in German Samoa* (Frankfurt a.M.: Peter Lang, 2002).
10. Ferdinand Wohltmann, *Samoa-Erkundung: Pflanzung und Siedlung auf Samoa. Erkundungsbericht* (Berlin: Verlag des Kolonial-Wirtschaftlichen Komitees, 1904), 104.
11. Hiery, *Das Deutsche Reich*, 83f., 88f.
12. See, for example, Ehlers, *Samoa*, 81f., 134, who stated that among coolie workers he did not see any belles like among the Samoans: "Schönheiten wie unter den Samoanern habe ich unter den sämtlichen mir zu Gesicht gekommenen eingeführten Arbeitern nicht gefunden, und auch nur halbwegs sympathische Gesichtszüge gehörten zu den Seltenheiten." For Ehlers, see Gabriele Dürbeck, *Stereotype Paradiese: Ozeanismus in der deutschen Südseeliteratur 1815–1914* (Tübingen: Max Niemeyer Verlag, 2007), 192ff.
13. George Steinmetz, "The Uncontrollable Afterlives of Ethnography: Lessons from 'Salvage Colonialism' in the German Overseas Empire," *Ethnography* 5 (2004), 262; George Steinmetz, *The Devil's Handwriting: Precoloniality and the German Colonial State in Qingdao, Samoa, and Southwest Africa* (Chicago, IL: University of Chicago Press, 2007), 302ff. The author Sophie Wörishöffer described the Samoans as "*hübsche, hellfarbige Ozeanier*" (pretty, light-colored Oceanians): Sophie Wörishöffer, *Das Naturforscherschiff oder Fahrt der jungen Hamburger mit der "Hammonia" nach den Besitzungen ihres Vaters in der Südsee*, 4th edition (Bielefeld: Verlag von Velhagen & Klasing, [1880] 1888), 447.
14. Dürbeck, *Stereotype Paradiese*, 43f.
15. Franz Reinecke, "Samoa," in *Das Überseeische Deutschland: Die deutschen Kolonien in Wort und Bild* (Stuttgart: Union Deutsche Verlagsanstalt, 1903), 633.
16. "Alle Versuche, die Samoaner an regelmäßige Arbeit zu gewöhnen, scheiterten an der diesen liebenswürdigen Menschen angeborenen Trägheit" (Ehlers, *Samoa*, 126).
17. Richard Deeken, *Manuia Samoa! Samoanische Reiseskizzen und Beobachtungen* (Oldenburg: Gerhard Stalling, 1902), 151f.: "Die Samoaner (besitzen) durchweg alles im Überflusse, was ihnen zur Befriedigung ihrer Bedürfnisse erforderlich ist, und (verspüren) infolgedessen zu einer geregelten, andauernden Arbeit keine Neigung."
18. Wohltmann, *Samoa-Erkundung*, 111.
19. Schwarz, *Ozeanische Affekte*, 176; Hempenstall, "Grundzüge," 704; see, for example, Frieda Zieschank, *Ein Jahrzehnt in Samoa (1906–1916)* (Leipzig: E. Haberland, 1918): "Bis jetzt ist es eben noch nicht ernsthaft versucht worden, die Samoaner zur Arbeit zu erziehen" (Until now there has been no sincere effort to educate the Samoans for work, p. 96). With the help of the German administration and government, Zieschank saw another possibility: she suggested that whole communities should be condemned to work and not to fines ("So sollten Bestrafungen von Ortschaften—sie kommen nicht häufig vor!—nicht in Geldbußen, sondern in Arbeitsleistungen, besonders im Bau von guten Straßen bestehen", p. 97). But, on the other side, education to work should be conducted without any violation of the Samoan people and only little by little by systematic cooperation of all involved forces ("müßte ohne jede Vergewaltigung des Volkes nach und nach durch systematisches Zusammenwirken aller beteiligten Kräfte erfolgen", ibid.).
20. Hiery, "Deutsche Verwaltung," 657f.; quotation ibid. (my translation from German); see other English translations from this document in Arthur J. Knoll and Hermann J. Hiery, eds., *The German Colonial Experience: Selected Documents on German Rule in Africa, China, and the Pacific 1884–1914* (Lanham, MD: University Press of America, 2010), 190.
21. Hiery, *Das Deutsche Reich*, 203; Götz Mackensen, *Zum Beispiel Samoa: Der sozio-ökonomische Wandel Samoas vom Beginn der kolonialen Penetration im Jahre 1830 bis zur Gründung des unabhängigen Staates im Jahre 1962, mit einem Exkurs über die Planungstätigkeit des unabhängigen Staates in den Jahren 1962–1970* (Bremen: Übersee-Museum, 1977), 226f.
22. Ehlers, *Samoa*, 121; Wohltmann, *Samoa-Erkundung*, 72f.

23. Schwarz, *Ozeanische Affekte*, 139; Hiery, *Das Deutsche Reich*, 202f.
24. Schwarz, *Ozeanische Affekte*, 136f.; Hiery, "Deutsche Verwaltung," 658. In a letter to the Colonial Office in Berlin in 1902, a plantation society complained that the situation on the labor market had deteriorated, "especially due to the refusal of the Samoans to work for economic prices (*zu einem rationellen Preise*)." They claimed "energetic and purposeful action" to solve this problem (Deutsche Samoa-Gesellschaft to Colonial Office, 3 July 1902, Bundesarchiv [hereafter "BA"] Berlin-Lichterfelde R 1001/2319, fol. 33f.).
25. Hiery, *Das Deutsche Reich*, 106.
26. Christian Kracht, *Imperium: Roman* (Cologne: Kiepenheuer & Witsch, 2012). English translation: New York: Farrar, Straus and Giroux, 2015.
27. Quoted in Claus Gossler, "Der Kaufmann August Unshelm (1824–1864)," *Zeitschrift des Vereins für Hamburgische Geschichte* 95 (2009): 33f.
28. Siegfried Genthe, *Samoa: Reiseschilderungen*, edited by Georg Wegener. 2nd ed. (Berlin: Allgemeiner Verein für Deutsche Literatur, 1908), 33f.
29. Deeken, *Samoa*, 164.
30. "Der gute McFarlan hat seine Rechnung mit der Welt fertig. Er lebt nur seiner Familie [*sic*]. Keine Zeitung, keine Briefe geben ihm Nachricht von dem, was draußen vorgeht, und er hat in seiner langen Einsamkeit gelernt, nach seiner Art glücklich zu sein. Er ist Samoaner geworden." Ernst von Hesse-Wartegg, *Samoa, Bismarckarchipel und Neuguinea: Drei deutsche Kolonien in der Südsee* (Leipzig: Verlagsbuchhandlung J. J. Weber, 1902), 280.
31. Reinecke, "Samoa," 616; Kracht, *Imperium*. See also Dieter Klein, "Neuguinea als deutsches Utopia: August Engelhardt und sein Sonnenorden," in *Deutsche Südsee 1884–1914*, ed. Hermann Joseph Hiery (Paderborn, 2001), 450–58.
32. Reinhardt Klein-Arendt, "Die Nachrichtenübermittlung in den deutschen Südseekolonien," in *Deutsche Südsee 1884–1914*, ed. Hermann Joseph Hiery (Paderborn, 2001), 187.
33. "[G]eochst, wie bei uns, wird hier nicht, vielmehr wird die Arbeitszeit nur den Erfordernissen angemessen." Quoted in Gossler, "Unshelm," 25; see also 51, 53ff.
34. Hiery, *Das Deutsche Reich*, 36f.; Zieschank, *Jahrzehnt*, 53; Genthe, *Samoa*, 33f.
35. Health Report, 14 November 1912, BA Berlin-Lichterfelde, R 1001/2328, fol. 54–56 ("ständigen Bureaudienst gezwungen ist, sondern sich viel in der freien Luft aufhalten kann").
36. Sebastian Conrad, *Globalisierung und Nation im deutschen Kaiserreich* (Munich: Beck, 2006), 279ff.; in general, see Alf Lüdtke, *Eigen-Sinn, Fabrikalltag, Arbeitererfahrungen und Politik vom Kaiserreich bis in den Faschismus* (Hamburg: Ergebnisse Verlag, 1993).
37. For a critic on Deeken's optimism, see especially Wohltmann, *Samoa-Erkundung*, 68ff.
38. Stewart Firth, "Governors versus Settlers: The Dispute over Chinese Labour in German Samoa," *The New Zealand Journal of History* 11 (1977), 164f.
39. Gustav Schloetelberg to Colonial Office, 31 January 1902, BA Berlin-Lichterfelde, R 1001/2319, no fol.: "Das Ausw[ärtige Amt] ist doch nicht dazu da Privatstellungen zu vermitteln."
40. For the coolie trading system with China, see Andreas Steen, "Deutschland, China und die Kuli-Frage: Transfer, Anwerbung und Widerstand, 1850–1914," *Preußen, Deutschland und China: Entwicklungslinien und Akteure (1842–1911)*, ed. Mechthild Leutner et al. (Berlin: LIT Verlag, 2014), 231–93, for Samoa esp. 276ff.; Bill Willmott, "Chinese Contract Labour in the Pacific Islands during the Nineteenth Century," *The Journal of Pacific Studies* 27 (2004): 161–76; for research on coolies in general: Nitin Varma, *Coolies of Capitalism: Assam Tea and the Making of Coolie Labour* (Berlin: de Gruyter Oldenbourg, 2017). Although "coolie" is historically a derogatory term, it is used today in labor history as an analytical term and as a critical approach.
41. BA Berlin-Lichterfelde, R 1001/2016, passim; number of coolies according ibid., fol. 50; the death rate between 1879 and 1884 lay between 5 and 10 percent per year (ibid., fol. 73r).
42. Report of the Imperial District Officer to Imperial Government, 23 August 1912, BA Berlin-Lichterfelde, R 1001/2313, fol. 9f.

43. British Consulate in Apia to German Consulate, 4 April 1895, BA Berlin-Lichterfelde, R 1001/2317, fol. 69f.
44. Zieschank, *Jahrzehnt*, 98; see ibid., 99f., where she makes further racist graduations: in her opinion the "African worker" was even below the Chinese one.
45. Governor Solf to Colonial Office, 24 May 1903, BA Berlin-Lichterfelde, R 1001/2319, fol. 145 ("von den Chinesen das abzusparen, was sie vorher unwillig den Samoanern haben geben müssen").
46. *Samoanische Zeitung*, 2 May 1903, quoted in: ibid., fol. 158. In general: Conrad, *Kolonialgeschichte*, 54–61.
47. Hans Mosolff, *Die chinesische Auswanderung (Ursachen, Wesen, Wirkungen), unter besonderer Berücksichtigung der Hauptauswanderungsgebiete und mit einem ausführlichen Bericht über die chinesische Arbeiterbeschaffung für Samoa unter der deutschen Verwaltung* (Rostock: Carl Hinstorff, 1932), 412.
48. In 1908, the only days they did not have to work were six Chinese holidays (Official Announcement, 21 December 1908, BA Berlin-Lichterfelde, R 1001/2324, fol. 150); see also: ibid., R 1001/2325, fol. 78, 101; R 1001/2326, fol. 272.; R 1001/2327, fol. 82ff.
49. Colonial Office to State Secretary in the Foreign Office, 19 July 1913, BA Berlin-Lichterfelde, R 1001/2328, fol. 227r.
50. Chinese Verbal Note, 4 July 1914, BA Berlin-Lichterfelde R 1001/2328, fol. 127r.
51. Wohltmann, *Samoa-Erkundung*, 112.
52. "[S]tellt sich allgemeine Schläfrigkeit ein, von der nur unsere Ruderer nicht befallen werden. Sie arbeiten in der tollsten Hitze weiter, ohne auch nur eine Minute zu rasten, und tragen durch die Gleichmäßigkeit ihrer Bewegungen, dazu bei, uns vollends einzuschläfern" (Ehlers, *Samoa*, 122f.).

Bibliography

Beckert, Sven. *King Cotton: Eine Globalgeschichte des Kapitalismus*. Munich: Beck, 2013.
Conrad, Sebastian. *Deutsche Kolonialgeschichte*. Munich: Beck, 2012.
———. *Globalisierung und Nation im deutschen Kaiserreich*. Munich: Beck, 2006.
Deeken, Richard. *Manuia Samoa! Samoanische Reiseskizzen und Beobachtungen*. Oldenburg: Gerhard Stalling, 1902.
Dürbeck, Gabriele. *Stereotype Paradiese: Ozeanismus in der deutschen Südseeliteratur 1815–1914*. Tübingen: Max Niemeyer Verlag, 2007.
Ehlers, Otto E. *Samoa, die Perle der Südsee, à jour gefaßt*. Berlin: Verlag von Hermann Paetel, 1895.
Firth, Stewart. "Governors versus Settlers: The Dispute over Chinese Labour in German Samoa." *The New Zealand Journal of History* 11 (1977): 155–79.
Fitzpatrick, Matthew P. *Liberal Imperialism in Germany: Expansionism and Nationalism, 1848–1884*. Oxford: Berghahn Books, 2008.
Flaßpöhler, Svenja. *Wir Genussarbeiter: Über Freiheit und Zwang in der Leistungsgesellschaft*. Munich: Deutsche Verlags-Anstalt, 2011.
Genthe, Siegfried. *Samoa: Reiseschilderungen*, edited by Georg Wegener. 2nd ed. Berlin: Allgemeiner Verein für Deutsche Literatur, 1908.
Gorz, André. *Reclaiming Work: Beyond the Wage-Based Society*. London: Polity Press, 1999.
Gossler, Claus. "Der Kaufmann August Unshelm (1824–1864)." *Zeitschrift des Vereins für Hamburgische Geschichte* 95 (2009): 23–67.

Hempenstall, Peter. "Grundzüge der samoanischen Geschichte in der Zeit der deutschen Herrschaft." In *Die deutsche Südsee 1884–1914*, edited by Hermann Joseph Hiery, 690–710. Paderborn: Schöningh, 2001.

Hiery, Hermann Joseph. *Das Deutsche Reich in der Südsee (1900–1921): Eine Annäherung an die Erfahrungen verschiedener Kulturen*. Göttingen: Vandenhoeck & Ruprecht, 1995.

———, ed. *Die deutsche Südsee 1884–1914: Ein Handbuch*. Paderborn: Schöningh, 2001.

———. "Die deutsche Verwaltung Samoas 1900–1914." In *Die deutsche Südsee 1884–1914*, edited by Hermann Joseph Hiery, 649–75. Paderborn: Schöningh, 2001.

Klein, Dieter. "Neuguinea als deutsches Utopia: August Engelhardt und sein Sonnenorden." In *Die deutsche Südsee 1884–1914*, edited by Hermann Joseph Hiery, 450–58. Paderborn: Schöningh, 2001.

Klein-Arendt, Reinhardt. "Die Nachrichtenübermittlung in den deutschen Südseekolonien." In *Die deutsche Südsee 1884–1914*, edited by Hermann Joseph Hiery, 177–97. Paderborn: Schöningh, 2001.

Knoll, Arthur J., and Hermann J. Hiery, eds. *The German Colonial Experience: Selected Documents on German Rule in Africa, China, and the Pacific 1884–1914*. Lanham, MD: University Press of America, 2010.

Komlosy, Andrea. *Arbeit: Eine globalhistorische Perspektive. 13. bis 21. Jahrhundert*. Vienna: Promedia, 2014.

Kracht, Christian. *Imperium: Roman*. Cologne: Kiepenheuer & Witsch, 2012 (English translation New York: Farrar, Straus and Giroux, 2015).

Loosen, Livia. *Deutsche Frauen in den Südsee-Kolonien des Kaiserreichs: Alltag und Beziehungen zur indigenen Bevölkerung, 1884–1919*. Bielefeld: transcript, 2014.

Lüdtke, Alf. *Eigen-Sinn, Fabrikalltag, Arbeitererfahrungen und Politik vom Kaiserreich bis in den Faschismus*. Hamburg: Ergebnisse Verlag, 1993.

Mackensen, Götz. *Zum Beispiel Samoa: Der sozio-ökonomische Wandel Samoas vom Beginn der kolonialen Penetration im Jahre 1830 bis zur Gründung des unabhängigen Staates im Jahre 1962, mit einem Exkurs über die Planungstätigkeit des unabhängigen Staates in den Jahren 1962–1970*. Bremen: Übersee-Museum, 1977.

Meleisea, Malama. *The Making of Modern Samoa: Traditional Authority and Colonial Administration in the Modern History of Western Samoa*. Suva, Fiji: Institute of Pacific Studies of the University of the South Pacific, 1987.

Mosolff, Hans. *Die chinesische Auswanderung (Ursachen, Wesen, Wirkungen), unter besonderer Berücksichtigung der Hauptauswanderungsgebiete und mit einem ausführlichen Bericht über die chinesische Arbeiterbeschaffung für Samoa unter der deutschen Verwaltung*. Rostock: Carl Hinstorff, 1932.

Reinecke, Franz. "Samoa." In *Das Überseeische Deutschland: Die deutschen Kolonien in Wort und Bild*, 601–69. Stuttgart: Union Deutsche Verlagsanstalt, 1903.

Rojek, Chris. *The Labour of Leisure: The Culture of Free Time*. London: SAGE, 2010.

Samulski, Roland. "Die Sünde im Auge des Betrachters—Rassenmischung und deutsche Rassenpolitik im Schutzgebiet Samoa 1900 bis 1914." In *Rassenmischehen—Mischlinge—Rassentrennung: Zur Politik der Rasse im deutschen Kolonialreich*, edited by Frank Becker, 329–56. Stuttgart: Franz Steiner Verlag, 2004.

Schmidt, Jürgen. *Arbeiter in der Moderne: Arbeitsbedingungen Lebenswelten, Organisationen*. New York: Campus, 2015.

Schwarz, Thomas. *Ozeanische Affekte: Die literarische Modellierung Samoas im kolonialen Diskurs*. Berlin: TEIA, 2013.

Skrivan, Aleš. "Das hamburgische Handelshaus Johann Cesar Godeffroy & Sohn und die Frage der deutschen Handelsinteressen in der Südsee." *Zeitschrift des Vereins für Hamburgische Geschichte* 81 (1995): 129–55.

Speitkamp, Winfried. *Deutsche Kolonialgeschichte*. Stuttgart: Reclam, 2014.

Steen, Andreas. "Deutschland, China und die Kuli-Frage: Transfer, Anwerbung und Widerstand, 1850–1914." In *Preußen, Deutschland und China: Entwicklungslinien und Akteure (1842–1911)*, edited by Mechthild Leutner et al., 231–93. Berlin: LIT Verlag, 2014.

Steinmetz, George. *The Devil's Handwriting: Precoloniality and the German Colonial State in Qingdao, Samoa, and Southwest Africa*. Chicago, IL: University of Chicago Press, 2007.

———. "The Uncontrollable Afterlives of Ethnography: Lessons from 'Salvage Colonialism' in the German Overseas Empire," *Ethnography* 5 (2004): 251–88.

van der Linden, Marcel. *Workers of the World: Essays toward a Global Labor History*. Leiden: Brill, 2008.

Varma, Nitin. *Coolies of Capitalism: Assam Tea and the Making of Coolie Labour*. Berlin: de Gruyter Oldenbourg, 2017.

von Hesse-Wartegg, Ernst. *Samoa, Bismarckarchipel und Neuguinea: Drei deutsche Kolonien in der Südsee*. Leipzig: Verlagsbuchhandlung J. J. Weber, 1902.

Wareham, Evelyn. *Race and Realpolitic: The Politics of Colonisation in German Samoa*. Frankfurt a.M.: Peter Lang, 2002.

Weeks, Kathi. *The Problem with Work: Feminism, Marxism, Antiwork Politics, and Postwork Imaginaries*. Durham, NC: Duke University Press, 2011.

Wendt, Reinhard. "Die Südsee." In *Kein Platz an der Sonne: Erinnerungsorte der deutschen Kolonialgeschichte*, edited by Jürgen Zimmerer, 41–55. Frankfurt a.M.: Campus, 2013.

Willmott, Bill. "Chinese Contract Labour in the Pacific Islands during the Nineteenth Century." *The Journal of Pacific Studies* 27 (2004): 161–76.

Wohltmann, Ferdinand. *Samoa-Erkundung: Pflanzung und Siedlung auf Samoa. Erkundungsbericht*. Berlin: Verlag des Kolonial-Wirtschaftlichen Komitees, 1904.

Wörishöffer, Sophie. *Das Naturforscherschiff oder Fahrt der jungen Hamburger mit der "Hammonia" nach den Besitzungen ihres Vaters in der Südsee*, 4th edition. Bielefeld: Verlag von Velhagen & Klasing, (1880) 1888.

Zieschank, Frieda. *Ein Jahrzehnt in Samoa (1906–1916)*. Leipzig: E. Haberland, 1918.

Chapter 9

GERMAN WOMEN IN THE SOUTH SEA COLONIES, 1884–1919

Livia Rigotti

Introduction

If our possessions in the Pacific, despite their enormous natural beauty, get so much less public interest than our African colonies, and if they are mostly just superficially known even in educated colonial circles, the natural reasons for this are the far distance to the mother country, the difficulties of communication and development, and last but not least a certain mistrust with regard to the health conditions.

—"Ein deutsches Gouverneursheim in der Südsee"
(A German governor's home in the South Seas)

This quotation[1] from the colonial press in 1914 explained why the so-called "German South Sea Colonies" received comparatively little attention from contemporaries. To this day, historical studies rarely discuss the fact that, from the end of nineteenth century until the start of World War I, the northeastern part of New Guinea with the Bismarck Archipelago, the northeastern Solomon Islands, the Caroline Islands, Palau, the Mariana Islands, the Marshall Islands, Nauru, and the Samoa Islands of Upolu and Savai'i were under German administration.[2] German colonial history is often limited to the colonies in Africa, but even those studies that do discuss German colonization of the South Sea neglect one section of the population: women. In addition, in general texts concerning colonial history, women are still represented as marginal. There are several reasons for this late and still unsatisfactory consideration of women's contribution to this chapter of history. First, significantly fewer women than men migrated to the colonies,

---

Notes from this chapter begin on page 227.

Table 9.1 Number of Germans over the age of fifteen in the South Sea colonies and in South West Africa as at 1 January 1913.

	Men	Women	Total
New Guinea	514	164	678
Micronesia	192	53	245
Samoa	222	63	285
South Sea colonies in total	928	**280**	1,208
South West Africa	7,336	**2,522**	9,858

Source: Reichskolonialamt (ed.), *Die deutschen Schutzgebiete in Afrika und in der Südsee 1912/13: Amtliche Jahresberichte* (Berlin, 1914).

especially to the South Sea colonies. Table 9.1 lists the population of the colonies in the Pacific in comparison to the German colony of South West Africa.

Even at the end of the German era, only 280 German women lived in the South Sea colonies, and there were more than three times that number of German men. Secondly, women were forced into passive, domestic roles, so they are very rarely found as decision makers or independent operators in the source material. Thirdly, women wrote down their experiences much less frequently than men, and hence it is quite hard to find suitable source material.[3] Nevertheless, it is worth the effort; my extended research brought to light numerous traces of these women, and the mark they left on the German colonial era.[4] My focus on the female population reveals a new perspective on the history of the South Sea colonies. Women came out with different expectations and different aims than men, had different tasks to fulfill, experienced a different daily life, and last but not least they had different access to the indigenous population. Therefore, looking at the events through the eyes of women is an important way to reconsider German history of the South Sea colonies, which has hitherto concentrated on men.

Ego-documents of German women who knew the territories and documented their experience provide the core of the study. Inspired by gender studies and postcolonial theories, such as Critical Whiteness Studies, the following research questions were applied to the source material:[5]

1. What motives did German women have for staying in the South Sea colonies?
2. What was expected from these women?
3. Did the social position of the German women in the South Sea colonies change in comparison with the motherland?
4. What were the interactions like between German women and the indigenous population and 'half-castes'? What kinds of relationships developed?

The analysis of the source base revealed that the situation of German women in the South Sea colonies was completely different than those in the much more widely researched colony of South West Africa. Therefore, it is not appropriate to transfer the results of historical research concerning women in South West Africa to other German colonies, as has been done at times. This will be illustrated by the example of the so-called "mixed marriage debate" later in this chapter. But firstly, the question of the motives for departure to the colonies arose, which also shaped the search for further source material.

Motives for Departure to the Colonies

Why did women make the decision to leave the German Empire in order to settle in the colonies? What reasons motivated them to leave their homes and loved ones, and undertake a journey several weeks long to take up a new challenge thousands of miles away from home?

To answers these questions, it is useful to distinguish between the migration to the colonies that was supported by institutions on the one hand, and individual migration on the other. In the first case, associations or missions took care of the organization and financing of the trip, whereas this was not the case for individual voyages. This distinction is important because the institutions defined women's tasks with reference to a predetermined role. In these cases, the women came to the colony due to a specific agenda of the institution. The activism of these associations may have aroused or confirmed the wish of many women to move to the colonies.

In the context of the departure of German women to the colonies, the Women's League of the German Colonial Society (Frauenbund der Deutschen Kolonialgesellschaft) was of central importance. It was founded in 1907, and within ten years it already had 18,680 members.[6] The most important aims of the association were "to interest women of all social positions in colonial questions," and "to assist German women and girls who want to settle in the colonies with help and advice."[7] The Women's League supported the voyages, both organizationally and financially. Ideally, women were to marry German settlers in the colony and start families to prevent so-called mixed marriages (*Mischehen*) between Germans and indigenous women.[8] The historian Birthe Kundrus calls this concept "a public arrangement of marriages, only poorly camouflaged as labor market policy."[9] The following conviction was more or less the consensus among colonial circles: "Indeed it must be obvious to everyone ... that the only thing that matters is to bring German girls into the country to keep a pure population, and that the establishment of an employment contract for the girls only serves as a means to an end for this purpose."[10] With this obviously racist intent, the Women's League organized the departure of 561 women and other employees to the colonies between 1908 and 1914.[11] But these women were sent exclusively to South West Africa whereas the Women's League did not organize voyages to the South Sea colonies. Still, the organization's publication *Kolonie und Heimat* (Colony and Homeland) published articles about everyday life in the South Sea colonies, sometimes written by women living there. Reading this magazine might therefore have influenced German women settling in these colonies and might have shaped their image of their future home. *Kolonie und Heimat* was known as the most popular colonial magazine and had one hundred thousand subscribers three years after the first issue.[12] This magazine was also read in the South Sea colonies.[13] *Kolonie und Heimat* is an important source for revealing the dominant role models for women in the colonies, and it illustrates the expectations that were set for them.[14]

Although the Women's League concentrated its activities on South West Africa, it also entailed a "section New Guinea" in Rabaul in northern New Britain from 1909 onward. German women consulted this section for advice when they were searching for a job in the colony or if they needed information or support. The chairperson of this section until 1914 was Luise Hahl, the governor's wife. In Samoa, by contrast, the Women's League could not gain a foothold.[15]

Twenty years before the Women's League was established, the German National Women's League (Deutschnationaler Frauenbund) was founded in order to organize nursing in German East Africa.[16] In 1888, it was renamed the German Women's Association for Nursing in the Colonies (Deutscher Frauenverein für die Krankenpflege in den Kolonien). In 1909, it gained a closer affiliation with the Red Cross and changed its name to German Women's Red Cross Association for the Colonies (Deutscher Frauenverein vom Roten Kreuz für die Kolonien). The association trained nurses and financed their voyage to the colonies, where they worked in government or private hospitals. When it was founded in 1888 its membership was 250, but this had increased to 20,000 by 1914.[17] Up until that point, the association had been expanding its work in other colonies. In 1891, Auguste Hertzer and Hedwig Saul were the first nurses in the service of the association to travel to New Guinea.[18] In 1903, Else Langenbeck and Anna Stein departed as the first nurses to Samoa.[19] The nurses signed up to stay for a certain service period in the colonies: three years for New Guinea and Samoa. Afterwards they traveled back home and had the possibility to volunteer to be sent abroad again.[20]

The association not only paid for the nurses' training and travel allowance but also their salary, their uniform, and their equipment.[21] In addition, the women got free room and board in the colony and free medical treatment.[22] Therefore, the association enabled the women to learn a socially valued profession and to have a secure income.[23] The possibility of working in exotic surroundings where nurses were badly needed and, in doing so, to serve their fatherland, provided further incentives to travel to the colonies with the support of the German Women's Red Cross Association.[24]

From 1896, there was a section of this association in Apia in Samoa, and from 1906 in Kokopo in New Guinea.[25] The number of nurses in the different South Sea colonies varied slightly, corresponding to the need for staff and the state of the nurses' health at the time. At the outbreak of World War I, sixty-six nurses of the association worked in the German colonies altogether. Eight of them worked in the South Sea colonies: three in Apia, one in Kokopo, one in Madang, two in Rabaul, and one in Jaluit.[26] The most important source for information on the development of the association is its publication *Unter dem roten Kreuz* (Under the Red Cross), which came out for the first time in 1899; regular reports of the nurses living in the South Sea colonies were published there.

Mission societies played an important role among the institutions sending German women to the colonies. The first women, and by far the most who came to the South Sea colonies, were in the service of missionary societies: about half of the 280 German women who lived in the German South Sea Colonies in 1913 were members of missionary societies.[27] Depending on their denomination, there were different possibilities for women working for a missionary society in the South Sea colonies: they could be Catholic sisters, wives of Protestant missionaries, or they could practice as a Protestant sister or *Missionsgehilfin* (helper of the mission). The latter supported the missionary society as a midwife, nurse, teacher, or home help.[28] Often these helpers married a missionary during their stay in the field, and if so then their status within the missionary society and their tasks may have changed.[29]

For women in missionary service, the most important motive for moving to the South Sea colonies was generally a wish to spread Christian thinking and to work "for the good of so many poor, unhappy pagans."[30] Their aim was the conversion of as many indigenous people as possible to Christianity. For those women who did not have to practice celibacy, such as helpers of the mission or other Protestant women, an expected marriage could be a reason for departure to the colony.[31] Some missionary women accompanied their husbands to the South Sea after they had married at home. Nevertheless, most of them were fiancées when they left their home country, awaiting their marriage in the mission field.[32] If the missionaries were not already engaged when they left Germany, they had to court their future bride from the missionary field.[33] Therefore, missionaries often begged friends and family at home or even the Mission Board to search for a wife for them.[34] Very often, the so-called *Missionsbräute* (mission brides) departed to the field without actually knowing their future husband.[35]

Among the individually traveling women, marriage and the search for employment were the most important motives for choosing a life in the South Sea colonies. Most of them accompanied or followed their husbands to the colony where they were working—as traders, planters, officials, doctors, or seamen, for example. Unmarried women traveling individually to the colonies were often fiancées of men who had searched for a bride in the homeland, sometimes via a personal advertisement in one of the colonial magazines.[36] Some of the unmarried women who came to the colonies planned to work there as teachers in a school or kindergarten, as educators, secretaries, home helps, or cooks. Employment advertisements were published both in the colonial press in Germany and in the newspapers in the colonies, for instance the *Samoanische Zeitung*.[37] Furthermore, letters of women searching for employment in the colonies can be found in files of colonial administrations.[38] In the German Empire, there were few possibilities for bourgeois women to practice a profession. To secure their own financial situation by a marriage was often difficult too, as there were more women of marriageable age than men.[39] Nevertheless the source material reveals that some women did not search for a partner or employment in a colony but were driven by wanderlust and thirst for adventure when they decided to go abroad. This applies, for example, to those women who came to the island of Kabakon in the Bismarck Archipelago to become a member of the so-called "Sonnenorden" (Order of the sun).[40] The founder of this group, a pharmacist from Nuremberg named August Engelhardt, propagated an alternative lifestyle in order to leave the "errors of modern life" behind: his followers should praise the sun naked and eat nothing but coconuts. However, based on analysis of the journal *Kolonie und Heimat* as well as other colonial publications, neither these adventurous dropouts nor women living alone and exercising a profession were corresponding with the ideal of the German colonial woman (*Deutsche Kolonialfrau*).

The Expected Role of German Colonial Women

The task of women should primarily be to guarantee German family life away from home.[41] Women who had chosen another way of life were underrepresented in colonial publications. Occupational activities were only tolerated as a transitional stage before marriage; the real aim was to be a good housewife and mother.[42] To fulfill their purpose, women were not only expected to master domestic duties in unfamiliar surroundings, they also needed specific character traits in order to represent their nation in the alien land.[43] The chairperson of the Women's League, Freifrau von Liliencron, stressed: "It is a serious task, which the girls who go to the colonies need to master. They must prove not only a practical ability, but the colony also expects them to work on behalf of high ideals. They should be bearers of German education, German discipline and custom, and through their influence a blessed family life should develop."[44]

The women should be prepared to make sacrifices in daily colonial life and be willing to incur any inconvenience without complaint. They should have willpower and be eager to fulfill their assigned tasks. For that purpose, a strong sense of duty was required. The ideal characteristics of the German women going abroad were hardworking, conscientious, well behaved, tidy, patient, gentle, and devoted.[45] Furthermore, she should be "a loyal employee for the man."[46] According to the prevailing concept, German men, through the influence of German women, should be prevented from becoming barbarized or degraded to the cultural level of the indigenous people.[47] It was the contemporary consensus that the cultivating effect of the German women upon the men would not only upgrade the standards of the colonial society but also the value of the whole colony.[48]

Features of the Social Fabric in the German South Sea Colonies

While colonial publications stressed the high value of a German wife for the success of the colonial project, there was an important difference between the South Sea colonies and German South West Africa. As already mentioned, no guided mass transmission of marriage-seeking women took place in the South Sea colonies, whereas this section of the population strongly influenced the social structure of German South West Africa. Most of the women sent out by the Women's League as maidservants and household assistants to South West Africa came from a so-called "humble background" (that is, from the working class).[49] In the colony, they found themselves among many women from the middle class and a few from the upper class.[50] Since every German woman was welcomed in the colonies as a potential bride, the social position of women who had come to Africa as maidservants could change fast. Due to the large surplus of men, even a large class distinction was, unlike in the homeland, no barrier to marriage. Social mobility in the colony was very high, and upper-class women tried to dissociate themselves from these "parvenues" by demonstrating a strong class consciousness. This led to many conflicts; malicious gossip and intrigues were prevalent and poisoned the social climate.[51] These kinds of conflicts were almost absent in the South Sea colonies. The newly arriving women were mostly already married or engaged—or, as missionary sisters, were not candidates for the marriage market. Moreover, the female proportion of the population was even lower in the German population in the South Sea colonies than in German South West Africa. Table 9.2 provides figures regarding the proportion of single and widowed missionary members among adult German women in these colonies at the beginning of 1913. This category was not further specified in official statistics, but celibate sisters made up the largest part. Furthermore, the table shows the number of single and widowed nurses, teachers, and "other professions," who all represented potential marriage candidates among the women.

Table 9.2: White inhabitants over the age of fifteen in German South West Africa and German South Sea Colonies as at 1 January 1913.

	Women				Men
	Married	Single or widowed missionary members	Single or widowed nurses, teachers, and other professions	Total	Total
German South West Africa	1,793 (71%)	36 (1.5%)	693 (27.5%)	2,522	7,336
German New Guinea (incl. island territory)	93 (43%)	103 (47%)	21 (10%)	217	706
Samoa	44 (70%)	5 (8%)	14 (22%)	63	222
Total	1,930 (69%)	144 (5%)	728 (26%)	2,802	8,264

Source: See Reichskolonialamt (ed.), *Die deutschen Schutzgebiete in Afrika und in der Südsee 1912/13, Amtliche Jahresberichte* (Berlin, 1914).

The figures make it clear that in the South Sea colonies the proportion of missionary members among single women was much higher. The remaining single women had no reason to compete for suitable marriage candidates.

The comparison of the social situation in the German South Sea Colonies and German South West Africa is also instructive in another way: historical research on South West Africa suggests that, in the first years of the German colonial administration, social relations developed informally and without any problems. The initial social climate could evolve due to a low number of white colonists, the simple way of life, and the large distances between the single settlement areas.[52]

They got more complicated with more and more white settlers moving in, especially white women.[53]

By contrast, South Sea colonies remained at a stage that resembled to some extent the early years of South West Africa until the end of German rule: there were only a few white settlers and, above all, very few white women; the few urban settlements were small; and the infrastructure was in relatively bad condition. Missions and plantations were remotely located. More complex social relationships could develop only with an increasing number of white settlers. But the settlement in the South Sea regions never reached the numbers of those in German South West Africa.[54] Thus, the relationships among the white settlers in the South Sea colonies remained relatively uncomplicated with rather flat hierarchies. The fact that so few whites lived in the South Sea colonies made it hard for the Germans in many places to be particular about their social contacts. Not having as much choice in society as in the homeland, the settlers learned fast to "take and appreciate [people] as they are," wrote Frieda Zieschank, who lived as a doctor's wife in Samoa.[55] The local circumstances dictated a certain degree of tolerance if one did not want to be socially isolated. The highly important class consciousness in the German Empire became less important in the South Pacific. Besides the fewer number of white settlers, relative homogeneity further explains a less developed class consciousness in the South Pacific as compared to German South West Africa. In contrast to South West Africa, aristocrats and the military were almost absent in the South Pacific. Governor Solf openly addressed this issue in a letter to the Imperial Colonial Office, stating that the military was not well received in Samoa.[56] The white colonial society in the South Pacific was primarily from the bourgeois middle class.[57] These differences between the German South Sea Colonies and German South West Africa regarding the composition of German settlers not only influenced the relations of the German women to the remaining whites but also shaped their attitudes toward indigenous women and to the so-called "mixed marriages" between indigenous women and white men.

The Position of Women in the Mixed Marriage Debate

Although only 166 such mixed marriages were registered in all German colonial territories during the years of German rule, they were regarded as a growing offense to "Germanness" (*Deutschtum*).[58] Most of the mixed marriages were concluded in Samoa. In spite of the relatively low number of white residents, a total of ninety of them were validly married to locals.[59]

For the year 1907, Frieda Zischank noted: "By far most men are married to half-castes or full-blood Samoan women—the officials of the government and the company [i.e., the *Deutsche Handels- und Plantagengesellschaft der Südsee-Inseln*] even to a larger extent than the planters. The remaining ones live for the most part *fa'a* Samoa (i.e., in wild marriage with Samoan women)."[60]

The fact that the Samoan women were, in comparison to the inhabitants of the other German colonies, regarded as more attractive and culturally further developed, supported the participation in mixed marriages.[61] Apart from that, in general, only the marriage of white men to local women was a subject of discussion: any connections of white women with local men is hardly mentioned in the sources. This type of relationship was seen as even more execrable and was stigmatized by the German public as "a perversion."[62] In fact, the available sources do not provide any hint regarding a romantic relationship between a white woman and an indigenous man.[63] Frieda Zieschank stated in her book *Ein Jahrzehnt in Samoa* (A Decade in Samoa) "That a white woman does not bond with same blood is precluded".[64] Even if one may doubt that these relations were really excluded, this remark proves how strong the social taboo was. In any case, relations between German men and indigenous women were very frequent, not only in Samoa, but also in the other South Sea Colonies. The historian Hermann Hiery stresses that the living together of white men and local women was the rule, not the exception, in many parts of the South Sea Colonies.[65] The governor of New Guinea, Albert Hahl, his successor the imperial judge, Paul Boether, and the station leaders of Kieta, Morobe, and Palau all lived with local women. The same was true for the majority of traders and many other German colonists in Melanesia and Micronesia.[66] Unlike in Samoa, in the remaining German South Sea areas, sexual relations between white men and indigenous women seldom led to an officially approved marriage. In the Bismarck Archipelago and in Kaiser-Wilhelmsland (the northern mainland of Papua New Guinea) the number of white men officially married to indigenous women always remained under ten and, under twenty in the Micronesian area.[67] Due to the low number of mixed marriages and because Governor Hahl apparently saw no need to prevent them, these relationships were never an object of discussion as they were in Samoa. In Samoa, the results of widespread sexual relations between white and indigenous people were very evident. The group of "half-castes" was growing rapidly: at the beginning of 1912, according to official statistics, this group consisted of 996 individuals, whereas the white section of the population numbered only 500, of which 294 were Germans.[68] Thus, the half-caste population exceeded the German population numerically. Critics of the 'race mixing' saw this situation as a threat to the power structures.[69] They feared that the half-castes could gain too much influence in the colony and threaten the dominance of "Germanness."[70] This was based, inter alia, on the fact that the existence of mixed marriages had far-reaching legal consequences: following the German Law of Citizenship of 1870, every foreign woman married to a German man could claim his citizenship, which was also handed down to the descendants of this couple.[71] Furthermore, German men could acknowledge their illegitimate children with foreign women, which meant that they became German citizens too.[72] Therefore, indigenous women and children could become "colored Germans," and were no longer subject to the law for indigenous people. By their equal legal status, colored Germans were allowed to take up a career in the civil or military services and could become a German's superior.[73] Besides this fear of social advancement of the half-castes, there was a very popular racist conviction: it was claimed that the descendants of mixed couples would only inherit the bad qualities from both "races."[74]

As already mentioned, there was the prevailing idea that white men who lived together with indigenous women and may even have decided to start a family would "descend to the level of the indigenous way of life."[75] Therefore, these men could not fulfill their colonial duties and would damage the reputation of the white "race."[76]

Based on this argument, mixed marriages began to be regarded as a problem from the mid-1890s onward, and were increasingly discussed from the turn of the century.[77] In 1905, the local colonial administration of German South West Africa forbade civil weddings of mixed couples.[78] In 1908, even legal mixed marriages (dating back before 1905) were retrospectively annulled in this colony.[79] Also, in German East Africa, mixed marriages were forbidden from 1906 onward, even though there was only one known case.[80]

The prohibition of mixed marriages in the colonies in Africa was debated fiercely in the homeland. The colonial press published plenty of articles on this subject.[81] But the peak of the debate was not reached until 1912 when Wilhelm Solf issued a general prohibition of mixed marriages in Samoa. At this time, Solf was no longer governor of this colony but state secretary of the Imperial Colonial Office. Unlike in South West Africa and East Africa, the prohibition of mixed marriages in Samoa was, for the first time, not just a measure of the local administration but a governmental decision taken in Germany without considering parliament.[82] In a letter to the governor in Apia, the state secretary listed new principles for marriage in Samoa. The first principle was: "Foreigners and indigenous people are no longer allowed to marry."[83] Although Solf had tolerated mixed couples when he was governor in Samoa, the fast-growing population group of half-castes had apparently troubled him for a long time.[84] Even before the prohibition became known, officials sometimes made marriages between German men and indigenous women more difficult. The uncertain legal situation was interpreted differently and left many questions unanswered until 1912.[85]

Among the whites living in Samoa, only a minority firmly opposed mixed marriages.[86] It was even claimed that the mixture with Samoan blood would have positive consequences for the constitution of the descendants, who would cope better with the tropical climate than the German settlers.[87] Already in 1904, the *Koloniale Zeitschrift* stated, "In Samoa many whites marry Samoan women or half-castes without anybody criticizing this fact."[88] In 1906, under the impression of the prohibition of mixed marriages in Africa, there was outrage in the German colonial press about the "indifference toward the result of the ongoing race mixing in Samoa, where it is claimed, no one would see any danger in the increase of the half-caste population."[89] In fact, in the colony, most settlers could not understand the increasing criticism from outside. They warned about the dangers of these inflammatory articles for the social life of the colony.[90]

Consequently, the prohibition of mixed marriages for Samoa only received a little support in the colony. Many of the white settlers reacted with a lack of understanding; there was even some strong resistance.[91] Evelyn Wareham stresses that "[t]he administration's measures against mixed marriage resulted in protests, which demonstrated that its legislation was not simply a reflection of existing social and cultural conditions." That is, the demand for a prohibition of mixed marriages did not originate from the colonies.[92]

But even those who defended mixed marriages always argued within the racial concepts of the time. For instance, the *Samoanische Zeitung* stressed that it was "not fair to put the descendants of the mixed marriages in Samoa on the same level as Mulattos or Mestizos" because Samoans would "be much higher than Negros or Indians."[93] Opponents of the prohibition mostly claimed that it would restrict the German man's right to choose his bride freely. Furthermore, it was feared that the prohibition would be followed by an increase in prostitution and concubinage. The fate of the offspring of these sexual relations would be uncertain.[94] In addition, it was claimed that the category of "race" was legally unclear.[95] Nevertheless, at that time even most critics and opponents of the prohibition disapproved in principle of "race mixing" (i.e., sexual relations between Germans and indigenous people). No one considered white and indigenous partners to be of equal value.[96]

The colonial women's movement used the debate on mixed marriages for its own purposes. After all, the increasing threat (or so it was claimed) to the "German Race" from mixed marriages provided the basis for the activism of the Women's League.[97] This threat scenario provided the justification for the main activity of the Women's League, namely "to find a remedy for the urgent lack of women by purposeful supplies of German white women."[98] In the colonial press, members of the colonial women's movement took positions against mixed marriages and never grew tired of stressing the high value of German women for a successful colonization process.[99]

Unlike in the South Sea colonies, in South West Africa, those Germans married to indigenous women were discriminated against by the other white settlers, at least from 1906 onward. They were systematically excluded from colonial social life; for instance, they were not allowed to join sports clubs or the farmers' associations. Men living in a mixed marriage were not granted loans, and so they could not buy a farm. In 1909, they even lost their right to vote for the municipal council. Half-caste children were not allowed to visit the new governmental school in Windhuk, or even some kindergartens. In East Africa, mixed couples and their descendants were discriminated against as well.[100]

Concerning the different European colonial powers, historical research has repeatedly shown that the increasing immigration of women from the motherland intensified racial segregation in the colonies and hence the objections to "race mixing."[101] Despite occasional exceptions, the historian Karen Smidt confirms this result for most of the German women in South West Africa:

> Owing to the increasing immigration of German women in South West Africa, especially of those sent by the Women's League, the racist and nationalistic opinions intensified … The systematic exclusion of Germans who were married to Africans or half-castes increased under the influence of German women. The latter made the distance between the African and the white population grow, created and deepened prejudices, and partly showed themselves more racist than German men.[102]

The source material concerning the South Sea colonies does not entail such undisguised racist commentaries by German women on mixed marriages. The fact that women in the South Sea colonies had not been sent by the Women's League proved to be important for the social relationships in this regard too. As already mentioned, the women sent by the Women's League mostly came from humble backgrounds and had a great interest in improving their social status. Therefore it was not only important for them to assert themselves against the other white competitors in the marriage market but also to stress the advantages of a German wife compared to an indigenous woman: only white women could give birth to white children and it was claimed that only they could keep house in the "proper" way and be a real partner to their husbands. The spread of racist ideas served to protect their own social status.[103]

In the South Sea colonies, where fewer whites lived compared with South West Africa, this competitive thinking by the few German women was not as strong as in South West Africa. The relaxed dealings of many German women with half-caste women in the South Sea colonies reveals a much more tolerant attitude toward mixed couples and their descendants than in the African colonies. German women mentioned half-castes in their texts more often than they mentioned indigenous women. This can be explained by the fact that there were nearly no German women at the beginning of the German colonization in the South Sea colonies. They only arrived there in later years, when the second generation descending from mixed couples had already been born.[104] German men preferred to choose a bride from these, who had often been educated in a European way and could be mediators between the indigenous and the European world. For instance, Antonie Brandeis, who lived as the wife of an official on the Marshall Island of Jaluit, mentioned a little party in her house "visited by all white settlers and their partly half-caste women."[105] Apparently for her this was nothing unusual or offensive. Also, Elisabeth Krämer-Bannow, a member of an expedition to the Bismarck Archipelago, reported on a visit to the house of a planter living in a mixed marriage without adding any negative commentary: "His wife, a dark curly-haired half-Samoan, helped him with skill and endurance in her quiet way. Notably she was very good in dealing with the black workers."[106] Gretel Kuhn, who lived during World War I in Rabaul in New Guinea, remembered very positively the wife of a planter she had met: "His wife was extraordinary likeable, she was a half-caste."[107] In Kokopo in the Bismarck Archipelago, a half-caste with her numerous relatives was even the center of social life. At the legendary dinner parties of the Samoan-American plantation owner Emma Forsayth, known as "Queen Emma," guests of various ethnic and national origins always gathered, but the sources do not contain a single critical voice about this fact.[108] Even concerning the governor of German New Guinea, Albert Hahl, a missionary wife named Johanna Fellmann wrote in a letter to her mother: "[B]y the way one is not that formal here. He is married to an indigenous girl in indigenous manner like all the others are."[109] The "race mixing" in Samoa is not criticized by the missionary Valesca Schulze, who wrote, for instance, of a German trader who "had a very nice and capable half-caste wife."[110]

In her numerous colonial publications, Frida Zieschank referred repeatedly to "race mixing" in Samoa. In her autobiographical book *Ein Jahrzehnt in Samoa*, which was published after the prohibition of mixed marriages, she told the reader that she would not approve of race mixing and therefore considered the prohibition as appropriate.[111] Nevertheless, she deemed it understandable that men entered into mixed marriages at the beginning of the colonization process. She understood that the sudden change in the acceptance of these relations angered the persons affected,[112] and gave a very positive image of the half-caste women who descended from these relationships and often lived together with white men themselves:

> Undoubtedly some of these young girls are very attractive creatures. You can find charming beauties among them … All of them are intelligent and capable of being educated; their basic character does not show any considerable difference from ours … Nearly all of them—there are always exceptions—are faithful wives to their men and caring mothers to their children.[113]

Zieschank stressed that "colored women" in Samoa were considered as "socially fully accepted" (*gesellschaftlich voll berechtigt*).[114] Although she was confident that "the German woman naturally belonged" to the German man, she urged a sensible handling of the "problem with the half-castes":[115] "The fact is, they exist, these children of German men, and therefore we should not just see the brown, but also the white blood inside them, and that's partly of the best kind! … Not by any stretch of the imagination, can I see a danger to the community in these Samoan half-castes."[116] Also in her letter to "a colonial bride" published in 1913 in *Kolonie und Heimat*, she predicted to the departing women that "You will meet many nice half-caste housewives as well."[117] According to Zieschank, the half-caste women welcomed German women in a friendly fashion from the beginning, and were on good terms with them. She argued that the debate on "race purity" that had been brought into the colony from the outside was destroying this harmonious relationship.[118]

Conclusion

The example of the debate on mixed marriages demonstrates that the South Sea colonies cannot easily be equated with the other German colonies. The comparison with South West Africa shows that the preconditions for German women living in the South Sea colonies were very different: the more isolated setting of the latter, and therefore the comparatively weaker influence of the motherland as well as the relative homogeneity of the few German inhabitants of these Pacific colonies, created a special social climate.

Above all, research has shown that the lack of women sent by the Women's League to the South Sea colonies in order to marry had far-reaching consequences for the social relationships among the white population as well as for those between the colonists and the indigenous people. As the decisive motive for departure to the South Sea colonies was not, in general, to find a husband, competing for suitable marriage candidates was not of importance for most of the German women there. This fact lowered the conflict potential among the white population and also led to a tolerant attitude of the German women toward the so-called mixed marriages. Unlike in South West Africa, mixed couples and their descendants were common social players and were mostly depicted in a positive or neutral light in the source texts written by German women.

The situation in the German South Sea Colonies had many characteristics that make further studies of this less recognized area worthwhile and exciting, especially regarding women, and their contribution to its history should not be overlooked.

Livia Rigotti (has published under the name Livia Loosen before) was a PhD student at the Max Weber Center for Advanced Cultural and Social Studies, University of Erfurt, Germany. Her thesis focused on German women in the South Sea colonies of the German Empire ("Deutsche Frauen in den Südsee-Kolonien des Kaiserreichs. Alltag und Beziehungen zur indigenen Bevölkerung, 1884–1919," Bielefeld, 2014). She is now working in the field of public relations in Mainz, Germany.

Notes

1. All quotations in this chapter are my own translations.
2. For more information concerning these colonies, see Hermann Hiery, ed., *Die deutsche Südsee 1884–1914: Ein Handbuch* (Paderborn: Schöningh, 2002).
3. See Anna Pytlik, *Die schöne Fremde: Frauen entdecken die Welt* (Stuttgart: Württembergische Landesbibliothek, 1991), 96; Karen Hagemann, "'Ich glaub' nicht, daß ich Wichtiges zu erzählen hab'…: Oral History und historische Frauenforschung," in *Oral History*, ed. Herwart Vorländer (Göttingen: Vandenhoek & Ruprecht, 1990), 33.
4. Livia Loosen, *Deutsche Frauen in den Südsee-Kolonien des Kaiserreiches: Alltag und Beziehungen zur indigenen Bevölkerung, 1884–1919* (Bielefeld: transcript Verlag, 2014).
5. With respect to quantity and quality, letters and diaries take up a very important position within this source material. These were found partly in private possession, and partly in different national and missionary archives, and this is the first time most of them have been analyzed. Besides these unpublished documents, various printed source texts form the basis

of the study. Significant importance is attached here to the different colonial magazines and publications of associations and missions. A very few women also wrote a book about their experiences in the Pacific colonies and, of course, these books were also used as sources. For more details, see Loosen, *Deutsche Frauen*, 29–39.
6. For more information concerning the history and development of the Women's League, see Karen Smidt, "'Germania führt die deutsche Frau nach Südwest': Auswanderung, Leben und soziale Konflikte deutscher Frauen in der ehemaligen Kolonie Deutch-Südwestafrika 1884–1920." Dissertation, University of Magdeburg, 1997, 55–74.
7. *Kolonie und Heimat* 1 (1907/8), 1: 13.
8. Hedwig Heyl to Herzog Johann Albrecht zu Mecklenburg, Berlin, 24 October 1913, BArch, R 8023/156; *Kolonie und Heimat* 7 (1913/14), 44: 8; Katharina Walgenbach, *"Die weiße Frau als Trägerin deutscher Kultur": Koloniale Diskurse über Geschlecht, "Rasse" und Klasse im Kaiserreich* (Frankfurt a.M.: Campus, 2007), 88.
9. Birthe Kundrus, *Moderne Imperialisten: Das Kaiserreich im Spiegel seiner Kolonien* (Cologne: Böhlau, 2003), 83.
10. *Deutsche Kolonialzeitung*, N.F. 12 (1899), 28: 249.
11. Lora Wildenthal, *German Women for Empire, 1884–1945* (Durham, NC: Duke University Press, 2001), 163.
12. Kundrus, *Moderne Imperialisten*, 12n34.
13. Loosen, *Deutsche Frauen*, 105f.
14. Walgenbach, *"Die weiße Frau als Trägerin,"* 83; Katharina Walgenbach, "Zwischen Selbstaffirmation und Distinktion: Weiße Identität, Geschlecht und Klasse in der Zeitschrift Kolonie und Heimat," in *Medienidentitäten: Identität von Globalisierung und Medienkultur*, ed. Carsten Winter, Tanja Thomas, and Andreas Hepp (Cologne: von Halem, 2003), 139.
15. Loosen, *Deutsche Frauen*, 104f.
16. Smidt, "Germania führt die deutsche Frau," 34–41; see also: *Unter dem roten Kreuz* [Under the Red Cross] 18 (1907), 5: 49f.
17. Number of members given in the publications *Unter dem roten Kreuz* and *Deutsches Kolonialblatt*.
18. *Unter dem roten Kreuz* 2 (1891), 2: 10; 3: 17; 4: 27; see also Margrit Davies, *Public Health and Colonialism: The Case of German New Guinea 1884–1914* (Wiesbaden: Harrasowitz, 2002), 77.
19. *Unter dem roten Kreuz* 14 (1903), 12: 145; Foreign Office/Colonial Department to the Governor in Apia, Berlin 12 August 1903, MESC(AU), S15-IG86-F4.
20. Contract between the "Deutscher Frauenverein für Krankenpflege" and its nurses, Berlin, ca. August 1903, MESC(AU), S15-IG86-F4; Leonore Niessen-Deiters, *Die deutsche Frau im Auslande und in den Schutzgebieten: Nach Originalberichten aus fünf Erdteilen* (Berlin: Fleischel, 1913), 75.
21. Contract between the "Deutscher Frauenverein für Krankenpflege" and its nurses, Berlin, ca. August 1903, MESC(AU), S15-IG86-F4; see also Käthe Schrey, *100 Berufe für Frauen und Mädchen des deutschen Mittelstandes* (Leipzig: Beyer, 1915), 133.
22. Treaty between the board of the "Deutscher Frauenverein für Krankenpflege in den Kolonien" and the Foreign Office/Colonial Department, Berlin 21 August 1903, MESC(AU), S15-IG86-F4; *Unter dem roten Kreuz* 23 (1912), 2: 19; see Schrey, *100 Berufe*, 133.
23. Smidt, "Germania führt die deutsche Frau," 188.
24. See *Unter dem roten Kreuz* 13 (1902), 8: 80; Schrey, *100 Berufe*, 134.
25. Newspaper cutting from *Samoanische Zeitung*, 3 October 1913, in MESC(AU), S15-IG86-F4; *Unter dem roten Kreuz* 8 (1897), 2: 15f. and 8: 70; 9 (1898), 5: 36; Bernhard Naarmann, "Koloniale Arbeit unter dem Roten Kreuz: Der Deutsche Frauenverein vom roten Kreuz für die Kolonien 1888–1917." Dissertation, University of Münster, 1986, 16f.; Schlossmuseum

Sondershausen / James N. Bade (ed.), *Zehn Jahre auf den Inseln der Südsee 1887–1897: Aus dem Tagebuch der Paula David*, entry 14 November 1896, 36.
26. *Unter dem roten Kreuz* 23 (1912), 2: 16; 24 (1913), 2: 15; 4: 40; 8: 80; 27 (1916), 4. Special edition, 3.
27. Reichskolonialamt (ed.), *Die deutschen Schutzgebiete in Afrika und in der Südsee 1912/13: Amtliche Jahresberichte* (Berlin: Mittler, 1914), Statistischer Teil, 30–35.
28. See Paul Steffen, *Missionsbeginn in Neuguinea: Die Anfänge der Rheinischen, Neuendettelsauer und Steyler Missionsarbeit in Neuguinea* (Nettetal: Steyler Verlag, 1995), 161.
29. See Johann Flierl to the Missionsinspektor, Sattelberg, 2 January 1903, AMEW, Vorl. Nr. 4.9.
30. Sr. Stanisla to her family, Hiltrup, 6 April 1902, AHM, single file "Briefe von und über Schwester Stanisla aus dem Besitz der Familie," not listed.
31. See Line Nyhagen Predelli and Jon Miller, "Piety and Patriarchy: Contested Gender Regimes in Nineteenth-Century Evangelical Missions," in *Gendered Missions: Women and Men in Missionary Discourse and Practice*, ed. Mary T. Huber and Nancy C. Lutkehaus (Ann Arbor: University of Michigan Press, 1999), 71f.
32. Smidt, "Germania führt die deutsche Frau," 285; see also Dagmar Konrad, *Missionsbräute: Pietistinnen des 19. Jahrhunderts in der Basler Mission* (Münster: Waxmann Verlag, 2001), 64–67.
33. See Albert Hoffmann, *Lebenserinnerungen eines Rheinischen Missionars: Vol. I* (Wuppertal-Barmen: Verlag der RMG, 1948), 181–85.
34. For instance, Georg Eiffert to the Missionsinspektor, Bogadjim, 14 February 1913 and 22 June 1913, RMG 2.159; Johannes Barkemeyer to the Missionsinspektor, Siar, 6 June 1895, RMG 2.147.
35. Dieter Klein, "Introduction to Jehova se nami nami," in *Die Tagebücher der Johanna Diehl*, ed. Dieter Klein (Wiesbaden: Harrassowitz, 2005), X; Mathilde Wagner to the Missionsinspektor, Speyer, September 1910, AMEW, Vorl. Nr. 4. 26; 4.34/3; 4.39/1; Smidt, "Germania führt die deutsche Frau," 179.
36. For instance, *Kolonie und Heimat* 3 (1909/10), 25: news section, 4.
37. For instance, *Kolonie und Heimat* 6 (1912/13), 17: 15; *Samoanische Zeitung* 2 (1902/03), 1: 3.
38. For instance, different inquiries of German women to the governor in Apia in ANZ(W), AGCA 6051/0119.
39. Angelika Schaser, *Frauenbewegung in Deutschland 1815–1933* (Darmstadt: WBG, 2006), 17; Christine Keim, *Frauenmission und Frauenemanzipation: Eine Diskussion im Kontext der frühen ökumenischen Bewegung 1901–1928* (Münster: Lit-Verlag, 2005), 80; see also *Kolonie und Heimat* 3 (1909/10), 2: 8. Concerning the statistical surplus of women of marriageable age, see: Statistisches Reichsamt (ed.): *Statistisches Jahrbuch für das Deutsche Reich* (Berlin: Schmidt, 1880–1914).
40. See Loosen, *Deutsche Frauen*, 136–42.
41. Walgenbach, *"Die weiße Frau als Trägerin,"* 88; see Hedwig Heyl to Herzog Johann Albrecht zu Mecklenburg, Berlin, 24 October 1913, BArch, R 8023/156.
42. See *Deutsche Kolonialzeitung*, N.F. 12. (1899), 28: 249; Kundrus, *Moderne Imperialisten*, 83.
43. See *Kolonie und Heimat* 6 (1912/13), 45: 8.
44. Adda Liliencron, "Ein Wort über den Deutschkolonialen Frauenbund und seine Aufgaben," *Kolonie und Heimat* 1 (1907/08), 20: 9.
45. See *Kolonie und Heimat* 2 (1908/9), 6: 8; Liliencron, "Ein Wort," 9; Pauline Montgelas, "Die Frau in den Kolonien," *Kolonie und Heimat* 3 (1909/10), 1: 8.
46. See *Kolonie und Heimat* 2 (1908/09), 6: 8; Schrey, *100 Berufe*, 57.
47. See Dag Henrichsen, "'…unerwünscht im Schutzgebiet … nicht schlechthin unsittlich': 'Mischehen' und deren Nachkommen im Visier der Kolonialverwaltung in Deutsch-Südwestafrika," in *Frauen in den deutschen Kolonien*, ed. Marianne Bechhaus-Gerst and

Mechthild Leutner (Berlin: Links, 2009), 82; Wildenthal, *German Women*, 95; Katharina Walgenbach, "Rassenpolitik und Geschlecht in Deutsch-Südwestafrika," in *Rassenmischehen—Mischlinge—Rassentrennung: Zur Politik der Rasse im deutschen Kolonialreich*, ed. Frank Becker (Stuttgart: Franz Steiner Verlag, 2004), 172f., 176.
48. See Richard Deeken, *Manuia Samoa!: Samoanische Reiseskizzen und Beobachtungen* (Berlin: Stalling, 1901), 188; Ludwig Külz, "Zur Frauenfrage in den deutschen Kolonien," *Koloniale Monatsblätter* 15 (1913), 2: 62.
49. Smidt, "Germania führt die deutsche Frau," 192f.; see also 66, 193; Martha Mamozai, *Schwarze Frau, weiße Herrin: Frauenleben in den deutschen Kolonien* (Reinbek bei Hamburg: Rowohlt, 1989), 144.
50. Smidt, "Germania führt die deutsche Frau," 193.
51. Ibid., 221f.; see also Mamozai, *Schwarze Frau*, 189f.
52. Smidt, "Germania führt die deutsche Frau," 289f.; Mamozai, *Schwarze Frau*, 148.
53. Smidt, "Germania führt die deutsche Frau," 178; Wildenthal, *German Women*, 79; Mamozai, *Schwarze Frau*, 148.
54. See Frieda Zieschank, *Ein Jahrzehnt in Samoa 1906–1916* (Leipzig: Haberland, 1918), 115f.
55. Zieschank, *Ein Jahrzehnt in Samoa*, 113.
56. Solf to the State Secretary of the Imperial Colonial Office, Apia, 14 November 1909, BArch, R 1001/2514; see also Hermann Hiery, *Das Deutsche Reich in der Südsee 1900–1921: Eine Annäherung an die Erfahrungen verschiedener Kulturen* (Göttingen: Vandenhoek & Ruprecht, 1995), 143.
57. See Hiery, *Das Deutsche Reich in der Südsee*, 143f.; Hermann Hiery, "Eliten im Elysium? Anmerkungen zur deutschen Kolonialelite," in *Deutsche Eliten in Übersee (16. bis frühes 20. Jh.)*, ed. Markus Denzel (St. Katharinen: Scripta-Mercatura-Verlag, 2007), 431f.
58. Walgenbach, *"Die weiße Frau als Trägerin,"* 78; Horst Gründer, *"...da und dort ein junges Deutschland gründen": Rassismus, Kolonien und kolonialer Gedanke vom 16. bis zum 20. Jahrhundert"* (Munich: Deutscher Taschenbuch Verlag, 2006), 230; Cornelia Essner, "'Wo Rauch ist, da ist auch Feuer': Zu den Ansätzen eines Rassenrechts für die deutschen Kolonien," in *Rassendiskriminierung, Kolonialpolitik und ethnisch-nationale Identität*, ed. Wilfried Wagner et al. (Münster: Lit, 1992), 145.
59. Concerning the development of the number of mixed marriages, see Reichskolonialamt (ed.), *Die deutschen Schutzgebiete in Afrika und in der Südsee 1912/13: Amtliche Jahresberichte 1909/10–1912/13*; see also: Walgenbach, *"Die weiße Frau als Trägerin,"* S. 78; Essner, "Wo Rauch ist," 147.
60. Zieschank, *Ein Jahrzehnt in Samoa*, 50.
61. See Theodor Grentrup, "Die Rassenmischehen in den deutschen Kolonien," *Görresgesellschaft zur Pflege der Wissenschaft im katholischen Deutschland: Veröffentlichungen der Sektion für Rechts—und Sozialwissenschaft* 25 (1914): 33.
62. Iros, "Koloniale Sexualpolitik," *Die neue Generation* 8 (1912), 6: 317.
63. Hermann Hiery mentions two cases of relationships between European women and Melanesian men: see Hermann Hiery, "Germans, Pacific Islanders and Sexuality: German and Indigenous Influence in Melanesia and Micronesia," in *European Impact and Pacific Influence: British and German Colonial Policy in the Pacific Islands and the Indigenous Response*, ed. Hermann Hiery and John MacKenzie (London: Tauris Academic Studies, 1997), 301, 318; Hiery, *Das Deutsche Reich in der Südsee*, 41; but see also Evelyn Wareham, *Race and Realpolitik: The Politics of Colonisation in German Samoa* (Frankfurt a.M.: Lang, 2002), 127: "No white women were recorded as married to coloured men."
64. Zieschank, *Ein Jahrzehnt in Samoa*, 108.
65. Hiery, *Das Deutsche Reich in der Südsee*, 40.

66. Hiery, *Das Deutsche Reich in der Südsee*, 42f., 54f.; Hermann Hiery, "Die deutsche Verwaltung Neuguineas 1884–1914," in *Die deutsche Südsee*, ed. Hiery, 300f.; Hiery, "Germans, Pacific Islanders and Sexuality," 301; Hermann Hiery, *The Neglected War: The German South Pacific and the Influence of World War I* (Honolulu: University of Hawaii Press, 1995), 3; Helmut Christmann, Peter Hempenstall, and Dirk Ballendorf, *Die Karolinen-Inseln in deutscher Zeit: Eine kolonialgeschichtliche Fallstudie* (Münster: Lit, 1991), 90; Karl Baumann, Dieter Klein, and Wolfgang Apitzsch, *Biographisches Handbuch Deutsch-Neuguinea 1882–1922: Kurzlebensläufe ehemaliger Kolonisten, Forscher, Missionare und Reisender* (Fassberg: Baumann, 2002), 127.
67. Reichskolonialamt (ed.), *Die deutschen Schutzgebiete in Afrika und in der Südsee 1909/10–1912/13*, Statistischer Teil, table A. I. 2, A. II. 2.
68. Reichskolonialamt (ed.), *Die deutschen Schutzgebiete in Afrika und in der Südsee 1911/12–1912/13*, Statistischer Teil, table A. II. 2, A. II. 3b.
69. See Richard Deeken, "Die Rassenmischung auf Samoa," *Koloniale Monatsblätter* 16 (1914), 3: 122–35; Maria Kuhn, "Die Stellung der Frau in den Kolonien," in *Verhandlungen des Deutschen Kolonialkongresses 1910*, ed. Deutscher Kolonialkongress (Berlin: Verlag Kolonialkriegerdank, 1910), 953.
70. Carl von Stengel, "Zur Frage der Mischehen in den deutschen Schutzgebieten," *Zeitschrift für Kolonialpolitik, Kolonialrecht und Kolonialwirtschaft* 14 (1912), 10: 745, 773; Smidt, "Germania führt die deutsche Frau," 152; Essner, "Wo Rauch ist," 146f.
71. Pascal Grosse, *Kolonialismus, Eugenik und bürgerliche Gesellschaft in Deutschland 1850–1918* (Frankfurt a.M.: Campus, 2000), 161f.; see also *Samoanisches Gouvernements-Blatt* 3 (1912), 3: 2.
72. Grosse, *Kolonialismus*, 162.
73. Ibid.; Wildenthal, *German Women*, 95.
74. See, for instance, *Kolonie und Heimat* 2 (1908/9), 25: 8; *Deutsche Kolonialzeitung* N.F. 10 (1897), supplement XIV, 57; Niessen-Deiters, *Die deutsche Frau*, 24; Stengel, "Zur Frage der Mischehen," 774; see also Fatima El-Tayeb, *Schwarze Deutsche: Der Diskurs um "Rasse" und nationale Identität 1890–1933* (Frankfurt a.M.: Campus, 2001), 53; Wildenthal, *German Women*, 95.
75. "Ein Urteil über den kolonialen Frauenbund," *Kolonie und Heimat* 7 (1913/14), 44: 8; cf. Henrichsen, "'…unerwünscht im Schutzgebiet'", 82.
76. Wildenthal, *German Women*, 95; Walgenbach, "Rassenpolitik und Geschlecht," 172f., 176.
77. Grosse, *Kolonialismus*, 152.
78. Wildenthal, *German Women*, 105; Grosse, *Kolonialismus*, 152.
79. Smidt, "Germania führt die deutsche Frau," 150; Walgenbach, *"Die weiße Frau als Trägerin,"* 79.
80. Walgenbach, *"Die weiße Frau als Trägerin,"* S. 79; Wildenthal, *German Women*, 108f.; Grosse, *Kolonialismus*, 152.
81. For instance, H. Edler von Hoffmann, "Die Mischehenfrage," *Deutsche Kolonialzeitung* 26 (1909), 48: 793f; Dr Friedrich, "Die rechtliche Beurteilung der Mischehen nach deutschem Kolonialrecht," *Koloniale Rundschau* 1 (1909), 361–368; V. Fuchs, "Nochmals zur Frage der Mischehe in den deutschen Schutzgebieten," *Koloniale Rundschau* 1 (1909), 493–497.
82. Wildenthal, *German Women*, 122; Walgenbach, *"Die weiße Frau als Trägerin,"* 81.
83. State Secretary Solf to the Governor in Apia, Berlin, 17 January 1912, ANZ(W), Samoa-BMO4 94; copy in ANZ(W), AGCA 6051/0408.
84. See also memorandum by Solf concerning newspaper cutting of the *Hamburger Nachrichten*, 21 July 1908, and draft of a decree, 3 October 1911, BArch, R 1001/5432; see also Hermann Hiery, "Die deutsche Verwaltung Samoas 1900–1914," in *Die deutsche Südsee*, ed. Hiery, 667f.
85. Schultz to Schlettwein, Apia, 27 September 1910, ANZ(W), AGCA 6051/0408; Schlettwein to the Governor, Apia, 19 June 1910, ANZ(W), AGCA 6051/0408 and Samoa-BMO4 94; announcement by the Governor, Apia, 2 August 1912, ANZ(W), AGCA 6051/0408.

86. See Robert Samulski, "Die 'Sünde' im Auge des Betrachters—Rassenmischung und deutsche Rassenpolitik im Schutzgebiet Samoa 1900 bis 1914," in *Rassenmischehen—Mischlinge—Rassentrennung*, ed. Frank Becker (Stuttgart: Franz Steiner Verlag, 2004), 343.
87. "Zur Rassenfrage in Samoa," *Samoanische Zeitung* 11 (1911), 15: 1.
88. "Die Mischehe in den Kolonien," *Koloniale Zeitschrift* 5 (1904), 24, quoted from *Samoanische Zeitung* 5 (1905), 10: 1.
89. A. Herfurth, "Wieder einmal die Rassenfrage," *Koloniale Zeitschrift* 7 (1906), 12: 202.
90. Copy of a letter from Samoa (unknown author), *Koloniale Zeitschrift* 7 (1906), 24: 409f.
91. See Barts, "Mischlingssorgen in Samoa," *Koloniale Zeitschrift* 13 (1912), 32: 502; Wildenthal, *German Women*, 121f.; Samulski, "Die 'Sünde,'" 355.
92. Wareham, *Race and Realpolitik*, 144.
93. *Samoanische Zeitung* 5 (1905), 10: 1.
94. See Walgenbach, *"Die weiße Frau als Trägerin,"* 81f.; Samulski, "Die 'Sünde,'" 347; Kathrin Roller, "'Wir sind Deutsche, wir sind Weiße und wir wollen Weiße bleiben'—Reichstagsdebatten über koloniale 'Rassenmischung,'" in *Kolonialmetropole Berlin: Eine Spurensuche*, ed. Ullrich van der Heyden and Joachim Zeller (Berlin: Berlin-Ed., 2002), 73.
95. The term "race" is not mentioned in the Civil Code for the German Empire; see Birthe Kundrus, "'Weiß und herrlich': Überlegungen zu einer Geschlechtergeschichte des Kolonialismus," in *Projektionen: Rassismus und Sexismus in der Visuellen Kultur*, ed. Annegret Friedrich et al. (Marburg: Jonas-Verlag, 1997), 44; Wildenthal, *German Women*, 85, 90, 127.
96. See Walgenbach, *"Die weiße Frau als Trägerin,"* 82f.; Wildentahl, *German Women*, 128; Roller, "Wir sind Deutsche," 77.
97. See Walgenbach, *Zwischen Selbstaffirmation und Distinktion*, 142; Grosse, *Kolonialismus*, 168–76.
98. Leonore Niessen-Deiters, "Rassenreinheit! Eine deutsche Frau über die Mischehen in den Kolonien," *Kolonie und Heimat* 5 (1911/12), 36: news supplement, 1.
99. For instance, ibid.
100. Smidt, "Germania führt die deutsche Frau," 155; Wildenthal, *German Women*, 99, 104, 118; Kundrus, *Moderne Imperialisten*, 260.
101. Smidt, "Germania führt die deutsche Frau," 154; Walgenbach, "Zwischen Selbstaffirmation und Distinktion," 146; Frances Gouda, "Das 'unterlegene' Geschlecht der 'überlegenen' Rasse: Kolonialgeschichte und Geschlechterverhältnisse," in *Geschlechterverhältnisse im historischen Wandel*, ed. Hanna Schissler (Frankfurt a.M.: Campus, 1993), 196; Wildenthal, *German Women*, 79.
102. Smidt, "Germania führt die deutsche Frau," 155. Worthy of mention are the numerous quotations on the following pages that show the racist attitudes of the German women in South West Africa.
103. See Smidt, "Germania führt die deutsche Frau," 154–56; Mamozai, *Schwarze Frau*, 154f.
104. See Zieschank, *Ein Jahrzehnt in Samoa*, 107f.
105. Antonie Brandeis, "Südsee-Erinnerungen," *Deutsche Kolonialzeitung* 25 (1908), 1: 6.
106. Elisabeth Krämer-Bannow, *Bei kunstsinnigen Kannibalen der Südsee: Wanderungen auf Neu-Mecklenburg 1908–1909* (Berlin: D. Reimer, 1916), S. 251.
107. Gretel Kuhn, *Erinnerungen an Rabaul 1914–1921*, unpublished transcript, in private hands, 80.
108. Concerning "Queen Emma," see Hermann Mückler, *Kolonialismus in Ozeanien: Kulturgeschichte Ozeaniens*, Vol. 3 (Vienna: facultas, 2012), 183f.; Andreas Blauert, "Queen Emma of the South Seas: Die Karriere der Emma Forsayth (1850–1913)," in *Bad Girls: Unangepasste Frauen von der Antike bis heute*, ed. Anke Väth (Konstanz: UVK-Verl.-Ges., 2003), 135–37; see also Lily and Karl Rechinger, *Streifzüge in Deutsch-Neu-Guinea und auf den Salomons-Inseln: Eine botanische Forschungsreise* (Berlin: Reimer, 1908), 91f.

109. Copy of a letter by Johanna Fellmann to her mother, 2 December 1901, in Helmuth Steenken, *Die frühe Südsee: Lebensläufe aus dem "Paradis der Wilden"* (Oldenburg: Isensee, 1997), 173.
110. Valesca Schultze, Tagebuch, entry 5 June 1882, in private hands.
111. Zieschank, *Ein Jahrzehnt in Samoa*, 108f.
112. Ibid., 111.
113. Ibid., 108.
114. Ibid., 50.
115. Ibid., 108f.
116. Ibid., 108f.
117. Frieda Zieschank, "Briefe an eine Kolonialbraut," *Kolonie und Heimat* 6 (1913), 45: 8.
118. Zieschank, *Ein Jahrzehnt in Samoa*, 110–12.

Bibliography

Bade, James N., ed. *Zehn Jahre auf den Inseln der Südsee 1887–1897: Aus dem Tagebuch der Paula David*. Dresden: Sandstein, 2011.

Baumann, Karl, Dieter Klein, and Wolfgang Apitzsch. *Biographisches Handbuch Deutsch-Neuguinea 1882–1922: Kurzlebensläufe ehemaliger Kolonisten, Forscher, Missionare und Reisender*. Fassberg: Baumann, 2002.

Blauert, Andreas. "Queen Emma of the South Seas: Die Karriere der Emma Forsayth (1850–1913)." In *Bad Girls: Unangepasste Frauen von der Antike bis heute*, edited by Anke Väth, 135–53. Konstanz: UVK-Verl.-Ges., 2003.

Brandeis, Antonie. "Südsee-Erinnerungen." *Deutsche Kolonialzeitung* 25, no. 1 (1908): 6–7.

Christmann, Helmut, Peter Hempenstall, and Dirk Ballendorf. *Die Karolinen-Inseln in deutscher Zeit: Eine kolonialgeschichtliche Fallstudie*. Münster: Lit, 1991.

Davies, Margrit. *Public Health and Colonialism: The Case of German New Guinea 1884–1914*. Wiesbaden: Harrasowitz, 2002.

Deeken, Richard. *Manuia Samoa!: Samoanische Reiseskizzen und Beobachtungen*. Berlin: Stalling, 1901.

———. "Die Rassenmischung auf Samoa." *Koloniale Monatsblätter* 16, no. 3 (1914): 122–35.

El-Tayeb, Fatima. *Schwarze Deutsche: Der Diskurs um "Rasse" und nationale Identität 1890–1933*. Frankfurt a.M.: Campus, 2001.

Essner, Cornelia. "'Wo Rauch ist, da ist auch Feuer': Zu den Ansätzen eines Rassenrechts für die deutschen Kolonien." In *Rassendiskriminierung, Kolonialpolitik und ethnisch-nationale Identität*, edited by Wilfried Wagner et al., 145–60. Münster: Lit, 1992.

Friedrich, Dr. "Die rechtliche Beurteilung der Mischehe nach deutschem Kolonialrecht," *Koloniale Rundschau* 1 (1909): 361–238.

Fuchs, V. "Nochmals zur Frage der Mischehe in den deutschen Schutzgebieten", *Koloniale Rundschau* 1 (1909): 493–497.

Gouda, Frances. "Das 'unterlegene' Geschlecht der 'überlegenen' Rasse: Kolonialgeschichte und Geschlechterverhältnisse." In *Geschlechterverhältnisse im historischen Wandel*, edited by Hanna Schissler, 185–203. Frankfurt a.M.: Campus, 1993.

Grentrup, Theodor. "Die Rassenmischehen in den deutschen Kolonien." *Görresgesellschaft zur Pflege der Wissenschaft im katholischen Deutschland: Veröffentlichungen der Sektion für Rechts—und Sozialwissenschaft* 25 (1914): 33.

Grosse, Pascal. *Kolonialismus, Eugenik und bürgerliche Gesellschaft in Deutschland 1850–1918*. Frankfurt a.M.: Campus, 2000.

Gründer, Horst. *"...da und dort ein junges Deutschland gründen": Rassismus, Kolonien und kolonialer Gedanke vom 16. bis zum 20. Jahrhundert*. Munich: Deutscher Taschenbuch Verlag, 2006.

Hagemann, Karen. "'Ich glaub' nicht, daß ich Wichtiges zu erzählen hab'…: Oral History und historische Frauenforschung." In *Oral History*, edited by Herwart Vorländer, 29–48. Göttingen: Vandenhoek & Ruprecht, 1990.

Henrichsen, Dag. "'…unerwünscht im Schutzgebiet … nicht schlechthin unsittlich': 'Mischehen' und deren Nachkommen im Visier der Kolonialverwaltung in Deutsch-Südwestafrika." In *Frauen in den deutschen Kolonien*, edited by Marianne Bechhaus-Gerst and Mechthild Leutner, 80–90. Berlin: Links, 2009.

Hiery, Hermann. *Das Deutsche Reich in der Südsee 1900–1921: Eine Annäherung an die Erfahrungen verschiedener Kulturen*. Göttingen: Vandenhoek & Ruprecht, 1995.

———, ed., *Die deutsche Südsee, 1884–1914: Ein Handbuch*. Paderborn: Schöningh, 2002.

———. "Die deutsche Verwaltung Neuguineas, 1884–1914." In *Die deutsche Südsee*, edited by Hermann Hiery, 277–311.

———. "Die deutsche Verwaltung Samoas 1900–1914." In *Die deutsche Südsee*, edited by Hermann Hiery, 649–76.

———. "Eliten im Elysium? Anmerkungen zur deutschen Kolonialelite." In *Deutsche Eliten in Übersee (16. bis frühes 20. Jh.)*, edited by Markus Denzel. St. Katharinen: Scripta-Mercatura-Verlag, 2007.

———. "Germans, Pacific Islanders and Sexuality." In *European Impact and Pacific Influence*, edited by Hermann Hiery and John MacKenzie, 299–323. London: Tauris Academic Studies, 1997.

———. *The Neglected War: The German South Pacific and the Influence of World War I*. Honolulu: University of Hawaii Press, 1995.

Hoffmann, Albert. *Lebenserinnerungen eines Rheinischen Missionars: Vol. I*. Wuppertal-Barmen: Verlag der RMG, 1948.

Iros. "Koloniale Sexualpolitik." *Die neue Generation* 8, no. 6 (1912): 317.

Keim, Christine. *Frauenmission und Frauenemanzipation: Eine Diskussion im Kontext der frühen ökumenischen Bewegung 1901–1928*. Münster: Lit-Verlag, 2005.

Klein, Dieter. "Introduction to Jehova se nami nami." In *Die Tagebücher der Johanna Diehl*, edited by Dieter Klein. Wiesbaden: Harrassowitz, 2005.

Konrad, Dagmar. *Missionsbräute: Pietistinnen des 19. Jahrhunderts in der Basler Mission*. Münster: Waxmann Verlag, 2001.

Krämer-Bannow, Elisabeth. *Bei kunstsinnigen Kannibalen der Südsee: Wanderungen auf Neu-Mecklenburg 1908–1909*. Berlin: D. Reimer, 1916.

Kuhn, Gretel. "Erinnerungen an Rabaul 1914–1921." Unpublished transcript, in private hands.

Kuhn, Maria. "Die Stellung der Frau in den Kolonien." In *Verhandlungen des Deutschen Kolonialkongresses 1910, Deutscher Kolonialkongress*, 945–64. Berlin: Verlag Kolonialkriegerdank, 1910.

Külz, Ludwig. "Zur Frauenfrage in den deutschen Kolonien." *Koloniale Monatsblätter* 15, no. 2 (1913): 62.

Kundrus, Birthe. *Moderne Imperialisten: Das Kaiserreich im Spiegel seiner Kolonien*. Cologne: Böhlau, 2003.

———. "'Weiß und herrlich': Überlegungen zu einer Geschlechtergeschichte des Kolonialismus." In *Projektionen: Rassismus und Sexismus in der Visuellen Kultur*, edited by Annegret Friedrich et al., 41–50. Marburg: Jonas-Verlag, 1997.

Liliencron, Adda. "Ein Wort über den Deutschkolonialen Frauenbund und seine Aufgaben." *Kolonie und Heimat* 1, no. 20 (1907/8): 9.

Loosen, Livia. *Deutsche Frauen in den Südsee-Kolonien des Kaiserreiches: Alltag und Beziehungen zur indigenen Bevölkerung, 1884–1919*. Bielefeld: transcript Verlag, 2014.

Mamozai, Martha. *Schwarze Frau, weiße Herrin: Frauenleben in den deutschen Kolonien*. Reinbek bei Hamburg: Rowohlt, 1989.

Montgelas, Pauline. "Die Frau in den Kolonien." *Kolonie und Heimat* 3, no. 1 (1909/10): 8.

Mückler, Hermann. *Kolonialismus in Ozeanien: Kulturgeschichte Ozeaniens*, Vol. 3. Vienna: Facultas, 2012.

Naarmann, Bernhard. "Koloniale Arbeit unter dem Roten Kreuz: Der Deutsche Frauenverein vom roten Kreuz für die Kolonien 1888–1917." Dissertation. University of Münster, 1986.

Niessen-Deiters, Leonore. *Die deutsche Frau im Auslande und in den Schutzgebieten: Nach Originalberichten aus fünf Erdteilen*. Berlin: Fleischel, 1913.

———. "Rassenreinheit! Eine deutsche Frau über die Mischehen in den Kolonien." *Kolonie und Heimat* 5, no. 36 (1911/12): news supplement, 1.

Nyhagen Predelli, Line, and Jon Miller. "Piety and Patriarchy: Contested Gender Regimes in Nineteenth-Century Evangelical Missions." In *Gendered Missions: Women and Men in Missionary Discourse and Practice*, edited by Mary T. Huber and Nancy C. Lutkehaus, 67–111. Ann Arbor: University of Michigan Press, 1999.

Pytlik, Anna. *Die schöne Fremde: Frauen entdecken die Welt*. Stuttgart: Württembergische Landesbibliothek, 1991.

Rechinger, Lily, and Karl Rechinger. *Streifzüge in Deutsch-Neu-Guinea und auf den Salomons-Inseln: Eine botanische Forschungsreise*. Berlin: Reimer, 1908.

Reichskolonialamt [Imperial Colonial Office], ed. *Die deutschen Schutzgebiete in Afrika und in der Südsee 1912/13: Amtliche Jahresberichte*. Statistischer Teil 26f, 30–35. Berlin: Mittler, 1914.

Roller, Kathrin. "'Wir sind Deutsche, wir sind Weiße und wir wollen Weiße bleiben'—Reichstagsdebatten über koloniale 'Rassenmischung.'" In *Kolonialmetropole Berlin: Eine Spurensuche*, edited by Ullrich van der Heyden and Joachim Zeller, 73–79. Berlin: Berlin-Ed., 2002.

Samulski, Robert. "Die 'Sünde' im Auge des Betrachters—Rassenmischung und deutsche Rassenpolitik im Schutzgebiet Samoa 1900 bis 1914." In *Rassenmischehen—Mischlinge—Rassentrennung*, edited by Frank Becker, 329–56. Stuttgart: Franz Steiner Verlag, 2004.

Schaser, Angelika. *Frauenbewegung in Deutschland 1815–1933*. Darmstadt: WBG, 2006.

Schrey, Käthe. *100 Berufe für Frauen und Mädchen des deutschen Mittelstandes*. Leipzig: Beyer, 1915.

Smidt, Karen. "'Germania führt die deutsche Frau nach Südwest': Auswanderung, Leben und soziale Konflikte deutscher Frauen in der ehemaligen Kolonie Deutch-Südwestafrika 1884–1920." Dissertation. University of Magdeburg, 1997.

Steenken, Helmuth. *Die frühe Südsee: Lebensläufe aus dem "Paradies der Wilden."* Oldenburg: Isensee, 1997.

Steffen, Paul. *Missionsbeginn in Neuguinea: Die Anfänge der Rheinischen, Neuendettelsauer und Steyler Missionsarbeit in Neuguinea*. Nettetal: Steyler Verlag, 1995.

von Hoffmann, H. Edler. "Die Mischehenfrage." *Deutsche Kolonialzeitung* 26, no. 48 (1909): 793–94.
von Stengel, Carl. "Zur Frage der Mischehen in den deutschen Schutzgebieten." *Zeitschrift für Kolonialpolitik, Kolonialrecht und Kolonialwirtschaft* 14 (1912): 738–80.
Walgenbach, Katharina. "Rassenpolitik und Geschlecht in Deutsch-Südwestafrika." In *Rassenmischehen—Mischlinge—Rassentrennung: Zur Politik der Rasse im deutschen Kolonialreich*, edited by Frank Becker, 165–83. Stuttgart: Franz Steiner Verlag, 2004.
———. *"Die weiße Frau als Trägerin deutscher Kultur": Koloniale Diskurse über Geschlecht, "Rasse" und Klasse im Kaiserreich*. Frankfurt a.M.: Campus, 2007.
———. "Zwischen Selbstaffirmation und Distinktion: Weiße Identität, Geschlecht und Klasse in der Zeitschrift Kolonie und Heimat." In *Medienidentitäten: Identität von Globalisierung und Medienkultur*, edited by Carsten Winter, Tanja Thomas, and Andreas Hepp, 136–52. Cologne: von Halem, 2003.
Wareham, Evelyn. *Race and Realpolitik: The Politics of Colonisation in German Samoa*. Frankfurt a.M.: Lang, 2002.
Wildenthal, Lora. *German Women for Empire, 1884–1945*. Durham, NC: Duke University Press, 2001.
Zieschank, Frieda. *Ein Jahrzehnt in Samoa 1906–1916*. Leipzig: Haberland, 1918.

Chapter 10

SACRIFICE, HEROISM, PROFESSIONALIZATION, AND EMPOWERMENT
Colonial New Guinea in the Lives of German Religious Women, 1899–1919

Katharina Stornig

In 1924, the German missionary periodical *Missionsgrüße* (Missionary Greetings),[1] the publication of a Catholic congregation of missionary nuns called the Servants of the Holy Spirit, printed a three-page article with the title "Twenty-Five Years of Missionary Work in New Guinea."[2] The article gave a comprehensive overview of the congregation's missionary engagement in northern New Guinea, which began in 1899 and extended through the German colonial period into present times. The article particularly emphasized the activities of a pioneer generation of nuns from Germany, who, after encountering a "wild and stony field of work" and a "bulwark" of "heathendom,"[3] had taken on the tasks of instructing New Guinean children and youth, caring for the sick, and supporting the spiritual works of missionary priests. Indeed, the Holy Spirit Congregation had been established in 1889 to complement the evangelizing activities of an affiliated German missionary order of priests and brothers, the Society of the Divine Word (1875).[4] Overall, the anniversary article from 1924 depicted female missionary work in New Guinea as a hard and demanding, yet spiritually rewarding, enterprise for religious women. Interestingly enough, the text was accompanied by a photograph, which had been taken seven years earlier in Alexishafen, the Catholic missionary headquarters in the region (Figure 10.1). The photograph showed the laid out body of Sister Valeria Dietzen (1872–1917) surrounded by five indigenous girls and another nun from Germany, all praying over her.[5]

Sister Valeria was born in 1872 close to the German town of Trier as Anna Maria Dietzen.[6] In 1894, she entered the Holy Spirit Congregation, and two years later she took her first vows. In 1899, Sister Valeria was one of the first group of four nuns who migrated to Kaiser Wilhelmsland in order to assist the Divine Word Missionaries, who had already arrived in 1896. Over the following

---

Notes from this chapter begin on page 250.

Figure 10.1: "Sr. Valeria Dietzen in the coffin, 1917, PNG." Courtesy of the Servants of the Holy Spirit's Archives.

years, Sister Valeria Dietzen became a leading nun in New Guinea; she contributed considerably to the development of Catholic schooling in the prefecture, and became head of all local nuns in 1905. As such, she regularly visited all local women's convents, and, staying in close touch with the Servants of the Holy

Sacrifice, Heroism, Professionalization, and Empowerment | 239

An der Bahre der Missionsschwester.
Die verstorbene Schwester Valeria, frühere Regionaloberin in Neuguinea betrauert von eingebornen Mädchen und ihrer leiblichen Schwester Schwester Ehrentrudis.

Figure 10.2: "On the stretcher of the missionary nun" (*An der Bahre der Missionsschwester*). Courtesy of the Servants of the Holy Spirit's Archives.

Spirit's Motherhouse in Europe, negotiated the adaptation of the congregation's religious rule to the New Guinea cultural setting. In 1913, Sister Valeria particularly cheered up, for her younger sister, Katharina Dietzen (1884–1944), who had also joined the congregation and become Sister Ehrentrudis in 1908, arrived in New Guinea.⁷ Yet, while both sisters enjoyed their reunion,⁸ it did not last long. In June 1917, Sister Valeria contracted blackwater fever and passed away at the age of forty-five.

Considering Sister Valeria's high status within the ranks of the congregation, the existence of the photograph at Figure 10.1 might not surprise us. Yet, at that time, to take such a photograph was quite unusual. As Hermann Hiery has pointed out in the introduction to his published collection of photographs from German New Guinea, picturing sick or dead "white" bodies there generally constituted a taboo.⁹ According to his analysis of more than five thousand images, the death of Europeans did not feature in the German colonial imagery, because such images would have nurtured the ever-present fears of serious sickness, and threatened the vision of a well-functioning colony in both New Guinea and Germany.¹⁰ Nevertheless, Sister Valeria's fellow sisters still produced a photograph of her laid out body and posted a print to Europe. In Germany, the Servants of the Holy Spirit not only filed it carefully in the archives of their Motherhouse,¹¹ but also reproduced it several times and printed it as an illustration in the quoted article (figure 10.2). Thus, they actively contributed to the distribution of the image to Catholic households in Germany and Austria. The question consequently emerges as to why the New Guinea-based missionaries had this photograph taken and what they hoped to achieve by posting it to Europe? Why did the nuns in Germany represent female missionary work in New Guinea to larger audiences by means of a photograph of the laid out body of a nun? What did "New Guinea" mean to these women and their supporting groups in Germany?

This chapter discusses these questions. Analyzing the activities and experiences of German missionary nuns in what was then German New Guinea, I particularly question the expectations and imaginations they connected to migration. Given that historical narratives of colonizing and missionizing still tend to privilege male voices and experiences, the chapter will largely focus on the published and non-published writings of religious women. In contrast to many of the recent historical studies that, whether explicitly or not, have tended to depict the Pacific Ocean as a space of exchange and imagination marked by high male mobility and female locality, I privilege a focus on the movements of women.¹² This, moreover, implies that rather than focusing on the male missionary elites who also engaged in, for instance, scientific work as ethnographers or linguists, I focus on nuns who formed the bottom end of the gendered ecclesiastical and colonial hierarchies. Yet, I argue that the nuns' activities and perceptions were nonetheless significant, for they involved socially and spiritually rewarding roles as teachers, nurses, and evangelists. Besides, women missionaries not only featured in missionary texts and photographs but also acted as writers and publishers. This, in turn, shows that they occupied an important space in the German imperial imagination. The nuns actively contributed to the construction and dissemination of an image of

New Guinea as a site where men—and particularly religious women—could lead meaningful lives.

New Guinea as a Mission Field

As has been widely argued, the South Seas already occupied an important place in the European imagination before its systematic exploration in the late eighteenth century.[13] Since the early modern period, constructions of Oceania inspired activities among both religious and secular groups. While first attempts to missionize Oceania date back to Jesuit activities in the seventeenth century, it was particularly in the early nineteenth century that the Christian churches again took great interest in the region. Around 1800, the newly founded Protestant mission-sending societies, such as the London Missionary Society (1795) and the Wesleyan Methodist Missionary Society (1813), promoted the systematic Christianization of Polynesia.[14]

In turn, Catholic missionaries, such as the Marist Brothers and the Sacred Heart Missionaries, moved to Oceania in larger numbers, but only in the second half of the nineteenth century. In the 1880s, Spanish Capuchins settled on the Caroline Islands and established missionary stations in Pohnpei and Palau, both situated in areas that were to become part of German New Guinea in 1899. For the context of this chapter, it must be noted that the greater presence of German missionaries in the area started with the onset of German colonialism in 1884, and was marked by a complex relationship of joint as well as conflicting interests between missionaries, traders, and politicians.[15] In some cases, the onset of German colonialism involved Germans replacing the missionaries of other nationalities.[16] On the Protestant side, it was particularly the Wuppertal-based Rhenisch Missionary Society and the Bavarian Neuendettelsauer Mission that sent workers to what had become Kaiser Wilhelmsland in the second half of the 1880s.[17] Moreover, German colonialism inspired the Vatican to create new prefectures, which were handed over to German missionary orders. In New Guinea, Pope Leo XIII erected the prefecture apostolic Kaiser Wilhelmsland on the homonymous German part of the mainland and offshore islands, and assigned it to the German Society of the Divine Word in 1896.

However, although German colonialism fueled the involvement of German missionaries in New Guinea, it is important to note that the missionary fascination with this region had a long-standing tradition. Since the eighteenth century, Christian missionaries in Europe had likewise received the many reports of other missionaries, travelers, explorers, and later traders with great interest. Consequently, some religious groups began to develop high expectations with regard to the Christianization of the region. Many missionaries envisioned the littleness of the territories and the geography of the island world as factors that allowed them to work among manageable population groups.[18] In addition, they generally considered the absence of large numbers of secular settlers as favorable to evangelizing efforts. Yet, the region, with its cultural, linguistic, and religious/spiritual diversity also presented the missionaries with many challenges, among them large geographic distances, tropical diseases, long shipping routes to Europe, and psychological and logistic problems connected to isolation.[19]

Also, the first Divine Word Missionaries, who settled in Tumleo, a small offshore island without European or colonial infrastructure, faced many difficulties. They made great efforts to provide what they considered proper food and lodging, founding new missionary stations and establishing connections between them.[20] The priests and brothers built stations and churches, founded plantations, and shipped along the coast. However, the missionaries also faced a range of other problems, some of which related to local gender arrangements and the limited access they had to indigenous girls and women. According to their view, female co-workers were needed in order to reach local girls and women, who, in their (future) capacity as mothers, were increasingly seen as the key to religious change. Just like most missionary orders at that time, the Society of the Divine Word's priests soon called for female co-workers to come over from Germany.[21] These calls found sympathetic ears in Germany; already by the beginning of 1899, the first group of four Servants of the Holy Spirit had departed. Many others followed, and, prior to 1914, the nuns set up ten women's convents along the north coast of Kaiser Wilhelmsland.[22] There they acted as teachers, nurses, workers, farmers, and housekeepers. In all settings, the nuns lived in close proximity to the indigenous population and, contracting indigenous girls or young women as boarders or housemaids, interacted with them on a daily basis.[23]

Gendering the New Guinean Mission Field

Since the Servants of the Holy Spirit considered writing, together with praying, as the most effective means to maintain a sense of religious sisterhood despite the large geographic distances, the departing nuns were instructed to take every opportunity to send letters and detailed reports to home-staying fellows and superiors. These travel reports bear witness to the fact that most New Guinea missionaries departed with ambivalent sentiments. On the one hand, given that the nuns, in contrast to their male colleagues, were not granted home leave, departure was irrevocable and implied both pain of separation and some natural worries about their new missionary life. On the other hand, the nuns were leaving for religious reasons. They referred to departure as a "long-standing wish" and an active response to what they perceived as God's call.[24] For instance, Sister Fridolina Vökt (1857–1926) recollected her parting from the Motherhouse in a retrospective report as follows:

Who can describe the feelings that overcame us when the first beam of light announced the dawning of this memorable day? Joy filled our hearts when we thought of the fulfillment of our long-standing wish to participate immediately in the great venture of evangelization. ... It was essential now for us to rise above nature, to direct our eyes up [and] to direct our steps afar in good spirits, resting our whole fate in the hand of the Almighty. ... Joy and grief fought for mastery; and if not bloody, the struggle was still hard.[25]

The passage shows that the migration of nuns cannot by seen in isolation from their religious subjectivities, as well as the perception of the Christian missionary venture as the most meaningful venture accessible to them.

In any case, for these women, who mostly came from Catholic milieus in rural Germany, departure involved the experience of transcontinental mobility. Sister Fridolina and her colleagues first traveled south by train. In Genoa, they boarded a steamship that took them via Port Said, Aden, and Colombo to Singapore, where they disembarked. Staying for eight days at the convent of the French Sisters of the Infant Jesus in Singapore, they visited churches, gardens, and Catholic institutions.[26] Obviously, the travelers attempted to share their experiences with their fellow sisters who had stayed back home. In several letters, they commented on the diverse people they met, lauded the "beautiful nature," and reported on the ways in which the local nuns organized religious life and missionary work.[27] Apart from dealing with their French hosts, they reported having met "Chinese" children and "very few blacks" in the boarding school and orphanage operated by the French nuns.[28] Sister Valeria Dietzen proudly reported on her first tastes of the "sweet fruits of this country," such as banana, mango, pineapple, coconut, lemon, and several more.[29] In addition, they informed their fellow sisters in Europe about the many "exotic trees" and animals (e.g., tigers, lamas, monkeys, pelicans, crocodiles, and snakes) they had seen during a visit to the botanic garden.[30] However, the travelers also criticized the streets of Singapore as being dirty, the city dwellers as "going about in old rags," and the houses as "miserable huts."[31]

Altogether, it must be noted that this first group of German nuns, on their way to New Guinea, had already encountered a range of experiences that connected them to the Pacific as an exchange network of people, goods, and ideas. Apart from their stay in Singapore, they reported on their multiple encounters with diverse people, be they missionaries, colonial administrators, or other travelers, both European and non-European. For instance, the nuns claimed to have met not only religious and secular travelers from England, Germany, and Italy on the cruise, but also three envoys of the Chinese emperor.[32] The same thing applied for their colleagues who followed in later years. Depending on timetables and shipping routes, the nuns from Germany met many people from diverse backgrounds en route to New Guinea, and made stopovers in towns such as Melbourne, Sydney, Freemantle, Penang, Batavia (Jakarta), Banda, and Herbertshöhe (Kokopo).[33] They visited places such as convents, Catholic institutions, gardens, and plantations. Besides, after the passage, high mobility also constituted a regular feature of missionary life; in New Guinea, most nuns in the course of their careers operated in more than one convent of the Servants of the Holy Spirit, and thus came to know several parts of the prefecture Kaiser Wilhelmsland. Irrespective of their missionary training and field of work, the nuns experienced missionary life in different settings. However, those nuns who had gone through the more sophisticated training as teachers or nurses were more likely to act in public and thus to also get to know the villages that surrounded the various convents that had been established in what was then Kaiser Wilhelmsland.

Female Missionary Lives

Sister Valeria Dietzen, as well as several others after her, took on teaching immediately upon arrival on Tumleo Island in April 1899. In particular, she started to give elementary education to children of both sexes, and religious instruction to girls and women. Significantly, even though the learning progress in these early classes must be questioned for several reasons,[34] Sister Valeria represented herself as a confident teacher from the outset. In the early twentieth century, she co-founded a boarding school and a nursery school on Tumleo, which were to set examples for the development of Catholic education in the whole prefecture. Later on, she contributed to the production of teaching materials,[35] and, like some nuns after her, translated passages of the catechism into native languages.[36] Most importantly for our context, Sister Valeria was recognized as a successful teacher not only by her fellow sisters but also by the priests. The ecclesiastical head of the prefecture, the Westphalia-born former missionary to China, Eberhard Limbrock (1859–1939), repeatedly lauded the nuns' aptitude in school, stating in 1906 that they "can dedicate themselves more to education, for which they have more patience and perseverance, prepare themselves with more zeal, and so achieve more and better results than most priests do." Overall, Limbrock concluded in 1906, the "sisters in this mission are of extraordinary importance."[37]

However, this perception was of course illicitly one-sided, for the nuns' activities largely rested on the collaboration of indigenous women. The nuns from Germany not only needed language assistance but also depended on local knowledge about everyday life and on the labor of indigenous women, who moved in at the convents. The sources suggest that these cross-cultural female communities were marked by both collaboration and conflict in day-to-day life.[38] Besides, read against the grain, the letters also show that indigenous girls followed their own agenda when staying with the nuns, and never stopped complaining about the behavior of Christianized women. For instance, in May 1902 (and thus after about two years in Tumleo), a somewhat disillusioned nun wrote about the prospect of remaking New Guinean girls in the face of European Christianity: "Not even one of our girls remained upright, even though we have attempted to protect them from dangers."[39] Hence, even the converted girls did not act in ways the nuns considered proper. Besides, particularly during the early years of missionary presence, the often coercive and violent methods applied by the missionary teachers and educators not only harmed the relationship between the nuns and the nearby villagers but also led to some serious disputes within the religious communities.[40] In these disputes, Sister Valeria took the position of a hardliner who emphasized the need to prevent the indigenous girls from engaging in what the Catholic missionaries considered to be immoral activities. In that, she received broad support from the priests, who likewise promoted corporeal punishment as a sign of what they called loving care.[41]

Overall, the nuns' intensive involvement in education and childcare was also acknowledged in Germany. Without doubt, for Sister Valeria, teaching constituted a basic and highly valued contribution to female missionary work. After her death in 1917, all New Guinea-based missionaries agreed that her contributions to the mission venture had been of great importance. On this occasion, several New Guinea-based nuns and priests wrote to Europe, describing Sister Valeria's last days on earth and referring to her death as a "most painful loss"[42] that had "affected all sisters and the mission deeply."[43] However, most of them found solace in the fact that, during the previous two decades, Sister Valeria "had devoted all her energies and entire life to the mission and the well-being of the … sisters."[44] A leading priest in New Guinea described her as "a mother" for all local nuns and Catholics, for she had "worked, sacrificed, and prayed for the mission with constant commitment."[45] Another nun stated that, praying at Sister Valeria's deathbed, "I recalled the Holy Scripture, where there is mention of the strong woman."[46] All New Guinea-based missionaries from Germany shared the conviction that Sister Valeria had led a meaningful life agreeable to God, and, having sacrificed herself to the redemption of New Guinea, she was now to receive the spiritual rewards for that.

However, not all nuns received some sort of teacher training before departing for New Guinea. In fact, quite the contrary was the case. The majority of female missionaries were trained as what the congregation classified as "working sisters" (*Arbeitsschwestern*). This implied that their missionary tasks were primarily defined by domestic labor, and involved, for instance, cooking, washing, bleaching, ironing, sewing, and stitching. In New Guinea, working sisters also engaged in gardening and farming. However, while such a job description does not appear to be like that of a religious emissary, the working nuns' letters nonetheless show that they perceived of their lifelong stay in New Guinea as contributing to the redemption of the country. The activities and writings of Sister Martha Siefering (1864–1914) provide a good example of that.

Coming from a small town close to Münster, Sister Martha had joined the Holy Spirit congregation in 1891 and moved to New Guinea in 1899. According to her status as a working sister, her tasks primarily involved washing, gardening, and chicken farming. Since some indigenous girls and women lived and worked with the nuns at all convents, working sisters also interacted with them on a regular basis. However, for Sister Martha, who was an advocate of hard work, strict discipline, and religious practices of suffering and self-mortification, the collaboration with New Guinean women often turned out to be disillusioning.[47] Worrying for the moral conduct of the local population, she repeatedly expressed her conviction that European Catholics had to engage in practices of suffering and mortification if they were to eventually save them. Many missionary nuns mentioned the ascetic concept of suffering as a way to do penance, which had a long-standing tradition in female religious life.[48] Suffering, in this context, referred to God's redemptive activity in the sufferings of Christ, and meant the striving of an individual for a share in it.[49] However, while most nuns believed in the practical force of suffering, and many of them tended to turn the psychological hardships they experienced in New Guinea (e.g., homesickness, isolation, depression) into a spiritual sacrifice, Sister Martha openly longed for it. In her letter to Europe, she envied the Catholic martyrs who had died during the Boxer Rebellion in China, and expressed her hopes that similar acts of religious heroism would be demanded once in New Guinea.[50] Her writings suggest that her missionary identity rested on this belief in the practical force of suffering. For instance, after seven years in New Guinea, she wrote:

> I am happy, and the only wish I have is to live and to die here, among the poor heathens, and to be granted to shed my blood for the poor heathens or at least to suffer as much as possible for them out of love for Jesus. … Oh yes, to imitate Jesus in His suffering and loving – that's the aspiration of my heart.[51]

Hardly surprisingly, Sister Martha not only wrote about suffering but she also practiced it—for instance, by overworking, fasting, or refusing to wear lighter dress. In the eyes of her fellows, she exaggerated, putting at risk her own health and that of others. For instance, when she refused to reduce her workload despite having a seriously injured leg for years, her superiors vehemently obliged her to stop.[52] However, this seems to have come too late, because her state of health soon faded. Yet, she continued to work and suffer until her death in 1914. Fellow nuns had observed during her last years that Sister Martha tried to "keep herself upright by all means,"[53] and individual admirers called her "a saint-like soul."[54] We may conclude that Sister Martha Sieferding's gendered missionary identity rested on suffering. For her, in New Guinea, her suffering body had become the prime site of her missionary vocation.

Yet, suffering bodies also inspired the nuns in another way. In New Guinea, nursing became an important field of female missionary work, which received much recognition by fellow religious as well as secular groups. Although the nuns' early nursing activities cannot be separated from their desire to provide moribund patients with emergency baptism or extreme unction, the field soon started to undergo a gradual professionalization.[55] This is most clearly shown by the activities of Sister Barnaba Zirkel (1877–1944). Growing up in a small village in the Pfälzer Wald, she had already received some limited medical training before she took her first vows at the age of twenty-eight. In 1908, she was appointed to New Guinea, where she contributed considerably to the development of the early Catholic health system.

Up to 1930, Sister Barnaba, whom her colleagues proudly titled "our doctor,"[56] was the best-trained nurse in the prefecture. Soon after her arrival, she was already managing a considerable part of the nursing activities at the first dispensary on Tumleo.[57] In addition, Sister Barnaba also visited the ill villagers nearby in order to "bring them relief and [to arrange that] they were provided with the holy sacraments in case of danger."[58] The sources show that the extension of her activities during subsequent years considerably depended on the demands of the indigenous people, who showed up at the convents asking for treatment for ulcers and wounds.[59] Although most of Sister Barnaba's writing conceptualized nursing as rooted in Christian charity, a feminine caring role, and religious attendance, it also contained medical details. Her letters bear witness to the ambiguity that marked the way in which she understood her profession. While she bemoaned and commented on patients' deaths from a medical point of view, she also remarked that "thank God" all of them died "provided with the holy sacraments."[60] Yet, Sister Barnaba Zirkel also proudly reported on having completed lifesaving operations.[61] Indeed, both her fellows in New Guinea and her superiors in Europe recognized her medical achievements. For Sister Barnaba, colonial New Guinea became the space where she was able to develop her religious medical program, according to which caring for souls and bodies went hand in hand.

Cross-cultural Transfers: Writing and Publishing on New Guinea

Through the nuns' letters and reports, as well as the massive use of print media by the Servants of the Holy Spirits in Germany, the nuns' involvement with nursing and education also became widely acknowledged in Catholic circles there. Already in 1899, a first article on the activities and experiences of the nuns appeared in the Divine Word Missionary's periodical, which the priests circulated among their regular supporters. Significantly, the text, which was titled "What do our sisters do at the Papuas' in German New Guinea?", not only emphasized that the nuns had adapted well to the local cultural setting but also stated that they were "very popular" among the indigenous people.⁶² Besides, the article quoted extensively from the letters of missionary nuns, who consequently started to act as authors and to write for larger audiences.

From 1899, New Guinea-based nuns increasingly authored published reports on missionary work, which, although selected, corrected, and edited by the priests, were signed with their names and distributed in Catholic circles in Germany and Austria. In the following years, articles written by female missionaries became a frequent feature in missionary journals. In this context, it must be noted that in the nineteenth- and twentieth-century missionary movement, which—unlike its early modern counterpart—was largely funded by lay people, the periodicals issued by the various religious institutions became of tremendous importance.⁶³ The growing participation of nuns, again, shaped the gendered outlook of missionary publishing in Europe. Several nuns authored histories of the congregation, and, from 1922, the Servants of the Holy Spirit launched their own female-centered missionary periodical entitled *Missionsgrüße*.⁶⁴

The anniversary article, mentioned at the beginning of the chapter, provides a good example of female missionary publishing on New Guinea at that time. While the text introduces the nuns' roles in mission as rewarding for religious and secular reasons, the photograph (figure 10.2) established a visible connection between the works and sufferings of German missionary nuns and the Christianization of the female population of New Guinea. Printed in the *Missionsgrüße*, the image suggested a spiritual closeness between Catholic women of different origins in striking contrast to the text, which introduced New Guinea as a "fortress of heathendom" inhabited by "savage brown people," and described the missionary encounter as twenty-five years of struggle between good (Christian) and evil (heathen) forces. Overall, the text left no doubt that missionary nuns from Germany played a crucial role in this struggle as teachers and nurses, but also as selfless sufferers and intrepid evangelizers. The photograph became valuable in this context, for it visibly linked what was constructed as the heroic missionary sacrifice of German nuns with religious change in geographically distant New Guinea.

The article constructed a narrative in which the arrival of the first missionaries constituted a crucial turning point in the history of New Guinea. Accordingly, while Kaiser Wilhelmsland had not encountered a single Catholic before 1896, by 1922 it had thousands of baptized people, and clear signs of Catholicism in society at large. This, as we learn from the article, was also due to German nuns whose teaching, educating, and nursing activities were particularly emphasized. Most importantly, the article promoted the idea of a type of causal connection existing between German Catholics and New Guinean people. On the one hand, this connection referred to the missionaries, who, according to this logic had left Germany and given their lives in order to save souls and to build a church. On the other hand, however, the article also encouraged the development of a sense of connection between the people in New Guinea and the readers in Germany, who supported this venture with their prayers and donations. Hardly surprisingly, the article closed with a charity appeal. On the whole, the nuns' extensive publishing activities point to the great role that missionary media played in the creation and shaping of a transnational space of communication between their diverse fields of missionary work and Catholic Germany. In contrast to those in other former German colonies, the German missionaries in New Guinea were allowed to stay during World War I, and the subsequent period under Australian colonial administration. Even though the interwar years witnessed a gradual Americanization of the missionary personnel in the region, the Catholic mission received a bishop from Germany and continued to be largely recognized as a German religious enterprise.

Conclusion

We may thus conclude that the photograph at the beginning of the chapter (Figure 10.1), with its particular arrangement of bodies and objects, was aimed at bearing witness to both missionary sacrifice and religious change in New Guinea, linking both to the Christian promise of resurrection and eternal life. While missionary texts often constructed New Guinea as a highly sexualized space that posed multiple threats to Christian morality,[65] the nuns' gendered bodies, modestly covered with shiny white habits, appear perfectly pure. Similarly, the indigenous girls, immersed in prayer poses, indicated religious and cultural change to spectators in Germany. Without doubt, a special emotional quality was evoked by the visual presence of Sister Ehrentrudis, mourning over the death of her spiritual and biological sister, who according to the German missionary logic had given her life for the salvation of New Guinea. The text introduced both nuns as biological sisters, and the image thus spoke to those German audiences who regularly supported the mission venture through donations and prayers. In addition, it particularly addressed those men and women in Germany who had sacrificed their children or siblings to the missionary venture. Overall, the article and the photograph point to the transnational space of communication created between Imperial Germany and New Guinea, as well as drawing our attention to the ways in which religious women shaped and were shaped by both the missionary encounter in New Guinea and its representation in Germany.

German missionary endeavors not only brought about religiously motivated migration to New Guinea but also involved the establishment of multiple transnational connections and the circulation of letters, objects, and ideas. As a consequence, in the eyes of many Catholics in Germany, New Guinea became a site where "ordinary" men and women could live what they perceived to be meaningful and spiritually rewarding lives. The presence of nuns in New Guinea was significant for at least two reasons. First, whether they wanted to or not, they introduced a new model of femininity to northern New Guinea, namely that of the celibate sister who privileged religious sisterhood over marriage and motherhood.[66] Second, the letters, reports, and images they posted to Germany gradually introduced new ideas on what it meant to be a missionary nun. Through missionary mass media, large groups of lay Catholics in imperial Germany not only read about the New Guinea mission and consumed imagery from there on a regular basis, but also supported this venture by giving money, goods, and prayers. This, in turn, suggests that New Guinea (or better a mission-mediated image of New Guinea, which differed considerably from other often highly sexualized representations) in some way became part of their world. During German colonialism and beyond, texts and image objects not only found their way into ethnographic collections, museums, and scientific institutions, but also into monasteries, rural and urban parishes, and ordinary Catholic households.

Katharina Stornig is junior professor of cultural history at the University of Giessen. She is the author of *Sisters Crossing Boundaries: German Missionary Nuns in Colonial Togo and New Guinea, 1897–1960* (Göttingen: Vandenhoeck & Ruprecht, 2013). Currently, she is working on the history of transnational aid for children.

Notes

1. The full title referenced the Servants of the Holy Spirit's colloquial name, which, according the location of their first Motherhouse in the small town of Steyl, gave them the name Steylan Missionary Sisters: *Missionsgrüße der Steyler Missionsschwestern Dienerinnen des Heiligen Geistes: Organ des Hilfswerks vom Heiligen Geist zur Unterstützung der Schwesternseminare und Noviziate der Steyler Missionsschwestern* (Missionary Greetings of the Steylean Missionary Sisters Servants of the Holy Spirit. Organ of the aid organisation of the Holy Spirit to support the seminaries and novitiates of the Steylean Missionary Sisters).
2. Missionsgrüße der Steyler Missionsschwestern Dienerinnen des Heiligen Geistes 2 (1924): 20–23.
3. Ibid., 20.
4. The Society of the Divine Word was one of the first and largest Catholic mission-sending societies in Germany.
5. The *Missionsgrüße* appeared in slightly different versions in Germany and Austria. However, Figure 10.1 featured as an illustration in both versions of the New Guinea anniversary article.
6. Basic biographic references to 1,072 Christian missionaries in Oceania are provided in Hermann Mückler, *Missionare in der Südsee: Pioniere, Forscher, Märtyrer. Ein biographisches Nachschlagewerk* (Wiesbaden: Harrassowitz, 2014). On Sister Anna Maria Valeria Dietzen, see p. 155.
7. Mückler, *Missionare in der Südsee*, 128.
8. AG SSpS PNG 601 Korrespondenz 1899–1917, Sr. Ehrentrudis Dietzen.

9. Hermann J. Hiery, *Bilder aus der deutschen Südsee: Fotografien 1884–1914* (Paderborn: Ferdinand Schöningh, 2005), 10.
10. Ibid., 7 and 10.
11. See "Sr. Valeria Dietzen in the coffin, 1917, PNG", in Historical Archives SSpS Steyl; Folder 5 "Tod, Begräbnis, Friedhof."
12. For example, see: Hermann J. Hiery and John McKenzie, eds., *European Impact and Pacific Influence: British and German Colonial Policy in the Pacific and the Indigenous Response* (London: I.B.Tauris, 1997); David Igler, *The Great Ocean: Pacific Worlds from Captain Cook to the Gold Rush* (New York: Oxford University Press, 2013); Claire Laux, *Le Pacifique aux XVIIIe et XIXe siècles, une Confrontation Franco-Britannique: Enjeux économiques, politiques, et culturels (1763–1914)* (Paris: Karthala, 2011); Matt K. Matsuda, *Pacific Worlds: A History of Seas, Peoples, and Cultures* (Cambridge: Cambridge University Press, 2012).
13. See Johannes Paulmann, "Ritual, Macht, Natur: Zur Einführung in die europäisch-ozeanische Beziehungswelten," in Ritual – Macht – Natur. Europäisch-ozeanische Beziehungswelten in der Neuzeit, ed. Johannes Paulmann (Bremen: Rasch, Bramsche, 2005), 7–12; Joachim Meißner, *Mythos Südsee: Das Bild von der Südsee im Europa des 18. Jahrhunderts* (Hildesheim: Olms, 2006), 203–72; Hermann Mückler, *Einführung in die Ethnologie Ozeaniens* (Vienna: Facultas, 2009), 20f.
14. Hermann Mückler, *Mission in Ozeanien* (Vienna: Facultas, 2010), 45.
15. Klaus J. Bade, "Colonial Missions and Imperialism: The Background to the Fiasco of the Rhenish Mission in New Guinea," in *Germany in the Pacific and Far East, 1870–1914*, ed. John A. Moses and Paul M. Kennedy (St. Lucia: University of Queensland Press, 1977), 313–46.
16. For instance, after the German acquisition of the Caroline Islands, Germans replaced the Spanish Capuchins. See Mückler, *Mission*, 56.
17. An overview is provided by Paul Steffen, "Die katholischen Missionen in Deutsch-Neuguinea," in Die deutsche Südsee 1884–1914. Ein Handbuch, ed. Hermann Joseph Hiery (Paderborn: Ferdinand Schöningh, 2002), 343–83; Rufus Pech, "Deutsche evangelische Missionen in Deutsch-Neuguinea 1886–1921," in Hiery (ed.), *Die deutsche Südsee*, 384–416.
18. Mückler, *Mission*, 37.
19. Ibid., 48.
20. Nancy Lutkehaus, "Introduction," in *The Life of Some Island People of New Guinea: A Missionary Observation of the Volcanic Islands of Manam, Boesa, Biem, and Urub*, ed. Karl Böhm (Berlin: D. Reimer, 1983), 13–69; Mary Taylor Huber, "Constituting the Church: Catholic Missionaries on the Sepik Frontier," *American Ethnologist* 14 (1987): 107–25.
21. In the late nineteenth century, priests in all settings of German New Guinea called for female support. See Livia Loosen, *Deutsche Frauen in den Südsee-Kolonien des Kaiserreichs: Alltag und Beziehungen zur indigenen Bevölkerung, 1884–1919* (Bielefeld: Transcript, 2014), 123–25.
22. Prior to 1914, the nuns had established convents in Tumleo (1899), Monumbo (1902), Bogia (1905), Ali (1906), Mugil (1906), Alexishafen (1907), Walman (1908), Malol (1911), Leming (1912), and Boikin (1912).
23. An analysis of the missionary encounter between women in the context of gender and race is presented in Stornig, *Sisters Crossing Boundaries: German Missionary Nuns in Colonial Togo and New Guinea, 1897–1960* (Göttingen: Vandenhoeck & Ruprecht, 2013).
24. See Archivio Generalis SSpS Rome (in the following AG SSpS Rome) PNG Reiseberichte 1899–1907, Sr. Fridolina Vökt, 5.3.1899.
25. "Wer vermag zu schildern mit welchen Gefühlen wir den ersten Lichtstrahl, der uns den Anbruch dieses für uns so denkwürdigen Tages verkündete, begrüßt haben? Freude erfüllte das Herz bei dem Gedanken an die nunmehrige Erfüllung des so lange gehegten Wunsches, an dem großen Werke der Glaubensverbreitung unmittelbarerweise mitzuwirken. ... Es galt nun für uns, sich über die Natur zu erheben, den Blick nach Oben zu richten, unser ganzes zukünftiges

Schicksal in des Allmächtigen Hand legend, frohen Mutes unsere Schritte nach der Ferne zu lenken. … Freude und Trauer rangen im Wettkampf um den Sieg; wenngleich nicht blutig, so war doch hart der Kampf." AG SSpS PNG Reiseberichte 1899–1907, Sr. Fridolina Vökt, 14.3.1899.
26. AG SSpS PNG Reiseberichte 1899–1907, Sr. Valeria Dietzen, 2.3.1899.
27. AG SSpS PNG Reiseberichte 1899–1907, Sr. Valeria Dietzen, 6.3.1899.
28. AG SSpS PNG Reiseberichte 1899–1907, Sr. Martha Sieferding, 5.3.1899.
29. AG SSpS PNG Reiseberichte 1899–1907, Sr. Valeria Dietzen, 6.3.1899.
30. AG SSpS PNG Reiseberichte 1899–1907, Sr. Ursula Sensen, 14.3.1899.
31. AG SSpS PNG Reiseberichte 1899–1907, Sr. Valeria Dietzen, 13.10.1899.
32. AG SSpS PNG Reiseberichte 1899–1907, gemeinsamer Bericht, 14.3.1899.
33. AG SSpS PNG Reiseberichte 1899–1907 and Reiseberichte 1908–1913.
34. For instance, since the comprehensive study of non-European languages started only in New Guinea, Sister Valeria at first had almost no command of the Tumleo vernacular.
35. See Paul Steffen, *Die Anfänge der Rheinischen, Neuendettelsauer und Steyler Missionsarbeit in Neuguinea* (Rome: Tipografia Poliglotta della Pontificia Università Gregoriana, 1993), 40f.
36. For instance, teacher Sister Hermengilde Simbürger (1891–1934) even translated parts of the Bible. See AG SSpS PNG 6201 Korrespondenz 1911–1975, Sr. Hermengilde Simbürger, 27.12.1924 and 5.9.1926.
37. Limbrock to Janssen, 19.5.1906, in Joseph Alt, ed., *Arnold Janssen – Letters to New Guinea and Australia* (Nettetal: Steyler Verlag, 2001), 342f.
38. Stornig, *Sisters Crossing Boundaries*, 277–339.
39. "Am schwersten fiel es mir, daß noch nicht eines unserer Mädchen brav geblieben ist, trotzdem wir sie vor Gefahren zu schützen suchten." AG SSpS PNG 6201 Korrespondenz 1899–1910, Sr. Fridolina Vökt, 18.5.1902.
40. Stornig, *Sisters Crossing Boundaries*, 326f.
41. AG SSpS PNG 6201 Korrespondenz 1899–1910, Sister Valeria Dietzen, 11.12.1902.
42. AG SSpS PNG 601 Korrespondenz 1899–1917, Sr. Humildis Klöckner, 24.6.1917.
43. AG SSpS PNG 6201 Korrespondenz 1911–1975, Sr. Ehrentrudis Dietzen, 22.6.1917.
44. AG SSpS PNG 6201 Korrespondenz 1911–1975, Sr. Philomena Herzog, 2.7.1917.
45. AG SSpS PNG 6201 Korrespondenz 1911–1975, Fr. Andreas Puff, August 1917.
46. AG SSpS PNG 6201 6201 Korrespondenz 1911–1975, Sr. Heriberta Jöris, 24.7.1917.
47. Stornig, *Sisters Crossing Boundaries*, 133–43.
48. Jo Ann Kay McNamara, *Sisters in Arms: Catholic Nuns through Two Millennia* (Cambridge, MA: Harvard University Press, 1996), e.g., 493ff.
49. See Walter Sparn, "Leiden IV. Historisch/Systematisch/Ethisch," in *Theologische Realenzyklopädie 20* (Berlin, 1990), 688–707.
50. AG SSpS PNG 601 Korrespondenz 1899–1917, Sr. Martha Sieferding, 2.6.1901.
51. "Was die Zufriedenheit mit meinem Stande und Beruf betrifft, so bin ich glücklich und habe nur den einen Wunsch, hier unter den armen Heiden zu leben und zu sterben, und wenn es mir gegönnt wäre, für die armen Heiden mein Blut vergießen zu dürfen oder doch wenigstens aus Liebe zu Jesus recht vieles für dieselben leiden zu dürfen." AG SSpS PNG 6201 Korrespondenz 1899–1910, Sr. Martha Sieferding, January 1906.
52. Stornig, *Sisters Crossing Boundaries*, 144–48.
53. AG SSpS PNG 601 Korrespondenz 1899–1917, Sr. Veronika König, 31.5.1911 and Sr. Ehrentrudis Dietzen, 20.12.1913.
54. AG SSpS PNG 6201 Korrespondenz 1911–1975, Sr. Pacifica Schmitz, 6.1.1911.
55. Besides, in early twentieth-century New Guinea, mother and child health care developed as an important part of the missionary medical system, even though by then clerics viewed the engagement of nuns in the field of childbirth with great suspicion. See Katharina Stornig,

"Cultural Conceptions of Purity and Pollution: Childbirth and Midwifery in a New Guinean Catholic Mission, 1896–c.1930," in *European Missions in Contact Zones: Transformation through Interaction in a (Post-)Colonial World*, ed. Judith Becker (Göttingen: Vandenhoeck & Ruprecht, 2015), 107–23.
56. AG SSpS PNG 6201 Korrespondenz 1911–1975, Sr. Hermengilde Simbürger, 15.8.1919.
57. Wolfgang Eckardt, *Medizin und Kolonialimperialismus: Deutschland 1884–1945* (Paderborn: Ferdinand Schöningh, 1997), 415.
58. AG SSpS PNG 6201 Korrespondenz 1899–1910, Sr. Barnaba Zirkel, 14.4.1909.
59. Ibid.
60. Ibid.
61. Ibid.
62. "Was machen unsere Schwestern bei den Papuas in Deutsch Neu-Guinea," in Kleiner Herz Jesu Bote 12 (1899): 53.
63. See Felicity Jensz and Hanna Acke, eds., *Missions and Media: The Politics of Missionary Periodicals in the Long Nineteenth Century* (Stuttgart: Franz Steiner Verlag, 2013).
64. The first widely circulated publication by a Servant of the Holy Spirit, which was also cited by male missiologists, appeared on the occasion of the congregation's twenty-fifth anniversary: Perboyre Neuß, *Die Steyler Missionsschwestern "Dienerinnen des Heiligen Geistes": Ein schlichter Kranz zu ihrem silbernen Jubelfest* (Steyl: self-published 1914).
65. In the German Empire, this construction of New Guinea paralleled another biased representation of the South Seas. Accordingly, Samoa constituted the paradisiacal and New Guinea the dark and archaic part of the South Seas. See Reinhard Wendt, "Einleitung: Der Pazifische Ozean und die Europäer. Ambitionen, Erfahrungen, Transfers," *Saeculum: Jahrbuch für Universalgeschichte* 64, no. 1 (2014): 6.
66. See Nancy Lutkehaus, "Missionary Maternalism: Gendered Images of the Holy Spirit Sisters in Colonial New Guinea," in *Gendered Missions: Women and Men in Missionary Discourse and Practice*, ed. Mary T. Huber and Nancy Lutkehaus (Ann Arbor, MI: University of Michigan Press, 1999), 207–36.

Bibliography

Alt, Joseph, ed. *Arnold Janssen – Letters to New Guinea and Australia*. Nettetal: Steyler Verlag, 2001.
Bade, Klaus J. "Colonial Missions and Imperialism: The Background to the Fiasco of the Rhenish Mission in New Guinea." In *Germany in the Pacific and Far East, 1870–1914*, edited by John A. Moses and Paul M. Kennedy, 313–46. St. Lucia: University of Queensland Press, 1977.
Eckardt, Wolfgang. *Medizin und Kolonialimperialismus: Deutschland 1884–1945*. Paderborn: Ferdinand Schöningh, 1997.
Hiery, Hermann J. *Bilder aus der deutschen Südsee: Fotografien 1884–1914*. Paderborn: Ferdinand Schöningh, 2005.
Hiery, Hermann J., and John McKenzie, eds. *European Impact and Pacific Influence: British and German Colonial Policy in the Pacific and the Indigenous Response*. London: I.B.Tauris, 1997.
Huber, Mary T. "Constituting the Church: Catholic Missionaries on the Sepik Frontier." *American Ethnologist* 14 (1987): 107–25.
Igler, David. *The Great Ocean: Pacific Worlds from Captain Cook to the Gold Rush*. New York: Oxford University Press, 2013.

Jensz, Felicity, and Hanna Acke, eds. *Missions and Media: The Politics of Missionary Periodicals in the Long Nineteenth Century*. Stuttgart: Franz Steiner Verlag, 2013.

Laux, Claire. *Le Pacifique aux XVIIIe et XIXe siècles, une Confrontation Franco-Britannique: Enjeux économiques, politiques, et culturels (1763–1914)*. Paris: Karthala, 2011.

Loosen, Livia. *Deutsche Frauen in den Südsee-Kolonien des Kaiserreichs: Alltag und Beziehungen zur indigenen Bevölkerung, 1884–1919*. Bielefeld: Transcript, 2014.

Lutkehaus, Nancy. "Introduction." In *The Life of Some Island People of New Guinea: A Missionary Observation of the Volcanic Islands of Manam, Boesa, Biem, and Urub*, edited by Karl Böhm, 13–69. Berlin: D. Reimer, 1983.

———. "Missionary Maternalism: Gendered Images of the Holy Spirit Sisters in Colonial New Guinea." In *Gendered Missions: Women and Men in Missionary Discourse and Practice*, ed. Mary T. Huber and Nancy Lutkehaus, 207–36. Ann Arbor, MI: University of Michigan Press, 1999.

Matsuda, Matt K. *Pacific Worlds: A History of Seas, Peoples, and Cultures*. Cambridge: Cambridge University Press, 2012.

McNamara, Jo Ann Kay. *Sisters in Arms: Catholic Nuns through Two Millennia*. Cambridge, MA: Harvard University Press, 1996.

Meißner, Joachim. *Mythos Südsee: Das Bild von der Südsee im Europa des 18. Jahrhunderts*. Hildesheim: Olms, 2006.

Mückler, Hermann. *Einführung in die Ethnologie Ozeaniens*. Vienna: Facultas, 2009.

———. *Missionare in der Südsee: Pioniere, Forscher, Märtyrer. Ein biographisches Nachschlagewerk*. Wiesbaden: Harrassowitz, 2014.

———. *Mission in Ozeanien*. Vienna: Facultas, 2010.

Neuß, Perboyre. *Die Steyler Missionsschwestern "Dienerinnen des Heiligen Geistes": Ein schlichter Kranz zu ihrem silbernen Jubelfest*. Steyl: self-published, 1914.

Paulmann, Johannes. "Ritual, Macht, Natur: Zur Einführung in die europäisch-ozeanische Beziehungswelten." In *Ritual – Macht – Natur: Europäisch-ozeanische Beziehungswelten in der Neuzeit*, edited by Johannes Paulmann, 7–12. Bremen: Rasch, Bramsche, 2005.

Pech, Rufus. "Deutsche evangelische Missionen in Deutsch-Neuguinea 1886–1921." In *Die deutsche Südsee 1884–1914. Ein Handbuch*, edited by Hermann J. Hiery, 384–416. Paderborn: Ferdinand Schöningh, 2002.

Sparn, Walter. "Leiden IV. Historisch/Systematisch/Ethisch." In *Theologische Realenzyklopädie 20*, 688–707. Berlin, 1990.

Steffen, Paul. *Die Anfänge der Rheinischen, Neuendettelsauer und Steyler Missionsarbeit in Neuguinea*. Rome: Tipografia Poliglotta della Pontifica Università Gregoriana, 1993.

———. "Die katholischen Missionen in Deutsch-Neuguinea." In *Die deutsche Südsee 1884–1914. Ein Handbuch*, edited by Hermann J. Hiery, 343–83. Paderborn: Ferdinand Schöningh, 2002.

Stornig, Katharina. "Cultural Conceptions of Purity and Pollution: Childbirth and Midwifery in a New Guinean Catholic Mission, 1896–c.1930." In *European Missions in Contact Zones: Transformation through Interaction in a (Post-)Colonial World*, edited by Judith Becker, 107–23. Göttingen: Vandenhoeck & Ruprecht, 2015.

———. *Sisters Crossing Boundaries: German Missionary Nuns in Colonial Togo and New Guinea, 1897–1960*. Göttingen: Vandenhoeck & Ruprecht, 2013.

Wendt, Reinhard. "Einleitung: Der Pazifische Ozean und die Europäer. Ambitionen, Erfahrungen, Transfers." *Saeculum: Jahrbuch für Universalgeschichte* 64, no. 1 (2014): 1–7.

Chapter 11

RAPE, INDENTURE, AND THE COLONIAL COURTS IN GERMAN NEW GUINEA

Emma Thomas

In 1911, Tapilai,[1] a Neu Hannover (Lavongai) woman, appeared with her husband and brother before the German imperial authorities in Rabaul, then the capital of German colonial New Guinea. The three worked as indentured laborers on a plantation in Neu Pommern (New Britain) in the New Guinean archipelago that still bears the name of imperial Germany's first Chancellor, Bismarck. Tapilai was employed by the plantation's owners as a laundress. Together with Tapilai's two-month-old child, they had walked some sixty miles to the capital to lodge a complaint with representatives of the imperial administration against their employers, the German brothers Wilhelm and Hermann Bolten, both of whom they charged with having repeatedly raped Tapilai.[2]

Tapilai and her family were participants in a system of "cheap" migrant labor, recruited to serve expanding European economic and imperial interests across the Pacific Ocean in the nineteenth and twentieth centuries.[3] An estimated 1.5 million Pacific Islanders and a further 0.5 million Asians worked as indentured laborers in the Pacific between 1863 and the outbreak of World War II.[4] They were transported from their homes principally to provide labor for European-owned plantations in Fiji, Queensland, New Caledonia, and Samoa. Like the larger Pacific labor trade, the German colonial indenture in New Guinea was a system based on labor migration, relocating New Guineans from their local villages predominantly to work on copra plantations in other parts of the colony. From the outset, the labor trade had its European critics, who saw it as little other than an extension of the slave trade, a view that has found support among some subsequent historians.[5] Others, however, have critiqued this image for its failure to take Pacific Islanders' role in the labor trade into account. These scholars have argued that kidnapping and trickery were not enduring features of the trade,

---

Notes from this chapter begin on page 268.

and that Islanders voluntarily signed on as indentured laborers in ever-greater numbers, attracted by promises of adventure and trade goods.[6] Their works have productively challenged Eurocentric narratives of imperial activity, instead placing Pacific Islanders' agency at the center of their analyses.

As the historical anthropologist Margaret Jolly has pointed out, however, this central debate in historiographies of the Pacific labor trade has been "constructed from the viewpoint of the male recruit," despite evidence that women constituted a significant minority of indentured Melanesians.[7] Focusing on female recruits, this chapter builds upon insights provided by Jolly and others whose works have challenged the marginalization of Pacific Islander women within historiographies of indentured labor. These works have demonstrated the need to bring gendered analyses to bear upon prevailing conceptions of voluntarism and violence that are central to scholarly debate about the indenture.[8] Adopting such an approach, I suggest, sheds new light on the Melanesian territories of German New Guinea and the indenture system that formed the economic, social, and political basis of German colonial rule.[9] In this chapter, I seek to demonstrate that shifting attention to indentured women helps to reveal the gendered forms of exploitation that indisputably characterized the German colonial indenture and its inherent potential for violence. While these dimensions of the labor indenture in German New Guinea too often remain eclipsed within historiographies that focus on normatively male plantation laborers, they are essential to demonstrating how the German colonial labor system not only conditioned relations of race, but those of gender and sexuality as well.[10]

This chapter analyzes several legal cases in which indentured New Guinean women and those close to them brought charges of rape against their white, male employers before German colonial courts. The testimonies of indentured women and men contained in the courts' records speak not only to gendered forms of violence produced by the German colonial indenture system, but also to the ways in which New Guinean laborers contested the terms of their indenture, and the claims white, European men laid to women's productive, domestic, and sexual labors. Colonial courts were sites where such contestations sometimes played out, and the records they produced contain the mediated stories of indentured New Guinean women and men that are invaluable to illuminating the everyday practices and experiences that shaped this colonial situation.[11]

Court cases also reveal much about assumptions that were made by colonists—both commercial planters and government officials—regarding indentured women. Animated by colonial fantasies about the Pacific, and about Pacific Islander women in particular, white, male colonists frequently characterized New Guinean women as licentious and promiscuous.[12] They also equated women's participation in the wage economy of the indenture with prostitution, indicating that many understood the indenture to provide them not only access to New Guineans' productive and domestic labors, but to the sexual labors of New

Guinean women as well. German colonial courts, I will argue, played a crucial role in the codification and normalization of discourses linking New Guinean women's laboring bodies to their purported sexual promiscuity and proclivities for prostitution. In seeking out New Guinean women and men's words in colonial court files, this chapter interrogates colonial tropes that worked to exculpate white, European men accused of perpetrating sexual violence against indentured women.

Background: New Guinean Women and the German Colonial Indenture

In its first annual report for the year 1886-1887, the German New Guinea Company identified "the native tribes" of its new colony as a great, untapped resource.[13] Upon annexing the northeastern part of New Guinea, then called Kaiser Wilhelmsland, and neighboring islands in 1884, the New Guinea Company closed off its possession to labor recruiters from rival empires and sought increasingly to transform New Guineans into a labor force for use within the colony and in German Samoa.[14] "[T]he task of educating them to labour" was of paramount importance to the chartered company,[15] and "constituted the central political-economic problem" for both the New Guinea Company and the imperial administration after 1899, as historian John Moses has noted.[16] By the effective end of German rule in 1914, at least 85,000 New Guineans had served as indentured laborers in the German colony, working for plantation and trading companies, the administration, and the missions, typically on a three-year contract. About another 15,000 had worked as day laborers.[17] The vast majority of these laborers were recruited during the period of imperial governance, from 1899 to 1914. This was a period marked by the establishment of new government stations, the spread of foreign-owned plantations and concomitant alienation of New Guinean lands, and increased efforts to "pacify" local populations in and around Germany's expanding colonial settlements. As historian Stewart Firth has shown, the imperial administration, particularly under the governorship of Albert Hahl (1902–13), implemented systems of taxation, mandatory and *corvee* labor, and appointed village middlemen, known as *luluais* and *tultuls*, in order to recruit ever-greater numbers of New Guineans into the indentured labor force. As German colonial demands for New Guinean laborers grew, efforts to recruit became increasingly coercive.[18]

In German New Guinea, as in Melanesia more generally, women were recruited into the colonial labor indenture in much smaller numbers than men.[19] As German colonial reports did not differentiate laborers according to gender, precise figures for the number of New Guinean women recruited are unknown.[20] Reports on German colonial recruitment efforts from the New Guinea Company period indicate that "a few women" were among the first laborers recruited from the Bismarck Archipelago and the northern Solomon Islands to work for German interests on Kaiser Wilhelmsland.[21] Yet the New Guinea Company's 1888 labor ordinance acknowledged the presence of female laborers only with regards to their accommodations in the colony's labor depots. Unmarried women and "girls over twelve years of age" were to be provided with separate houses, or compartments sectioned off from the men's and families' quarters with "thick walls."[22] It is possible that the "thirty women and girls" who were among the 227 laborers contracted at to work in Friedrich Wilhelmshafen (Madang) in the early 1890s passed through such accommodations on their way to being "chiefly employed for cleaning and in road maintenance."[23] By the effective end of German rule in 1914, at least 4,900 New Guinean women had worked for foreign interests in the colony, laboring on plantations, at trading, government, and mission stations, and in the homes of white colonists, mostly under indenture contracts. The number was likely much higher.[24]

Archival evidence provides only fleeting insights into the reasons that New Guinean women became indentured laborers under German colonial rule. Trickery, kidnapping, and violent episodes persisted throughout the German colonial period, and coercion on the part of plantation owners, labor recruiters, and village middlemen were also factors.[25] For example, Lanthe, a woman from Lihir who was recruited in 1913, reported that she had not wished to sign on but had been "strongly encouraged" to do so by the local *tultul* who received the ten marks "beach payment" for her recruitment.[26] Some women signed on with their partners or husbands, especially as Hahl's administration began to prohibit the recruitment of single women from parts of the colony amid colonial anxieties about depopulation in the years prior to World War I.[27] One girl recruited in 1913, whom the recruiter himself noted was "still a child," apparently signed on willingly with her husband, though the authorities in Rabaul refused to recognize her marital status on account of her age.[28] Conversely, a woman named Mante might have used a recruiter's visit to her home on Tanga to escape from her husband, whom she claimed beat her (a claim he denied when he appeared in a court in Rabaul and successfully demanded her return).[29] In some villages small groups of women signed on together, without village men, but perhaps motivated by the same promises of adventure and opportunity that also drew New Guinean men into indenture.[30]

An existing labor recruitment contract reveals that European planters were prepared to pay recruiters a premium for "*single* women"—120 marks compared with ninety marks for a (presumably male) laborer on a three-year contract.[31] As Dorothy Shineberg has demonstrated in the case of New Caledonia, indentured women were valued by colonists not only as domestic and plantation laborers, but also for their sexual labors in the service of the predominantly male colonial society, both European and Melanesian.[32] In German New Guinea, where New

Guinean men constituted somewhere between 90 and 95 percent of the indentured labor force, planters spoke openly about the need to recruit women for the "thousands of male laborers" indentured on the plantations, many of whom, planters said, signed on "in order to get a woman from [their] employer."[33] In 1914, one German official declared the colony's indentured women to be "actually nothing other than prostitutes."[34] But in a colonial context where, in 1913, single white women numbered 161 compared with 826 single white men, European men, too, sought New Guinean women to satisfy their sexual urges.[35]

European travel writings provide insights into the ways in which male colonists understood the indenture as providing access to New Guinean women's bodies, often understood to mean their productive, domestic, and sexual labors. The Hungarian naturalist, Lajos Biró, who resided in German New Guinea from 1896 to 1902, reminisced about the arrival of "a major fresh transport" of laborers from Neu Mecklenburg (New Ireland): "I chose my Saghan from among thirty-five companions of her."[36] In addition to providing sex to male colonists, temporary "wives" like Saghan "were expected to do the chores, to keep our clothes in order, to see to it that the dirty linen were washed in time and clean dresses were always on hand."[37] To describe these women as "more sexual partners and local advisors than laborers," as one historian has, overlooks their subordinate legal status as indentured laborers as well as the multiple labors indentured women were tasked with, on and off the plantations.[38] The German naturalist Carl Ribbe provided perhaps a more accurate description of the complex position New Guinean women occupied as "concubines" in the homes of European colonists. Going under the "official names" of "laundress, cook, gardener, house girl, and chambermaid," he wrote, these "black women" offered multiple "advantages" to white men: they could be taught to take care of housework, provide local knowledge, and, as such women would be obtained from distant locales, her relatives would not be around to pose a nuisance. "[I]f the black better half no longer wants to comply," Ribbe continued, "she does not take it badly if her husband [*Gemahl*] reminds her that she is to obey with the help of the cane"—a rare acknowledgement from a colonist of racial and gender hierarchies and the violence they produce.[39]

Whether New Guinean women and men were recruited voluntarily or otherwise, the indenture was a system of labor exploitation through which colonial power structures were configured and maintained. For indentured New Guinean women, these relations were drawn along the axes of gender as well as race. Always a numerical minority on the plantations and colonial stations, and often receiving lower wages than their male counterparts—four marks compared to six marks per month for government laborers in 1904, for instance[40]—colonial indenture rendered them particularly vulnerable.[41] Demographic and economic aspects of the colonial labor regime may have compelled some to engage in prostitution or to enter into relations with white overseers, as Ann Laura Stoler has shown happened in the neighboring Dutch East Indies.[42] As I seek to demonstrate below, however, colonial discourses that characterized indentured women as "prostitutes," whether or not they received remuneration for sex, worked to obfuscate the sexual exploitation and violence that women faced in the indenture. They also often bore little resemblance to New Guinean women and men's own accounts of their experiences as indentured laborers.

Rape in the Indenture and before the Courts

In order to access New Guinean women and men's stories about sexual violence in the indenture, I turn to three cases that came before imperial district courts in the colonial capitals of Herbertshöhe (Kokopo) and Rabaul, on the Gazelle Peninsula of Neu Pommern. As seats of colonial governance, Peter Hempenstall has aptly described these towns as "staging posts for the activities of all administrators, from the Governor down."[43] My focus, however, is on those colonial administrators in the district courts charged with the decision making that constituted the rule of law in German New Guinea. Colonial courts provided sites where indentured New Guineans could and did contest the terms of their labor and the violence inflicted upon them. They were also, I argue, key sites in which tropes of indentured women's "promiscuity" and "prostitution" worked to exculpate individual colonists accused of rape, and to deny justice to New Guinean laborers. As such, colonial courts were instrumental in establishing and maintaining racial and gender hierarchies that defined the colonial situation. Unlike cases limited to disputes involving "natives" that were tried at station courts, cases brought before the district courts were tried under German law.[44] And whereas New Guinean men charged with the rape of New Guinean women were variously sentenced to imprisonment with forced labor,[45] fined for compensation in local shell money (*diwarra* or *tambu*),[46] and sometimes acquitted,[47] I know of no case in which a European man charged with raping a New Guinean woman was convicted of that crime in German New Guinea's colonial courts.[48]

The relative paucity of source materials chronicling sexual assault is likely a result of the colony's judicial system and the imperial and patriarchal power structures that informed it and were informed by it.[49] As no criminal police force operated in German New Guinea, only cases brought to the courts' attention were investigated.[50] Colonial courts were often located great distances from the plantations and stations where indentured New Guineans were employed. Some laborers walked miles to have their complaints heard while others may have been unwilling or unable to do so.[51] Available court records also reveal that New Guineans often reported sexual assaults to overseers who then failed to act upon the complaints.[52] Court records also speak to the fear that New Guinean women and their family members had of reporting sexual assault. Some women remained silent for shame or fear of their husbands' reactions, while others resisted reporting these crimes fearing retaliatory violence from their assailants.[53] The cases discussed here, therefore, are in many ways exceptional, but traces left in the colonial archives indicate that the violence they describe was less exceptional.

Pulus's Story

Pulus worked as an indentured laborer for the German colonial government in Herbertshöhe. She was married to Kinela, who also worked as an indentured laborer in Herbertshöhe. Her story was recorded by the imperial district court in the colonial capital on 12 February 1906, when she reported that she had been sexually assaulted by a German storehouse foreman named Waldemar Kolbe while carrying out her daily labors for the colonial government. As was typical for New Guineans appearing before German colonial courts, she gave her testimony in Tok Pisin, the lingua franca of (Papua) New Guinea. Her statement was recorded in German and Tok Pisin (italicized here) by a German court official as follows:

> At noon yesterday, as I approached the [government] storehouse to fetch rice, the storehouse foreman, Kolbe, grabbed me near the huts and dragged me into the storehouse. I told him that he should leave me alone. He said: "*never mind by and by me give you money.*" I tried to get away, but he held onto me tightly, he threw me over the sacks of rice and used me sexually.

Kolbe had then given Pulus trade goods—two *lavalavas* (waist cloths), two knives, and five sticks of tobacco—and four marks in cash. She told the court that she initially refused these items, but Kolbe had stuck them into her belt. She left the storehouse with the goods and money and went to find her husband, Kinela.[54]

Kinela was also called to testify before the court. His statement reveals indentured laborers' familiarity with the structures of German colonial governance, and how they used them to make claims as colonial subjects. He told the court that upon hearing from Pulus about the assault, he discussed the incident with "the other boys"—his fellow laborers—who told him that he "should go to Doctor Hahl and report the matter," which he did. Indeed, it was Governor Albert Hahl, himself a trained lawyer and former imperial judge in Herbertshöhe, who brought this case to the district court, requesting that it make an inquiry.[55] The court then summoned Kolbe to appear on rape charges.

Kolbe's testimony gives a sense of both the gendered nature of colonial violence and the colonial logics that worked to obscure it. Kolbe did not deny having had sex with Pulus. He told the court: "As Pulus was opening a sack of rice, I grabbed her on the genitals. She easily acquiesced. I bent her over the sacks of rice and used her sexually. Then I finished weighing the rice and gave her two marks from my wallet." The violence of the assault is suggested in Kolbe's own language—his admission that he "grabbed her on the genitals" and "used her sexually." However, the violence so explicitly depicted in Pulus's testimony is distorted in Kolbe's statement by the colonist's lascivious gaze. He did not "throw" her, he "bent" her over the sacks of rice (he described the position in some detail for the court), and, he added, Pulus had "smiled cheerily" at him later that day.[56] His description of routinely weighing the rice renders the incident mundane, while his assertions that "she easily acquiesced," and that he had paid her, rationalize his actions by rendering Pulus "easy" and a prostitute.

Many scholars have noted Europeans' tendency in the age of empire to characterize non-European women as sexually promiscuous, a trait that supposedly separated them from Europeans and worked to legitimize colonial control.[57] While Germans did not afford the "black" women of New Guinea the same standards of beauty that they attributed to Polynesian women in Samoa, they nevertheless characterized them licentious for their apparent failure to conform to European gender norms and notions of sexual propriety.[58] Moreover, as indentured women, their laboring bodies were not only sexualized "in the eyes of [the] colonizer," as Philippa Levine argued, but made available to European men.[59] Kolbe's defense relied on his mobilization of precisely these tropes: Pulus's purported promiscuity and sexual availability coalesced with fantasies that linked her participation in the wage economy to prostitution and that held the monetization of sex to preclude the possibility of rape.[60] As John Kelly reminds us, white, male colonists acted upon racialized and gendered fantasies in lived colonial spaces, often in highly tangible and embodied ways, the violence of which becomes obscured when colonial tropes of non-European women's "licentiousness" are taken at face value. Pulus's testimony draws attention to the violence of the "grasp" rather than assuming the inscribing powers of the colonial gaze. Yet, in the everyday exercise of colonial power, as Kelly has shown, the courts were critical in transforming colonists' understandings of non-Europeans "from fantasy to legal presumption."[61] It is unclear whether the district court in Herbertshöhe understood the trade goods and money laid out before it as evidence enough of Kolbe's versions of events. The judge's ruling was brief: stating simply that the court lacked "reasonable suspicion" of rape, he brought legal proceedings against Kolbe to a close.

Minni's Story

Minni was pregnant when she was allegedly raped by Gustav Thurm,[62] an employee of one of the colony's major trading and plantation firms, Hernsheim & Co. Minni and her husband Willi, from the island of Neu Mecklenburg, worked as indentured laborers on the Hernsheim trading station in Kieta, on Bougainville. On 24 January 1910, Willi appeared before Kieta's imperial station chief, August Doellinger, and reported the following to him:

> In early December or late November, Herr Class sent me off to Faisi by boat. When I came back, my wife Minni told me that she had been raped by Thurm, a European working for Class, in his house. The Buka boy, Rabes, who works for Hernsheim & Co., and the Neu Mecklenburg boy, Annes, who works for the Bismarck Archipel Gesellschaft, witnessed the incident. Afterwards, Thurm wanted to pay Minni but she didn't accept any payment. Minni was heavily pregnant. A few days ago, my wife went back to hospital, the child died last night. I didn't report the incident to my boss, but my wife did. [Later] I spoke with Herr Class about it and he sent me away.[63]

Almost one month later, when she was out of hospital where she had been recovering from pneumonia, Minni told Doellinger that at the time of the incident:

> Thurm sent me into his house to take his dirty laundry off to be washed. I told him that he should put his laundry on the veranda, whereupon he told me yet again that I should fetch his laundry from the house. I went into the house. Thurm followed me at once, grabbed hold of me, chucked me onto the bed, and had sex with me. I struggled and told him I didn't want to have it. I screamed loudly, I couldn't shake him off, he was too strong for me. A boy from the Bismarck Archipel Gesellschaft, Annes, witnessed the event. When I came back out of the house, I went to Herr Class and told him what had happened. Class didn't tell me that I should make a report to the court. Rather, he went to Thurm and spoke with him. I received neither payment nor an apology from Thurm.[64]

Willi and Minni's testimonies speak to the limitations that New Guineans faced as indentured laborers: limitations on their ability to determine their whereabouts, to protect loved ones and themselves from harm, to control the ways in which white, European "masters" would exploit their labors. Like Pulus's testimony, Minni's similarly draws attention to the potentially quotidian nature of colonial sexual violence, as the daily routine of performing one's labor brought New Guinean women into male-dominated German "colonial enclaves," into storehouses with male overseers, and into the homes of white, male colonists.[65] Yet they also speak to the ways in which indentured New Guineans could and did contest Europeans' claims to their bodies—laboring, gendered, and sexualized. When Minni and Willi's complaints to their boss fell on deaf ears, they took their case to Doellinger, who had since 1905 served as the local representative of the German colonial government in Kieta.

Testimonies reveal other things too. Doellinger's questions to them, not recorded in the case file, can be inferred from the witnesses' statements. There were questions about remuneration and questions about resistance. Motivating these questions were the same assumptions about indentured New Guinean women that Kolbe had rallied to his defense four years earlier. The extent to which Minni had resisted Thurm's advances had apparently occupied Doellinger as he questioned the witness, Annes. Annes largely corroborated Minni's version of events, but suggested that had she screamed louder, "Herr Class and the other people would have had to hear." According to his statement, Minni's initial screams as Thurm "dragged her to the bed" soon gave way to silence.[66] Doellinger went a step further, however, and put down in writing his assumptions about the indentured New Guinean woman accusing a white man of rape. In a note dated 1 March, he declared Minni to be "a very promiscuous woman" who had been known "to gallivant about in the bush with other workers."[67] He forwarded his note with the case file to his colleagues in Herbertshöhe, where he presumed Thurm then to be residing.

Thurm was in fact in Friedrich Wilhelmshafen, where the district judge questioned him on 27 April. Like Kolbe, Thurm did not deny that he had had sex with Minni, but contested the charge of rape, since, he informed the court, she had agreed to exchange sex for money and he had paid her two marks (a claim that Minni and her husband had already disputed). By May, Thurm was residing in Neu Pommern, where the judge, Georg Stuebel, ruled to acquit Thurm of the rape charges. His ruling ostensibly rested on the evidence of Thurm's statement, claiming he had not raped Minni, and on that part of Annes's testimony that suggested, as Stuebel put it, "that Minni did not struggle or scream *during* sex."[68]

It is impossible to say whether Doellinger's assessment of Minni's character might have played into the judge's ruling. It is clear, however, that Stuebel himself did not question the individuals involved, but rather based his ruling on a selective reading of the statements provided to him by his colleagues in Kieta and Friedrich Wilhelmshafen. The judge mentioned neither Minni's nor Willi's testimonies detailing the violence of the assault, nor the death of Minni's child, nor her refusal to accept payment. Nor did he mention the witness's testimony describing how Minni had screamed as Thurm "dragged" her to his bed. Rather, he reduced the contradictions of the case to a narrative in which Minni had in all likelihood "acquiesced" to Thurm's advances—a narrative that rested upon the assumption that Minni was indeed a "promiscuous woman." Perhaps Willi, too, believed this, for when the court's verdict was eventually returned to the Kieta station in mid-May, he had since been repatriated to Neu Mecklenburg. There was no further mention of Minni in the legal correspondence.

Tapilai's Story

I now return to Tapilai, with whose story I opened this chapter. On 27 November 1911, she appeared with her husband and brother before the district court in Rabaul, having absconded from the plantation in the Baining Mountains where they worked as indentured laborers and made the sixty-mile trek to the colonial capital. The three were originally from Neu Hannover, and neither Tapilai nor her husband, Laimasung, presumably both first-time laborers, were conversant in Tok Pisin. It was thus Bago, Tapilai's brother, who told Stuebel, the same judge who had acquitted Thurm the previous year, "we walked all the way here from

Baining to make our complaint." Their complaint was that their employers, the German brothers Wilhelm and Hermann, had repeatedly raped Tapilai and had beaten her and Laimasung with a cane. They did not want to stay at the plantation, but rather to return to their home in Neu Hannover.[69]

Unlike the cases discussed thus far, Tapilai's alleged assailants never admitted that they had had sex with Tapilai—Hermann, who was married to a white, German woman, explicitly denied it, telling the court: "I never so much as touched the woman."[70] However, though both contested the rape charges that Tapilai and her family had brought against them, they did not deny Hermann's use of physical violence against her and her husband. Testifying on 14 December, Hermann claimed that Tapilai and Laimasung had brought the rape charges against him as "an act of revenge" because he had "clobbered [them] with a cane."[71] Wilhelm concurred that the allegations of rape were false, brought by the laborers "because Tapilai wanted to get away from my brother." He added that Tapilai had previously made similar complaints to Hermann in which she claimed to have been raped by male laborers on the plantation, allegations that he equally dismissed as fabricated. Further, he added, "Tapilai's husband is very jealous."[72] Hermann was ultimately convicted and fined forty marks on charges of bodily harm for beating his laborers, not because corporal punishment of laborers was illegal per se, but because he lacked the official authorization to administer such "disciplinary punishment." Further, as the deciding judge put it, "under no circumstance may female natives be punished with flogging."[73] Neither brother was convicted of rape.

Much like Pulus and Minni, Tapilai claimed to have been raped by her employers as she was carrying out her daily labors—in Tapilai's case, as a laundress. With a government laborer from Neu Hannover acting as her interpreter, Tapilai told the court:

> One evening, the accused Hermann Bolten called me into his room, to his bed where he was lying. First, he told me to fetch some water for the washstand. When I returned with the water, he came up behind me, pulled off my *lavalava* from behind, and pulled me into his bed, whereupon he had sex with me. He violently raped me twice more besides.

She claimed the assaults had taken place when Frau Bolten was away in Rabaul to give birth, and shortly after Tapilai herself had given birth.[74] According to her testimony, Wilhelm Bolten had also twice ordered another female laborer to "bring him a woman." Both times, the female laborer instructed Tapilai to go to Wilhelm, and both times he had grabbed her by the arm and raped her, she told the court.[75]

From the outset, the court's attention seems to have been focused less on ascertaining the veracity of the rape charges than with the allegations that Hermann had physically assaulted his laborers with a cane. Noting welts on Laimasung's back and arm, the court had immediately sought the expert opinion of government physician Dr. Karl Kopp. The doctor confirmed that there were "superficial" injuries on Laimasung's arm and torso that had been caused by a blow from a cane. On Tapilai's right upper arm he observed a "small skin ulcer." There was also an abrasion on her lower back. Were these injuries sustained when Wilhelm grabbed her by the arm, when she was sexually assaulted? Were they marks left by the cane? In Kopp's assessment, the cause of these injuries could not be determined.[76] But Hermann's testimony of 14 December provided the court with an explanation. According to Hermann, he beat Tapilai because she had been disobedient, had arrived late for work and then "lazed about" instead of working. He had beaten Laimasung in self-defense, as the latter, upon hearing Tapilai's screams, had come running over "with a bearing that suggested he wanted to attack me."[77] Having established this matter, the judge in charge of the case, Eugen Grundler, promptly approved Hermann's request to return Tapilai, Laimasung, and Bago to his plantation in Baining.

Early the next year, Hermann signed a summons for Tapilai and Laimasung to reappear in the court in Rabaul as witnesses in the trial against him on charges of bodily harm. The trial date had been set for 25 January, but was postponed until 19 February as stormy seas prevented travel from Baining to Rabaul by boat. In the meantime, on 10 February, the court noted that Tapilai had withdrawn her earlier claim that Hermann had "used force against her," as the district judge Gustav Weber, now trying the case, put it. The judge concluded from this that none of her allegations of sexual assault were to be believed.[78] However, the record of the case suggests that the court had already abandoned its investigation of the rape charges, without making a formal ruling, as from late December onward the case file only referenced the charge of bodily harm. The file made no mention of why Tapilai, then back on the Bolten plantation, might have withdrawn her charges against Hermann. That she fabricated the claims in an attempt to free herself and her husband of their indentures to an abusive employer, as Wilhelm himself suggested, is one possible explanation. It perhaps does not adequately explain the charges Tapilai brought against Wilhelm, her claim to having also been raped by male laborers, or Wilhelm's reference to Laimasung's "jealousy."

Indeed, there is much within the sixty-two pages of this case file that remains unexplained and was doubtless beyond the court's grasp. Drawing again on Kelly, however, I propose that in constructing coherent narratives out of contradictory ones, in choosing when and when not "to act or even to look,"[79] German colonial courts in New Guinea sought their answers in the familiar tropes of New Guinean women's licentiousness and their propensity to engage in prostitution on the colony's plantations. Consider judge Weber's choice of words: Hermann had not "used force" against Tapilai. Already on 27 November 1911, as the court read back Tapilai's original statement to her, it is apparent that judge Grundler, like station chief Doellinger in Kieta, asked questions pertaining to payment, jotting down Tapilai's answers in the page margin of the case file. According to these notes, Hermann had asked Tapilai if she had wanted money in exchange for sex: "He didn't give me any anyway," was Tapilai's recorded reply. When the court questioned Bago, Grundler asked (and the question is recorded) "whether the witness [Tapilai] willingly had sex" with the defendants. When Bago replied that the defendants had used force against Tapilai, Grundler noted that "the witness gives the impression that he is untrustworthy."[80]

The court's questioning of the claimants and Weber's concluding remarks on the charges of rape suggest that while these German colonial judges refused to believe New Guinean laborers' rape claims, they did not doubt that indentured women "willingly" engaged in sex with white, male overseers, for money or otherwise. What is noteworthy in this case is that legal presumptions of indentured women's promiscuity and engagement in prostitution persist despite the defendants'—or at least Hermann's—own claims to the contrary. I suggest that the defendants' claims to what might be considered sexual propriety mattered less to the court than the judges' own assumptions that held Tapilai, Pulus, Minni, and other indentured women to be sexually available to white, European men.[81] Unlike the beatings that Hermann had given Tapilai and Laimasung, the sexual "use" of indentured women's bodies not only failed to contravene official labor regulations, it received tacit official sanction in colonial courts. Within a prevailing discourse that held indentured women to be "promiscuous" and "prostitutes," it was easy enough for colonial judges to overlook claims like that made by Laimasung, who told the court that the beatings had taken place because "the master was cross because my wife wouldn't allow him to do as he pleased with her."[82]

Conclusion

This chapter has drawn attention to an often-overlooked "modality of violence" in German colonial New Guinea—the rape of indentured New Guinean women by white, male colonists—and the colonial logics that worked to obscure it.[83] These logics characterized indentured women as "willing" participants in the violence that male colonists perpetrated against them. Attentiveness to indentured New Guinean women's and men's testimonies of sexual violence prompts a reconsideration of the categories of voluntarism and violence that have dominated debates on the Pacific labor trade. Appearing before German colonial courts, women and men contested the terms of their indentures and, as I have argued, white, European men's assumptions that understood the indenture to grant them access to women's productive, domestic, and sexual labors. In their accounts of struggle and resistance, their denial of accusations of prostitution, and their refutation of the assumption that remuneration precluded the possibility of rape, their stories contrast starkly with those that colonists told the courts, and that the courts told themselves.

Colonial courts were thus crucial in transforming fantasies of indentured New Guinean women's "promiscuity" and sexual availability into legal presumptions. In perpetuating these tropes, German colonial courts worked to efface the complex position of women in the indenture, and the multiple labors they were expected to perform. As gestured to above and worthy of further examination are the ways in which colonists' assumptions about indentured women worked not only to obscure their multiple roles as laborers, but also as wives, partners, mothers, and sisters. In depicting indentured women as "actually nothing other than prostitutes," German colonial officials rendered them knowable at the same time as they allowed themselves to remain largely ignorant of the violence indenture inflicted upon New Guinean families and societies.[84] By exploiting gendered and racialized tropes of indentured New Guinean women, colonial judges not only exculpated individual male colonists accused of sexual violence, but worked to obscure the larger structures of violence inherent in the German colonial indenture itself.

Emma Thomas is a PhD candidate in history at the University of Michigan. Grounded in research conducted in Australia, Germany, and Papua New Guinea, her doctoral dissertation examines the social, cultural, and political worlds occupied by indentured New Guinean women under German colonial rule.

Notes

1. The spelling of New Guineans' names in the German records is often highly inconsistent. For the sake of clarity, I have applied one spelling consistently throughout. I have also used the spellings Doellinger and Stuebel, sometimes rendered as Döllinger and Stübel in the colonial records and secondary literature.
2. This and subsequent references to this case come from the National Archives of Australia, Canberra (NAA): Imperial Government of German New Guinea; G255, Correspondence files; 325: Kaiserliches Bezirksgericht zu Rabaul. Akten in der Strafsache gegen Bolten, Wilhelm, und Bolten, Hermann, wegen Notzucht (1911–12).
3. There is a significant body of scholarship on the Pacific "labor trade," the bulk of which focuses on the trade in Melanesian laborers to colonial Queensland. For overviews, see Clive Moore, "Revising the Revisionists: The Historiography of Immigrant Melanesians in Australia," *Pacific Studies* 15, no. 2 (1992): 61–86; Doug Munro "The Labor Trade in Melanesians to Queensland: An Historiographic Essay," *The Journal of Pacific History* 28, no. 3 (1995): 609–27.
4. Doug Munro, "The Origins of Labourers in the South Pacific: Commentary and Statistics," in *Labour in the South Pacific*, eds. Clive Moore, Jacqueline Leckie, and Doug Munro (Townsville, QLD: James Cook University, 1990), xxxix–li.

5. For example, John M. Ward, *British Policy in the South Pacific, 1786–1893: A Study in British Policy towards the South Pacific Islands prior to the Establishment of Governments by the Great Powers* (Sydney: Australasian Publishing Co., 1948). A notable history of the trade in indentured Indian laborers that adopts this view is Hugh Tinker, *A New System of Slavery: The Export of Indian Labour Overseas, 1830–1920* (London: Oxford University Press, 1974).
6. The seminal texts are Deryck Scarr, "Recruits and Recruiters: A Portrait of the Pacific Islands Labour Trade," *The Journal of Pacific History* 2 (1967): 5–24; Peter Corris, *Passage, Port and Plantation: A History of Solomon Islands Labour Migration, 1870–1914* (Carlton: Melbourne University Press, 1973).
7. Margaret Jolly, "The Forgotten Women: A History of Migrant Labour and Gender Relations in Vanuatu," *Oceania* 58, no. 2 (1987): 119–39, quotation 124.
8. On indentured Melanesian women in the British and French Pacific, see ibid.; Kay Saunders, "Melanesian Women in Queensland, 1863–1907: Some Methodological Problems Involving the Relationship between Racism and Sexism," *Pacific Studies* 4, no. 1 (1980): 26–44; Dorothy Shineberg, *The People Trade: Pacific Island Laborers and New Caledonia, 1865–1930* (Honolulu: University of Hawai'i Press, 1999), 90-115. On indentured Indian women in British Fiji, see Brij V. Lal, "Kunti's Cry: Indentured Women in Fiji Plantations," *Indian Economic and Social History Review* 20, no. 3 (1985): 55–71; Vicki Luker, "A Tale of Two Mothers: Colonial Constructions of Indian and Fijian Maternity," *Gender Issues in Fiji*, ed. Jacqueline Leckie, special issue, *Fijian Studies: A Journal of Contemporary Fiji* 3, no. 2 (2005): 357-74.
9. Specifically, the northeastern part of New Guinea, the islands of the Bismarck Archipelago, principally Neu Pommern, Neu Mecklenburg, and Neu Hannover, the northern Solomon Islands of Buka and Bougainville, and smaller outlying islands, as distinct from the "Island Territories" of Micronesia.
10. The most thorough and insightful study of the indenture in German New Guinea is Stewart Firth, *New Guinea under the Germans* (Carlton: Melbourne University Press, 1983), but indentured women still occupy a marginal place in this study, appearing primarily as objects of imperial policy debates (see especially 112–35).
11. For an instructive treatment of colonial court records as historical sources, see Megan Vaughan, *Creating the Creole Island: Slavery in Eighteenth-Century Mauritius* (Durham, NC: Duke University Press, 2005). On the "colonial situation," see Georges Balandier, "The Colonial Situation: A Theoretical Approach," in *Social Change: The Colonial Situation*, ed. Immanuel Wallerstein (New York: Wiley, 1966), 34–61.
12. Susanne Zantop, *Colonial Fantasies: Conquest, Family, and Nation in Precolonial Germany, 1770–1870* (Durham, NC: Duke University Press, 1997); Serge Tcherkézoff, "A Reconsideration of the Role of Polynesian Women in Early Encounters with Europeans: Supplement to Marshall Sahlins' Voyage around the Islands of History," in *Oceanic Encounters: Exchange, Desire, Violence*, eds. Margaret Jolly, Serge Tcherkézoff, and Darrell Tryon (Canberra: ANU E Press, 2009), 113–60; Robert Tobin, "*Venus von Samoa*: Rasse und Sexualität im deutschen Südpazifik," in *Kolonialismus als Kultur: Literatur, Medien, Wissenschaft in der deutschen Gründerzeit des Fremden*, eds. Alexander Honold and Oliver Simons (Tubingen: A. Francke Verlag, 2002), 192–220; Margaret Jolly, "Women of the East, Women of the West: Region and Race, Gender and Sexuality on Cook's Voyages," in *The Atlantic World in the Antipodes: Effects and Transformations since the Eighteenth Century*, ed. Kate Fullagar (Newcastle upon Tyne, UK: Cambridge Scholars, 2012), 2–23.
13. Peter Sack and Dymphna Clark, eds. and trans. *German New Guinea: The Annual Reports* (Canberra: Australian National University Press, 1979), 19.
14. Heinrich Schnee, *Bilder aus der Südsee: Unter den kannibalischen Stämmen des Bismarck-Archipels* (Berlin: D. Reimer, 1904), 59–60; Stewart Firth, "German Labour Policy and the Partition of

the Western Pacific: The View from Samoa," *The Journal of Pacific History* 25, no. 1 (1990): 85–102.
15. Sack and Clark, *German New Guinea*, 19.
16. John Moses, "Imperial Priorities in New Guinea, 1885–1914," in *Papua New Guinea: A Century of Colonial Impact, 1884–1984*, ed. Sione Lātūkefu (Port Moresby: National Research Institute and the University of Papua New Guinea, 1989), 165. As Sebastian Conrad has demonstrated, the task of "educating to work" was central to imperial Germany's ambitions both at home and in the colonies. Sebastian Conrad, *Globalisation and the Nation in Imperial Germany* (Cambridge: Cambridge University Press, 2010), 77–143.
17. Stewart Firth, "The Transformation of the Labour Trade in German New Guinea, 1899–1914," *The Journal of Pacific History* 11, no. 2 (1976): 51.
18. Ibid., 51–65.
19. Historians estimate that women made up between 4 and 10 percent of indentured Melanesian laborers. The lower estimate comes from Clive Moore's study of Solomon Islanders in Queensland. See Clive Moore, *Kanaka: A History of Melanesian Mackay* (Port Moresby: Institute of Papua New Guinea Studies and University of Papua New Guinea Press, 1985), 49. Shineberg (*The People Trade*, 92) gives the higher figure in her study of laborers transported to New Caledonia, most of whom were ni-Vanuatu. The numbers given by Corris for Queensland fall inside this range at 6.2–8.7 percent (*Port, Passage and Plantation*, 46), as do those provided by Jeff Siegel, who suggests that women constituted 5.5 percent of Melanesians transported to Fiji from Vanuatu, the Solomons, and the Bismarck Archipelago between 1876 and 1911. See Jeff Siegel, "Origins of Pacific Islands Labourers in Fiji," *The Journal of Pacific History* 20, no. 1 (1985): 54.
20. German colonial officials' own estimates of numbers of women recruited into the indenture could differ considerably. For instance, the station chief at Käwieng, Franz Boluminski, estimated that 1,000 women had been recruited from Neu Mecklenburg between 1905 and 1907, whereas Hahl believed the number to be 625. See Boluminski, Käwieng, to Hahl, Herbertshöhe, 19 October 1907, Bundesarchiv Berlin (BArch): Reichskolonialamt; R 1001/2310, 88; Hahl, "Betrifft: Bevölkerungsrückgang in Neu-Mecklenburg," Herbertshöhe, to the State Secretary of the Imperial Colonial Office, Berlin, 25 October 1908, BArch: R 1001/2311, 52.
21. *Nachrichten über Kaiser Wilhelms-Land und den Bismarck-Archipel* 3 (1888): 154, and 9 (1893): 29.
22. "Verordnung betreffend die Arbeiter-Depôts im Schutzgebiet der Neu Guinea Compagnie. Vom 16. August 1888," *Nachrichten* 3 (1888): 140–44, § 4.
23. Sack and Clark, *German New Guinea*, 73.
24. The lower estimate of 4,900 draws on Siegel's calculation that women constituted 4.9 percent of laborers recruited from the New Guinea islands (prior to German annexation) for British colonial Fiji. See Siegel, "Origins of Pacific Islands Labourers," 53. Given his much higher figure (17.3 percent) for women recruited from New Ireland (Neu Mecklenburg), and intensive recruiting there under the Germans, that figure is likely too conservative. The Australian officer J. J. Cummins estimated in 1921 that New Guinean women never constituted more than 10 percent of indentured laborers during the period of German colonial administration, suggesting a maximum number of around 8,500 indentured women. See NAA: Department of Foreign Affairs and Trade, Central Office; A4, Correspondence files; NG8: Letter to the Prime Minister, 24 November 1921.
25. See, for example, NAA: G255, 572: Stationsgericht zu [Rabaul]. Akten gegen Tom Miller in Makurapan wegen Zuwiderhandlung gegen die Arbeiterverordnung (1911); NAA: G255, 1098: Kaiserliches Bezirksgericht zu Friedrich-Wilhelmshafen. Akten in der Strafsache gegen den Pflanzungsleiter Emil Hofmann, Siar, wegen Vergehens gegen die Anwerberverordnung (1914). Oral histories corroborate this. See Otto Manganau, "My Grandfather's Experience

with the Germans," *Oral History* [Port Moresby] 1, no. 6 (1973): 8–9; Richard Scaglion, "Multiple Voices, Multiple Truths: Labour Recruitment in the Sepik Foothills of German New Guinea," *The Journal of Pacific History* 42, no. 3 (2007): 345–60.
26. Lanthe's statement, Rabaul, 28 July 1913, NAA: G255, 331: Kaiserliches Bezirksgericht zu Rabaul. Akten in der Strafsache gegen Paulsen wegen Vergehens gegen [die] Anwerberverordnung (1913).
27. On the policy debate concerning the recruitment of unmarried women, see Firth, *New Guinea under the Germans*, 112–35.
28. Richard Paulsen's statement, Rabaul, 31 July 1913, Tinmara's statement, Rabaul, 28 July 1913, and Richard Gebhard's ruling, 31 July 1913, Rabaul, NAA: G255, 331.
29. Kuangkake's statement, Rabaul, 29 June 1911, and Georg Stuebel's ruling, 21 July 1911, NAA: G255, 572.
30. See for example, existing lists of laborers recruited for the New Guinea Company in 1902, NAA: G255, 565; and for Forsayth & Co. in 1904, NAA: G255, 566.
31. Recruiting contract made between Curt A. Schultze and Adolf Jahn, Lebrechtshof, 2 February 1916, NAA: Military Administration of the German New Guinea Possessions; G261, General Correspondence; 6. My emphasis.
32. Shineberg, *The People Trade*, 107.
33. See statements made by Maximilian Thiel of Hernsheim & Co., in "Protokoll zur Gouvernementsratssitzung der IV. Sitzungsperiode, Herbertshöhe, den 27. Dezember 1909," *Amtsblatt für das Schutzgebiet Deutsch-Neuguinea* 2, no. 2 (15 January 1910): 14; and Wilhelm Mirow of Forsayth & Co. in "Sitzungsbericht zur 10. Gouvernementsratssitzung der IV. Sitzungsperiode am 10. November 1911 im Gouvernementsgebäude zu Rabaul," *Amtsblatt* 3, no. 23 (1 December 1911): 258.
34. Dr. Wick, "Arbeiterfürsorge in Deutsch-Neuguinea," 1914, BArch: R 1001/5773, 38.
35. Hans Rodatz, Eitapé, to Albert Hahl, Herbertshöhe, 15 May 1909, BArch: R 1001/2311, 174–75; Hahl, Herbertshöhe, to the State Secretary of the Imperial Colonial Office, Berlin, 5 July 1909, BArch: R 1001/2311, 169–70. For the German colonies more generally, see Daniel Walther, *Sex and Control: Venereal Disease, Colonial Physicians, and Indigenous Agency in German Colonialism, 1884–1914* (New York: Berghahn Books, 2015), 26.
36. Gábon Vargyas, *Data on the Pictorial History of North-East Papua New Guinea* (Budapest: Ethnographical Institute of the Hungarian Academy of Sciences, 1986), 44.
37. Ibid., 46.
38. Hermann Joseph Hiery, *Das Deutsche Reich in der Südsee (1900–1921): Eine Annäherung an die Erfahrungen verschiedener Kulturen* (Göttingen: Vandenhoeck & Ruprecht, 1995), 41. "Concubines," or "house girls," had been legally classed as laborers since 1890 in an effort by Imperial Commissioner Fritz Rose to extend them a degree of protection under the labor ordinance. See Rose, Finschhafen, to Chancellor Otto von Bismarck, Berlin, 13 February 1890, BArch: R 1001/2960, 66. For a critical appraisal of similar colonial relations, see Ann Laura Stoler, *Carnal Knowledge and Imperial Power: Race and the Intimate in Colonial Rule* (Berkeley: University of California Press, 2002), 49.
39. Carl Ribbe, *Zwei Jahre unter den Kannibalen der Salomo-Inseln: Reiseerlebnisse und Schilderungen von Land und Leuten* (Dresden: Elbgau-Buchdruckerei, 1903), 81–82.
40. Verzeichnis der von dem Kapitän Komine, Schiffe Zabra, angeworbenen farbigen Arbeiter, NAA: G255, 566.
41. As Luker has argued of British Fiji in "A Tale of Two Mothers," 361. In German New Guinea, the gender disparity in the indenture was much more acute than in Fiji, where British labor regulations mandated that women constitute at least 40 percent of indentured laborers.
42. Ann Laura Stoler, *Capitalism and Confrontation in Sumatra's Plantation Belt, 1870–1979* (New Haven, CT: Yale University Press, 1985), 31–33. Luise White has demonstrated the close rela-

tionship between women's sex work and colonial labor regimes in Kenya. See Luise White, *The Comforts of Home: Prostitution in Colonial Nairobi* (Chicago, IL: University of Chicago Press, 1990).

43. Peter Hempenstall, "The Neglected Empire: The Superstructure of the Colonial State in German Melanesia," in *Papua New Guinea: A Century of Colonial Impact, 1884–1984*, ed. Sione Lātūkefu (Port Moresby: National Research Institute and the University of Papua New Guinea, 1989), 140.

44. For a comprehensive treatment of law in German New Guinea, see Peter Sack, *Phantom History, the Rule of Law, and the Colonial State: The Case of German New Guinea* (Canberra: Research School of Pacific and Asian Studies, Australian National University, 2001).

45. Heinrich Schnee's ruling, Herbertshöhe, 15 April 1899, NAA: G255, 202: Stationsgericht Herbertshöhe. Strafsache gegen Toreren von Wunamamie wegen Notzucht (1899); Schnee's ruling, Herbertshöhe, 28 January 1899, NAA: G255, 205: Stationsgericht Herbertshöhe. Strafsache gegen den Hausjungen Kuka in Herbertshöhe aus Neu Hannover wegen Notzucht (1899).

46. Schnee's ruling, Herbertshöhe, 6 May 1899, NAA: G255, 201: Stationsgericht zu Herbertshöhe. Strafsache gegen Tokarambele von Kakunai wegen Notzucht (1899).

47. Schnee's ruling, Herbertshöhe, 29 August 1899, NAA: G255, 191: Stationsgericht Herbertshöhe. Strafsache gegen Diwito von Neu Hannover wegen Notzucht (1899); Schnee's ruling, 30 August 1899, NAA: G255, 192: Stationsgericht Herbertshöhe. Strafsache gegen Ignalangai von Neu Hannover wegen Notzucht (1899).

48. In addition to the cases discussed here, see for example, NAA: 255, 1070: Kaiserliches Bezirksgericht zu Friedrich Wilhelmshafen. Akten in der Strafsache gegen den Assistenten Arthur Sacchi wegen Menschenraubes (1903–4); NAA: G255, 1071: Kaiserliches Bezirksgericht zu Friedrich Wilhelmshafen. Akten in der Strafsache gegen den Offizier der Handelsmarien Jüdtz wegen Körperverletzung und Hausfriedensbruchs (1903–5); NAA: Imperial District Court and Office; G254, Administrative records of German New Guinea; 108: Kaiserliches Bezirksgericht zu Herbertshöhe. Akten in der Strafsache gegen den Handlungsgehilfen Louis Patterson wegen [Notzucht] (1906). Other cases appear not to have proceeded to trial, or the court files have been lost. See, for example, correspondence of 21 November 1913 concerning Albert Stehr in NAA: G255, 896: Akten der Kaiserlichen Station Käwieng betreffend Haftbefehle. In one 1913 case (NAA: G255, 33), a European man convicted of statutory rape in Ponape (Pohnpei) had his conviction overturned by the Supreme Court in Rabaul.

49. Patricia Hayes is instructive on the ways in which androcentric, and, I would add, Eurocentric, "attitudes and archives" have worked to obscure colonial histories of sexual violence. See Patricia Hayes, "'Cocky' Hahn and the 'Black Venus': The Making of a Native Commissioner in South West Africa, 1915–46," *Gender & History* 8, no. 3 (1996): 364–92. Catherine Komisaruk reaches a similar conclusion in her study of rape cases in colonial Guatemala. See Catherine Komisaruk, "Rape Narratives, Rape Silences: Sexual Violence and Judicial Testimony in Colonial Guatemala," *Biography* 31, no. 3 (2008): 369–96.

50. Hermann J. Hiery, "Traditional and European Concepts of 'Justice' and their Influence on One Another," in *European Impact and Pacific Influence: British and German Colonial Policy in the Pacific Islands and the Indigenous Response*, eds. Hermann J. Hiery and John M. MacKenzie (London: I.B. Tauris, 1997), 172.

51. Firth, *New Guinea under the Germans*, 124.

52. Minni's statement, Kieta, 18 February 1910, NAA: G254, 75: Kaiserliches Bezirksgericht zu Herbertshöhe. Akten in der Strafsache gegen Thurm, G., Händler, zuletzt in Kieta wegen Notzucht (1910).

53. Waneri's statement, Herbertshöhe, 29 August 1899, NAA: G255, 191; Tawui's statement, Herbertshöhe, 28 August 1899, NAA: G255, 192.

54. Puluss's statement, Herbertshöhe, 12 February 1906, NAA: G254, 106: Kaiserliches Bezirksgericht zu Herbertshöhe. Akten in der Strafsache gegen den Lageraufseher Waldemar Kolbe zu Herbertshöhe wegen Notzucht und Unterschlagung (1906).
55. Kinela's statement, Herbertshöhe, 12 February 1906, ibid. On Hahl's career in German New Guinea, see Peter Biskup, "Dr Albert Hahl—Sketch of a German Colonial Official," *Australian Journal of Politics and History* 14, no. 3 (1968): 342–57.
56. Waldemar Kolbe's statement, Herbertshöhe, 12 February 1906, NAA: G254, 106.
57. Sander Gilman, *Difference and Pathology: Stereotypes of Sexuality, Race, and Madness* (Ithaca, NY: Cornell University Press, 1985), 76–108; Barbara Bush, "Gender and Empire: The Twentieth Century," in *Gender and Empire*, ed. Philippa Levine (Oxford: Oxford University Press, 2004), 98.
58. Tobin, "*Venus von Samoa*"; Jolly, "Women of the East."
59. Philippa Levine, "Sexuality, Gender, and Empire," in *Gender and Empire*, ed. Philippa Levine (Oxford: Oxford University Press), 142.
60. On how the monetization of sex has been used as a "justification" for rape, see Koni Benson and Joyce M. Chadya, "Ukubhinya: Gender and Sexual Violence in Bulawayo, Colonial Zimbabwe, 1946–1956," *Journal of Southern African Studies* 31, no. 3 (2005): 587–610.
61. John D. Kelly, "Gaze and Grasp: Plantations, Desires, Indentured Indians and Colonial Law in Fiji," in *Sites of Desire, Economies of Pleasure: Sexualities in Asia and the Pacific*, eds. Lenore Manderson and Margaret Jolly (Chicago, IL: University of Chicago Press, 1997), 72–98, quotation 95.
62. Erroneously referred to as Georg Thurm by colonial officials throughout the file. See NAA: G254, 75.
63. Willy's statement, Kieta, 24 January 1910, ibid.
64. Minni's statement, Kieta, 18 February 1910, ibid.
65. On "colonial enclaves" as gendered spaces, see Anne Dickson-Waiko, "Colonial Enclaves and Domestic Spaces in British New Guinea," in *Britishness Abroad: Transnational Movements and Imperial Cultures*, eds. Kate Darian Smith, Patricia Grimshaw, and Stuart Macintyre (Carlton: Melbourne University Press, 2007), 205–30.
66. Annes's statement, Kieta, 26 February 1910, NAA: G254, 75.
67. Doellinger, Kieta, to the Imperial District Court, Herbertshöhe, 1 March 1910, ibid.
68. Stuebel's ruling, Herbertshöhe, 12 May 1910, ibid. My emphasis.
69. Bago's statement, Rabaul, 27 November 1911, NAA: G255, 325.
70. Hermann Bolten's statement, Rabaul, 14 December 1911, ibid.
71. Ibid.
72. Wilhelm Bolten's statement, Rabaul, (incorrectly dated) 6 November 1911, ibid.
73. Gustav Weber's ruling, Rabaul, 19 February 1912, ibid. On colonists' casual use of corporal punishment, see Firth, *New Guinea under the Germans*, 109–10.
74. Hermann and Amalie Bolten's daughter was born in October 1911, which corresponds with Tapilai's estimate of when the rapes took place: "not more than two months ago." See Karl Baumann, Dieter Klein, and Wolfgang Apitzsch, *Biographisches Handbuch Deutsch-Neuguinea, 1882–1922: Kurzlebensläufe ehemaliger Kolonisten, Forscher, Missionare und Reisender* (Fassberg: Baumann, 2002), 41. Further biographical information on the Europeans mentioned in this chapter can also be found in this volume.
75. Tapilai's statement, Rabaul, 27 November 1911, NAA: G255, 325.
76. Kopp's "Ärztliches Gutachten," Rabaul, 30 November 1911, ibid.
77. Hermann's Bolten's statement, Rabaul 14 December 1911, ibid.
78. Weber's ruling, Rabaul, 19 February 1912, ibid.
79. Kelly, "Gaze and Grasp," 91.

80. Tapilai and Bago's statements, and Grundler's note, Rabaul, 27 November 1911, NAA: G255, 325.
81. On the imperial emphasis on notions of respectability and sexual propriety, see Ann L. Stoler, "Making Empire Respectable: The Politics of Race and Sexual Morality in 20th-Century Colonial Cultures," *American Ethnologist* 16, no. 4 (1989): 634–60.
82. Laimasung's statement, Rabaul, 19 February 1912, NAA: G255, 325.
83. I borrow this term from Nancy Rose Hunt, "An Acoustic Register, Tenacious Images, and Congolese Scenes of Rape and Repetition," *Cultural Anthropology* 23, no. 2 (2008): 223.
84. Wick, "Arbeiterfürsorge in Deutsch-Neuguinea," 38.

Bibliography

Amtsblatt für das Schutzgebiet Deutsch-Neuguinea. Rabaul: Kaiserliches Gouvernement in Rabaul, 1909–1914.

Balandier, Georges. "The Colonial Situation: A Theoretical Approach." In *Social Change: The Colonial Situation*, edited by Immanuel Wallerstein, 34–61. New York: Wiley, 1966.

Baumann, Karl, Dieter Klein, and Wolfgang Apitzsch. *Biographisches Handbuch Deutsch-Neuguinea, 1882–1922: Kurzlebensläufe ehemaliger Kolonisten, Forscher, Missionare und Reisender*. Fassberg: Baumann, 2002.

Benson, Koni, and Joyce M. Chadya. "Ukubhinya: Gender and Sexual Violence in Bulawayo, Colonial Zimbabwe, 1946–1956." *Journal of Southern African Studies* 31, no. 3 (2005): 587–610.

Biskup, Peter. "Dr Albert Hahl—Sketch of a German Colonial Official." *Australian Journal of Politics and History* 14, no. 3 (1968): 342–57.

Bush, Barbara. "Gender and Empire: The Twentieth Century." In *Gender and Empire*, edited by Philippa Levine, 77–111. Oxford: Oxford University Press, 2004.

Conrad, Sebastian. *Globalisation and the Nation in Imperial Germany*. Cambridge: Cambridge University Press, 2010.

Corris, Peter. *Passage, Port and Plantation: A History of Solomon Islands Labour Migration, 1870–1914*. Carlton: Melbourne University Press, 1973.

Dickson-Waiko, Anne. "Colonial Enclaves and Domestic Spaces in British New Guinea." In *Britishness Abroad: Transnational Movements and Imperial Cultures*, edited by Kate Darian Smith, Patricia Grimshaw, and Stuart Macintyre, 205–30. Carlton: Melbourne University Press, 2007.

Firth, Stewart. "German Labour Policy and the Partition of the Western Pacific: The View from Samoa." *The Journal of Pacific History* 25, no. 1 (1990): 85–102.

———. *New Guinea under the Germans*. Carlton: Melbourne University Press, 1983.

———. "The Transformation of the Labour Trade in German New Guinea, 1899–1914." *The Journal of Pacific History* 11, no. 2 (1976): 51–65.

Gilman, Sander. *Difference and Pathology: Stereotypes of Sexuality, Race, and Madness*. Ithaca, NY: Cornell University Press, 1985.

Hayes, Patricia. "'Cocky' Hahn and the 'Black Venus': The Making of a Native Commissioner in South West Africa, 1915–46." *Gender & History* 8, no. 3 (1996): 364–92.

Hempenstall, Peter. "The Neglected Empire: The Superstructure of the Colonial State in German Melanesia." In *Papua New Guinea: A Century of Colonial Impact, 1884–1984*, edited by Sione Lātūkefu, 133–62. Port Moresby: National Research Institute and the University of Papua New Guinea, 1989.

Hiery, Hermann Joseph. *Das Deutsche Reich in der Südsee (1900–1921): Eine Annäherung an die Erfahrungen verschiedener Kulturen.* Göttingen: Vandenhoeck & Ruprecht, 1995.

———. "Traditional and European Concepts of 'Justice' and their Influence on One Another." In *European Impact and Pacific Influence: British and German Colonial Policy in the Pacific Islands and the Indigenous Response*, edited by Hermann J. Hiery and John M. MacKenzie, 169–76. London: I.B. Tauris, 1997.

Hunt, Nancy Rose. "An Acoustic Register, Tenacious Images, and Congolese Scenes of Rape and Repetition." *Cultural Anthropology* 23, no. 2 (2008): 220–53.

Jolly, Margaret. "The Forgotten Women: A History of Migrant Labour and Gender Relations in Vanuatu." *Oceania* 58, no. 2 (1987): 119–39.

———. "Women of the East, Women of the West: Region and Race, Gender and Sexuality on Cook's Voyages." In *The Atlantic World in the Antipodes: Effects and Transformations since the Eighteenth Century*, edited by Kate Fullagar, 2–23. Newcastle upon Tyne, UK: Cambridge Scholars, 2012.

Kelly, John D. "Gaze and Grasp: Plantations, Desires, Indentured Indians and Colonial Law in Fiji." In *Sites of Desire, Economies of Pleasure: Sexualities in Asia and the Pacific*, edited by Lenore Manderson and Margaret Jolly, 72–98. Chicago, IL: University of Chicago Press, 1997.

Komisaruk, Catherine. "Rape Narratives, Rape Silences: Sexual Violence and Judicial Testimony in Colonial Guatemala." *Biography* 31, no. 3 (2008): 369–96.

Lal, Brij V. "Kunti's Cry: Indentured Women in Fiji Plantations." *Indian Economic and Social History Review* 20, no. 3 (1985): 55–71.

Levine, Philippa. "Sexuality, Gender, and Empire." In *Gender and Empire*, edited by Philippa Levine, 134–55. Oxford: Oxford University Press, 2004.

Luker, Vicki. "A Tale of Two Mothers: Colonial Constructions of Indian and Fijian Maternity." *Gender Issues in Fiji*, edited by Jacqueline Leckie, special issue, *Fijian Studies: A Journal of Contemporary Fiji* 3, no. 2 (2005): 357–74.

Manganau, Otto. "My Grandfather's Experience with the Germans." *Oral History* [Port Moresby] 1, no. 6 (1973): 8–9.

Moore, Clive. *Kanaka: A History of Melanesian Mackay.* Port Moresby: Institute of Papua New Guinea Studies and University of Papua New Guinea Press, 1985.

———. "Revising the Revisionists: The Historiography of Immigrant Melanesians in Australia." *Pacific Studies* 15, no. 2 (1992): 61–86.

Moses, John. "Imperial Priorities in New Guinea, 1885–1914." In *Papua New Guinea: A Century of Colonial Impact, 1884–1984*, edited by Sione Lātūkefu, 163–75. Port Moresby: National Research Institute and the University of Papua New Guinea, 1989.

Munro, Doug. "The Labor Trade in Melanesians to Queensland: An Historiographic Essay." *The Journal of Pacific History* 28, no. 3 (1995): 609–27.

———. "The Origins of Labourers in the South Pacific: Commentary and Statistics." In *Labour in the South Pacific*, edited by Clive Moore, Jacqueline Leckie, and Doug Munro, xxxix–li. Townsville, QLD: James Cook University, 1990.

Nachrichten über Kaiser Wilhelms-Land und den Bismarck-Archipel. Berlin: Neu Guinea Compagnie, 1885–98.

Ribbe, Carl. *Zwei Jahre unter den Kannibalen der Salomo-Inseln: Reiseerlebnisse und Schilderungen von Land und Leuten.* Dresden: Elbgau-Buchdruckerei, 1903.

Sack, Peter. *Phantom History, the Rule of Law, and the Colonial State: The Case of German New Guinea*. Canberra: Research School of Pacific and Asian Studies, Australian National University, 2001.

Sack, Peter, and Dymphna Clark, eds. and trans. *German New Guinea: The Annual Reports*. Canberra: Australian National University Press, 1979.

Saunders, Kay. "Melanesian Women in Queensland, 1863–1907: Some Methodological Problems Involving the Relationship between Racism and Sexism." *Pacific Studies* 4, no. 1 (1980): 26–44.

Scaglion, Richard. "Multiple Voices, Multiple Truths: Labour Recruitment in the Sepik Foothills of German New Guinea." *The Journal of Pacific History* 42, no. 3 (2007): 345–60.

Scarr, Deryck. "Recruits and Recruiters: A Portrait of the Pacific Islands Labour Trade." *The Journal of Pacific History* 2 (1967): 5–24.

Schnee, Heinrich. *Bilder aus der Südsee: Unter den kannibalischen Stämmen des Bismarck-Archipels*. Berlin: D. Reimer, 1904.

Shineberg, Dorothy. *The People Trade: Pacific Island Laborers and New Caledonia, 1865–1930*. Honolulu: University of Hawai'i Press, 1999.

Siegel, Jeff. "Origins of Pacific Islands Labourers in Fiji." *The Journal of Pacific History* 20, no. 1 (1985): 42–54.

Stoler, Ann Laura. *Capitalism and Confrontation in Sumatra's Plantation Belt, 1870–1979*. New Haven, CT: Yale University Press, 1985.

———. *Carnal Knowledge and Imperial Power: Race and the Intimate in Colonial Rule*. Berkeley: University of California Press, 2002.

———. "Making Empire Respectable: The Politics of Race and Sexual Morality in 20th-Century Colonial Cultures." *American Ethnologist* 16, no. 4 (1989): 634–60.

Tcherkézoff, Serge. "A Reconsideration of the Role of Polynesian Women in Early Encounters with Europeans: Supplement to Marshall Sahlins' Voyage around the Islands of History." In *Oceanic Encounters: Exchange, Desire, Violence*, edited by Margaret Jolly, Serge Tcherkézoff, and Darrell Tryon, 113–60. Canberra: ANU E Press, 2009.

Tinker, Hugh. *A New System of Slavery: The Export of Indian Labour Overseas, 1830–1920*. London: Oxford University Press, 1974.

Tobin, Robert. "*Venus von Samoa*: Rasse und Sexualität im deutschen Südpazifik." In *Kolonialismus als Kultur: Literatur, Medien, Wissenschaft in der deutschen Gründerzeit des Fremden*, edited by Alexander Honold and Oliver Simons, 192–220. Tubingen: A. Francke Verlag, 2002.

Vargyas, Gábon. *Data on the Pictorial History of North-East Papua New Guinea*. Budapest: Ethnographical Institute of the Hungarian Academy of Sciences, 1986.

Vaughan, Megan. *Creating the Creole Island: Slavery in Eighteenth-Century Mauritius*. Durham, NC: Duke University Press, 2005.

Walther, Daniel. *Sex and Control: Venereal Disease, Colonial Physicians, and Indigenous Agency in German Colonialism, 1884–1914*. New York: Berghahn Books, 2015.

Ward, John M. *British Policy in the South Pacific, 1786–1893: A Study in British Policy towards the South Pacific Islands prior to the Establishment of Governments by the Great Powers*. Sydney: Australasian Publishing Co., 1948.

White, Luise. *The Comforts of Home: Prostitution in Colonial Nairobi*. Chicago, IL: University of Chicago Press, 1990.

Zantop, Susanne. *Colonial Fantasies: Conquest, Family, and Nation in Precolonial Germany, 1770–1870*. Durham, NC: Duke University Press, 1997.

Chapter 12

The Trans-Pacific "Ghadar" Movement
The Role of the Pacific in the Indo-German Plot to Overthrow the British Empire during World War I

Douglas T. McGetchin

The Pacific provided an important conduit for Indo-German revolutionary activity during World War I. Indian revolutionaries and German agents operated not just in the capitals of Central Europe, but also along the west coast of North America, and especially in San Francisco, with networks and activities stretching across the Pacific to Batavia, Singapore, the Philippines, Bangkok, Shanghai, and Tokyo. Indians used German contacts in these Pacific sites as staging areas to promote the overthrow of the British in India. These Indo-German activities organized men, arms, and explosives from the United States, which was neutral until 1917. Ghadar (or Ghadr), Urdu for "mutiny" or "rebellion," revolutionaries sent fellow Indians, mostly Sikhs, living on the west coast of North America to support revolutionary activities against the British in India.

When one considers the role of Germans in the Ghadar activities, focusing particularly on the international networks of contact between Indians and Germans as they stretched their activities from North America to India itself, this case shows at least five interacting and "entangled" webs across the Pacific.[1] The main spy–counterspy protagonists were the upstart Indian revolutionaries and the British counterintelligence operatives trying to stifle them. A third group were German diaspora colonists, immigrants and their agents who helped their Ersatz allies the Indians. A fourth group were sympathizers on both sides in the United States, including its overseas Pacific empire in the Philippines, who hindered or aided the main antagonists when the United States became a British ally in 1917. A fifth group was neutral Japan, which negotiated between the Indians and British, serving both as a surreptitious base for rebel Indians whom some pan-Asian Japanese favored while the official position favored the British, whom they successfully placated to make imperial gains of their own in the Pacific.

Notes from this chapter begin on page 287.

The willingness to use violence, and debates around the most effective way to engage on both sides of these struggles, provides a litmus test for each of these groups. How individual actors and forces negotiated these far-flung trans-Pacific struggles allows one to momentarily disentangle and analyze the threads of empire and anti-imperialism during World War I. The ability and willingness of Ghadar proponents to state anti-British rhetoric and conduct anticolonial activities had to do with the degree of support they had from the friendliness of the locale and how safe they felt from the long arms of British counterrevolutionary forces. Likewise, the willingness of the British to use force against their Ghadar opponents also was proportionate to their own proximity to friendly territory.[2]

The first group were the Indian immigrant diaspora flung out across the Pacific. The relatively smaller wave of South Asian immigrants to North America followed earlier generations of Chinese and Japanese immigrants. Sikh soldiers in the British Indian Army became aware of the economic promise of North America, ironically after helping to crush the Boxer Rebellion (1898–1900) in China and making contact with the Americans involved.[3] Less than a hundred South Asians had immigrated to the United States by 1904, but immigration mushroomed in the second half of the decade, reaching close to six thousand by 1910.[4] Others settled in Canada as former soldiers and adventurers, pushing the numbers of South Asians, primarily Sikhs, on the Pacific Coast of the United States and Canada to more than ten thousand by 1910.[5] In the decade before World War I, the United States had been a safe harbor for South Asians dissatisfied with the British rule in India. With the repressive response to the 1909 assassination in London of Sir Curzon Wyllie by Madan Lal Dhingra, many South Asian students started to prefer to study in the United States instead of submitting to the rigorous government surveillance in England. One of these students in Canada was Taraknath Das (1884–1956), whom the British watched because he published the monthly newspaper *Free Hindustan* from 1908 to 1911.[6]

The views of these Indian immigrants toward the British and their North American white culture was soured by an ugly incident in 1914 on the eve of the war. On 24 March 1914 in Hong Kong, Sardar Gurdit Singh chartered the *Komagata Maru* to challenge the Canadian immigration laws that had a "continuous journey" clause requirement specifically designed to thwart direct South Asian immigration to Canada, as no shipping lines had such direct routes.[7] Arriving in Vancouver on 23 May 1914, Canadian immigration officials only allowed a handful of the 347 Sikh passengers to debark—only those who had previously lived in Canada.[8] After a two-month standoff, the ship departed for Japan. The blatantly racist rhetoric associated with this incident led to an angry backlash from those South Asians already living in North America who had tremendous support for the Ghadar movement.[9] A key figure in the debacle was William C. Hopkinson, who had lived in India as a youth and had partly Indian heritage, a background that helped him learn Hindi and serve as a Calcutta police inspector. He moved to Vancouver in 1907 where he became an immigration inspector. He was married with children, and lived in a middle-class suburb, but he had a secret double-life in a poor immigrant neighborhood, living part-time in a shack as "Narain Singh," wearing a turban and fake beard, and pretending to be a poor worker from Lahore. His part in the *Komagata Maru* challenge unraveled a few months later when he was attending the trial of Bela Singh. Mewa Singh, a Sikh gurdwara priest, killed Hopkinson in the courtroom, reinforcing a familiar pattern of violent resistance.[10]

Ghadar was deliberately reminiscent of the bloody 1857 Indian revolt against British rule, and significantly was the name the San Francisco revolutionaries picked for both their newspaper and movement.[11] The leader of the California Ghadar rebels was Har Dayal, who with revolutionary credentials arrived in the United States in 1911, and became a lecturer in South Asian philosophy at Stanford University until administrators dismissed him, as they disapproved of his politics as an anarchist and labor organizer. In November 1913, Har Dayal and friends in San Francisco founded the *Ghadr* (Rebellion) newspaper and the Yugantar (New Era) ashram to foment revolution in India. After his arrest in March 1914 as an undesirable alien, he jumped bail and fled to Switzerland.[12] The US government arrested Har Dayal not because of pressure from the British, who were unwilling to press the United States on the South Asian immigrant agitation issue for fear of alienating an important friendly neutral power, but rather because the US government considered Har Dayal an anarchist.[13]

The second group in this trans-Pacific struggle, the Indians' antagonists, were the British who worked diligently to unravel the efforts of the South Asian revolutionaries. Before the war British counterintelligence included carefully watching the far-flung flotsam of seditious Indians. After the war started, the British applied diplomatic pressure on the United States government, but with only mixed results, belatedly gaining the active help of US officials by mid-1916 to investigate and eventually prosecute the South Asians.[14] Nevertheless, the British had a far-reaching network of surveillance operatives and informers, as well as stout legal defenses erected at the beginning of the war, such as the Ingress of South Asian Ordinance in India, which allowed British authorities to arrest suspects and hold them without trial.[15] British activities included representing the South Asians in the most unfavorable light they could, highlighting sedition, violence, massacre, and bomb making.[16]

The third group were German officials living abroad who helped the South Asian Ghadar conspirators as part of an overall strategy in World War I to unsettle the British Empire. At the end of July 1914, Kaiser Wilhelm told his advisors about the need to stir up colonial unrest against the British: "Our consuls in Turkey and India, agents, etc., must get a conflagration going throughout the whole Mohammedan world against this hated, unscrupulous, dishonest nation of shopkeepers—since if we are going to bleed to death, England must at least lose India."[17] The chief officials working on this plan included Count Johann von Bernstorff, the imperial German ambassador to the United States, and Constantin Theodor Dumba, the Austro-Hungarian ambassador. The consulates of Germany and Austria-Hungary across the United States proved useful bases of operation for those involved in the plot, such as the military attaché and future prime minister Captain Franz von Papen, as well as the naval attaché Captain Karl Boy-Ed, the commercial attaché Dr. Heinrich F. Albert, and diplomat Wolf von Igel.[18]

The Germans generously supported the Ghadar operations, as the South Asians would be helpful to Germany's war aims. Although the Indians did not have the means to contribute much financially, they did put their lives on the line, thus replicating the usual colonial division of labor. The South Asians accepted German aid for a variety of reasons, including pragmatism, and German funding kept South Asians involved in the secret work of resistance; some examples include the substantial payments of $20,000 to Chakravarty in May 1916, followed by $30,000, and he asked for $15,000 more in August. The San Francisco German consulate paid another Ghadar leader, Ram Chandra, $1,000 monthly.[19] In the first year of the war, the German work with the Ghadar was part of a wider collaboration with Mexicans to keep the American war-making capacity out of the hands of the western European allies by purchasing it. Military attaché von Papen "concluded that for twenty million dollars Germany could buy up the entire American munitions capacity for one year ($420 million in today's value)."[20]

The fourth group were those in the United States who sympathized with either the Germans or the Indians. The Germans benefited from German-American and Irish-American sympathies and help, as well as an anti-imperialist strain in US politics of Americans who felt an affinity with downtrodden nationalities. The British had faced an uphill battle for decades trying to get the American government to suppress Irish-American sympathies for resistance to British rule in Ireland. The United States was the haven of other groups as well, including Russian revolutionaries and Chinese nationalists. One British report stated: "On the Pacific coast the Germans and the Irish together exercise a strong control over local politics, and this control is exercised to our disadvantage. As a general rule the action of the local authorities has a strong anti-British bias, [as newspapers] on the West Coast are controlled by Mr. Hearst."[21] The role of the United States as a haven for foreign revolutionaries reflected widespread anti-imperial sentiment during the era, and only changed as a result of British diplomatic pressure and the influence of the US entry into the war.

The fifth and final group was the Japanese, who had reasons to support both sides. By acting as a minor British ally, Japan had much to gain in the Pacific, as they did after the war, winning former German colonies like the Mariana Islands. Yet some Japanese, as fellow Asians, were sympathetic to Indian nationalism.

Japanese art critic Kakuzo Okakura, who advocated a pan-Asian cultural identity, had founded the Fine Arts Academy of Japan and visited India in 1900–1 to investigate Indian antiquities and make contact with Indian cultural figures like Rabindranath Tagore. Okakura's book, *The Ideals of the East*, begins "Asia is one," which was particularly inspiring as the book emerged when the Japanese were winning a stunning victory during the Russo-Japanese war of 1904–5, which fired nationalist sentiment across Asia. It particularly moved Indian nationalists in Bengal as they protested against the British partition of their province during the Swadeshi movement, with the boycott of British goods and the purchase of Indian-made items, especially clothing.[22] During and after World War I, Japan was also an important haven for key Indian revolutionaries, such as Rash Behari Bose, instrumental in the 1912 Delhi bombing assassination attempt against British Viceroy Charles Hardinge.[23] If the British had captured Bose while he was operating in India in 1915, they would have executed him like those they had convicted in the First Lahore Conspiracy Case of 1915, a result of the failed uprising that year.[24] Nevertheless, he escaped to Japan where he lived for the rest of his life.[25] His presence helped to provide a pan-Asian nucleus of resistance that laid the groundwork for Subhas Chandra Bose's pro-Axis Indian National Army during World War II.[26]

These five main groups—Indians, British, Germans living abroad, American sympathizers, and the Japanese—would interact surreptitiously and sometimes violently in a series of covert actions and campaigns across the Pacific during World War I. An important base for the Ghadar insurgency was the west coast of North America. The provocative Ghadar pamphlets they started printing in 1913 featured Germans prominently. One pamphlet at the beginning of the war entitled "Indian Soldiers! Do Not Fight with Germany," urged its readers to take action against the British, with the knowledge that Germans were on their side: "Now Germany has got our enemy in her power, [and] therefore this is a very good time *to raise a mutiny and kill the English*, and *take our revenge*. Strike them and turn them out of India. Liberate India."[27] Dissuading Indians from fighting on behalf of the English was a major concern of the Ghadar movement, which sought to undermine Indian loyalty to the British. The pamphlet continued: "The Germans are not our enemies. They are our friends who have got our great enemy—the English—into their power … You also should unite with the Germans and [by] fighting against the English *secure the independence of India*." The Indo-German mutual self-interest became apparent in a symbiotic relationship. "All intelligent people know that Germany is an enemy of Great Britain. We also are the mortal enemy of the British Government, so an enemy of my enemy is my friend."[28]

There was an emphasis on the Ghadar movement being a struggle that spanned the globe, as did the British Empire. "We should not fight against the Germans in China for the British," one pamphlet urged, emphasizing the connections this struggle in China had throughout the world: "We should turn around and mutiny and so prevent the British from sending troops to India, and having started a big mutiny, to grind the British in India, so that their tyranny shall forever cease in India, Turkey, Nepal, Persia, Egypt, China and Morocco, and that the Hindus should class themselves free as other nations."[29] The Ghadar thus saw themselves as part of a wider pan-Asian and even larger global anti-imperial struggle.

Once the war started, Indians abroad sought to return home to India to fight the British in person, including a thousand from western North America and a further seven thousand from Panama, the Philippines, Shanghai, and Hong Kong.[30] Because the war in Europe drained India of British garrison troops, revolutionaries hoped the thinned forces there would be susceptible to surprise attack, followed by a mass uprising.[31] During summer 1914, Ghadar advocates in the US held public meetings up and down the west coast, including in Seattle, Portland, Astoria, Sacramento, Stockton, Fresno, Oxnard, and Los Angeles, recruiting hundreds of volunteers and thousands of dollars.[32] The first expedition of approximately sixty South Asians left San Francisco on 29 August 1914 on the steamer *Korea*.[33] The organizing continued onboard as the ship picked up additional Indians in Honolulu, Yokohama, and Manila before landing in Hong Kong where they transferred to the *Tosa Maru*. These 173 Ghadarites landed in Calcutta on 29 October 1914, where British officials immediately interned a hundred, and hung six.[34] Of all the eight thousand emigrants who returned to India from October 1914 to December 1917, the British killed 22 (0.2%), interned 331 (4.1%), and restricted 2,576 to their villages (32.2%).[35] Militants were also involved in a Ghadar uprising in Lahore in March 1915 that the British infiltrated and stopped, although isolated bombings and armed robberies (dacoity, banditry) continued throughout the war.[36]

The Germans were helpful in the abortive Ghadar effort to smuggle weapons into India early in the war. The Berlin Committee had sent out Heramba Lal Gupta, who recruited men and tried to get weapons. The prospect of buying a million rifles in China seemed good until they learned that most were antiquated muzzle-loading models.[37] The German ambassador Count Bernstorff denied he was involved with smuggling arms shipments, but his colleagues were implicated. The military attaché and future German chancellor Franz von Papen, and the German consul in San Francisco, Franz Bopp, who had coordinated with Ram Chandra, admitted deep involvement.[38] By December 1914, von Papen had used his connections with the Krupp arms company representative Hans Tauscher, to secure 8,080 rifles, 2,400 carbines, 410 repeating rifles, 500 revolvers, 250 Mauser pistols, 4 million rounds of rifle ammunition, and 100,000 pistol cartridges. They smuggled the arms out of the United States on the schooner *Annie Larsen*, with the plan to rendezvous at the Mexican island of Socorro, and transfer the arms onto an oil tanker, the *Maverick*. When the two ships failed to make contact, despite several attempts, the *Maverick* made for Java without the weapons. The US government impounded the *Annie Larsen* when it returned to Seattle.[39] But even if the ships had made their rendezvous, the British already knew about the plot and were waiting when it arrived in Batavia.[40]

Other sites of resistance to the British across the Pacific included Singapore, which had only a light defense as the British had shipped most of their garrison to Europe in 1914. On 15 February 1915, about half the Indian garrison of 850 revolted. One of the three groups of rebels quickly freed German prisoners of war from the camp at Tanglin, and killed fourteen British and Indian loyalist soldiers.[41] German prisoners of war had told rebel Indian Ali Ulla that, in exchange for releasing them, they could escape within a few hours on a German ship. Once freed, however, seventeen *Emden* sailors immediately departed, eleven never to be recaptured, not sticking around long enough to help the Indian mutineers they had inspired to revolt.[42] The rebellion was over quickly as the British received help from local militias and a Russian navy ship. On 22 March 1915, the British convicted almost all of the 203 Indian troops they tried, hanging 41, transporting 63 for life, imprisoning 69 for 10–20 years, and 24 for six weeks to seven years.[43] Revealing the official Japanese position when forced to choose sides, the Japanese consul in Singapore was very active in suppressing the uprising, recruiting an impromptu militia of nearly two hundred to patrol the city, and sending a request to the Japanese government for naval reinforcements, although Russian and French ships arrived in Singapore to fill the need first.[44]

Hong Kong also was a site of Ghadar activity. The Ghadar publications noted a bombing incident across the Pacific, filtered through the Irish-American paper *Gaelic* in a notice entitled "Unrest in Hong Kong," which revealed the British had moved Germans to the south shore to separate them from British Indian Army troops there who were "trying to create a disturbance" by being "turbulent and disobedient to their officers."[45] The disturbance culminated in an assassination attempt, as "somebody had thrown a bomb at the Governor of Hong Kong … the man who threw the bomb had escaped, leaving no trace. Well done."[46]

Unlike British-held Hong Kong, the Philippines, as an American colony, was a useful neutral base in the Asian Pacific, more than halfway to India from California. From San Francisco, the Berlin Committee operative Jodh Singh went to Manila in the Philippines where, he later related in court, he had a conversation with the German Captain Boehm about the purchase of weapons.[47] Boehm "said he was going to buy arms and ammunition from a German firm in Manila and charter a boat and send them to Siam—Bangkok." The Americans were able to catch up with Boehm, however, finding him and several codefendants "guilty on October 20, 1917, of conspiracy and of violating the neutrality of the United States," sentencing him "to imprisonment in the Federal penitentiary at Leavenworth, Kansas, for two years, and to pay a fine of $10,000."[48]

By the end of the war, with the United States having entered on the Allied side, there was less room for even Americans with German heritage to move freely in the Far East. For example, an American consul in Batavia wrote in 1918 to officials in Manila, warning them about a German-American citizen, William Kessel, who was on a ship on his way there. Kessel was "a naturalized American citizen and by profession a Master Mariner ... [who] hopes on arrival in Manila to be able to obtain a berth on an American vessel, due to the shortage of officers to man our merchant fleet." Kessel, who had been in Batavia for several months, was a suspect because he had "been on terms of intimacy with German subjects [there,] and his conduct in this respect has been complained of a number of times. The undersigned has himself personally seen him in company with the German consul and other prominent Germans in Batavia during the past few days." Born in Germany and living twenty-nine years in California from 1888 to 1917, Kessel had become a naturalized citizen in 1895.[49] Thus even Germans who had lived in the United States for decades could not be trusted, especially if they were seen in German company. Yet there was good reason for this suspicion as seditious Indians and Germans did work together and shared common goals.

German contributions to joint wartime operations nevertheless suffered from many challenges. One was overoptimism based on a lack of accurate knowledge among Germans about modern South Asia. For example, the information the German Foreign Office had heard from the former Austro-Hungarian consul general in Calcutta, Count Thurn, was overoptimistic; he believed there were 250 South Asian secret revolutionary societies ready to spring into action.[50] The *Kreuz-Zeitung* received embellished reports of Indian revolutionaries from the Irish Sinn Fein leader George Freeman.[51] Another problem was that although German officials did their work reasonably well, when captured in their espionage work they had a tendency to talk easily.[52]

The Indians had their share of similar problems. Their vast distance from India caused confusion as many of the revolutionaries had been absent from home for years and were unaware of the current political developments there. In San Francisco, internal divisions emerged among the Ghadar leadership. These included the absent Har Dayal's successor Ram Chandra, who continued the Yugantar ashram and the *Ghadr* newspaper, facing down rivals Heramba Lal Gupta, who left for Japan to secure weapons, and Chandra K. Chakravarty, who arrived in February 1916 from Berlin.[53] Another challenge was the inexperience of the revolutionaries, which made them prone to carelessness. In New York City, they neglected to post a guard at night at their office, and Czech agents posing as employees broke in, infiltrating their organization and passing on the intelligence to the British.[54]

The wartime British had a difficult time getting the neutral American government to move against the Ghadar revolutionaries because of widespread Indian sympathies, especially among Americans of Irish and German descent.

The British efforts gained a boost when the anti-imperialist Secretary of State Williams Jennings Bryan resigned in June 1915.⁵⁵ The British made progress against the Indo-German network when the US Department of Justice raided German diplomatic offices in 1916 and then secured a conviction in January 1917 of the German consul general in San Francisco, Franz Bopp, for violating neutrality laws.⁵⁶ Ghadar leader Chakravarty confessed to being an agent of the German Berlin Committee.⁵⁷ The pendulum of state prosecution increasingly swung in favor of the British.

The United States entry into the war on 7 April 1917 provided the opportunity to bring an end to South Asian plots by making further arrests, including Chandra and sixteen South Asians in San Francisco, and a further seven, including three South Asians, in Chicago.⁵⁸ The Chicago trial was a test case that helped to set a precedent.⁵⁹ An even larger trial, the greatest in US legal history to that point, convened in San Francisco. On 1 May 1917, a grand jury indicted Chandra and seven other South Asians, while on 7 July the San Francisco grand jury returned secret indictments for conspiracy and violating neutrality against 105 men, and on 12 July they indicted 19 more.⁶⁰ Authorities apprehended only 35 of the 105 accused, including nine Germans, nine US citizens—four of whom were German immigrants—and seventeen South Asians.⁶¹ There was a history of the United States using the 1794 military expedition law to prosecute those who used its soil to organize foreign expeditions, including Irish Fenian revolutionaries and Cuban and Mexican *insurrectos*. Convictions were difficult, however, as there was public support for these foreign movements.⁶²

The San Francisco "Hindu Conspiracy" trial began on 20 November 1917, the government using many advantages to obtain a conviction against the defendants, who all pleaded not guilty.⁶³ The trial lasted five months, ending literally with a bang on 23 April 1918.⁶⁴ On the last day of the trial the defendant Ram Singh secretly brought a pistol into the courtroom after the midday break, approached the government witness Chandra, and shot him four times; then "Chandra staggered back and dropped dead at the foot of the witness stand." A court guard then shot Ram Singh, killing the assassin.⁶⁵ This dramatic ending did not inhibit the swift judgment, as the jury only took from that afternoon until midnight to return guilty verdicts for the defendants. Other than the two who were dead, one who was adjudged insane, and one who was found not guilty, there were twenty-nine convictions, the remainder of the 105 defendants either having fled abroad or were working as witnesses for the prosecution.⁶⁶ Among those convicted were most of the German diplomatic staff in North America, including San Francisco consul Franz Bopp, Eckhart H. von Schack, William von Brincken, Hans Tauscher, Franz von Papen, von Papen's assistant Wolf von Igel, the German consul in Honolulu George Rodiek, and Earnest Sekunna.⁶⁷

The "Hindu Conspiracy" trial contributed to changing perceptions in the United States about South Asians, leading to stricter immigration restrictions and inhibiting South Asian revolutionary activities. In 1923 the Supreme Court excluded "Hindus" from citizenship, invalidating the citizenship of almost sixty naturalized South Asians.[68] As Joan Jensen has argued, "[w]hat the trial had done was to make the United States less a land of liberty. It openly arrayed the United States government against the movement for political liberation in India, and put a seal of disapproval on participation by Americans in that movement."[69] The work of Germans such as von Papen and Bopp, who supplied South Asians with resources to carry out their revolutionary activities, and the context of wartime hatred contributed to these shifting perceptions. The Americans and British worked together on the global repression of Ghadar, which corresponded to the emergence of a greater economic and political postwar threat: the Red Scare and the suppression of Bolsheviks.[70] The trial would have a larger significance and lasting impact as part of a crackdown on subversion, eclipsing the United States as a base for revolutionary and rebel forces like it had been before World War I.

Although not successful in the short run, parts of the liberation ideology of these overseas Indians across the Pacific during World War I would play a crucial role in eventual Indian independence, and in inspiring anticolonial movements around the world. It is important to look beyond the Indian or German nationalist frame, and seek the international dimensions of these Indian revolutionaries in key cities around the Pacific Rim such as San Francisco, Vancouver, Tokyo, Hong Kong, and Singapore.[71] Indians shared international experiences first as soldiers in the British Empire, and then as laborers in North America, where they faced racist North American hostility, epitomized by the 1914 *Komagatu Maru* incident of refused immigration entry to Canada. Indians saw Japanese treated with more respect in North America, they believed, because there was a Japanese Empire looking out for them, while Indians were subjugated by the British.[72] The international space where the Ghadar movement operated with German help forged tools for eventual independence. Before Gandhi returned to India from South Africa, cosmopolitan Punjabis had realized a secular approach to uniting Indians that eventually informed mass movements. The German role was crucial in providing material support and encouragement to Indian nationalists during both world wars. Germany's defeat and humiliation at Versailles in 1919 meant that the relationship of mutual adversaries to a rival global British Empire would continue through the interwar era and into the Second World War. Weimar Berlin was a meeting place for Indian nationalists, including young Jawaharlal Nehru, and, during World War II, for Subhas Chandra Bose.[73] Bose organized a "Free" Indian legion among Indian prisoners of war in Germany and met Hitler, gaining transportation on a U-boat back to Asia to support the Japanese war effort in Burma.[74] Through support for the Ghadar and subsequent Indian nationalists, Germans contributed to eventual Indian independence mediated through trans-Pacific links.

Douglas T. McGetchin is associate professor of history at Florida Atlantic University. He is the author of *Indology, Indomania, Orientalism: Ancient India's Rebirth in Modern Germany* (Fairleigh Dickinson University Press, 2009), and co-editor with Joanne Miyang Cho of *Gendered Encounters between Germany and Asia* (Palgrave Macmillan, 2017). He received a Fulbright-Nehru Senior Scholar Research Award in 2013/14 to conduct research in Kolkata (Calcutta) India.

Notes

1. For more on the idea of entanglement and Indo-European cultural exchange in the nineteenth and twentieth centuries, see Kris Manjapra, *Age of Entanglement: German and Indian Intellectuals across Empire* (Cambridge, MA: Harvard University Press, 2013).
2. Historical assessments of the South Asian activities during the war began at the trials toward the end of World War I, as formulated by the prosecuting United States attorney, who presented the South Asian defendants as "reprehensible but relatively ineffectual," although paradoxically their conspiracy had "permeated and encircled the whole globe" in coordination with Germans. Joan M. Jensen, "The 'Hindu Conspiracy': A Reassessment," *The Pacific Historical Review* 48, no. 1 (1979): 65. Newly available archival sources in the late 1950s undermined this first version as scholars such as Arun Coomer Bose questioned these negative interpretations, choosing instead to interpret the movement positively as a "prelude to national self-determination" (ibid.: 66). Don K. Dignan, "The Hindu Conspiracy in Anglo-American Relations during World War I," *Pacific Historical Review* 40, no. 1 (1971): 57–76.
3. Harold Gould, *Sikhs, Swamis, Students, and Spies: The India Lobby in the United States, 1900–1946* (New Delhi: Sage, 2006), 78.
4. Immigration of Indians to the United States: less than 100 up to 1904; 5,762 (577/year) 1901–10; 1,562 (156/year) 1911–20; 1,177 (118/year) 1921–30; 131 (13/year) 1931–41; total 8,632 plus up to another 100. Gould, *Sikhs*, 90–91.
5. Harish K. Puri, *Ghadar Movement to Bhagat Singh: A Collection of Essays* (Ludhiana, India: Unistar, 2012), 53.
6. Dignan, "Hindu Conspiracy," 61.
7. This modification to Canadian immigration law had occurred in 1910. Baba Gurdit Singh, *Voyage of Komagata Maru or India's Slavery Abroad*, edited by Darshan S. Tatla (Chandigarh, India: Unistar Books, [1928] 2007), 11.
8. The total of 376 onboard included passengers from Hong Kong (150), Shanghai (111), Moji, Japan (86), and Yokohama (11). There were 24 Muslims, 12 Hindus, and 340 Sikhs. Singh, *Voyage of Komagata Maru*, 50.
9. Maia Ramnath, *Haj to Utopia: How the Ghadar Movement Charted Global Radicalism and Attempted to Overthrow the British Empire* (Berkeley: University of California Press, 2011), 3.
10. Gould, *Sikhs*, 135–37.
11. Dignan, "Hindu Conspiracy," 64.
12. Nirode K. Barooah, *India and the Official Germany* (Frankfurt a.M.: Peter Lang, 1977), 183.
13. Dignan, "Hindu Conspiracy," 61–62.
14. Jensen, "Hindu Conspiracy," 70.
15. Ibid., 73.
16. Ibid., 74.
17. Night of 30/31 July 1914. Michael Leonard Graham Balfour, *The Kaiser and His Times* (New York: Norton, 1972), 352. There was a Berlin to Baghdad railroad project linking Germany to

the Ottoman Empire. James Joll and Gordon Martel, *The Origins of the First World War*, 3rd ed. (New York: Pearson Longman, 2006), 236–41.
18. Earl E. Sperry and Willis M. West, *German Plots and Intrigues in the United States during the Period of Our Neutrality* (Washington, DC: Committee on Public Information, 1918), 8. The authors were history professors at Syracuse University (Sperry) and the University of Minnesota (West).
19. Giles T. Brown, "The Hindu Conspiracy, 1914–1917," *Pacific Historical Review* 17, no. 3 (1948): 306.
20. Heribert von Feilitzsch, *The Secret War Council: The German Fight against the Entente in America in 1914* (Amissville, VA: Henselstone Verlag, 2015), 181.
21. Dignan, "Hindu Conspiracy," 65.
22. Sister Nivedita (the Irish Margaret Noble) wrote the introduction for Okakura's *Ideals of the East*. Kakuzo Okakura, *The Ideals of the East with Special Reference to the Art of Japan*, 2nd ed. (New York: E. P. Dutton, 1904); Arun Bose, *Indian Revolutionaries Abroad, 1905–1922, in the Background of International Developments* (Patna, India: Bharati Bhawan, 1971), 9n28; Hiren Chakrabarti, *Political Protest in Bengal: Boycott and Terrorism 1905–18* (Calcutta, India: Papyrus, 1992), 46–47, 72; Peter Heehs, *Nationalism, Terrorism, Communalism: Essays in Modern Indian History* (Delhi: Oxford University Press, 1998), 2–3, 72.
23. Seema Sohi, *Echoes of Mutiny: Race, Surveillance and Indian Anticolonialism in North America* (Oxford: Oxford University Press, 2014), 158.
24. The British named Bose as an "arch conspirator" who had "absconded." Malwinderjit Singh Waraich and Harish Jain, eds., *First Lahore Conspiracy Case: Mercy Petition* (Chandigarh, India: Unistar, 2010), 16.
25. Sohi, *Echoes of Mutiny*, 163.
26. Peter Ward Fay, *The Forgotten Army: India's Armed Struggle for Independence 1942–1945* (Ann Arbor: University of Michigan Press, 1995), 202.
27. Emphasis in original. "Indian Soldiers! Do Not Fight with Germany," pamphlet, United States National Archives, San Francisco (San Bruno, California), RG118, Box 1, Folder 2.
28. "Ghadr" Extracts Issue of 21 July 1914, United States National Archives, San Francisco (San Bruno, California), RG118, Box 1, Folder 2.
29. "Opportunity for Mutiny in India," United States National Archives, San Francisco (San Bruno, California), RG118, Box 1, Folder 2.
30. Sohi, *Echoes of Mutiny*, 153.
31. Bose, *Indian Revolutionaries Abroad*, 168.
32. Sohi, *Echoes of Mutiny*, 155–56.
33. Brown, "Hindu Conspiracy," 300.
34. Typically, two became witnesses for the British government. Sohi, *Echoes of Mutiny*, 156–57.
35. Ibid.; Thomas G. Fraser, "Germany and Indian Revolution, 1914–18," *Journal of Contemporary History* 12, no. 2 (1977): 260.
36. Bose, *Indian Revolutionaries Abroad*, 224.
37. Brown, "Hindu Conspiracy," 301.
38. Fraser, "Germany and Indian Revolution," 261–63. The first Sanskrit professor appointed to the University of Berlin in 1821 was also named Franz Bopp. Franz von Papen, *Memoirs*, trans. Brian Connell (New York: E. P. Dutton, 1953).
39. Nirode K. Barooah, *Chatto: The Life and Times of an Indian Anti-Imperialist in Europe* (New Delhi: Oxford University Press, 2004), 77. Heribert von Feilitzsch, *The Secret War Council: The German Fight against the Entente in America in 1914* (Amissville, VA: Henselstone Verlag, 2015), 207, 219.
40. Jensen, "Hindu Conspiracy," 73.

41. Heather Streets-Salter, "The Local Was Global: The Singapore Mutiny of 1915," *Journal of World History* 24, no. 3 (September 2013): 540. Dignan, "Hindu Conspiracy," 64.
42. Streets-Salter, "Local Was Global," 558.
43. Ibid., 539–540.
44. Ibid., 565–66, 570.
45. "Ghadr" Extracts, Issue of 29 August 1915 [*sic*: 1914], United States National Archives, San Francisco (San Bruno, California), RG118, Box 1, Folder 2.
46. Ibid.
47. For Jodh Singh's wider activities, see Sohi, *Echoes of Mutiny*, 168–70.
48. The other defendants were Jacobsen, Wehde, and Gupta. Sperry and West, *German Plots*, 50–51.
49. Copy of letter, Horace J. Dickinson, American Consul, American Consular Service, Batavia, Java, 1 March 1918, to the Insular Collector or Customs, Manila, Philippine Islands. United States National Archives, San Francisco (San Bruno, California), RG118, Box 4, Folder 2.
50. Fraser, "Germany and Indian Revolution," 259.
51. Barooah, *Chatto*, 35.
52. Bose, *Indian Revolutionaries Abroad*, 230.
53. Barooah, *India and the Official Germany*, 183. Brown, "Hindu Conspiracy," 300–1, 305.
54. Bose, *Indian Revolutionaries Abroad*, 232–33. Fraser, "Germany and Indian Revolution," 257. The American investigators used a new system of surveillance that appeared as "Phone Dope," or telephone conversation wiretaps, most likely by having someone listen in and take shorthand notes, as telephone recording equipment was extremely rudimentary if not nonexistent. United States National Archives, San Francisco (San Bruno, California), RG 118, Box 11, Folder 4b.
55. Dignan, "Hindu Conspiracy," 64.
56. Dignan, "Hindu Conspiracy," 71. Jensen, "Hindu Conspiracy," 78. United States v. Bopp, 230 Fed. 723 (1916).
57. Dignan, "Hindu Conspiracy," 73. Brown, "Hindu Conspiracy," 307.
58. Brown, "Hindu Conspiracy," 308.
59. Sohi, *Echoes of Mutiny*, 185.
60. Jensen, "Hindu Conspiracy," 80–81. Brown, "Hindu Conspiracy," 308.
61. Dignan, "Hindu Conspiracy," 57.
62. Jensen, "Hindu Conspiracy," 68.
63. Jensen, "Hindu Conspiracy," 81. Brown, "Hindu Conspiracy," 308.
64. Dignan, "Hindu Conspiracy," 58.
65. Brown, "Hindu Conspiracy," 309.
66. Ibid., 310.
67. Sperry and West, *German Plots*, 47.
68. Dignan, "Hindu Conspiracy," 76.
69. Jensen, "Hindu Conspiracy," 83.
70. Sohi, *Echoes of Mutiny*, 210.
71. Harald Fischer-Tiné, "Indian Nationalism and the 'World Forces': Transnational and Diasporic Dimensions of the Indian Freedom Movement on the Eve of the First World War," *Journal of Global History* 2 (2007): 325. Streets-Salter, "The Local Was Global," 542, 576.
72. Puri, *Ghadar Movement*, 22.
73. Michele Louro, *Comrades against Imperialism: Nehru, India, and Interwar Internationalism* (Cambridge: Cambridge University Press, 2018), 29–30.
74. Sugata Bose, *His Majesty's Opponent: Subhas Chandra Bose and India's Struggle against Empire* (Cambridge, MA: Harvard University Press, 2011), 201. Michele Louro, *Comrades against Imperialism: Nehru, India, and Interwar Internationalism* (Cambridge: Cambridge University Press, 2018).

Bibliography

Balfour, Michael Leonard Graham. *The Kaiser and His Times*. New York: Norton, 1972.

Barooah, Nirode K. *Chatto: The Life and Times of an Indian Anti-Imperialist in Europe*. New Delhi: Oxford University Press, 2004.

Barooah, Nirode K. *India and the Official Germany*. Frankfurt a.M.: Peter Lang, 1977.

Bose, Arun. *Indian Revolutionaries Abroad, 1905–1922, in the Background of International Developments*. Patna, India: Bharati Bhawan, 1971.

Bose, Sugata. *His Majesty's Opponent: Subhas Chandra Bose and India's Struggle against Empire*. Cambridge, MA: Harvard University Press, 2011.

Brown, Giles T. "The Hindu Conspiracy, 1914–1917." *Pacific Historical Review* 17, no. 3 (1948): 299–310. http://www.jstor.org/stable/3634258. Accessed 29 June 2018.

Chakrabarti, Hiren. *Political Protest in Bengal: Boycott and Terrorism 1905–18*. Calcutta, India: Papyrus, 1992.

Dignan, Don K. "The Hindu Conspiracy in Anglo-American Relations during World War I." *Pacific Historical Review* 40, no. 1 (1971): 57–76.

Fay, Peter Ward. *The Forgotten Army: India's Armed Struggle for Independence 1942–1945*. Ann Arbor: University of Michigan Press, 1995.

Fischer-Tiné, Harald. "Indian Nationalism and the 'World Forces': Transnational and Diasporic Dimensions of the Indian Freedom Movement on the Eve of the First World War." *Journal of Global History* 2 (2007): 325–44.

Fraser, Thomas G. "Germany and Indian Revolution, 1914–18." *Journal of Contemporary History* 12, no. 2 (1977): 255–72.

Gould, Harold. *Sikhs, Swamis, Students, and Spies: The India Lobby in the United States, 1900–1946*. New Delhi: Sage, 2006.

Heehs, Peter. *Nationalism, Terrorism, Communalism: Essays in Modern Indian History*. Delhi: Oxford University Press, 1998.

Jensen, Joan M. "The 'Hindu Conspiracy': A Reassessment." *The Pacific Historical Review* 48, no. 1 (1979): 65–83.

Joll, James, and Gordon Martel. *The Origins of the First World War*, 3rd ed. New York: Pearson Longman, 2006.

Louro, Michele. *Comrades against Imperialism: Nehru, India, and Interwar Internationalism* Cambridge: Cambridge University Press, 2018.

Manjapra, Kris. *Age of Entanglement: German and Indian Intellectuals across Empire*. Cambridge, MA: Harvard University Press, 2013.

Okakura, Kakuzo. *The Ideals of the East with Special Reference to the Art of Japan*. 2nd ed. New York: E. P. Dutton, 1904.

Puri, Harish K. *Ghadar Movement to Bhagat Singh: A Collection of Essays*. Ludhiana, India: Unistar, 2012.

Ramnath, Maia. *Haj to Utopia: How the Ghadar Movement Charted Global Radicalism and Attempted to Overthrow the British Empire*. Berkeley: University of California Press, 2011.

Singh, Baba Gurdit. *Voyage of Komagata Maru or India's Slavery Abroad*, edited by Darshan S. Tatla. Chandigarh, India: Unistar Books, [1928] 2007.

Sohi, Seema. *Echoes of Mutiny: Race, Surveillance and Indian Anticolonialism in North America*. Oxford: Oxford University Press, 2014.

Sperry, Earl E., and Willis M. West. *German Plots and Intrigues in the United States during the Period of Our Neutrality*. Washington, DC: Committee on Public Information, 1918. https://archive.org/details/germanplotsintri00sper. Accessed 1 March 2015.

Streets-Salter, Heather. "The Local Was Global: The Singapore Mutiny of 1915." *Journal of World History* 24, no. 3 (September 2013): 539–76.

von Feilitzsch, Heribert. *The Secret War Council: The German Fight against the Entente in America in 1914*. Amissville, VA: Henselstone Verlag, 2015.

von Papen, Franz. *Memoirs*, trans. Brian Connell. New York: E. P. Dutton, 1953.

Waraich, Malwinderjit Singh, and Harish Jain, eds. *First Lahore Conspiracy Case: Mercy Petition*. Chandigarh, India: Unistar, 2010.

Chapter 13

THE VAVA'U GERMANS

History and Identity Construction of a Transcultural Community with Tongan and Pomeranian Roots

Reinhard Wendt

On 11 January 2014, Makanesi Wolfgramm died in Salt Lake City at the age of 89. He had been born in Vava'u, a group of islands in the north of the Tongan archipelago, as the son of Charles Fredrick Wolfgramm and Salome Fo'ou Afu, and the grandson of a German immigrant from Pyritz in Pomerania. At his memorial service, not only the outpouring of compassion and sympathy were remarkable, but also the impressive number of symbols referring back to the Pacific Islands. The most striking of these was the "fahu throne," a seat embellished with fine mats, embroidered plaiting, and shell jewelry, upon which the fahu, the dignitary presiding over the ceremony, sat. In Tongan tradition, the position of fahu is always held by a woman—specifically, by the oldest daughter or sister in the family clan.[1] On this occasion, as the oldest daughter of Makanesi's oldest paternal aunt, Liahoni Moleni—who herself has German, Tongan, Maori, and British roots—held that role.[2]

In October 2011, I had the opportunity to interview Makanesi at his home in the company of his cousin, Malina Wolfgramm Henderson. When I entered his living room, my attention was caught by three portraits on display on one of the walls. On the far left was a photo of Friedrich Gustav Ludwig Wolfgramm, Makanesi's German grandfather; in the middle, a picture of Kisaea Sisifa Tu'inahoki, Friedrich's first wife and Makanesi's grandmother; and on the right, a portrait of Martha Emilie Sanft, Friedrich's second wife and once-removed cousin, who had a German father and a Tongan mother. Martha was also Liahona's grandmother. During the interview, I asked Makanesi what this German grandfather meant to him. Both Makanesi and Malina replied that they were proud of their German heritage. Makanesi further explained that the Tongans had always attributed German traits to him and his family: "Tongan

---

Notes from this chapter begin on page 305.

people, they look to us, and we do something good, and they say 'oh, that's your German blood' … They look to us working hard all the time, and they know, oh, working hard because you are German."³

Already these few clues from the memorial service and the interview suffice to reveal the contours of this group of people, who, although they live in the United States, are rooted in different cultures and still cultivate practices and use symbols that connect them with Tonga and Tongan traditions. Concomitantly, they also maintain the awareness of a German facet to their identity. I have thus called them "the Vava'u Germans."

In the first part of this chapter, I describe this group's history for the period between the mid-nineteenth century, when the first pioneers set out to Vava'u from Pyritz, and the start of World War I, when the political and economic situation took a turn for the worse for them and second-and third-generation members looked for a better life beyond the borders of Tonga, somewhere else in the Pacific region. These historical developments are highlighted in three points: I start by sketching the biography of Makanesi's grandfather, Friedrich Wolfgramm, to exemplify a first-generation German in Vava'u; then, I place him in the context of the chain migration he was part of, and which brought him and other fortune seekers from Pyritz to Vava'u. As the third point, I illustrate what life was like in Oceania, which culminated in a "golden era" in the years before World War I.⁴ Remembrance of this history helped, and still helps, this group not to dissipate across the vastness of the Pacific, but to foster a cultural memory that unites them across time and space, and maintains their identity as "Vava'u Germans."

The second part deals with this selective and evaluative use of the past. Here, I first touch on their dispersion, to illustrate the significance and strength of this cultural memory as a force capable of maintaining cohesion across huge distances. While the relationship to Tonga plays a decisive role in this respect, remembrance of Germany and a sense of having a certain "Germanness" is also always present, and constitutes a further identity marker. I will, therefore, conclude by focusing on this important facet of the Vava'u Germans' self-perception.

Neither their ancestors' migration to the Pacific, nor their integration into the local society, nor the identity-endowing factor of having a multicultural heritage make this group exceptional. Similar cases can be found on many other islands in the region. They all represent a distinct and important part of the history of Germans in the Pacific, especially when seen under transcultural aspects—and, hence, perhaps are often overlooked. The Vava'u Germans, who arose from a handful of immigrants and now constitute a community of many thousands, are part of this history.⁵

The Vava'u Germans and Their History

Friedrich Gustav Ludwig Wolfgramm

Friedrich Wolfgramm, also called "Fritz" or "Feleti," was born in 1856, in a rural settlement just outside Pyritz proper. His father and his grandfather were farmers, but neither Fritz nor any of his brothers continued in this family tradition. Despite the fact that the agricultural sector as a whole flourished after the manorial system had been abolished throughout Germany and the growing towns offered good marketing potential, smaller farmers—as we must assume the Wolfgramms to have been—gained little from this upswing. From 1875 on, better quality grain was imported into the German market at lower prices.[6] This was an unfavorable situation even for large landowners, and it is not surprising that Fritz chose to be trained as a watchmaker instead. He never really worked in his trade, however, as he already left Germany for Vava'u on 14 March 1881, sailing from Hamburg onboard the German sailing vessel *Taikun*. He was accompanied by his younger brother, Franz Otto. After a tempestuous crossing via Australia and New Zealand, the brothers arrived in Apia, Samoa on 3 August. Only a day later, they boarded the *Daphne*, a schooner under the command of Captain Schröder, and shortly afterwards landed in Neiafu, the capital of the Vava'u islands.[7]

Several relatives from Pyritz already lived there and had established trading footholds. Initially, Fritz worked for some of them, but soon started an import–export business of his own. He became a successful trader with the export of copra, the dried meat of coconuts, and the import of goods from Europe, Australia, and the United States. His main store was in Neiafu, but he also maintained several branches and outposts.[8] He also ran plantations on which he primarily grew coconuts, as well as oranges, lemons, and tangerines. From New Zealand, he imported sheep and cattle to stock his farms, along with chickens and pigs. With horse carts and boats, he delivered goods to his trading stations and brought other products back to Neiafu. In part, he produced copra himself, but he largely obtained it from the locals, whom he encouraged to plant more coconut trees, conceivably not only to strengthen Vava'u's economy, but also his own position. Fritz thus played a leading role in the business world of Vava'u.

When World War I broke out, Fritz, like the other Vava'u Germans, had to give up his business and was declared an "enemy alien."[9] Because he had a Tongan wife and children, he was allowed to resume his work after 1918. In the interim, however, he had lost much ground to business competitors from Australia and New Zealand. Although he remained comfortably situated, the days of the "golden era" were past.

Fritz married twice, and both times chose his wife cleverly. His first wife, Kisaea, opened the gates to the local elite for him. After her death in 1898, he married Martha Sanft, who was his junior by thirty years, and thus joined the two most prosperous Vava'u German families and bundled their potential. Martha was active in business matters and is said to have been both spirited and assertive. In the period of religious reorientation that all the Vava'u Germans had to go through because the Lutheran Church was not represented on Vava'u, she was one of the first to join the Mormon Church—against the will of her husband, who would rather have seen her as a Catholic.[10]

Fritz's magnificent home, overlooking the harbor of Neiafu, reflected his social and economic status. It bore the name Vaha'akeli, and had business and residential functions. While the ground floor encompassed the shop and storage rooms, the upper floor was used as the living quarter. A verandah of sorts abutted the private rooms, which were furnished and decorated in the European style. Louvre windows provided shade, let air circulate, and kept the rooms cool. It is even said that a tennis court had been built on the rooftop terrace for the convenience of those inclined to play. At the waterfront, there was a shed and a jetty. Fritz hosted dinner parties and dances, served drinks to friends and relatives from his extensive assortment of alcoholic beverages, and made Vaha'akeli the center of social life in Neiafu.

Out of his two marriages and a relationship, Fritz had a total of fourteen children. Of those who lived to adulthood, only one remained in Tonga. Initially, some of Fritz's children were sent to Pyritz for schooling, but all save one soon died there because they could not withstand the rough climate. The others eventually left Tonga for New Zealand or the United States. Fritz died in 1937 and is buried in the European cemetery in Neiafu along with Martha, who outlived him until 1942. A simple headstone carved out of red granite still marks their grave.[11]

The Chain Migration from Pyritz to Vava'u

Fritz Wolfgramm was part of a clearly delineated group of twenty-five immigrants—twenty-two men and three women—who were closely linked to each other in numerous ways. Nineteen of these people were related to each other by family ties; twenty-one were from Pyritz and, in one way or another, they were all involved in the import–export business I described for Fritz Wolfgramm's case.

At the beginning of every chain migration there is a successful "pioneer." In this case, the pioneer was August Sanft, a baker born in Pyritz in 1822. In convoluted ways that are not fully clear to me, he ended up in the South Pacific. The first record I have for him there dates to 1862. At that time, he had already established a successful trading business in Neiafu.[12]

August Sanft soon saw himself in a position to be able keep a family; he sent for his fiancée, Sophie Dörner, to join him, and they married in 1864. It is likely that he also wrote to friends and relatives at home about the opportunities the

South Pacific offered, because only a short time later, in 1866, his nephew, Carl Friedrich Wolfgramm—a cousin of Makanesi's grandfather, Fritz—also traveled to Tonga.

In the period before 1914, the other twenty-two people gradually joined the chain migration. Their fathers had been craftsmen, tradesmen, or farmers. Although some, like Fritz Wolfgramm, did not take over their fathers' businesses, all remained within their parents' socioeconomic stratum. Most had been trained as craftsmen and were bakers, butchers, coopers, watchmakers, carpenters, or smiths. We only find two people with agricultural training and three with commercial or accounting skills. With the exception of one Catholic woman and one Jewish man, all of the others were Lutherans. They all spoke German, flavored predominantly with a Pomeranian accent or, maybe, interspersed with smatterings of *Platt* (Low German).

Evidence suggests that the reasons for this migration to the South Pacific were less economic "push" than the "pull" factor of opportunities in Vava'u. For these, the immigrants traded a moderate climate, changing seasons, and the softly undulating hills of the Weizacker region around Pyritz, with its fertile fields and meadows. At the time, Pyritz was a romantic town of about five thousand inhabitants. It was encircled by a wall with towers and gates, and half-timbered houses lined the narrow alleys and two main streets.[13] Although the immigrants sought their fortunes in the South Pacific, they were not fleeing poverty or disaffection. On the contrary, there is much to suggest that they carried a positive image of their hometown along with them.

Emigration files document that these people knew exactly where they were heading, and named the "Friendly Islands" or Vava'u as their destination. This observation is supported by the fact that Fritz Wolfgramm sailed straight to Neaifu without any long stopovers. He and others of the group organized the trips themselves, without resorting to the services of an agent.[14] The journey to the Pacific was thus less adventurous and less unusual than one may assume today.

German captains not only sailed their ships along routes from the North Sea to the South Seas, they also operated a network of shipping lines between the islands of the South Pacific. This infrastructure was based on the circumstance that, since the first half of the nineteenth century, Germans settled on all of the larger and many of the smaller islands of the Pacific region. They were a colorful crowd, encompassing everything from former whalers, sailors, beachcombers, fortune seekers, and missionaries to planters, traders, and captains, who were not only intrepid and venturous, but definitely also had an entrepreneurial mindset.[15] In terms of socioeconomic status, they usually came in second to the British, but occasionally held the leading position. All in all, the German presence grew to be quite significant and extended far beyond the area of the later colonies. Pro-colonialists therefore liked to refer to the South Pacific as a "German Sea."[16] The Vava'u Germans were part of this crowd and held the lion's share of the trade business in the northern Tongan Islands until 1914. Their contemporaries already noted that these Germans were closely connected families from Pyritz "whose ranks were constantly being replenished by the arrival of further relatives."[17]

There were consistent endeavors to encourage initially Prussia, and later the German Reich, to take a more active stand in the region to protect the interests of these Germans. In 1881, Hugo Zöller, a journalist and colonial propagandist, wrote that the South Pacific could be seen as "a small continent, albeit one that was made up of hundreds of islands," in which there was ample room for German colonies, and he appealed that appropriate steps be taken in this direction.[18] Such calls for action did not meet with success until 1884, when the flag of the German Reich was hoisted over the northwestern corner of New Guinea. In 1885, the Marshall Islands became German, and, in 1899, the Caroline Islands and Western Samoa also. Great Britain had relinquished its Samoan claims when Germany gave up her interests in part of the Solomon Islands and in Tonga.[19]

Life in the Islands

Thirteen of the people who participated in this chain migration remained in Vava'u for the rest of their lives. Others stayed for many years before returning to Germany or moving on to New Zealand. The jump from Pomerania to Polynesia led to profound changes in their daily lives and in their businesses. On the one hand, the standards, values, and rules of conduct of the Tongan society became increasingly dominant; on the other, the immigrants were also children of their time, and they likely took for granted that Europe dominated the world. They may also have considered European culture to be the most highly developed and progressive, even if they—in accordance with the spirit of the nineteenth century—may also have held a romanticized image of the South Pacific in their minds.[20]

Home was now a place that, in the 1870s, consisted of only a few small European houses and local *fales* scattered over the slopes of a hill in the shade of palms and other trees. August Sanft initially lived in such a Tongan *fale* with his family, and the first people to have followed him would at first also have found a home in housing of this kind. Such *fales* had an oval floor plan and walls constructed of wooden posts and braided palm fronds. Their saddle-back roofs were also thatched with palm leaves, and the floors were strewn coral limestone pebbles, covered with woven Pandanus mats.[21]

The immigrants were now no longer craftsmen or farmers, but traders. The most pressing task at first would have been to get to know the details of the copra business. To some extent, they bought copra from locals, and it was, therefore, crucial for them to be able to recognize its quality. Some immigrants, however, produced the copra themselves. To this end, they had to learn how to build and operate wood-fired drying kilns. Further, in order to properly stock and run their stores, they had to understand customer needs and marketing strategies.

The typical assortment of goods that could be found in a German store in Vava'u were salted meat, canned corned beef, fish, bread, biscuits, butter in tins, cooking oil, flour, salt, sugar, tea, tobacco, sweets, medicines, seeds, matches, kerosene, bowls, shoes, clothing, scarves, various textiles made of silk or cashmere wool, draperies, ribbons, umbrellas, nails, spades, axes, building materials for houses including zinc sheets for roofs, sewing machines, card decks, harmonicas, exercise books, and slates. Standard supplies were spiced up with modern, hitherto unknown commodities. Some of the Vava'u Germans also tapped into new business sectors in which they fell back on skills they had acquired in Germany, and worked as bakers, butchers, or carpenters. They planted orchards, bred animals, and established a hotel.[22]

Some married Europeans, but most chose women of mixed Western–Polynesian, Samoan, and especially Tongan descent as partners. Such relations were economically favorable because immigrants were barred from owning land by Tongan law.[23] Marriages into leading families made it easier to lease plantations or be preferentially supplied with coconuts. However, by taking such a step, they—in the diction of the racist-colonialist discourse of the time—"went native," ceased being German, and "sank" to the cultural level of their wives.[24] In contrast, the Germans were seen as good matches from a Tongan perspective because they facilitated access to Western technological innovations and goods. The women introduced their German husbands to Polynesian standards and norms, and familiarized them with the fact that Tongan society had its set social strata, that family interests took priority over those of the individual, and that a person's status was defined largely by kinship and ancestry.[25]

The second generation of Vava'u Germans already comprised about one hundred people. Their skin color was no longer white, but brown in various shades. In the eyes of the Tongans, they were quarter- or half-castes. Thus, although their fathers were integrated in the local society as friends, spouses, or business partners, they were not considered to be "truly" Tongan. However, although the Tongans saw them as being different and foreign, they did not discriminate against them. In contrast, the racist European ideology of the time considered children of mixed descent to have inherited the worst traits from both parents.[26]

The Vava'u Germans stood and lived between and across cultures. To be able to compete in the business world, they had to learn English and Tongan, with the latter as the dominant language in their private domain. German, they now only spoke among themselves. As the example of Fritz Wolfgramm elucidates, the Vava'u Germans also had to reorient themselves in terms of religion. Some joined the Wesleyan community, while others became Catholics. It is conspicuous that many of them felt drawn to newly developed religious movements that were only marginally represented in Europe, such as the Seventh Day Adventists,

Jehovah's Witnesses, and, especially, the Mormons. Besides their mother tongue and religion, they also lost their nationality if they failed to register at a consulate within ten years of leaving Germany. Many therefore became stateless.

The history of the Vava'u Germans should not, however, be understood as a tale of loss or parting. Many of the immigrants from Pyritz settled in quickly. Overall, they were economically successful and enjoyed a social status they could never have attained in Pyritz. They demonstrated their status and success by building new, European-style houses, for they did not care to live in Tongan *fales* longer than necessary. To them, modern, "civilized" Western standards were indispensable, even in the tropics. The only adaptations they made to the architecture of their houses were concessions to the climate, as Fritz Wolfgramm's home, Vaha'akeli, showed.

Through their economic activities and cultural innovations, the Germans contributed to Neiafu's development and growth. A main road, lined with the homes and stores of the Germans, was built parallel to the harbor. Tongans followed their example and also started building Western houses. In the European cemetery—which they most likely helped found—many of the Vava'u Germans were laid to rest.[27]

Although Neiafu had by no means ever been an isolated place, and maintained close contacts not only within the Tongan Islands but also with Samoa and Fiji, the Vava'u Germans were still instrumental in opening the town up to the world market. They used, developed, and intensified the trade routes that linked Neiafu with harbors, both near and faraway. In the beginning, Apia, in Samoa, played the most prominent role. However, when British influence grew in Tonga after 1900, Fiji gained importance and the Vava'u Germans procured goods from there as well as from Sydney; but over time, Auckland became the place with which they had the most intense contact. They also maintained ties back to Pyritz, and it may be assumed that there was a steady flow of correspondence back and forth, of which, unfortunately, only fragments have survived. Several journeys of Vava'u Germans to Pyritz and back are, however, documented.[28]

In economic respects, the Vava'u Germans helped put Neiafu on the map with regional and transregional business contacts, and, in sociocultural respects, contributed to listing Neiafu among the places where white expatriates lived. They were part of the audience the *Pacific Islands Monthly* wrote for. This periodical supplied white residents in the central and southern parts of the Pacific Ocean with news, biographical information, obituaries, wedding and birth announcements, printed passenger lists, and social event reports.[29] In keeping with this lifestyle, the Vava'u Germans sent their children abroad for schooling—in the early years, to Pyritz, and later, primarily to Auckland. The Vava'u Germans wanted their sons and daughters to be able to take over their businesses and to succeed in a world beyond the borders of Vava'u. Auckland also became a destination for Vava'u Germans to seek medical treatment or to enjoy the European-influenced culture.

A new social environment developed around the Vava'u Germans, to which their wives adapted and into which their sons and daughters grew. Although they assimilated Polynesian values and traditions, they also saw themselves as a group of internationally minded people, committed to the Western values of their time. When they invited people to their homes for receptions or dances, or when they met informally in the Vava'u Club in Neiafu, they publicly demonstrated Western social behavior. The new products they offered in their stores and the new businesses they started influenced the people of Neiafu in their eating habits, fashions, and cultural ways. A small group of Pomeranians transformed into a transcultural community and, at the same time, triggered sociocultural change in Vava'u.

Recalling History: Cultural Memory and Identity Construction of the Vava'u Germans

Formation of a Transcultural Community across the Pacific

When World War I broke out, the situation for the Vava'u Germans changed dramatically: they became "enemy aliens" and some were even interned.[30] As mentioned in Fritz Wolfgramm's case, they experienced economic disadvantages. These difficulties deepened when the world market prices for copra sank.[31] The already strained relations with the British authorities became even tenser in the 1930s, when some of the Vava'u Germans were reputed to hold sympathies for the Third Reich. At the outbreak of World War II, some of them were again interned.[32] An additional push factor can be seen in the fact that they set great store in educating their children, although there were few opportunities for well-trained young people in Tonga. More and more of them thus looked beyond Tonga for a future, and left. The places with which they had maintained business contacts developed into destinations for an onward migration: first Samoa, Fiji, and, in greater measure, New Zealand; later, Australia and the United States.

Today, the Vava'u Germans live scattered between Sydney and San Francisco, between Auckland and Anchorage, and they add a facet to the Pacific worlds, to the "multiple seas, cultures, and peoples and especially the overlapping transits between them."[33] They are at home in manifold cultural settings and constitute what Paul Spickard calls a "transnational or diasporic" community. They migrated to numerous destinations instead of just one, they did not fully merge with their new resident societies, and they stayed connected with their original home—either directly or through reminiscence.[34]

The Vava'u Germans dispersed without losing sight of their heritage, and they carried their history and experiences with them. The remembrance of their past became a central uniting bond that helped assure them of their identity. On the other hand, in the societies they now lived in, they were continuously confronted with both their Tongan and their German heritages. A cultural memory—to use Jan Assmann's terminology—developed.[35] This not only gave the Vava'u Germans coherence, it also delineated them from others.

Memories and Experiences of the Past

The ties of memory that bound together needed to be kept alive. Communication, friendships, visits, family reunions, and marriages all helped serve this purpose. "Specialists" played a central role in its development—for example, collectors of genealogical data, organizers of reunions, and activists in the social media, who fostered this cultural memory, and, in doing so, also substantially decided what was remembered.

Five key points can be distinguished in which the history of the Vava'u Germans crystalized—core elements of their cultural memory, or, to use Pierre Nora's mnemonic term, "lieux de mémoire."[36] The first and most important of these was the reality of constantly living on the interface between two cultures and the experience of belonging to a transcultural minority. Vika Lataheanga Tu'ua, for example, recalls that the Tongans did not acknowledge her as one of their own: "In Tonga, I was half-caste. They call us *hafakasi*, you know, or quarter-caste or whatever it was. No, I wasn't a Tongan."[37] In the course of the interview, however, it became clear, as well, that she herself also questioned her status as a true member of Tongan society. As will become evident later on, there were barriers on her side that did not allow her to behave like a full Tongan.

The question of who they were, and to what extent they belonged to the society in which they lived, is a recurrent theme that threads its way through the history of the Vava'u Germans. This question was manifest not only in Tonga, but it also followed them to every other country in their transpacific migration. The "lieux de mémoire" of being a "transcultural minority" emerged time and again in their minds. Central to this perception is the experience that their identity was conferred by the interplay of outside- and self-attribution. Lata illuminates this when she explains that the way they were seen, and who they were considered to be, changed fundamentally when her family moved to New Zealand: "And then we went to New Zealand; now we're Tongans."

In New Zealand, the Vava'u Germans slipped into the role of being Tongans. This came easily to them, as they had built a strong relationship to Tongan traditions. This attachment not only kept them linked to Tonga, it also allowed them to carve out a niche in the societies they now resided in. This is the second core element in their cultural memory. Lata again illustrates this when she speaks of the Tongan dances she loved so much, but could or would not perform while she still lived in Tonga: "I remember every time they do the dances, you know

…, I love to dance, but because I'm half-caste, you know, I don't participate in those things." This changed fundamentally in New Zealand, where people saw them as being Tongan, and where they themselves embraced being Tongan: "We were taught all the Tongan dances, all of us half-caste girls … They taught all those half-caste girls to represent Tonga in New Zealand." Lata and the other girls performed Polynesian dances and used the money they earned to create the first financial basis for their life in the new environment. A similar example can be seen in Lata's cousin Bill Wolfgramm. In the fifties and sixties, he ranked among New Zealand's most popular musicians. He played the steel guitar and performed South Sea rhythms with his band, the *Islanders*.[38]

The feeling of living in a cultural transition zone was a lasting reality for the Vava'u Germans. Since the time they first settled in Tonga, they learned that identities are flexible, and this insight became deeply imprinted in their memory. This is the third "lieux de mémoire," and it continued to be a shaping factor also after their dispersal. The Vava'u Germans, in the words of one of them, "can adapt their identity to whichever audience it suits … They move fluidly between different worlds."[39] And the German-Tongan-Fijian-Australian sociologist and author Robert Wolfgramm told me that he is convinced of a general "plasticity (of) ethnic identity."[40]

This fluid identity, conferred through historical experiences and memory, allows the Vava'u Germans to easily move back and forth between their old home and the new, a capability that is seen as a central characteristic of transnational or diasporic ways of life.[41] Just as Lata became Tongan in New Zealand, other Vava'u Germans embraced German attributes that had been passed down to them from their fathers and grandfathers after leaving Vava'u, without, however, renouncing all cultural ties to Tonga. Yet again others, who returned to Tonga, had internalized the skills and attitudes they had learned while living in New Zealand or the United States, and brought back values and views that were foreign to Tongans. A young man I interviewed put it this way: "The businesses I kind of see Tongans running is – I hate to sound like I'm, uh, putting them down – but the Tongans would only run a business they see someone else doing … I would say Tongans are not really pioneers … Over here you're taught to stay on your own level … You're not supposed to try to surpass people who rank above you … And so maybe it was a blessing that I grew up somewhere else."[42]

The importance of history as an identity-forming bond was strengthened by the quintessential role that genealogical knowledge plays in Tongan society. The Vava'u Germans learned that one's status was defined by where one came from and who one's ancestors were. This genealogical awareness is the fourth core element in the cultural memory of the Vava'u Germans, as reflected in the fact that the graves of their ancestors in Vava'u, are still, to this day, being tended by those who remained in Tonga. For Vava'u Germans coming for a visit from abroad, it is an essential part of their itinerary to pay tribute at these graves.

The Vava'u Germans were—as they see and remember it—generous and, in a certain sense, patriarchal. The shops in which they sold their imported wares figure strongly in many of the interviews and have become another key point in their memory, a fifth "lieu de mémoire." The shops represent the development and civilization that the Vava'u Germans brought to the islands; the profit that they did not put into their own pockets, but instead invested in the further development of Vava'u; and the generosity with which they helped out the local population in hard times, sometimes to their own financial detriment.

Germanness

Wherever they may be living, the Vava'u Germans feel bonded to Tonga because it is the place from which they dispersed. This place of origin is, as I have just elaborated, very present in their minds and memories. Its importance was also evident at Makanesi's memorial service. Nevertheless Makanesi also always remained aware of his German roots. A certain brand of "Germanness" thus appears to be part of the Vava'u Germans identity, both to outsiders and in their own perception. It is, above all, this aspect of their identity that separates the Vava'u Germans from other Pacific Islanders who have migrated to similar places. This Germanness is not marked by nationality, language, religion, or skin color. Central aspects are, rather, historical experiences and, in particular, certain traits that delineated the Vava'u Germans from other people, both in the past and in the present.

An essential aspect of the transcultural history of the Vava'u Germans is that they were not seen as simply being foreign or different; they were actually often perceived as being German. This was harmful when they were declared "enemy aliens" and interned. At other times, it could have a respectful connotation as Makanesi recalled, or sometimes be disparaging. Robert Wolfgramm, for example, told me that his Australian class mates "did call me ... squarehead or kraut."

The Vava'u Germans found a number of symbolic ways to remind themselves of their "Germanness." Before World War I, they celebrated the Kaiser's birthday, and Wilhelm II's portrait hung in many homes. A number of households possessed various German flags—also those of the Third Reich. Nowadays, logos developed for family reunions frequently use symbols that refer back to Pyritz and Germany, such as the coat of arms of Pyritz, or the German national colors—usually black, red, and gold, but also sometimes historically correct (for the time of the chain migration) black, white, and red.

The store, which, in memory, stands out as a symbol of the hands-on approach and innovative spirit of the Vava'u Germans, gains a particularly German connotation when it is remembered in relation to bread. Baker and miller were common vocations in the families that the first immigrants hailed from, and some of them started baking bread, which they sold in their stores. This tradition was passed on to the following generations. One of the Vava'u Germans who recently visited Pyritz stumbled across a Polish bakery there and posted a photo of it on facebook with the following comment: "Since Great-grandpa Emil was a baker, it was interesting that the first shop I set foot on in Pyrzyce was the bakery. I enjoyed their fresh baked bread and pastries; it was the best in all the worlds."[43]

All in all, it would be safe to say that the Vava'u Germans mainly see their German heritage reflected in certain traits, such as the willingness to work hard, humbleness, self-reliance, faith in one's own skills and competence, and the ability to overcome hardship and obstacles on the way to success. That was how Makanesi defined his German heritage; and also a young German-Tongan New Zealander told me that everything his parents and grandparents had achieved "came out of their own hard work and spirit"—something he understood as German "work ethic."[44]

The Cultural Memory of the Vava'u Germans and Art: The Bottom Line

Dagmar Dyck, a prestigious young New Zealand artist of Vava'u-German background, combines the expressivity of modern painting with stylistic Polynesian elements, such as the modular structure and iconography used for designing tapa, the traditional Tongan bark cloth.[45] In one of her latest works, an installation titled "Which side are you on?", she portrays the history of the Vava'u Germans. Differently sized discs that emulate elements from the decorative belts (*Kiekie*) worn by Tongan women on festive occasions represent individual immigrants and their stories.

In her art, she not only draws on one of the central Vava'u German "Lieux de mémoire," namely, Tongan traditions, but also evokes the history of this transcultural minority with the help of "visual metaphors." Using symbols, she represents the historical roots that define the Vava'u German identity: the discs refer to Pyritz when they bear the griffin from that town's coat of arms; a coconut shell reminds of the copra trade that brought wealth to the Vava'u Germans and aided Neifau's development; and the logo of a boatbuilding company again stresses the impulses the Vava'u Germans gave to the society they lived in, and also refers to the modernity the Vava'u Germans brought to Neiafu. The combination of Tongan forms of artistic expression with references to the history and identity of the Vava'u Germans symbolizes both their transcultural identity and their sense of connectedness with Germany.

Reinhard Wendt, retired professor for modern European and non-European history at the FernUniversität at Hagen, Germany, dealt in his academic work with cultural contacts, conflicts, and transfers between Western and non-Western societies. His views and interpretations are summarized in his book *Vom Kolonialismus zur Globalisierung: Europa und die Welt seit 1500*, second edition (Ferdinand Schöningh, 2016).

Notes

1. Edward Winslow Gifford, *Tongan Society* (Honolulu, 1921. Reprint New York: Kraus, 1971), 22–26.
2. Facebook posting and correspondence with Tisina Wolfgramm Gerber.
3. Interview with Makanesi Wolfgramm (28 October 2011).
4. Tony Muller uses this term to denote the period of peace and prosperity between the end of the nineteenth century and 1914. Tony Muller, *From Prussia to the Pacific: The Guttenbeil Family of Tonga* (Auckland: Tony Muller, 2013), 49.
5. Unless otherwise mentioned, the information presented in this chapter is based on a genealogical databank with more than 5,000 entries and about 150 interviews with Vava'u Germans.
6. Hans-Ulrich Wehler, *Deutsche Gesellschaftsgeschichte 1849–1914* (Munich: Beck, 1995), 39–59, 179–85.
7. Databank Ballinstadt, Hamburger Passagierlisten 1850–1934; StAH, 373–77, VIII A 3 Band 001, p. 180; *Auckland Star*, 22 July 1881: 2; *Samoa Times and South Sea Gazette*, 6 August 1881: 2.
8. *The Cyclopedia of Fiji, Samoa, Tonga, Tahiti, and the Cook Islands* (Sydney: McCarron, Steward & Co. 1907), 63.
9. Christine Liava'a, *Enemy Aliens in Tonga, May 1916: As Listed by the British Consul in Tonga* (Auckland: C. Liava'a, 2005).
10. M. Vernon Coombs, A Partial History of the Tongan Mission, unpublished manuscript, Church History Library, Salt Lake City, Ms d 3766, 13–14.
11. Reinhard Wendt, "Deutsche Gräber auf dem europäischen Friedhof in Neiafu, Vava'u, Tonga-Inseln: Erinnerungsort zu Auswanderung und Transkulturation," *Saeculum* (2014): 100.
12. Alfred O. Bretschneider, *Gottfried Wilhelm August Unshelm*, unpublished manuscript, Staatsarchiv Hamburg, 731-1, Handschriftensammlung 2737, 197.
13. For a townscape, see Robert Holsten, *Heimatkunde von Pyltz und Umgegend* (Pyritz: Verlag der Backeschen Buchdruckerei, 1921).
14. Archiwum Pánstwowe w Szczecinie, Regierung Stettin, 9684, Auswanderung nach Australien.
15. Hermann Mückler, *Kolonialismus in Ozeanien* (Vienna: Facultas, 2012), 167–69.
16. Hermann Roskoschny, *Europas Kolonien: Die Deutschen in der Südsee* (Leipzig: Gressner & Schramm, 1886), 149.
17. Moritz Schanz, *Australien und die Südsee an der Jahrhundertwende* (Berlin: Süsserott, 1901), 198.
18. Hugo Zöller, *Rund um die Erde. 2 Bde*: Limbach (Cologne: DuMont-Schauberg, 1881), vol. 2, 446–47.
19. Mückler, *Kolonialismus*, 71, 110, 137–38, 170–82.
20. Reinhard Wendt, *Vom Kolonialismus zur Globalisierung: Europa und die Welt seit 1500* (Paderborn: Ferdinand Schöningh, 2016), 225–31.
21. Bartholomäus von Werner, *Ein deutsches Kriegsschiff in der Südsee* (Leipzig: F. A. Brockhaus, 1889), 491; Studer, "Die Tonga-Inseln," *Deutsche Geographische Blätter* 1 (1877): 27–28.
22. Muller, *From Prussia to the Pacific*, 43.

23. Gerd Koch, *Südsee—gestern und heute* (Braunschweig: Limbach, 1955), 116–22.
24. Mückler, *Kolonialismus*, 46; Livia Loosen, *Deutsche Frauen in den Südsee-Kolonien des Kaiserreichs: Alltag und Beziehungen zur indigenen Bevölkerung, 1884–1919* (Bielefeld: transcript, 2014), 385, 396.
25. Gifford, *Tongan Society*, 19–20, 29–30.
26. See Loosen, *Deutsche Frauen*, 384–85.
27. Wendt, "Deutsche Gräber," 92, 98.
28. Passenger lists available on portals such as ancestry.com, familysearch, trove, and paperspast allow the partial reconstruction of journies taken by Vava'u Germans within the Pacific and to Europe and the USA.
29. https://fragmentedidentities.wordpress.com /2015/03/02/pacific-islands-monthly/ (last visited 26 July 2015). Although the idea for this periodical was born in 1914, its first edition was not published until 1930; Vava'u Germans were among its subcribers (Interview with Martha Meredith, 28 October 2011).
30. The plight of one these internees is described in: Reinhard Wendt, "Die Internierung des Gustav Kronfeld in Neuseeland: German Pacific Islanders, Transkulturalität und Kategorien des Nationalen im Ersten Weltkrieg," in *Der Erste Weltkrieg im Geschichtsunterricht. Grenzen – Grenzüberschreitungen – Medialisierung von Grenzen*, ed. Bärbel Kuhn and Astrid Windus (St. Ingbert: Röhrig, 2014), 83–104. Gustav Kronfeld was interned in the camp on Motuihe Island, which was relatively acceptable compared to other camps. A publication about Motuihe has just been released: Leilani Tamu, *Restricted: Motuihe Island Internment Camp 1914–1918* (Auckland: Leilani Tamu, 2015).
31. Between 1914 and 1939, the price for a ton of copra fell from 39£ to 9£. Clara B. Wilpert, *Südsee: Inseln, Völker und Kulturen* (Hamburg: Christians, 1987), 25.
32. See Reinhard Wendt, "Deutschsein in der Südsee: Berichte des Schweizerischen Konsuls in Neuseeland über Internierte aus Vava'u während des Zweiten Weltkriegs." http://www.europa.clio-online.de/2013/Article=609.
33. Matt K. Matsuda, *Pacific Worlds* (Cambridge: Cambridge University Press, 2012), 2.
34. Paul Spickard, "Introduction: Pacific Diaspora," in *Pacific Diaspora: Island People in the United States and Across the Pacific*, ed. Paul Spickard, Joanne L. Rondilla and Debbie Hippolite Wright (Honolulu: University of Hawaii Press, 2002), 11–12.
35. Jan Assmann, "Kollektives Gedächtnis und kulturelle Identität," in *Kultur und Gedächtnis*, ed. Jan Assmann and Tonio Hölscher (Frankfurt a.M.: Suhrkamp, 1988), 15.
36. For a short introduction, see Etienne François, "Vorwort," in *Erinnerungsorte Frankreichs*, ed. Pierre Nora (Munich: Beck, 2005), 7–14.
37. Interview with Vika Lataheanga Tu'ua (26 September 2010). Lata, as she is called in short, was born as one of Charles Ataongo Wolfgramm's daughters in 1933. She first moved to New Zealand with her father, and then to the USA.
38. Nick Bollinger, *100 Essential New Zealand Albums* (Wellington: Awa Press, 2009), 5–7.
39. E-mail from Tony Muller to the author (17 January 2012).
40. Interview with Robert Wolfgramm (23 August 2011).
41. Spickard, "Introduction," 11–12.
42. Interview with anonymous Wolfgramm (identity known to author) (7 October 2012).
43. Mitch Vuki, "My German Roots." Wolfgramm and Sanft Reunion 2012. Posted on facebook, 6 August 2012.
44. Interview with Bjorn Guttenbeil (16 September 2010).
45. Caroline Vercoe and Nina Tonga, "Tapa in der zeitgenössischen pazifischen Kunst Neuseelands," in *Made in Oceania*, ed. Peter Mesenhöller and Oliver Lueb (Cologne: Rautenstrauch-Joest-Museum, 2013), 66–81.

Bibliography

Assmann, Jan. "Kollektives Gedächtnis und kulturelle Identität." In *Kultur und Gedächtnis*, edited by Jan Assmann and Tonio Hölscher, 9–19. Frankfurt a.M.: Suhrkamp, 1988.
Auckland Star, 22 July 1881: 2.
Bollinger, Nick. *100 Essential New Zealand Albums*. Wellington: Awa Press, 2009.
The Cyclopedia of Fiji, Samoa, Tonga, Tahiti, and the Cook Islands. Sydney: McCarron, Steward & Co., 1907.
Bretschneider, Alfred O. Gottfried Wilhelm August Unshelm, unpublished manuscript, Staatsarchiv Hamburg, 731-1, Handschriftensammlung 2737.
Coombs, M. Vernon. A Partial History of the Tongan Mission, unpublished manuscript, Church History Library, Salt Lake City, Ms d 3766.
François, Etienne. "Vorwort." In *Erinnerungsorte Frankreichs*, ed. Pierre Nora, 7–14. Munich: Beck, 2005.
Gifford, Edward Winslow. *Tongan Society*. Honolulu, 1921. Reprint New York: Kraus,1971.
Holsten, Robert. *Heimatkunde von Pyritz und Umgegend*. Pyritz: Verlag der Backeschen Buchdruckerei, 1921.
Koch, Gerd. *Südsee—gestern und heute*. Braunschweig: Limbach, 1955.
Liava'a, Christine. *Enemy Aliens in Tonga, May 1916: As Listed by the British Consul in Tonga*. Auckland: C. Liava'a, 2005.
Loosen, Livia. *Deutsche Frauen in den Südsee-Kolonien des Kaiserreichs: Alltag und Beziehungen zur indigenen Bevölkerung, 1884–1919*. Bielefeld: transcript, 2014.
Matsuda, Matt K. *Pacific Worlds*. Cambridge: Cambridge University Press, 2012.
Mückler, Hermann. *Kolonialismus in Ozeanien*. Vienna: Facultas, 2012.
Muller, Tony. *From Prussia to the Pacific: The Guttenbeil Family of Tonga*. Auckland: Tony Muller, 2013.
Roskoschny, Hermann. *Europas Kolonien: Die Deutschen in der Südsee*. Leipzig: Gressner & Schramm, 1886.
Samoa Times and South Sea Gazette, 6 August 1881: 2.
Schanz, Moritz. *Australien und die Südsee an der Jahrhundertwende*. Berlin: Süsserott, 1901.
Spickard, Paul. "Introduction: Pacific Diaspora." In *Pacific Diaspora: Island People in the United States and Across the Pacific*, edited by Paul Spickard, Joanne L. Rondilla, and Debbie Hippolite Wright, 1–27. Honolulu: University of Hawaii Press, 2002.
Studer. "Die Tonga-Inseln." *Deutsche Geographische Blätter* 1 (1877): 18–31.
Tamu, Leilani. *Restricted: Motuihe Island Internment Camp 1914–1918*. Auckland: Leilani Tamu, 2015.
Vercoe, Caroline, and Nina Tonga. "Tapa in der zeitgenössischen pazifischen Kunst Neuseelands." In *Made in Oceania*, edited by Peter Mesenhöller and Oliver Lueb, 66–81. Cologne: Rautenstrauch-Joest-Museum, 2013.
von Werner, Bartholomäus. *Ein deutsches Kriegsschiff in der Südsee*. Leipzig: F. A. Brockhaus, 1889.
Wehler, Hans-Ulrich. *Deutsche Gesellschaftsgeschichte 1849–1914*. Munich: Beck, 1995.
Wendt, Reinhard. "Deutsche Gräber auf dem europäischen Friedhof in Neiafu, Vava'u, Tonga-Inseln: Erinnerungsort zu Auswanderung und Transkulturation." *Saeculum* (2014): 91–107.

———. "Deutschsein in der Südsee: Berichte des Schweizerischen Konsuls in Neuseeland über Internierte aus Vava'u während des Zweiten Weltkriegs." Retrieved 25 August 2015 from http://www.europa.clio-online.de/2013/Article=609.

———. "Die Internierung des Gustav Kronfeld in Neuseeland: German Pacific Islanders, Transkulturalität und Kategorien des Nationalen im Ersten Weltkrieg." In *Der Erste Weltkrieg im Geschichtsunterricht: Grenzen – Grenzüberschreitungen – Medialisierung von Grenzen*, edited by Bärbel Kuhn and Astrid Windus, 83–104. St. Ingbert: Röhrig, 2014.

———. *Vom Kolonialismus zur Globalisierung: Europa und die Welt seit 1500*. Paderborn: Ferdinand Schöningh, 2016.

Wilpert, Clara B. *Südsee: Inseln, Völker und Kulturen*. Hamburg: Christians, 1987.

Zöller, Hugo. *Rund um die Erde*. Vol. 2. Cologne: DuMont-Schauberg, 1881.

Epilogue

GERMAN HISTORIES AND PACIFIC HISTORIES
New Directions

Matt Matsuda

This volume, ranging across centuries from Europe to Asia, Oceania, and the Americas, has proposed investigations that are as much questions as they are answers regarding the entwined histories of the German and Pacific worlds. Indeed, the editors and authors have made this their challenge. It would be ambitious, but perhaps misdirected, to write about "the German Pacific," as if it were simply a scholarly category to be filled with analyses and archival narratives. For here are cases whose authors make clear that they are themselves wrestling with the definitions of both "German" and "Pacific." Without a nationally identifiable German state before the late nineteenth century, and a Pacific where engagements were only fitfully colonial, and only for a generation, where does one even locate the subjects? Whether by diving deeply into botany, maps, industrial agreements, work cultures, immigration, or marriage policies, the scholars in this volume are all organized around this question.

The title captures this: *Explorations and Entanglements: Germans in Pacific Worlds*—not one subsumed to or a subset of the other, but a set of parallelisms and interactions, of engagements that nominally involve "German" figures in "Pacific" places; but just as much an interrogation of each category in mutual construction and deconstruction. Thus, "German" becomes an identity principle to a culture of transglobal expertise in natural history at a time when politics was dynastic and academic knowledge the privilege of erudites, or a disputed quantum of blood, culture, and civilization in a mixed marriage. Or, again, here are stories that trace a yearning to find a place for a "German" heritage in islander society, or to likewise assert islander sovereignty against European encroachments.

These studies are precisely not simply narratives attempting to find a place for a "German" presence along with those of Spanish, Portuguese, Chinese, Dutch, British, French, Japanese, American, or other global or regional "empires," such as those of Tonga or Yap. Rather, the work is dialectical, full of contractions, contingencies, negotiations, and accommodations. Whether gaining local knowledge from native informants in New Guinea, establishing regimes of contract and indentured labor in Samoa, or negotiating industrial and railway projects in China, the authors have presented a German presence in the Pacific as a set of transits and assays in search of plants, animals, and specimens; unstable and shifting boundaries in establishing mapping conventions with the help of Oceanian navigators; constantly challenged notions of patrimony, and of female authority in the legal status of mixed-race children, and claims for justice and protection against sexual violence. These are not Rankean prescriptions of things that happened, but frank uncertainties and wrestling with cultures and situations often in dispute and collision.

This matters, for the volume promises not only stalwart research and storytelling, but a commitment to "new directions." By engaging multiple disciplines, the volume also launches into newer edges of historical scholarship, crossing over anthropology and linguistics, religion, labor studies, politics and politics activism, legal and juridical studies, as well as significantly engaging domains that—in academic terms—have long been the realm of professional schools: civil engineering, topography, and cartography; environmental, marine, and coastal science; botany and pharmacology, as well as biology and chemistry. There is no master methodology for what took place, or for what the stories all mean. A reading of the chapters indicates that they embrace a number of other categories and thematically pull the volume along different currents: epistemologies for generating science; professional expertise at the service of states and profits; the social and phenomenological experience of immigrants and local peoples within new regimes of law, labor, and ideology.

We see the natural-historical thoughts and actions of Andreas Cleyer and Englebert Kaempfer; the geographical vision of Paul Klein; the expertise of Georg Forster and Georg Wilhelm Streller. We see German engineers helping to enable a technological empire of infrastructure in China; the grand shipping strategies of the Spreckels family; the inversion of family ideologies in examinations of labor and work-ethic politics, or the affective interventions into "mixed marriages" and liaisons—nuns committed to good works and ideals of discipline; female islanders seeking justice in the face of sexual assault framed by ideologies of promiscuity; German agents working in support of Indian nationalists against the British Empire; Pomeranian ethnic Germans migrating to Tonga, looking to understand their own identities as both Pacific-Oceanian and German peoples.

Out of these stories, greater narratives do take shape. The volume has been assembled in two different sections, the first concerned with agents of knowledge transfer, largely in the early modern period, and the second with legacies developing more directly from sustained encounters, developing contacts, and colonial projects over the nineteenth century. In all cases, readers are exposed to a new generation of the ways historical narratives are being rewritten by current scholars, and here we see the contours of their efforts to wrestle original analyses into shape, imagining what scholarship might mean after a number of national, postnational, global, and postcolonial turns. In this instance, one of the key generalities is the embrace of a fitfully evolving, rather than mythically invoked, Germany and Germanic culture. German histories as Pacific histories are pieced together, rather than declared or annexed to a national narrative.

These narrations crosscut not only thematically, but spatially. They are emplotted into specific places, and this gives the volume its claim to engaging both European and Pacific traditions. German voyagers and Pacific Islanders and Asians travel from New Guinea to Fiji and Samoa, from Chinese ports to the Philippines, from the Bering Strait to the Indian subcontinent and around again. This might have resulted in a set of contingent and dispersed case studies; instead, the studies are linked together by their own undertones of networks, connection, and interaction. Commercial deals link Honolulu and San Francisco; marriage policies and practices in South Seas colonies are measured against those of settler colonies in Southwest Africa; workforce politics in Samoa are unsettled by the presence of Melanesian and Chinese laborers.

The authors approached their subjects with global visions very much in mind—whether the cartographical and navigational visions of Germanic savants on Russian ships, Pomeranian immigrants building communities in Samoa, or anti-British agents on an Oceanian-wide circuit—the contributors offer finely detailed examinations of localities and actors while contributing broadly to globally defined historiographies of both the Pacific and of German studies. Each chapter unrolls with a scholarly expertise, while also connecting like a web of inter-island archipelagic transits over centuries of nested chronologies and wide geographies.

In this way, the volume is an invitation to imagine and reconsider the boundaries and borders of German histories not in "Germany," and a Pacific intersected by a European power not generally woven into narratives that strongly emphasize Spanish, British, French, and American perspectives. The result is work that demonstrates how states, communities, and peoples do not so much define themselves, as constantly refigure their identities against the peoples and cultures and knowledge they encounter—or, as in many cases, how they in fact do not refigure themselves, while holding on to frameworks brought from other worlds and lives—with consequences for territorial claims, laborers under indenture regimes, or victims of violence and exploitation.

Importantly, this set of shifting and contested scenarios presented as a German and Pacific history helps to interrogate the ways that other European historical traditions in the Pacific have long been shaped by established critical frameworks. If an Iberian vision of the Pacific led oceanic geographies to be denominated "The Spanish Lake" in the age of the Manila Galleon transits and empire in the Americas, the authors here describe the ways that German erudites like Humboldt were part of the natural-historical, cartographic, and political teams that assayed and defined those domains.

If the British Pacific is built upon the storied legacies of James Cook's staggering voyages for the admiralty, the authors here illuminate how Johann Reinhold Forster was not only an accompanying figure of science on such voyages, but himself a German influence, bringing specific cultural and intellectual training. Likewise, American expansionism, especially after the Spanish–American War, has found its historians in scholars of colonialism, strategic control, and militarism in the Philippines, the Hawaiian Islands, and what would become the trust territories of the Micronesian Islands. Less visible, until now, have been the activities propelled by capital and commodity interests like those of the German Spreckels family from the eastern seaboard of the United States to major influences in California and Hawaii. The German and Pacific histories problematize the elegant simplicity of dynastic or national metropoles and colonial prizes.

In this volume, "Germany" figures much less than a "German presence," perhaps aligned with a state, but just as likely embodied in sets of individual actors and characters, whether men of science and cartography, women of faith and labor, or agents of political change and technical expertise. Each chapter has a key exploration, whether labor, gender, business relations, natural history, or clandestine politics. How are they all arrayed in a single collection so as to be composed of more than a set of interestingly distinctive pieces? Once again, this is found in the interrogation of both "German" and Pacific," set across a broad canvas. What this volume has aimed to provide is not just a set of peregrinations, but a narrative of history as simultaneously episodic and interconnected. The German presence and impact in the Pacific is alternately grand—as with the power of trade, shipping, and copra commercial dominion—and contingent—as with individual botanists and collectors, or nuns strategizing the appeal of their deceased sisters.

As such, German histories and Pacific histories are explorations of boundaries, as in the cartographic studies here—from early modern surveys and assays, to business and spiritual projects, to imperial exploitation and settler colonialism, to identity fashioning and sovereignty struggles. All of these make claims to what can properly be defined and maintained as German, while relentlessly being transformed or challenged in pursuit of what can be imagined as the Pacific.

Matt Matsuda is professor of history at Rutgers University–New Brunswick, and teaches Modern European and Asia-Pacific global and comparative histories. He is the author of *The Memory of the Modern*, *Empire of Love*, and *Pacific Worlds*. He is the founder and coeditor of the *Palgrave Studies in Pacific History* series.

Index

NOTE: Page numbers with an *f* are figures; Page numbers with a *t* are tables.

Academy of Science (Russia), 104, 105, 106, 116
Aceh War (1873–1903), 10
Africa, 213, 214; German imperialism in, 13
Afu, Salome Fo'ou, 292
Age of Empire, 171
The Age of Exploration, 153
Alaska, 104, 106–12
Albert, Heinrich F., 280
Aleutian Islands, 104, 110, 113
aliens, 294
The Ambonese Curiosity Cabinet (*D'Amboinsche Rariteitkamer* [Rumpf, 1705)]), 46
Ambonese Herbal (*Het Amboinsche kruidboek* or *Herbarium Amboinense* [Rumpf, 1741-50]), 46
American Civil War (1860-1865), 196
American Sugar Refining Company, 174
Amoenitatum Exoticarum (1712), 45
ancestry, 298
Andersson, J. G., 164
Annie Larsen, 282, 283
annulments, 223
Antarctic, 128
anti-British rhetoric, 278
anti-imperialism, 278
aphrodisiacs, 44
apothecaries, 35–48
Arbeitsschwestern (working sisters), 245
Archive of the Russian Academy of Science, 105
Arctic region, 103
assault, sexual, 260–67
Assmann, Jan, 301
Astrolabe, 114

audiences for maps (Klein), 64–69
Australia, 8, 81, 294, 300
Australian Brigade, 12
Austria-Hungary, 280, 284
Austrian Habsburgs, 57, 58
Aztecs, 44

Bacon, Francis, 131; *Novum organum scientiarum*, 132*f*
Baltic Sea, 2
Banks, Joseph, 81, 82, 127, 131, 139
Baret, Jeanne, 81
Batavia, 40; *medicinale winkel*, 40–42
Baudin, Nicolas, 85
Bay Sugar Refining Company, 172
beachcombers, 200–201
Behrens, Carl Friedrich, 83, 84
Bellingshausen, Fabian Gottlieb von, 86, 91
Berghaus, Heinrich, 88
Berghoff, Hartmut, 188, 191, 194
beri-beri, 40
Bering, Vitus Jonassen, 20, 105, 106, 109
Bering Island, 111
Bering Strait, 115
Berlin, Weimar, 24
Berlin Committee, 282, 283, 285
Bernstorff (Count), 282
Bildung, 21
Billings, Joseph, 113, 116, 117
Billings-Sarychev expedition (1785-1794), 20, 112–16
bioprospecting in the Pacific, 139–42
Biró, Lajos, 259
bironovshchina, 106
Bismarck Archipelago, 203, 213, 218, 225
Bismarck, Otto von, 3, 11, 155, 161

blue clitoris flower, 47
Boether, Paul, 222
Bolsheviks, 286
Bonpland, Aimé, 85
Bontius, Jacobus, 38, 40
Booth-Tucker, Frederick, 177
Bopp, Franz, 282, 285, 286
Borsig, August, 154
Bose, Subhas Chandra, 286
Botanical Gardens, 130
botanists, 35–48; botanical prospecting, 37, 39; global botanizing, 36–40
botany, 81; Colonial Politics of Botany, 134; Linnaean method of classification, 135
Bougainville, Louis Antoine de, 8, 80, 85, 90
Boussole, 114
Boxer Rebellion (1898–1900), 278
Boym, Michal, 40
Braive, Emile, 158
Brandt, Max von, 155, 158, 160, 162
Breve Noticia, 64
British Empire, 18. *See also* Great Britain
British Indian Army, 278
Brooke, James, 10
Brown, Robert, 81
building master *(Regierungsbaumeister),* 157
Burschenschaft songs, 198

California (USA), 9
California Gold Rush (1848), 10
California Sugar Refinery Company, 172
Camel, Georg Josef, 19, 35, 42–47
Canada, 278
Cantova, Antonio, 68, 69
Cape of Good Hope, 133
Caroline Islands, 55, 56, 213, 297
Carte de France, 65
cartography, 56, 65. *See also* maps
Catherine II, 85, 113, 130
Catherine the Great, 113
Catholicism, 3, 248, 295, 296, 298; education, 245; in Germany, 249; missionaries, 38
celibacy, 219
chain migration from Pyritz to Vava'u, 295–97

Chakravarty, Chandra K., 284, 285
Chamisso, Adalbert von, 14, 69, 91
Chandra, Ram, 280, 282
children, half-castes, 224
Chile, 12
Chilean Civil War, 184
China, 6, 9, 12, 18, 243, 310; coolies, 203–4; German influence on industrialization, 153–66; herbs, 43; invasion of Hawaii (fears of), 176*f*; *Specimen Medicinae Sinicae* (1862), 40; trade products from, 37
China Geological Survey, 164
China Railway Company, 157, 158
Chinese-American Commercial Company, 182–84
Chirikov, Aleksei, 105, 106, 109, 112
Christianity, 217, 243; charities, 247; expansion of, 57. *See also* Catholicism; missionaries
cinchona, 37
City of Paris, 176
Clain, Pablo, 43
classification, Linnaean method of, 135
Claudius, Hendrik (or Heinrich), 41
Clerke, Charles, 113
Cleyer, Andreas, 19, 42, 310; *medicinale winkel,* 40–42
Cleyer, Andries, 35
Clitoris Principissae, 47
coal, 160
Cobo, Juan, 43
coke, 160
colonialism, 13–18, 240; Germany, 2; Samoa, 196–97
Colonial Politics of Botany, 134
colonization efforts of Russia, 130
Colony and Homeland *(Kolonie und Heimat),* 216, 218, 226
Columbus, Christopher, 36
commerce, 36–40
Commerçon, Philibert, 81
Conrad, Sebastian, 17
contact zones, 81
contracts, indenture, 258
convents, 244

Cook, James, 8, 20, 21, 80, 82, 84, 90, 113, 127; European participants of Cook's voyages, 129; social hierarchies on ships, 127
coolies, 203–4
Cooper, Robert, 136
Coronado Tent City, 181
corvee labor, 257
cotton, Samoa, 196, 197
counterintelligence operatives, 277
Couplet, Philippe, 40
Critical Whiteness Studies, 214
cultural memory of Vava'u Germans, 304

D'Amboinsche Rariteitkamer (The Ambonese Curiosity Cabinet [Rumpf, 1705]), 46
Daphne, 294
Darwin, Charles, 8
Das, Taraknath, 278
Daum, Andreas, 14, 15, 20, 21
Dayal, Har, 279, 284
Daye Iron Mines, 157
de Brosses, Charles, 68
A Decade in Samoa (*Ein Jahrzehnt in Samoa* [Zischank]), 221, 222
Deeken, Richard, 199, 201, 202
Defense of India Force, 12
de Freycinet, Louis, 81
Delisle, Guillaume, 103, 108
Delisle, Joseph-Nicolas, 108, 112
de Loaísa, García, 83
Deshima Island, 8
Detring, Gustav, 164
Deutsche Handels- und Plantagen-Gesellschaft (DHPG, German Trade and Plantation Society), 197, 200, 202, 206
Deutsche Kolonialfrau (German colonial woman), 218–19
Deutschnationaler Frauenbund (German National Women's League), 216
Deutschtum (Germanness), 221
Dhingra, Madan Lal, 278
diary (Georg Wilhelm Steller), 105
Dietzen, Katharina, 239
Dietzen, Valeria (Sister), 238, 239*f*, 240, 243, 244, 245

Divine Word Missionaries, 238, 242, 247
diwarra (shell money), 257
Dohm, Christian Wilhelm von, 83
Dörner, Sophie, 295
Douglas, Brownen, 60
Drakenstein, Hendrik Adriaan van Reede tot, 38
drugs, 41
Duan Fang, 154
Duperrey, Louis, 81
Dutch East Indies, 10, 260
Dutch East India Company (VOC), 7, 8, 14, 35
Dutch Republic, 38
Dutch VOC, 14
dysentery, 40

East Asia, 155
economic background (of Somoa), 196–97
Edgcumbe, John, 135
education: Catholicism, 245; Jesuit missionaries, 57; Klein, Paul, 58, 59
Ehlers, Otto, 199, 206
Eley, Geoff, 17, 18
Emden, 283
empires, 36–40
employment of women (German), 218
enemy aliens, 294
Engelhardt, August, 201, 218
engineering, 154–66; development of, 153; mining, 160
England, 130
the Enlightenment, 8, 103
Euclidian geometry, 62
Europe: audiences for maps (Klein), 64–69; imaginings of oceanic spaces, 60–63; maps, 55, 60, 68; maritime powers of, 80
European Pacific, 4, 5
European project, Pacific as, 5–13
European voyages (in the Pacific), 92*t*–93*t*
Evreinov, Ivan M., 103
expeditions: Billings–Sarychev Expedition, 112–16; naturalists (around 1800), 92*t*–93*t*; Second Kamchatka Expedition, 105–6

316 | Index

explorers: in the North Pacific, 103–18; in the Pacific, 83–87
Exportmusterlager, 182
exports from Somoa, 197

fact-finding missions (Paul Klein), 63
fahu throne, 292
fales, 297, 299
Fellmann, Johanna, 225
female locality, 240
Fiji, 311
First Lahore Conspiracy Case of 1915, 281
First Lord of the Admiralty, 127
First Opium War (1839-1842), 155
Firth, Stewart, 257
Flos Clitoridis, 47
foreigners, suspicion of, 57
Forsayth, Emma, 225
Forster, Georg, 20, 82, 83, 84, 85, 89, 90, 91, 310; Voyage around the World *(Reise um die Welt),* 129, 143
Forster, Johann Reinhold, 15, 21, 69, 70, 82, 84, 85, 127–45, 312; actor of Eighteenth-century natural history, 129–31; knowledge production aboard HMS *Resolution,* 131–42; *Resolution Journal,* 129, 134, 137, 140, 141
Foucault, Michel, 90, 128
France, 65, 80
Frauenbund der Deutschen Kolonialgesellschaft (Women's League of the German Colonial Society), 215, 216
Free Hindustan, 278
Freeman, George, 284
free wage laborers, 195
French Sisters of the Infant Jesus, 243
French–Tahitian Wars (1843–46), 10
Friendly Islands, 296
frontiers, German-American penetration of the Pacific, 171–87
Frost, Alan, 55
Frost, Orcutt, 108
fuel shortages, 163
Furneaux, Tobias, 138

Gama, Vasco de, 6, 36
Garbanzo islands, 63

gender in the New Guinean mission field, 242–44
Gen'emon Eisei, Imamura, 46
Genthe, Siegfried, 200
gentleman soldiers, 46
Gentlemen Seventeen, 38
Geographica (Ptolemy), 56
geography, 56
geology, 81
geometry, 62
German-American penetration of the Pacific, 171–87
German colonial woman *(Deutsche Kolonialfrau),* 218–19
German connection, 36
German Enlightenment, 36
German Foreign Ministry, 155
German Imperial District Officer, 204
German laborers, 175
German Law of Citizenship of 1870, 222
German National Women's League (Deutschnationaler Frauenbund), 216
Germanness *(Deutschtum),* 221
German Women's Red Cross Association, 217
Germany, 35; apothecaries *(see* apothecaries); botanists *(see* botanists); Catholicism in, 249; colonialism, 2; contribution to knowledge of the Pacific, 5; dynamics of naturalist networks, 87–91; explorers in the Pacific, 83–87; geographical features, 2; Germans in the Pacific, 13–18; histories, 1–18, 309–12; historiography, 2; indentured women (New Guinea), 257–60; Indo-German Plot to Overthrow the British Empire, 277–87; influence on Chinese industrialization, 153–66; nation-state, 3; naturalists (around 1800), 79–96; role in the world, 1; Vava'u Germans, 292–305; women (German), 213–27
Gesindeordnung ("Servant's law"), 205
Gibson, Samuel, 136
global botanizing, 36–40
global history, 1, 4, 5
globalization, 17
Gmelin, Johan Georg, 84, 107, 108

Godeffroy Trading Company, 196, 197, 201, 203
God's eye, 62
Goethe, Johann Wolfgang von, 114
Golder, Frank A., 105
Gothaer Tageblatt, 175
governance, 2
Gradmann, Robert, 108
Great Britain, 10, 80; anti-British rhetoric, 278; Indo-German Plot to Overthrow the British Empire, 277–87; Royal Society, 104
Great Cabin, 127
Great Instauration, 131
Great Race, 165
Great Southern Continent, 8
guandu shangban system, 156
Gupta, Heramba Lal, 282, 284

Habsburg Empire, 84
Hackfeld & Co., 175, 176
Haenke, Thaddäus, 84
hafakasi, 301
Hahl, Albert, 222, 257, 258
half-castes, 222, 224, 226, 301
Hallesche Berichte, 67
Halle the International Society of Georg Wilhelm Steller, 107
Hanyang Iron Foundry, 157
Hardinge, Charles, 281
Hau'ofa, Epeli, 62
Hawaii (USA), 12; Chinese invasion of, 176f; multicultural repopulation of, 175–78; sugaring of, 172–75; tourism, 181
Hawaiian Commercial and Sugar Company, 173, 176
Hawley, George T., 182, 183f
headhunters in New Guinea, 198
Hearst Press, 186, 280
heathendom, 238
helper of the mission *(Missionsgehilfin),* 217
Hempenstall, Peter, 257
Henderson, Malina Wolfgramm, 292
herbs, 41, 43
Hermann, Paulus, 41
Hernsheim & Co., 262

Hertzer, Auguste, 216
Hesse-Wartegg, Ernst von, 201
Het Amboinsche kruid-boek or *Herbarium Amboinense* (Ambonese Herbal [Rumpf, 1741–50]), 46
Hiery, Hermann Josef, 13
Hildebrand, Heinrich, 159, 160, 161, 162
Histoire de Navigation aux Terre Australes (1736), 69
historía, 38
Historia Plantarum (1704), 43
histories: European Pacific, 4; Germany, 1–18, 309–12; imperial, 5–13; Pacific, 1–18, 309–12; Vava'u Germans, 294–300
historiography, Germany, 2
History of Japan (Sloane, 1727), 45
Hititi, 138
HMS *Adventure,* 133, 136
HMS *Discovery,* 136
HMS *Endeavor,* 136
HMS *Resolution,* 127–45. See also Cook, James
Ho-Chi Minh, 13
Hofmann, Ernst R., 87
holiness, 142
höllisch viel zu thun ("to work like hell"), 202
Holy Roman Empire of the German Nation, 3, 15, 16
Holy Spirit Congregation, 238
homogeneity of German inhabitants, 227
Hong Kong, 282, 283
Hongkong Telegraph, 164
Honolulu Music Hall, 181
Hopkinson, William C., 278, 279
Horner, Johann Kaspar, 86, 91
Hotel del Coronado, 181
Ho Yow, 182, 183f
Humboldt, Alexander von, 20, 83, 85, 88, 89, 90, 91
hydrology, 81

The Ideals of the East (Okakura), 281
Igel, Wolf von, 280
Igler, David, 10, 16
illustrations, 131
imbruted whites *(verwilderten Weißen),* 200
Imperial Colonial Office, 221

imperial expansion, 17
imperial histories, 5–13
Imperium (Kracht), 200
"incorrectness" *(Ungehörigkeiten),* 204
indentured women (New Guinea), 257–60; rape, 260–67
India, 277, 279, 282, 286; revolutionaries, 277
Indo-German Plot to Overthrow the British Empire, 277–87
Indonesia, 35
industrialization: foundations for, 153; German influence on Chinese, 153
Insulae Laos seu novae Philippinae, 68*f*
Ireland, Sinn Fein, 284, 285
Irwin, William G., 175, 181
islas encantadas (mystery islands), 63
Italy, 65

Jacob, Margaret, 153
Ein Jahrzehnt in Samoa (A Decade in Samoa [Zischank]), 221, 222, 226
Japan, 6, 7, 11, 35, 41, 45, 83, 277
J. C. Goddefroy and Son, 11
J. D. Spreckels & Bros., 184
Jehovah's Witnesses, 299
Jensen, Joan, 286
Jesuit missionaries, 6, 7, 16, 55, 56; education, 57. *See also* Klein, Paul
John D. Spreckels & Bros., 178
Johnston, Harry, 12

Kadu, 14
Kaempfer, Engelbert, 19, 35, 42–47, 83, 310
Kaiping Mines, 157
Kaiser-Wilhelmsland, 222, 238, 242, 244, 248. *See also* New Guinea
Kalakaua (King), 173
Kamchatka, 111, 116
Kayak Island, 109
Kearney, Dennis, 177
Kelly, John, 262
Kessel, William, 284
kinderpoxkens, 40
Kindrus, Birthe, 215
kinship, 298

Kittlitz, Johann von, 88, 89
Klein, Paul, 19, 55–71, 56, 70, 310; audiences for maps, 64–69; *carta* of the Palaos, 56–60; education, 58, 59; factfinding missions, 63; imaginings of oceanic spaces, 60–63; in Manilla, Philippines, 58; maps, 61*f*, 63; Palaos map, 67; Philippines, 56; travels to the Pacific, 58
Klein, Paulus. *See* Clain, Pablo
knowledge production aboard HMS *Resolution,* 131–42
Kolbe, Waldemar, 261
Kölnische Zeitung, 165
Koloniale Zeitschrift, 223
Kolonie und Heimat (Colony and Homeland), 216, 218, 226
Komagatu Maru incident (1914), 278, 279, 286
Kotzebue, Otto von, 69, 86, 87, 89, 91
Kracht, Charles, 200, 201
Krämer-Bannow, Elisabeth, 225
Krupp, Friedrich, 154, 162
Krusenstern, Adam von, 85, 86, 90, 91
kuangwu ju (official bureau), 157
Kuhn, Gretel, 225
Küntzel-Witt, Kristina, 14, 15, 20
Kurile Islands, 102, 113

labor, 195; camps, 203; in Melanesia, 198. *See also* work in the South Sea
Ladrones, 7
laissez faire, 199
Langsdorff, Georg Heinrich von, 86
Latour, Bruno, 128
laws, Tonga, 298
Leavenworth, Kansas, 283
Legazpi, Miguel Lopez de, 6
Le Gobien, Charles, 66
Leibniz, Gottfried Wilhelm, 103
Leinung, Gustav, 162, 163
Lenz, Emil von, 87, 89
Leonen aan de Vecht, 39
leprosy, 43
Lettres Edifiantes et Curieuses, 66, 67
Li Hongzhang, 156, 157, 160, 162
Liliencron, Freifrau von, 218

Limbrock, Eberhard, 245
Linnaean method of classification, 135
locomotive factories, 154
Lomonosov, Mikhail V., 104
longue durée, 2, 13–18
Louis XIV, 64, 65
lovers' trysts *(Schäferstündchen feiern)*, 201
Low German *(Platt)*, 296
Ludwig, Friedrich Gustav, 292
luluais, 257
Lutheran Church, 295, 296
Luzhin, Fedor F., 103

Magellan, Ferdinand, 3, 6, 83
Mai, 139
Maier, Charles, 184
malaria, 159
Malaspina, Alejandro, 38
Malaspina, Alessandro, 85
male mobility, 240
malnutrition, 39
Malog, 62
Maltzan, Von, 164
Map of the New Philippines Discovered under the Patronage of Philip V, 64
maps, 55–71; audiences for (Klein), 64–69; Cantova, Antonio, 69; Caroline Islands, 56; Europe, 60, 68; geographic knowledge, 70; Insulae Laos seu novae Philippinae, 68f; Klein, Paul, 61f, 63, 70 (*see also* Klein, Paul)
Maria Anna of Austria, 58
Mariana Islands, 62, 213
Mariss, Anne, 14, 15, 21
the Marquesas, 8
marriage: annulments, 223; markets, 219; mixed marriage debates, 221–26
Marshall Islands, 213, 297
Matsuda, Matt, 4
Maui (Hawaii), 175. *See also* Hawaii
Maverick, 282, 283
McGetchin, Douglas T., 18, 24, 25
mechanical view of the world, 153
Medici, Anna Maria Luisa de, 44
medicinale winkel, 40–42
Meister, Georg, 41, 42
Melanesia, 8, 198

Mentzel, Christian, 41
Merck, Carl H., 20, 103–18, 117; Billings–Sarychev Expedition, 112–16; death of, 116
Merck, Heinrich, 20
Merian, Maria Sybilla, 38
Mertens, Karl Heinrich, 90
Messerschmidt, Daniel Gottlieb, 39, 102, 104
Mestizos, 224
Mignolo, Walter, 65
migration: chain migration from Pyritz to Vava'u, 295–97; to the Pacific, 293
mining academy, 163
mining engineers, 160
Ministry of Agriculture and Commerce, 163
Ministry of Public Works, 155
Mischehen (mixed marriages), 215
Misericordia, 43
missionaries, 18; female lives, 244–47; gender in the New Guinean mission field, 242–44; New Guinea, 240, 241–42, 250 (*see also* New Guinea)
Missionsbräute (mission brides), 217
Missionsgehilfin (helper of the mission), 217
Missionsgrüße (Missionary Greetings), 238, 248
mixed marriage debates, 215, 221–26, 227
modernity, 196
Moleni, Liahoni, 292
Moluccas, 36, 64. *See also* Spice Islands
Monkhouse, William Brougham, 136
Mormon Church, 295, 299
Moses, John, 257
Motherhouse, 240, 242
Mueller, Gerhard Friedrich, 104, 106, 107, 112, 115
Muir, John, 108
Mulattos, 224
multicultural repopulation of Hawaii, 175–78
Murillo Velarde, Pedro, 42, 44, 45
museums, 39
mystery islands *(islas encantadas)*, 63

Nadeshda, 86
Nagai Island, 110

Napoleonic Wars (1799–1815), 9
Napoleon III, 10
Nassenhuben (Mokry Dwór), 130
nationhood, 14
nation-state, Germany, 3
natural history, 131
naturalists, 18, 19, 79–96, 94*t*–95*t*;
  dynamics of networks, 87–91;
  expeditions, 92*t*–93*t*; identity, 91–96;
  transnatural networks of, 80–83
Nauru, 213
Naval Industrial Complex, 184–86
Naval Reserve Committee, 186
networks: dynamics of naturalist, 87–91;
  transnatural of naturalists (around 1800),
  80–83
Der Neue Welt-Bott, 66, 67
Neu Mecklenburg (New Ireland), 259, 262
New Caledonia, 258
New Era (Yugantar) ashram, 279
New Guinea, 213, 216, 238–50, 310, 311;
  female missionary lives, 244–47; gender
  in the New Guinean mission field,
  242–44; headhunters, 198; indentured
  women, 257–60; missionaries, 240,
  241–42, 250; rape of indentured women,
  260–67; taboos, 240; women and the
  German colonial indenture, 257–60;
  writing and publishing in, 247–49
New Guinea Company, 257, 258
the New Hebrides, 8
New Philippines, 64
New Worlds, 8, 141
New York Chamber of Commerce, 186
New Zealand, 8, 135, 294, 295, 297, 300,
  301, 302
non-work in the South Sea, 195–207
North America, 282
North Pacific: Billings–Sarychev Expedition,
  112–16; explorers in the, 103–18; Second
  Kamchatka Expedition, 105–6
Novum organum scientiarum (Bacon), 132*f*

Oceanic Steamship Company, 178, 179,
  180*f*, 181*f*, 186. *See also* Spreckels
  family
official bureau *(kuangwu ju)*, 157

Okakura, Kakuzo, 281
Old World, 140, 141
onderkoopman, 46
Opium Wars (1839–42, 1856–60), 9
Ordubadi, Diana, 116
Otto, Johann Friedrich Wilhelm, 88

Pacific: bioprospecting in the, 139–42;
  Chinese-American Commercial
  Company, 182–84; dynamics of naturalist
  networks, 87–91; as European project,
  5–13; European voyages in, 92*t*–93*t*;
  explorations (naturalists around 1800),
  80–83; explorers in the North Pacific,
  103–18; German-American penetration
  of, 171–87; German explorers in,
  83–87; German naturalists (around
  1800), 79–96; Germans in the, 13–18;
  histories, 1–18, 309–12; homogeneity of
  German inhabitants, 227; Indo-German
  Plot to Overthrow the British Empire,
  277–87; maps, 55–71; migration to, 293;
  multicultural repopulation of Hawaii,
  175–78; Naval Industrial Complex,
  184–86; Pomerania, 292–305; role
  of Germans in, 16; Somoa, 195–207;
  Spreckels family shipping lines, 178–81;
  sugaring of Hawaii, 172–75; Tonga,
  292–305. *See also* North Pacific
Pacific Century, 3
Pacific Commercial Museum, 182
Pacific Foreign Trade Council, 186
Pacific Islanders, 15
Pacific Islands Monthly, 299
Palaos islands, 56, 66
Palau, 213
Pallas, Peter Simon, 115, 116
Panama, 282
Papen, Franz von, 282, 286
paradise island. *See* Saomoa
Paris Peace conference (1919), 13
Paulus Klein, 43
Peace of Westphalia, 16
Peking University, 163
Pérouse, Jean-François de Galaup de La,
  114
Perry, Matthew C., 11

Persia, 45
Peru, 12
Peter Schlemihl (Chamisso), 87
Peter the Great, 39, 103, 104
Petiver, James, 43
philanthropy, 141
Philippines, 35, 186; imaginings of oceanic spaces, 60–63; Klein, Paul, 56
Philosophical Transactions, 66
Pickersgill, Richard, 136
Pingxiang Coalmines, 157
placeless places, 128
plant collecting, 37, 39
plants, hunt for, 134
Platt (Low German), 296
pluralism, 15
politics, Colonial Politics of Botany, 134
Polynesia, 8
Polytechnic School, 172
Pomerania, 292–305, 297
populations: half-castes, 222; whites in the South Sea, 220
porcelain, 37
Portugal, 6, 7
post-Westphalian early modern era, 14
Pradella, Francesco, 60
Preuss, Ernst Wilhelm, 87
private curiosity cabinets, 39
Proctor, Robert, 142
promiscuity, 262
promyshlenniki, 111, 112
Prussian Geological Institute, 164, 165
Prussian Ministry of Culture, 154
publishing in New Guinea, 247–49

quarter-castes, 301
Queen Charlotte Sound (New Zealand), 139

race mixing, 226. *See also* mixed marriage debates
racism, 177
railroads: building, 155; engineers, 161
Railway Administration of Saarbrücken, 159
rape of indentured women (New Guinea), 260–67
ratio studiorum, 56

Ray, John, 43
Red Cross, 216
Reformation period, 3, 16
Regierungsbaumeister (state building master), 157
Reichskolonialamt, 203
Reinecke, Franz, 198, 201
Reinhold, Johann, 20, 84
Reise um die Welt (*Voyage around the World* [Forster]), 129, 143
Resolution Journal (Forster), 129, 134, 137, 140, 141
revolutionaries, 277, 279. *See also* Indo-German Plot to Overthrow the British Empire
Reyes, Raquel, 14, 19
Ribbe, Carl, 259
Richthofen Institute for German China Research, 165
Rigotti, Livia Maria, 18, 23
Robinson Crusoe (Defoe), 90
Rodiek, George, 285
roles: of German colonial woman *(Deutsche Kolonialfrau),* 218–19; of German women in the South Seas, 214
Roosevelt, Theodore, 184
Royal Society (Great Britain), 81, 88, 104
Rumpf, Georg Everard, 19, 35, 42–47
Rumphius. *See* Rumpf, Georg Everard
Rurik expedition, 87, 89
Russia, 80; Academy of Science, 20, 105, 106, 116; colonization efforts of, 130; explorers in the North Pacific, 103–18
Russo-Japanese war of 1904-5, 11, 281

Said, Edward, 90
salpa tunicate, 87
Samoa, 12, 195–207, 213, 221, 297, 311; beachcombers, 200–201; coolies, 203–4; cotton, 196, 197; exports, 197; German employees, 201–2; under German rule, 196; German settlers, 202–3; history of, 196–97; segregation, 198; self-administration, 196; types of work in, 198–205; wages, 200
Samoanische Zeitung, 218, 224
Sandwich (Lord), 127

322 | Index

Sandwich Islands, 179
San Francisco Call, 186
San Francisco Panama–Pacific International Exposition (1915), 183
Sanft, August, 295
Sanft, Martha Emilie, 292, 294
Santo, Ignacia del Espiritu, 59
Sarychev, Gavriil, 116
Sauer, Martin, 116
Saul, Hedwig, 216
Scandinavia, 35
Schäferstündchen feiern (lovers' trysts), 201
Scheidtweiler, Peter, 157, 158, 159, 160, 161, 162
Scherer, Johann Benedict, 112
Schiebinger, Londa, 134
Schmidt, Jürgen, 18, 22
Scholient, Ernst, 133
Schulze, Valesca, 226
Schüssler, Hermann, 173
Scientific Revolution, 36
scurvy, 39, 108
Second Age of Discovery, 80
Second Kamchatka Expedition, 105–6
segregation, 198, 224
Sekunna, Earnest, 285
self-administration, 196
Serrano, Andres, 55, 61, 63, 64, 65, 66, 70
"Servant's law" *(Gesindeordnung),* 205
Servants of the Holy Spirit, 238, 239, 240, 242, 244, 247
Seventh Day Adventists, 298
Seven Years' War, 80
sexual assault, 260–67
Shanghai Mercury, 162
shell money *(diwarra* or *tambu),* 257
Shineberg, Dorothy, 258
shipping lines, Spreckels family, 178–81
Shiva, Vandana, 140
Shumagin, Nikita, 110
Siefering, Martha (Sister), 246
Sight of Strangers, 141
Sikhs, 278
silks, 37
Singh, Bela, 279
Singh, Mewa, 279

Singh, Ram, 285
Singh, Sardar Gurdit, 278
Sinn Fein, 284, 285
Sino-Japanese War (1894-1895), 11, 161
Slava Rossii, 115
Smidt, Karen, 224
Smith, Isaac, 136
Smith, Vanessa, 139
Smithsonian Institution, 105
soccum capas tree, 47
social background (of Somoa), 196–97
social fabric of South Sea colonies, 219–21
Society of Jesus, 42
Society of the Divine Word, 238
Solander, Daniel, 82
Solf, Wilhelm, 199, 202, 203, 221, 223
Solger, Friedrich, 163, 164, 165
Solomon Islands, 8, 213
South America, 9
South Manchurian Railroad, 154
South New Britain (Südneupommern), 204
South Sea, 131; motives of women (German) for departure to, 215–18; populations, 220; social fabric of South Sea colonies, 219–21; Somoa, 195–207; women (German), 213–27
South West Africa, 214, 215, 216, 219
sovereignty, 312
Spain, 7, 80
Spanish–American War of 1898, 11, 186, 312
Spanish Crown, 37, 38, 85
The Spanish Lake, 7, 14
Sparrman, Anders, 134
Spate, Oskar, 3, 4
Specimen Medicinae Sinicae (1862), 40
Spice Islands, 6, 19, 36
spices, 37
Spickard, Paul, 300
Spiekermann, Uwe, 16, 22
Spöring, Herman, 82
Spreckels, Adolph B., 179, 184
Spreckels, Claus, 172, 175, 177, 185*f*
Spreckels, John D., 172, 178, 179, 184
Spreckels, Peter, 172
Spreckels, Rudolph, 182, 183

Spreckels family: Chinese-American Commercial Company, 182–84; German-American penetration of the Pacific, 171–87; multicultural repopulation of Hawaii, 175–78; Naval Industrial Complex, 184–86; shipping lines, 178–81; sugaring of Hawaii, 172–75
Spreckelsville Mill, 174f, 175
Sprengel, Matthias Christian, 69
Spring Valley Water Works, 173
star compasses, 62
Stein, Anna, 216
Steinmetz, George, 198
Stejneger, Leonhard, 105, 106
Steller, Georg Wilhelm, 20, 84, 88, 91, 103–18, 117, 310; death of, 107; diary, 105; passage to Alaska, 106–12
stereotypes, racist, 177
St. Ignatius' bean (*Strychnos Ignatii* Berg), 44
St. Louis World's Fair, 1902, 182, 183f
Stöcklein, Joseph, 67, 68, 69
Stoler, Ann Laura, 259
Stornig, Katharina, 18, 23, 24
St. Paul, 108, 109
St. Peter, 111
Strahlenberg, Johann Tabbert von, 103–4
Strasser, Ulrike, 14, 19
Strychnos Ignatii Berg (St. Ignatius' bean), 44
Südneupommern (South New Britain), 204
sugaring of Hawaii, 172–75
Sugar Trust, 174
Swan, Claudia, 134
Swedish National Geological Survey, 164
taboos in New Guinea, 240

Taikun, 294
Taiping Rebellion (1850–62), 156
tambu (shell money), 257
Tang dynasty (618–907), 163
tapu, 142
Tasmania, 8
Ten Rhijne, Willem, 40, 43
Thailand, 12
Thirty Years War, 3
Thomas, Emma, 18, 24
Thoreau, Henry David, 108
Thurn (Count), 284

Tianjin Railroad, 161
Tierra del Fuego, 141
Tilesius, Wilhelm Gottlieb von, 86
Tonga, 292–305, 298, 309
Tosa Maru, 282
total war campaigns, 36
tourism in Hawaii, 181
trade: products from China, 37; Somoa, 196
traditional cultures, 196
translators, 59
transnatural networks of naturalists, 80–83
Trans-Pacific galleon trade, 36, 37
Trans-Pacific "Ghadar" movement, 277–87
Treaty of Paris (1763), 80
Treaty of Nanking (1842), 9
Tu'inahoki, Kisaea Sisifa, 292
tultuls, 257, 258
Tupaia, 138, 139
typhus, 39

U-boats, 286
Ulla, Ali, 283
Ungehörigkeiten ("incorrectness"), 204
United States, 81, 277, 285, 300, 302
University of Dorpat, 88
Unshelm, August, 197, 201
Urdaneta, Andrés de, 7, 36
US Pacific Northwest, 9

Vava'u Germans, 292–305; chain migration from Pyritz to Vava'u, 295–97; cultural memory of, 304; formation of community, 300–301; Germanness of, 303–4; history of, 294–300; identity construction of, 300–304; life in the islands, 297–300; memories and experiences of the past, 301–3; Wolfgramm, Friedrich, 294–95
Velasco, Juan Lopez de, 65
verwilderten Weißen (imbruted whites), 200
VOC *(Vereenigde Oost-indische Compagnie)*, 35, 36; in Batavia, 40, 41, 45; factory in Deshima, 45; gentleman soldiers, 46; global botanizing, 38

vocabulario tagala, 59
Vökt, Fridolina (Sister), 242
Vostok, 86
Voyage around the World (*Reise um die Welt* [Forster]), 90, 129, 143

wages in Saomoa, 200
Wareham, Evelyn, 223
Waxell, Sven, 110
Weber, Theodor, 197
Wendt, Reinhard, 25
"Western" epistemology, 82
whaling, 9
White Fleet, 184
white supremacy, 177
Wilhelm (Kaiser), 279
Wilson, Henry, 69
Wilson, Woodrow, 13
Winkler, Martina, 114
Wolfgramm, Carl Friedrich, 296
Wolfgramm, Charles Fredrick, 292
Wolfgramm, Friedrich, 293, 294–95, 298, 299, 300
Wolfgramm, Robert, 302
women (German), 213–27; employment, 218; female missionary lives, 244–47; German colonial woman *(Deutsche Kolonialfrau),* 218–19; marriage markets, 219; mixed marriage debates, 221–26; motives for departure to South Seas, 215–18; movements of, 240; in New Guinea, 238–50; social fabric of South Sea colonies, 219–21
women (indentured): background of, 257–60; rape of, 260–67
Women's League of the German Colonial Society (Frauenbund der Deutschen Kolonialgesellschaft), 215, 216, 224
Workingmen's Party, 177
working sisters *(Arbeitsschwestern),* 245
work in the South Sea, 195–207; beachcombers, 200–201; coolies, 203–4; German employees, 201–2; German settlers, 202–3; Samoans, 198–200
World War I, 1, 12, 18, 249, 258, 281, 293; anti-imperialism, 278; Indo-German Plot to Overthrow the British Empire, 277–87; United States entry into, 285; Vava'u Germans in, 294
World War II, 286
Wormskjold, Morten, 82
writing in New Guinea, 247–49
Wu, Shellen, 18, 21
Wyllie, Curzon (Sir), 278

Yuan Shikai, 163
Yugantar (New Era) ashram, 279

Zhang Zhidong, 156, 157, 158, 159, 160, 161, 164
Zieschank, Frieda, 199, 202, 204, 221, 226
Zirkel, Barnaba (Sister), 247
Zischank, Frieda, 221
Zöller, Hugo, 297
zoology, 81
Zuo Zongtang, 156

Studies in German History

Published in association with the German Historical Institute, Washington, DC

General Editor:
Simone Lässig, Director of the German Historical Institute, Washington, DC, with the assistance of **Patricia Sutcliffe**, Editor, German Historical Institute

Volume 1
Nature in German History
Edited by Christof Mauch

Volume 2
Coping with the Nazi Past: West German Debates on Nazism and Generational Conflict, 1955–1975
Edited by Philipp Gassert and Alan E. Steinweis

Volume 3
Adolf Cluss, Architect: From Germany to America
Edited by Alan Lessoff and Christof Mauch

Volume 4
Two Lives in Uncertain Times: Facing the Challenges of the 20th Century as Scholars and Citizens
Wilma Iggers and Georg Iggers

Volume 5
Driving Germany: The Landscape of the German Autobahn, 1930–1970
Thomas Zeller

Volume 6
The Pleasure of a Surplus Income: Part-Time Work, Gender Politics, and Social Change in West Germany, 1955–1969
Christine von Oertzen

Volume 7
Between Mass Death and Individual Loss: The Place of the Dead in Twentieth-Century Germany
Edited by Alon Confino, Paul Betts, and Dirk Schumann

Volume 8
Nature of the Miracle Years: Conservation in West Germany, 1945–1975
Sandra Chaney

Volume 9
Biography between Structure and Agency: Central European Lives in International Historiography
Edited by Volker R. Berghahn and Simone Lässig

Volume 10
Political Violence in the Weimar Republic, 1918–1933: Battle for the Streets and Fears of Civil War
Dirk Schumann

Volume 11
The East German State and the Catholic Church, 1945–1989
Bernd Schaefer

Volume 12
Raising Citizens in the "Century of the Child": Child-Rearing in the United States and German Central Europe in Comparative Perspective
Edited by Dirk Schumann

Volume 13
The Plans that Failed: An Economic History of the GDR
André Steiner

Volume 14
Max Liebermann and International Modernism: An Artist's Career from Empire to Third Reich
Edited by Marion Deshmukh, Françoise Forster-Hahn, and Barbara Gaehtgens

Volume 15
Germany and the Black Diaspora: Points of Contact, 1250–1914
Edited by Mischa Honeck, Martin Klimke, and Anne Kuhlmann-Smirnov

Volume 16
Crime and Criminal Justice in Modern Germany
Edited by Richard F. Wetzell

Volume 17
Encounters with Modernity: The Catholic Church in the Federal Republic, 1945–1975
Benjamin Ziemann

Volume 18
Fellow Tribesmen: The Image of Native Americans, National Identity, and Nazi Ideology in Germany
Frank Usbeck

Volume 19
The Respectable Career of Fritz K: The Making and Remaking of a Provincial Nazi Leader
Hartmut Berghoff and Cornelia Rauh
Translated by Casey Butterfield

Volume 20
The Second Generation: Émigrés from Nazi Germany as Historians in the Transatlantic World
Edited by Andreas W. Daum, Hartmut Lehmann, and James J. Sheehan

Volume 21
The Ethics of Seeing: Photography and Twentieth-Century German History
Edited by Jennifer Evans, Paul Betts, and Stefan-Ludwig Hoffmann

Volume 22
Explorations and Entanglements: Germans in Pacific Worlds from the Early Modern Period to World War I
Edited by Hartmut Berghoff, Frank Biess, and Ulrike Strasser

www.ingramcontent.com/pod-product-compliance
Lightning Source LLC
Chambersburg PA
CBHW071333080526
44587CB00017B/2817